LIVY

BOOKS XXXI–XXXIII

A COMMENTARY ON
LIVY

BOOKS XXXI–XXXIII

BY

JOHN BRISCOE

Lecturer in Greek and Latin
University of Manchester

OXFORD
AT THE CLARENDON PRESS
1973

Oxford University Press, Ely House, London W. 1

GLASGOW NEW YORK TORONTO MELBOURNE WELLINGTON
CAPE TOWN IBADAN NAIROBI DAR ES SALAAM LUSAKA ADDIS ABABA
DELHI BOMBAY CALCUTTA MADRAS KARACHI LAHORE DACCA
KUALA LUMPUR SINGAPORE HONG KONG TOKYO

ISBN 0 19 8144423

*Printed in Great Britain
at the University Press, Oxford
by Vivian Ridler
Printer to the University*

TO

MY PARENTS

PREFACE

In writing this commentary I have been very conscious that I was treading a path blazed for me by others—in the case of Livy by Dr. Ogilvie in his commentary on the first pentad, in the case of the period of the Second Macedonian War by Professor Walbank in the relevant parts of his commentary on Polybius. On a considerable number of matters Ogilvie or Walbank have already said all that is necessary and in these cases I have been content simply to refer to their discussions. This is especially so in those places where Polybius' account survives, since on these occasions my main purpose has been to illuminate the way in which Livy utilized his source, not to discuss again all the historical problems raised by the narrative of Polybius.

In one particular field, that of Greek topography, the commentary is more second-hand than some will feel it should be. It would, however, have been impossible to visit those campaign areas which now lie within Albania, and, for the rest, I have not felt able to visit Greece under present conditions. Fortunately there are full discussions of the main campaigns (with maps) by Hammond and Walbank respectively. Statements about Italian topography, on the other hand, are usually based on autopsy.

The commentary was conceived and begun in Oxford, and its historical approach is the fruit of my years in Oxford as undergraduate, research student, and teacher. It would, however, have been very one-sided to attempt to write a purely historical commentary on so literary and artistic a historian as Livy. For the greater part of nearly eight years I had the good fortune to be in almost daily contact with Eduard Fraenkel, and though I cannot claim that he had any direct influence on what I have written, I have throughout been extremely conscious of Fraenkel's emphasis on the indivisibility of Classical Scholarship. Without what I learnt from Fraenkel I should have been far more hesitant about committing myself on questions of style and language.

The bulk of the commentary was written, however, in

Manchester, and if the inspiration of the book belongs to Oxford, it is appropriate that it should have been brought to completion in the University where Robert Seymour Conway made so great a contribution to Livian studies.

I have constantly picked the brains of colleagues, both at Oxford and Manchester: I trust they will forgive me for not acknowledging their contributions by name. My greatest single debt, however, is to Professor Robin Nisbet, who taught me Latin as an undergraduate, and who has given me every help and encouragement at all stages of my career. He has discussed with me innumerable points of Latinity in these books of Livy, and has saved me from many errors: only occasionally have I ventured to persevere in an opinion with which he has disagreed. As if this were not enough, he offered to read the proofs and detected many mistakes which I would not have noticed.

I am extremely grateful to the staff of the Clarendon Press and the Printer to the University of Oxford for their helpfulness and courtesy at all stages of the production of the book, from its original conception in 1965 to its final translation into print. I must also express my thanks to the Craven Committee at Oxford and the Grants Assessment Committee at Manchester for assistance with travelling expenses, to the University of Manchester Library for their constant helpfulness and for their diligence in obtaining for me copies or microfilms of a number of foreign dissertations, and to Mrs. Kathleen Moore for typing a large portion of the manuscript.

One of the purposes of a commentary is to serve as a repository of references to relevant modern literature, and with this in mind I have tried to keep the references as up to date as possible. The final typing of the manuscript was begun in August 1971 and I have not been able to give full consideration to works which I read after that date. I have, however, inserted references to works which were available to me in Manchester up to the end of January 1972 and have included in the *addenda* some further references to works which came to my notice between then and September 1972.

J. B.

Manchester
October 1972

CONTENTS

LIST OF ABBREVIATIONS   xi

INTRODUCTION
1. Sources and Methods of Composition   1
2. Language and Style   12
3. The Speeches   17
4. Flamininus and Roman Politics   22
5. Livy's Account of the Outbreak of the Second Macedonian War   36
6. Text   47

COMMENTARY

BOOK XXXI   49

BOOK XXXII   166

BOOK XXXIII   248

ADDENDA   342

INDEXES
1. General   349
2. Authors and passages   362
3. Latin   368
4. Greek   370

ABBREVIATIONS

THIS is a list of modern works referred to in the Introduction and Commentary in an abbreviated form. It is not a bibliography. Abbreviations of periodicals are, in general, those of *L'Année Philologique*. The numbers in brackets following the names of individual Romans in the Commentary are those of the articles on the persons concerned in *RE*.

Accame, *Espansione romana*	S. Accame, *L'espansione romana in Grecia* (Naples, 1961).
Ashby, *Campagna*	T. Ashby, *The Roman Campagna in Classical Times* (London, 1927; republished London, 1970).
Astin, *Scipio Aemilianus*	A. E. Astin, *Scipio Aemilianus* (Oxford, 1967).
Aymard, *Assemblées*	A. Aymard, *Les Assemblées de la confédération achaienne* (Bordeaux–Paris, 1938).
Aymard, *ÉHA*	A. Aymard, *Études d'histoire ancienne* (Paris, 1967).
Aymard, *PR*	A. Aymard, *Les Premiers Rapports de Rome et de la confédération achaienne* (Bordeaux–Paris, 1938).
Badian, *FC*	E. Badian, *Foreign Clientelae, 264–70 B.C.* (Oxford, 1958).
Badian, *Flamininus*	E. Badian, *Titus Quinctius Flamininus, Philhellenism and Realpolitik* (Cincinnati, Ohio, 1970).
Badian, *Studies*	E. Badian, *Studies in Greek and Roman History* (Oxford, 1964).
Bellezza	A. Bellezza, *L'ombra di un'antica alleanza* (Genoa, 1962).
Bleicken	J. Bleicken, *Das Volkstribunat der klassischen Republik* (Munich, 1955).
Bornecque	H. Bornecque, *Tite-Live* (Paris, 1933).
Bredehorn	U. Bredehorn, *Senatsakten in der republikanischen Annalistik* (Marburg, 1968).
Brueggmann	H. Brueggmann, *Komposition und Entwicklungstendenzen der Bücher 31–35 des Titus Livius* (Kiel, 1955).
Brunt	P. A. Brunt, *Italian Manpower, 225 B.C.–A.D. 14* (Oxford, 1971).
Burck, *Erzählungskunst*	E. Burck, *Die Erzählungskunst des T. Livius* (Berlin, 1934).
CAH	*Cambridge Ancient History.*

Cassola, *GP*   F. Cassola, *I gruppi politici romani nel III secolo a. C.* (Trieste, 1962).

Catin   L. Catin, *En lisant Tite-Live* (Paris, 1944).

Chausserie-Laprée   J. P. Chausserie-Laprée, *L'Expression narrative chez les historiens latins* (Paris, 1969).

CIL   *Corpus Inscriptionum Latinarum.*

Dahlheim   W. Dahlheim, *Struktur und Entwicklung des römischen Völkerrechts im dritten und zweiten Jahrhundert v. Chr.* (Munich, 1968. This is a revised version of the author's *Deditio und Societas*, Munich, 1965: references are given only to the later version.)

Deininger   J. Deininger, *Der politische Widerstand gegen Rom in Griechenland, 217–86 v. Chr.* (Berlin–New York, 1971).

De Sanctis   G. De Sanctis, *Storia dei romani* (Turin–Florence, 1907–64).

Ducrey   P. Ducrey, *Le Traitement des prisonniers de guerre dans la Grèce antique* (Paris, 1968).

Economic Survey   *An Economic Survey of Ancient Rome* (ed. T. Frank) (Baltimore, Md., 1933–40).

Errington, *Philopoemen*   R. M. Errington, *Philopoemen* (Oxford, 1969).

Ferguson, *Hellenistic Athens*   W. S. Ferguson, *Hellenistic Athens* (London, 1911).

Ferro   B. Ferro, *Le origini della seconda guerra macedonica* (Atti dell'Accademia di Scienze, Lettere e Arti di Palermo, serie IV^a, vol. xix, pt. 2, 1958/9; Palermo, 1960).

Feyel   M. Feyel, *Polybe et l'histoire de Béotie au IIIe siècle avant notre ère* (Paris, 1942).

FGH   *Die Fragmente der griechischen Historiker*, ed. F. Jacoby (Berlin–Leiden, 1923–).

FHG   *Fragmenta Historicorum Graecorum*, ed. C. and Th. Müller (Paris, 1841–70).

FIRA, i   *Fontes Iuris Romani Anteiustiniani*, i, ed. S. Riccobono (2nd edn., Florence, 1941).

Flacelière   R. Flacelière, *Les Aitoliens à Delphes* (Paris, 1937).

Flurl   W. Flurl, *Deditio in Fidem* (Munich, 1969).

Fraccaro, *Opuscula*   P. Fraccaro, *Opuscula* (Pavia, 1956–7).

Fraser and Bean, *RPI*   P. M. Fraser and G. E. Bean, *The Rhodian Peraea and Islands* (London, 1954).

Gelzer, *Kleine Schriften*   M. Gelzer, *Kleine Schriften* (Wiesbaden, 1962–4).

GGM   *Geographici Graeci Minores*, ed. C. Müller (Paris, 1855–61).

Habicht, *Gottmensch-entum*	Chr. Habicht, *Gottmenschentum und griechische Städte* (2nd edn., Munich, 1970).
Hammond, *Epirus*	N. G. L. Hammond, *Epirus* (Oxford, 1967).
Hansen, *Attalids*	E. V. Hansen, *The Attalids of Pergamon* (2nd edn., Ithaca, N.Y., 1971).
Heidemann	M.-L. Heidemann, *Die Freiheitsparole in der griechisch-römischen Auseinandersetzung, 200–188 v. Chr.* (Bonn, 1966).
Hellmann	F. Hellmann, *Livius-Interpretationen* (Berlin, 1939).
Heuss, *Stadt u. Herrscher*	A. Heuss, *Stadt und Herrscher des Hellenismus* (*Klio*, Bhft. xxxix; Leipzig, 1937).
Hoch	H. Hoch, *Die Darstellung der politischen Sendung Roms bei Livius* (Berlin-Schöneberg, 1951).
Holleaux, *Études*	M. Holleaux, *Études d'épigraphie et d'histoire grecques* (Paris, 1938–68: articles in this collection are not cited by their original publication).
Holleaux, *Rome*	M. Holleaux, *Rome, la Grèce et les monarchies hellénistiques au III*^{e} *siècle avant J.-C.* (*273–205*) (Paris, 1920).
HRR	*Historicorum Romanorum Reliquiae*, ed. C. Peter, (Leipzig: vol. i, 2nd edn., 1914, vol. ii, 1906).
H–S	J. B. Hofmann and A. Szantyr, *Lateinische Syntax und Stilistik* (Munich, 1965).
IG	*Inscriptiones Graecae.*
I.I.	*Inscriptiones Italiae.*
ILLRP	*Inscriptiones Latinae Liberae Rei Publicae*, ed. A. Degrassi (Florence: vol. i, 2nd edn., 1965: vol. ii. 1963).
ISE	*Iscrizioni storiche ellenistiche*, i, ed. L. Moretti (Florence, 1967).
Judeich	W. Judeich, *Topographie von Athen* (2nd edn., Munich, 1931).
Kahrstedt	U. Kahrstedt, *Die Annalistik von Livius, B. XXXI–XLV* (Berlin, 1913).
Kajanto	I. Kajanto, *God and Fate in Livy* (Turku, 1957).
Klotz, *Livius*	A. Klotz, *Livius und seine Vorgänger*, (Stuttgart, 1940; republished Amsterdam, 1964).
Krauss	F. B. Krauss, *An Interpretation of the Omens, Portents, and Prodigies recorded by Livy, Tacitus and Suetonius* (Philadelphia, Pa., 1930).
Kromayer	J. Kromayer and G. Veith, *Antike Schlachtfelder in Griechenland* (Berlin, 1903–31).
Kromayer–Veith	J. Kromayer and G. Veith, *Heerwesen und Kriegführung der Griechen und Römer* (Munich, 1928).

K–St	R. Kühner and C. Stegmann, *Ausführliche Grammatik der lateinischen Sprache: Satzlehre* (3rd edn. revised by A. Thierfelder, Leverkusen, 1955).
Kühnast	L. Kühnast, *Die Hauptpunkte der Livianischen Syntax* (Berlin, 1872).
Laistner	M. L. W. Laistner, *The Greater Roman Historians* (Berkeley, Cal., 1947).
Lambert	A. Lambert, *Die indirekte Rede als künstlerisches Stilmittel des Livius* (Rüschlikon, 1946).
Larsen, *Greek Federal States*	J. A. O. Larsen, *Greek Federal States* (Oxford, 1968).
Larsen, *Representative Government*	J. A. O. Larsen, *Representative Government in Greek and Roman History* (Berkeley and Los Angeles, Cal., 1955).
Latte, *RRG*	K. Latte, *Römische Religionsgeschichte* (Munich, 1960).
Launey	M. Launey, *Recherches sur les armées hellénistiques* (Paris, 1949–50).
Lebek	W. D. Lebek, *Verba Prisca* (Göttingen, 1970).
Lehmann	G. A. Lehmann, *Untersuchungen zur historischen Glaubwürdigkeit des Polybios* (Münster, 1967).
Lévêque, *Pyrrhos*	P. Lévêque, *Pyrrhos* (Paris, 1957).
Lippold	A. Lippold, *Consules* (Bonn, 1963).
Löfstedt, *Syntactica*	E. Löfstedt, *Syntactica* (Lund; vol. i, 2nd edn., 1942, vol. ii, 1933).
L–S	C. T. Lewis and C. Short, *A Latin Dictionary* (Oxford, 1879).
Luterbacher	F. Luterbacher, *Der Prodigienglaube und Prodigienstil der Römer* (2nd edn., Burgdorf, 1904).
McDonald	A. H. McDonald, *Titi Livi ab urbe condita tomus v, libri xxxi–xxxv* (Oxford, 1965).
McShane	R. B. McShane, *The Foreign Policy of the Attalids of Pergamum* (Urbana, Ill., 1964).
Madvig, *Emendationes*	J. N. Madvig, *Emendationes Livianae* (2nd edn., Copenhagen, 1877).
Magie, *RRAM*	D. Magie, *Roman Rule in Asia Minor* (Princeton, N.J., 1950).
Marquardt, *StV*	J. Marquardt, *Römische Staatsverwaltung* (2nd edn., Leipzig, 1881–5).
Meloni, *Perseo*	P. Meloni, *Perseo e la fine della monarchia macedone* (Rome, 1953).
Meloni, *Valore storico*	P. Meloni, *Il valore storico e le fonti del libro macedonico di Appiano* (Rome, 1955).

xiv

Meltzer–Kahrstedt	O. Meltzer and U. Kahrstedt, *Geschichte der Karthager* (Berlin, 1879–1913).
Merten	M.-L. Merten, *Fides Romana bei Livius* (Frankfurt, 1965).
Mommsen, *RF*	Th. Mommsen, *Römische Forschungen* (Berlin, 1864–79).
Mommsen, *StR*	Th. Mommsen, *Römisches Staatsrecht* (Leipzig: vols. i–ii, 3rd edn., 1887, vol. iii, 1887–8).
Mommsen, *Strafrecht*	Th. Mommsen, *Römisches Strafrecht* (Leipzig, 1899).
MRR	T. R. S. Broughton, *The Magistrates of the Roman Republic* (New York, 1951–60).
Münzer, *RA*	F. Münzer, *Römische Adelsparteien und Adelsfamilien* (Stuttgart, 1920).
Nash	E. Nash, *Pictorial Dictionary of Ancient Rome* (London, 1961–2).
Neue–Wagener	F. Neue and C. Wagener, *Formenlehre der lateinischen Sprache* (3rd edn., Leipzig, 1892–1905).
Niese	B. Niese, *Geschichte der griechischen und makedonischen Staaten seit der Schlacht bei Chaeronea* (Gotha, 1893–1903).
Nisbet and Hubbard	R. G. M. Nisbet and M. Hubbard, *A Commentary on Horace: Odes book i* (Oxford, 1970).
Nissen, *IL*	H. Nissen, *Italische Landeskunde* (Berlin, 1883–1902).
Nissen, *KU*	H. Nissen, *Kritische Untersuchungen über die Quellen der vierten und fünften Dekade des Livius* (Berlin, 1863).
Ogilvie	R. M. Ogilvie, *A Commentary on Livy, books 1–5,* (Oxford, 1965).
Ogilvie, *Phoenix*	R. M. Ogilvie, Review of McDonald, *Phoenix,* xx (1966), 343–7.
OGIS	*Orientis Graeci Inscriptiones Selectae,* ed. W. Dittenberger (Leipzig, 1903–5).
Oost, *RPEA*	S. I. Oost, *Roman Policy in Epirus and Acarnania in the Age of the Roman Conquest of Greece* (Dallas, Tex., 1954).
*ORF*²	*Oratorum Romanorum Fragmenta,* ed. H. Malcovati (2nd edn., Pavia, 1955; cf. also the 3rd edn., Pavia, 1967).
Packard	D. W. Packard, *A Concordance to Livy* (Cambridge, Mass., 1968).
Paschkowski	I. Paschkowski, *Die Kunst der Reden in der 4. u. 5. Dekade des Livius* (Kiel, 1966).
Pédech	P. Pédech, *La Méthode historique de Polybe* (Paris, 1964).

Pettersson   O. Pettersson, *Commentationes Livianae* (Uppsala, 1930).

Petzold   K.-E. Petzold, *Die Eröffnung des zweiten römisch-makedonischen Krieges* (Berlin, 1940).

Pianezzola   E. Pianezzola, *Traduzione e ideologia: Livio interprete di Polibio* (Bologna, 1969).

P–K   A. Philippson and E. Kirsten, *Die griechische Landschaften* (Frankfurt, 1950–9).

Plathner   H. G. Plathner, *Die Schlachtschilderungen bei Livius* (Breslau, 1934).

Platner–Ashby   S. B. Platner and T. Ashby, *A Topographical Dictionary of Ancient Rome* (London, 1929).

Preuss   S. Preuss, *De bimembris dissoluti apud scriptores Romanos usu sollemni* (Edenkoben, 1881).

RE   *Real-Encyclopädie der classischen Altertumswissenschaft.*

Riemann   O. Riemann, *Études sur la langue et la grammaire de Tite-Live* (Paris, 1884).

Roesch   P. Roesch, *Thespies et la confédération béotienne* (Paris, 1965).

Rostovtzeff, *SEEHW*   M. I. Rostovtzeff, *Social and Economic History of the Hellenistic World* (Oxford, 1941).

Sage   E. T. Sage, *Livy with an English Translation, ix, books xxxi–xxxiv* (Loeb Classical Library; Cambridge, Mass., and London, 1935).

Salmon, *Colonization*   E. T. Salmon, *Roman Colonization under the Republic* (London, 1969).

Salmon, *Samnium*   E. T. Salmon, *Samnium and the Samnites* (Cambridge, 1967).

Schlag   U. Schlag, *Regnum in Senatu* (Stuttgart, 1968).

Schmitt, *Antiochos*   H. H. Schmitt, *Untersuchungen zur Geschichte Antiochos' des Grossen und seiner Zeit* (*Historia*, Einzelschriften, 6, Wiesbaden, 1964).

Schmitt, *Rom und Rhodos*   H. H. Schmitt, *Rom und Rhodos* (Munich, 1957).

Schmitt, *StV*, iii   H. H. Schmitt, *Die Staatsverträge des Altertums*, iii (Munich, 1969).

Schur, *SA*   W. Schur, *Scipio Africanus und die Begründung der römischen Weltherrschaft* (Leipzig, 1927).

Scullard, *RP*   H. H. Scullard, *Roman Politics, 220–150 B.C.* (Oxford, 1951).

SEG   *Supplementum Epigraphicum Graecum.*

Seibert   J. Seibert, *Historische Beiträge zu den dynastischen Verbindungen in Hellenistischer Zeit* (*Historia*, Einzelschriften, 10, Wiesbaden, 1967).

SGDI	*Sammlung der griechischen Dialektinschriften*, ed. H. Collitz and F. Bechtel (Göttingen, 1884–1915).
Sherk	R. K. Sherk, *Roman Documents from the Greek East* (Baltimore, Md., 1969).
Sherwin-White, *RC*	A. N. Sherwin-White, *The Roman Citizenship* (Oxford, 1939)
Skard	E. Skard, *Sallust und seine Vorgänger* (Oslo, 1956).
Stählin, *HTh*	F. Stählin, *Das hellenische Thessalien* (Stuttgart, 1924).
Stübler	G. Stübler, *Die Religiosität des Livius* (Stuttgart, 1941).
StV, iii	cf. Schmitt, *StV*, iii.
*Syll.*³	*Sylloge Inscriptionum Graecarum* (3rd edn., ed. W. Dittenberger, Leipzig, 1915–24).
Täubler	E. Täubler, *Imperium Romanum*, i (Leipzig, 1913).
Taylor, *RVA*	L. R. Taylor, *Roman Voting Assemblies* (Ann Arbor, Mich., 1966).
Thiel	J. H. Thiel, *Studies on the History of Roman Seapower in Republican Times* (Amsterdam, 1946).
TLL	*Thesaurus Linguae Latinae*
Toynbee	A. J. Toynbee, *Hannibal's Legacy* (London, 1965).
Tränkle, *Gnomon*	H. Tränkle, review of McDonald, *Gnomon* xxxix (1967), 365–80.
Tränkle, *WS*	H. Tränkle, 'Beobachtungen und Erwägungen zum Wandel der livianischen Sprache', *WS* lxxxi (1968), 103–52.
Travlos, *Bildlexikon*	J. Travlos, *Bildlexikon zur Topographie des antiken Athen* (Tübingen, 1971: the English version of this work was not available to me until after the Commentary was completed.)
Ullmann, *Étude*	R. Ullmann, *Étude sur le style des discours de Tite Live* (Oslo, 1929).
Volkmann	H. Volkmann, *Die Massenversklavungen der Einwohner eroberter Städte in der hellenistisch-römischen Zeit* (Abhandlungen der geistes- und sozialwissenschaftlichen Klasse, Akademie der Wissenschaften und der Literatur in Mainz, 1961 nr. 3; Wiesbaden, 1961).
Walbank, *Aratus*	F. W. Walbank, *Aratus of Sicyon* (Cambridge, 1933).
Walbank, *Commentary*	F. W. Walbank, *A Historical Commentary on Polybius* (Oxford, 1957–67).
Walbank, *Livy*	F. W. Walbank, 'The Fourth and Fifth Decades', *Livy*, ed. T. A. Dorey (London, 1971).

Walbank, *Philip V*	F. W. Walbank, *Philip V of Macedon* (Cambridge, 1940).
Walker, *Supplementary Annotations*	J. Walker, *Supplementary Annotations on Livy* (London, 1822).
Walsh, *CR*	P. G. Walsh, review of McDonald, *CR* N.S. xvii (1967), 53–6.
Walsh, *Livy*	P. G. Walsh, *Livy, His Historical Aims and Methods* (Cambridge, 1961).
Wege zu Livius	*Wege zu Livius*, ed. E. Burck (Darmstadt, 1967).
Wegner	M. Wegner, *Untersuchungen zu den lateinischen Begriffen Socius und Societas* (Göttingen, 1969).
Welwei	K.-W. Welwei, *Könige und Königtum im Urteil des Polybius* (Cologne, 1963).
Will, *HP*	E. Will, *Histoire politique du monde hellénistique* (Nancy, 1966–7).
Willems, *Le Sénat*	P. Willems, *Le Sénat de la république romaine* (Paris, 1878–83).
Wissowa, *RuK²*	G. Wissowa, *Religion und Kultus der Römer* (2nd edn., Munich, 1912).
Witte	K. Witte, 'Über die Form der Darstellung in Livius' Geschichtswerk', *RhM* lxv (1910), 270–305, 359–419.
W–M	W. Weissenborn and H. J. Müller, *Titi Livi ab urbe condita libri* (Berlin, 1880–1911: I refer to notes in this edition as 'W–M', whether they are the original notes of Weissenborn or fresh contributions by Müller: a reference to 'Weissenborn' alone refers to a note in one of the earlier editions [1853–78]).
Wülker	L. Wülker, *Die geschichtliche Entwicklung des Prodigienwesens bei den Römern* (Leipzig, 1903).
Zancan	P. Zancan, *Tito Livio* (Milan, 1940).

INTRODUCTION

I. SOURCES AND METHODS OF COMPOSITION

SINCE the publication of Nissen's *Kritische Untersuchungen über die Quellen der vierten und fünften Dekade des Livius* in 1863 it has been clear that it is possible to divide Livy's narrative into those sections which derive from Polybius and those which do not. The surviving fragments of Polybius allow this to be demonstrated for those sections of L. to which they correspond. The Polybian origin of those sections of L. to which no surviving fragments of Polybius correspond can be deduced in various ways[1]—they form part of a continuous narrative, other parts of which do correspond to surviving fragments of Polybius; they contain explanations of Greek terms,[2] thus indicating a Greek origin; they have detailed information on military matters or criticism of military tactics, a sphere in which Polybius was particularly interested and qualified;[3] they contain allusions to points of earlier Greek history which would not have been common knowledge in Rome.[4]

In books xxxi–xxxiii the following sections correspond to surviving portions of Polybius:

LIVY	POLYBIUS
xxxi. 14. 11–18. 8	xvi. 25–6, 28–34
xxxii. 32. 9–37. 5	xviii. 1–12
xxxii. 40. 8–11	xviii. 16–17. 5
xxxiii. 2. 1	xviii. 17. 6
xxxiii. 5. 4–13. 15	xviii. 18–27, 33–4, 36–9
xxxiii. 20. 2–3	xviii. 41a. 1
xxxiii. 21. 1–5	xviii. 41
xxxiii. 27. 5—28	xviii. 43, 40. 1–4
xxxiii. 30–5	xviii. 44–8
xxxiii. 39–40	xviii. 49–51

The further criteria allow us to see that Polybius' account of the campaign of Sulpicius by land and Apustius by sea is represented by

---

[1] On these criteria cf. especially Nissen, *KU*, ch. iv.

[2] On the *vocant* formula cf. xxxi. 24. 4 n.

[3] Cf. xxxi. 38 n.

[4] Cf. e.g. xxxiii. 20. 2. Omission of *cognomina* in most cases is another sign of Polybian origin.

xxxi. 22. 4–47. 3, that of the campaign of Villius in 199 by xxxii. 3–6. 4, that of the campaign of Flamininus in 198 by xxxii. 9. 6–25. 12, that of the events of winter 198/7 by xxxii. 32–40, that of the campaign of 197 by xxxiii. 1–17, that of other events in the Greek world in 197 by xxxiii. 18–21. 5, that of the events of winter 197/6 and summer 196 by xxxiii. 27. 5–35. 12, and that of the negotiations with Antiochus by xxxiii. 38–41.[1]

There remain the sections for which a Polybian origin cannot be deduced—xxxi. 1–13, 19–22. 3, 47. 4—50, xxxii. 1–2, 7–9. 5, 26–31, xxxiii. 21. 6–27. 5, 36–7, 42–45. 5. These sections deal with events in Rome and Italy—elections, decisions of the senate on various matters, accounts of prodigies, slave revolts, etc.—and also contain accounts of wars in northern Italy and Spain. These are matters with which Polybius did not concern himself in great detail although he did relate important senatorial decisions. It seems clear, then, that all these sections contain material which L. found in the works of his predecessors in writing the history of Rome, whom we usually call 'annalists'.[2] That conclusion is made even clearer by consideration of the way in which the Polybian and non-Polybian sections are joined together. Polybius' chronology was based on Olympiad years, running from late summer to late summer.[3] The annalists, on the other hand, used Roman consular years. At the time of the Second Macedonian War the consuls entered office on the Ides of March: but since in fact the Roman calendar was some two and a half months ahead of the corresponding Julian dates, the consular year began in the middle of winter.[4] L. evidently found difficulty in marrying these two systems together. His account of the consular year 200 runs from xxxi. 5. 1 to the end of book xxxi. He makes it clear that Sulpicius arrived late in the campaigning season (xxxi. 22. 4): it is thus obvious that the campaigns described in chapters 33–47 must in fact belong to the year 199. They had been related by Polybius in his (completely lost) book xvii under the Olympiad year 200/199. Since the events of the Olympiad year began in the consular year 200, L. put the whole account under that year. Villius' campaign was very short, and is therefore correctly assigned to the year 199: if he had campaigned in 198, no doubt L. would equally have put his campaign in 199. But Flamininus, consul in 198, went out much earlier (xxxii. 9. 6) and, though his initial campaign would have been described by Polybius under the

---

[1] On xxxi. 14–18 cf. pp. 7, 10, 46–7. On the sources of xxxii. 3 and xxxiii. 45. 6–49. 8 cf. nn. ad locc.

[2] I shall use the term, though really it is misleading. Polybius wrote equally annalistically.

[3] Cf. Walbank, *Commentary*, i. 35–7.   [4] On the calendar cf. p. 42.

Olympiad year 199/8, the connection with Flamininus' election to the consulship made it possible for L. to date the campaign correctly. Polybius began his book xviii with the Olympiad year 198/7. xxxii. 32–40 are placed by L. in the consular year 197, though they in fact belong to the winter of 198/7. So L. relates the continuation of Flamininus' command (xxxii. 28. 3–9) before the events that in fact preceded it. In this case L. has made the reverse error to that made in respect of the campaign of 199.[1] The events of summer 197 were continuous with the preceding section in Polybius and hence are correctly dated by L. The events of winter 197/6 (xxxiii. 27–9) are dated in 196, although in this case the events described in fact belong to the latter part of the winter, and so little inaccuracy is involved.[2] The events described in xxxiii. 38, however, are again misdated. L. writes as if the activities of Antiochus in northern Asia Minor belong to 196. In fact they almost certainly took place in autumn and winter 197/6. They were described by Polybius under the Olympiad year 197/6 and placed by L. in 196.[3]

Thus far there is little disagreement among scholars. But the situation is very different when we come to inquire more closely into L.'s sources in the non-Polybian sections. Nissen, with a few exceptions, did not attempt any further sub-divisions of the annalistic sections. But in the years that followed—the peak period of *Quellenforschung*—such attempts were made. Soltau,[4] on the basis of some *a priori* assumptions about the nature of the historical work of Piso, Valerius Antias, and Claudius Quadrigarius, divided the annalistic sections between them. With more attention to detail, Unger,[5] and later Kahrstedt,[6] adduced a number of alleged discrepancies in the annalistic sections and on this basis divided them between Valerius Antias and Claudius Quadrigarius. Reacting against this sort of procedure, Klotz[7] argued that many of the alleged discrepancies did not exist, and that Livy used Antias as his main source for books xxxi–xxxviii, only using Claudius as a check on him. Antias' treatment of the trials of the Scipios, however, so dismayed L. that in book xxxix and thereafter Claudius became the main source, with Antias used as the control. Since Klotz there has been little interest in *Quellenforschung*, though Zimmerer in her dissertation on Claudius used methods similar to those of Kahrstedt.[8]

---

[1] For cases of both types of dislocation in the third decade cf. De Sanctis, iii. 2. 327 ff., 440 ff.

[2] Cf. xxxiii. 30. 1 n. [3] Cf. xxxiii. 38. 1 n.

[4] *Philologus* lii (1894), 664–702, *Livius' Geschichtswerk* (Leipzig, 1897), ch. iv.

[5] *Philologus* Suppbd. iii (1878).

[6] *Die Annalistik von Livius, B. XXXI–XLV.*

[7] *Hermes* l (1915), 481–536, *Livius*, 1–100.

[8] M. Zimmerer, *Qu. Claudius Quadrigarius* (Munich, 1937). Cf. the review by

All attempts to divide L. into his sources on the basis of inconsistencies are doomed to failure. If L. was capable of including in his
history elements which contradicted one another, there is no reason
why one of his predecessors should not have done so. Even the first
person to write the history of an event may receive conflicting
information and, if he is not careful, fail to resolve the conflict.
Thus it was as unjustified for Kahrstedt to deduce different sources
from inconsistencies as it was unnecessary for Klotz to deny the
inconsistencies to refute Kahrstedt's view.[1]

It is, however, worth considering the alleged discrepancies in more
detail.[2] Some are not inconsistencies at all. There is nothing particularly odd about the fact that the appointment of C. Cornelius
Cethegus to Spain (xxxi. 49. 7) had not been previously mentioned.
The alleged aedileship of Flamininus in 201 (xxxi. 4. 5), which would
conflict with the statement in xxxii. 7. 10, stems only from a manuscript corruption of the *praenomen*. There is no inconsistency between
the placing of Carthaginian hostages at Signia and Ferentinum in
xxxii. 2. 4 and their presence at Setia in xxxii. 26. xxxi. 21. 10 does
not refer to the official number of a legion, and there is thus no
inconsistency with xxxiii. 22. 8 and xxxiii. 36. 5. There is no problem
in the addition of Spanish veterans at xxxi. 49. 5 to the African
veterans entitled to receive land by the provisions reported at xxxi.
4. 1. The colonies planned at xxxii. 29. 3 are settled at xxxiv. 45. 1—
the passages are not doublets. The fact that at xxxi. 8. 7 and 10. 1
trouble in Gaul is not expected does not prove that the war reported
at xxxi. 2. 5 ff. is an invention.[3] xxxi. 10. 3 does not imply that
Placentia was destroyed and thus conflict with xxxi. 21. 18. xxxiii.
22. 7 reports the comments of a hostile tribune, and it is not strange
that nothing corresponds to it in L.'s account of the Gallic campaign
in xxxii. 30 ff. The apparent conflict between xxxii. 29. 7 and 31. 4
on Clastidium can be explained without difficulty.

In other places, however, there are undeniable contradictions.
Some are small, and could easily be slips by L. himself or have stood
as such in his source. In this category are the facts that at xxxii. 28. 2
M. Sergius Silus is *praetor urbanus*, at xxxiii. 21. 9 *praetor peregrinus*,
and that the Spanish governor described as Cn. Cornelius Lentulus
at xxxi. 50. 11 has become Cn. Cornelius Blasio in xxxiii. 27. 1.

Klotz, *RhM* xci (1942), 268 ff. Similar methods are used for L.'s account of
Ligurian affairs by G. Mezzar-Zerbi, *RSC* vi (1958), 5–15, vii (1959), 152–62, viii
(1960), 329–40, xiii (1965), 66–78, 287–99, xiv (1966), 211–24.

[1] On a number of issues Klotz does allow the inconsistency to have stood in the
source. Zimmerer, 24, sees the principle correctly, but fails to apply it.
[2] Cf. in particular Kahrstedt, 38 ff. On all these matters see the notes on the
passages concerned.
[3] On this and the following points cf. Zimmerer, 26 ff.

The repetition at xxxii. 26. 1–2 of the information contained in xxxii. 9. 5 may be due only to L.'s carelessness. In other cases it is more likely that the variant accounts do stem from different sources. This must be true of the different versions on the fate of Pleminius at xxxi. 12. 7 and xxxiv. 44. 7,[1] and is probably the case with the different foundation dates at xxxi. 1. 4 and 5. 1 (cf. xxxiv. 54. 6), the apparent confusion between the events of 200 and 197 at xxxiii. 23. 1–2, and the conflict on the death of Hamilcar (xxxi. 21. 18, xxxii. 30. 12, xxxiii. 23. 5).[2]

The titulature of the governors of the Spanish provinces is a more complex problem. L. describes them variously as praetors, propraetors, and proconsuls. Kahrstedt believed that this was due to the use of two sources, one who referred to them as praetors or propraetors, the other who called them proconsuls. Klotz accepted that the variation between propraetor and proconsul reflected different sources, and to accommodate the evidence to his view that L. used first Antias and later Claudius as his main source, he claimed that cases of governors being called proconsuls in his 'Claudius section' were textual errors. His arguments for emendation in these cases, however, are extremely implausible. When governors appear as praetors in his 'Antias section', Klotz argued, they are still in their year of office and the usage does not conflict with his thesis. When C. Sempronius Tuditanus, praetor in 197 (xxxii. 27. 7, 28. 2), appears as proconsul in xxxiii. 25. 9, that is because the latter passage in fact refers to the following year. Klotz's conclusion is unnecessary. The evidence of the *Fasti* shows that the praetors governed as *praetor pro consule* in their year of office and as *pro consule* thereafter.[3] In the year of office, therefore, either *praetor* or *pro consule* is a correct title. But neither Kahrstedt nor Klotz commented on the fact that at

---

[1] At xxix. 22. 9 L. refers to the versions as variants, one coming from Clodius Licinus. Klotz's view (*Appians Darstellung des zweiten Punischen Krieges* [Paderborn, 1936], 68) that the version reported by Licinus also stood in Antias is absurd: cf. F. Grosso, *GIF* v (1952), 246.

[2] On the alleged conflicts between xxxiii. 43. 2 ff. and 44. 4 and between xxxi. 49. 7 and xxxiii. 26. 5 see xxxiii. 21. 6–9 n.

It is interesting to note the difficulties into which Kahrstedt's approach could lead him (61 ff.). In xxxi. 21. 18 Hamilcar is killed in 200, in xxxii. 30. 12 his capture in 197 is reported as a variant. Therefore the source of the main account of xxxii. 29–30 is the same as that of xxxi. 21. But xxxiii. 22–3, which has other conflicts with xxxii. 29–30, also has Hamilcar's death in 197 as a variant. But according to Kahrstedt's scheme, xxxiii. 22–3 must come from a source other than that of xxxii. 29–30. Kahrstedt weakly concludes that the variant in xxxiii. 23. 5 is only 'apparent'.

[3] Cf. W. F. Jashemski, *The Origins and History of the Proconsular and the Propraetorian Imperium to 27 B.C.* (Chicago, Ill., 1950), 40 ff., McDonald, *JRS* xliii (1953), 143–4.

xxxiii. 42. 5 Sempronius is called *praetor*, and on balance it does seem likely that the different titles in the two passages come from different sources.

It is clear enough that L. consulted at least two sources for his non-Polybian sections. At xxxiii. 36. 13 he quotes Antias and Claudius on the numbers of enemy dead and the amount of booty taken in the battle with the Gauls. But are these the only two Roman historians used throughout, and in what way did L. use his predecessors? It will be easier to answer this question if we first return to the Polybian sections and consider the way in which L. makes use of the material he found in Polybius.[1]

L. was far from simply translating Polybius. Sometimes, indeed, he appears to have mistranslated him. Such howlers as taking καταβαλοῦσι τὰς σαρίσας as *hastis positis* (xxxiii. 8. 13) are well known.[2] Other misunderstandings of the Greek in passages where Polybius survives can be seen at xxxii. 36. 8, xxxiii. 5. 9, 7. 3, 13. 7 ff., 30. 2, 34. 11, 35. 8, 40. 3: possible cases occur at xxxi. 15. 7, xxxiii. 6. 3, 12. 6. Similarly in Polybian sections where Polybius himself does not survive, misunderstanding of the Greek appears to have occurred at xxxi. 22. 4, 24. 4, 25. 2, 28. 1, 32. 4, 33. 6, 39. 6, xxxii. 5. 4, 40. 11, xxxiii. 17. 6, 18. 7, 18. 10, 41. 5. More doubtful cases occur at xxxii. 14. 5, 19. 9, 23. 9, 40. 4, xxxiii. 19. 9.

But apart from these, which are all matters of detail, it is clear that L. adapted Polybius to suit his own purposes. He introduces descriptions of emotions, ascribes motives, rearranges the order of points in speeches reported by Polybius, omits passages which seem to him of less importance.[3] Of his additions to Polybius a number can easily be regarded as no more than comments or interpretations by L. himself. In this category come such passages as xxxi. 15. 6, xxxii. 35. 1, xxxiii. 5. 12, 6. 7, 9. 11, 11. 2, 30. 4, 31. 10, 32. 5, 32. 6, 33. 5 ff. Some of these additions make sense, others introduce mistakes. They do not, however, affect matters of substance and there is no difficulty in attributing them to L. But there is also a number of places where there are significant additions, omissions, or alterations in the account of L. as compared with the corresponding passage of Polybius. In some cases the additions may convey information contained in other passages of Polybius read by L. but now

---

[1] Many of the important points about L.'s use of Polybius were noticed by Nissen, *KU*, ch. ii. Detailed study of L.'s adaptations of Polybius began with Witte, *RhM* lxv (1910), 270–305, 359–419. Cf. also Lambert, 58 ff., Walsh, *RhM* xcvii (1954), 97–114, McDonald, *JRS* xlvii (1957), 155–72.

[2] Cf. Walsh, *G & R* v (1958), 83–8. On the points that follow see the relevant notes.

[3] All these matters are analysed in the notes on the sections corresponding to the surviving passages of Polybius.

lost—this is probable for xxxi. 15. 5 and possible for xxxi. 15. 7, 15. 10, and xxxiii. 34. 2–3. We are left with a group of passages where more serious changes have occurred. The most striking of these are the suppression of the part played by the Roman ambassadors at Athens and the alterations to the account of the ultimatum delivered by M. Aemilius Lepidus at Abydus (xxxi. 14–18) and the series of alterations which have the effect of removing comments in Polybius which appear derogatory to Flamininus—including the possible suppression of the expulsion of the inhabitants of Elatia at xxxii. 24.[1] We must also take into account the alterations to xxxiii. 10. 5–6 to suppress indications of brutality and greed on the part of the Roman army, passages ascribing fear and panic to Philip (xxxiii. 7. 8, 10. 6), L.'s explanatory comment on the Isthmian games in xxxiii. 33. 1–2, and his information on the age of Flamininus at xxxiii. 33. 2.[2] It would be possible to hold that all these changes are due to L. himself. Most of the changes would be the result of L.'s desire to avoid criticism of Rome and Roman commanders, and to portray Philip in a bad light. The information on the Isthmian games would result from his reading of a handbook on the subject, that concerning Flamininus' age could be a false recollection of earlier information in Polybius. But it is equally possible that many of these changes reflect the version given by Roman annalists. We know that L. read both Claudius and Antias for events in the East: he refers to the discrepancies between them and Polybius at xxxii. 6. 5–8, xxxiii. 10. 8–10, 30. 8–11. But it is clear that L. can introduce non-Polybian material without acknowledging it as a variant. That is shown by the false addition of two clauses to the peace-terms with Philip in xxxiii. 30. 6.[3] It thus seems quite conceivable that some of the other variations also stem from the annalists. This would certainly make excellent sense for the consistent alterations in the account of the prelude to the Second Macedonian War. The mission of the Roman ambassadors is misrepresented in the annalistic section, and alterations to accord with this misrepresentation are made in the Polybian section. The motive for the change, as we shall see, is one that would have been far less likely to have influenced L. than his annalistic predecessors.[4] It also seems quite likely that the alterations in connection with Flamininus stem from the different picture of him painted by the annalists, and the information on

---

[1] Cf. xxxii. 24. 7 n. On the events at Athens and the Abydos ultimatum, cf. pp. 41–7, on Flamininus pp. 22–3 n. 4.

[2] Cf. also xxxi. 40. 6 n.

[3] Cf. n. ad loc.

[4] Similarly, it is very hard to believe that L. himself would have been responsible for such recherché alterations to Polybius as are alleged by Flurl (*Deditio in Fidem*, *passim*) in his claim that L. rejected Polybius' equation of *deditio* and *deditio in fidem*.

Flamininus' age may equally come from an annalistic source. If this is accepted, it becomes possible that some of the passages where I have attributed the alterations to L. himself, or to an otherwise lost passage of Polybius, are also of annalistic origin. Possible candidates are xxxiii. 33. 5 ff. and 34. 2–3.[1]

There can be no serious doubt that L. read Polybius for himself.[2] The stylistic changes and verbal parallels can only be explained on that hypothesis. If that is not enough the case is proved by the fact that L. can quote Claudius and Antias as variants to the Polybian version. It would pass credibility that the annalists indicated their own inventions and additions to Polybius. It can, however, be argued that in cases where the alterations are particularly far-reaching the contamination of Polybius occurred in the annalists, and was not produced by L. combining Polybian and annalistic accounts.[3] The strongest case for such a possibility would be xxxi. 14–18 which is consistent with the annalistic account of the sending of the three *legati* to Egypt in xxxi. 2. 3–4. Yet it is still very difficult to believe that L. could have followed Polybius so closely in many details, yet embellished his account in the way he does, if he had only read an annalist who had read Polybius. It is, however, quite likely that the annalists themselves perverted Polybius, and that it was this perverted account which L. combined with Polybius himself.[4] If there are passages where Polybius has been altered by an annalist, and the annalist alone used by L., they must lie in places where there are no such close verbal parallels between L. and Polybius.

---

[1] L.'s information on Flamininus' age (xxxiii. 33. 2) could also come from the annalistic tradition. But I doubt if so obscure a detail as the exact relationship of Q. Fabius to Flamininus (cf. xxxii. 36. 10 n.) would have been found in the annalists. Hammond (*JRS* lvi [1966], 52) argued that the differences between Plutarch and L. at xxxii. 9 ff. are due to L.'s use of an annalist. This could be so, but the differences may be alterations by Plutarch himself, or caused by the use of another source by Plutarch (on Plutarch's sources cf. R. E. Smith, *CQ* xxxiv [1940], 1 ff., xxxviii [1944], 89 ff.). Petzold, 105, sees xxxiii. 39. 7 as an example, but this is probably just L.'s own alteration. The speeches are a separate problem (cf. pp. 17–22).

[2] Dahlheim, 166–7, does seem to contemplate the possibility, but he misrepresents the position of Gelzer (see next note).

[3] Gelzer, *Gnomon* xviii (1942), 226 = *Kleine Schriften*, iii. 275.

[4] The arguments of Klotz (*SIFC* xxv [1951], 243 ff.) only show that it cannot be proved that they did. Badian (*Latin Historians* [London, 1966], 19) argues from the fact that Claudius had only three or four books between the end of the Hannibalic War and the Gracchi that 'the author did not discover Polybius'. Certainly he cannot have used Polybius to anything like the extent that L. did, but he could still have read him. Moreover book numbers in quotations are extremely liable to corruption and it cannot be regarded as certain that fr. 73 (137 B.C.) comes from book ix.

We can now return to the annalistic sections. First, did L. use only Claudius and Antias, or other Roman writers as well? In the fourth decade, apart from Polybius, Claudius, and Antias, the only specific references are to Cato (xxxiv. 15. 9) and, on an individual point, Rutilius (xxxix. 52. 1). On occasion L. refers to sources in a general way as in *ceteri Graeci Latinique auctores quorum quidem ego legi annales* (xxxii. 6. 8, cf. xxxix. 50. 10 *ab scriptoribus rerum Graecis Latinisque*), or *quidam auctores sunt* (xxxii. 30. 11, xxxiii. 23. 5). Since Nissen[1] it has generally been held that these phrases are misleading, and that in fact L. consulted only two sources in annalistic sections, three for eastern events. Now certainly such phrases as *quidam auctores sunt* may only refer to a variant in one source, but the phrase at xxxii. 6. 8 is a different matter. It seems very hard to take it to mean just Polybius and Claudius. L. admits that he may not have read all the history books, but he cannot mean that he only read three, two of which differed from the version of Valerius Antias. The absence of specific references to sources other than those mentioned is not significant. L. quotes sources so rarely that nothing can be deduced from non-quotation. *Ceteri Graeci Latinique auctores* may not mean that he has read any Greek historian other than Polybius— though there may have been such Greek writers independent of Polybius, and L. could have read them.[2] But it does mean that he read other Latin historians, and these may have included the second-century writers Cassius Hemina, Piso, Gellius, and Sempronius Tuditanus.[3] That he had read all of these is uncertain, but it is quite possible.

But how did L. use these earlier historians, and how did he compose his own narrative? In the Polybian sections it is clear enough that he followed Polybius reasonably closely, adding or correcting in matters of substance only rarely. Hence it has been assumed that he must have followed the same procedure in the non-Polybian sections, and that a given passage—whether quite short, as for

---

[1] *KU*, 47–8. Cf. for the first decade, Ogilvie, 5 ff. Klotz, *Livius*, 34, regarded the citation from Cato as coming from Claudius. Cf. n. 3. For a complete list of L.'s references to sources cf. R. B. Steele, *AJP* xxv (1904), 15 ff.

[2] For the possibility of such a work as the source of Appian's *Macedonica* cf. Meloni, *Valore storico*, Balsdon, *JRS* xlvi (1956), 199–201; *contra* Gelzer, *BO* xiv (1957), 55 ff. = *Kleine Schriften*, iii. 280 ff.

[3] Cf. *HRR* i. 98 ff. (Cassius Hemina), 120 ff. (Piso), 143 ff. (Sempronius), 148 ff. (Gellius). Sempronius Asellio probably did not deal with this period in detail. Similarity of language between Piso fr. 34 and L. xxxix. 6. 7 cannot prove the use of Piso, as Soltau (*Livius' Geschichtswerk*, 30) argued.

For arguments that L. used Cato directly in the fourth and fifth decades cf. Tränkle, *Abh. Mainz Ak.* (geistes- und sozialwissenschaftlichen Klasse), 1971 nr. 4 (an enlarged version of his paper in *Forschungen zur römischen Literatur* [Wiesbaden, 1970], 274–85).

Soltau and Kahrstedt, or of considerable length, as for Klotz—can be assigned to a single source, the other source or sources being used only for variations and corrections. But it is by no means certain that the procedure was the same in Polybian and non-Polybian sections. L. knew that for Greek matters Polybius was pre-eminent.[1] But for Roman and Italian affairs no one author had such a pre-eminence. Moreover we must remember the constraints imposed by the difficulties of reading a book in the ancient world. The ancient writer of history could not, like a modern scholar, have a large number of books open on his desk. He could read, or have read to him, just one roll at a time. From it he could make, or have made, notes on what he had read.[2] When L. came to write his own account he would no doubt refer closely to Polybius for the Greek sections. But for other matters he may not have gone back directly to the books themselves—he may have used his notes or even relied on his memory. Hence in the non-Polybian sections it may be that L.'s narrative often represents his own account based on what he has read, and except for specific citations cannot be assigned to individual sources. Certainly alleged characteristics of the individual annalists cannot enable us to spot their influence in L. Even if we decide, for example, that the differing nomenclature of the Spanish provinces indicates different sources, it does not follow that one source alone has been used for the passage in which the indication occurs.[3]

As we have seen, there are clear breaks between the annalistic and Polybian sections. In most years L. gives first an annalistic section, then the material from Polybius, and finally another annalistic section (in 200 and 196 there are three annalistic sections, the second one dividing the Polybian section). It is wrong, however, to ask precisely where the divisions between the sections come. The history that L. gives us is his own and he adapts his material to suit his own purposes. The transitions are his way of linking his material together, and it is futile to seek for the origin of such passages as xxxi. 14. 1–5, xxxiii. 19. 6, 45. 5.[4] Again passages concerning

[1] Cf. xxx. 45. 5, xxxiii. 10. 10—deliberate meiosis, not lukewarm praise.

[2] Cf. the younger Pliny's description of his uncle's methods in *Ep.* iii. 5.

[3] There is no justification for Badian's statement (*Latin Historians*, 19) that 'Claudius' lack of interest in politics and personalities is phenomenal: he is not even cited for the trials of the Scipios'. The non-citation of Claudius does not mean that he did not deal with the trials. It is true that he described battles at length, but he clearly dealt with political matters also. A random selection of fragments from L. would contain a great deal of military material.

[4] It is wrong to assert, as do Nissen, *KU*, 105, and Klotz, *Livius*, 3, that the use of *Macedonia* to mean northern Greece as a whole indicates an annalistic source. L. naturally described it as *Macedonia*, and it was natural for him to use it in introducing Eastern sections, as at xxxi. 14. 2, xxxii. 3. 2.

elections, assignment of provinces, games, short notices from abroad, and so forth are often, and probably rightly, regarded as basic annalistic material stemming from the *annales maximi*. Yet even here we find such passages as xxxii. 27. 3 with moral comments on Cato, or xxxiii. 26. 5–6 with general remarks on the war in Spain. Whether these are due to L. or his source, however, is uncertain.

We have seen the presence of annalistic material in the Polybian sections. Are there conversely any Polybian passages in the annalistic sections? L. presumably read the whole of Polybius, yet in books xxxi–xxxiii[1] he clearly chose not to follow his account of events at Rome. His omission of Polybius' story of the senatorial decision not to relieve Flamininus of his command (xxxii. 37) is part of his suppression of the criticism of Flamininus in Polybius, but the same cannot be true of his use of an annalistic version of Marcellus' opposition to the making of peace in 196 (xxxiii. 25. 4–7) in preference to that of Polybius xviii. 42. It seems that just as he found Polybius superior to the annalists for Eastern events, so for domestic matters he found the detailed history of the annalists preferable to Polybius. In one passage, however, (xxxiii. 44. 8) there are echoes of Polybian language (*haerere et aliud in visceribus Graeciae ingens malum*) in what is clearly an annalistic passage. But again it is impossible to tell whether this is due to L. himself or to his annalistic predecessor.

How reliable was the information given by the annalists?[2] In many cases they are clearly guilty of invention. Antias created a victory of Villius in 199 (xxxii. 6. 5–6) and both he and Claudius made additions to the peace-treaty with Philip (xxxii. 30). Antias was often criticized by L. for his absurd exaggerations of the numbers of enemy dead (xxxiii. 10. 8, cf. iii. 5. 13, xxx. 19. 11, xxxvi. 19. 12, 38. 6–7, xxxviii. 23. 8, xxxix. 41. 6).[3] The events preceding the Second Macedonian War are violently distorted, and the reports of reinforcements for the army in Greece seem unacceptable (xxxii. 1. 2 n.). On the other hand a lot of their material is rightly seen as going back to the *annales maximi* or other archival material,[4] and

---

[1] Sometimes L. does follow Polybius on Roman matters: cf. e.g. xxxvii. 52–6, xlii. 47 ff.

[2] For a long time, following Nissen, 'annalistic' was regarded as almost equivalent to 'false'. Holleaux contributed a lot to this attitude, and it reached its peak in Petzold's wholesale rejection of the annalistic evidence for the beginning of the Second Macedonian War. The main defence of the annalistic tradition came from Klotz. In Britain Balsdon challenged the common view in *CQ* n.s. iii (1953), 158 ff., *JRS* xliv (1954), 30 ff. A good survey of approaches to the problem will be found in Bredehorn, 1 ff. But Bredehorn's own wholesale defence of almost everything in the annalists is absurd.

[3] Cf. Brunt, 695.

[4] Recently E. Rawson (*CQ* n.s. xxi [1971], 158–69) has argued that the *annales*

a number of passages which scholars have declared fabrications are probably authentic (e.g. xxx. 26. 2–4, 42. 1–10, xxxi. 3. 3–6, xxxii. 8. 9–16). In some cases the annalistic account is preferable to the Polybian (xxxiii. 45. 4 against xxxiv. 22. 5).[1] For the rest one must decide each case on historical grounds alone, and without general preconceptions about the reliability of the annalists. Thus the danger from Gaul in these years may be exaggerated, though that cannot be proved. As we have seen, some of the inconsistencies that have been detected in L.'s account of the Gallic wars are not such at all. Others remain; but that may indicate only uncertainty about what happened, not that the whole account is an invention. Where there are inventions, there is no need to ascribe them all to the annalists of the Sullan age. Piso was certainly not free from inventions.[2]

2. LANGUAGE AND STYLE

At the very beginning of the fourth decade Livy demonstrates his awareness of the vast ground he has still to cover.[3] With Polybius as his main source for Eastern events and plentiful detail on domestic affairs in his annalistic predecessors, he had an abundance of material for each year—embassies to and from foreign parts, details of campaigns, peace-treaties, and settlements. Though important, it might not have seemed very exciting—at least in comparison with the great episodes from the early centuries of the Republic. To many that has seemed a sufficient explanation of the difference in tone and style between the earlier and later books. That there is some such difference is prima facie apparent to the reader.[4] Its precise nature, however, is a matter of dispute.

maximi were not used by the annalists to any extent. Her principal arguments are (i) that inconsistencies in the prodigy lists suggest compilation from a number of sources, (ii) that Varro does not refer to the *annales* for prodigies, (iii) that when Cicero wanted to find out the names of the *x legati* of 146 (*ad Att.* xiii. 4, 5, 6, 30, 32, 33) he did not think of looking in the *annales*. But (i) the sorts of prodigies reported and accepted may in fact have varied from year to year, (ii) Rawson admits that most of Varro's prodigies are from the post-Gracchan period, after the publication of the *annales*, (iii) the fact that certain lists of *legati* were not included does not mean that all were not, or that lists occurring in L. do not come from the *annales*. (It is noticeable that L. does not list the names of the *x legati* for the settlements of 201 and 196.)

[1] The prime example of this is xxxvii. 56. 1–6, the *s.c.* for the settlement of Apamea. The detail of this is far superior to the general statements of xxxvii. 55. 4–6 = Pol. xxi. 24. 7–8.

[2] Cf. K. Latte, *SB Berl. Ak.* (1960), nr. 7, Badian, *Latin Historians*, 13. Klotz, *Livius*, 99, held that inventions began with the Sullan annalists.

[3] xxxi. 1. 1–5.

[4] Cf. the general comments of Norden and Löfstedt quoted by McDonald, *JRS* xlvii (1957), 167.

For long almost all scholars accepted the view, first adumbrated by Wölfflin,[1] and developed in detail by Stacey,[2] that in the earlier books L. made a deliberate effort to introduce a poetic flavour into his narrative by using words and phrases found in the poets but not used by Cicero. In the later books, Stacey argued, L. reverted closer to the norms of Ciceronian prose.

A frontal attack on Stacey's position was launched by Gries in 1949.[3] Gries claimed (i) that a large number of Stacey's alleged poeticisms were not poeticisms at all, (ii) that in many cases the occurrences of the usages concerned in the later books were as frequent as, or not significantly less frequent than those in the first decade. In many instances Gries had a strong case, but its impact was considerably lessened by his refusal to acknowledge the importance of the occasions where Stacey's case remained unchallenged,[4] and by his extremely simplistic approach to the early history of Latin literature—he regarded the language of Plautus and Terence as entirely colloquial and was apparently unaware of the development of the style of Latin historiography before L. Gries did not deny that in some instances L.'s style changed and that in some parts L. consciously imported an old-fashioned flavour: he claimed though that he merely 'adapts his style to the events and the atmosphere of the period with which he is currently dealing', but did not deliberately import words culled from his reading of the poets.[5]

Recent studies have tended towards a compromise position. In 1957 McDonald[6] argued that when L.'s attention was sufficiently engaged on a particular episode in the later books, he was quite capable of writing in a way reminiscent of the earlier books; at other times he was more straightforward. A similar position is taken by Walsh: 'such poetic expressions became naturally rarer in the more sober transactions of later years, but they are employed when apposite events demand them'.[7] McDonald seems to have arrived at his view largely intuitively—at least he adduces only L.'s account of the capture of Abydus (xxxi. 17–18). His case, however, has been given striking confirmation by Tränkle's fundamental study.[8] Tränkle emphasizes that in a large number of instances Stacey's

---

[1] *Livianische Kritik und livianischer Sprachgebrauch* (Berlin, 1864), 28–9 (= *Ausgewählte Schriften* [Leipzig, 1933], 18 ff.), *Antiochos von Syrakus und Coelius Antipater* (Winterthur, 1872), 85 ff.

[2] *ALL* x (1898), 17–82. For the acceptance of Stacey's position, cf. Tränkle *WS*, 106 n. 13.

[3] *Constancy in Livy's Latinity* (New York, 1949).

[4] Cf. Gries, 125–6, nn. 41 and 42.

[5] Gries, 4–5.

[6] *JRS* xlvii, 157–72.

[7] Walsh, *Livy*, 249.

[8] Tränkle, *WS*.

case stands fast, and indeed he adds to his list of non-classical usages which appear in the first decade. But he also produces examples of three other groups of usages not found in classical prose: (a) those which appear in all parts of the work, (b) those which appear in the beginning, disappear for many books, and reappear in the later books, (c) those which appear only in the later books. Tränkle gives further force to his case by showing that L.'s account of the death of Cicero, preserved in the elder Seneca,[1] contains a large number of poetic elements.

Tränkle's second great contribution was to set L. in his place in the historiographical tradition.[2] Latin historiography began with the elder Cato. It was Cato, too, who was probably responsible for the first consciously planned Latin oratory.[3] That was the beginning of stylistic Latin prose. Previously of course there were laws, *senatus consulta*, treaties, and religious formulas; speeches were made in lawsuits, the senate, or *contiones*. But the language of the former was largely formulaic, as we can see in the *s.c. de Bacchanalibus*, and of the second probably little different from the colloquial Latin of the time. Something more impressive was needed, above all in vocabulary. Cato built his vocabulary in two ways. First, he took over words used by the poets. Latin poetry had come into existence in the second half of the third century; the poets, too, needed impressive language and to a considerable extent, no doubt, coined the words they needed. Cato used some of these neologisms, but he also added his own. Horace refers to the way in which both Ennius and Cato enriched the Latin language by neologisms.[4] It seems probable that this process continued throughout the second century, not necessarily in imitation of Cato but still because of the need to expand the available vocabulary.[5]

---

[1] Seneca, *Suas.* vi. 17, 22.

[2] On the development of prose style cf. E. Norden, *Die Antike Kunstprosa* (Leipzig, 1898), i. 164 ff., W. Kroll, *Glotta* xxii (1934), 1 ff., A. D. Leeman, *Orationis Ratio* (Amsterdam, 1963), especially chs. i–iii, F. Kuntz, *Die Sprache des Tacitus und die Tradition der lateinischen Historikersprache* (Heidelberg, 1962), especially ch. iii, Lebek, *Verba Prisca*, especially 194–290.

[3] On the language of Cato cf. R. Till, *Philologus* Suppbd. xxviii, 2 (1935), Lebek, 48–51, 210–11.   [4] *AP* 56–9, cf. Fronto, p. 62N.

[5] Thus apparent oddities in e.g. Fannius and Coelius Antipater are not indicative of a deliberate 'historical style', as is argued by Badian, *Latin Historians*, 14 and 32 n. 63, 17 and 33 n. 77. For the 'oddities' are found also in oratory—*poteratur* in Gaius Gracchus (*ORF²*, fr. 35), *potestur* in Scipio Aemilianus (*ORF²*, fr. 27), adjectives in *-osus* in Scipio (fr. 17), nouns ending in *-mentum*, favoured later by Sallust, in Gaius Gracchus (fr. 43). Some of these instances may simply be forms in use at the time, others are neologisms (if, it seems, one needed to coin an adjective, one ended it in *-osus*, if an adverb, in *-im*). Since at the time oratory and historiography are the only forms of conscious prose—formal letters, philosophical discourses, rhetorical treatises do not yet exist in Latin—there can be no question

With the historians of the Sullan age, however, there begins a clear 'historical style', an attempt to write in the way in which history had been written in the past. This is seen particularly clearly in the cases of Claudius Quadrigarius and Cornelius Sisenna—both were noted for neologisms and for archaisms.[1] In this tradition comes Sallust—he is explicitly stated to have ransacked the works of Cato for archaisms.[2] In his peculiar sentence structure Sallust was unique, but in his vocabulary he was following a tradition.

That was the historiographical tradition as L. found it. He reacted against Sallust's excessive brevity and obscurity, but he could not altogether ignore his influence.[3] To begin with, then, his vocabulary is nearer to Sallust. There is a number of cases where usages common to Sallust and L. are not found in classical prose, and these are particularly common in the first decade.[4] Skard, indeed, collected a considerable number of such instances, but, convinced that L.'s antipathy to Sallust would not have permitted him to take over Sallustian words, he argued that both Sallust and L. derived them from their annalistic predecessors.[5] Tränkle plausibly argues that the changes in L.'s style can be seen, in part at least, as a moving away from the influence of Sallust.

In what precedes I have used the terms 'archaic' and 'poetical' indiscriminately. As has often been stressed they are not identical. It is easy to see, however, how both could be used by historical writers. If a historian looked to his predecessors for his vocabulary, he would find both words culled from the early poets, and others which, though not used by the poets, had gone out of common usage. The former often continued in poetic vocabulary, and were therefore both poetic and archaic, the latter merely archaic. In addition, Sallust and L. were aware of the borrowing from the poets by their

---

of a purely historical style. Even when Coelius used archaisms (on *topper* in fr. 47 cf. Lebek, 222) and tried to emulate Ennius (Fronto, p. 62N), his aim was to write impressively, not to display a specifically historical style. Cf. on the whole question Lebek, 194–290, who seems to me, however, to underestimate the degree of archaism in the Sullan annalists (see next note).

[1] Cf. Badian, *Latin Historians*, 20 and 26.

[2] Suet. *DA* 86, *de gramm.* 15. On the style of Sallust cf. R. Syme, *Sallust* (Berkeley and Los Angeles, Cal., 1964), 257 ff., Lebek, 291 ff., A. La Penna, *Sallustio e la rivoluzione romana* (Milan, 1968), 366 ff.

[3] Tränkle (*WS*, 149–52) rightly stresses that L.'s objections were only to Sallust's excesses. Seneca's report that 'Livius tam iniquus Sallustio fuit, ut hanc ipsam sententiam et tamquam translatam et tamquam corruptam dum transfertur obiceret Sallustio' (*Contr.* ix. 1. 14) should not be taken to indicate a complete antipathy, and the statements that L. urged the avoidance of archaic words (Sen. *Contr.* ix. 2. 26) and advised his son to read Demosthenes and Cicero (Quint. x. 1. 39) refer to oratory, not historiography. Cf. also Lebek, 199 ff.

[4] Cf. Tränkle, *WS*, 131 ff.   [5] Skard, ch. i.

15

predecessors, and themselves took words from poets of their own age which were not necessarily archaic.[1]

In the structure of his prose, of course, L. is very different from Sallust. As has often been said, L. fulfilled Cicero's ideal of historiography as an *opus oratorium*, as it had been in the hands of certain Greek historians, but not of any of L.'s Latin predecessors.[2] It was L. who introduced fully developed periodic structure into Latin historical writing.[3]

The fourth decade, then, does not differ from earlier books in exhibiting a variety of styles. The most powerful writing is kept for what L. regarded as the most important episodes—in books xxxi–xxxiii the siege of Abydus (xxxi. 17–18), the conference of Nicaea (xxxii. 32–7), the battle of Cynoscephalae (xxxiii. 6–10), the proclamation of the Isthmus (xxxiii. 32–3). There is a number of poetic usages—*letum* at xxxi. 18. 7, *interfari* at xxxii. 34. 2, xxxiii. 12. 12, *nimbus* at xxxiii. 6. 12, *mussare* at xxxiii. 31. 1, *marcescere* at xxxiii. 45. 7. At xxxiii. 20. 13 we have *non operae est*, a phrase which, apart from L., is used commonly only by Plautus. An archaism which had become part of the historiographical tradition can be seen in *virile ac muliebre secus* at xxxi. 44. 4, while *invicti animi* (xxxiii. 11. 7) and *paucis absolvit* (xxxiii. 12. 2) are unusual phrases which may have been suggested to L. by his reading of Sallust.[4] There are several examples of striking word-order, some to achieve emphasis, others the purpose of which is less clear.[5] And at xxxi. 30. 6 there is an anacoluthon unparalleled in the rest of his work.

Some passages—straight reports of elections, assignments of provinces and armies, games, prodigies, etc.—are reported in a flat matter-of-fact style. Some have argued that this is due to L.'s use of unadorned 'annalistic' material—he is not interested in it, and does

[1] In the case of neologisms L. showed considerable restraint—for examples cf. Gries, index s.v. *Livy, innovations and neologisms*, Walsh, *Livy*, 260, Badian, *Latin Historians*, 34 n. 96.

[2] Cicero thought that Coelius Antipater, Licinius Macer, and Sisenna had made some attempt at what was needed (*de or.* ii. 54, *legg.* i. 6–7). Cicero is thinking entirely in terms of sentence structure, not of vocabulary.

[3] On L.'s periodic style, cf. McDonald, *JRS* lvii (1957), 164 ff., Walsh, *Livy*, 250 ff., K. Lindemann, *Beobachtungen zur livianischen Periodenkunst* (Marburg, 1964), J. P. Chausserie-Laprée, *L'Expression narrative chez les historiens romains* (Paris, 1969), 1–338.   [4] On all these passages cf. nn. ad locc.

[5] See the notes to xxxi. 14. 9, 22. 6, xxxiii. 15. 2, 41. 7, 42. 10, 49. 5: cf. also xxxi. 3. 5 n., xxxiii. 18. 12 n. It has long been recognized that L.'s word order and syntax are not those of Cicero and that it is wrong to alter his text to make him conform to Ciceronian standards (as Madvig tended to, despite his awareness of the differences—cf. his *Kleine philologische Schriften*, ii. 356 ff.). But one must beware of going to the other extreme and defending MS. readings which are not Latin at all—as is done by Pettersson in his *Commentationes Livianae*. Where to draw the line must be a matter for judgement in each individual case.

not care to work it up. But it may be that L. knew that this was the kind of material found in the *annales*, and deliberately used the appropriate style.[1] In the case of prodigies, L.'s lists contain certain unusual stylistic features, such as omission of subject, but it is clear that the individual accounts have been carefully worked up by L.[2] For rapid action in battles, L. uses the crisp, military style partly to reflect the speed of the action, partly in imitation of military dispatches.[3]

Not all of L.'s work exhibits the same degree of polish. xxxi. 21–22. 3 has a number of signs of not having been worked up with L.'s usual care, and other indications of haste of composition may be seen in the looseness of construction at xxxi. 3. 5–6, xxxiii. 49. 3, the unstylistic repetitions at xxxi. 11. 3, 42. 6–7, 43. 2, xxxiii. 36. 4, 48. 4, and the obscurity of expression at xxxi. 46. 2. Some of these occur in passages of no great moment, but two come from the story of the flight of Hannibal from Carthage, which in other ways suggests, as one might expect, careful writing. There is highly poetical language at xxxiii. 45. 7, and the flight itself in xxxiii. 48 is narrated in a free-flowing, almost Herodotean style. Had he had time to revise the passage, one feels, the inelegancies would have been removed.

3. THE SPEECHES[4]

The importance of the speeches in L.'s work has long been recognized. Even if, following Taine, we regard the whole of his history as primarily the work of a skilled orator, it will be obvious that it is in the speeches above all that we should look for evidence of that skill.

Books xxxi–xxxiii contain four full-scale speeches in *oratio recta*—the speech of Sulpicius urging the *comitia centuriata* to reverse its decision to reject the proposal to go to war with Macedon (xxxi. 7), the speeches of the Macedonian and Roman envoys at the conference of the Aetolian League in spring 199[5] (xxxi. 29 and 31), and the speech of Aristaenus to the Achaean League in 198 (xxxii. 21). In addition there is the first short speech of Aristaenus in

---

[1] Cf. McDonald, *JRS* xlvii (1957), 155–6.

[2] Luterbacher, 57 ff. Cf. xxxii. 1. 10 n., 29. 1 n.

[3] Cf. xxxi. 23. 6–7 n.

[4] See especially on the speeches H. V. Canter, *AJP* xxxviii (1917), 125–51, R. Ullmann, *La Technique des discours dans Salluste, Tite-Live et Tacite* (Oslo, 1927), 133 ff., *Étude, passim*, Bornecque, 155 ff., Walsh, *Livy*, 219–44. On the speeches at the Aetolian conference (xxxi. 29–31), Burck, *Wege zu Livius*, 452–63. I. Paschkowski, *Die Kunst der Reden in der 4. u. 5. Dekade des Livius* (Kiel, 1966), does not deal specifically with the speeches in books xxxi–xxxiii.

[5] Not in 200 as Burck, l.c., states. Hence the Athenian speech in xxxi. 30 does not contain the chronological 'Unklarheiten' to which Burck refers.

xxxii. 20. 3–6 and—following Polybius—mixtures of direct and indirect speech in the appeal of Philip to the Achaean League (xxxi. 25)
and in the conferences of Antigonea (xxxii. 10), Nicaea (xxxii. 32–7),
and Tempe (xxxiii. 13). There is, of course, a very large number
of reported remarks in *oratio obliqua* but among these the Athenian
speech before the Aetolian League (xxxi. 30) and the speeches of the
Roman envoys and Antiochus at the conference of Lysimachia
(xxxiii. 39–40) can rank as the equivalent of full speeches, and
mention should also be made of the short speeches of Philip
and Flamininus before the battle of Cynoscephalae (xxxiii. 3. 11–
4. 3, 8. 4–5). L.'s rhetorical technique can certainly be discerned in
oratio obliqua speeches,[1] but the four main *oratio recta* speeches are of
greater length, and I propose to confine my attention to them.[2]

The first problem concerns the provenance of the speeches. It is
clear that their form is largely L.'s own creation. But did he find
speeches of any sort in his sources at the places where he inserted
them? *A priori*, we might expect that he did. The practice of inserting speeches in historical narrative went back, of course, to Herodotus, and had been followed by many of the Roman annalists. L.
was relatively restrained in his use of speeches, reserving them for
what he regarded as important occasions. It would thus be plausible
to think that on these occasions he found, if not a full-blown speech,
at least an indication of one. It is only in the surviving portions of
Polybius that such a supposition can be checked, and these do indeed
confirm it. There is a number of cases where both Polybius and L.
have a speech, and no case where it can be demonstrated that a
Livian speech did not have a counterpart in Polybius[3]—though it is
highly probable that such speeches before battle as xxxvi. 17 and
xxxviii. 17 are inspired by non-Polybian sources.[4] Direct comparison
is not possible for any of the *oratio recta* speeches in books xxxi–
xxxiii, though we do have the Polybian original for the mixture of
direct and indirect speech at the conferences of Nicaea and Tempe,
and for the indirect speeches at Lysimachia. Of the four direct
speeches, the speeches at the Achaean and Aetolian League meetings were clearly the sort of thing that would be of great interest to
Polybius.[5] Both occasions concern the taking of vitally important
decisions by the two confederations on whether or not to throw in

---

[1] Cf. Lambert, *passim*, Walsh, *Livy*, 243.

[2] For statistics on all forms of speeches in the fourth and fifth decades cf.
Paschkowski, 9.   [3] Cf. Pédech, 277.

[4] Cf. Ullmann, *La Technique*, 20, 147–8, 157–8.

[5] Cf. Pédech, 266. Burck's reasons (*Wege zu Livius*, 453, 455) for thinking that
the speeches at the Aetolian conference are entirely due to L. are unconvincing.
They are (i) the chronological difficulties, on which cf. p. 17 n. 5, (ii) the fact that
the Athenian and Macedonian speakers are not named at the beginning of their

their lot with Rome. On both occasions the true nature of Roman policy and Roman imperialism, matters which were always of concern to Polybius, were called into question. We cannot, of course, be certain that there were speeches in Polybius on these occasions, but it is highly probable.

The speech of Sulpicius, on the other hand, occurs in a non-Polybian section and L. may have found some sort of speech at this point in one, or more, of his annalistic sources. As with the speeches at the conferences of the Aetolian and Achaean Leagues, the decision to be taken was one of vital importance. The fresh introduction at the beginning of book xxxi shows that L. was aware of the big new step that was taken with Rome's decision to go to war with Macedon in 200. If the *comitia* had not reversed its decision, the whole story of the years covered by books xxxi–xlv might have been very different.

We turn now to the four speeches themselves. Ullmann has provided a detailed analysis of L.'s speeches. In *La Technique des discours* he is concerned with the structure of the speeches and the arrangements of their arguments, in *Étude sur le style* with the actual language and style, the way in which the arguments are expressed. The former the ancient rules of rhetoric subsumed under *inventio* and *dispositio*, the latter under *elocutio*. L. had views on oratory,[1] and may well have himself taken part in the declamations of the Augustan age. There can be no doubt that he was well acquainted with the principles and distinctions which formed part of ancient rhetorical theory. Ullmann, therefore, presents analyses of L.'s speeches which divide them, for the most part, into an introduction (*prooemium*), an argument (*tractatio*), and a peroration (*conclusio*). The *tractatio* is further divided into its detailed arguments, under the headings of the various τόποι indicated in ancient rhetorical writings—*tutum, utile, possibile, honestum, dignum*, etc.[2] Ullmann admits that there are cases in the fourth and fifth decades where L. appears to be following the order of a Polybian speech and not dividing it according to rhetorical principles. Such are the speech of the Roman envoy in 199 and those of Eumenes and the Rhodians before the senate in 189 (xxxvii. 53–4).[3] Ullmann is clearly right to refuse to

speeches. But L. often omits non-Roman names which do not interest him (cf. xxxi. 17. 2, xxxii. 32. 10–11, 36. 10, xxxiii. 7. 7–8, 7. 11, 12. 3–4, 34. 2, 39. 2, Nissen, *KU*, 28). But Burck is right to object to Ullmann's argument (*La Technique*, 135) that the sandwiching of the Athenian speech in *oratio obliqua* between the two direct speeches shows Polybian origin. For such a practice elsewhere in L. cf. iii. 44–8.

[1] Cf. p. 15 n. 3.
[2] Ullmann's analyses are followed by Ogilvie for the speeches in books i–v.
[3] *La Technique*, 17, Walsh, *Livy*, 221.

try to divide the *tractatio* in cases like these. The reason for the structure of such speeches is probably not so much that L.'s interest was not sufficiently engaged to produce a full rhetorical composition at these points as that the matter in hand was best dealt with by a point-by-point argument of the sort that Polybius had used. It is equally true that for a large number of speeches, particularly in the earlier books, Ullmann's analysis appears to be correct. It seems to me, however, that in a number of cases the divisions and distinctions introduced by Ullmann are not really to be found in the text of L. I believe this to be the case in some earlier speeches, but I restrict my discussion to the speeches in books xxxi–xxxiii.

First, the speech of Sulpicius. Ullmann divides it as follows.[1] (i) § 2 *prooemium*: your only choice is whether to fight Philip in Italy or in Macedonia. (ii) §§ 3–12 *tractatio*. (a) §§ 3–5 *possibile*: if we had helped Saguntum immediately, the Second Punic War could have been fought in Spain, not Italy. Even then we kept Philip in Macedon; are we not to do it now? (b) §§ 6–7 *prudens*: if we do not act, Philip will soon be in Italy. (c) §§ 8–12 *tutum*: Philip would be much more dangerous than Pyrrhus. (iii) §§ 13–15 *conclusio*. On the main divisions of the speech I have no quarrel with Ullmann. It is the sub-divisions of the *tractatio* which seem to me artificial. *Prudens* and *tutum* could describe any of the three sections. It would be fairer to say that the whole of the *tractatio* is an elaboration of the point made in the *prooemium*—invade Macedon now or you will have a war in Italy. The arguments for this are: (i) if you had invaded Spain, the Second Punic War, like the first, would not have been fought in Italy; (ii) you invaded Macedon even during the Hannibalic War: surely you can do it now with the Punic danger removed; (iii) give Philip any time, and he will be in Italy; (iv) he will be a far greater danger than Pyrrhus; (v) many Italian states will join him. All these arguments, if one wants to give them a name, are simply sub-divisions of the *utile*—which Aristotle regarded as the sole aim of deliberative orations.[2]

Much the same seems to me true of the Macedonian speech at the meeting of the Aetolian League. Ullmann analyses thus.[3] (i) §§ 4–5 *prooemium*: Rome is inconsistent in first rejecting an Aetolian appeal for help, then expecting the Aetolians to join them, and inconsistent also in claiming to have been acting on the Aetolians' behalf against Philip in the First Macedonian War, and now attempting to disturb the state of peace existing between Philip and the Aetolians; (ii) §§ 6–15 *tractatio*: (a) §§ 6–11 *tutum*: Italy and Sicily have been ruthlessly suppressed by Rome, (b) §§ 12–15 *utile*: it is madness to expect barbarians to leave Greek freedom un-

---

[1] *La Technique*, 135.   [2] *Rhet.* 1358 b 22.   [3] *La Technique*, 136.

impaired; (iii) § 16 *conclusio*: do not break the peace. Again, Ullmann's division of the *tractatio* is artificial. What we have is an abrupt transition from the *prooemium* to the onslaught on Roman imperialism, describing what has already happened in Italy and Sicily in §§ 6–11, and what will happen in Greece in §§ 12–16. To treat these as separate arguments for the *tutum* and the *utile* makes no sense.

The speech of Furius Purpurio causes less difficulty. Ullmann divides it as follows.[1] (i) §§ 1–4 *prooemium*: the Macedonian speech has made it necessary to defend Roman policy, the Athenian speech has made it unnecessary to describe Philip's outrages; (ii) §§ 5–17 *tractatio*: point-by-point answer to Macedonian charges; (iii) §§ 18–20 *conclusio*: appeal to the Aetolians. This seems right: one might add that the *prooemium* contains, as it were, a summary of Macedonian wrongs concealed in an *omissio*.

The speech of Aristaenus in xxxii. 21 is among the longer of L.'s speeches, and is the most careful and ornate construction of the four speeches which we are considering. Ullmann's analysis is as follows.[2] (i) §§ 1–3 *prooemium*: nobody else will speak, so I must do so; (ii) §§ 4–5 κατάστασις: statement of the decision that has to be made; (iii) §§ 6–29 *tractatio*: (a) §§ 6–11 *tutum*: the Romans are in a far stronger position than Philip; (b) §§ 12–20 *utile*: if, as the Macedonian envoy claims, Macedon will win, why are they unable to defend their own allies? The Romans are in a far stronger position than in the First Macedonian War; (c) §§ 21–5 *dignum*: let us forget Philip's outrages —what he asks we cannot perform; (d) §§ 26–9 *possibile*: we cannot defend ourselves: the Peloponnese is in a very weak position; (iv) §§ 30–7 *conclusio*. It is certainly easier to see divisions in this speech, and we have, unusually in a deliberative speech, a clear and concise statement of the question that has to be answered. But again, I find the distinction of *tutum* and *utile* forced. What we have in §§ 6–20 is a continuous argument to show the weakness of Macedon and the strength of Rome. §§ 21–5, it is true, deal with moral rather than prudential arguments, but they are introduced by way of an *omissio*, not as a direct argument. But §§ 26–9 certainly deal with the *possibile*, as is made clear in *quod fieri non possit* in § 25.

Less need be said on the *elocutio* of these speeches. Ullmann's analysis of the tropes, figures of speech, and arrangements of words and phrases is exhaustive, and comments will be found in the notes on some of the individual passages. Two general points, however, might be made here. First, the rhetorical features to which Ullmann draws attention are not unique to the speeches in L. Many are found in other parts of his work. It is true, though, that they occur, as one would expect, in greater number in the speeches. Secondly,

---

[1] *La Technique*, 136–7.   [2] *La Technique*, 137–9.

it is interesting to observe the results of using the points noted by Ullmann as a guide to the relative ornateness of the speeches.[1] The lengths of the four speeches, in terms of lines of Oxford text, are: xxxi. 7: 49 lines, xxxi. 29: 41 lines, xxxi. 31: 64 lines, xxxii. 21: 122 lines. The number of rhetorical points noted by Ullmann is: xxxi. 7: 12, xxxi. 29: 16, xxxi. 31: 8, xxxii. 21: 35. This confirms the impression which we would already have from the consideration of structure. The speech of Furius is the least ornate speech in style, and the simplest in structure. Aristaenus and the Macedonian at the Aetolian meeting are the most ornate, with Sulpicius in between. None of these speeches is of the greatest rhetorical ornamentation. All belong to the *genus medium* in Cicero's division of the types of speech,[2] and this again, not because L. was not sufficiently interested to compose orations in the *genus grande*, but because all these speeches were designed to persuade their audience to adopt a certain course of action when there were powerful arguments on the other side. The audience needed powerful persuasion, but not rhetorical bombast or high-flown purple passages.

4. FLAMININUS AND ROMAN POLITICS

Titus Quinctius Flamininus is the central figure of the Second Macedonian War, and a satisfactory picture of his policy and political position cannot be given in the confines of comments on individual passages of L. in which he is mentioned. The following discussion first analyses Flamininus' policy with particular reference to the events covered by books xxxi–xxxiii and then attempts to explain his relation to other leading politicians of the period.[3]

Polybius had little love lost for Flamininus. He admired his diplomatic and political ability and his skill at promoting his own interests without damaging those of Rome, but he regarded him as a man who used underhand methods and who fundamentally could not be trusted. On many occasions L. suppresses criticisms of Flamininus made by Polybius.[4] Polybius' view has been widely

[1] I am not, of course, suggesting that degrees of ornateness can be measured precisely in this way.

[2] Cf. Ullmann, *Étude*, 121 ff.

[3] A fuller version of my views will be found in *Latomus* xxxi (1972), 22–53. On Flamininus' career as a whole cf. H. Gundel, *RE* xxiv. 1047–1100, on his early career Badian, *JRS* lxi (1971), 102–11.

[4] He suppresses Polybius' comments on Flamininus' handling of the Nicaea negotiations and the machinations of Flamininus' friends at Rome (xxxii. 36. 10–37, Pol. xviii. 10–12), though he does admit that Flamininus was willing to settle with Philip if his command was not prorogued (xxxii. 32. 5–8). He omits references to Flamininus' jokes and laughter at Nicaea (xxxii. 34. 7, 9–10, 35. 1 nn.) and

accepted, particularly as it was reinforced by a magisterial article of Holleaux, analysing and bringing out the implications of Polybius' account of Flamininus' conduct of the negotiations with Philip at Nicaea in the autumn of 198.[1]

It is not difficult to argue that Polybius is biased against Flamininus.[2] Hostility to him could have derived from two possible sources, either from political opponents of Flamininus among the circle of Aemilius Paullus at Rome or through earlier connections with Philopoemen, with whom Flamininus had more than one clash.[3] For every occasion on which Polybius reports some incident damaging to Flamininus it is possible to argue that he is biased. But cumulatively the evidence is more difficult to reject and it becomes more impressive the more items we consider.[4]

The most discreditable episodes all come in 183. On his mission to Prusias of Bithynia, Flamininus was responsible for securing the suicide of Prusias' guest Hannibal.[5] On his way to Asia Flamininus stopped in the Peloponnese and attempted, quite unofficially, to influence events in Messene, now a member of the Achaean League, in the interests of Dinocrates, who had been intriguing with him at Rome.[6] Most serious of all was Flamininus' attempt to create divisions within the royal house of Macedon by intriguing with

removes an insinuation that Flamininus' report of the secret meeting might not be trustworthy (xxxii. 35. 8 n.). He fails to record the aggressive language used by Flamininus to the Aetolians after Cynoscephalae (xxxiii. 11. 5 n.), and suppresses Flamininus' connivance at the murder of Brachylles (xxxiii. 28. 1 n.), his fear of being superseded in 197 (xxxiii. 13. 15 n.), and his intrigues with Demetrius (xxxix. 47). For other possible suppressions cf. xxxii. 24. 7 n. and n. 5 below. See also Holleaux, *Études*, v. 46 n. 4, 100 n. 6, Walsh, *AJP* lxxvi (1955), 376.

[1] Holleaux, *Études*, v. 29–79.

[2] Cf. F. M. Wood, *TAPA* lxx (1939), 93–103, *AJP* lxii (1941), 277–88, M. Feyel, *RÉG* lvi (1943), 235–46, J. P. V. D. Balsdon, *Phoenix* xxi (1967), 177–90. For recent defences of Polybius cf. Lehmann, 165 ff., Badian, *Flamininus*. Schlag, 71–139, goes even further than Polybius and holds that Flamininus was preoccupied only with his own self-interest to the neglect even of the interests of Rome. Cf. also Aymard, *PR*, 114 ff.

[3] Plut. *Phil.* 16, Paus. viii. 51. 1–2, Pol. xxiii. 5. Cf. in general L. xxxv. 47. 4, Plut. *Phil.* 15, *Flam.* 13. On these matters see now Errington, *Philopoemen*, chs. vi and vii.

[4] Equally, if one accepts, as Balsdon does, the discreditable episodes of the later part of Flamininus' career, it becomes harder to interpret the earlier events in a way favourable to Flamininus.

[5] For the sources on the death of Hannibal, cf. *MRR*, i. 380. Plut. *Flam.* 20. 3 and App. *Syr.* 11 say that Flamininus was exceeding senatorial instructions, L. (xxxix. 51) that it was part of his mission. But L. may be defending Flamininus against charges levelled at him. Even if Flamininus was acting in accordance with senatorial instructions, it remains significant that Flamininus was the man chosen to carry out the task.

[6] Pol. xxiii. 5, Errington, *Philopoemen*, 124 ff., 183 ff., Lehmann, 179–94.

Philip's younger son Demetrius, and encouraging him to hope that Flamininus would secure for him the throne of Macedon in place of his half-brother Perseus. The result was the execution of Demetrius.[1] These events may be compared with Flamininus' conniving at the murder of Brachylles in Boeotia in 196.[2]

With this in mind, we may return to Flamininus' period of command in Greece, and begin with the conference of Nicaea.[3] The original demands of Flamininus and his Greek allies, made on the first day of the conference, were that Philip was to evacuate Greece completely. Philip eventually asked for a written statement of all the demands, and for a day in which to consider them. On the second day Philip asked for a private meeting with Flamininus. At this Flamininus was accompanied by Ap. Claudius, a *tribunus militum*, and subsequently reported Philip's reply, which agreed to some of the demands but rejected others. There was general discontent with this, but Philip secured another adjournment, and on the third day asked for the whole matter to be referred to the senate. The allies objected initially, but Flamininus persuaded them to agree, on the grounds that the senate would in any case have to approve a settlement, and that since it was now winter, there would be no military disadvantage in such a move. Polybius expresses his admiration for Flamininus' skill in both preserving his own interests and in protecting those of Rome by giving Philip no military advantage.

In Rome Flamininus' friends, once they had ascertained that Flamininus was not going to be succeeded in his command, wrecked the negotiations by pressing for an answer on one point only—would Philip surrender the three 'fetters of Greece', the Acrocorinth, Chalcis, and Demetrias? Polybius' view of Flamininus is made particularly clear. Apart from the comment I have mentioned, he refers to Amynander of Athamania whom Flamininus sent to Rome at this time as εὐάγωγον μὲν ὄντα καὶ ῥᾳδίως ἐξακολουθήσοντα τοῖς ἐκεῖ φίλοις, ἐφ' ὁπότερ' ἂν ἄγωσιν αὐτόν, φαντασίαν δὲ ποιήσοντα καὶ προσδοκίαν διὰ τὸ τῆς βασιλείας ὄνομα.[4]

It is necessary now to consider Balsdon's attack on Holleaux's interpretation of these events.[5] His discussion raises four problems, two connected with the interpretation of the evidence, two with the accuracy of what Polybius says. The first concerns Holleaux's argument that Flamininus' reluctance to agree to negotiations was

---

[1] Pol. xxiii. 1–3, 7–10, L. xxxix. 47, 53, xl. 5–16, 20–4, 54–5. Cf. C. F. Edson, *HSCP* xlvi (1935), 191–202, Walbank, *Philip V*, 238–52, Meloni, *Perseo*, 29–60, Badian, *FC*, 94.

[2] Cf. xxxiii. 27. 5—28 and nn.

[3] xxxii. 32–7, Pol. xviii. 1–12.

[4] Pol. xviii. 10. 7. Cf. K.-W. Welwei, *Historia* xiv (1965), 252–6.

[5] *Phoenix* xxi (1967), 177–85.

assumed, not real. In this matter Balsdon appears to have mis-interpreted what L. says at xxxii. 32. 5–8.[1]

On a second point, however, Holleaux probably went too far. He believed that at the secret meeting on the second day of the con-ference it was Flamininus who suggested to Philip that he should ask for the matter to be referred to the senate, thus laying the ground for his manœuvres.[2] There is certainly no evidence for this assump-tion. It would not have been fatal for Flamininus if such a request had not been made: he himself could have reported Philip's offer to the senate, and left it to his political friends to press for peace if his command was not prorogued. On the other hand, if Philip mentioned the possibility of a reference to the senate at the secret meeting, Flamininus will not have discouraged him.

These are the points of interpretation of the evidence. We now turn to those concerning its accuracy. The common objection to Polybius' account is that there would have been no advantage for Flamininus in trying to make peace on Philip's terms. If a majority of the senate had been opposed to the continuation of Flamininus' command, it is argued, they would simply have transferred the command to one of the new consuls, and would not have been willing to make peace on Flamininus' terms.[3] This, however, ignores the nature of the Roman senate.[4] It did not consist of friends and enemies of Flamininus, and different people would have been influenced by different arguments. It could well have happened that a majority believed in a system of annual commands and yet would still be ready to vote for peace on the terms that Flamininus recommended: that is what his φίλοι were ready to try to accomplish. In any case, if Flamininus' manœuvre had failed, and a successor had been appointed to continue the war, he would have been no worse off than if he had not made the attempt.

The second difficulty in Polybius' account detected by Balsdon concerns the status of the fetters in the discussion at Rome. They had not played any prominent part in the negotiations at Nicaea, and yet appear to be virtually the sole issue before the senate.

---

[1] Cf. n. ad. loc.

[2] Holleaux, *Études*, v. 59 ff., Walbank, *Philip V*, 162. Badian, *Flamininus*, 40 ff. It is hard to decide whether there is any significance in Flamininus' failure to reply when Philip inquired whether he was to abandon his inherited possessions in Greece as well as his own conquests (Pol. xviii. 7. 2: omitted by L.).

[3] Balsdon, 181, and the other works cited in p. 23 n. 2. I cannot understand Balsdon's objection that the mention of Flamininus' φίλοι indicates the 'invention of someone who . . . pictured Roman politics . . . in the image of a Hellenistic court'. Certainly the φίλοι are a defined group in certain Hellenistic courts, but the word is also the Greek for *amici* (cf. xxxii. 32. 7). In an age of slow communications who else but one's *amici* could protect one's political interests? Cf. Badian, *Flamininus*, 46 ff. [4] Cf. my comments in *Historia* xviii (1969), 61.

Schlag, on the other hand, uses the position of the fetters in the discussion at Rome as an indication that Flamininus, in order to secure renewal of his command, misrepresented what had been discussed at Nicaea. Feyel thought that Philip had in fact offered to abandon the fetters but retain control of Thessaly and Magnesia except Demetrias.[1] To the latter Balsdon's objection is decisive. If such an agreement had really been made, why did the Macedonian envoys say they had no instructions on the fetters?

Is the mention of the fetters really so puzzling? Balsdon thinks that Philip had indicated willingness to withdraw from the fetters: 'there was only one town in mainland Greece . . . which Philip refused to surrender—Phthiotic Thebes.' This is a misunderstanding of Polybius.[2] Phthiotic Thebes (plus Iasus and Bargylia in Asia Minor) is the only town which Philip explicitly refuses to surrender. There are others, including the fetters, which were included in the Roman demands but of which there was no specific mention in Philip's reply. The implication was that he was not ready to surrender them. When the envoys said they had 'no instructions' that was a diplomatic way of saying the fetters were not negotiable. On Balsdon's view their reply is as puzzling as it is on Feyel's hypothesis.[3]

Nor is there anything odd in the implication of the Greek envoys that if Philip surrendered the fetters, they would be content.[4] In part it is simply a rhetorical way of highlighting the fetters. In part, though, it is an indication of their minimum demands, if by any chance the senate were willing to seek a negotiated peace.

We turn next to the question of the prorogations of Flamininus' command for 196 and 195. In 197 the motif of Flamininus' fear of a successor reappears. After the battle of Cynoscephalae Polybius reports that Flamininus was eager to make peace because of the danger from Antiochus: this might result either in Philip seeking to prolong the war, or in another commander being appointed who would win the glory of completing the war.[5] Schlag argues that Flamininus, together with P. Sulpicius Galba and P. Villius Tappulus, who had been appointed as *legati* to Flamininus in 197,[6] had convinced the senate that there was a real danger from Antiochus. As a result of these reports a Seleucid embassy had been given a mild reply, but Rome was clearly hostile to Syria. But

[1] *RÉG* lvi (1943), 235–46, Balsdon, 184.

[2] Balsdon, 182. In Phthiotic Achaea the implication is that he refused to surrender Echinus (cf. Holleaux, *Études*, v. 54 n. 1, Walbank, *Commentary*, ii. 558).

[3] Badian (*Flamininus*, 42–3) may be right in thinking that the fetters as such were not discussed at the secret meeting.

[4] Pol. xviii. 11. 9.

[5] Pol. xviii. 39. 4. For the similar charge in 195 (xxxiv. 33. 14) cf. *Latomus* xxxi, 32.

[6] xxxii. 28. 12.

Flamininus, she claims, did not really believe in a danger from Antiochus, as is shown by his disagreement with the ten commissioners in 196 on the maintenance of control of the fetters and the fate of Oreus and Eretria.[1]

This argument is composed of a series of misapprehensions. Above all, there is nothing odd, as Schlag appears to think, in Flamininus' command being prorogued without it being made clear that this was only for the completion of the peace, and without a stipulation about the return of his army. It does not prove that Flamininus had made any representations about keeping his army there.[2] As the senate's instructions to the *legati* make clear, it is they who were concerned about Antiochus. They had by this time received an appeal from Lampsacus, and had heard of Antiochus' advances from other sources.[3] Nor do Flamininus' disagreements with the commissioners indicate that he had been dissembling his real views in his report to the senate. They show rather that Flamininus did not regard a continued Roman military presence in Greece as the best guarantee against Antiochus. Thirdly, Schlag has completely misunderstood xxxiii. 20 as indicating a Seleucid embassy to Rome in 197. The envoys in §9 of that chapter are those of the winter of 198/7 and are not identical with those mentioned in §10. The alleged evidence for Roman hostility to Antiochus in 197, therefore, does not exist.[4]

We come now to the prorogation for 195. The reasons are given by L. as *suspectis non solum Antiocho et Aetolis sed iam etiam Nabide*.[5] Nabis is the new factor here and Schlag argues that Flamininus sent representatives to Rome to report the danger from Nabis and exaggerate the strategic importance of Argos, which was in Nabis' possession. But L.'s reference to Argos occurs in the report of the ten *legati* who had returned between the decision to prolong Flamininus' command and the further decision to give Flamininus discretion to go to war with Nabis if he saw fit.[6] Of course it is true that Roman policy towards Nabis altered remarkably. He had been an ally of Rome since the end of 198.[7] But it was obvious that Nabis' continued possession of Argos made a nonsense of Rome's declared profession of Greek freedom. Flamininus found himself forced to undertake the war: we shall see that he had no desire to eradicate Nabis completely. Misrepresentation did not come into it.

---

[1] Pol. xviii. 45. 10–12, 47. 10–11, L. xxxiii. 31. 8–11, 34. 10.

[2] Cf. the prorogation of Manlius Vulso's command in 188 (xxxviii. 35. 3).

[3] *Syll.*[3] 591: for the possibility of a further Pergamene embassy in 197, cf. Schlag, 91 n. 67.

[4] L.'s implication that the senate in 198 was biding its time with Antiochus is simply an interpretation (perhaps L.'s own) made with the benefit of hindsight.

[5] xxxiii. 43. 6.   [6] xxxiii. 44. 9.   [7] xxxii. 39–40.

It is now time to evaluate Flamininus' policy and behaviour as a whole. His flamboyant display in proclaiming Greek freedom at the Isthmus in 196, his dedications in the Greek world and the honours given to him by Greeks, his obvious ability to get on with Greeks have often led to his being called a philhellenist.[1] But such things tell us little about his actual policy. Dedications by and to other Roman nobles are found in Greece at this period[2] and Greek culture was by now widespread among the Roman governing classes. Even Cato was by no means hostile to all aspects of Hellenism.

What, then, was Flamininus' policy in Greece? McDonald held that he concerned himself exclusively with the interests of the Greek city-states;[3] he called this policy 'Hellenic' and contrasted it with the 'Hellenistic' policy of Scipio, who was more willing to work with kings and federations.[4] But it is not the case that Flamininus had a doctrinaire attachment to the city-states. It may be true that Flamininus' original attraction towards the Greeks and Greek culture led him to formulate a policy of independence for the city-states. But he also conceived such a policy as suiting Rome's best interests, and he did not push it to extremes. His aim, rather, was to achieve a balance of power, to prevent any one state, be it city-state, federation, or kingdom, from becoming too powerful, and thus to make Roman military presence or intervention unnecessary. He also wanted, of course, to enhance his own *dignitas*. In the pursuit of these aims Flamininus sometimes had recourse to the underhand methods which we have already considered; on other occasions his method was no worse than subtle diplomacy.

Flamininus, like any Roman *nobilis*, had a natural predilection for the upper classes, and on occasion he indulged this predilection, as with the sanctioning of the murder of Brachylles in Boeotia or the reorganization of Thessaly on timocratic lines.[5] But this policy, too, was not pushed to excess. When the murder of Brachylles led to a

[1] For dedications by and honours to Flamininus see Plut. *Flam.* 12, *Syll.*[3] 585. 46, 616 (Delphi), Plut. *Flam.* 16. 4, *IG* xii. 9. 931 cf. L. xxxv. 49. 6 (Chalcis), *SGDI* 3656 = *IGRR* iv. 1049 (Cos), *Syll.*[3] 592, *SEG* xi. 923 (Gytheum), *MRR* i. 330 (Delos), *BCH* lxxxviii (1964), 569 ff. (Argos), 607 ff. (Corinth), *RÉA* lxvi (1964), 309 ff. (Scotoussa). Cf. Heidemann, 36–9, Walbank, *Commentary*, ii. 613–14. On the gold staters issued by Flamininus in Greece cf. A. A. Boyce, *Hommages Grenier* (Brussels, 1962), i. 342 ff. For an attempt to identify a portrait head of Flamininus at Delphi, cf. F. Chamoux, *BCH* lxxxix (1965), 214 ff.

[2] The Scipios: *SEG* i. 144, L. xxviii. 45. 12 (Delphi), *Syll.*[3] 617, *MRR*, i. 356, 358 (Delos), *IC* ii. 3. 5 (Crete). Acilius Glabrio: *Syll.*[3] 607 ff. (Delphi): cf. L. Acilius in *Syll.*[3] 585. 47 and Acilii in Acarnania (*IG* ix.[2] 1. 208). For other dedicators at Delos cf. *MRR* i. 350 (Atilius), 353, 357 (Livius Salinator), 360 (Manlius Vulso), 361 (Fabius Labeo). [3] *JRS* xxviii (1938), 153–64.

[4] For arguments against this description of Scipio's policy cf. *Latomus* xxxi, 38–9.

[5] Cf. *Past and Present* xxxvi (Apr. 1967), 10–11, J. Touloumakos, *Der Einfluss*

violent reaction against Rome, he made no attempt to secure the recall of Zeuxippus who had been exiled following the murder. He was quite willing to accept the aid of the left-wing tyrant Nabis. As we saw, the inconsistency of allowing Nabis to remain in control of Argos meant that he had little alternative to war with him. But even now he refused the Achaean demand to remove Nabis from control of Sparta itself.[1] That would have left the Achaean League too powerful. In 192/1, again, he tried to limit Achaean expansionism, though he could not afford to be too restrictive, as Achaean loyalty in the struggle against Antiochus was vital for Rome.[2] Similarly, in 197, he resisted Aetolian demands for the eradication of Philip from Macedon for fear that Aetolia would take his place.[3] But in 191 he was equally afraid that if too much energy were devoted to attacking Aetolia, Philip would again become a potential danger.[4] He was willing to come to a compromise with the *legati* on the control of the fetters in 196: and while he insisted that Oreus and Eretria should be free, and not given to Pergamum, he made no attempt to remove Aegina and Andros which were already in Eumenes' possession.[5] It would have been madness to offend Rome's principal ally.

Flamininus' policy thus remained flexible to meet the needs of the time and his own *dignitas*.[6] It should be mentioned, though, that despite his generally gentle approach Flamininus could be harsh and cruel on occasions. His punishment of the Boeotians following the outbreak after the murder of Brachylles was far from mild, and in 198, it seems, he expelled all the inhabitants of Elatea after he had captured the town.[7]

We can now try to relate Flamininus to other leading politicians of the time.[8] The period is one that presents new problems, and new

Roms auf die Staatsform der griechischen Stadtstaaten des Festlandes und der Inseln im ersten und zweiten Jhdt. v. Chr. (Göttingen, 1967), 63 ff.

[1] xxxiv. 33 ff., Plut. *Flam.* 13.

[2] xxxv. 25 ff., xxxvi. 31–2, 35, Plut. *Phil.* 16. 1–3, Paus. viii. 51. 1–2. Cf. Aymard, *PR*, 212 ff., 294 ff., Errington, *Philopoemen*, chs. vi and vii.

[3] xxxiii. 11. 9, Pol. xviii. 34. 1, Dio fr. 60. Flamininus' declared fear of barbarian invasions (xxxiii. 12. 10–11, Pol. xviii. 39. 1) cannot be the real reason.

[4] xxxvi. 34. 7 ff., Plut. *Flam.* 15. 4–5, Dio fr. 62. 1a, Zon. ix. 19. 14.

[5] On Andros cf. xxxi. 45. 7 n., on Aegina xxxi. 14. 11 n., on Oreus and Eretria xxxiii. 31. 3 n. See also xxxiii. 34. 10 n. on Carystus.

[6] It is just this flexibility that is visible in his conduct of the negotiations with the representatives of Antiochus in 193. Cf. xxxiv. 57. 4–59, *Latomus* xxxi, 35–6.

[7] Cf. xxxii. 24. 7 n.

[8] Apart from Schlag, works dealing primarily or specifically with the politics of this period are Schur, *SA*, 69 ff., 131 ff., R. M. Haywood, *Studies on Scipio Africanus* (Baltimore, Md., 1933), 59 ff., McDonald, *JRS* xxviii (1938), 153 ff., Scullard, *RP*, 89 ff., T. A. Dorey, *PACA* ii (1959), 9–10, *Klio* xxxix (1961), 191–8, F. Cassola, *Labeo* vi (1960), 105 ff. Balsdon does not attempt prosopographical analysis, but

individuals rise to prominence. It must therefore be considered in its own terms and against the background of the questions which confronted the senate at the time. Some earlier attempts at prosopographical analysis have described the 190s in terms that were applicable to the Second Punic War. Then it is reasonable to distinguish three main groupings, one centring on the Scipios, another on Q. Fabius Maximus, and a third consisting of persons opposed to both Fabius and the Scipios. In the last years of the Second Punic War the main conflict was between Scipio and his opponents. Both Q. Fabius Maximus and Q. Fulvius Flaccus opposed Scipio's proposal to invade Africa in 205.[1] Both Scipio and members of the third group—whom I call the 'Fulvians'[2]—are still active in the second century, but the great Cunctator died in 203 and from then on it is very misleading to talk of a Fabian group. Such facts as that both the Fabii and the Quinctii are *gentes lupercales*[3] or that Quinctii in the late third century may have had fairly close connections with the 'Fabian' M. Claudius Marcellus[4] or even that Flamininus himself may have married a Fabia[5] are irrelevant. The concept of the Fabian group and its policy of attrition belong to the period of the Hannibalic War. Its members, or relatives of its members, may be active in the second century, but we must examine their political position in this period, not attempt to deduce it from earlier events.[6]

argues that Sulpicius and Villius always co-operated with Flamininus (185-6). Balsdon seems to me to ignore the general political context and to underestimate the disagreement between Flamininus and the commissioners in 196. The fact that on other occasions there was no disagreement is not necessarily an indication of political agreement.

[1] xxviii. 40. 3, 45. 2. I agree with the main lines of the analysis of Scullard, *RP*, 39–88. But I avoid the label 'Fulvio-Claudian' as it seems to me that the consuls of 212 were linked by nothing more than opposition to both the Scipios and Fabius, and that at other times the Claudii are not part of the Fulvian group. For other views of the politics of the Second Punic War cf. M. Patterson, *TAPA* lxxiii (1942), 319–40, J. E. A. Crake, *Phoenix* xvii (1963), 123–30, Cassola, *GP*, 259 ff., Lippold, 147 ff., J. Jahn, *Interregnum und Wahldiktatur* (Kallmunz, 1970), 116 ff. For the correct method of prosopographical inquiry cf. *CR* N.S. xiii (1963), 321 ff., *Latomus* xxvii (1968), 156.

[2] For some of the links between these men cf. *Historia* xviii (1969), 65. Among the Fulvii, Sulpicii, Postumii, and Valerii Laevini I believe it is possible to trace a continuous tradition of opposition to the Scipios, and unity among themselves for more than half a century. Hence I use the label 'Fulvian' even though there are at some periods no Fulvii particularly active and though at different times members of other *gentes* are also involved. I hope to elaborate on this matter elsewhere.

[3] Münzer, *RA*, 114.

[4] Münzer, *RA*, 114–18, Scullard, *RP*, 98.

[5] Cf. xxxii. 36. 10 n.

[6] The uselessness of continuing to talk of the old Fabian group is illustrated by statements of Schur and Scullard. Schur (*SA*, 71) talks of 'die aufstrebenden Führer

A second unprofitable line of analysis is the attempt to deduce political relationships from a common interest in matters Greek.[1] We have seen already that 'philhellenism' is not a sufficient description of the policy of Flamininus. Nor is evidence of such interest a reason for associating Flamininus with Scipio, or other politicians with either of them. For example, Cn. Manlius Vulso and M. Fulvius Nobilior succeeded the Scipios in Asia and Greece respectively in 189: they met with bitter opposition from friends of the Scipios.[2] Yet Fulvius took the poet Ennius with him to Ambracia, and Manlius made dedications at Delos.[3] Poets do not necessarily have fixed political allegiances, and there is nothing odd in Ennius having been brought to Rome by Cato, being on joking terms with Scipio Nasica, and writing both a eulogy of Africanus and an account of the deeds of Fulvius in Ambracia.[4] Conversely M'. Acilius Glabrio was certainly a supporter of Scipio and showed a certain amount of sympathy for Greek aspirations. Yet at other times he showed himself insensitive to Greek feelings.[5]

Freed, then, from these preconceptions we may attempt a positive account of the politics of the Second Macedonian War. It will be argued in the next section that the war was sponsored by Scipio's opponents, the Fulvians, and that Scipio himself was opposed to the declaration of war.[6] P. Sulpicius Galba was elected consul for 200, and was in Greece by the autumn of that year. He failed to achieve any real break-through in 199, though his campaign was not as unsuccessful as has sometimes been claimed.[7] The Aetolians had eventually joined Rome, though Sulpicius had not undertaken any

der ehemals fabischen Partei, die patrizier T. Quinctius Flamininus und L. Valerius Flaccus und die plebeier M. Porcius Cato und M. Claudius Marcellus', Scullard (*RP*, 118) of 'the two very different sections of the old Fabian party, represented by Cato and Flamininus'. If the sections are so different that they are led by Cato and Flamininus, then it has become useless to talk of such a party. Cassola (*Labeo* vi [1960], 105 ff.) discusses the 190s in their own terms, but his analysis is vitiated by his refusal to use orthodox prosopographical arguments. On Cassola's methods cf. my comments in *CR* N.S. xiii (1963), 321–4.

[1] Haywood, op. cit.

[2] Cf. *Latomus* xxxi, 52

[3] Fulvius and Ennius: Cic. *Tusc.* i. 3, Manlius: cf. p. 28 n. 2. In 187 Fulvius dedicated a temple to Hercules of the Muses (*MRR* i. 369). Even so callous a character as M. Popillius Laenas (on whom cf. *JRS* liv [1964], 74) wrote poetry (Suet. *Vita Ter.* 4).

[4] For all this cf. Schanz–Hosius, *Römische Literatur-Geschichte* i⁴ (Munich, 1927), 86–8. Ennius' *Ambracia* may have been a *tragoedia praetextata*.

[5] Cf. p. 28 n. 2 for his relations with Delphi. He restored the Elateans expelled by Flamininus (cf. xxxii. 24. 7 n.). For his support of Scipio cf. xxx. 40. 9–16, 43. 2–3, for his insensitivity Pol. xx. 10, L. xxxvi. 27–8, Plut. *Flam.* 16. 2.

[6] Cf. pp. 45–6.

[7] Cf. e.g. Walbank, *Philip V*, 147, Scullard, *RP*, 96.

other diplomatic initiatives. His reputation among the Greeks was bad: they remembered his cruelty during the First Macedonian War.[1] His successor was P. Villius Tappulus, who came to Greece late in 199 and was quickly succeeded by Flamininus. There is no certain evidence for his political position. Scullard saw the fact that he came out late as an indication of an agreement between Villius and Sulpicius to allow Sulpicius a full year's campaigning.[2] Scullard's interpretation of the date of Villius' arrival is not necessary, but the general political situation does suggest that Villius was a supporter of the Fulvians. Nothing, at least, contradicts such a hypothesis.[3] Villius' colleague, L. Cornelius Lentulus is the brother of the consul of 201 who had shown clear opposition to Scipio, and may also be ranked with the Fulvians.[4]

Flamininus' campaign for the consulship will have begun before Villius reached Greece. I believe that this was one of the moments in Republican history when an individual sought office with a definite policy: a bold strategy, both militarily and diplomatically, in the war and a clear idea of what would follow victory—the freedom of Greece. Though of course no Roman *nobilis* would be without some electoral support which came from traditional allegiances, in this case Flamininus' appeal was broader. It is just this sort of situation that produces political fluidity. It is no surprise to find, for example, that a M. Fulvius opposed the validity of Flamininus' candidature,[5] whilst a Q. Fulvius, tribune of 197, supported Flamininus when the consuls of that year wanted to succeed Flamininus in Greece,[6] and another Q. Fulvius was sent to Rome to work with Flamininus' friends after the conference of Nicaea.[7] Scipio too may have given Flamininus his support.[8] This did not mean that Flamininus joined the Scipionic group or became a protégé of Scipio. Scipio was opposed to the negative policy of the Fulvians, and will have welcomed the new initiative of Flamininus.

---

[1] App. *Mac.* 7, cf. Pol. ix. 42.   [2] Scullard, *RP*, 96.

[3] For Schlag's attempt (104–10) to show that Villius was an opponent of Sulpicius and an ally of Flamininus cf. *Latomus* xxxi, 41–2. She argues, *inter alia*, that by reporting a prodigy (xxxii. 1. 12) Sulpicius was deliberately preventing Villius from going to Greece early. But Sulpicius could not possibly have foreseen that his report would delay the consul. In any case we do not know in what part of the year the report came, or what sort of delay was involved.

[4] On the facts cf. Scullard, *RP*, 81. On the position of C. Aurelius Cotta, Sulpicius' colleague in 200, and L. Furius Purpurio, praetor in 200 and consul in 196, cf. xxxi. 47. 4—49. 3, 49. 8–11 n.

[5] xxxii. 7. 8, Plut. *Flam.* 2. 1.   [6] xxxii. 28. 3.

[7] xxxii. 36. 10, Pol. xviii. 10. 8.

[8] Scipionic veterans supported his candidature for the consulship and volunteered to join his army (Plut. *Flam.* 2. 1, 3. 1). Flamininus had been a *xvir* for the assignation of land to Scipionic veterans in 200 (xxxi. 4. 3).

But if it was only Flamininus' policy, and not Flamininus personally that Scipio was backing, there is nothing surprising in Scipionic consuls of 197 wanting to succeed him.[1]

The glamour and novelty of Flamininus' policy will have attracted to him men from diverse groups—some perhaps seeing him as a counterweight to Scipio, others merely breaking away from their own former allegiances. The latter would include the young Q. Fabius, Q. Fulvius, and Ap. Claudius Nero whom Flamininus sent to Rome after Nicaea. But news of Flamininus' methods may soon have begun to alienate Scipio. Scipio would still back a settlement in Greece based on respect for Greek independence and a method of achieving it based on tact and understanding. He will not necessarily have agreed that Flamininus was the only man capable of executing such a policy.[2]

When Philip was defeated, Scipio will not have disagreed with the need to make peace. After Cynoscephalae we can, I believe, discern two sources of opposition to Flamininus. First, Scipio and his friends, and secondly those Fulvians who did not share Flamininus' approach towards policy in Greece. On some issues—whether or not troops should be kept in Greece, for example—Scipio and the Fulvians were opposed to Flamininus. On the general approach to the war and its settlement, on the other hand, Scipio and Flamininus were united in opposition to the Fulvians.

The test was to come with the settlement that followed the battle

---

[1] xxxii. 28. 3–9, cf. Pol. xviii. 11. 1. The consuls gave way fairly readily, but Flamininus' efforts indicate that he could not rely on them. Cassola (op. cit., 110) doubts whether they were Scipionic consuls. But one was a Cornelius Cethegus, and there is no case of a Cethegus acting in opposition to the Scipios and a lot of evidence pointing to collaboration. On Minucius Rufus, cf. xxxi. 4. 4 n.

[2] This fluid situation may perhaps explain the activities of P. and Sex. Aelius Paetus. Publius Paetus was *magister equitum* in the indubitably anti-Scipionic dictatorship of 202 (cf. Scullard, *RP*, 80–1: *contra* Lippold, 215–16, Jahn, op. cit., 144 ff.) and consul in 201. He was censor with Africanus in 199. His brother Sextus was consul with Flamininus in 198 and censor with C. Cornelius Cethegus in 194. Scullard (*RP*, 97) thinks that Publius was anti-Scipionic until 'he came under the spell of Scipio's personality' in 199. But the *concordia* of the censors (xxxii. 7. 3) does not prove any political alliance, and there is nothing remarkable in the nomination of Scipio as *princeps senatus* by his colleague. He may have been the senior member of the patrician *gentes maiores*, who alone qualified for the position. On the other hand, the censorship of Sextus Paetus in 194, a year when Scipionic supporters really swept the board, makes it hard to think that he was an enemy of the Scipios. The two Paeti were distinguished jurists (cf. Schlag, 145–7, Douglas, *Commentary on Cicero: Brutus*, 67) and it could be that this enabled them to remain outside factional disputes. I suspect, though, that they started as Fulvians, but were later attracted by the programme of Flamininus, and then found that they preferred Scipio to Flamininus. On the Aelii Paeti cf. Dorey, *Klio* xxxix, 191–8, who, however, seems to me to exaggerate their importance and influence.

of Cynoscephalae. Philip accepted all the demands which had been made previously, but the details were left for the senate to settle,[1] and it was the treaty approved by the senate that was finally ratified by the *comitia*.[2]

The conclusion of peace was opposed by the consul of 196, M. Claudius Marcellus, who wanted the command in Macedon for himself.[3] The extent of his support is unclear, and it may be that only Marcellus' personal position was involved. There are, however, strong grounds for regarding him as a Fulvian in 189, and it may be that some Fulvians supported him in the belief that the terms being recommended by Flamininus were too lenient.

But there was little disagreement between the senate and Flamininus on the terms to be imposed on Philip.[4] The main field of disagreement was the settlement of Greece. The activities of Antiochus were already causing alarm in 197, and Flamininus was aware of the danger.[5] His view, however, was that a free Greece was the best defence against Antiochus. Scipio, as we shall see, probably took the opposite view. The Fulvians were also opposed to the complete withdrawal of the Roman army from Greece, partly through fear of Antiochus, but also because they did not share Flamininus' advanced views, and preferred to maintain some kind of direct control. It should be stressed, however, that no one was in favour of completely subjugating Greece to Roman domination.

The majority of the commissioners who had been appointed to supervise the settlement of 196 were in favour of giving Oreus and Eretria to Eumenes. Flamininus opposed this, and his stand was supported by the senate.[6] But as we have seen, he made no attempt to remove the existing Pergamene possessions of Aegina and Andros.

The other disputes concerned the fetters. Flamininus wanted to free all of them, the commissioners thought that garrisons should be maintained. A compromise was reached.[7] Compromise was not alien to Flamininus, but we may still feel that he genuinely believed it would be best to free the cities. The discontent which was already rife among the Aetolians will have reinforced this belief.[8]

---

[1] xxxiii. 13. 4, Pol. xviii. 39. 5.   [2] xxxiii. 25. 7, Pol. xviii. 42. 4.

[3] xxxiii. 25. 4 ff., Pol. xviii. 42. 3.

[4] On Appian's claim (*Mac.* 9. 3) that the senate imposed far harsher terms cf. xxxiii. 30. 5, 7 nn.

[5] xxxiii. 13. 15, 27. 6, Pol. xviii. 39. 3, 43. 2. A. Passerini (*Ath.* N.S. x [1932], 111 ff., cf. *Ath.* N.S. xxiii [1945], 114 ff.) held that the commissioners were aware of the danger and Flamininus was not.

[6] xxxiii. 34. 10, Pol. xviii. 47. 10–11. Cf. p. 29 n. 5.

[7] xxxiii. 31. 11, Pol. xviii. 45. 12. I do not understand Balsdon's statement (186 n. 47) that this was a 'dilemma, not a disagreement'.

[8] xxxiii. 31. 1 ff., Pol. xviii. 45. 1.

The commissioners, on the other hand, seem to have been more interested in keeping the larger units happy. Thus Cn. Cornelius Lentulus encouraged Philip to ask the senate for an alliance and tried, with less success, to placate the Aetolians.[1]

Is it possible to determine the political composition of the board of commissioners?[2] There are two Cornelii Lentuli amongst the *legati*, whilst L. Cornelius Lentulus, the consul of 199, joined the conference of Lysimachia as a special envoy from the senate.[3] If the Lentuli are to be regarded as opposed to Scipio,[4] then the only two *legati* who might be regarded as supporters of Scipio are L. Terentius Massaliota and—if he was in fact a commissioner[5]— M. Caecilius Metellus. In neither case, however, is certainty possible. The position of Massaliota can only be assumed from that of two other Terentii—the consul of 216 and Terentius Culleo, the praetor of 187.[6] M. Metellus is probably the brother of Q. Caecilius Metellus, the consul of 206, but while the latter's earlier allegiance to Scipio is beyond doubt, there are reasons for thinking that this allegiance did not continue into the period we are now considering.[7]

The chief opposition to Flamininus, then, would appear to have come from the Fulvians on the commission. It was they, too, who were mainly responsible for the negotiations with Antiochus at Lysimachia.[8] On this, however, there seems to have been no conflict with Flamininus, and the demands of Lentulus at Lysimachia are exactly the same as those expressed by Flamininus at Corinth. Nor is there any evidence of disagreements over the war with Nabis. There was a long debate in the senate over whether to declare war immediately or leave the matter with Flamininus. It may be that some of Flamininus' opponents wanted to tie his hands, but uncertainty about Antiochus' intentions probably made the majority decide to leave the situation flexible.[9]

---

[1] xxxiii. 35. 3–9, Pol. xviii. 48. 4–9.

[2] The list is never given in full. Cf. *MRR*, i. 337 and supp. 2. The fact that the senate seems to have backed Flamininus on the matters that were referred to it does not mean that a majority of Flamininus' supporters would have been included on the commission. Similar situations seem to occur in 189 (*Latomus* xxxi, 53) and 168 (*JRS* liv [1964], 75).

[3] xxxiii. 39. 2, Pol. xviii. 49. 2.

[4] Cf. p. 32.   [5] *MRR*, i. 337.

[6] For Varro cf. Scullard, *RP*, 49 ff., for Culleo xxx. 45. 5.

[7] For earlier support cf. xxxi. 4. 3 n. But in 193 he criticized the consul Cornelius Merula (xxxv. 8. 4.) and in 179 he reconciled the two censors M. Fulvius Nobilior and M. Aemilius Lepidus (xl. 45. 6 ff., cf. Scullard, *RP*, 180–1), an action which seems to have marked the end of Lepidus' associations with the Scipionic group.

[8] xxxiii. 39. 1–2, Pol. xviii. 49. 2–50. 1.

[9] Cf. xxxiii. 45. 3 n. For Flamininus' political position in the years following 196 cf. *Latomus* xxxi, 47 ff.

5. LIVY'S ACCOUNT OF THE OUTBREAK OF THE SECOND MACEDONIAN WAR

(a) *Philip's activities from the Peace of Phoenice until 201*[1]

The First Macedonian War was concluded by the Peace of Phoenice in 205. In that year Cretan piracy led the Rhodians to declare war on them. Polybius relates that Philip sent Heraclides of Tarentum to Rhodes to destroy the Rhodian fleet, and also sent ambassadors to Crete to stir up the Cretans to make war on Rhodes.[2] Help was also given to the Cretans by Dicaearchus, another of Philip's henchmen: the latter, in addition, attacked various places in the Aegean and Hellespont.[3] Philip was not acting overtly at this time—he was himself engaged in operations in Thrace and against the Dardanians.[4]

By the autumn of 203, at the latest,[5] it was known that Ptolemy IV Philopator was dead. In 202 came Philip's first major expedition in the Aegean. He advanced to the Propontis and captured Lysimacheia, Perinthus, and Chalcedon.[6] He then captured Cius and

[1] The basic work on these difficult years was done by Holleaux in a series of articles now collected together in *Études*, iv. Walbank, *Philip V*, 108 ff., gives the clearest complete narrative. Cf. also Magie, *RRAM*, 746 nn. 36 ff., Ferro, 35 ff., Dahlheim, 234 ff., Will, *HP*, ii. 80 ff.

[2] Pol. xiii. 4–5, cf. Diod. xxviii. 1, Polyaenus v. 17. 2, Holleaux, *Études*, iv. 124–45, Walbank, *Philip V*, 109 ff., *Commentary*, ii. 417–18. The outbreak of the war is in 205, as in Diodorus xxvii. 3 it immediately precedes the activities of Pleminius at Locri. Philip may have stirred up the Cretans to renew their piracy, rather than only encouraging them to resist Rhodian opposition, as Holleaux and Walbank believe. Nabis was also involved (Pol. xiii. 8: cf. on this Errington, *Philopoemen*, ch. iii and my review in *JRS* lx [1970], 209).

[3] Pol. xviii. 54, Diod. xxviii. 1. For the date cf. Holleaux, *Études*, iv. 131 ff. Polybius mentions him in a back reference and Diodorus' account belongs to 202. But Diodorus goes on to mention Heraclides in what is clearly a back reference (xxviii. 2) and it is best to assume that his whole discussion is a summary of earlier events, designed to serve as an introduction to the major misdeeds of Philip and Antiochus.

[4] Walbank, *Philip V*, 111–12, *CQ* xxxvi (1942), 138. Holleaux ingeniously argued that an inscription from Iasos (*IBM*, iii. 441) referred to an attack on Iasos at this time, instigated by Philip. A recently discovered inscription, however, makes it clear that the Iasos inscription cannot refer to these years (Holleaux, *Études*, iv. 146–62, with Robert's note on p. 162, Walbank, *Commentary*, i. 621–2, ii. 645, J. Crampa, *Labraunda* iii. 1 (Lund, 1969), 93–6: Ferro, 43–4, Will, *HP*, ii. 105, oddly think that the new inscription makes no difference. Cf. also J. and L. Robert, *RÉG* lxxiv [1961], 235 no. 673, lxxviii [1965], 160 no. 368).

[5] This would not be the place for a full discussion of the date of the death of Philopator. For my own view (death on 28 Nov. 205, announcement on 8 Sept. 203) cf. my review of Schmitt, *Antiochos*, in *CR* N.S. xvi (1966), 98–100. The most recent discussion is by K. Abel, *Hermes* xcv (1967), 72–90.

[6] Pol. xv. 23. 9, xviii. 2. 4, 3. 11, 4. 5, L. xxxii. 33. 15, 34. 6. On the date of the capture of Sestus (200) cf. xxxii. 33. 7 n.

gave it to his relative Prusias of Bithynia, who refounded it under the name of Prusa.[1] Rhodes now declared Philip an enemy, and the latter proceeded to capture Thasos.[2]

At the beginning of 201 Philip occupied many of the Cyclades.[3] There follow three events whose relative chronology is disputed— the battle of Lade, in which Philip defeated the Rhodian fleet, the battle of Chios, in which Philip was defeated by a joint Rhodio–Pergamene fleet, and Philip's invasion of Pergamum. My own view is that the order was Lade, invasion of Pergamum, Chios.[4] Some time before the battle of Chios, probably in fact before the battle of Lade, Philip had occupied Samos and taken control of the Egyptian fleet stationed there: there was, however, violent resistance to the Macedonian takeover, and soon afterwards the Macedonians were expelled, and the island reverted to Egyptian control.[5]

After the battle of Chios, Philip advanced on Caria and captured Prinassus, Iasus, Bargylia, Euromus, Pedasa, and Stratonicea.[6] The Rhodian and Pergamene fleets finally blockaded him in Bargylia.[7]

Epigraphic evidence provides further information on the events of 201. The Cretan war with Rhodes came to an end shortly before the conflict between Rhodes and Philip. We also know that Philip attacked Cos in that year and that Nisyros was in his possession.[8]

(b) *The Pact of the Kings and Philip's motives 203–200* [9]

The ancient sources refer to an agreement between Philip and Antiochus to partition the Ptolemaic kingdom between them.[10]

[1] Cf. xxxi. 31. 4 n.

[2] Pol. xv. 23. 6, 24, cf. L. xxxi. 31. 4, xxxiii. 30. 3.

[3] Cf. xxxi. 15. 8, 31. 4.

[4] The original view of Walbank (*Philip V*, 307–8, cf. 117 ff.). Walbank now agrees with Holleaux (*Études*, iv. 213–22) that Chios precedes Lade, but places the invasion of Pergamum between the battles (*CR* N.S. xii [1962], 273–4, *Commentary*, ii. 497–500, cf. McDonald, *JRS* liii [1963], 188). I still believe that Polybius' phrase τὸν δ' Ἄτταλον μηδέπω συμμεμιχέναι (xvi. 10) cannot be translated 'had not yet rejoined the fight' and hence that Chios cannot antedate Lade.

[5] Pol. xvi. 2. 4, 2. 9, 7. 5, Chr. Habicht, *MDAI(A)* lxxii (1957), 233 ff. The inscription makes it clear that Holleaux (*Études*, iv. 233–4, 312) was wrong in his argument that Philip was concerned only to incorporate the Egyptian ships in his fleet, that he did not occupy Samos, and voluntarily abandoned it at the end of the summer's campaign. Both L. (xxxi. 31. 4) and Appian (*Mac.* 4. 1) imply a capture, though without the inscription little trust could be put in either.

[6] The evidence for the Carian expedition is meticulously assembled and examined by Holleaux, *Études*, iv. 222–4, 255–63.

[7] Pol. xvi. 24. See further below.

[8] *Syll.*[3] 569, Holleaux, *Études*, iv. 163 ff.: for the treaty between Rhodes and Hierapytna, *SGDI* 3749. Cos: *Syll.*[3] 568–9, Paton–Hicks, *Inscriptions of Cos*, 10–11. Nisyros, *Syll.*[3] 572. (*Syll.*[3] 570 and 673 probably refer to the Second Cretan War of 155–3: cf. M. Segre, *RFIC* lxi (1933), 379–82, Fraser and Bean, *RPI*, 148–51, Robert *ap.* Holleaux, *Études*, iv. 164 n. 4). [*Notes 9 and 10 overleaf*]

Holleaux and his followers thought that the news of this pact was the primary motive in inducing the senate to determine to go to war with Philip. Such a view could, of course, be true whether or not there really was such a pact, but it remains necessary to investigate Philip's motives for his aggressive actions at this time.

The evidence about the pact would lead us to expect that both Philip and Antiochus would immediately attack the possessions of Ptolemy. In fact it is only Antiochus who does so, invading Koile Syria in 202.[1] In 203 Ptolemy, the son of Sosibius, had been sent as an ambassador from Egypt to Macedon, with instructions to request Philip's help in the event of an attack on Egypt by Antiochus.[2] Ptolemy did not return until 201, which suggests that Philip had deliberately kept him waiting for a reply.[3] Philip was evidently concealing his intentions.

Other evidence shows that there was no close collaboration between Philip and Antiochus. In 201 Philip seems to have had great difficulty in getting help from Antiochus' satrap Zeuxis.[4] In that year Philip attacked Alabanda, whose integrity had been recently guaranteed by Antiochus: and if Stratonicea belonged to Antiochus at this time, it would be another example of a Seleucid possession being attacked by Philip.[5]

Holleaux proved beyond doubt that, of the Asiatic cities attacked by Philip in 201, Iasos, Bargylia, Euromus, and Pedasa were not Ptolemaic, and also that several Egyptian possessions in Caria were not attacked.[6] On the other hand, Philip did attack Samos, and Cos had close ties with Egypt.[7] But there was clearly no all-out assault

[9] The authenticity of the pact was denied by D. Magie, *JRS* xxix (1939), 32–44, L. De Regibus, *Aegyptus* xxxii (1952), 97–100, A. Bellezza, *L'ombra di un' antica alleanza* (Genoa, 1962). For the most recent discussions cf. Schmitt, *Antiochos*, 237–61, Walbank, *Commentary*, ii. 471–3, Dahlheim, 235–7 n. 6.

[10] Pol. xv. 20, App. *Mac.* 4, Trogus, *prol.* xxx, Just. xxx. 2. 8, Hier. *in Dan.* xi. 13 (= *FGH* 260 F45). L. only refers to the pact at xxxi. 14. 5 (cf. below and n. ad loc.).

[1] For the details of the Fifth Syrian War cf. Holleaux, *Études*, iii. 317–35.

[2] Pol. xv. 25. 13.

[3] Pol. xvi. 22. 3. Schmitt's view (*Antiochos*, 233 ff., 257) that he returned in 202 depends on his chronology for the death of Philopator, on which cf. my comments in *CR* N.S. xvi (1966), 99–100.

[4] Pol. xv. 20. 6, xvi. 1. 8–9.

[5] Alabanda: *OGIS* 234 (cf. Holleaux, *Études*, iii. 141 ff.), Pol. xvi. 24. 8. Mylasa may also be Seleucid (Holleaux, *Études*, iv. 262). On Stratonicea cf. xxxiii. 18. 22 n. and for Philip at Panamara Holleaux, *Études*, iv. 204–10.

[6] *Études*, iv. 298 ff. Samos apart, it is unlikely that any places captured in 201 were lost before the conference of Nicaea (cf. Pol. xviii. 2. 4, Holleaux, *Études*, iv. 308).

[7] M. Segre, *Tituli Calymnii* (Bergamo, 1952), xii, G. Klaffenbach, *Gnomon* xxv (1953), 455–7, P. Herrmann, *Der römische Kaisereid* (Göttingen, 1968), 36–7.

on Ptolemy's possessions, and in some cases he seems to have deliberately left them alone.

What, then, was Philip doing? In the latter part of the third century Macedon and Egypt had been on far better terms than they were earlier.[1] As we have seen, the Egyptian court could hope for Philip's aid in the event of an attack by Antiochus. In these circumstances Antiochus may well have wanted to secure Philip's benevolent neutrality before embarking on his invasion of Koile Syria, and it seems possible that the pact was no more than a mutual agreement to obstruct each other's aggressive designs. How the pact became known remains a mystery. But the very fact that Philip and Antiochus were both engaged in aggression, and were not in open conflict with each other, would be bound to raise suspicions.

(c) *Livy's account of the outbreak of the War*

There has been a great variety of modern explanations of the Roman decision to go to war with Philip.[2] Some see the war as a case of Rome's aggressive imperialism,[3] others as revenge for the First Macedonian War.[4] A third view is that the war was undertaken through love of Greece and the desire to defend Greek freedom.[5] Then there is the view that Rome felt herself bound to go to war because of Philip's aggressions against Rome's friends.[6] Lastly, there is the view that the war was a case of 'defensive imperialism', that it was undertaken as a 'pre-emptive strike' in fear of what Philip might do, either by himself or in concert with Antiochus.[7]

---

[1] Holleaux, *Rome*, 78 ff. (though his argument from the Egyptian mediation in the First Macedonian War is invalid).

[2] I do not propose here to discuss all these views in detail, but rather to set out my own position.

[3] G. Colin, *Rome et la Grèce de 200 à 146 av. J.-C.* (Paris, 1905), 69–70, 89–95, De Sanctis, iv. 1. 25–6, T. Walek, *RPh* n.s. xlix (1925), 28–54, 118–42, J. Carcopino, *Les Étapes de l'impérialisme romain* (Paris, 1961), ch. ii, Petzold, *passim*, Will, *HP*, ii. 116 ff. (senate, not people), Pédech, 113–23. For further references cf. Cassola, *GP*, 25 n. 2, 26 n. 4, Dahlheim, 239–41 n. 20, Will, *HP*, ii. 125–8.

[4] Balsdon, *JRS* xliv (1954), 30–42. Badian, *FC*, 64 ff. also inclines in this direction, although he rightly sees a complex mesh of overlapping motives.

[5] Tenney Frank, *Roman Imperialism* (New York, 1914), 138–51—though he too recognized that other motives may have played a part. Cf. also H. E. Stier, *Roms Aufstieg zur Weltmacht und die griechische Welt* (Cologne and Opladen, 1957), 114 ff.

[6] This would be the consequence of E. Bikerman's view (*RPh*, série III, ix [1935], 59–81, 161–76) that the war was legally justified on the basis of the Peace of Phoenice. Though Rome could always claim that her wars were justified because of appeals made to her, without any treaty being involved. The ultimatum of Abydos, in fact, has only very loose connections with the Peace of Phoenice: Rome's *amici* had called for her protection and that was sufficient for her intervention. Cf. especially Dahlheim, 248 ff.

[7] Holleaux, *CAH*, viii. 155 ff., *Rome*, 306 ff., A. Passerini, *Ath.* n.s. ix (1931), 260–90, 542–62, G. T. Griffith, *CHJ* v (1935), 1–14, J. A. O. Larsen, *CPh* xxxii

L. gives no comprehensive, coherent account either of the actual events leading to the outbreak of war or of Roman motives in undertaking it.[1] In the first eleven chapters of book xxxi, however, he makes a number of statements which appear to correspond with the revenge, morally justified, and defensive imperialism views of the war. Thus 1. 9 'infensos Philippo cum ob infidam adversus Aetolos aliosque regionis eiusdem socios pacem, tum ob auxilia cum pecunia nuper in Africam missa Hannibali' suggests both revenge and moral justification.[2] In chapter 2, the message to Egypt 'si coacti iniuriis bellum adversus Philippum suscepissent' is again moral justification. In chapter 3, Aurelius warns Laevinus that war is urgent 'ne cunctantibus iis auderet Philippus quod Pyrrhus prius ausus ex aliquanto minore regno esset', which is the pre-emptive strike. The proposal of Sulpicius to the assembly to declare war on Philip 'ob iniurias armaque inlata sociis populi Romani' (6. 1) is moral justification, and perhaps revenge. But the whole argument of Sulpicius' speech in chapter 7 is one of defensive imperialism, whilst the letter to Massinissa in chapter 11, 'quod Carthaginienses auxiliis iuvisset iniuriasque inferendo sociis populi Romani flagrante bello Italia coegisset classes exercitusque in Graeciam mitti et distinendo copias causa in primis fuisset serius in Africam traiciendi', is pure revenge.

But there is no consistent claim that Rome was morally bound to go to the help of the Greeks, and it cannot be shown that there is any consistent attempt to mislead the reader and hide the facts of Roman aggressive imperialism: nor is there any trace of philhellenism as such. Athens, in particular, has only a contributory role.[3]

Equally L. does not give a continuous account of the events leading to the war, and what he does say involves serious difficulties. In chapter 1, §§ 9–10, he appears to be giving a general summary of the causes of the war.[4] Chapter 2 reports the embassy from Rhodes and Attalus, bringing news of Philip's aggressions in Asia. The matter is referred to the consuls. An embassy is sent to Egypt to explain that Rome might be forced to go to war with Philip. In

(1937), 15–31, McDonald, *JRS* xxvii (1937), 180–207, Magie, *JRS* xxix (1939), 32–44, Walbank, *Philip V*, 127–37. Further references in Cassola, *GP*, 26 n. 3, Dahlheim, 239–41 n. 20.

[1] Bikerman's view (*CPh* xl [1945], 138 ff.) that this is a consistent and carefully worked-out causation account seems to me untenable. The whole thing is far too much of a rag-bag. Consistency is also assumed by Hoch, 77.

[2] For the truth of these charges cf. nn. ad loc.

[3] It is only the epitomator who gives prominence to Athens. This is a strong argument against Holleaux's view that the Athenian embassies in L. were invented to provide a justification for Roman action, or that Athens' inclusion in the Peace of Phoenice (xxix. 12. 14) was part of that invention. Cf. Balsdon, *JRS* xliv, 33 and xxxi. 5. 8 n.

[4] Cf. n. ad loc.

chapter 3 the senate authorizes the dispatch of a preliminary naval expedition under M. Valerius Laevinus, and the latter is told by Aurelius of Philip's aggressive activities; Laevinus authorizes Aurelius to report these matters to the senate. All these events are related under the consular year 201.

Under 200, L. reports the arrival of letters from Aurelius and Valerius, and of an Athenian embassy, which says that Philip is approaching Attica and Athens itself would soon be in his power. The senate authorizes P. Sulpicius Galba, who had drawn Macedon as his province, to propose to the *comitia* that war be declared on Philip. The *comitia centuriata* reject the proposal and there follows a speech by Galba which was successful in persuading the assembly to change its mind. Next come details of the arrangements for war, during which an embassy from Egypt arrives, promising help to Rome. In chapter 14 L. reports Galba's departure for Greece. An Athenian embassy meets him, and requests help against Philip; a force under Claudius Centho is sent (14. 3). Philip is at that time besieging Abydus.

At this point L. digresses to explain the causes of the hostility between Philip and Athens and the events leading to the siege of Abydus (chs. 14–18). Two Acarnanians had been executed by Athens for profaning the Eleusinian mysteries. Acarnania appealed to Philip who sanctioned an Acarnanian raid on Attica with Macedonian support. Later Athens declared war, inspired by Attalus and the Rhodians. This was followed by a major Macedonian invasion of Attica under Philocles. Philip himself began to attack Ptolemaic possessions in Thrace, and finally laid siege to Abydus. Here he was met by a Roman *legatus* M. Aemilius Lepidus, who told him that if he did not desist from his aggressions, he would be at war with Rome.

Little survives of Polybius' account of these events,[1] but it is sufficient to show that there are very serious omissions and distortions in L.'s narrative. Polybius' account of the visit of Attalus and the Rhodians to Athens (xvi. 25–7) includes a description of the presence of Roman ambassadors and of the ultimatum delivered by them to the Macedonian commander Nicanor, all of which is completely suppressed by L. These are clearly the same ambassadors as those who sent Lepidus to deliver the ultimatum to Philip at Abydus (xvi. 34).[2] They are also clearly identical with the *legati* whom L. (xxxi. 2) had described as being dispatched to Egypt in the autumn of 201. L. has, it seems, systematically obliterated

---

[1] xvi. 24–34 is the relevant section.

[2] They are not named in xvi. 25–7 but the reference to their mission to Antiochus and Ptolemy in both 27 and 34 proves the identification.

references to the activities of the *legati* in Greece, and also to their instructions to attempt to make peace between Antiochus and Ptolemy. Their brief is mis-stated in chapter 2, and their presence at Athens is suppressed in chapters 14 and 15. In chapter 18 there are two significant differences from the account of Polybius in xvi. 34. L. implies that the decision to send Lepidus to Philip at Abydos was taken by the *legati* themselves, whilst Polybius makes it clear that they were acting on the instructions of the senate (κατὰ τὰς ἐντολάς). Secondly in Polybius Lepidus complains specifically of Philip's attacks on Athens, Cius, and Abydus. L. refers to Abydus alone.

(d) *The course of events*

Before attempting to explain the reasons for these distortions it will be as well to establish the details of the actual events between autumn 201 and the siege of Abydus, as this will involve discussion of further errors in L.'s account.

Philip was besieged at Bargylia in the autumn of 201.[1] How long he remained there is crucial to the chronology of what follows. Polybius describes the beginning of the blockade as being τοῦ χει-μῶνος ἤδη καταρχομένου, καθ' ὃν Πόπλιος Σολπίκιος ὕπατος κατεστάθη ἐν 'Ρώμῃ.[2] From this it is often assumed that Philip remained at Bargylia all winter, and that while he was there he was incom-municado.[3] It follows that the Acarnanian raid on Athens cannot antedate the spring of 200, and that the Athenian embassies men-tioned by L. in xxxi. 1 and 5 must be rejected. The assumptions, however, seem to me indefensible. All that Polybius says is that the winter was beginning when the blockade began and that Sulpicius entered office in the course of that winter. The consular year at this time began on the Ides of March, and Polybius' statement indicates that the Roman calendar was running ahead of the Julian at this time. How far ahead it is not possible to say, but the evidence would support a working hypothesis that Sulpicius entered office some time in December.[4]

---

[1] See above.

[2] Pol. xvi. 24. 1, cf. Holleaux, *Études*, iv. 286–7.

[3] McDonald, *JRS* xxvii, 187, cf. *JRS* liii (1963), 189, Walbank, *Philip V*, 312. Holleaux, *Études*, v. 18–19, does envisage the possibility of the Acarnanian raid as preceding Philip's return from Asia: in *CAH*, viii. 161 he appears to leave the position open. Cf. Pédech, *RÉG* lxxv (1962), 227–30. The view was attacked by P. Culmann, *Die römische Orientgesandtschaft vom Jahre 201–200* (Giessen, 1922), 11, Ferro, 73–9.

[4] Cf. Holleaux, *Études*, iv. 336–48. On the calendar, De Sanctis, iv. 1. 376 ff. A. K. Michels, *The Calendar of the Roman Republic* (Princeton, 1967), does not deal

There thus seems no reason why the Acarnanian raid on Athens should not come in the early winter of 201/200.[1] The Eleusinian mysteries took place in the month of Boedromion—about September.[2] In which case either Philip received the news of the executions at Bargylia, or he was already back in Greece. In fact the first alternative is almost certainly correct, for at xxxi. 14. 11, a passage which must derive from Polybius, L. implies that the Acarnanian raid on Attica preceded Philip's return across the Aegean.[3] The raid, then, is at the end of October at the earliest. This would appear to rule out the Athenian embassy reported by L. in xxxi. 1. 10, for that embassy precedes the consular elections. There has to be an interval between the elections and the entry of the consuls into office, and it seems impossible for all this to follow an Athenian embassy which itself follows the Acarnanian raid.

The second embassy reported by L. comes just after the consuls had entered office, but before the first meeting of the *comitia*, the meeting which rejected the motion for war (5. 6). If this was in December, it is still rather early, though just possible for it to have arrived by this time. L.'s language, however, makes far better sense as a description of the invasion of Philocles than of the Acarnanian raid, and it is very tempting to alter its position, and allow it to be

with this year. I see no justification for the view of R. Knapowski, *Beiträge zur alten Geschichte und deren Nachleben*, i (Berlin, 1969), 325, that only two intercalations had been omitted before 200.

[1] The calendar changes at Athens at this time, while not confirming this chronology, do not conflict with it. When Attalus visited Athens, the Athenians created the tribe of Attalis in his honour (Pol. xvi. 25. 9, L. xxxi. 15. 6). Shortly before this Athens had abolished the two Macedonian tribes Antigonis and Demetrias. An inscription (*IG* ii². 2362) records the division of the demes into eleven tribes, but the list was left unfinished, which suggests that the gap between the abolition of Antigonis and Demetrias and the creation of Attalis was only a short one (cf. W. K. Pritchett, *TAPA* lxxxv [1954], 159–67). The year also saw a break in the secretary cycle. 201/0 should have produced a secretary from tribe 11 (Aiantis) but instead a new cycle started with tribe 5 (Ptolemais). Since Ptolemais did not replace one of the Macedonian tribes, and the deme list in any case shows that the abolition of the Macedonian tribes is later than the beginning of the Attic year, the change of secretary can have nothing to do with the Acarnanian raid. It was probably intended as a sign of sympathy for Egypt in its struggle with Antiochus. I follow the orthodox dating of the Athenian archons. Ferro, 81 ff., accepts the system of E. Manni (*Ath.* n.s. xxxiii [1955], 253 ff.) which eliminates a break in the cycle. Manni's views seem to me completely unacceptable(cf. *JHS* lxxxiv [1964], 307–8).

[2] Bikerman's attempt (*CPh* xl [1945], 142) to place the episode at the mysteries of 202 is quite impossible.

[3] Admittedly it could be argued that since there are other distortions in this section, we cannot trust any detail not specifically found in Polybius. But it is hard to see any motive for a change on this point.

one of the factors in persuading the *comitia* to change its mind.[1] If so, we can proceed to attempt to fit it into the pattern of events in Greece.

When the Roman envoys reached Athens, their reception was very cordial, though not quite as rapturous as that accorded to Attalus.[2] But their treatment is quite consistent with the supposition that Athens had as yet made no approach to Rome, and I would suggest that the Athenian embassy was dispatched, with the approval of the Roman *legati*, after the invasion of Philocles, which is probably itself subsequent to the invasion of Nicanor which is mentioned by Polybius in xvi. 27. This embassy was probably the same as the embassy of Cephisodorus mentioned by Pausanias.[3]

Such a view has two important consequences. First, the ultimatum delivered to Nicanor by the Roman *legati* had no formal status, as the war-vote had not yet been passed. Secondly we can accept that the Roman *legati* left Rome in the autumn of 201, where L. places their dispatch to Alexandria.

Before proceeding, it may be as well to suggest a working chronology. The blockade of Bargylia began in September, and it was at this time that Rhodes and Attalus sent ambassadors to Rome.[4] At this same period the Eleusinian mysteries were taking place, and soon afterwards the two Acarnanians were executed. There followed the Acarnanian appeal to Philip, and we might put the Acarnanian raid in November. Meanwhile the three Roman ambassadors had been dispatched: they first went to north-west Greece, Aetolia, and Achaea.[5] In October or November the consular elections were held at Rome. In December or January Philip escaped from Bargylia, and was pursued across the Aegean by Attalus and the Rhodians. At Athens the latter were joined by the Roman *legati*. There followed the raids of Nicanor and Philocles, and an Athenian embassy was sent to Rome. Sulpicius had entered his consulship in December,

---

[1] Thus De Sanctis, iv. 1. 32 n. 65, S. Accame, *RFIC* lxix (1941–2), 183.

[2] Pol. xvi. 26. 6. Holleaux's view (*Études*, v. 20, *CAH*, viii. 162) that their reception was cool is ridiculous.

[3] Paus. i. 36. 6. The chronology fits other details of Pausanias' account. Help from Egypt and Attalus had not yet arrived—Attalus had not brought his army—and the Rhodian ships were no use against Macedonian troops. The main Rhodian fleet had indeed returned across the Aegean (xxxi. 15. 8) but some remained behind (xxxi. 22. 8 n.). The appeal to Egypt also fits in with the Egyptian embassy to Rome (xxxi. 9). Petzold's doubts (75 ff.) about the authenticity of Pausanias' account are not convincing (cf. Accame, *Espansione romana*, 130 ff.). McDonald, *JRS* liii, 189, retracts his earlier view (*JRS* xxvii, 198) that the embassy belongs to the late summer of 200.

[4] Pol. xvi. 24. 3, L. xxxi. 2. 1. The embassy of the Rhodians (alone) in App. *Mac.* 4. 2 will have the same reference.

[5] Pol. xvi. 27.

and the assembly had rejected his motion for war with Philip. The Athenian ambassadors reached Rome about March, and the war-vote followed soon afterwards.[1]

(e) *Roman motives for war*

We are now in a position to answer the main questions—what were the Roman motives for going to war with Philip, and why is L.'s account of these events so distorted? I believe that Holleaux was fundamentally right in thinking that the news brought by the Rhodian and Pergamene ambassadors in the autumn of 201 had a serious effect on the senate, though they were as much affected by the news of Philip's actual aggressions as by his reported pact with Antiochus, which Holleaux regarded as the decisive factor. But any senatorial decision had to be promoted, and argued for, by a smaller number of people. It was the opponents of Scipio Africanus who held the chief magistracies in the last few years of the third century, and who were usually able to command a majority in the senate.[2] It was they who seem to have been particularly affected by the news: the second commander in the First Macedonian War, P. Sulpicius Galba, was qualified to hold a second consulship in 200, and it was decided to promote his candidature: the first commander, M. Valerius Laevinus, was dispatched with a preliminary expedition.[3] And the group persuaded the senate to dispatch three *legati* to stir up support for Rome's cause in Greece, to secure the neutrality of Antiochus,[4] and to deliver the *indictio belli* to Philip as soon as the *comitia* had passed the motion for war. Now Sulpicius, Laevinus, and their friends had conceived and fought the First Macedonian War as a purely defensive operation: their mandate had been to keep Philip out of Italy, and their conduct of it had been desultory and ineffective.[5] It seems entirely plausible that they should have been frightened of a possible invasion of Italy by Philip. They had already heard of Philip's alleged aggressions in Illyria, and perhaps in Aetolia, and of his supposed help to the Carthaginians at Zama,[6] but these had not posed as powerful a threat as now seemed to be the case.

---

[1] The dates are only approximate. If the war-vote was passed in April, the gap between this and Sulpicius' arrival in Greece at the end of the campaigning season (cf. xxxi. 18. 9, 22. 4) will not be too long.

[2] Cf. p. 30, Scullard, *RP*, 78 ff.   [3] Cf. xxxi. 3 n.

[4] This was clearly the real purpose of the visit to Antiochus: as a result *amicitia* was established. Cf. xxxii. 8. 13 n.

[5] For the mandate cf. xxiii. 38. 11, and for the character of the war Holleaux, *Rome*, 217 ff.

[6] For the truth of these allegations, and the Aetolian appeal to Rome, cf. xxxi. 1. 9–10, 29. 4 nn.

In addition, the fact that these senators were the political opponents of Scipio can rightly be seen as a contributory cause of the war. Scipio had won great glory in Africa, and they wanted a command to counterbalance his influence. But that does not mean that they wanted war for imperialistic reasons.

There are good reasons for thinking that Scipio himself was opposed, initially at least, to the war proposal.[1] What was the reason for this opposition? In part, sheer war-weariness may have been the answer. But Scipio's *dignitas* is also important. He did not want to fight, and did not want his opponents to have the glory of fighting. Scipio, moreover, had not fought Philip before and may have been instrumental in bringing the First Macedonian War to an end.[2] The new war was going to be conducted by those who had shown so little initiative in the old one. If they were going to display the same lack of vision, the same defensive spirit, Scipio would want none of it. He was a man who liked to be clear where he was going.

At first Scipio's view prevailed with the *comitia*. They were persuaded to change their minds by the news of the fresh attacks in Attica, by the concessions to Scipio's veterans,[3] and no doubt by some vigorous lobbying of the right people.

(f) *The reasons for Livy's distortions*

Why did L. fail to report these facts accurately? Let us first consider his sources. As we have seen, chapters 1–13 are of annalistic origin, while 14. 6–18 must derive from Polybius xvi. 25–34.[4] Yet the suppression of all mention of the Roman ambassadors at Athens occurs in the annalistic chapter 2, as well as the Polybian chapters 14–18. Either L. himself distorted the truth, as related by Polybius and his Roman predecessors, or he read an annalist who had done this, and being impressed by this annalistic account, combined it with what he read in Polybius as best he could.

---

[1] Cf. xxxi. 6. 3–4 n.
[2] Scullard, *RP*, 77: but cf. xxxi. 2. 3 n.
[3] xxxi. 8. 6.
[4] Cf. p. 8. Modern explanations of L.'s distortions have been inadequate. Nissen, *KU*, 125, said that L. had already narrated the outbreak of the war from the Roman point of view. De Sanctis, iv. 1. 32 n. 65, thought that L. was ashamed of the humble role of the Roman *legati* in the events at Athens. Holleaux (*Études*, v. 24) that he was embarrassed to discover that Polybius' description of the Athenian episode conflicted with the annalistic account of the Athenian embassies to Rome. Both these views depend on misunderstandings of what actually happened at Athens (cf. p. 44 n. 2). McDonald (*JRS* xxvii, 190 n. 63) held that L. omitted the visit of the *legati* to Athens because he had originally sent them to Alexandria: that merely pushes the problem one stage further back. Walsh (*Livy*, 149) talks merely of 'chronological inconsistency' while Balsdon (*JRS* xliv, 40–1) thinks that L. regarded the Romans' presence at Athens as of little importance.

Consideration of the reasons for the distortion suggests that the latter is in fact what happened. The distortions have the effect of divorcing events in Greece in the winter of 201/0 from the vital decisions in Rome, and also of divorcing events east of the Aegean from those decisions.[1] What the senate had done was to anticipate the decision of the *comitia* to go to war. The *legati* were assuring the Greeks of Rome's intentions; they delivered an ultimatum to Nicanor which had all the appearance of an *indictio belli*, but in fact lacked formal sanction. They could only deliver a proper *indictio* when informed that the *comitia* had passed the war-vote.[2] If there was one right which everyone agreed belonged to the *populus*, it was that of making peace and war.[3] The senate was clearly acting *ultra vires* and probably kept its decision secret.[4] Now this sort of procedure may not have worried L. himself: but it could well have troubled those earlier annalists who wanted to show that the senate's actions had always been based on respect for the (limited) prerogatives of the people. The distortion could have occurred at the time of Sulla, and if so Valerius Antias could well be the culprit. But it could equally as well have taken place earlier.[5] It follows that chapters 14–18 are neither annalistic nor Polybian. They are L.'s own reworking of two discordant accounts.

6. TEXT

The lemmata give the reading of the Oxford text, even in cases where the note proceeds to argue for a different reading. The sigla are also those of the Oxford text. I have collated B myself, but relied on McDonald's reports of the χ group.

One aspect of the relationship between B and χ deserves special comment. There is a large number of passages in books xxxi and xxxii where B omits a word or words found in χ. In many of these χ's addition seems correct—xxxi. 2. 2, 4. 1, 4. 3, 7. 14, 11. 17, 31. 4, 31. 9, 32. 3, 33. 8, 34. 5, 37. 5, 38. 5, 47. 1, 49. 2, xxxii. 4. 4, 10. 2,

---

[1] Cf. Bikerman, *CPh* xl, 140. The news of the pact of the kings brought by Rhodes and Pergamum, and the mission of the Roman *legati* to Antiochus were closely connected with the senate's anticipation of the people's decision on Macedon, and are thus also suppressed.

[2] For the form of the fetial procedure at this time cf. Walbank, *JRS* xxvii (1937), 194–7, *CPh* xliv (1949), 15 ff.: the latter article argues convincingly against Bikerman's view (*RPh* série III, ix, 173 ff.) that the Abydos ultimatum was not an *indictio belli*.

[3] Cf. Pol. vi. 14. 10.

[4] For senatorial secrecy cf. Pol. iii. 20. 3, Willems, *Le Sénat*, ii. 164, Gelzer, *SB Heid. Ak.*, 1956, 3, 11. Cf. also *JRS* liv (1964), 67 n. 18.

[5] Cf. p. 12.

10. 8, 10. 12, 11. 7, 14. 6, 15. 7, 16. 14, 16. 15, 17. 2, 17. 10, 17. 15, 18. 1, 18. 4, 18. 8, 21. 5, 21. 11, 21. 36, 22. 10, 24. 5, 25. 8, 26. 15, 29. 3, 29. 4, 30. 1, 31. 4, 34. 2, 35. 1, 36. 5, 38. 2, 39. 8, 39. 9, 39. 11.

In a few passages McDonald does not accept χ's addition—xxxi. 18. 4, 40. 6, 41. 12, xxxii. 19. 4—apart from such obvious slips as xxxi. 17. 9, 18. 8, 29. 13.

In a number of other passages, however, where χ's reading is accepted by McDonald, it seems to me probable or possible that B is right—see the notes to xxxi. 3. 5, 7. 3, 18. 1, 19. 1, 24. 2, 24. 12, 31. 6, 31. 11, 41. 10, 41. 14, 43. 1, 43. 2, xxxii. 2. 7, 8. 1, 12. 1, 18. 6, 21. 36, 30. 5, 35. 3, 40. 11.

On the general tendency of χ to make additions to complete what he regarded as the sense cf. Tränkle, *Gnomon*, 373.

BOOK XXXI

1. 1–5		Introduction
1. 6—4	201 B.C.	Events in Rome and Italy
	(continued)	
5–13	200 B.C.	Events in Rome and Italy
14–18		Events in Greece and the East
19–22. 3		Events in Rome and Italy
22. 4–47. 3		The campaign in Greece 200/199
47. 4—50		Events in Rome and Italy: warfare in Spain

1. 1–5. *Introduction*

L. has a fresh introduction at the beginning of books vi, xxi, and xxxi. The placing of these introductions suggests that L. tried to divide his work into groups of five or ten books with clear breaks in subject-matter. Thus book v ends with the sack of Rome by the Gauls, book xvi begins the First Punic War, book xxi begins the Second Punic War, and book xxxi the Second Macedonian War. Book xxxvi marks the beginning of the war with Antiochus, xli the beginning of the reign of Perseus, and xlv the end of the Third Macedonian War. On the other hand there is no obvious unit beginning with books xi or xxvi and the system appears to have broken down completely in the later books; cf. Bornecque, 13 ff., Zancan, 17, R. Syme, *HSCP* lxiv (1959), 27–88. Walsh, *Livy*, 5 ff., 173 ff., distorts the evidence in trying to find pentad division throughout L.'s work.

1. 1. quoque: with reference to the relief felt in Rome and Italy at the end of the war with Carthage. Cf. xxx. 45. 2 *laetam pace non minus quam victoria Italiam.*

3. tres et sexaginta annos: the First Punic War began in 264 and ended in 201, which by normal Roman inclusive reckoning would be 64 years. It is unlikely that L. was reckoning to the battle of Zama in 202 rather than to the peace in 201, and it appears that in this case he counted exclusively. He divides the whole period from the foundation of the city to the end of the Second Punic War into two sections, the first ending in 264, the second from 263 until 201. The year 264 was not to be counted twice, and the second period is therefore 63 years. It would have been more logical for L. to have ended his first period in 265, since the First Punic War in fact began in 264. For a similar case of exclusive reckoning cf. xxx. 44. 2.

4. duodenonaginta: the numeral appears in the MSS. as lxxviii. 478 A.U.C. = 264 B.C. produces a date for the foundation of the city of 742/1 B.C. With one exception, however, the A.U.C. dates given elsewhere by L. indicate a foundation date of 751/0 B.C. (iii. 33. 1, iv. 7. 1, v. 54. 5, vii. 18. 1, *per.* xlvii, xlix). After 300 B.C. the Livian dates are three years less than the Varronian dates based on a foundation date of 754/3 B.C. Before 300 the relations between the two systems are accounted for by the fact that the Livian system omits Varr. 247 and the four 'dictator-years' (Varr. 421, 430, 445, 453) but allows three years for the decemvirate, against the two in the Varronian system (Ogilvie's denial of this [455] appears to be based on a miscalculation), and includes the consuls omitted by L. in his list of eponymous magistrates but included by Licinius Macer (cf. iv. 7. 10–12). To make the present passage accord with this system one would have to emend to *lxxxvii* (thus C. Peter, *Zeit. f. Alt.* vi [1839], 631, and Mommsen, *Römische Chronologie* [2nd edn., Berlin, 1859], 121 n. 210). Corruption of numerals is very easy: at xxxiv. 54. 6, however, we find a passage giving a foundation date of 752/1 (194 B.C. = 558 A.U.C.), and it may be that the present passage should be emended to *lxxxviii*. Both this passage and xxxiv. 54. 6 concern periods of years rather than A.U.C. dates for individual events, and L. may have used in these two cases a source who had adopted a foundation date different to that used by L. for the rest of his A.U.C. dates.

On the whole question see especially R. Werner, *Der Beginn der römischen Republik* (Munich, 1963), 145–56. (Unfortunately Werner is not aware of the MSS. reading in the present passage. At p. 152 he regards *per.* xlix as another exception to the 751/0 system: but the epitomator's methods are so bizarre that it is quite uncertain whether he regards 150 or 149 as the beginning of the Third Punic War.) The account of J. Bayet, *Tite-Live*, tome i (Paris, 1947), cxii–cxxvi is incomplete and deficient. On the question of foundation dates in general, cf. Walbank, *Commentary*, i. 665 ff.

Ap. Claudium consulem: (102). Ap. Claudius Caudex, known only for his consulship in 264. For the sources on his invasion of Sicily cf. *MRR*, i. 203.

5. The motif is similar to that in the *Prooemium* to Quintilian xii: 'mox velut aura sollicitante provecti longius, dum tamen nota illa et plerisque artium scriptoribus tractata praecipimus, nec adhuc a litore procul videbamur et multos circa velut isdem se ventis credere ausos habebamus.' Cf. T. Janson, *Latin Prose Prefaces* (Stockholm, 1964), 71, R. G. Austin, *Quintiliani Institutionis Oratoriae liber xii* (Oxford, 1948), 48. L.'s simile is a variation on the common comparison between work and a sea-voyage, on which cf. G. Lieberg, *GIF* xxi (1969), 209 ff. The idea is precisely the opposite of the view that 'well begun is half done'; cf. Hor. *Ep.* i. 2. 40.

As early as the *praefatio* L. was aware of the size of his task (*praef.* 4, 13, Ogilvie, 24). But the present statement is more gloomy, and suggests that L. had no clear conception of the economy of his whole work when he embarked on it. (Cf. Klotz, *RE*, xiii. 819–20: *contra* Hellmann, 19 n. 2). See also xxxiii. 20. 13 n. and Tränkle, *WS*, 136.

It is quite wrong to think that L. intends *vada* to refer to the period before the First Punic War, the *vastior altitudo* to the years from 264–201 and the *profundum* to what he has still to relate (thus Kallenbach, *Über T. Livius in Verhältnis zu seinem Werke und zu seinem Zeit* (Quedlinburg, 1860), quoted by Bornecque, 15–16.

proximis litori vadis : B has *proximi litori*, which makes no sense, and χ *proximi litoris*. Professor Nisbet has suggested to me that χ's reading is correct and that *litus* should be taken as meaning 'that part of the sea nearest to the shore' (for which cf. E. Wistrand, *Nach Innen oder nach Aussen* [Göteborg, 1946], 36–42, E. Löfstedt, *Coniectanea* [Uppsala and Stockholm, 1950], 84–9). There does not, however, seem to be any case of *litus* being used in this sense elsewhere in L., and it seems safest to accept Carbach's emendation.

201 B.C.

1. 6—4. Events in Rome and Italy

1. 6–10. Causes of the Second Macedonian War

7. claritate . . . imperii : L. is apparently thinking of the fame of the Macedonian royal house more in relation to his own time than to the period about which he is writing. The greatest extent of the Macedonian empire, under Alexander the Great, was only 130 years before the Second Macedonian War. At ix. 17–19 L. digresses on the theme of whether Rome would have defeated Alexander if the latter had invaded Italy. On the theme cf. W. B. Anderson, *TAPA* xxxix (1908), 94 ff., P. Treves, *Il mito di Alessandro e la Roma di Augusto* (Milan, 1953), L. Alfonsi, *Hermes* xc (1962), 505–6, A. Rostagni, *Scritti minori*, ii. 2. 234–9, H. R. Breitenbach, *MH* xxvi (1969), 146–57.

quo : the MSS. reading. It has been doubted on the grounds that one could say *imperio obtinere* 'to hold in one's empire' or *armis obtinere* 'to obtain by force of arms', but that since *obtinere* is used in different senses the two cannot be combined. There is indeed a zeugma here but since *imperium* contains the sense both of 'the power to gain an empire' and of the empire when gained, it is a natural enough expression and emendation is undesirable.

51

8. decem . . . depositum erat: the First Macedonian War is regarded as beginning with the alliance with the Aetolian League, dated by L. in the winter of 211/0 (xxvi. 24. 1), though probably belonging to 212/1. For bibliography on this, cf. Schmitt, *StV*, iii. no. 536, add Badian, *HZ* ccix (1969), 638–9.

For other matters concerned with the treaty cf. xxxiii. 13. 9–12 n.

triennio: the peace of Phoenice was in 205 (xxix. 12). *triennio* means that a full three years (204–2) elapsed between the peace and the events preceding the second war in 201. Cf. 12. 3 and for a similar use of *biennio ante* Cic. *leg. agr.* ii. 49, *pro Sulla* 67. In the same way the rules in the *leges annales* that a *biennium* or a *decennium* had to elapse between two offices meant that a full two or ten years' interval was required. At xliii. 2. 8, however, *triennio* and *biennio* are used to refer to intervals of only two and one full years respectively. For a similar use of *triduo* cf. Nisbet, *Commentary on Cicero, in Pisonem*, 67, P. Grimal, *Études de chronologie cicéronienne* (Paris, 1967), 18–19. At 29. 16 the phrase recurs in the Macedonian speech at the meeting of the Aetolian League, although it is there inaccurate as the year of the speech is 200 (on L.'s chronology, 199 in fact).

Aetoli . . . causa: the statement is false and unfair to the Aetolians. Rome had begun the First Macedonian War against Philip V as a result of Philip's treaty with Hannibal in 215 (xxiii. 33. 1–34. 9, 38. 1–39. 4, 48. 3, Pol. vii. 9, App. *Mac.* 1, Just. xxix. 4. 4, Eut. iii. 12. 4, Flor. i. 23. 4, Zon. ix. 4. 2; cf. 7. 4 n.) and had themselves sought an alliance with the Aetolians (cf. xxv. 23. 9). Nor were the Aetolians really to blame for making peace. Technically, it is true, they broke the treaty which forbade the making of a separate peace by either Rome or Aetolia (xxvi. 24. 12), and it was on these grounds that the Romans declared that the treaty was at an end (29. 5, xxxiii. 13. 11). But in fact the Aetolians had been left little alternative. Rome lost interest in Greece in 207 and 206— *neglectae eo biennio res in Graecia erant* (xxix. 12. 1.)—and the Aetolians suffered a devastating attack by Philip (Pol. xi. 7. 2). L. makes some attempt to excuse the Romans by suggesting that if only the Aetolians had waited a little longer new Roman forces would have been able to help them (cf. Holleaux, *Rome*, 256 n. 1, Walbank, *Philip V*, 102 n. 2). Cf. also 29. 5, 31. 18, xxxii. 21. 18, xxxiii. 35. 10–11 nn.

9–10. Summary of Roman motives for going to war with Philip. For the relation of these to the actual causes of the war, see pp. 45–6. All of the complaints here specified give rise to serious difficulties.

ob infidam adversus Aetolos aliosque regionis eiusdem socios pacem: the Aetolians were not included in the peace of

Phoenice, and the peace concerned must be that of the Aetolians with Philip in 206: as far as that was concerned, Rome had no *locus standi*. Rome probably regarded their defection in 206 as a breach not only of the treaty of 212 but also of the general state of *amicitia*: in that case the Aetolians were not at this time *socii* of Rome. (*socius* can refer to the existence of *amicitia* as well as to the possession of a *foedus*: on these terms cf. L. E. Matthaei, *CQ* i [1907], 182–204, H. Horn, *Foederati*, [Frankfurt, 1930], A. Heuss, *Die Völkerrechtlichen Grundlagen der römischen Aussenpolitik in republikanischer Zeit, Klio* Bhft. xxxi [1933], Dahlheim, esp. chs. iii and iv, Wegner, 72 ff., D. Kienast, *ZRG* lxxxv [1968], 330 ff. On the status of the Aetolians after 206, cf. Petzold, 17, Lehmann, 78.) It is improbable that L. is here using the idiom where *alii socii* would mean 'and others, being *socii*' (cf. iv. 41. 8, v. 39. 3, xxi. 27. 5, xxxii. 36. 8, xxxiii. 37. 4, K–St, i. 651 n. 16).

For L.'s usage of *fidus* and *infidus* of peaces faithfully or unfaithfully observed, cf. ii. 15. 7, iv. 10. 4, v. 4. 13, v. 17. 9, viii. 21. 4, ix. 45. 5, xxxiv. 33. 12. The phrase *pax infida* may have been coined by Sallust (Hist. i. fr. 11, cf. W. V. Clausen, *AJP* lxviii [1947], 301). What were the aggressions?

(a) *The Aetolians.* The reference could be simply to Philip's capture of Lysimachia, Chalcedon, and Cius in 202, all of them allies of Aetolia (cf. pp. 36–7, 31. 4 n.). There may also have been aggressions in Phthiotic Achaea. Echinus, Larisa Cremaste and Phthiotic Thebes together with Pharsalus (which lay outside Phthiotic Achaea itself) are often mentioned as towns in Philip's possession claimed by the Aetolians (xxxii. 33. 16, xxxiii. 13. 6 ff., 34. 7, 49. 8, cf. xxxi. 31. 4, Pol. xviii. 3. 12, 8. 9, 38). Phthiotic Thebes was captured by Philip in 217 and Pharsalus was also Macedonian at this time (Pol. v. 99). Echinus, and probably Larisa also, was captured by Philip in 210 (Pol. ix. 41). If, then, to justify the Aetolian claims, one assumes that the four towns were Aetolian in 206, and again captured by Philip between 206 and 200, one has to find a time when they were restored to the Aetolians.

Some have held that they were recaptured by Aetolia between 210 and 206, others that they were ceded in the peace of 206. Alternatively, it has been argued that the towns were promised either in the peace of 206, or soon after, to prevent the Romans from persuading Aetolia to restart the war, but never handed over. Again, it has been held that the Aetolian claims were not justified and that they were merely demanding places held by them a long time previously.

There are objections to all these views. The first two depend on the assumption that the four towns did belong to Aetolia some time between 206 and 200. The argument for this assumption is that the presence of delegates from Phthiotic Thebes as Aetolian representatives at the Delphic amphictiony in this period (*Syll.*³ 564, *OGIS* 234) shows that Thebes must have been Aetolian at the time, and hence was recaptured by Philip before 200. The inference, however, is far from certain: the presence of the Theban delegate may represent merely the propaganda of the anti-Macedonian party at Thebes.

Against the view that the towns were recaptured by the Aetolians between 210 and 206, one can argue that it is hard to see when during this period the Aetolians could have recaptured them. But it is equally hard to think that Philip in 206, when he was in an immensely strong position, would have ceded, or even offered to cede, such important possessions. On the other hand it seems very strange that the Aetolians should have laid claim to cities whose status had been regularized by the peace of 206.

The suggestion that the offer was made after the peace to ensure Aetolian loyalty to the peace is more attractive, but there does not seem to have been any real likelihood of the Aetolians being willing to break the treaty when Roman reinforcements arrived.

It is impossible to find a solution. All one can say is that it is not impossible that Philip attacked these towns of Phthiotic Achaea some time in 202 or 201. For references for the views mentioned see Walbank, *Commentary*, ii. 555–6; add R. G. Hopital, *RD* xlii (1964), 205 n. 5, Lehmann, 67–78, Dahlheim, 195 n. 43.

For the Aetolian appeal to Rome cf. 29. 4 n.

(b) *The other allies.* These can only be Illyrians. At the conference of Nicaea in 198 Philip was asked τοὺς δὲ κατὰ τὴν Ἰλλυρίδα τόπους παραδοῦναι Ῥωμαίοις, ὧν γέγονε κύριος μετὰ τὰς ἐν Ἠπείρῳ διαλύσεις. (Pol. xviii. 1. 14 cf. L. xxxii. 33. 3). Holleaux (*Rome*, 278 n. 1, following G. Zippel, *Die römische Herrschaft in Illyrien bis auf Augustus* [Leipzig, 1877], 73) denied that Polybius meant that Philip had captured places in Illyria, and translated μετὰ τὰς ἐν Ἠπείρῳ διαλύσεις as 'in accordance with the terms of the peace of Phoenice'. Holleaux held that the Illyrian cities were handed over to Philip by the terms of the peace.

Holleaux's interpretation is quite unacceptable. The sentence goes on to refer to Egyptian possessions taken μετὰ τὸν Πτολεμαίου τοῦ Φιλοπάτορος θάνατον. This cannot possibly mean 'in accordance with the death of Philopator', and it is very awkward for the preposition to have a different meaning in the two phrases. It should be accepted that Philip did seize certain places in Illyria (but not the Parthini—cf. xxxiii. 34. 11 n.): it was these seizures that Roman *legati* were sent to investigate in 203 (xxx. 26. 2–4, 42 cf. 3. 4 below).

The fact that Philip was ordered to surrender his conquests to Rome suggests that the places involved were part of the Roman protectorate, not areas under the control of Pleuratus (or lands which had no previous connection with Rome, as urged by Walbank, *Commentary*, ii. 551). On the authenticity of the embassy of 203 cf. *MRR*, i. 315 n. 7, J. P. V. D. Balsdon, *CQ* n.s. iii (1953), 162 ff., Bredehorn, 100 ff.: *contra* Petzold, 44 ff., Dahlheim, 219–21 n. 99. Against the view of Holleaux, cf. E. Badian, *PBSR* xx (1952), 91 n. 102, Balsdon, l.c., *JRS* xliv (1954), 35, Walbank, *JRS* liii (1963), 4, *Commentary*, ii. 551, retracting *Philip V*, 103 n. 4. The controversy between Badian, S. I. Oost, and T. A. Dorey (*CPh* liv [1959], 158–64, lv [1960], 180 ff.) has not added much of value.

10. ob auxilia . . . Poenisque: the allegation that Macedonian troops fought at Zama is repeated in xxx. 33. 5, 40. 4, 42, xxxiv. 22. 8, xlv. 22. 6, cf. Front. *Str.* ii. 3. 16, Sil. It. xvii. 418 ff. There is no mention of them in Polybius' list of the mercenaries at Zama (xv. 11. 1 ff.) and in L. they do not appear to play any part in the battle. On the other hand Philip is later said to have demanded the return of Sopater, the leader of the mercenaries (xxx. 42). This looks far less like the sort of detail that would be invented, and it may be that some mercenaries were present, but had not been sent officially by Philip. Philip could still demand the return of a Macedonian subject. Cf. Petzold, 52, Balsdon, *JRS* xliv, 34, Dorey, *AJP* lxxviii (1957), 185–7, Bredehorn, 120–1.

preces Atheniensium: an Athenian embassy before the consular elections is impossible on chronological grounds; cf. p. 43. At first sight, this might appear to be part of L.'s general summary of the causes of the war and not a reference to a particular request from Athens (cf. Bellezza, 45). This, however, is excluded by *sub idem tempus* (2. 1) and *nova Atheniensium legatio* (5. 5). Nevertheless it may be that L.'s source referred to the Athenians in a general way, and L. himself mistakenly took the reference to be to a specific embassy.

2. 1–2. *Embassies from Rhodes and Attalus*

These embassies came to Rome in the autumn of 201 and will have brought news to Rome of Philip's aggressions in 201, and probably also news of the alleged 'pact of the Kings'. (On these matters cf. pp. 36–9.) News of the pact is mentioned explicitly by Appian, *Mac.* 4. 2, who refers only to a Rhodian embassy. (Bellezza, 33, thinks that the two embassies came separately, but this seems unnecessary.) Philip at this time was besieged in Bargylia, and was aware of the embassies being dispatched to Rome (Pol. xvi. 24. 3). There is not the slightest reason for rejecting the embassy as an annalistic fabrication (cf. Schmitt, *Antiochos*, 259 n. 4, against Pédech, *RÉA* lx [1958], 242, *Polybe*, 114 n. 73).

Attalus had been an ally of Rome since 210 though there was no formal *foedus* (Pol. ix. 30. 7, L. xxix. 11. 2, cf. Niese, ii. 484 n. 5, Hansen, *Attalids*, 47 n. 102, Dahlheim, 224 ff.). The Rhodians had probably been *amici* since the end of the fourth century. (Pol. xxx. 5. 6: on this passage see Schmitt, *Rom und Rhodos*, 1–49.)

2. 2. ad consules: the consuls of 201, Cn. Cornelius Lentulus (176) and P. Aelius Paetus (101). Lentulus was in charge of the fleet (sources in *MRR*, i. 319), Aelius in Gaul (below 5–11). For the delay of important decisions to await the return of a consul or consuls, cf. iii. 24. 2, xxx. 23. 2, xxxi. 48. 4 n., xxxix. 4. 3.

2. 3–4. *The embassy to Egypt*

This embassy in fact made a tour of Greece to stir up support for Rome against Philip, and delivered an ultimatum to Philip's general Nicanor at Athens; it was also charged with mediating in the war between Antiochus III and Ptolemy Epiphanes (Pol. xvi. 25–7). They delivered the ultimatum to Philip at Abydos (18. 1–4 and Pol. xvi. 34). L. distorts the facts by making the embassy go on a purely formal mission to Egypt and suppressing many of its other activities. For the reasons for this distortion and the chronology involved, see pp. 42–7.

3. ad Ptolomaeum: Ptolemy V Epiphanes: he was only ten years old at the time (Walbank, *Commentary*, ii. 625). For the problem of the date of his accession cf. p. 36 n. 5. The form *Ptolomaeus* is found in the MSS. of the third and fourth decade, though the Vienna uncial MS. of books xli–xlv has *Ptolemaeus*. *Ptolomaeus* also occurs in MSS. of other Latin authors, in a Latin inscription of 2 B.C., and in a few Greek inscriptions of the Imperial age, in reference to private individuals. The form became common, appearing as *Tolommeo* in Italian. On the other hand the correct form appears in some early MSS., and this makes it very hard to decide whether L. himself spelt the name incorrectly or not. There is no Greek evidence for such a form in the Hellenistic period. Cf. K. Keil, *RhM* xviii (1863), 267–8, A. Fleckeisen, *N.J. für Phil.* xciii (1866), 3 ff., Housman on Lucan v. 59, W. Schulze, *Orthographica et Graeca Latina* (Rome, 1958), 76.

C. Claudius Nero: (246). He was praetor in 212, with command prorogued in 211 and 210. He served under Marcellus in 209, and was consul in 207. He was censor in 204.

M. Aemilius Lepidus: (68). He was curule aedile in 193, praetor in 191, with command prorogued in 190: he was consul in

187, censor in 179, and held a second consulship in 175. He was a *pontifex* from 199 until his death in 152, and *pontifex maximus* from 180. He was *princeps senatus* from 179 until his death.

Lepidus presented the ultimatum to Philip at Abydos (18. 1–4, Pol. xvi. 34: see also addenda). Val. Max. vi. 6. 1 and Just. xxx. 3. 4 (cf. Tac. *Ann.* ii. 67) say that Lepidus was sent to Egypt to be *tutor* of the young Ptolemy and later coins of the Aemilii portray Lepidus as *tutor regis* (E. A. Sydenham, *The Coinage of the Roman Republic* [London, 1952], nos. 831, 832). The story is highly unlikely and its origins problematical. It is clear that Lepidus later developed a close interest in Egypt and this was retrojected to the time of his first contact with the kingdom. Cf. W. Otto, *Zur Geschichte der Zeit des 6. Ptolemaers, ABAW* 1934, 11, 28 ff., 122, Scullard, *RP*, 237 n. 3, Badian, *FC*, 110 n. 3, De Sanctis, iv. 3. 101 n. 49, Briscoe, *Historia* xviii (1969), 69 n. 142.

P. Sempronius Tuditanus: (96). He had been curule aedile in 214, praetor in 213, with command prorogued in 212–211, and censor in 209. In 205 he had been responsible for the conclusion of the peace of Phoenice, and was elected to the consulship for 204: his command was prorogued in 203. He is the only one of the three *legati* with previous experience of Eastern affairs. The other two commanders of the First Macedonian War, P. Sulpicius Galba and M. Valerius Laevinus, were being used in the military field.

The political composition of this embassy is uncertain. Lepidus may be counted as pro-Scipionic, Claudius as an opponent of Scipio. The position of Sempronius is unclear. (Scullard, *RP*, 77, makes him Scipionic, but by p. 94 he has become a member of the Claudian group: cf. Lippold, 207, J. Jahn, *Interregnum und Wahl-diktatur* [Kallmünz, 1970], 141.) Two Scipionic supporters on the embassy might appear strange, but the decision to send *legati* and their actual selection are different matters (cf. p. 35). Although Scipio now opposed going to war (cf. 6. 3–4 n.) he would not have been averse to having his supporters on the embassy. Though they would have to carry out senatorial policy, Scipio would at least have some control over what was happening.

The order of the names is unusual. One would have expected Sempronius, as a consular, to have preceded Lepidus: cf. Münzer, *RE*, iiA. 1445.

4. in fide mansissent: Egypt had been in a relationship of *amicitia* with Rome since 273 (D.H. xx. 14, L. *per.* xiv, Val. Max. iv. 3. 9, App. *Sic.* 1, Just. xviii. 2. 9, Dio fr. 41, Eut. ii. 15, Zon. viii. 6, Holleaux, *Rome*, 60–83, with bibliography to date, T. Walek, *RPh* N.S. xlix (1925) 118 ff., Otto, *Zur Geschichte der Zeit des 6. Ptolemaers,*

104 n. 5, A. Passerini, *Ath.* N.S. xiii (1935), 317–30, E. Manni, *RFIC* xxvii (1949), 79–87, L. H. Neatby, *TAPA* lxxxi (1950), 89–98, H. Mattingly, *AJA* liv (1950), 126–8, G. Nenci, *Pirro* (Turin, 1953), 182 ff., Cassola, *GP*, 45, Dahlheim, 141 ff. *Amicitia* was renewed in 210 (xxvii. 4. 10) and about the same time the senate asked Ptolemy Philopator to permit the export of corn to Italy (Pol. ix. 11a: for the date, Holleaux, *Rome*, 67 n. 2).

In the First Macedonian War Egypt attempted to mediate (cf. xxvii. 30. 4, xxviii. 7. 13, App. *Mac.* 3, Schmitt, *Rom und Rhodos*, 204 ff., Meloni, *Valore storico*, 9–20). Holleaux (*Rome*, 39 ff.) and Täubler (49 ff.) are quite wrong in their view that an *amicus* of Rome was bound to neutrality in Roman wars and could not have mediated. Holleaux concluded from this that Rome and Egypt could not have been *amici* (*Rome*, 74 ff.).

2. 5–11. *Events in Gaul*

5. P. Aelius: P. Aelius Paetus (101). He was plebeian aedile in 204, praetor in 203, and *magister equitum* in 202. In 199 he was censor and *iiivir* for the colony at Narnia. He may have been a member of the commission for the settlement of Greece in 196 (cf. xxxiii. 39. 2 n.), and was *legatus* to Antiochus in 193. He was an augur from 208 until his death in 174 and a distinguished jurisconsult. See also 4. 3, xxxii. 2. 6 and for his political position p. 33 n. 2.

Boiis: the Boii had occupied the land between the Po and the Appennines, Felsina (mod. Bologna) being their chief town (v. 35. 2). They had attacked Roman forces and been defeated in 283/2 (Pol. ii. 20). They joined the Gallic rising in the 220s and were reduced in 224 (Pol. ii. 22–31). In 218 they captured Roman commissioners who were settling colonies at Placentia and Cremona (10. 2 n.).

See Ihm, *RE*, iii. 630–2, Walbank, *Commentary*, i. 183, Ogilvie, 715.

subitariis tumultus eius causa: 'hastily levied for the emergency': the use of *subitarius* in a military context appears to be limited to L.; cf. Ogilvie, 401. *tumultuaria* in § 6 has the same meaning.

Originally *capite censi* could be enrolled in the case of a *tumultus* (Gell. xvi. 10. 11) but it appears that this was not the case in the second-century instances of emergency levies. Cf. Gabba, *Ath.* N.S. xxvii (1949), 189, Toynbee, i. 463, Brunt, 629–30. For other instances of *tumultus* cf. Toynbee, i. 471, ii. 92. It is not clear whether these two legions were enrolled at Rome or formed from citizens in the area, as argued by Brunt, 392.

6. exercitu suo: cf. xxx. 40. 16.

C. Ampium: (not in *RE*). He is not mentioned elsewhere. The *praefectus socium* was always a Roman citizen (Mommsen, *StR*, iii.

539, Walbank, *Commentary*, i. 709, Kromayer–Veith, 276). D. Kienast, *Cato der Zensor* (Heidelberg, 1954), 149 n. 66 oddly quotes Kromayer–Veith in support of the opposite view.

qua: *quam* MSS. Madvig (*Emendationes*, 462), rightly argued that the MSS. reading cannot be interpreted as 'that part of Umbria which is called the *tribus Sapinia*', and his emendation *qua* gives the sense required. For the usage of *vocare* he compared, amongst other passages, xxxii. 39. 6.

tribum Sapiniam: the only other references to the *tribus Sapinia* and the fort of Mutilum (§ 7) are in xxxiii. 37. 1–2. The name *Sapinia* suggests a connection with the River Sapis, the modern Savio, which runs into the sea between Ravenna and Rimini. We must assume that Aelius divided his forces when in the neighbourhood of Faesulae (*in Gallia* need not be taken too strictly). Thus he himself will have marched due north towards Bologna, whilst Ampius will have gone over the Mandrioli pass into the valley of the Savio (thus De Sanctis, iv. 1. 412, cf. Phillip, *RE*, iA. 2323). Toynbee, i. 485–7, objects that the upper Savio valley was in fact part of the land of the Sarsinates and identifying Mutilum with Modigliana he places the *tribus Sapinia* in the valley of the Marzeno, which flows down to Faenza.

This is not likely; there seems no reason why the *tribus Sapinia* and the Sarsinates should not exist in the same neighbourhood (cf. Walbank, *Commentary*, i. 200) and the divorcing of the Sapinia from the river Sapis is most improbable. But the identification of Mutilum with Modigliana has a lot in its favour. The town was called *Mutiliana* in the Middle Ages and the Renaissance and there is no difficulty in thinking that Ampius moved northwestwards from the Savio towards Modigliana. Cf. G. C. Susini, *Atti e memorie della deputazione di storia patria per le province di Romagna* N.S. v. (1953–4), 1 ff., G. Mezzar-Zerbi, *RSC* vi (1958), 8 n. 22. (I am very grateful to Professor Susini for information about Modigliana.)

tribus here has the meaning of district. Umbrian tribes—*trifu*—are mentioned in the Iguvine tablets (cf. E. Täubler, *SB Heid. Ak.* 1929/30, 4. Abh., L. R. Taylor, *Voting Districts of the Roman Republic* [Rome, 1960], 4 n. 4, Ogilvie, 176).

9. cepit: for L.'s fondness for using states of mind as subjects of *capere* cf. Tränkle, *WS*, 144–5.

palata: as often in L.'s brief mentions of Roman defeats, the Roman troops are not fighting in proper formation. Cf. xxxv. 51. 4, xlii. 65. 2, xliii. 10. 4, xliv. 10. 9, 12. 3, H. Bruckmann, *Die römischen Niederlagen im Geschichtswerk des T. Livius* (Bochum-Langendreer, 1936), 121.

11. **Ingaunis Liguribus**: Cf. xxviii. 46. 9, xxx. 19. 1, xxxix. 32. 4, xl. 25. 1, 28. 6, 41. 6. The state of *Albingaunum* (cf. xxix. 5. 2) is often mentioned in inscriptions. It is the modern Albenga, 56 miles west of Genoa (cf. Nissen, *IL*, ii. 1. 141, Hülsen, *RE*, i. 1336, N. Lamboglia, *Per l'archeologia di Albingaunum* [Albenga, 1934], *Liguria Romana* [Alassio, 1939], 119 ff.).

3. *The mission of M. Valerius Laevinus*

The mission of Laevinus has been doubted on two grounds (Holleaux, *CAH*, viii. 156 n. 1, Petzold, 71, Walbank, *Philip V*, 127 n. 7, De Sanctis, iv. 1. 21 n. 55, *MRR*, i. 322 n. 3, Dahlheim, 243).

(a) It is a doublet of Laevinus' similar expedition in 215 (xxiii. 38. 11). This is more of an explanation for the existence of the story than an argument for rejecting it. In reply it can be said that the senate was viewing the war very much in the pattern of the First Macedonian War and this makes it quite intelligible that they should take the same precautionary measures under the same commander. On the senate's attitude see pp. 45–6.

(b) It is inconsistent with other passages in L. dealing with the fleet. At xxx. 44. 13 Scipio orders Cn. Octavius to take the fleet to Sicily and hand it over to the consul Cn. Cornelius Lentulus. This seems to be confirmed when Sulpicius takes ships from Lentulus at Brundisium (14. 2). This argument is best dealt with by Thiel, 212 ff. In 201 the senate gave instructions concerning the fleet (xxx. 41. 6–8). Lentulus was to have a fleet of 50 ships, to be selected from the fleets of Octavius and Villius. The rest of the existing fleet, if Scipio did not want Octavius in charge of the 40 ships that Scipio was to retain himself, were to be taken back to Rome by Octavius. At xxx. 44. 13 Scipio is telling Octavius to comply with the first part of the senate's instructions. We are to assume that Octavius later brought the ships not wanted by Lentulus back to Rome. Thus the fleet of Laevinus came from the ships brought back by Octavius, that of Sulpicius from those taken over by Lentulus, and later brought by Lentulus to Brundisium.

See Thiel, 219 ff. for further arguments in favour of the authenticity of Laevinus' expedition.

3. 1. habuit: sc. Aelius.

2. Cn. Octavius: (16). Praetor in 205, and had his *imperium* prorogued year by year up to this point. In 200 he was a *legatus* to Africa (11. 18). In 194 he was a *iiivir* for the settlement of Croton, and a *legatus* to Greece, under the leadership of Flamininus, in 192/1.

in Macedoniam: not at this point to Macedon itself, but rather to the territory of Rome's allies in Illyria, the so-called 'Roman protectorate'. (Cf. Holleaux, *Rome*, 105–12; for a different view, Badian, *PBSR* xx [1952], 78 = *Studies*, 6–7.)

3. M. Valerius Laevinus: (211). He was probably elected to the consulship for 220, but was declared *vitio creatus* and resigned (Degrassi, *I.I.* xiii. 1. 118, *MRR*, i. 235). He was praetor in 215 and appointed as commander in the First Macedonian War, a post he held until 211. He was consul in 210 and proconsul in charge of the fleet from 209 to 207. In 205 he was one of the *legati* sent to bring the Magna Mater from Pessinus to Rome. He died in 200 (50. 4).

propraetor: the technical term is *pro praetore* (cf. Mommsen, *StR*, ii³. 240 n. 5) but L. regularly uses both *propraetor* and *proconsul* as nouns (cf. Packard, iii. 1146, 1188: for his use of *pro praetore* id. 1135, 1139, and below 8. 10 n.). Tacitus uses *proconsul* but always *pro praetore*. Though a consular, Valerius is given only propraetorian imperium. In the late republic a man appointed to a command not continuous with a magistracy at Rome was normally given the rank of his last Roman office (cf. Balsdon, *JRS* lii [1962], 134, but see also Badian, *JRS* lv [1965], 111–12).

Vibonem: Vibo is on the western coast of the toe of Italy, about 60 miles north of Reggio di Calabria. A colony was established there in 192 (xxxv. 40. 5) and the town was then known as Vibo Valentia. Cf. Nissen, *IL*, ii. 2. 956, Radke, *RE*, viiiA. 2000–7.

4. M. Aurelius: he had been in Greece since 203 (cf. 1. 9–10 n.). His identification with the M. Aurelius Cotta of 50. 5 (Klebs, *RE*, ii. 2487, *MRR*, i. 313) is far from certain.

quantos . . . numerum: there is probably a certain amount of exaggeration here. Philip decided in 208 to build his own fleet (xxviii. 8. 14).

5. et quemadmodum: B omits *et* and asyndeton would be quite possible here.

non continentis . . . per legatos: examples are Philip's use of Heraclides of Tarentum to set fire to the Rhodian fleet in 205, and of other ambassadors to stir up the Cretans to war with Rhodes. Dicaearchus also helped the Cretans and attacked various places in the Aegean and Hellespont (cf. p. 36). But the charge is exaggerated; there is no evidence for Philip stirring up war in mainland cities.

ipse adeundo: for L.'s use of nominative pronouns in ablative absolutes or with ablative gerunds and gerundives cf. xxxii. 24. 4, xxxiii. 9. 11, 35. 1, Madvig, *Kleine philologische Schriften* (Leipzig, 1875), 356 ff., K–St, i. 784–5.

6. For the Pyrrhus motif cf. 7. 8 ff.

ex aliquanto minore regno: Epirus as compared with Macedon. For a brief period from 288 to 285 Pyrrhus himself had shared the throne of Macedon (Niese, i. 375 ff., Lévêque, *Pyrrhos*, 158–68, Kienast, *RE*, xxiv. 124–7).

placuit: sc. *Laevino*. Sage's translation 'the two agreed that the Romans must undertake the war with greater vigour' is misleading.

4. 1–3. *Provision for Scipionic veterans*

This is the first occasion on which the state had to make public provision of land for a returning army. It was one of the few instances in the second century when the senate did take action to distribute the *ager publicus*: the result was that much of it was occupied by illegal squatters, producing the situation with which Tiberius Gracchus attempted to deal. Cf. in general McDonald, *CHJ* vi (1939), 124 ff., Toynbee, ii. 195 ff.

4. 1. ductu atque auspicio: for the phrase cf. *TLL*, v. 2170, Packard, i. 1333–4, Nisbet and Hubbard, 106. Only a magistrate or pro-magistrate with *imperium* confirmed by the people was able to campaign *suis auspiciis*. Cf. Wissowa, *RE*, ii. 2582–3, M. A. Levi, *Rend. Ist. Lomb.* lxxi (1938), 101–18, E. S. Staveley, *Historia* v (1956), 89–90, Ogilvie, 392. (This, however, was not the reason for the inability of *privati cum imperio* to triumph [xxviii. 38. 4, xxxi. 20 3 n.]; Scipio had conducted affairs in Spain *suis auspiciis*—xxviii. 38. 1). See also 47. 4 n.

2. M. Iunius: sc. Pennus (121). He had been plebeian aedile in 205. For his appointment as *praetor urbanus* cf. xxx. 40. 5. For cases of a praetor presiding at elections of such commissions cf. xxv. 7. 5, xxxiv. 53. 2.

si ei videretur: the phrase is added because in theory the senate is only in the position of offering advice to a magistrate with *imperium*. For parallels cf. Mommsen, *StR*, iii. 1027 n. 2, Ogilvie, 379.

quod . . . esset: land confiscated from rebels during the Second Punic War, but not yet divided. There is no direct evidence for this confiscation, but it may be included in the measures subsumed at xxx. 24. 4 (thus W–M, cf. Toynbee, ii. 118 n. 4, 659–660). For the defection of Samnium and Apulia, cf. xxii. 61. 11, xxiv. 20. 4, Pol. iii. 118. 1–3. For the legal phrase cf. the Lex Agraria of 111 (*FIRA*, i. 104, line 4) *quei ager publicus populei Romani in terra Italia . . .*, Ogilvie, 709.

crearet: 'hold an election', not 'nominate' as held by Scullard, *RP*, 83.

3. **P. Servilius**: (23). Not otherwise known.

Q. Caecilius Metellus: (81). He held the plebeian and curule aedileships in 209 and 208 respectively. He was consul in 206 and dictator in charge of the elections in 205: in 204 he was one of the commissioners sent to investigate the conduct of Pleminius. He was a *legatus* to Greece and Macedonia in 185. In the Second Punic War he was a strong supporter of Scipio Africanus (xxix. 20. 1–5, xxx. 23. 3 ff., 27. 2, Scullard, *RP*, 77–8, Cassola, *GP*, 408). Cf. p. 35 n. 7.

C. et M. . . . erat: B has *et M. Servilius*, and the singular is also found in two MSS. of the χ group. The correct reading is not in doubt—it is two Servilii who have the *cognomen* Geminus, not one Servilius and Caecilius Metellus. The survival of the singular in the two χ MSS. may be coincidence, but it is possible that the variant form was included both in F and χ. In the case of the Hostilii below, however, it seems likely that *Hostiliis* was read by F, and that the nominative forms are the result of emendation.

The *cognomen* Geminus arose from the twin sons of an otherwise unknown Q. Servilius. One was P. Servilius Geminus (62), consul in 252 and 248. The two Servilii here are the latter's grandsons, their father being the *iiivir* captured by the Boii in 218 (2. 5, 10. 2 nn.: cf. *MRR*, i. 240, 241 n. 12). The Servilii were patrician by origin, but the father of our Servilii evidently made a *transitio ad plebem*, thus enabling two Servilii to hold the consulship together in 203, in defiance of the *Lex Genucia* of 342. See Münzer, *RA*, 132 ff., A. Aymard, *RÉA* xlv (1943), 199 ff.

Caius (60) was a *legatus* to Etruria in 212, tribune in 211, plebeian aedile in 209, curule aedile and *magister equitum* under the dictator T. Manlius Torquatus in 208, praetor in 206 and consul in 203. His command was prorogued in 202, and in the same year he was dictator: in 194 he was a *iiivir* for the dedication of a temple to Jupiter. He was a *pontifex* from 210 until his death in 180, and *pontifex maximus* from 183 to 180.

Marcus (78) was curule aedile in 204, *magister equitum* under the dictator P. Sulpicius Galba in 203, and consul in 202. His command was prorogued in 201. He was a *iiivir* for Campanian colonies from 197–4 (xxxii. 29. 4).

L. . . . Catones: L. Hostilius Cato (12) is only known otherwise as a *legatus* in 190 (the statement in *MRR*, i. 322 that he was a praetor in 207 is an error).

A. Hostilius Cato (10) was praetor in 207 and a *legatus* under L. Scipio in 190. They were both accused of *peculatus* at the same time as L. Scipio, and it is reasonable to regard them as Scipionic supporters (Toynbee, ii. 201). For later connections between the

Hostilii and Apulia cf. Münzer, *RE*, viii. 2505–6, T. P. Wiseman, *New Men in the Roman Senate 139 B.C.–A.D. 14* (Oxford, 1971), 54–5.

P. Villius Tappulus: (10). Plebeian aedile in 204, praetor in 203, with command prorogued in 202, and consul in 199. On his command against Philip in 199 and his activities as a member of the commission to administer the settlement with Philip in 196 see 49. 12, xxxii. 1, 3, 6, xxxiii. 24. 7, 35. 2, 39. 2. In 193 he was an ambassador to Antiochus. The form of the *cognomen* is assured by the *Fasti Capitolini* for the consul of 199. At 49. 12 the MSS. have *t. appulus*, though they give it correctly in the case of L. Villius Tappulus in the same section. For his political position cf. p. 32.

M. Fulvius Flaccus: (56). He is perhaps to be identified with the tribune of 198 (cf. xxxii. 7. 8 n.).

P. Aelius Paetus: (101). Cf. 2. 5 n.

T. Quinctius Flamininus: (45). For the earlier career of Flamininus see xxxii. 7. 9 n. and for his political position pp. 22–35.

It is noticeable that of the ten commissioners only three can be regarded with any certainty as supporters of Africanus (Toynbee, ii. 201 adds Aelius Paetus, but cf. p. 32).

4. 4. *Elections*

P. Sulpicius Galba: (64). Consul in 211 and proconsul in charge of the First Macedonian War from 210 until 206. His cruelty was long remembered by the Greeks (cf. Pol. ix. 42. 5–8, App. *Mac.* 7). He was dictator in 203. On his membership of the commission for the settlement with Philip see xxxiii. 24. 7. He was a *legatus* to Antiochus in 193 (the entry *leg. amb.* 205–4 in *MRR*, ii. 623 is an error). Sulpicius is to be regarded as a member of the Fulvian group responsible for the renewal of the conflict with Philip. See p. 45.

C. Aurelius Cotta: (95). He had been praetor in 202 (whether *ILLRP* 75 refers to him is uncertain). For his political position cf. 47. 4–49. 3, 49. 8–11 n. For the view of Toynbee, ii. 660–1, that he was responsible for the building of the *Via Aurelia* cf. xxxiii. 43. 5 n.

Q. Minucius Rufus: (22, 55). He had served at Capua in 211 and was plebeian aedile in 201 (see § 7 n.). His praetorian *imperium* was prorogued for 199 (xxxii. 1. 7). He became consul in 197 (xxxii. 27. 5, 28–31, xxxiii. 22–3) and was a member of the commission for the settlement at Apamea in 189/8, and a *legatus* in Gaul in 183. He can be presumed to be a supporter of Scipio on two grounds.

(a) Q. Minucius Thermus, *tr. pl.* 201, was a strong supporter of Scipio (xxx. 40. 9–16, 43. 2–3).

(b) He has the same filiation as M. Minucius Rufus, consul in 221 and *magister equitum* in 217, and it is not impossible that the two men were brothers. The latter can be regarded as being supported by the Scipios at the time. (I would in general accept the views of Scullard, *RP*, 44–9, cf. Cassola, *GP*, 361–73, Lippold, 154.)

L. Furius Purpurio: (86). He was military tribune in 210 under Marcellus, and consul in 196. He was a *xvir* for the Apamea settlement and a *legatus* in Gaul in 183. See 6. 2, 8. 7, 10. 5 ff., 21. 2 ff., 29. 1 n., 47. 6 ff., xxxiii. 24. 1, 25. 4, 37. 1 ff. On his political position see 47. 4–49. 3, 49. 8–11 n.

Q. Fulvius Gillo: (69). He was a *legatus* bringing the Carthaginian ambassadors to Rome in 203, and perhaps curule aedile in 202 (*MRR*, i. 319 n. 2). His is the only known example of this *cognomen* in the Republic, though three are known in the Flavian period (*RE* (68) (70) (71)). Groag (*RE*, vii. 250) suggests that they are all descended from this Fulvius, and belonged to the Sabine nobility especially favoured by Vespasian. Cf. also Syme, *Historia* xiii (1964), 116.

C. Sergius Plautus: (36). Apart from his praetorship and its prorogation in 199 (xxxii. 1. 6) nothing is known of him. The statement in *MRR*, i. 326 n. 2 that B reads *Plancus* for *Plautus* is incorrect.

4. 5–7. *Aedilician activities*

5. Ludi Romani scaenici: on the *Ludi Romani*, held in September, see 9. 5–10 n. Dramatic performances of Greek plays had first appeared in the *ludi* in 240 (Cic. *Brut.* 72, *de sen.* 50, *TD* i. 3, Gell. xvii. 21. 42) though representations of Etruscan mimes went back as far as the fourth century (cf. vii. 2. 3 ff.).

magnifice apparateque: both words are regularly applied to *ludi* (Packard, i. 437–8, iii. 170) and are combined in xxxiii. 42. 9, Cic. *Sest.* 116 *qui ludos apparatissimos magnificentissimosque fecisti*, *Pis.* 65 *instant . . . apparatissimi magnificentissimique ludi.*

ab aedilibus curulibus: i.e. those of 201.

L. Valerio Flacco: (173). The patron of the elder Cato. He was a *legatus* in Gaul in 200 (21. 8), praetor in 199, and consul in 195 with command prorogued in 194: he was a *legatus* in Greece in 191 and *iiivir* for the settlement of additional colonists at Placentia and Cremona in 190–189. He was censor in 184, and a *pontifex* from 196 until his death in 180.

L. Quinctio Flaminino: (43). The MSS. read *T.*—i.e. the consul of 198. But Titus is said to have stood for the consulship *ex quaestura* (xxxii. 7. 9) and the reference must be to his brother Lucius. *praenomina* are regularly corrupted in the MSS. Failure to realize this led Klotz (*Livius*, 96) to think that there was a conflict between this passage and xxxii. 7. 9 and that the latter was due to the Sullan annalists' belief that a man of 30 could not have been an aedile. He was praetor in 199 (49. 12) and served under his brother in

Greece (cf. xxxii. 16. 2, 19. 5, 23. 3, 28. 11, 39. 4, xxxiii. 16. 1, 17. 2). He was consul in 192, and a *legatus* under Acilius Glabrio in 191. He was an *augur* from 213 until his death in 170. On the question whether Titus or Lucius was the elder cf. Badian, *JRS* lxi (1971), 110–11.

biduum instauratum est: 'was repeated for a second period of two days'. *Instauratio* was the procedure followed when there had been a flaw in the original performance of a ceremony and it had to be repeated: cf. Habel, *RE*, supp. v. 612, S. P. C. Tromp, *De Romanorum piaculis* (Lyons, 1921), 66 ff., Latte, *RRG*, 250 n. 4, Ogilvie, 327 (with further bibliography). The *ludi Romani* lasted four days at this period (Habel, *RE*, supp. v. 619) and the repetition was therefore only partial.

6. frumenti: there is no previous mention of this dispatch of corn by Scipio.

quaternis aeris: i.e. 4 *asses* per *modius*. *c*. 210 the price, at a time of scarcity, was $2\frac{1}{2}$ *denarii* (= 25 *asses*) per *modius* (Pol. ix. 11a. 3). 4 *asses* had also been charged for a distribution by the aediles in 203 (xxx. 26. 6), whilst in 200 the aediles distributed African corn at only 2 *asses* per *modius* (50. 1), and the same applied for Sicilian corn in 196 (xxxiii. 42. 8). The price established for the state selling of corn by C. Gracchus in 123 was $6\frac{1}{3}$ *asses* per *modius*.

Under 439 B.C. L. reports a price of 1 *as* per *modius* for distribution of the corn collected by Sp. Maelius (iv. 16. 2). But this passage cannot be used as evidence, for coinage had not then been introduced.

The low price of Gallic corn (equivalent to $1\frac{1}{6}$ *asses* per *modius*) indicated by Polybius ii. 15 is a local price, caused by the difficulties of exporting it (Walbank, *Commentary*, i. 176, Toynbee, ii. 182, Brunt, 180).

These public distributions are not found after 196. The instances in 203, 201 and 200 were due to the exceptional circumstances of the requisitioning—or in the case of 200, the gift (cf. 50. 1 n.)—of large quantities of corn in Spain and Africa, at a time when military needs were declining. A further consequence of this was that Sicilian and Sardinian corn, over and above the tithe, was not needed for military purposes, and was released on to the market, severely depressing the price (xxx. 38. 5: Toynbee, ii. 338 wrongly takes this to refer to tithe-corn).

The corn price fluctuated wildly at Rome, and its level was often more a reflection of the confidence of the corn-dealers in the general political and economic situation than an actual 'supply and demand' price. The dealers probably hoarded when it suited them. For sudden changes in price cf. Cic. *de imp.* 44, *de domo* 14, *post red. ad*

Quir. 18. On the Roman corn trade, see T. Frank, *Economic Survey*, i. 97–8, 158–60, 191–2, 402–3, Rostovtzeff, *RE*, vii. 143–50, Toynbee, ii. 337–9, Brunt, 376 n. 3, 703–6, *Past and Present* xxxv (1966) 25 ff., and on the Hellenistic trade, Heichelheim, *RE*, supp. vi. 844 ff., especially 856–60 on prices, Rostovtzeff, *SEEHW*, 1249–52, 1354 n. 41. On the Roman Empire cf. R. Duncan-Jones, *PBSR* xxxiii (1965), 221 ff., M. H. Crawford, *JRS* lx (1970), 41.

7. plebei ludi: these were probably instituted about 220, and celebrated in November; cf. Latte, *RRG*, 248 n. 4, Habel, *RE*, supp. v. 620–1, Lippold, 97 n. 82, *contra* W. K. Quinn-Schofield, *Latomus* xxvi (1967), 677–85.

ter toti instaurati: in this case the complete ceremony is repeated. Cf. xxxii. 27. 8 n.

L. Apustio Fullone: (5). He was a *legatus* in Greece in 200 and 199 (cf. 27. 1 n., 44. 1, 46. 5, 47. 1, xxxii. 16. 5) and praetor in 196 (xxxiii. 24. 2, 26. 1). He was a *iiivir* for colonies in the *Ager Thurinus* from 194 to 192: he was probably a *legatus* under L. Scipio in 190.

Q. Minucio Rufo: cf. § 4 n.

ex aedilitate: between 207 and 196 17 men proceeded directly from the plebeian aedileship to the praetorship, whilst after that date no examples are known. As a plebeian office, it was not part of the official *cursus* and so not subject to the *leges annales* (Mommsen, *StR*, i³. 534, A. E. Astin, *Latomus* xvii [1958], 64 n. 1 = *The Lex Annalis before Sulla* [Brussels, 1958], 46 n. 1), but it seems that the *nobiles* came to accept unwritten rules in the early years of the second century, and that many of these were codified in the *Lex Villia Annalis* of 180 (cf. G. Roegler, *Klio* xl [1962], 76–123, especially 103 on plebeian aediles).

Iovis epulum: this formed a regular part of the *ludi plebei* at this period (xxix. 38. 8, xxxii. 7. 13, xxxiii. 42. 11) but it is unlikely that it was a feature only of these games (thus Mommsen, *RF*, ii. 45 n. 4, A. Piganiol, *Recherches sur les jeux romains* [Strasbourg, 1923], 88 n. 1; *contra* Wissowa, *RuK²*, 127 n. 11, Habel, *RE*, supp. v. 621, De Sanctis, iv. 2. 1. 317, Ogilvie, 745). The *epulum* appears to have developed into a banquet for the senate: cf. xxxviii. 57. 5, Gell. xii. 8. 2, Marquardt, *StV*, iii. 348–9.

200 B.C.
5–13. *Events in Rome and Italy*
5. *Preparations for war*

5. 1. anno quingentesimo quinquagesimo primo: cf. 1. 4 n. The MSS., as in 1. 4, give a figure ten years too small (*quadragesimo*).

The giving of an A.U.C. date is rare in L. and indicates an 'epoch date' for important events—here the beginning of a major war. Cf. *per.* xlix, the beginning of the Third Punic War, and Ogilvie, 455–6.

P. Sulpicio Galba C. Aurelio consulibus: on the consuls cf. 4. 4 n. Their names are probably given in the order of election. Cf. L. R. Taylor and T. R. S. Broughton, *MAAR* xix (1949), 1–11, *Historia* xvii (1968), 166–72. (Though Taylor and Broughton's assumptions about the connection between the holding of the *fasces* and the right to presidency in the senate and the assemblies seem to me open to grave doubt: cf. *Gnomon* xli [1969], 756.)

paucis mensibus: in fact the peace with Carthage was probably concluded in the spring of 201 (cf. the table in De Sanctis, iii. 2. 688) and the war with Philip did not begin until the end of summer 200 (22. 4 cf. p. 45 n. 1). But L. is probably thinking of the interval between the peace and the events here described in the winter of 201–200.

2. idibus Martiis . . . inibatur: the ides of March were the date of entry to the consulate until 153, when 1 January was established. For changes in the date of entry cf. Mommsen, *StR*, i³. 599, Kübler, *RE*, iv. 1116, Ogilvie, 404–5, A. K. Michels, *The Calendar of the Roman Republic* (Princeton, 1967), 97 ff.

consul rettulit senatusque decrevit: these are the technical terms for senatorial procedure. The consul put a subject for debate before the senate (*relatio*), individual senators framed motions (*sententiae*), and the result was a decision of the senate (*consultum* or *decretum*). Mommsen (*StR*, iii. 952–3), followed by O'Brien-Moore (*RE*, supp. vi. 709) argues that *relatio* is only properly used where the end product is a *patrum auctoritas* and a reference to the people: for a *consultum* the correct term is *senatum consulere*. It seems to me that this is an arbitrary distinction not based on the evidence.

3. maioribus hostiis: sacrificial victims were divided into *lactentes* and *maiores* according to their age. Cf. Gell. iv. 6. 2, Wissowa, *RuK²*, 412, 415, Latte, *RRG*, 210; see also xxxii. 1. 13, xxxiii. 26. 9. The ablative is regularly used of sacrificial victims: e.g. Hor. *Od.* i. 4. 12 *seu poscat agna sive malit haedo.* Cf. K–St, i. 384–5.

4. quod . . . eveniret: for the formula cf. 7. 15, 8. 2, xxi. 17. 4, xxxvi. 1. 2, xl. 46. 9, Cic. *pro Mur.* 1, G. Appel, *De Romanorum precationibus* (Giessen, 1909) 130–1, Toynbee, ii. 409.

de re publica . . . consulerent: a *relatio de re publica* allowed a general debate in the senate. Cf. xxi. 6. 3, xxii. 1. 5, xxvi. 10. 2, 27. 17, Cic. *Cat.* iii. 13, Caes. *BC* i. 1. 2, Willems, *Le Sénat*, ii. 176 n. 3, Mommsen, *StR*, iii. 956–7, O'Brien-Moore, *RE*, supp. vi. 709.

5. M. Aurelio . . . propraetore : cf. 3. 3–6.

6. Atheniensium nova legatio : L.'s second Athenian embassy which is probably misplaced. For its authenticity and the chronology cf. pp. 43–4.

regem : not necessarily Philip himself: the reference is probably to the invasion of Philocles: cf. 16. 2 and p. 43.

finibus suis : 'the borders of Athens'; clearly not 'his own borders' as Ferro, 75, believes.

nisi . . . auxilii foret : for the phrase, cf. Ogilvie, 619.

7. laetaque exta fuisse : for the inspection of the entrails of the sacrificial victims by the *haruspices* cf. Ogilvie, 675–6.

prolationem finium : cf. xxxvi. 1. 3, xlii. 20. 4, 30. 9, Tac. *Hist.* 78. ii. The phrase is rather unsuitable in the passages of L., since in all these cases Rome is claiming not to be fighting a war for the enlargement of her empire. The phrase looks at first sight as if it is part of an archaic formula belonging to the wars in Italy, but it does not occur in the early books, and may reflect Augustus' interest in the extension of the boundaries of the Empire. Cf. *RG* 26, Tac. *Ann.* xii. 23. The surviving *elogia* fail to confirm Cicero's statement (*de r.p.* iii. 24) that Rome's greatest generals had *fines imperii propagavit* inscribed on their monuments.

8. sociis : Athens had been visited by Roman ambassadors in 228 (Pol. ii. 12. 8) and this probably led to the establishment of *amicitia* (cf. 1. 9–10 n.: *contra* Dahlheim, 219 n. 98 with bibliography). Her inclusion in the peace of Phoenice (xxix. 12. 14) has often been rejected mainly on the grounds that her name was inserted as part of the justification for going to war in 200. Athens is, however, not prominent in L.'s account of the outbreak of the war. Cf. p. 40 n. 3. For bibliography, cf. Robert in Holleaux, *Études*, v. 28 n. 3.

6. *The* comitia's *rejection of the war-vote*

Dahlheim (242–4 n. 23) rejects the whole account, and believes there was no proposal for war at this time. He holds (1) that it is connected with the Athenian Embassy and the report of Laevinus, both of which are false; (2) there are no *socii* in Greece at the time who could suffer *iniuriae*; (3) the events are too early. On the Athenian Embassy and the chronology, cf. pp. 43–4, on Laevinus 3 n. As for point (2), there is no reason why *socii* should not include *amici* even in an official declaration of war, cf. n. on *ob iniurias* below.

6. 1. sorti : for L.'s usage of *sorti* and *sorte* as ablative of *sors* cf. Ogilvie, 682. It was intended from the beginning that Sulpicius should have the command against Philip (cf. p. 45) and one is therefore led to the suspicion that the lot was not entirely arbitrary in its operation.

vellent iuberent: *velitis iubeatis* is the regular formula used by the magistrate presiding over an assembly when taking a vote. Cf. Mommsen, *StR*, iii. 312 n. 2, Ogilvie, 187.

Philippo regi Macedonibusque: this is the full and correct formula for the Macedonians—Βασιλεὺς Φίλιππος καὶ Μακεδόνες— cf. Walbank, *Philip V*, 4 n. 1, E. Bikerman, *CPh* xl (1945), 137 n. 6, A. Aymard, *RIDA* iv (1950), 75 ff. = *ÉHA*, 109 ff. The use of the formula is a further argument for the authenticity of Galba's motion.

ob iniurias: the declaration of war is based on the wrongs done by Philip—i.e. those in 1. 9–10 (cf. nn. ad loc.) together with those reported by Rhodes and Attalus (2. 1) and Athens (5. 6). All these are *socii* in the broadest sense of the term (1. 9–10 n., 5. 8 n.). Notice that there is no mention of the peace of Phoenice (cf. p. 39 n. 6).

2. urbanam: though L. does not say so explicitly, the *praetor urbanus* in this year and the two following ones probably also took the duties normally carried out by the *praetor peregrinus*. This happened when all the other praetors were required for military duties. Cf. xxv. 3. 1, xxxv. 41. 6, Mommsen, *StR*, ii³. 210.

Bruttios: Bruttium had defected to Hannibal in 216, and was the scene of many of the operations against him in the latter part of the Punic War. It was a separate praetorian province on several occasions after the departure of Hannibal (202–200, 192–188), partly because it was a key area for defensive action against possible invasion from the East, partly because there were still dissident elements in the area. For Bruttium's character and the frequency of brigandage there, cf. T. P. Wiseman, *PBSR* xxxii (1964), 34 ff. For Minucius' activities, cf. 12. 1–4, 13. 1, xxxii. 1. 7.

3–4. *The rejection of the war-vote.* There are good reasons for thinking that the rejection owed something to the influence of Scipio.

(i) The Tribune involved is Q. Baebius (20), and the Baebii are a *gens* who appear linked to the Scipios over a long period of years. Q. Baebius Tamphilus (45) was a *legatus* to Saguntum and Carthage in 220 and 218 respectively: apart from one Fabius, the second of these embassies appears to have been heavily weighted with supporters of the Scipios (*MRR*, i. 239: for the identity of the Fabius cf. Scullard, *RP*, 274, *MRR*, i. 241 n. 7, Walbank, *Commentary*, i. 333–4). Q. Baebius Herennius (26), *tr. pl.* in 216, strongly supported Varro in his candidacy for the consulship, and was in fact related to him (xxii. 34. 3–11): there are good reasons for linking Varro with the Scipionic group (cf. Scullard, *RP*, 49–55, Cassola, *GP*, 365–73). Cn. Baebius Tamphilus (41), tribune in 204, plebeian aedile in 200 (cf. 50. 3) and praetor in 199 (50. 3, xxxii. 1. 2, 7. 5), was a candidate for the consulship of 184, and eventually elected for 182 with L. Aemilius Paullus, the brother-in-law of Africanus. L. Baebius (14, 25) was a *legatus* under Scipio in 203, M. Baebius Tamphilus (44), praetor in 192, was consul with P. Cornelius Cethegus in 181. Cn. Baebius (42, 43) was praetor in 168, the year of Paullus' second consulship. A. Baebius (8) was left in charge of Demetrias by Paullus in 167—though he was punished by Paullus for allowing Roman soldiers to take part in internal Aetolian disputes (xlv. 31. 2). This is an occasion where the accumulation of evidence over a long period constitutes a valid prosopographical argument.

(ii) It appears that the unwillingness of Scipio's veterans to serve played a considerable part in the rejection of the motion. Concessions appear to have been made to them between the two meetings of the *comitia* (cf. 8. 6, 14. 2, xxxii. 3. 3; it is they particularly who are referred to in *fessi . . . fecerant*).

For the reasons for Scipio's opposition, cf. p. 46.

3. ab omnibus ferme centuriis : declarations of war were always made by the centuriate assembly (Mommsen, *StR*, iii. 343, Walbank, *Commentary*, i. 687–8). For the procedure for declaring war at this time cf. 8. 3–4 n.

omnibus cannot be literally true, since the voting stopped once an absolute majority was reached. For similar exaggeration cf. Cic. *de imp. Pomp.* 2, *Pis.* 2. On voting procedure in the assemblies, see most recently U. Hall, *Historia* xiii (1964), 267–306, Taylor, *RVA*, *passim*; *ferme* gives very little indication of the actual size of the minority.

4. viam antiquam : perhaps in reference to the speech of Baebius Herennius in 216 (see above), but more probably in general to such speeches in the period of the struggle of the orders as iv. 58. 12, vi. 27. 7 (thus W–M). For the phrase *bella ex bellis* cf. ii. 18. 10, xxi. 10. 4, Ogilvie, 283.

5–6 : these words conceal, no doubt, some vigorous political per-suasion and manœuvring. They also conceal a considerable time-lag between the two assemblies; cf. pp. 44–5.

damno dedecorique: for the alliteration cf. iv. 13. 14, Lambert, 26.

7. *The speech of Sulpicius*

On this speech, cf. p. 20. The theme of the speech is 'war will come whether you like it or not: strike first before Philip strikes'.

There is no mention of the danger from Antiochus (cf. Bellezza, 46 and p. 47).

7. 2. contione advocata : a *contio* is an informal gathering of the people meeting to hear a magistrate speak before a vote is taken. The *comitia* as such could only decide issues, and could not debate them; cf. Mommsen, *StR*, i³. 197–202, G. W. Botsford, *The Roman Assemblies* (New York, 1909), 139–51, Taylor, *RVA*, ch. ii.

bellum molitur : on the phrase cf. Tränkle, *Gnomon*, 374 n. 1, and xxxiii. 19. 6, 26. 5, 45. 5 nn.

3. ante alias : B omits *ante*. *ante alias* and *alias ante* occur seven times in L. (Packard, i. 325, 413). For omission of *ante* W–M quote vi. 42. 12, viii. 6. 14, but the latter does not have *alias*. It is possible that *ante* is an addition, but decision is difficult.

proximo certe Punico bello : the MSS. have *Punico proximo certe bello*. The collocation of the two adjectives is harsh, and gives an undesirable emphasis to *Punico*, making Sulpicius say 'your evidence is in the Punic war—the second one'. Madvig (*Emendationes*, 463) deleted *Punico*. McDonald defends M. Müller's transposition by referring to xlv. 37. 12. The latter passage, however, is really only giving a dating reference 'the Second Punic War', while here the point is that it is the war just ended that is to be considered. The MSS. reading suggests that *Punico* was added as an explanatory gloss at an early stage of transmission.

Saguntinis . . . opem : Hannibal began the siege of Saguntum in the spring of 219 and it fell eight months later (Pol. iii. 17, Walbank, *Commentary*, i. 327–8). Roman ambassadors did not go to Carthage until the spring of 218 (Walbank, *Commentary*, i. 333–4, Scullard, *RP*, 39–41). This means that Polybius' claim (iii. 20) that there was no delay or hesitation after the news of the fall of Saguntum must be rejected. L. compressed all the events into 218—though he recognized the difficulties involved (xxi. 15)—and followed Polybius in holding that there was no delay after the fall of Saguntum. There is no conflict between this version and Sulpicius' comments here, for Sulpicius is referring to the lack of Roman action before the fall of Saguntum. Saguntum had made many appeals to Rome even before Hannibal had attacked it and these the senate had ignored (Pol. iii. 15). Even immediate action after the fall of Saguntum would have been too late to keep Hannibal in Spain. That this is Sulpicius' view is confirmed by § 6 *Sagunto expugnando*, not *expugnato*. For other criticism of Rome's failure to help Saguntum cf. xxi. 16. 2, 19. 9, Merten, 12.

For full bibliography on issues connected with the outbreak of the Second Punic War, see Cassola, *GP*, 245–58.

sicut . . . tulerant: the Mamertines were Campanian mercenaries who captured Messana *c.* 283 (Walbank, *Commentary*, i. 52). They ravaged much of Sicily, but were eventually defeated, *c.* 265, by Hiero of Syracuse. One party in Messana then appealed to Carthage, another to Rome. Carthage garrisoned Messana, and the Romans, after much debate, decided to send forces of their own to Messana. Hence the First Punic War. The main narrative is Pol. i. 7 ff.; for the other sources cf. *MRR*, i. 203. For the details, see Walbank, *Commentary*, i. 52 ff., Cassola, *GP*, 204–7 with bibliography, Badian, *FC*, 33–6, Lippold, 113.

Sulpicius' claim is exaggerated. Roman inaction in 264 would not have precipitated a Carthaginian invasion of Italy (cf. Walbank, *Commentary*, i. 57).

aversuri fuerimus: for this use of the perfect subjunctive cf. K–St, ii. 409(b).

4. pactum . . . ut . . . traiceret: B. χ has *traicere*: the infinitive is defended by Tränkle, *Gnomon*, 372 n. 1, as a rarer usage found in xxi. 41. 9, xliii. 21. 3: he holds that B altered to the more usual form. Tränkle could be right, but alterations of this sort are unusual in B, and it does not seem very likely that the infinitive would have seemed so odd to B as to produce correction in this case. The treaty between Philip and Hannibal was concluded in 215; cf. 1. 8 n. L.'s version (xxiii. 33. 11–12), repeated here, is that there was specific provision for Philip to cross to Italy and, after the defeat of Rome, for Hannibal to help Philip in Greece. The falsity of this is demonstrated by the authentic text of the treaty preserved in Polybius (vii. 9). The latter does, however, provide for co-operation βοηθήσετε δὲ ἡμῖν, ὡς ἂν χρεία ᾖ καὶ ὡς ἂν συμφωνήσωμεν (ibid., § 11), and it is reasonable to interpret this as looking to Philip's eventual coming to Italy. It is unnecessary to think that Philip's activities were to be confined to Greece (thus De Sanctis, iii. 2. 407, Walbank, *Philip V*, 71, E. Manni, *Mem. Acc. di sci. di Bologna, classe di scienze morali*, serie iv. 3 [1941], 7–26). There is no case for regarding L.'s version either as the definitive form of the treaty when finally ratified, or as the second treaty concluded after the original text had been captured by the Romans (xxiii. 39). Cf. Niese, ii. 467 n. 4, G. Egelhaaf, *HZ* xvii (1885), 456 ff., Holleaux, *Rome*, 183 n. 1, De Sanctis, iii. 2. 407 n. 22, Walbank, *Philip V*, 71: further bibliography in Schmitt, *StV*, iii. 245–50.

Laevino: M. Valerius Laevinus (211); cf. 3. 3 n. For his mission xxiii. 38. 10–11. His mandate was *ut Philippum in regno contineret* (cf. p. 45).

6. Athenis: Athens is here emphasized as a leading example of

Philip's aggressions, not as a legal or moral justification for going to war.

7. quinto . . . mense : xxi. 38. 1, Pol. iii. 56. 3, Walbank, *Commentary*, i. 365, 391. Hannibal left Carthage in April 218, and reached Italy in September.

quinto [inde] die : as Madvig argued (*Emendationes*, 463–4), the conjunction of *inde* with a relative clause is not a possible construction. Even if it were, the repetition of *quinto inde* would be extremely harsh.

8. Ne aequaveritis : for this use of *ne* cf. K–St, i. 190(b).

aequabitis; ⟨aequabitis⟩ : the second *aequabitis* is omitted in all MSS. by haplography. For this rhetorical figure—called *correctio*— cf. R. Volkmann, *Die Rhetorik der griechen und römer* (2nd edn., Leipzig, 1885), 496.

9. Epirus : apart from a short period from 330–323, Epirus had remained nominally independent of Macedon. But their fortunes had been inextricably mixed, and with the exception of the reign of Pyrrhus, rulers of Epirus had not been in a position to pursue a policy unpleasing to the rulers of Macedon. Macedon had often interfered in the internal affairs of Epirus, and their ruling families had been linked by the marriage of Philip II to the Epirote princess Olympias. About 231 a republican revolution had deposed the Epirote royal family. Epirus joined the symmachy of Antigonus Doson (Pol. iv. 9. 4). In the First Macedonian War, Epirus, though nominally an ally of Philip, in fact adopted a position of neutrality (cf. Holleaux, *Rome*, 214, Walbank, *Philip V*, 86 n. 6, Oost, *RPEA*, 30–2, R. G. Hopital, *RD*, ive série, xlii [1964], 21 n. 10, 42 n. 16: *contra* Hammond, *Epirus*, 610 n. 2).

On the history of Epirus cf. G. N. Cross, *Epirus* (Cambridge, 1932), Oost, *RPEA*, 2 ff., P. R. Franke, *Alt Epirus und das Königtum der Molosser* (Kallmunz, 1955), Lévêque, *Pyrrhos*, 89 ff., Hammond, *Epirus*. See further xxxii. 10. 1, 14. 5 nn.

Peloponnesum . . . ipsos : an exaggeration. The Achaean League was an ally of Philip, but only the Acrocorinth (involving control of Corinth), Orchomenus, Heraea, Triphylia and Aliphera were actually in Philip's possession at this time. The Acrocorinth had been handed over as the price for Doson's alliance in 224 (Pol. ii. 52. 4, Plut. *Arat.* 42, *Cleom.* 19). On the other towns cf. xxxii. 5. 4 n. On Corinth and the Acrocorinth cf. 22. 6 n. For the relations of leading Argives with Philip xxxii. 22. 11.

morte Pyrrhi : Pyrrhus died in street fighting in Argos in 272: Plut. *Pyrr.* 32 ff., Just. xxv. 5. 1, Strabo viii. p. 376c, Paus. i. 13. 8, Polyaenus viii. 68, Schol. Ov. *Ibis* 303, Zon. viii. 6, *Vir. Ill.* 35. 10,

Oros. iv. 2. 7, Quint. v. 11. 10, Serv. *in Aen.* vi. 839, Val. Max. v. i. ext. 4, Aelian *NA* vii. 41, Amp. 28. 3, Niese ii. 60 n. 3, Lévêque, *Pyrrhos*, 622 ff., Kienast, *RE*, xxiv. 159–61.

10. ad ipsam urbem Romanam : another exaggeration. After the battle of Heraclea in 280 Pyrrhus marched towards Rome, but got no further than Anagni, or, according to some accounts, Praeneste. (Anagni, App. *Samn.* 10, cf. Plut. *Pyrr.* 17. 5; Praeneste, Eut. ii. 12. 1, Flor. i. 13. 24, cf. Amp. 45. 2, *Vir. Ill.* 35. 6, Lévêque, *Pyrrhos*, 334–40, Kienast, *RE*, xxiv. 139.)

11. Tarentini : Tarentum had been an ally of Rome since her surrender in 272. On her capture by Hannibal in the Second Punic War and subsequent status cf. 29. 10–11 n.

maiorem Graeciam vocant : on the origin of the name cf. Walbank, *Commentary*, i. 222.

ut . . . crederes : 'so that you would not be surprised that they followed one who spoke the Greek language and bore a Greek name.'

L. often uses the second person singular of the imperfect subjunctive in this way (e.g. ii. 43. 9, xxix. 28. 3, xli. 13. 8): the usage is idiomatic (cf. K–St, i. 179), and though it occurs here in a speech to the people, L. naturally keeps the verb in the singular.

12. Lucanus et Bruttius et Samnis : on the non-Greek allies of Pyrrhus, cf. Plut. *Pyrr.* 13. 6, Just. xviii. 1. 1, Flor. i. 13. 1, De Sanctis, ii. 383, Lévêque, *Pyrrhos*, 303–7, Kienast, *RE*, xxiv. 129–30. Only this passage mentions Bruttium, but they were involved in the later fighting (*I.I.* xiii. 1. 73–5) and Rome took punitive action against them (cf. Lévêque, 304).

For the use of the singular in the sense of a plural, particularly common in historical writers, cf. Löfstedt, *Syntactica*, i. 14 ff., K–St, i. 67.

manserunt : highly ironical, for these peoples did revolt to Hannibal in 216 (xxii. 61. 11–12). Sage wrongly translates ' "Yes", you say, "for they did in the later Punic War" '.

numquam . . . deficient : although they did not rebel at the time of the Gallic threat in 225 (cf. Salmon, *Samnium*, 294–5).

bene iuvantibus divis : L. uses the form *divus* in religious formulae. Cf. vi. 29. 9, viii. 9. 6, xxii. 10. 8, xxiii. 11. 1, 4, xxix. 27. 1, Sall. *Or. Lep.* 27, Lebek, 282.

15 : cf. 5. 4–7.

sed etiam : χ. B has *iam*. McDonald thinks the *et* was omitted after *sed*. But *non modo . . . sed iam* is the more unusual collocation (cf. vii. 12. 14, viii. 29. 12, xxi. 63. 6, xxii. 15. 1) and has more point here. The goodwill of the gods was manifested after the senate had authorized the consul to propose the war motion (cf. 5. 4).

8. 1. *The vote for war*

8. 1. uti rogaret: this is the reading of all the MSS. Sigonius and Madvig wanted to read *uti rogas*, the usual formula for the people agreeing to a motion put before them by the presiding magistrate. Here, however, there is a subordinate clause in *oratio obliqua*—*bellum* (sc. *fieri*), *uti rogaret, iusserunt*, and the MSS. reading should be retained. (This appears to be the argument of McDonald also.)

8. 2. Supplicationes *for victory*

2. supplicatio . . . pulvinaria: *pulvinaria* are couches on which images of the gods were placed. They were specially used in the *lectisternium* which was first performed in 399 (v. 13. 6, D. H. xii. 9, Aug. *CD* iii. 17). The *supplicatio*, though probably existing before then (cf. iii. 7. 7, 63. 5), appears to have been assimilated to the *lectisternium*. We hear on many occasions of *supplicationes ad* (or *circa*) *omnia pulvinaria* (see the list in Wissowa, *RE*, ivA. 944): on many occasions *supplicationes* were instituted by the *xviri sacris faciundis* after consultation of the Sibylline books: the *xviri* were specially concerned with the *Graecus ritus*, which included the *lectisternium* (cf. Varro *L.L.* vii. 88, A. A. Boyce, *TAPA* lxix (1938), 161–87, Latte, *RRG*, 397–8: on the *lectisternium*, Ogilvie, 655–7).

This is the orthodox view of *supplicationes*. (See Wissowa, *RE*, ivA. 942–51, *RuK*[2], 423–6, Latte, *RRG*, 245–6.) W. Hoffmann, however (*Phil.* supp. xxvii, 1 [1934], 135–8), argues that the forms of the *supplicatio* were not assimilated to those of the *lectisternium* until 218, when we first hear of *pulvinaria* in connection with a *supplicatio* (xxi. 62. 9), and that even after this some unassimilated *supplicationes* occurred. He argues that we cannot assume *supplicationes ad pulvinaria* or initiation by the *xviri* where these are not specifically attested. This is true, but it is equally dangerous to argue *ex silentio* that where *pulvinaria* or *xviri* are not mentioned, they were not involved. L. is quite capable of mentioning sometimes the *xviri* as initiators, sometimes the senate, without the one necessarily excluding the other. And as Latte stresses (*RRG*, 245 n. 2) the senate's authorization was needed for a consultation of the Sibylline books by the *xviri*.

Agnes Lake (*Quantulacumque*, Studies presented to Kirsopp Lake [London, 1937], 243–51) goes even further than Hoffmann and denies any connection between *supplicatio* and *lectisternium*: she believes that it was only occasionally that the *xviri* ordered a *supplicatio* and that they had no special connection with it. Apart from the defect in the *ex silentio* argument (which is made far more positive by Lake) her case is based on an unconvincing attempt to cull from Ps.-Acro *ad* Hor. *Od.* i. 37. 3 an original meaning for *pulvinar* of 'elevation on which cult objects were placed'. The *supplicatio* as a preliminary to war is probably a later development from the *supplicatio* as an expiation after disasters: cf. L. Halkin, *La Supplication d'action de grâces chez les Romains* (Paris, 1953), 10–12, Ogilvie, 512–13.

8. 3–4. *Consultation of the* Fetiales

The original procedure for declaring war at Rome had been to send *fetiales* to the offending people to demand satisfaction (*ad res repetundas*). If satisfaction was not forthcoming the people voted for war, and a spear was cast into enemy territory (*belli indictio*). But by the present time the procedure had been modified; the vote of the *comitia* to seek satisfaction and that to declare war were combined and the people voted for war if satisfaction were not forthcoming. The difficulty for Sulpicius was that if the act of *belli indictio* were regarded as purely formal, and were not conveyed to Philip himself, then strictly Philip was not being given a chance to satisfy the conditions. On the other hand Philip had ignored the earlier unofficial ultimatum delivered to Nicanor at Athens (Pol. xvi. 27, cf. pp. 41 ff.) and the full procedure would only give him time to prepare for the war. The *fetiales* did not commit themselves, perhaps because they did not want either to sanction or to condemn the senate's action in sending out ambassadors without the authority of the people—or maybe they were split on the issue.

See Walbank, *JRS* xxvii (1937), 192–7, xxxi (1941), 82–93, *CPh* xliv (1949), 15–19, Ogilvie, 128–9, Dahlheim, 171–80. On L.'s interest in fetial procedure, W. Liebeschuetz, *JRS* lvii (1967), 46.

8. 5–11. *Military arrangements*

5. veteres dimittere exercitus: the legions serving in Gaul, Bruttium, Sicily, Sardinia, and Etruria, as well as the army brought back by Scipio from Africa. For the armies in 201 cf. xxx. 40. 16 ff. On the Spanish army cf. xxx. 41. 5, xxxii. 28. 11 n.

6. voluntarios . . . esset: cf. 6. 3–4 n.

7. praetoribus: cf. 6. 2 for the assignation of praetorian provinces.
socium Latini nominis: strictly the Italian *socii* and the *nomen Latinum* should be distinguished (Mommsen, *StR*, iii. 611). But L. regards the forms *socii ac nomen Latinum* and *socii nominis Latini* (and variants on them) as interchangeable (cf. Packard, iv. 709–16), and no conclusions can be drawn as to whether Latins alone are meant on any particular occasion (cf. Wegner, 95–104, but Wegner's view

that the origin of the phrase is an asyndetical expression [*milites*] *socium, Latini nominis* is not compelling). Where military contingents are involved, it is safe to assume that both Latins and Italians are included. For the position of the allies in the Roman army, cf. Marquardt, *StV*, ii. 389 ff., Sherwin-White, *RC*, 93, A. Afzelius, *Die römische Kriegsmacht* (Acta Jutlandica xvi [1944]), 62–77, Salmon, *Samnium*, 306, Toynbee, i. 424 ff., ii. 128 ff., Brunt, 677 ff.

8. P. Aelius consul: on this see McDonald, *PCPS* N.S. vi (1960), 47. Purpurio and Rufus are to be given 5,000 troops each to garrison Gaul and Bruttium respectively. Fulvius is told to keep 5,000 troops from the army which had belonged to P. Aelius Paetus in Gaul, and take it to Sicily. Yet there is already an army in Sicily (xxx. 41. 2). This seems an extraordinary procedure and we may add to McDonald's arguments that *is quoque de exercitu qui ibi esset* in § 10 indicates that Valerius in Sardinia is to do the same as Fulvius in Sicily in using troops already in his province.

It should be said, however, that the position envisaged by the MSS. reading is not quite so fantastic as McDonald thinks. Aelius, it seems, had brought his army home from Gaul, and that is why Furius had to be given troops by the consuls—i.e. he is in a different position from Fulvius and Valerius. This means that at 10. 5 *exercitu dimisso* must indicate that the army was dismissed in Rome, not by Furius when he reached Gaul, as McDonald states. Thus the MSS. reading does not involve taking Gallic troops to Sicily and fresh troops to Gaul.

We must agree with McDonald, however, that P. Aelius is in fact P. Aelius Tubero (152), the praetor of 201. McDonald prefers to regard the error as having been committed by L. himself. But he rightly agrees with Johnson's deletion of *praetor* at xxx. 41. 2, and it looks as if someone, knowing of the two Aelii, attempted in both places to distinguish them. In this case he got it wrong.

praesidii: the MSS. have *praesidio* which is a perfectly acceptable predicative dative and Madvig's change to *praesidii* is not necessary.

9. M. Valerio Faltoni: (153). In 201 he had been assigned Bruttium (xxx. 40. 5) and presumably moved to Campania during the year. He was a quaestor by 206, a *legatus* to collect the *magna mater* from Pessinus in 205, and curule aedile in 203.

10. pro praetore: B has *pro p̄r̄*, which χ expands into the meaning-less *pro populo Romano*. It may be that we should read *propraetor*: cf. 3. 3 n.

11. sex: i.e. four of the consuls (§ 5) and two *urbanae*. The praetors do not have Roman troops, and their armies do not therefore count as legions.

9. 1–5. *The Egyptian embassy*

For the chronological place of this embassy cf. p. 44 n. 3. Notice once again that there is no mention of Egypt's war with Antiochus, and Egypt herself is not appealing to Rome for help.

9. 1. Athenienses . . . petisse: cf. Paus. i. 36. 5 and p. 44.

2. communes socii: Athens and Egypt, *communes* meaning that they had reciprocal agreements with each other. It cannot mean that Egypt was a *socius* of both Rome and Athens, which would destroy the contrast *etsi . . . tamen*. Athenian policy, under the leadership of Euryclides and Micion, had been based on friendship for Egypt from 224 onwards: in 224/3 the new tribe of Ptolemais had been created in Egypt's honour. See Pol. v. 106. 6–7, Ferguson, *Hellenistic Athens*, 237 ff., McDonald and Walbank, *JRS* xxvii (1937), 191, Walbank, *Commentary*, i. 631, Briscoe, *JHS* lxxxiv (1964), 208.

3. passurum . . . missurum: it is fantastic to think that Egypt could have made such an offer while engaged in the Fifth Syrian War.

4. firma ac fidelia: on the alliteration cf. Lambert, 27.

5. munera: for Roman hospitality to foreign envoys cf. Mommsen, *RF*, i. 343–8.

9. 5–10. *The vowing of* ludi magni

Ludi magni votivi are to be distinguished from the annual *ludi Romani* (cf. 4. 5). They were *ludi* vowed in a crisis to be performed if the state survived for a certain period of years (cf. n. on *quinquennalia* below). It is probable that they were originally celebrated after victories as part of the triumphal celebrations, and that it was from these that the annual *ludi* developed during the fourth century. *Ludi votivi* continued to be performed on special occasions. (L. himself thought that the annual *ludi* were instituted by Tarquinius Priscus—i. 35. 8.)

For this, the orthodox view of the *ludi* see Mommsen, *RF*, ii. 42–57, Wissowa, *RuK*², 452–4, Habel, *RE*, supp. v. 618, Latte, *RRG*, 248, Ogilvie, 149, 327; the view of A. Piganiol (*Recherches sur les jeux romains* [Strasbourg, 1923], 75–91) that the *ludi Romani* were the continuation of early plebeian games is not convincing. I do not fully understand the position of W. K. Quinn-Schofield, *Latomus* xxvi (1967), 96–103.

5. civitas religiosa : L. believes that at times of crisis the people
are particularly concerned with religious matters. The phrase here,
however, (cf. vi. 5. 6) does not convey the critical tone of e.g. xxi.
62. 1, xxiv. 10. 6.

7. Licinius pontifex maximus : P. Licinius Crassus Dives (69).
He was curule aedile in 212, when he was elected *pontifex maximus*,
defeating two senior consulars, Q. Fulvius Flaccus and T. Manlius
Torquatus. He was *magister equitum* in 210 and censor in the same
year with L. Veturius Philo (19). He was praetor in 208 and
consul in 205 with Scipio Africanus. He refused offers from Fabius
to have the African command (xxviii. 44. 11, Plut. *Fab.* 25) and
there are thus good reasons for regarding him as a supporter of
Scipio. One may note that the son of his colleague in the censorship was consul with Scipio's supporter Q. Caecilius Metellus (81:
cf. 4. 3 n.) in 206. In that case Crassus' obstruction of the anti-
Scipionic Sulpicius is quite intelligible. The actual issue involved
is very legalistic, and this makes it extremely probable that Crassus'
motive was purely political. See Schur, *SA*, 15, Scullard, *RP*, 67,
75–7, 87–8, Münzer, *RA*, 189–91, Cassola, *GP*, 410, Lippold, 177,
301, Schlag, 149–51.

ex incerta pecunia voveri debere, quia ⟨ea⟩ : 'it was wrong to
vow an undetermined sum of money, because the money vowed
could not be spent on the war, but should be set aside at once and
not confused with other money'.

B reads *vovere debere quia pecunia*, χ *vovere debere si ea pecunia*. The
two changes adopted by McDonald seem necessary. A passive
infinitive is required—the active would need a subject—and *pecunia*
needs further definition. Madvig (*Emendationes*, 464) thought that
there was a *lacuna* after *vovere*, on the grounds that Crassus was
saying that a vow *ex incerta pecunia* was prohibited, not simply that
it ought not to be made: he also argued that the *quia* clause should
depend on a positive. He thus wanted to read *vovere ⟨licere: ex certa
voveri⟩ debere* . . . Mommsen (*StR*, iii. 1137 n. 1) followed Madvig,
but preferred *quae* for *quia ea*. Madvig's reasoning is unconvincing.
debere negavit does indicate a complete prohibition, and the *quia*
clause goes as well with *incerta* or *certa pecunia*. McDonald argues that
Madvig's reading is inappropriate, because a fixed sum of money
would already be 'set aside'; but vowing a fixed sum of money does
not entail physically setting it aside, and Madvig's text makes perfectly good sense in itself. *quia ea pecunia seponi deberet* can be used as
well to mean 'you must fix a sum of money, and that must be set
aside' as 'you must not vow an undetermined sum of money, because
the money vowed has to be set aside'.

The usual sum for *ludi* up to the Second Punic War had been 200,000 HS (D. H. vii. 71, Ps.-Asc. *in* Cic. *Verr.* i. 31 [p. 217St.]). In 217 333,333⅓ HS were vowed (xxii. 10. 7; the last 333 is a supplement; the figure in Plut. *Fab.* 4 is a complete confusion). In fact, of course, no vows in money can have been made before the introduction of coinage in the early third century.

8. posse . . . decreverunt: the *pontifex maximus* clearly could not convince his colleagues, who probably contained a majority of opponents of Scipio (Scullard, *RP*, 87 n. 3, Schlag, 150–1). Sulpicius' reason for wanting to vow an indeterminate sum of money was no doubt the fact that the *aerarium* was in dire straits, and a firm commitment would be impossible (cf. 13. 3, Schlag, 149).

9. quinquennalia: 'vows to be fulfilled after five years had elapsed'. The vow took the form that the games would be celebrated if the state survived and prospered for five years. Cf. xxii. 10. 2, xxvii. 33. 8, xxx. 2. 8; also xxi. 62. 10, xlii. 28. 8 (*decennium*). The present vow was redeemed in 194 (xxxiv. 44. 6).

10. octiens: the reading (Bψ except L) is certainly right against *totiens* (ϕ plus L). The interpretation is far more difficult. *ludi magni votivi* are mentioned by L. at iv. 27. 2, v. 19. 6 (celebrated in v. 31. 2), vii. 11. 4, xxii. 9. 10, xxvii. 33. 8 (celebration of the previous vow and making of a new one): celebration of the latter in xxx. 2. 8. This makes only five vows mentioned by L. but there are five possible instances which may be added:

ii. 36. 1: this is rather improbable as L. appears to regard them as an instance of the annual *ludi* which he thought had been instituted by Tarquinius Priscus.

iv. 12. 2, vii. 15. 12: *ludi votivi*, but not specifically said to be *magni*.

xxi. 62. 10: a vow *in decennium*, but not said to be for *ludi*.

xxvii. 33. 8: a suggestion that in 217 *ludi* were performed in fulfilment of an earlier vow (cf. Piganiol, *Recherches sur les jeux romains*, 80). The text states *ludos magnos facere dictatorem iussit quos M. Aemilius praetor urbanus C. Flaminio Cn. Servilio consulibus fecerat et in quinquennium voverat.* It is intolerable Latin for *quos* to refer to two different sets of games, one already performed. I suspect that *fecerat et* is an interpolation.

It is likely that L. is referring to eight of these instances, but precisely which is unclear. We must also reckon with the possibility that other instances were recorded in the second decade.

Piganiol (*Recherches sur les jeux romains*, 81) believes that the reference is to a series of *ludi votivi* begun during the third century, and vowed at regular five-yearly intervals. He suggests that they commenced in 242, and the other instances were in 237, 232, 227, 222, 218, 217, 208. To this view there are three objections:

(i) the impression we gain from xxii. 9. 10 is that measures are being taken for a crisis, and we should not expect these to include measures which had in fact been carried out at regular intervals.

(ii) it depends on the assumption that games were celebrated in 217 (see above).

(iii) L. knew of earlier *vota* and must have thought they were *de certa pecunia.*

For subsequent vows *de incerta pecunia* cf. xxxvi. 2. 4, xlii. 28. 9.

10–11. 3. *The Gallic rising*

Cf. 21–22. 3, 47. 4–49. 3, Dio fr. 58. 5, Zon. ix. 15, Oros. iv. 20. 4. Münzer (*RE*, vii. 362–3) regards the whole of the account of Furius' campaign in 200 as a doublet constructed from the campaigns of Cornelius Cethegus in 197 (xxxii. 29–30) and of Furius himself as consul in 196 (xxxiii. 37). He points to similarities in the number of Gallic dead (xxxi. 21. 17, xxxii. 30. 11), in the freeing of Placentine captives (xxxi. 21. 18, 48. 11, xxxiii. 23. 1–2, 6) and to discrepancies about the fate of Hamilcar (xxxi. 21. 18, xxxii. 30. 12, xxxiii. 23. 5). He also believes that the disputes about Furius' triumph (47. 4–49. 3) in reality belong to 196 (cf. xxxiii. 37. 8 n.) and that the notices about Furius' dedication of a temple or temples to Jupiter (xxxi. 21. 12, xxxiv. 53. 7, xxxv. 41. 8) also point to the falsity of the account of the 200 campaign.

It is probably true that various of the details of these campaigns have been confused, and elements belonging to one imported into another. But it is unnecessary to reject the campaign of 200 altogether. The discrepancy about Hamilcar reflects differences in the sources, and is not itself an argument against the authenticity of the campaign; cf. *MRR*, i. 326 n. 1. The discrepancies are discussed in the notes on the relevant passages. On Gallic affairs in this period cf. Schlag, 40 ff., Toynbee, ii. 268 ff.

10. 2. Insubres : their chief town was Mediolanium (Milan). They joined in the Gallic rising in the 220s and surrendered in 222 (Pol. ii. 34). They supported Hannibal (xxi. 25. 2, Pol. iii. 60. 8). Cf. Philipp, *RE*, ix. 1589–93, Ogilvie, 713.

Cenomani : they lived in the area around Brescia and Verona. They had previously been loyal to Rome—cf. v. 35. 1, xxi. 55. 4, Pol. ii. 23. 2, 24. 7, 32. 4, Strabo v, p. 216c, Ogilvie, 714 and references there cited, Toynbee, ii. 266 n. 3, 627.

Boii : 2. 5 n.

Celinibus : the tribe is otherwise unknown: it is unclear whether they are to be identified with the Celeiates mentioned at xxxii. 29. 7.

Ilvatibus: a Ligurian tribe, cf. xxxii. 29. 8, 31. 4. Toynbee (ii. 269 and elsewhere) identifies them with the Eleiates whose defeat is recorded in the *Fasti Triumphales* between 166 and 155. (They are called *Eleates* in the *Fasti Capitolini*, but *Veliates* in the *Fasti Urbisalvienses*.) The identification is uncertain.

Hamilcare Poeno . . . substiterat: Hasdrubal had invaded Italy from Spain in 207 and had been defeated and killed at the battle of the Metaurus (xxvii. 36–51, other sources *MRR*, i. 294). At 11. 5 L. says the senate were not sure whether Hamilcar had remained from the army of Hasdrubal or that of Mago, who had retreated from Italy in 203 (xxx. 18–19). It is possible that Hamilcar stayed after Hasdrubal's expedition, and then collaborated with Mago. The version of Dio (fr. 58. 5, Zon. ix. 15. 7) that Hamilcar and Mago collaborated in 202 is part of the variant version that Mago was still in N. Italy in 202 (App. *Lib.* 49, 59) and should be rejected. Cf. Ehrenberg, *RE*, xiv. 504, Lenschau, *RE*, vii. 2308–9, De Sanctis, iii. 2. 542 n. 151. On the possible identification of Hamilcar with the Carthaginian admiral in Spain in 217, cf. Walbank, *Commentary*, i. 431.

Placentiam: Placentia (mod. Piacenza) had been settled together with Cremona, as a Roman colony in 218, but the colonists had been attacked by the Boii and many had fled to Mutina. The Boii captured the commissioners responsible for settling the colony (Pol. iii. 40, L. *per.* xx, xxi. 25, Asc. p. 3c, Vell. Pat. i. 14. 8, Tac. *Hist.* iii. 34: on the names of the commissioners, *MRR*, i. 241, Scullard, *RP*, 273–4, 4. 3 n.). Placentia remained, however, in Roman possession, cf. Hanslik, *RE*, xx. 1898–1902, Walbank, *Commentary*, i. 374–5, Brunt, 190. For Kahrstedt's claim (Meltzer–Kahrstedt, iii. 400) that Placentia and Cremona cannot have survived during the Hannibalic war cf. De Sanctis, iii. 2. 102–4.

3. Cremonam: see above and Hülsen, *RE*, iv. 1702–3.

5. cetero . . . nominis: cf. 8. 7 n.

proxima regione provinciae: 'the part of the province nearest to Rome', not 'the part of the province nearest to Cremona', or 'the area nearest to the province'.

Ariminum: on Ariminum, mod. Rimini, cf. G. A. Mansuelli, *Ariminum* (Spoleto, 1941).

6. tempestatem belli: for the phrase cf. iii. 7. 3, Ogilvie, 407.

11. 1. exercitum: presumably the two legions previously enrolled by Aurelius (8. 5).

eadem die adesse iuberet: W–M argue that *eadem die* is to be taken with *iuberet*, not with *adesse*, on the grounds that it would be

impossible for the legions to march from their assembly point of
Arretium (cf. 21. 1) to Ariminum on the same day. But clearly the
order would be given in advance, not on the day itself. The army
were presumably to congregate at Arretium earlier than had originally been intended, and to reach Ariminum on the same day that
they were originally to be at Arretium.

3. Q. Minucio: at 8. 7 he is in charge of Bruttium and the praetor
in question must be Furius. McDonald ascribes the error to L.
himself, but L. has just been talking about Furius, and such a
mistake would be very strange, as at 12. 1 he again places Minucius
in Bruttium. As in 8. 8 *Q. Minucio* should be regarded as a gloss,
probably by the same glossator (thus M. Müller).

sociorum: cf. 8. 7 n.

Etruriae praesidio: the senate was still fearful of revolt in
Etruria: cf. A. J. Pfiffig, *Historia* xv (1966), 210.

proficisceretur ipse: the use of *ipse . . . proficisceretur* in § 2 to
refer to Aurelius, and *proficisceretur ipse* here to refer to the praetor
is ugly, and is a good example of L.'s lack of interest in presentation
in such matters as the reporting of senatorial decisions. See p. 17.

coloniam: Cremona.

11. 4–18. *Embassies to and from Africa*

Massinissa, son of the king of the Numidian tribe of the Massyli,
had served under the Carthaginians in Spain. But in his struggle
for the kingdom after the death of his father, he was opposed by
Syphax and the Carthaginians and joined Rome when Laelius
arrived in Africa in 205 (xxix. 4. 7 ff., 29. 4 ff.). Syphax had earlier
been an ally of Rome, but had allied himself with Carthage in 206.
Syphax had been captured and died in Italy shortly before Scipio's
triumph. On the details see Walsh, *JRS* lv (1965), 149 ff., Habel,
RE, ivA. 1472–7, Schur, *RE*, xiv. 2154 ff., Astin, *Scipio Aemilianus*,
49–50. The boundaries between Massinissa's kingdom and Carthage
remained a subject of dispute for the next fifty years (cf. § 12 n.). It
is clear from §§ 16–18 that the status of Syphax's son Vermina had
not been settled at the time of the peace with Carthage. He certainly
retained some parts of his father's former kingdom. Zonaras (ix. 13. 7)
wrongly says that Vermina was brought to Rome with Syphax and
then given the kingdom.

5. Hamilcarem: cf. 10. 2 n.

6. contra foedus: the peace treaty of 201. Hamilcar, as a Carthaginian citizen, was accused of being in breach of the clause
bellum neve . . . extra Africam gererent (xxx. 37. 4, Pol. xv. 18. 4).

7. perfugas : xxx. 37. 3, Pol. xv. 18. 3.

8. parte florentissima : indicating that parts of Syphax' former territory were not given to Massinissa; cf. Walsh, *JRS* lv, 151–2.

9–10. This is the strangest of all the reasons for going to war with Philip that are contained in this book. It appears to be a simple case of revenge—by his alliance with Hannibal in 215 Philip had been responsible for the prolongation of the Hannibalic War. The motive is improbable, the claim false. When Scipio wanted to invade Africa in 205 his plan was violently opposed by Fabius Maximus and Q. Fulvius Flaccus (xxviii. 40 ff.). Fabius and Flaccus had had the greatest influence over Roman policy in the preceding years, and never thought of invading Africa—such a move would have been entirely contrary to the Fabian policy of attrition.

10. sociis : the Illyrian protectorate, attacked by Philip in 216 and thereafter. The reference is not to the attacks on the Illyrians after 205 alluded to in 1. 9.

Numidarum equitum : for Massinissa's offer cf. 19. 3. We have no record of their playing any part in the actual fighting in Macedon.

11. dona ampla : the *toga praetexta* and the *sella curulis* are the signs of curule office at Rome. The purple toga, believed to have been worn by the kings of Rome, the *tunica palmata*, and the sceptre were part of the insignia of *triumphatores*. Cf. Ehlers, *RE*, viiA. 504–7, K.-W. Welwei, *Historia* xvi (1967), 62, L. B. Warren, *JRS* lx (1970), 59, M. Reinhold, *Purple as a status symbol in antiquity* (Brussels, 1970), 37 ff. For similar gifts cf. xxvii. 4. 8–10 (Syphax and Ptolemy IV), xxx. 15. 12, App. *Lib.* 32. 137 (recognition of Massinissa by Scipio in Africa: the present gift is the senate's confirmation of Scipio's action), xlii. 14. 10 (Eumenes), Pol. xxxii. 1 (Ariarathes), Caesar, *BG* i. 43 (Ariovistus), Tac. *Ann.* iv. 26 (Ptolemy of Mauretania), D. H. iii. 61, v. 35, Mommsen, *StR*, iii. 592, D. Kienast, *ZRG* lxxxv (1968), 335 ff.

12. ei⟨s⟩ : the MSS. read *ei*—that is, Massinissa—and this would be taken with *opus esse*. Gronovius kept this sense by reading *sibi*, but Madvig's *eis* (*Emendationes*, 464–5) has been accepted by the majority of subsequent editors. But the reflexive is regularly used to refer to the subject of the main verb, and *ei* to refer to Massinissa here is perfectly in order, and should be retained (cf. K–St, i. 607 ff.).

The senate seems to be indicating to Massinissa that it will take his side in any boundary disputes that arise between him and Carthage. Whether the senate would have made so open an indication of its policy may be doubted, and the passage may be an inference from what happened subsequently. On these disputes see Walsh, *JRS* lv, 156 ff., and below xxxiii. 47. 8 n.

13–15. On the facts see above.

15. ex socio et amico: it is uncertain whether or not there was ever a formal treaty with Syphax (cf. Dahlheim, 230 n. 122).

16. nominis . . . consuesse: see the parallel language in Caesar *BG* i. 43 *pro magnis hominum officiis consuesse tribui docebat* (cf. Klotz, *RhM* xcvi [1953], 62 ff.). The sentiment is somewhat anachronistic as Rome's contact with foreign kingdoms was as yet limited. The Ptolemies, Attalus, Hiero of Syracuse and, probably, Sparta were, or had been, *socii et amici*, but specific recognition as *rex*, involving the gifts described in § 12, is only attested in the cases of Massinissa, Syphax, and Ptolemy.

17. liberum arbitrium: Vermina is being asked to make what amounts to a modified form of *deditio*. The terms involved are to be entirely within Rome's judgement, but Vermina can object to them if he so desires, and this last element is alien to a complete *deditio*. On *deditio* cf. 27. 3 n.

18. C. Terentius Varro: (83). Cf. 49. 6. He is the consul of 216, defeated at Cannae. Despite his defeat he was subsequently used in various capacities (proconsul 215–213, propraetor 208–207, *legatus* to Philip in 203 [cf. 1. 9–10 n.]) and this suggests that Cannae was not so much due to his own incompetence and rashness as the sources suggest. Cf. Scullard, *RP*, 52.

Sp. Lucretius: (13). Plebeian aedile in 206, praetor in 205, and propraetor from 204–202.

Cn. Octavius: (16). Military tribune 216, plebeian aedile 206, praetor 205 and propraetor from 204–201. He was a *iiivir* for the foundation of Croton in 194 and a *legatus* to Greece in 192–191. He is the first Octavius to hold curule office, and father of the consul of 165.

12. 1–4. *Thefts from the temple of Proserpina at Locri*

12. 1. Q. Minuci . . . erat: cf. 11. 3 n.

Locris ex Proserpinae thesauris: Epizephyrian Locri is on the east coast of the toe of Italy, about 25 miles north of its tip and 2 miles south of modern Locri. Cf. P. Larizza, *Locri Epizephyrii* (Reggio di Calabria, 1930), Oldfather, *RE*, xiii. 1289–1363. Full bibliography to date in J. Bérard, *Bibliographie topographique des principales cités grecques de l'Italie méridionale et de la Sicile dans l'antiquité* (Paris, 1941), 62 ff. Add P. E. Arias, *Archivio storico per la Calabria e la Lucania* xv (1946), 71 ff., A. de Franciscis, *Archaeology* xi (1958), 206 ff. The temple of Proserpina, said by Diodorus (xxvii. 4) to be the most famous of all temples in Italy, lay outside the city on the hills to its west (cf. xxix. 18. 16, Oldfather, *RE*, xiii. 1301–2, L. A. Springer, *Temple Treasures* [Philadelphia, 1949], 66–8, P. Zancani Montuoro *RAL* serie 8, xiv [1959], 225–32).

2. Pleminium : (2). Q. Pleminius. He was put in charge of Locri by Scipio after its capture in 205 as *legatus pro praetore*. He indulged in a number of acts of extreme cruelty towards the citizens, including the theft from the temple referred to here. He was also involved in a dispute with two of his own military tribunes, and as a result was almost murdered by Roman soldiers. Scipio took his part in an inquiry into this, but in the following year complaints were made in the senate by the Locrians. Scipio's negligence in the matter was attacked by his political opponents, and Fabius Maximus proposed that Scipio himself should be recalled from Sicily where he was about to embark on his invasion of Africa. But the senate decided that the praetor M. Pomponius Matho (see § 3) should head a commission of inquiry (*quaestio*) into the allegations against Pleminius. The Locrians desisted from pressing their charges against Scipio, but the *quaestio* sent Pleminius and others alleged guilty to Rome to await formal trial. Scipio was allowed to proceed with his military tasks. According to L. (xxix. 22. 9) Pleminius died at Rome before his trial could take place, but L. reports a variant version of Clodius Licinus, according to which in 194 Pleminius was implicated in an attempt to set fire to the city and thus to escape from prison: as a result he was executed. This is repeated at xxxiv. 44. 6–8 without mention of the inconsistency. *poenae* here implies L.'s first version.

Sources on Pleminius: xxix. 8–9, 16–22, Diod. xxvii. 4, Val. Max. i. 1. 21, App. *Hann.* 55, Dio fr. 57. 62, Zon. ix. 11, Lippold, 61–2, 201–2, Toynbee, ii. 613 ff. On the version of Licinus see Münzer, *Hermes* xlvii (1912), 162–6, *RE*, xxi. 222, arguing that the version of Pleminius' death in Licinus is an anticipation of later examples of execution in the Tullianum, F. Grosso, *GIF* v (1952), 119–35, 234–53, arguing in favour of Licinus' account.

3. quaestionem : this is an example of the semi-judicial inquiries which were often set up by the senate in the early part of the second century. The senate was in many cases authorizing actions in allied territories which went beyond what was envisaged by the *foedera* with the allied states involved. Cf. McDonald, *JRS* xxxiv (1944), 11–33, especially 14 n. 23 on this episode. The *quaestio* to investigate the complaints against Pleminius consisted of ten senators chosen by the consuls, two tribunes, and an aedile (xxix. 20. 4). It is not clear whether there was to be a similar *consilium* on this occasion.

M. Pomponius : (19). M. Pomponius Matho was plebeian aedile in 207, a *legatus* to Delphi in 205 and praetor in 204. His command in Sicily was prorogued in 203. He was probably the nephew of Scipio's mother (cf. Münzer, *RA*, 161–2, Cassola, *GP*, 386, 407–8) and the appointment was in itself a victory for Scipio.

triennio ante: cf. 1. 8 n.

4. expleri: cf. 13. 1 *ex bonis noxiorum*—i.e. in addition to the actual stolen money found in their possession.

piacularia: for the *piacula* in 204 cf. xxix. 19. 8, 21. 4; for this occasion cf. xxxii. 1. 8. See Tromp, *De Romanorum piaculis* (cf. 4. 5 n.), 87–8.

12. 5–10. *Prodigies*

Lists of prodigies are given by L. for all except seven years between books xxi and xlv. They probably stem from the *annales maximi* (for the arguments of E. Rawson, *CQ* xxi (1971), 158 ff. against this cf. p. 11 n. 4). L.'s style in these accounts of prodigies is terse, and the language often differs from L.'s normal usage. This no doubt reflects the style of the notices in the *annales*, though L. has often worked over them in his own way. Thus in the present passage L. works up from the lesser prodigies to the deformities of nature in §§ 6 ff.

L. regarded attention given to prodigies as historically important, even though he was aware that many could be explained in non-religious ways. Cf. xliii. 13, compared with the sceptical comments of xxi. 62. 1, xxiv. 10. 6, xxvii. 23. 2, xxix. 14. 2.

For other lists in books xxxi–xxxiii, see xxxii. 1, xxxii. 9, xxxii. 29, xxxiii. 26. Cicero, *de natura deorum* ii. 14, gives a catalogue of prodigies.

For bibliography, cf. Ogilvie, 403–4, to which add L. Wülker, *Die geschichtliche Entwicklung des Prodigienwesens* (Leipzig, 1903), Krauss, *An Interpretation of the Omens, Portents and Prodigies recorded by Livy, Tacitus and Suetonius* (Philadelphia, 1930), Bornecque 59–60, Laistner, 69 ff., Kajanto, 47 ff., Latte, *RRG*, 203–4, Walsh, *Livy*, 62–4, R. Bloch, *Les Prodiges dans l'antiquité classique* (Paris, 1963), R. Günther, *Klio* xlii (1964), 209 ff. The second edition (1904) of F. Luterbacher's *Der Prodigienglaube und Prodigienstil der Römer* has been republished (Darmstadt, 1967). Wülker analyses the known prodigies by type, place of origin, cure effected, and so forth, and much of what follows is drawn from him.

5. caelum arsisse: for similar prodigies cf. Wülker, 8, Luterbacher, 22 n. 27, Krauss, 78 n. 119, Ogilvie, 403.

adferebant: for the non-expression of the subject in reports of prodigies cf. v. 15. 1, xxviii. 11. 3, xxxii. 9. 3, Luterbacher, 44–5.

Priverni: the Volscian town was on the site of the modern

Priverno, about 50 miles south of Rome, but after the Roman con-
quest it was probably rebuilt in the valley to the north of Priverno.
Cf. Nissen, *IL*, ii. 2. 646, H. H. Armstrong, *AJA* xv (1911), 44–59,
170–94, 386–402, Radke, *RE*, xxiii. 15–17. For other prodigies at
Privernum xxvii. 11. 4, xlii. 2. 4, Obs. 14, 36, 38, Cic. *de div.* i. 97,
Wülker, 99.

   rubrum solem : cf. xxv. 7. 8, Wülker, 8, Luterbacher, 20.

6. Lanuvi i⟨n⟩ : the MSS. read *Lanuvii*. Walsh (*CR*, 54) appears
to want to retain the MSS. reading as a 'local ablative'. L. certainly uses the ablative without *in* far more often than previous
writers, but I cannot see a case similar to the present passage, where
there is no verb denoting action or motion. It seems preferable to
follow the traditional emendation. See Riemann, 271–2, K–St, i.
353–4.
   Lanuvium is modern Lanuvio on the Via Appia some 15 miles
south of Rome. Cf. Nissen, *IL*, ii. 2. 592, Ashby, *Campagna*, 199 ff.,
G. E. Colburn, *AJA* xviii (1914), 18–31, 185–98, 363–80, Philipp,
RE, xii. 694–5. For other prodigies at Lanuvium: xxi. 62. 4, xxiii.
31. 15, xxiv. 10. 6, xxix. 14. 3, xxxii. 9. 2, xxxv. 9. 4, xl. 19. 2, xli.
21. 13, xlii. 2. 4, xlv. 16. 5, Obs. 6, 11, 12, 20, 46, Cic. *de div.* i. 99,
Pliny *NH* viii. 221, Wülker, 98.

   Sospitae Iunonis : this was a famous Latin temple; cf. Cic. *de
n. d.* i. 82, A. E. Gordon, *The Cults of Lanuvium* (Berkeley, 1938),
23 ff. For the vowing of a temple to Juno Sospita to be built at Rome
cf. xxxii. 30. 10.

   nocte strepitum : cf. xxix. 14. 3, Wülker, 19, Krauss, 163.

   in Sabinis : for other prodigies in Sabine country cf. xxii. 36. 7,
xxiv. 10. 9, xli. 28. 2, Gran. Lic. p. 21, Wülker, 99.

   incertus . . . inventus : for examples of hermaphrodites see
xxvii. 11. 4, 37. 6, xxxix. 22. 5, Obs. 22, 27a, 32, 34, 36, 47, 48, 50,
53, Phlegon *FGH* 257 F 36(x), Oros. v. 4. 8, Dio fr. 47, Diod.
xxxii. 12, Pliny *NH* vii. 15–16, 34–6. They were regarded in
republican times as a major abomination (cf. § 8). The case of the
16-year-old is one of a 'change of sex' rather than a true hermaphrodite (cf. xxiv. 10. 10). On the Roman attitude to hermaphrodites
see M. Delcourt, *Hermaphrodite* (London, 1961), 43 ff. See further
Wülker, 14, Luterbacher, 25–26, Krauss, 130–2.

7. Frusinone : modern Frosinone on the Via Latina some 50
miles south-east of Rome, cf. Nissen, *IL*, ii. 2. 655, Weiss, *RE*, vii.
188. For other prodigies at Frusino: xxvii. 37. 5, xxx. 2. 12, xxx.
38. 9, xxxii. 29. 2, Obs. 15, 20, Wülker, 97.

   Sinuessae : on the coast about 100 miles south of Rome near modern Mondragone, on the borders between Latium and Campania, cf. Nissen, *IL*, ii. 2. 664, Philipp, *RE*, iiiA. 259–60. For other prodigies at Sinuessa: xxiii. 31. 15, xxvii. 11. 4, xxxii. 9. 3, xli. 21. 12, Wülker, 100.

porcus cum capite humano: cf. xxvii. 4. 14, xxxii. 9. 3, Val. Max. i. 6. 5, Obs. 14, Wülker, 15, Luterbacher, 27, Krauss, 126.

in agro publico: the prodigy is the more important for occurring on land belonging to the *populus romanus*. At xliii. 13. 6 (169) L. reports prodigies not being accepted as they occurred *in loco privato* or *loco peregrino*. But it is clear enough from other years that such a restriction was not normally applied, cf. Luterbacher, 29 ff.: *contra* Wülker, 2, Latte, *RRG*, 204, Rawson, *CQ* xxi (1971), 161 ff.

eculeus cum quinque pedibus: cf. xxviii. 11. 3, xxx. 2. 11, xxxii. 1. 11, xxxii. 9. 3, xxxii. 29. 2, Obs. 24, 28, 31, 32, 50, 53, Wülker, 15–16, Luterbacher, 27, Krauss, 123.

8. in mare . . . erat: in 207 when C. Claudius Nero (cf. 2. 3 n.) and M. Livius Salinator were consuls. For the episode cf. xxvii. 37. 6 ff.

M. Livio: (33). M. Livius Salinator was consul in 219 and *legatus* to Carthage in the following year: he was then convicted of *peculatus* in his expedition against the Illyrians, and went into exile. He returned in 210 and became consul in 207, with command prorogued in 206–4. He was censor in 204.

For similar cases of drowning hermaphrodites cf. xxvii. 37. 6, Obs. 22, 27a, 32, 34, 36, 47, 48, 50, Wülker, 39.

9. decemviros: the *xviri sacris faciundis* who had charge of the Sibylline books. For cases of consultation of the *libri* following prodigies cf. Wülker, 33, Luterbacher, 35–6, Wissowa, *RuK*², 538.

Carmen . . . iusserunt: for the *carmen* in expiation cf. xxvii. 37. 11 ff., Obs. 27a, 34, 36, 43, 46, 48, 53, Wissowa, *RuK*², 426.

It seems to have been customary for the *carmen* to be sung by the girls alone, cf. Schol. ad Hor. *Carm. Saec.*, xxvii. 37. 7, E. Fraenkel, *Horace* (Oxford, 1957), 380–1 n. 3.

praeterea: strictly speaking, this was included in the acts of expiation which had been performed, on the order of the *pontifices*, in 207 (xxvii. 37. 7). But it seems unnecessary to emend to *propterea* (M. Gitlbauer, *Z̄. f. öst. Gymn.* xxix [1878], 933). L. is simply being a little inaccurate in his mode of expression. (McDonald's argument that it is paralleled by *item* in xxvii. 37. 7 misses what I take to be the logic of Gitlbauer's emendation.)

donum . . . ferri: on the site of Juno's temple on the Aventine, cf. Ogilvie, 694–5. For such gifts cf. xxii. 1. 18, xxvii. 37. 9, xl. 37. 2, Obs. 28, 46, Phlegon *FGH* 257 F 36 (x), Wülker, 45.

10. sicut patrum memoria Livius: clearly a reference to the poem of Livius Andronicus in 207 (xxvii. 37. 7, Festus, p. 446L) and not to the Secular Games in 249. *patrum memoria*, that is, means 'as the senators remembered', not 'as their ancestors remembered'. Cf. F. Leo, *Geschichte der römischen Literatur* (Berlin, 1913), 58 n. 2, Fraenkel, *RE*, supp. v. 600.

Livius: he came from Tarentum, presumably at the time of its capture in 272, and was the freedman of a Livius Salinator (Eus. ed. Schöne, ii p. 125). He produced Rome's first play in 240. The present passage suggests that he was dead by 200. For this, the orthodox chronology of his life, cf. Fraenkel, *RE*, supp. v. 598 ff., H. J. Mette, *Lustrum* ix (1964), 41 ff., W. Suerbaum, *Untersuchungen zur Selbstdarstellung älterer römischer Dichter* (Hildesheim, 1968), 297–9: *contra* H. B. Mattingly, *CQ* N.S. vii (1957), 159–63, *Gnomon* xliii (1971), 680 ff., G. Marconi, *MAL* serie 8, xii (1966), 125 ff.: see also A. E. Douglas, *Commentary on Cicero's Brutus* (Oxford, 1966), 62–4.

P. Licinius Tegula: (168). He is otherwise unknown, and is not to be identified with the Licinius Imbrex referred to by Gell. xiii. 23. 16 (cf. Leo, l.c., Münzer, *RE*, xiii. 371). Münzer (*RE*, xiii. 485) plausibly suggests that he owed his position in 200 to the influence of the *pontifex maximus* P. Licinius Crassus.

13. *Public debt and public land*

This is one of the few detailed pieces of information on economic matters in these books. It gives us a valuable glimpse into economic conditions and attitudes at the beginning of the second century. For literature on the *trientabula* see L. Labruna, *Vim Fieri Veto* (Camerino, 1971), 251 n. 423.

13. 1. Cf. 12. 4 n.

2. quibus ex pecunia . . . dederant: in 210 the consul M. Valerius Laevinus urged all classes of the Roman people to make voluntary contributions to the war effort (xxvi. 35–6, Flor. i. 22. 25, Festus, p. 500L, Oros. iv. 17. 14). L.'s account of the episode does not indicate that the payments were a loan. These payments are not to be confused with the loans made by *publicani* on other occasions, when they agreed to delay payment for contracts (cf. xxiii. 49. 1–3, xxiv. 18. 10–11, Cassola, *GP*, 67–8, 71 ff., Lippold, 99–100).

M. Valerio: Laevinus (211); cf. 3. 3 n.

M. Claudio: (220). M. Claudius Marcellus. He held the curule aedileship and praetorship, and was consul in 222: he held a second praetorship in 216; he was proconsul in 215, and consul again in

214. From 213 till 211 he was in Sicily, and captured Syracuse in 211. He was consul again in 210, proconsul in 209 and consul for the fourth time in 208, when he was killed in an ambush. He was an augur for several years.

tertia pensio: in 204 Laevinus raised in the senate the question of repayment and it was agreed that it should be repaid in three parts, the first immediately and the second and third in the years of the *tertii et quinti consules* (xxix. 16. 1–3). This clearly indicates the consuls of 202 and 200, and this therefore is the year for the final payment. W–M argue that in fact this must be the second payment, because at xxxiii. 42. 3 L. says that the final payment was made, and interprets *tertia pensio* here as 'payment of a third' which is very forced. In fact xxxiii. 42. 3 is easily explained. No payment was made in 200 (the arrangements described in §§ 5–9 being optional and interim) and the final payment, reasonably enough, was made in 196 when the war with Macedon was over.

4. aliis ex aliis orientibus bellis: cf. 6. 4 n.

ob noxiam: B reads *noxiam*, χ *ob noxam*. Weissenborn reads *noxia*, understanding *pro*, Rossbach *obnoxiam*, and Bessler *ob noxiam*. χ's reading makes perfectly good sense, but if it were right, it would be hard to explain the corruption in B. Weissenborn's reading is rather strained, and not really paralleled by v. 41. 9 and xxi. 28. 8 which he adduces. *ob noxiam* and *obnoxiam* (palaeographically, of course, the same reading) explain the MSS. reading well. I prefer *obnoxiam*.

5. aere: thus all the MSS., though the normal dative of *aes* is *aeri*. Weissenborn and McDonald defend it as a 'formular phrase' paralleled by *iure dicundo* (xlii. 28. 6) and *aere* in Cic. *ad fam.* vii. 13. 2; Ogilvie (*Phoenix*, 345) objects that *aere* occurs in only one title (Cic. loc. cit. and *CIL* iii. 6076). But *iure dicundo* is regular in inscriptions and the parallels seem to me sufficient to justify the retention of *aere*. Cf. Neue–Wagener, i. 297–300.

solvendo . . . esset: for this use of the predicative dative, cf. K–St, i. 747(b).

medium . . . utile: the conflict between duty and interest is an old one in Greek philosophy. It played a part in Stoic doctrine, and was discussed by Cicero in book iii of the *de officiis*. The issue here is semi-legal, hence the use of *aequum*. The idea of a mean between extremes also has a long pedigree, probably going back to Pythagoras. Toynbee (ii. 249) points out that while L.'s intended meaning is that the solution was *aequum* for the creditors and *utile* for the senate, the result was something that was extremely *utile* for the creditors (cf. also Schlag, 155, Laistner, 71–2).

6. The argument is somewhat complex. The creditors say that there is a lot of land for sale, and that they want to buy it. The implication is that they need repayment of their money in order to do this. As a compromise the senate gives them the usufruct of *ager publicus*.

agros . . . esse: these are privately owned lands. No doubt their owners are small landowners whose property was severely ravaged by the Hannibalic war, and who now lack the capital to improve it. The price was probably low, and that is why the creditors are so keen to acquire it.

sibimet emptis opus esse: 'they needed to buy it'. Sage mistranslates 'to purchase which cash was needed'.

agri . . . fieret: it is a little surprising that there was sufficient unallocated *ager publicus* so near to Rome. Most of the land confiscated from rebels during the Hannibalic war was not within this radius. It is not clear whether there were any illegal squatters who had to be turned off the land. If so, the low price of land will have prevented trouble. The creditors, of course, did extremely well out of the transaction. They received valuable land, and if it was valued at the prevailing low market price, they received a lot of land. They probably, in time, increased their holdings by buying up neighbouring *ager privatus* (cf. App. *BC* i. 7. 29) or squatting on vacant *ager publicus*. The senate's action in 200 thus considerably helped the movement towards *latifundia* and the agrarian crisis with which the Gracchi attempted to deal.

On the situation cf. McDonald, *CHJ* vi (1939), 124 ff., Toynbee, ii. 174–5 n. 5, 203–4, 248–51, Gabba, *Commentary on Appian BC* i (Florence, 1958), 16 and works there cited.

7. in iugera asses: one *as* per *iugerum* is a purely nominal rent, to assert ownership on behalf of the state. Tenney Frank (*Economic Survey*, i. 125) estimates (by some rather doubtful calculations) that the capital value of land at this time was 100 *denarii* per *iugerum*. In the second century A.D. Columella gave the value of unimproved land as 1,000 *sestertii* per *iugerum* (Frank, op. cit., 168). On the vectigal cf. G. Tibiletti, *Ath.* N.S. xxvi (1948), 185.

9. trientabulumque: although the MSS. did not understand the word they in fact give the correct reading, the abbreviation mark over the *n* being an attempt at an emendation, which was happily carried no further.

In the *Lex Agraria* of 111, the *trientabula* are converted into *ager privatus*, probably with the provision that they did not exceed the limits laid down in the law of Tiberius Gracchus; cf. *FIRA*, i. 110, ll. 31–2.

14–18. *Events in Greece and the East*

14. 1–5 describe Sulpicius' departure for the East and explain what Philip is doing at the time. 14. 6–18 are a digression to explain what has happened prior to these events. Verbal correspondences (noted in the commentary on the individual passages) indicate that the basic source is Polybius. But it is a very perverted form of Polybius—in particular because of the deletion of all reference to the Roman ambassadors. For the truth, and possible reasons for this cf. pp. 39 ff. It is wrong to ask whether the transition to the digression (14. 3–5) is Polybian or Annalistic. Clearly it refers to matters which L. has read in Polybius—the conflicts of 201 and the pact of the kings—but they are mentioned very briefly. It is L.'s own summary of the events, based on his reading of his sources, but in no way 'copied' from them, and presented in a way which does not conflict with the distortions derived from annalistic sources.

14. 1. vota in Capitolio nuncupata : *votum nuncupare* is the technical term for the vow made by a commander before setting out on a campaign (Varro *L.L.* vi. 60, Wissowa, *RuK*², 382, Mommsen, *StR*, i³. 244). For the vow cf. 9. 6–10. L.'s narrative suggests that the senatorial decisions described in the preceding chapters all preceded the taking of the vows. Whether this is the real order of events is more doubtful.

paludatis lictoribus : Varro (*L.L.* vii. 37) says that when the lictors put on *paludamenta*, the *imperator* is said to set out *paludatus*. Thus it is quite natural to describe the lictors as *paludati* and gratuitous to alter the text to *paludatus cum lictoribus*. McDonald rightly quotes xli. 10. 5 (and cf. xli. 10. 7, 10. 13) and xlv. 39. 11.

2. veteribus militibus voluntariis : the Scipionic veterans who had volunteered to serve. Cf. 6. 3–4 n. and 8. 6. There were 2,000 of them (xxxii. 3. 3).

ex classe : on the fleet cf. 3 n.

Cn. Corneli : Lentulus (176). He was military tribune in 216, quaestor in 212, curule aedile in 205, and consul in 201, when he attempted to continue the war with Carthage (cf. Scullard, *RP*, 81) showing that though a Cornelius, he was no friend of Scipio. He was a *iiivir* for the increasing of the size of the colony at Narnia (xxxii. 2. 7) and a member of the *xviri* for the settlement with Macedonia in 196 (xxxiii. 35. 2).

altero die . . . traiecit : Klotz (*Livius*, 3) sees this as a conflation of *altero die pervenit* and *duobus diebus traiecit*. But L. uses *traicere* so frequently that it comes to have the meaning of 'arrive by sea at a place', and the expression is perfectly natural. For a similar usage with *transmisit* cf. xlii. 48. 9. There is certainly no case for using the phrase to posit a change in source, as Klotz seems to suggest.

a Brundisio: the usual port of embarkation for the East. On its topography cf. Ch. Picard, *RÉL* xxxv (1957), 285–303.

in Macedoniam: cf. 3. 2 n.

3. Atheniensium legati: this embassy is in no way connected with the main problem of the Athenian embassies, and since it meets Sulpicius in Greece cannot possibly be that of Cephisodorus which went to Rome itself, cf. p. 44 and McDonald, *JRS* xxvii (1937), 200 n. 134.

obsidione eximeret: siege activities following the raid of Philocles (16. 3).

C. Claudius Cento: (105) presumably a *legatus*, cf. 22. 5 ff. He is probably son of the consul of 240 and grandson of Appius Claudius Caecus.

longis navibus: they were triremes cf. 22. 5: hence L. uses *naves longae*, instead of *tectae* or *constratae*, cf. Nissen, *KU*, 109, Thiel, 198–9.

4. neque enim . . . obsidebat: i.e. the Macedonian forces (those of Philocles) were too small to warrant a major force. In fact Sulpicius may not have wanted to stake too much on an assault on Philip's forces at Athens at this point.

Abydum: 16. 6 ff. L. thus gives a clear chronological correspondence between this paragraph and the digression.

iam . . . proelio: the battles of Lade and Chios in 201. On the order of the battles cf. p. 37. In fact Lade was a victory for Philip, cf. Pol. xvi. 10. 1, 14. 5, 15. On Chios cf. xxxii. 33. 5.

5. sed . . . imminebant: the alleged pact of the kings between Philip and Antiochus the Great to partition the Egyptian kingdom between them. On its authenticity see pp. 37–9.

divisaeque iam: in theory. It is wrong to take the passage to mean that L. thought that the plan had already been carried into effect (thus D. Magie, *JRS* xxix [1939], 33).

cui morte audita: the death of Ptolemy Philopator. For the date of his death cf. p. 36 n. 5. L. here indicates a very close relation between his death and the pact of the kings (cf. Schmitt, *Antiochos*, 226 n. 4).

6. dum . . . servant: the anti-Athenian tone of this sentence is certainly due to Polybius who took a poor view of Athens at this time. Cf. 44. 2 ff., Pol. v. 106. 6 ff., vi. 43–4, ix. 23, xxx. 20.

7. Acarnanes duo iuvenes: L. gives a summary of the events leading to the Acarnanian raid, probably condensed from Polybius.

The surviving section of Polybius (xvi. 25–7) begins with the arrival of Attalus (§ 11 in L.).

Acarnania had been an ally of Philip in the First Macedonian War, having been a member of the Hellenic symmachy formed in 224. Attacks on Acarnania were part of the provisions of the Romano–Aetolian treaty of 212–11 (xxvi. 24. 11). An Acarnanian made a speech at Sparta urging the Spartans not to join the Romano–Aetolian alliance (Pol. ix. 32–9). They are included in the *adscripti* on Philip's side in the peace of Phoenice (xxix. 12. 14). The story of Justin (xxviii. 1. 1 ff.) that Rome had interceded with Aetolia on behalf of the Acarnanians *c.* 240 is to be rejected: cf. Holleaux, *Rome*, 5–22, P. Treves, *RAL* serie vi, 8 (1932), 197 n. 1, G. Walser, *Historia* ii (1953/4), 315, Oost, *RPEA*, 92–7, E. Manni, *PP* xi (1956), 185 ff., Cassola, *GP*, 48. In general cf. Oost, *RPEA*, 16–39.

per initiorum dies: for the details of the proceedings at the Eleusinian mysteries see L. Deubner, *Attische Feste* (Berlin, 1932), 91 ff., M. P. Nilsson, *Geschichte der griechischen Religion*, i³. 653 ff., J. Pollard, *Seers, Shrines and Sirens* (London, 1965), 65 ff., G. E. Mylonas, *Eleusis and the Eleusinian Mysteries* (Princeton and London, 1961), 224 ff.

8. sermo: what they said rather than their dialect.

9. gens Acarnanum factum: thus the MSS. The striking word order is used to emphasize *tam foede atque hostiliter* and should not be altered. (The parallels quoted in W–M, 182, are not all relevant: but *praefatio* 5 is a clear example, cf. Ogilvie, 26.)

ad Philippum: see p. 43, where it is argued that Philip is still in Bargylia. § 11 implies that the Acarnanian raid preceded Philip's return across the Aegean.

10–11. postea . . . Attalus enim: the actual decision is described in 15. 5, and *enim* introduces the story of the events leading up to the decision.

Attalus . . . Rhodiique: 2. 1–2 n.

cedentem in Macedoniam: after he has broken out from Bargylia.

rex Piraeum . . . traiecit: cf. Polybius xvi. 25. 1–5, according to which the Athenians ask Attalus to come to Athens. He crosses to Piraeus and there confers with the Roman ambassadors. Polybius has no mention of the renewal of *amicitia*. Walbank, *Philip V*, 130, thinks that the Rhodian fleet began immediately the recovery of the Cyclades. But it seems to have stayed at Ceos or Aegina for some time (cf. 15. 8 n.).

Aeginam : bought by Attalus from the Aetolians after it had been captured by Roman forces in 210 (Pol. ix. 42. 5, xi. 5. 8, xxii. 8. 9). **confirmandaeque :** thus B. χ reads *firmandae*. Tränkle, *Gnomon*, 372 n. 1 argues for *firmandae* adducing ix. 3. 10, xxxii. 5. 5. But the latter example is a case of strengthening the dubious allegiance of the Achaeans, while the former refers to a new alliance. Here, with *renovandae*, we need *confirmandae* to give the sense of confirm.

For Attalus' previous connections with Athens (mainly gifts) cf. Ferguson, *Hellenistic Athens*, 209, 239–40, Hansen, *Attalids*, 59, 306–14, McShane, 60, 94, 103, Walbank, *Commentary*, ii. 535. It is uncertain whether the famous gift of statues on the Acropolis is connected with this occasion, or comes earlier.

12. civitas . . . acceperunt : Pol. xvi. 25. 5–7: οὐ γὰρ μόνον οἱ τὰς ἀρχὰς ἔχοντες μετὰ τῶν ἱππέων, ἀλλὰ καὶ πάντες οἱ πολῖται μετὰ τῶν τέκνων καὶ γυναικῶν ἀπήντων αὐτοῖς. ὡς δὲ συνέμιξαν, τοιαύτη παρὰ τῶν πολλῶν ἐγένετο κατὰ τὴν ἀπάντησιν φιλανθρωπία πρός τε ῾Ρωμαίους καὶ ἔτι μᾶλλον πρὸς τὸν Ἄτταλον ὥσθ᾽ ὑπερβολὴν μὴ καταλιπεῖν. ἐπεὶ δ᾽ εἰσῄει κατὰ τὸ Δίπυλον, ἐξ ἑκατέρου τοῦ μέρους παρέστησαν τὰς ἱερείας καὶ τοὺς ἱερεῖς. μετὰ δὲ ταῦτα πάντας μὲν τοὺς ναοὺς ἀνέῳξαν, ἐπὶ δὲ πᾶσι θύματα τοῖς βωμοῖς παραστήσαντες ἠξίωσαν αὐτὸν θῦσαι. *di prope ipsi exciti sedibus suis acceperunt* appears to be a phrase of L.'s own, to give added drama to the situation.

15. 1–7. This section is based reasonably closely on Polybius xvi. 26.

1–2. In contionem . . . onerantis : Pol. xvi. 26. 1–3: Μετὰ δὲ ταῦτα συναγαγόντες ἐκκλησίαν ἐκάλουν τὸν προειρημένον. παραιτουμένου δὲ καὶ φάσκοντος εἶναι φορτικὸν τὸ κατὰ πρόσωπον εἰσελθόντα διαπορεύεσθαι τὰς εὐεργεσίας τὰς αὑτοῦ τοῖς εὖ πεπονθόσι, τῆς εἰσόδου παρῆκαν, γράψαντα δ᾽ αὐτὸν ἠξίουν ἐκδοῦναι περὶ ὧν ὑπολαμβάνει συμφέρειν πρὸς τοὺς ἐνεστῶτας καιρούς. Polybius simply says that it would be φορτικόν for Attalus to appear in person. L. uses the Roman concept of *dignitas* and adds vividness with *erubescere* and *significationibus acclamationibusque* (cf. McDonald, *JRS* xlvii [1957], 162). *Onerantis* suggests that L. took φορτικόν in its literal sense of 'burdensome', though Polybius meant it in its metaphorical use as 'vulgar'.

3–4. In litteris . . . quaesituros : Pol. xvi. 26. 4–6: τοῦ δὲ πεισθέντος καὶ γράψαντος εἰσήνεγκαν τὴν ἐπιστολὴν οἱ προεστῶτες. ἦν δὲ τὰ κεφάλαια τῶν γεγραμμένων ἀνάμνησις τῶν πρότερον ἐξ αὐτοῦ γεγονότων εὐεργετημάτων εἰς τὸν δῆμον, ἐξαρίθμησις τῶν πεπραγμένων αὐτῷ πρὸς Φίλιππον κατὰ τοὺς ἐνεστῶτας καιρούς, τελευταία δὲ παράκλησις εἰς τὸν κατὰ Φιλίππου πόλεμον, καὶ διορκισμός, ὡς ἐὰν μὴ νῦν ἕλωνται συνεμβαίνειν εὐγενῶς εἰς τὴν ἀπέχθειαν ἅμα ῾Ροδίοις καὶ ῾Ρωμαίοις καὶ αὐτῷ, μετὰ δὲ ταῦτα παρέντες τοὺς καιροὺς κοινωνεῖν βούλωνται τῆς εἰρήνης, ἄλλων αὐτὴν κατεργασαμένων, ἀστοχήσειν αὐτοὺς τοῦ τῇ πατρίδι συμφέροντος.

3. beneficiorum: cf. 14. 11 n.

quas . . . gessisset: the events of 201.

4. dum etiam Romanos: here L. does not exclude Polybius' mention of the Romans. If challenged, he would no doubt say that Attalus knew that Rome had now decided to go to war with Philip. In fact these incidents preceded the war-vote at Rome. Cf. pp. 43–5.

nequiquam . . . quaesituros: Polybius says that Athens will desert her own interest if she fails to take part in the war and later wants to join in the peace which has been obtained by the efforts of others.

5. Rhodii . . . decretum: Pol. xvi. 26. 8: οὐ μὴν ἀλλὰ καὶ τῶν Ῥοδίων ἐπεισελθόντων καὶ πολλοὺς πρὸς τὴν αὐτὴν ὑπόθεσιν διαθεμένων λόγους, ἔδοξε τοῖς Ἀθηναίοις ἐκφέρειν τῷ Φιλίππῳ τὸν πόλεμον. Cf. § 9 τάς τε ναῦς ἀποκαταστῆσαι. There is no mention of the number of ships involved in Polybius, but it is probably authentic, and L. read it in a section of Polybius which no longer survives.

itaque ingenti consensu: L. embroiders Polybius' simple statement ἔδοξε τοῖς Ἀθηναίοις ἐκφέρειν τῷ Φιλίππῳ τὸν πόλεμον.

6. Honores: in Polybius the honours for Attalus preceded his letter, only those for the Rhodians coming at this stage.

de tribu quam Attalida: Pol. xvi. 25. 9: πρὸς γὰρ τοῖς ἄλλοις καὶ φυλὴν ἐπώνυμον ἐποίησαν Ἀττάλῳ, καὶ κατένειμαν αὐτὸν εἰς τοὺς ἐπωνύμους τῶν ἀρχηγετῶν. On the changes in the tribes cf. p. 43 n. 1.

ad decem veteres: L. is unaware that in fact the ten Clisthenic tribes had been increased to 12 in 307 by the addition of Antigonis and Demetrias, and to 13 by the institution of Ptolemais in 224. L. is not to be blamed: our own information on the Athenian tribes derives almost entirely from inscriptions. On the tribes cf. Ferguson, *Hellenistic Athens*, 64, 242, W. B. Dinsmoor, *The Archons of Athens in the Hellenistic Age* (Cambridge, Mass., 1931), *The Athenian Archon List in the light of recent discoveries* (New York, 1939), Ferguson, *Athenian tribal cycles in the Hellenistic Age* (Cambridge, Mass., 1932), W. K. Pritchett, *The Five Attic tribes after Kleisthenes* (Baltimore, 1943), Pritchett and B. D. Meritt, *The Chronology of Hellenistic Athens* (Boston, 1940), Meritt, *The Athenian Year* (Berkeley and Los Angeles, 1961). (The arguments of these books hang so closely together that it is not practicable to give more specific references.)

7. et Rhodiorum . . . dederant: Pol. xvi. 26. 9: ἀπεδέξαντο δὲ καὶ τοὺς ῾Ροδίους μεγαλομερῶς καὶ τόν τε δῆμον ἐστεφάνωσαν ἀριστείων στεφάνῳ καὶ πᾶσι ῾Ροδίοις ἰσοπολιτείαν ἐψηφίσαντο. On the crown cf. Walbank, *Commentary*, ii. 535–6. Inscriptions granting ἰσοπολιτεία to the citizens of another state are common between the third and first centuries. The grant of ἰσοπολιτεία involved admitting all the citizens of another state to full citizen rights. It was often specifically stated that they had the right of contracting legal marriages with citizens of the state granting ἰσοπολιτεία (ἐπιγαμία). Cf. G. Busolt, *Griechische Staatskunde*[3] (Munich, 1920), i. 223 n. 2, 225, Oehler, *RE*, ix. 2227 ff., Toynbee, i. 199.

quemadmodum . . . dederant: there is no mention of this in Polybius, and Oehler (l.c.) suggests that L. has misunderstood ἰσοπολιτεία to refer to a reciprocal agreement, when in fact the ἰσο- indicates that the citizen-rights of the grantees are to be equal to those of the citizens of the granting state. But it is possible that a Rhodian grant of ἰσοπολιτεία to Athens was mentioned in a portion of Polybius no longer surviving.

8. Rhodii . . . Aegina: Pol. xvi. 26. 10: οἱ μὲν οὖν πρέσβεις οἱ παρὰ τῶν ῾Ροδίων ταῦτα διαπράξαντες ἀνήχθησαν εἰς τὴν Κέων ἐπὶ τὰς νήσους μετὰ τοῦ στόλου. The sentence is probably abbreviated by the excerptor of Polybius. Thus L. may be right in making the fleet as a whole stay at Aegina, even though our text of Polybius suggests it was at Ceos.

Ceam: the name is guaranteed by Polybius, despite the confusion in the MSS. of L. Ceos is about 25 miles south-east of Attica.

inde per insulas . . . acceptis: Philip had probably occupied those of the Cyclades which he did not already control at the beginning of his expedition in 201 (Holleaux, *Études*, iv. 126). The history of the Cyclades in the third century is extremely obscure. The Ptolemaic control of the islands disintegrated in the middle of the century, and Macedon obtained control of some of them. But Rhodes' influence in the Cyclades was considerable, though it had no formal basis. Cf. Holleaux, *Études*, iii. 72–3, Fraser and Bean, *RPI*, 155 ff. (Ferro, 27–30, has a very obscure account). Fraser and Bean stress that *insulas* cannot mean all the Aegean islands, and must refer only to the Cycladic group.

quae praesidiis Macedonum tenebantur: it does not follow that the other islands did not have garrisons. But only those on Andros, Paros, and Cythnos held out against the Rhodians.

9. Attalum . . . tenuere: Attalus had long had good relations with Aetolia. Before 219 he had fortified Elaus for them (Pol. iv. 65. 4) and his portico at Delphi may date from that time (cf.

McShane, 100–2). He joined the Romano–Aetolian alliance against Philip in 210 (cf. 2. 1–2 n.) and appears to have had a formal treaty with the Aetolians (cf. 46. 3 n.) which survived the peace.

The Aetolians had appealed to Rome for help against Philip in 201; cf. 29. 4 n. Their unwillingness to join now is a sign of their annoyance at Rome's response and is not an argument against the authenticity of the Aetolian appeal.

10. pace: cf. 1. 8 n.

10–11: these remarks are a shortened version of the criticism of Rhodes and Attalus in Pol. xvi. 28. The criticism is rather unfair as Rhodes and Attalus did not have sufficient forces to move on the offensive against Philip, at least by land. That they were suspicious of each other and hence did nothing seems less probable (cf. Walbank, *Commentary*, ii. 538).

That the statement about the glory being left to Rome is an addition by L. (thus Hoch, 86) is not certain: the idea may have occurred in a lost section of Polybius preceding ch. 28.

11. Thraeciae: the MSS. read *Graeciae*, but it is in Thrace that Philip makes advances, and a general reference to Greece is inappropriate. Weissenborn's emendation is clearly right: the corruption, easy enough in itself, was assisted by *Graeciae* in the previous line.

16. 1. regio animo: again from Pol. xvi. 28: see especially § 3 τὸ δὲ Φιλίππου βασιλικὸν καὶ μεγαλόψυχον (cf. Welwei, 48). For a similar favourable comment on Philip cf. 43. 4, Hoch, 46, and for L.'s picture of Philip as a whole Catin, 66 ff.

non sustinuisset: i.e. in the expedition of 201.

2. Philocle quodam: L. omits the expedition of Nicanor referred to in Pol. xvi. 27. That of Philocles is subsequent to, and not identical with, that of Nicanor (cf. p. 44). On Philocles cf. 26. 6, xxxii. 16. 12, 23. 11, 25. 1, 25. 9, 38. 2, 40. 1, 40. 5. He was one of Philip's close advisers, but was involved in the disputes that led to the death of Demetrius in 182 and was subsequently himself put to death. Cf. Schoch, *RE*, xix. 2491–2.

3. Heraclidi: cf. 33. 2, 46. 8, xxxii. 5. 7. Heraclides of Tarentum, one of Philip's unsavoury henchmen. For his character cf. Pol. xiii. 4–5. In 205 he was sent by Philip to destroy the Rhodian fleet: cf. p. 36. He was probably in charge of Philip's fleet at Lade (Pol. xvi. 15. 6). See further Walbank, *Commentary*, ii. 417.

4–5. Philip's attack on the Thracian towns is his first full-scale assault on Ptolemaic possessions. For previous incidents, cf. pp. 38–9.

This region of Thrace came into Ptolemaic possession *c.* 241 after the Laodicean war. Cf. xxxiii. 40. 5, Pol. v. 34. 7, xviii. 51. 5, Walbank, *Commentary*, i. 565, ii. 622, Will, *HP*, i. 226 ff.

L. appears to be intending to give the exact order in which Philip took these places. If so, there are difficulties. Maronea is *c.* 30 miles west of the Hebrus, Aenus just to the east of the gulf where the Hebrus joins the Aegean. Cypsela is inland, about 23 miles from the mouth of the Hebrus. All this is quite intelligible, but Doriscus and Serrheum lie to the west of the Hebrus, and it is odd that they were not captured by Philip on the way from Maronea to Aenus. It may be that Polybius mentioned the more important towns first and L. took him to be giving the actual order of Philip's campaign.

cum magno labore: the phrase implies unsuccessful efforts and has led many editors to supply a verb or verbal phrase after *labore* since it appears to go inappropriately with *cepit* (cf. McDonald's appendix). McDonald compares xxiii. 15. 3 *saepe vi, saepe sollici-tandis nequiquam nunc plebe nunc principibus, fame demum in deditionem accepit*. There, however, the phrase is preceded by *cum aliquamdiu circumsedisset*, and *saepe . . . principibus* goes closely with that. Nevertheless the MSS. text can stand as meaning 'it was taken with a great amount of toil, but finally fell through the treachery of Callimedes'. The asyndeton is perfectly natural. Cf. also Pettersson, 85 n. 3. (Tränkle, *Gnomon*, 379, disagrees, but without giving any reasons.)

Callimedis: as with Callipolis in § 6 the MSS. read *Galli-*. Callimedes is not otherwise known.

5–6. ad Chersonesum . . . ignobilia: Elaeus is on the southern tip of the Chersonese, Alopeconnesus on the west coast, Madytus and Callipolis on the east coast. The *castella ignobilia* probably include Sestus, whose capture is to be dated to this time (Holleaux, *Rome*, 290 n. 1, *Études*, iv. 129, Walbank, *Philip V*, 306).

Abydeni: Abydus was a free city. There is no evidence that it was Egyptian, cf. Magie, *RRAM*, ii. 1012, Walbank, *Commentary*, ii. 539. L. omits the description of the site of Abydus given by Polybius, xvi. 29.

7. cum ad Tenedum staret: presumably the Rhodian fleet had come here after its journey through the Cyclades (15. 8). Here again L. repeats the criticism of Rhodes and Attalus found in Pol. xvi. 28 (cf. 15. 10–11 n.). For Attalus at Tenedos cf. Pol. xvi. 34. 1.

8. neque . . . sociis: Madvig (*Emendationes*, 465) holds that such a negative absolute, indicating what did not happen at the same time as the action described in a main clause, is impossible. He holds that the punctuation is wrong, and that the correct reading should be a stop after *ostendit* followed by *Neque terra neque mari adiuti a sociis Abydeni primo*. . . . This is quite unnecessary: the ablative absolute can perfectly well express such a negative, and in any case *neque* . . . *adiutis* refers to the effect of Rhodian and Attalid inactivity as a whole, not just to Attalus' crossing to Tenedos.

17–18. These two chapters are a shortened version of Polybius' account of the siege of Abydus (Pol. xvi. 29–34). On L.'s style and method in this section cf. Witte, 290–4, 304–5, Walsh, *RhM* xcvii (1954), 97–8, Brueggmann, 16 ff., McDonald, *JRS* xlvii (1957), 168–70, Pianezzola, 30–5, Walbank, *Livy*, 60.

17. 1. Abydeni primo . . . faciebant: Pol. xvi. 30. 4–5: τὰς μὲν γὰρ ἀρχὰς πιστεύοντες αὑτοῖς οἱ τὴν Ἄβυδον κατοικοῦντες ὑπέμενον ἐρρωμένως τὰς τοῦ Φιλίππου παρασκευάς, καὶ τῶν τε κατὰ θάλατταν προσαχθέντων μηχανημάτων τὰ μὲν τοῖς πετροβόλοις τύπτοντες διεσάλευσαν, τὰ δὲ τῷ πυρὶ διέφθειραν, οὕτως ὥστε καὶ τὰς ναῦς μόλις ἀνασπάσαι τοὺς πολεμίους ἐκ τοῦ κινδύνου. τοῖς δὲ κατὰ γῆν ἔργοις ἕως μέν τινος προσαντεῖχον εὐψύχως, οὐκ ἀπελπίζοντες κατακρατήσειν τῶν πολεμίων. L. balances *non terra modo* with *navium quoque*, where Polybius simply mentions the two elements of the fighting separately.

2. cum . . . miserunt: Pol. xvi. 30. 6–7: ἐπειδὴ δὲ τὸ μὲν ἐκτὸς τοῦ τείχους ἔπεσε διὰ τῶν ὀρυγμάτων, μετὰ δὲ ταῦτα διὰ τῶν μετάλλων ἤγγιζον οἱ Μακεδόνες τῷ κατὰ τὸ πεπτωκὸς ὑπὸ τῶν ἔνδοθεν ἀντῳκοδομημένῳ τείχει, τὸ τηνικάδε πέμψαντες πρεσβευτὰς Ἰφιάδην καὶ Παντάγνωτον ἐκέλευον παραλαμβάνειν τὸν Φίλιππον τὴν πόλιν. L. omits the Greek names which are of little interest to him, cf. p. 18 n. 5.

3. Paciscebantur . . . vestimentis: Pol. xvi. 30. 7: τοὺς μὲν στρατιώτας ὑποσπόνδους ἀφέντα τοὺς παρὰ ῾Ροδίων καὶ παρ᾽ Ἀττάλου, τὰ δ᾽ ἐλεύθερα τῶν σωμάτων ἐάσαντα σῴζεσθαι κατὰ δύναμιν οὗ ποτ᾽ ἂν ἕκαστος προαιρῆται μετὰ τῆς ἐσθῆτος τῆς περὶ τὸ σῶμα.

Paciscebantur: 'They were willing to agree on terms that . . .': for the conative imperfect cf. K–St, i. 121–2.

quadriremem: Polybius may mean that the ship itself would be kept by Philip, in which case L. has misunderstood him.

cum singulis vestimentis: for similar provisions cf. 45. 6, xxi. 12. 5, 13. 7, xxii. 6. 11, 52. 3, xxiii. 15. 3, Thuc. ii. 70. 3, Xen. *Hell.* ii. 3. 6, Diod. xvi. 34. 5, E. S. McCartney, *CPh* xxiii (1928), 15–18, J. Vallejo, *Emerita* viii (1940), 42–7, Ducrey, 140 ff.

4. Quibus . . . respondisset: Pol. xvi. 30. 8: τοῦ δὲ Φιλίππου προστάττοντος περὶ πάντων ἐπιτρέπειν ἢ μάχεσθαι γενναίως. Philip demands complete surrender—the *deditio* so often demanded by the Romans.

adeo renuntiata . . . accendit: Pol. xvi. 31. 1: οἱ δ᾽ Ἀβυδηνοὶ πυθόμενοι τὰ λεγόμενα, συνελθόντες εἰς ἐκκλησίαν ἐβουλεύοντο περὶ τῶν ἐνεστώτων ἀπονοηθέντες ταῖς γνώμαις.

renuntiata haec legatio: renuntiare legationem, 'to report on an embassy', is found in xxiii. 6. 3, xxxv. 32. 8, xxxix. 33. 2, xlii. 47. 1 and xlv. 25. 5, and L. naturally uses it in the passive (ix. 4. 6, xxiii. 20. 7, xxxvi. 35. 6, 9. 8). In the phrase legatio means 'what happened on the embassy' rather than simply 'going on an embassy'.

ab indignatione . . . ac desperatione: L. embroiders for effect. P. merely says (31. 1) ἀπονοηθέντες ταῖς γνώμαις.

5. ad Saguntinam rabiem: Polybius does not refer to Saguntum in this context (just as his actual description of the fall of Saguntum in iii. 17 merely records the fact) but mentions in xvi. 32 two Greek parallels, that of the Phocians in a war against the Thessalians (Paus. x. 1. 6; the war is probably that referred to by Hdt. viii. 27–8) and of the Acarnanians against the Aetolians (cf. ix. 40). In fact Saguntum is not a particularly good parallel. There was not premeditated mass suicide there, though many did kill themselves: cf. xxi. 14.

It is pertinent to remark on the falsity of the popular view that the mass suicide of the Jewish zealots at Masada was unique. Cf. also the case of Astapa in xxviii. 22–3. (I do not think it necessary to believe that the latter passage was modelled on Polybius' account of Abydus, as is argued by Walbank, Livy, 71 n. 101.)

5–6. matronas . . . poni: Pol. xvi. 31. 2–3. ἔδοξεν οὖν αὐτοῖς πρῶτον μὲν τοὺς δούλους ἐλευθεροῦν, ἵνα συναγωνιστὰς ἔχοιεν ἀπροφασίστους, ἔπειτα συναθροῖσαι τὰς μὲν γυναῖκας εἰς τὸ τῆς Ἀρτέμιδος ἱερὸν ἁπάσας, τὰ δὲ τέκνα σὺν ταῖς τροφοῖς εἰς τὸ γυμνάσιον, ἑξῆς δὲ τούτοις τὸν ἄργυρον καὶ τόν χρυσὸν εἰς τὴν ἀγορὰν συναγαγεῖν, ὁμοίως δὲ καὶ τὸν ἱματισμὸν τὸν ἀξιόλογον εἰς τὴν τετρήρη τὴν τῶν Ῥοδίων καὶ τὴν τριήρη τὴν τῶν Κυζικηνῶν. Polybius makes it clear that the decision to do this was taken in an assembly. L. omits the fact that the slaves were freed, and adds the detail of altars and victims from Polybius' description of the oaths (31. 7). He expands Polybius' τὰ δὲ τέκνα σὺν ταῖς τροφοῖς for dramatic effect.

in gymnasio: gymnasium MSS. Madvig (Emendationes, 465) argued convincingly that the case must be the same as in templo above, and we must either read gymnasio here or templum in the former place. Weissenborn defends the MSS. readings by reference to xxxii. 21. 22, but the change of construction there occurs in a long sentence and is of a different character.

Cyzicenam: this is the first we have heard of the Cyzican ship, though it was probably mentioned in the lost part of Polybius. Cyzicus was a free ally of Attalus (Magie, RRAM, 81, 903 n. 117).

7–8. ibi delecti . . . subicerent: Pol. xvi. 31. 4–5: ταῦτα δὲ προθέμενοι καὶ πράξαντες ὁμοθυμαδὸν κατὰ τὸ δόγμα πάλιν συνηθροίσθησαν εἰς τὴν ἐκκλησίαν, καὶ πεντήκοντα προεχειρίσαντο τῶν πρεσβυτέρων ἀνδρῶν καὶ μάλιστα πιστευομένων, ἔτι δὲ τὴν σωματικὴν δύναμιν ἐχόντων πρὸς τὸ δύνασθαι τὸ κριθὲν ἐπιτελεῖν, καὶ τούτους ἐξώρκισαν ἐναντίον ἁπάντων τῶν πολιτῶν ἦ μήν, ἐὰν ἴδωσι τὸ διατείχισμα καταλαμβανόμενον ὑπὸ τῶν ἐχθρῶν, κατασφάξειν μὲν τὰ τέκνα καὶ τὰς γυναῖκας, ἐμπρήσειν δὲ τὰς προειρημένας ναῦς, ῥίψειν δὲ κατὰ τὰς ἀρὰς τὸν ἄργυρον καὶ τὸν χρυσὸν εἰς τὴν θάλατταν. Polybius mentions that this was done at a second assembly following the implementation of the earlier decisions. L. also omits the decision to burn the ships. The throwing of the clothes into the sea and the burning of the houses, however, appear to be L.'s own additions.

9. praeeuntibus exsecrabile carmen sacerdotibus: cf. § 6 n. In Polybius 31. 6 the priests supervise only the oath of the whole people, although they then pronounce imprecations which appear to cover both the selected elders and the people as a whole (32. 7).

exsecrabile carmen: a formula giving details of the consequences that should follow breaking of the oath, cf. x. 38. 10, 41. 3. Where texts of oaths survive, they often include such provisions. In Greek oaths they are usually expressed briefly, e.g. *OGIS* 229 ll. 69, 78, 266 l. 50, Diod. xxxvii. 11, cf. F. Cumont, *Studia Pontica*, iii (Brussels, 1910), 84; but for more ornate forms cf. *ILS* 190, *IGRR* iii 137.

tum militaris aetas . . . excessurum: Pol. xvi. 31. 6. ὤμνυον πάντες ἢ κρατήσειν τῶν ἐχθρῶν ἢ τελευτήσειν μαχόμενοι περὶ τῆς πατρίδος. L. restricts it to those of military age, as effectively they will do the fighting.

iurat: B. iurare χ: the latter is defended as a historical infinitive by Tränkle, *Gnomon*, 372 n. 1. It is certainly a possible reading, but this is the sort of case where there is no real way of making a decision between the two alternatives.

10–11. L. abbreviates Polybius' account of the fighting (xvi. 33) considerably.

10. Hi memores . . . abstiterit: Pol. xvi. 33. 1: κατὰ τοὺς ὅρκους διεμάχοντο τοῖς πολεμίοις οὕτω τετολμηκότως ὥστε τὸν Φίλιππον, καίπερ ἐκ διαδοχῆς προβαλόμενον τοὺς Μακεδόνας ἕως νυκτός, τέλος ἀποστῆναι τῆς μάχης and 33. 4 ἐπιγενομένης δὲ τῆς νυκτός.

rex prior, territus: Walsh, *Livy*, 162–3, makes this an example of L.'s habit of ascribing terror to commanders. But though L. uses dramatic language, the idea is present in Pol. xvi. 33. 1 Φίλιππον, . . . δυσελπιστήσαντα καὶ περὶ τῆς ὅλης ἐπιβολῆς. See further 34. 5 n.

11. principes . . . mittunt: Pol. xvi. 33. 4–5. τῶν μὲν πλείστων τεθνεώτων ἐπὶ τοῦ πτώματος, τῶν δὲ λοιπῶν ὑπὸ τοῦ κόπου καὶ τῶν τραυμάτων ἀδυνατούντων, συναγαγόντες ὀλίγους τινὰς τῶν πρεσβυτέρων Γλαυκίδης καὶ Θεόγνητος κατέβαλον τὸ σεμνὸν καὶ θαυμάσιον τῆς τῶν πολιτῶν προαιρέσεως διὰ τὰς ἰδίας ἐλπίδας· ἐβουλεύσαντο γὰρ τὰ μὲν τέκνα καὶ τὰς γυναῖκας ζωγρεῖν, ἅμα δὲ τῷ φωτὶ τοὺς ἱερεῖς καὶ τὰς ἱερείας ἐκπέμπειν μετὰ στεμμάτων πρὸς τὸν Φίλιππον, δεησομένους καὶ παραδιδόντας αὐτῷ τὴν πόλιν. L., recoiling from the horrible deed which they had sworn to perform, does not share Polybius' condemnation of their action. L. uses the simple but expressive *atrocior pars facinoris delegata erat* to show his feelings. The case is symptomatic of the difference of approach between the two historians (cf. xxxiii. 28. 14 n., Walbank, *JRS* lv [1965], 11).

principes: i.e. the *delecti* of § 7. *principes* as often means simply 'leaders', cf. *Past and Present* 36 (April, 1967), 6 n. 17. The objections of Deininger, 19 n. 15 are unconvincing.

18. 1. legatis Romanis: *Romanis* is in χ but not B. McDonald alleges that it is necessary for the context. But it would be quite clear that Lepidus was a Roman ambassador (cf. 19. 1). *Romanis* was added by a scribe who thought there might be some obscurity. Cf. Tränkle, *Gnomon*, 373.

qui Alexandream missi erant: cf. 2. 3 nn. and pp. 42–7. *Alexandream* is the reading of B, *Alexandriam* of χ. In general MSS. alternate between the two spellings, though -*eam* occurs in the oldest inscriptions (cf. *TLL*, i. 1534). In such circumstances it seems best to follow the oldest manuscript.

M. Aemilius: cf. 2. 3 n.

trium consensu . . . ad Philippum venit: Pol. xvi. 34. 1–2: Μάρκος Αἰμίλιος ὁ νεώτατος ἧκε καταπλέων εἰς αὐτὴν τὴν Ἄβυδον. οἱ γὰρ Ῥωμαῖοι τὸ σαφὲς ἀκούσαντες ἐν τῇ Ῥόδῳ περὶ τῆς τῶν Ἀβυδηνῶν πολιορκίας καὶ βουλόμενοι πρὸς αὐτὸν τὸν Φίλιππον ποιήσασθαι τοὺς λόγους κατὰ τὰς ἐντολάς, ἐπιστήσαντες τὴν πρὸς τοὺς βασιλέας ὁρμὴν ἐξέπεμψαν τὸν προειρημένον. The suppression of κατὰ τὰς ἐντολάς and its apparent replacement by *trium consensu* is the most striking of L.'s alterations to Polybius' account. Cf. pp. 42, 46–7. Any alteration to *trium* (cf. McDonald's apparatus) is quite otiose. Clearly the three *legati* decided which of them was to go to Abydus.

2. Qui questus: L. talks merely of a complaint and does not give the detailed *indictio belli* reported by Polybius (34. 3–4). He cannot do so, as his version implies that the *legati* were acting unofficially.

Attalo Rhodiisque: Pol. xvi. 34. 3: περὶ δὲ τῶν εἰς Ἄτταλον καὶ Ῥοδίους ἀδικημάτων. The events of 201: cf. p. 37.

cum rex . . . diceret: Pol. xvi. 34. 5: τοῦ δὲ Φιλίππου βουλομένου διδάσκειν ὅτι 'Ρόδιοι τὰς χεῖρας ἐπιβάλοιεν αὐτῷ. L. adds to Philip's claim that Attalus was the aggressor, a claim which Polybius makes Philip make at the conference of Nicaea (xviii. 6. 2 cf. L. xxxii. 34. 7). It is wrong to assume that Philip's claims are justified, and that hence the battle of Chios precedes Philip's attack on Pergamum (thus Holleaux, *Études*, iv. 213–14, Walbank, *Commentary*, ii. 499).

num Abydeni ... arma : Pol. xvi. 34. 5. "Τί δαὶ Ἀθηναῖοι; τί δαὶ Κιανοί; τί δαὶ νῦν Ἀβυδηνοί; καὶ τούτων τίς" ἔφη "σοὶ πρότερος ἐπέβαλε τὰς χεῖρας;" L. omits Lepidus' reference to the Athenians, in accordance with his suppression of the part played by the *legati* at Athens (cf. p. 42). But he also omits mention of Cius, and this has the dramatic effect, probably deliberate, of concentrating Lepidus' outburst on the siege of Abydus itself. Similarly with L.'s *quod tum maxime Abydum* above. For Polybius Abydus is subsumed under the general injunction μήτε τῶν 'Ελλήνων μηδενὶ πολεμεῖν (34. 3).

3. insueto vera audire ... esset : L.'s own comment. Polybius simply reports Philip's reply. (Cf. Walsh, *AJP* lxxvi [1955], 373 = *Wege zu Livius*, 186).

3–4. Aetas ... sentietis : Pol. xvi. 34. 6–7: ἔφησεν αὐτῷ συγγνώμην ἔχειν ὑπερηφάνως ὁμιλοῦντι, πρῶτον μὲν ὅτι νέος ἐστὶ καὶ πραγμάτων ἄπειρος, δεύτερον ὅτι κάλλιστος ὑπάρχει τῶν καθ' αὐτὸν—καὶ γὰρ ἦν τοῦτο κατ' ἀλήθειαν—⟨μάλιστα δ' ὅτι 'Ρωμαῖος. "ἐγὼ δὲ⟩ μάλιστα μὲν ἀξιῶ 'Ρωμαίους" ἔφη "μὴ παραβαίνειν τὰς συνθήκας μηδὲ πολεμεῖν ἡμῖν. ἐὰν δὲ καὶ τοῦτο ποιῶσιν, ἀμυνούμεθα γενναίως, παρακαλέσαντες τοὺς θεούς". L. omits Philip's statement that he would forgive Lepidus his outburst.

sin bello lacessitis : for the use of the present instead of the future or future perfect in a future conditional cf. K–St, i. 145–7.

mihi quoque animos facere : the MSS. have *animo est* which is nonsense, and emendations based on it (e.g. *in animo est ut . . .*) fail to yield satisfactory sense. *animos facere* was Madvig's convincing emendation (*Emendationes*, 465–6). He compared § 9 below and 14. 5, i. 34. 4, vi. 7. 5, xxxv. 36. 7, xxxvii. 37. 9, xxxviii. 15. 9, xlii. 50. 7. Translate, with Madvig's text, 'you will find that the name and kingdom of Macedon, no less noble than that of Rome, breeds confidence in me too', not as Sage 'you will find that I too have the resolution to make both the name and kingdom of Macedonia no less renowned than those of Rome'.

The language is considerably more florid than that of Polybius.

5. auro argento ... amisit : Pol. xvi. 34. 7–8: Οὗτοι μὲν οὖν ταῦτ' εἰπόντες διεχωρίσθησαν ἀπ' ἀλλήλων· ὁ δὲ Φίλιππος κυριεύσας τῆς πόλεως, τὴν ὕπαρξιν ἅπασαν καταλαβὼν συνηθροισμένην ὑπὸ τῶν Ἀβυδηνῶν ἐξ ἑτοίμου παρέλαβε. The MSS. read *auro argentoque quae* *coacervata erant accepto.* The plural is very harsh between the two singulars. McDonald defends H. J. Müller's reading (*Jahresberichte d. Berl. phil. Vereins* xi [1885], 123, xiv [1888], 87: not adopted in W–M) *quaeque alia* . . . *acceptis* on the grounds that L. has referred to *vestes* in 17. 6, and Polybius says τὴν ὕπαρξιν ἅπασαν. But L. might well refer simply to the gold and silver, the most important of the booty, and in that case the simplest emendation is just to change *accepto* to *acceptis*.

hominum . . . **amisit**: L. introduces his account of the self-destruction of the Abydenes with this vivid phrase. Polybius simply describes what happened.

6–7. Tanta enim rabies . . . interficerent: Pol. xvi. 34. 9: τὸ πλῆθος καὶ τὴν ὁρμὴν τῶν σφᾶς αὐτοὺς καὶ τὰ τέκνα καὶ τὰς γυναῖκας ἀποσφαττόντων, κατακαόντων, ἀπαγχόντων, εἰς τὰ φρέατα ῥιπτούντων, κατακρημνιζόντων ἀπὸ τῶν τεγῶν and 34. 11 νομίζοντες οἷον εἰ προδόται γίνεσθαι τῶν ὑπὲρ τῆς πατρίδος ἠγωνισμένων καὶ τεθνεώτων. Notice that L. describes the Abydenes' activities as *rabies*. Polybius just reports the facts; cf. 17. 11 n. The extract from Polybius breaks off at 34. 12, and it is therefore not possible to determine whether *periuriumque* . . . *hosti fecissent* occurred in Polybius or was added by L.

repente proditos: *repente* is repeated later in the sentence. W–M say the repetition is probably unintentional, and quote 38. 4, xxvi. 37. 1, xxxii. 21. 16, xliv. 29. 4 as parallels. But none of these involves repetition in the same clause. It is best to delete the first *repente*.

devovissent: not technically a *devotio*, but L. treats it as if it were one, as the Abydenes' case is hopeless. Cf. Stübler, 188 n. 47.

leti: thus χ. B's *laeti* is grotesque. *Letum* is a favourite word of L., but otherwise is found almost exclusively in verse (cf. Skard, 46, Tränkle, *WS*, 116, C. Brakman, *Mnemosyne* lv [1927], 54).

Obstupefactus . . . dixit: Pol. xvi. 34. 10: ἐκπλαγὴς ἦν, καὶ διαλγῶν ἐπὶ τοῖς γινομένοις παρήγγειλε διότι τρεῖς ἡμέρας ἀναστροφὴν δίδωσι τοῖς βουλομένοις ἀπάγχεσθαι καὶ σφάττειν αὐτούς. It is wrong to see *obstupefactus* as a deliberate omission by L. of Polybius' description of Philip's human emotions, as argued by Pianezzola, 73 n. 113.

8. Quo spatio . . . in potestatem venit: Pol. xvi. 34. 11–12: οὐδαμῶς ὑπέμενον τὸ ζῆν, ὅσοι μὴ δεσμοῖς ἢ τοιαύταις ἀνάγκαις προκατελήφθησαν· οἱ δὲ λοιποὶ πάντες ὥρμων ἀμελλήτως κατὰ συγγενείας ἐπὶ τὸν θάνατον. The contrast of *victi* . . . *victores* is probably L.'s own.

9. consulem: cf. 14. 2 and 4 n. L. thus makes the chronology clear. This section, with the reference to Saguntum (cf. 7. 6, 17. 5) is L.'s own way of rounding off his digression. Sage mistranslates 'When, as Hannibal's destruction of Saguntum had aroused the

Romans to war against him, so now the slaughter of the people of Abydos had roused them against Philip, ...'

in Epiro: not strictly Epirus itself which was not an ally of Rome (cf. 7. 9 n.). L. here uses Epirus to mean north-west Greece in general; cf. xxxv. 24. 7.

Apollonia and Corcyra are both part of the Roman protectorate, cf. 3. 2 n.

19–22. 3. *Events in Rome and Italy*

19. *The embassy to Africa*

For the dispatch of these *legati*, cf. 11. 4–18. For their names, 11. 18.

19. 1. Hamilcare: cf. 10. 2 n.

nihil ultra . . . publicarent: the words imply that this is the action that the Carthaginians promise to take, not that they have already taken it.

bonaque: B omits -*que*, and asyndeton is perfectly possible.

2. Ducenta . . . miserunt: a voluntary contribution, not one specified in the peace of 201. For its arrival cf. 50. 1 n.

ad reges: B. *regem* χ. χ has misunderstood the import of *tertia legatio* in § 5; in fact both Massinissa and Vermina are ruling over parts of Numidia.

3. Dona . . . edita: cf. 11. 8–11.

4. Ipse . . . misit: Massinissa himself pays for the transport, and presumably the ships are his own. Sage mistranslates *curavit* as 'supervised'.

For other contributions of grain by Massinissa cf. xxxii. 27. 2, xxxvi. 4. 8, xliii. 6. 13, Walsh, *JRS* lv (1965), 154, Toynbee, ii. 187.

5. ad Verminam: cf. 11. 13 ff. Vermina accepts the condition of a virtual *deditio*: cf. 11. 17.

6. iussusque . . . Romam: in 11. 17 L. says that the senate will have to be asked for any change from the terms laid down by the *legati* for which Vermina might seek. This does not imply, however, that if Vermina does not seek any changes, there would be no further reference to Rome, and there is thus no inconsistency between the two passages. In any case the people as well as the senate would have to ratify the terms.

20. *The* Ovatio *of L. Cornelius Lentulus*

20. 1. L. Cornelius Lentulus: (188). He had been proconsul in Spain since 206, having been given the command as a *privatus*. He had been elected curule aedile in his absence for 205. He was consul in 199 (cf. 49. 12, xxxii. 1. 2, 2. 6, 7. 1, 7. 7, 9. 5) and proconsul in 198 (xxxii. 26. 2). He was a *legatus* who met Antiochus at Lysimachia in 196 (xxxiii. 39. 1, 41. 2). He may have been a *xvir sacris faciundis* since 213.

ex Hispania rediit: at xxx. 41. 5 L. records a *senatus consultum* that the tribunes should consult the people as to who should command in Spain, and that an army should be provided for him. Lentulus and L. Manlius Acidinus, who had both been there for many years, should bring their armies home. In the event Lentulus appears to have been replaced by C. Cornelius Cethegus (cf. 49. 7), but Manlius remained until the end of 200 (cf. 50. 11, xxxii. 7. 4). The original *s.c.* provided, it seems, for a unified command in Spain, and it may have been later decided that this was impractical.

pro consule: *pro consul* χ. Cf. 3. 3 n. Technically *pro consule* is correct and as it is the reading of B here and in §4 it is safest to assume that that is what L. wrote.

2. fortiter feliciterque: for the phrase cf. v. 30. 5, xxviii. 9. 7, Ogilvie, 693. It is probably a standard formula used in the granting of triumphs.

3. res triumpho dignas: the requirement was that 5,000 of the enemy should have been killed in a single battle (Val. Max. ii. 8. 1), but it is possible that this requirement was introduced after this date, and that at this time the senate made its judgement as it saw fit (cf. Mommsen, *StR*, i³. 133, Schlag, 17–22, 56–70).

exemplum . . . obtinuisse: Scipio was in the same position after his Spanish campaigns, cf. xxviii. 38. 4, Val. Max. ii. 8. 5, Plut. *Pomp.* 14, Mommsen, *StR*, i³. 126–7.

5. ovans: on the *ovatio* and the differences between it and the full triumph, cf. Rohde, *RE*, xviii. 1890–1903, Ogilvie, 277, L. B. Warren, *JRS* lx (1970), 51, H. S. Versnel, *Triumphus* (Leiden, 1970), 165 ff.

Ti. Sempronio Longo: (67). The MSS. read *T.*; Titus is a very rare *praenomen* among the Sempronii, while Tib. is very common. It is attested, apart from the present passage and xxxiii. 36. 5, which should also be emended (cf. n. ad loc.) only for T. Sempronius Musca (xlv. 13. 11) and T. Sempronius Rutilus (xxxix. 9. 2). It would be a circular procedure to alter every occurrence of Titus on the grounds that it is not often found, but in this case there can be little doubt that the tribune is in fact Tib. Sempronius Longus, the consul of 194 (cf. xxxii. 27. 8, 29. 4, xxxiii. 24. 2, 26. 1, 43. 9: the MSS. have *T.* at all these passages). He was consul with Scipio in 194 and his father had been consul with Scipio's father in 218. Lentulus' brother Gnaeus, consul in 201, had opposed Scipio (cf.

14. 2 n.) and it is thus probable that Longus was acting in Scipio's interest in objecting to the *ovatio* (cf. Scullard, *RP*, 95).

6. victus consensu patrum: it is hardly likely that the whole of the senate was united and only one tribune objected. In fact what probably happened is that there was clearly a majority in favour of Lentulus, and Longus, after making his point, and probably on the advice of Scipio, withdrew. It would have been unwise to provoke a major conflict on what was essentially a minor matter.

7. [ex praeda]: the words make little sense here and are probably imported from the next sentence (Pettersson, 109, defends them unconvincingly).

For figures of booty and distributions to soldiers in the second century, cf. Tenney Frank, *Economic Survey*, i. 127 ff.

21–22. 3. *Gaul*

The story of the Gallic war is continued from ch. 11. This account bristles with difficulties. The description of the battle is inadequate and stereotyped, details of the formation of the Roman army are presented in a very obscure way, and the passage contains several examples of unusual syntax or idiom. The impression is that L. has taken this account from an annalistic source, and has not worked it up with his usual care. Much of the language may be taken almost verbatim from the source. But it is unnecessary to argue from this to the inauthenticity of the campaign as such: cf. 10–11. 3 n. On the description of the battle cf. Plathner, 53–4.

21. 1. iam exercitus . . . transierant: as the senate had instructed in 11. 1–3. Aurelius is carrying out the second of the two alternatives given to him, that of allowing the praetor to raise the siege of Cremona.

Arretio: Arretium was the original assembly point of the army in Etruria, though not specified as such in 11. 1. Arretium, mod. Arezzo, had been an ally of Rome since the early third century. Cf. H. H. Scullard, *The Etruscan Cities and Rome* (London, 1967), 165–7.

2. tum obsidentes: *tum* MSS. *etiam tum* (Weissenborn) is unnecessary. L. is reminding readers of the chronological connection with his account in 10–11. 3, not stressing that the siege was still continuing.

castra . . . posuit: L. is very imprecise here about the geography. He does not indicate whether Furius crossed the Po to march on Cremona, or whether the Gauls came south of the river to meet the Roman advance.

3. **egregie rei gerendae**: B and V have *egregiae*. L. always uses the adverb of *egregius*, never the adjective, with *res gerere* (Packard, ii. 45).

4. **lassitudini militum timuit**: this is the MSS. reading. The dative of the thing feared is unusual, and has attracted a variety of emendations (see McDonald's apparatus). It is, however, defended by E. J. Kenney (*CQ* N.S. ix [1959], 258) as parallel to Ovid, *Ars Amatoria*, iii. 455 *discite ab alterius vestris timuisse querelis* to which McDonald adds (apparently on Kenney's prompting) *Laus Pisonis* 245 . . . *quo praeside tuti* | *non umquam vates inopi timuere senectae*. To this G. P. Goold objects (*HSCP* lxix [1965], 88–9) that in our passage the *lassitudo* is a present object, in the Ovid passage the *querelae* are prospective. He thinks that the dative here is one of the object on behalf of which fear is felt, of which he quotes several examples. But it is not the *lassitudo* on behalf of which Furius is afraid and Goold's statement that the phrase equals '*timuit ne quid lassitudo militum pateretur* which the context invests with the meaning of *ne lassitudo efficeret ut milites vincerentur*' merely restates, and does not solve the problem.

One of Goold's parallels, however, comes closer to our passage. It is Caesar *BG* vii. 44 *vehementer huic illos loco timere*. The reference is to the siege of Gergovia, and the inhabitants fear an attack by the one way possible. Their fear is not 'for the hill' but 'about the hill, and the consequences that flow from it'. So here, Furius fears 'about the tiredness of the soldiers, and the consequences that might flow from it'.

To this it should be added that though Kenney's and Goold's examples are not strictly parallel, it is clear that *timere* was used with the dative in a variety of instances, and this is in itself a reason for accepting it.

I see no evidence for McDonald's assertion that the usage is colloquial (cf. Tränkle, *Gnomon*, 377).

5–6. **et postero die . . . pugnandi fecit**: Madvig (*Emendationes*, 265) deleted *et* and put a stop after *repetivere*, on the grounds that the events of two separate days should be clearly distinguished. But the MSS. reading with McDonald's punctuation makes perfectly good sense and should be retained. Walsh's suggestion (*CR*, 54) of a stop after *repetivere*, retention of *et* and a comma after *progressi* is intolerably harsh.

For the common omission of *sunt* cf. 25. 5 n., 26. 13 n., xxxii. 2. 7 n., 14. 2 n., K–St, i. 13, H–S, 422.

7. **dextra ala . . . habebat**: the allied troops present are the normal accompaniment of a Roman legion and there is no confusion with

the 5,000 allied troops which had been sent to Etruria. But the language here is quite extraordinary. It was normal for the allied contingents to be divided into two *alae*, and L. often refers to them (cf. Pol. vi. 26. 9, Kromayer–Veith, 267, Packard, i. 314–15). Here he refers only to the *dextra ala*, and that in several places (21. 8, 10, 12, 22. 2). There is no mention of the *sinistra ala*, though he appears to have given a complete catalogue of the Roman formation: several other passages, it is true, refer to only one of the two *alae*, but they are discussing only individual parts of the battles concerned.

Since L. was clearly well aware of the normal organization of the *socii*, *in alas socialem exercitum habebat* is a totally unnecessary addition, and *habebat*, though formally agreeing with *Romanus*, harsh. Were it not for the other difficulties in the chapter, one would be tempted to regard it as a gloss. As it is, it is best to hold that both the references to the *dextra ala* and the explanation are due to L.'s source being badly acquainted with some of the details of Roman military organization.

8. M. Furius: (56). Münzer (*RE*, vii. 353) tentatively identifies him with the *praetor* of 187 and 173 and with the *legatus* to Illyria in 201 (xxx. 42. 5). His relationship to the *praetor* is unknown. Cf. 47. 4–49. 3, 49. 8–11 n.

M. Caecilius: (15). Münzer (*RE*, iii. 1188) quotes only this passage in connection with him, but he could be M. Caecilius Metellus (praetor in 206) (*RE*, 76) and probably brother of Q. Caecilius Metellus (cf. 4. 3 n.). Cf. p. 35.

L. Valerius Flaccus: (173). Cf. 4. 5 n.

9. C. Laetorium: (2). Curule aedile in 216, a *legatus* from the senate to the consuls in Campania in 212, praetor in 210, a *legatus* under Sempronius Tuditanus in Greece in 205, a *iiivir* for the foundation of Croton in 194 and *xvir sacris faciundis* from 209.

P. Titinium: (16). Not otherwise known.

10. quae prima erat: unnecessarily repetitive, as L. has already given us this information (§ 7). He gives it again in § 12 though there it is somewhat more natural, as he has said *dextra laevaque* and to repeat *dextrae* would be ambiguous. (Kahrstedt, 59, strangely thought *prima* was the number of the *ala*: cf. p. 4).

12. aedemque Diiovi . . . fudisset: this statement is a major problem, and must be considered in conjunction with two other passages:

(194) xxxiv. 53. 7. *et in insula Iovis aedem C. Servilius iivir dedicavit: vota erat sex annis ante Gallico bello ab L. Furio Purpurione praetore, ab eodem postea consule locata.*

(192) xxxv. 41. 8. *Aedes duae Iovis eo anno in Capitolio dedicatae sunt: voverat L. Furius Purpurio praetor bello Gallico unam, alteram consul.*

The two passages are thus in conflict over the site of the temple vowed by Furius in 200, and the date of its dedication. The second involves the incredible situation of two separate temples on the Capitol. Münzer (*RE*, vii. 362–3) cut the knot by arguing that the whole of the 200 campaign is fictitious and that there was only one vow, in 196, fulfilled by the Capitoline temple dedicated in 192. Not only is his dismissal of the campaign improbable (cf. 10–11. 3 n.), but he fails to take account of other relevant evidence.

There was certainly a temple of Veiovis on the island. Vitruvius, iii. 2. 3 and Ovid, *Fasti* i. 293–4, call it a temple of Jupiter but the *Fasti Praenestini* and *Antiates* (*I.I.* xiii. 2. 2, 111) refer to a festival of *Vediovis in insula* on the Kalends of January. It is reasonable, as a first step, to assume that L.'s statement in xxxiv. 53. 7 is correct and that this was the temple vowed by Furius in 200. Now the MSS. at the present passage read *deo Iovi*, which makes little sense. Ogilvie (*Phoenix*, 345) suggests that *deo* is a gloss and we should read *Iovi* here. Such a simple solution is attractive, but the alleged gloss would be a most unilluminating one. The *Diiovi* of Valesius, printed by McDonald, is not otherwise attested (cf. Ogilvie, l.c.) and it seems to me that we should let the text follow the facts and return to the *Vediovi* of Merkel (introduction to edition of Ovid, *Fasti*, Berlin, 1841, cxxiv) or the *Veiovi* of Rossbach (*WKlPh* xxxiv [1917], 1129). McDonald's objection that the archetype would have had *aedemq.* not *aedemque* and that this makes the corruption of *Ve* less likely, is insufficient; the posited corruption is natural whatever the archetype read. At xxxiv. 53. 7 there is no such MSS. authority for reading *Vediovis* or *Veiovis* and it is best to keep *Iovis*. L. could well have been inconsistent over this, and the error is far less striking than the conflict between xxxiv. 53. 7 and xxxv. 41. 8. As we have seen Ovid and Vitruvius made the same mistake, and in any case Jupiter and Veiovis are very closely connected. (Cf. Latte, *RRG*, 79–83: the identification of Veiovis and Apollo—on which cf. Nisbet and Hubbard, 30—is a later development.)

What then of the book xxxv passage? It has usually been held that L.'s error (or his source's) was simply in thinking, at this point, that there were two temples on the Capitol, and that there was in fact one, vowed by Furius in 196 and dedicated in 192 (Wissowa, *RuK*², 237 n. 7, Latte, *RRG*, 82). Now there was a temple of Veiovis on the Capitol (Ovid, *Fasti* iii. 429–30, *Fasti Praen. Ant.* [*I.I.* xiii. 2. 6, 121]) and its dedication day was March 7 (for the remains cf. A. M. Colini, *Bull. Comm.* lxx [1942], 5–55). Pliny (*NH* xvi. 216) says that a statue was dedicated in this temple in 561 A.U.C. Now this would, on the Varronian reckoning, mean 193/2 and would conflict with a dedication in 192/1. Furthermore, the *iivir* of xxxv. 41. 7 Q. Marcius Ralla had been in office in 194 (xxxiv. 53. 5) and it is unlikely that a *iivir*, who was elected for a special dedication, would still be in office two years later. Hence G. Radke (*RhM* cvi [1963], 315–18) argues that the whole notice in book xxxv is to be rejected. The actual temple of Veiovis on the Capitol had been built before this time, and the statue referred to by Pliny was dedicated on the anniversary of the dedication of the temple on 7 March 193. This was in Varronian year 561 (calculated as beginning on 1 January) but in the Capitoline year 559 (which began with the date of entry into office of the consuls). The Varronian date was later misunderstood to be a Capitoline one, and the notice transferred to 192, and then confused with the dedication of the temple of Veiovis on the island.

Against this, however, it is far from clear that Pliny's source was working with a Varronian year beginning on 1 January, but even if he was, a misunderstanding of a Capitoline date as a Varronian one is just as possible; or it could be that the numeral in Pliny is corrupt and should read 562. It is perfectly possible that the temple and the statue were dedicated on the same day, and if so this could be in fulfilment of a vow made by Furius in 196, and Ralla could have been reappointed as a *iivir* in 192. It is no obstacle that L. does not mention such a vow in his account of Furius' campaign in 196.

Emendation of xxxv. 41. 8 is not desirable. The nonsensical *duae Iovis* is very similar to the *deo Iovi* in the present passage, but an emendation to fit the facts would require an original text of *aedes Veiovis eo anno in Capitolio dedicata est: voverat L. Furius Purpurio consul bello Gallico.* Such would represent the truth, but it is likely that the process of misunderstanding goes back to L. himself, if not to his source.

Cf. in addition to the works already quoted Platner–Ashby, 548–9, Degrassi, *I.I.* xiii. 2. 388, A. Stazio, *RAAN* xxiii (1946–8), 135–47 (denying that there was a temple of Veiovis *in insula* and defending the MSS. of L. in all three passages). Walsh, *Livy*, 148, is confused.

14. ut extenuatam . . . vidit : for other examples of this occurring in Livian battles, cf. Ogilvie, 307.

15. in omni parte : unique in L., who uses *ab omni parte* or *omni parte*. Again it may be due to the source, and emendation is unwise.

16–17. The Gallic losses are very large and probably exaggerated. On exaggerated figures for enemy losses in L. cf. Walsh, *Livy*, 120–1.

18. **Hamilcar dux . . . cecidit**: cf. 10. 2 n. According to xxxii. 30. 12 Hamilcar was captured after Cethegus' defeat of the Insubres in 197 and xxxiii. 23. 5 refers to his being led in Cethegus' triumph. In view of the other difficulties in the present chapter, the statement that he was killed should be rejected.

22. 1. **supplicatio**: the *supplicatio* as a thank-offering after a victory was probably a later development of the *supplicatio* praying for deliverance from plagues etc. (cf. 8. 2 n.). It is attested in iii. 63 and v. 23 but both instances are suspect (Ogilvie, 512–13, 679) and the first undisputed instance is in 296 (x. 21). For a list of *supplicationes* see Halkin, *La Supplication* (cf. 8. 2 n.).

in triduum: three day *supplicationes* were decreed after the battles of Metaurus (xxvii. 51. 8) and Zama (xxx. 40. 4). Four days are recorded for Scipio's victory over Syphax and the Carthaginians in 203 (xxx. 17. 3) and also for a victory over the Samnites in 293 (x. 45. 1), but in the latter case two commanders were involved. Similarly four days were decreed for the Gallic victories of the two consuls in 197 (xxxii. 31. 6). Five days were decreed for the victory at Cynoscephalae (xxxiii. 24. 4).

2. **duo milia**: for a list of Roman war losses in this period cf. Toynbee, ii. 71–2.

3. **C. Aurelius**: for the continuation of the story, and Aurelius' resentment of Furius' success, cf. 47. 4 ff.

22. 4–47. 3. *The campaign of 200/199 in Greece*

L.'s account is clearly taken from Polybius, though of the latter's version only a fragment survives (xvi. 38, cf. 25. 2–11 n.). The narrative covers events down to autumn 199 (cf. 47. 1) even though L. includes it under the consuls of the year 200, whose year of office ended on *Id. Mart.* 199, which was in fact *c.* Dec. 200 (Jul.) (cf. p. 42). L. has taken the events included by Polybius under the Olympiad year 200/199 and placed them under the consular year 199. For other cases of this (and the reverse) confusion cf. pp. 2–3.

22. 4—28. *Events of autumn and winter 200/199*

4. **cum autumno ferme exacto**: on the meaning of this phrase cf. Holleaux, *Études*, iv. 338–40, Walbank, *Philip V*, 317. To us the end of autumn would indicate the time around the beginning of November, and indeed the Roman *autumnus* lasted from the middle of August until the middle of November (cf. Holleaux, 338 n. 3). But L. must be dependent on Polybius, and the latter has no phrase

for autumn—his year is divided into χειμών and θερεία. For the period which we understand as autumn he uses such phrases as συνάπτοντος τοῦ χειμῶνος (ii. 54. 13) and these L. translates by *hiemps iam instabat* (xxxii. 4. 7, xxxiii. 41. 9). Here Polybius probably said that Sulpicius arrived at the beginning of winter and L. has taken this to mean the end of the Roman autumn. The true date is probably the beginning or middle of September.

Apolloniam: cf. 18. 9 n.

5. Corcyrae: cf. 18. 9 n.

C. Claudius . . . dictum est: 14. 3.

6. terrestres . . . incursiones: the word-order is designed to emphasize the contrast between the land attacks and those by sea (*praedonum . . . naves*).

ab Corintho quae per Megara: the Acrocorinth had been in Macedonian possession since the formation of the symmachy in 224 (cf. 7. 9 n.). Formally, Corinth itself remained a member of the league, but it is clear from the negotiations of these years that the garrison on the Acrocorinth exercised *de facto* control over the city, and that the league's writ did not run there. Megara had been a member of the Achaean League since 243 (E. L. Highbarger, *The History and Civilization of Ancient Megara* [Baltimore, 1927], 209, Walbank, *Aratus*, 182).

7. praedonum: as with Heraclides and Dicaearchus in 205/4, Philip was making semi-official use of privateers (cf. p. 36).

Chalcide: Chalcis, like the rest of Euboea, had been in Macedonian possession almost continuously since the battle of Chaeronea, cf. Geyer, *RE*, supp. iv. 442 ff. With the Acrocorinth and Demetrias it was one of the three 'fetters of Greece' (xxxii. 37. 4, Pol. xviii. 11. 5).

ne extra fretum ⟨quidem⟩: the MSS. have simply *ne*: the omission of *quidem* is odd and *nec* is palaeographically a far easier change. L. uses *nec* to equal *ne . . . quidem* on several occasions (Riemann, 277, K–St, ii. 44–5, Ogilvie, 493). McDonald objects that he particularly uses it with pronouns. But xl. 20. 6 *neque scribi sibi vellet* is a case where the *neque* does not go with the pronoun (it limits *scribi*, not *sibi*) and I would read *nec* here.

Euripi: the straits between Euboea and the mainland. At their narrowest, opposite Chalcis itself, they are only 30 m. wide. *aperto mari* probably refers to the area to the south of Marathon, where there is a large distance between Attica and Euboea. Cf. P–K, i. 2. 551–60, Philippson, *RE*, vi. 1281–3. See also 23. 3, 24. 3 nn.

8. supervenerunt . . . apertae naves: taken literally *super-*

venerunt would imply that the Rhodian ships arrived after those of Centho. It is possible, however, that L. has misunderstood Polybius on this point and that either these three ships stayed behind when the rest of the Rhodian fleet left Athens (15. 8) or returned before the Roman ships arrived. An inscription of Delos (*Syll.*³ 582) refers to Rhodian ships acting to defend the islands together with islanders and Athenian ἄφρακτοι (which must be the same as the *apertae naves* here—i.e. ships without decks and other protection, the opposite of κατάφρακτοι or *tectae*, cf. 46. 6). Hence Thiel, 224, assumes that the Athenian ships left Athens at the same time as the Rhodian fleet, and that the events referred to in the inscription fall in the period between then and that covered by the present passage. But it is incredible to think that the Athenian ships should have left Attica when Macedonian attacks were still imminent or actually taking place, and the events referred to in the inscription must fall after the danger to Attica had receded. In that case, the Rhodian ships too may have been at Athens before those of Centho.

This view is apparently taken by Walbank, *Philip V*, 138, and by McDonald, *JRS* xxvii (1937), 198.

23. *The assault on Chalcis.* The incident is also mentioned by Zonaras, ix. 15. 3.

23. 1. exules . . . pulsi: presumably an anti-Macedonian party had threatened Philip's control of Chalcis and been exiled. The *regii* are the supporters of Philip and Macedonian officials in Chalcis. Cf. the *praefecti* in Thessaly (xxxiv. 48. 2). It seems probable that such garrisons were maintained permanently, and not only in time of war, as is argued by Heidemann, 9–10.

3. Sunium: the fortification and harbour were on the west of the cape, and therefore invisible from Euboea: cf. Meyer, *RE*, ivA. 911–19, P–K, i. 3. 843.

ad primas angustias: i.e. north of what is described as *apertum mare* in 22. 7.

4–5. infrequentissima urbis . . . frequentia aedificiis loca: the unpopulated parts are probably those in the southern extremities of the town; the *frequentia loca* those nearer the Euripus bridge. The former will be those described by Aeneas Tacticus, 4, as τὸ ἐρημό-τατον τῆς πόλεως and being within the walls. This would exclude W–M's suggestion that it is the tongue of land projecting south-westwards into the Euripus just to the south of the town, cf. Oberhummer, *RE*, iii. 2088.

6–7. The short vivid sentences, the asyndeton, and the impersonal passive *discursum est* are typical of L.'s 'military style'. Cf. e.g. 33. 8, ii. 25–6, Ogilvie, 302. In part this reflects the language of military communiqués (cf. E. Fraenkel, *Eranos* liv [1956], 189 ff.) but it also serves to emphasize the speed of the action as the invasion reaches its climax.

8. Sopatro etiam Acarnane: not otherwise known. He is not to be identified with the Sopater who was captured in Africa in 202 (xxx. 26. 3, 42. 4, cf. 1. 10 n.).

9. carcer: for the imprisonment of captives in public prisons cf. Ducrey, 217–18.

11. quod . . . regi forent: De Sanctis (iv. 1. 47 n. 85) thinks that the numbers of Macedonians and supporters killed is exaggerated, and that if L. were right, the Romans would have made some attempt to hold Chalcis. But L.'s reason for their not so doing is convincing. Athens was far from adequately defended as it was.

12. nam . . . claudit: thus in 480 the Greeks took up position against Xerxes at Thermopylae and Artemisium respectively. Cf. Hdt. vii. 175. 2.

24–25. 1. *Philip's attack on Athens.* Referred to by Zon. ix. 15. 3.

24. 1. Demetriade: another of the 'fetters of Greece', cf. 22. 7 n. Demetrias was founded by synoecism of existing communities by Demetrius Poliorcetes *c.* 293 (cf. F. Stählin–E. Meyer–A. Heidner, *Pagasai und Demetrias* [Berlin–Leipzig, 1934], C. Wehrli, *Antigone et Demetrios* [Geneva, 1969], 196 ff.). Thessaly had been almost continuously under Macedonian control throughout the Hellenistic age.

   sociae: technically an ally, but in fact, as often, a subject.

   perditis ⟨rebus⟩: the supplement seems necessary. *res perditae* is often used by L., while he never uses *perditus* in an absolute sense (cf. Packard, iii. 860).

2. cum expeditis quinque milibus peditum: χ. B omits *peditum*. McDonald defends χ's reading, comparing 16. 3 *cum expeditis duo milibus peditum.* W–M, however, point to xxii. 16. 2 *cum expeditis equitibusque* and the fact that the present passage contains a numeral does not seem to me particularly important. I would keep B's text.

3. deforme . . . fumantis: L. here uses language reminiscent of his description of the Gallic sack of Rome. Cf. v. 49. 3–4 *solum patriae deforme . . . in semirutae solo urbis.*

   ponte: the bridge was a permanent structure, built in 411: cf. xxviii. 7. 2, Diod. xiii. 47, Strabo ix. p. 403c.

4. hemerodromos: ἡμεροδρόμος is not the Greek for *speculator*. ἡμεροδρόμος or ἡμεροδρόμης (see below) is used by Herodotus (vi. 105) of Philippides who ran from Athens to Sparta in 490 and (ix. 12) of an Argive messenger to Mardonius in 479. Neither is a spy, nor do any of the other uses of ἡμεροδρόμος quoted by LSJ refer to spies. The Greek for a spy is ἡμεροσκόπος and L. has probably confused the two. Such confusion was made easier by the fact that spies too had to be quick runners (cf. Hdt. vii. 183, 192, Aen. Tact. 6).

W–M suggest that L. used *speculator* here because imperial couriers were called *speculatores*. It seems unlikely, however, that *speculator* had come to mean 'messenger' as early as the time that L. was writing. (For the imperial *speculatores* cf. F. Lammert, *RE*, iiiA. 1585.) Such a view, moreover, would presuppose that Polybius wrote ἡμεροδρόμος and that L. used *speculator* as a translation of it. But it is clear from *e specula* that L. was quite well aware that he was talking about a spy, not a messenger, and we must therefore conclude either that L. has mis-remembered or miscopied Polybius, or that the text of Polybius was corrupt by L.'s time, or that Polybius said nothing about ἡμεροσκόποι or ἡμεροδρόμοι and L. added the gloss from his own knowledge.

The MSS. of Herodotus at vi. 105 read ἡμεροδρόμης and if L. had this passage in mind he may have written what B reads— *hemerodromas*.

vocant: used by L. to indicate he is translating a Greek term in Polybius. Cf. Nissen, *KU*, 74 ff.

5. idem . . . prodiderat: Walsh, *RhM* xcvii (1954), 113, points to this as an example of L.'s technique in connecting two episodes. His implication, however, that the comparison between the events at Chalcis and Athens did not stand in Polybius is unjustified.

6. praetor Atheniensium: the ten Athenian *strategoi* continued to be elected, but in the Hellenistic period they were assigned specific tasks. The leading one was the στρατηγὸς ἐπὶ τὰ ὅπλα and it is to him that L. is probably referring here. Cf. Ferguson, *Hellenistic Athens*, 9, Schwahn, *RE*, supp. vi. 1086 ff.

Dioxippus: not otherwise known.

mercede militantium: on the use of mercenaries in Athens in this period, cf. Ferguson, *Hellenistic Athens*, 74, 251, G. T. Griffith, *The Mercenaries of the Hellenistic World* (Cambridge, 1935), 80 ff.

9. ab Dipylo accessit: from the direction of the Dipylon, i.e. in fact towards the Dipylon. Cf. 46. 9, viii. 17. 9 *adversus regem escensionem a Paesto facientem* (which means 'landing at Paestum', not 'marching from Paestum', as is clear from L.'s other uses of *escensio*. Cf. *TLL*, v. 2. 858, Packard, ii. 175). W–M also quote 21. 11 and xxxviii. 32. 2 but these are not the same usage. The Dipylon gate was on the north-west side of Athens, leading to the Academy,

Colonus, and Eleusis. It consisted of two gates, one behind the other, with a space in between. Cf. Judeich, 135–9, Walbank, *Commentary*, ii. 534.

10. Academiae: for sources on the Academy, cf. Judeich, 412–14. L. says it is a Roman mile, but Cicero gives 6 stades (*fin.* v. 1) which is rather less. For the remains, R. E. Wycherley, *G & R* ix (1962) 5 ff., Travlos, *Bildlexikon*, 42 ff. The gymnasium was probably built by the Pisistratids but it was Cimon who laid out the area as a public park.

Attali praesidio: probably a very small force left at Athens when he returned to Aegina: it is not to be identified with the force sent over later from Aegina (25. 1).

11. neque . . . erat: especially so because of the overt anti-Macedonian action of abolishing the Macedonian tribes in 201 and the friendly reception given to Philip's enemies Rhodes and Attalus (cf. pp. 43–4).

⟨iram⟩ **expleturum:** some supplement or alteration is clearly necessary, as *se* is the subject of *habere se hostes* and cannot be understood as the object of *expleturum*. Palaeographically Madvig's *expletum iri* is an easier change than the insertion of *iram* or *odium*.

12. in hostes: χ: not in B and should be omitted. It is clearly an explanatory gloss, probably influenced by § 14. Thus Walsh, *CR*, 55, Tränkle, *Gnomon*, 373 and n. 2.

13. gloria elatus: the phrase is commonly used in military contexts. Cf. Ogilvie, 512.

17–18. Cf. Diod. xxviii. 7 who probably reflects the language of Polybius fairly closely.

17. Cynosarges: for its position in the area to the south of the Acropolis cf. Judeich, 422–4, Wycherley, *G & R* ix, 13 ff., Travlos, *Bildlexikon*, 340. For philosophical activity there, Wycherley, 14–15. The temple of Hercules here is mentioned by Herodotus v. 63.

18. Lycium: the gymnasium here was probably built by Pericles. For its position in the east of the city cf. Judeich, 415, Wycherley, *G & R* ix, 10, Travlos, *Bildlexikon*, 345.

et quidquid . . . servatum: one of the many passages where Polybius accuses Philip of offending against the normal canons in his actions in war. Cf. 26. 9 ff., 30. 1 ff., Pol. v. 9. 5 ff., iv. 62. 3, vii. 14. 3, xi. 7. 2, xvi. 1, Diod. xxviii. 7, Walbank, *Commentary*, i. 517. For Polybius Philip's last years were nemesis for these actions. Cf. Walbank, *JHS* lviii (1938), 55–68.

sepulcra : the main cemetery was the Ceramicus, just outside the Dipylon. But Philip seems to have devastated any tombs he came across, and the reference will not be to the Ceramicus alone. On cemeteries of Athens cf. Judeich, 400 ff.

25. 1. praesidium Attali : cf. 24. 10 n. It is presumably not the case that the whole of Attalus' garrison on Aegina came over to Attica. On Attalus' possession of Aegina cf. 14. 11 n.

25. 2–11. *Philip at the meeting of the Achaean League.* The fragment of Polybius, xvi. 38, refers to this episode.

2. Eleusinem : the MSS. read *Eleusinam. Eleusina* appears to be a later form of the name, and in classical authors the form is *Eleusin -inis.* This passage apart, where *Eleusina* occurs, it does so in inferior manuscripts. In ch. 26 the MSS. have various forms of *Eleusin* (at 26. 3 B has *Eleusino,* at 26. 4 *Elusinem*) and B's *Eleusiniae* at 30. 9 is clearly corrupt. At xlv. 12. 3 the uncial MS. has *adleunsinem.* Carbach's correction here should clearly be accepted.

templi : the famous shrine of Demeter where the mysteries (14. 7 n.) took place. On the site and its development cf. Mylonas, *Eleusis and the Eleusinian Mysteries* (14. 7 n.), *passim.*

castelli . . . circumdatum est : *castellum* can hardly designate the fortifications surrounding the temple, as W–M assert, but would have to refer to the fort on the western hill (cf. Mylonas, 152). On the other hand, that fort can scarcely be said to surround the temple. It is probable that L. has misunderstood Polybius, and either that Polybius referred to the fortifications of the temple and city, and not to a fort, or that he referred to the fort but did not say that it surrounded the temple. The references to the *castellum* in ch. 26 suggest that the latter is the case. The narrative suggests a separate fort, and its relief by a garrison landed from the sea makes particular sense of the fort's position overlooking the Saronic gulf. L. will have had little idea of the topography. (Perhaps Polybius used $\tau\epsilon\acute{\iota}\chi\iota\sigma\mu\alpha$ which could mean either fort or fortification.)

Megara . . . Corinthum : cf. 22. 6 n.

cum Argis . . . audisset : the Achaean League had been an ally of Macedon since the foundation of the symmachy in 224. Despite quarrels between Philip and Aratus, the Achaeans had remained on Philip's side in the First Macedonian War and were included among Philip's *adscripti* in the peace of Phoenice (xxix. 12. 14). There were two kinds of meeting of the Achaean League, the regular quarterly meetings, probably at this time consisting of the Council alone, called σύνοδοι, and irregular meetings of the whole people, probably called σύγκλητοι (though irregular meetings of the council were also called σύγκλητοι). Polybius uses σύγκλητος only once, no doubt because that was his word for the Roman senate but there is sufficient evidence to justify the nomenclature and I shall continue to use it. Σύγκλητοι were summoned to deal with matters of war or making alliance, or to deal with communications from the Roman senate. Until 188 σύνοδοι were regularly held at Aegium, but σύγκλητοι in various cities (cf. xxxii. 19. 5 at Sicyon). The present meeting is a σύγκλητος and hence the proposed correction of *Argis* to *Aegii* is quite unjustified.

On the Achaean assemblies, cf. Aymard, *Assemblées*, Larsen, *Representative Government*, 75–105, 165–88 (a list of all known meetings of League bodies), Walbank, *Commentary*, i. 219–20, Errington, *Philopoemen*, 6, A. Giovannini, *MH* xxvi (1969), 1–17, Walbank, *MH* xxvii (1970), 129–43.

contioni ipsi: i.e. without first presenting himself to the magistrates to ask for permission to address the assembly.

3. consultabant . . . Nabim tyrannum Lacedaemoniorum: Nabis became sole king of Sparta in 207, having first removed the legitimate heir Pelops (Diod. xxvii. 1). He instigated an extreme left-wing regime, involving suppression of the rich, distribution of land, and enfranchisement of helots. He is consistently called *tyrannus* in the sources which, based on Polybius, are very hostile towards him. As he was sole king, his rule could be represented as unconstitutional. But it is clear from xxxiv. 31. 13 that Rome recognized him as king of Sparta.

Nabis had come to power after his predecessor Machanidas had been killed in a battle by Philopoemen (Pol. xi. 18). War between Sparta and Achaea broke out again in 204 (Pol. xiii. 8) and was still continuing in 200 (Pol. xvi. 36–7). Cf. Errington, *Philopoemen*, 77–81, Walbank, *Commentary*, ii. 419–20.

Errington, *Philopoemen*, 78 and n. 3, follows Aymard, *PR*, 39 n. 51, in believing that this war was initially undeclared, and that the present passage concerns the actual declaration of war (Aymard himself put the official declaration at the beginning of 200). But *consultabant de bello* means that they were debating whether to continue to fight Nabis, and if so, how, not whether to declare war on him (cf. § 10 *de exercitu parando adversus Nabim*).

On Nabis see Aymard, *PR*, 32 ff., Ehrenberg, *RE*, xvi. 1471–82, K. M. T. Chrimes, *Ancient Sparta* (Manchester, 1949), 27 ff., C. Mossé, *Cahiers d'histoire* ix (1964), 313–23, *La Tyrannie dans la Grèce antique* (Paris, 1969), 179–92, B. Shimron, *CPh* lxi (1966), 1–7, my comments in *P & P* no. 36 (April 1967), 8 ff., W. G. Forrest, *History of Sparta 950–192 B.C.* (London, 1968), 148 ff.

tralato imperio a Philopoemene ad Cycliadan: Achaean *strategoi* at this time entered office in autumn (Larsen, *Representative Government*, 93).

This is the only reference in these three books to Philopoemen, the most significant Greek statesman of the period. He became *hipparchos* of the League in 210/9 and *strategos* in 208/7 when he reorganized the structure of the League and defeated Machanidas (v.s.). His second *strategia* was in 206/5 and his third in 201/0. From 200–193 he was in self-imposed semi-exile in Crete. Cf. Hoffmann, *RE*, xx. 76–95, Errington, *Philopoemen*, *passim*. (Errington, 250 ff., argues for a *strategia* in 204/3 or 203/2; but this is connected with his chronology of the years 188/7–184/3, on which cf. *JRS* lx [1970], 209).

Cycliadan: Cycliadas was a pro-Macedonian (§ 10): he was expelled after the end of his year of office and later fled to Philip (xxxii. 19. 1 n., 32. 10). He was first *strategos* in 210/9. Cf. Schoch, *RE*, xi. 2321, Lehmann, 207 ff. Here and in §9 the MSS. have created chaos of Cycliadas' name. At xxxii. 19. 2 B has it right and χ's only error is to end in -*m* rather than -*n*. At xxvii. 31. 10 and xxxii. 32. 10 the MSS. preserve the correct reading.

For the view of Errington, *Philopoemen*, 70 ff., that Philopoemen was in favour of alliance with Rome and that the election of Cycliadas was a blow to his policy cf. xxxii. 19–23. 3 n.

auxilia: possibly mercenaries; cf. Aymard, *PR*, 44 n. 71, xxxiii. 15. 3 n.

agrosque . . . terribilis: Aymard, *PR*, 48 n. 82 thinks that L. has condensed Polybius' account and that Nabis did not in fact make fresh military moves until the spring of 199. But if the Macedonians could fight at this time (ch. 26) there is no reason why Nabis could not also.

5. ⟨est⟩ pollicitus . . . tralaturum: Aymard (*RÉA* xlviii [1946], 109 = *ÉHA* 138) rightly stresses that Philip's promise was dictated purely by motives of expediency, and that there is no contradiction with his alliance with Nabis in 198.

McDonald follows Madvig and M. Müller in supplying *est*, and argues that xxiii. 10. 2 is not relevant. That is true enough, for the participle there is subordinate, but the MSS. again omit *est* with *pollicitus* at xxxvii. 36. 2 and for L.'s ellipse of *esse* cf. 21. 5–6 n. It is no objection that *est pollicitus* occurs at xxviii. 9. 17, xli. 20. 6, xliii. 3. 6, and xliv. 7. 5.

7. Oreum: Oreus is the later name of Histiaea on the northern coast of Euboea (cf. Geyer, *RE*, supp. iv. 749–57, P–K, i. 2. 575–6, B. Pace, *Annuario della Regia Scuola archeologica in Atene* iii [1921],

276–82). It was captured in 199 and given to Attalus (46. 6 ff.).
It was probably recaptured by Philip (xxxiii. 31. 3 n.). In 196
Flamininus persuaded the senate, against the advice of the com-
missioners, to grant it freedom (xxxiii. 34. 10, Pol. xviii. 47. 10–11).
The Greek is Ὠρεός and L. has the nominative *Oreus* at xxxiii. 31. 3.
Oreum appears as a nominative at xxviii. 7. 4.

8. pollicitatio: a word avoided by Cicero, but used by Caesar,
Sallust, and Asinius Pollio (cf. L–S s.v.).

9. id quidem . . . ratus: in § 10 L. notes that this is a unique
example of an apparently anti-Macedonian act on the part of
Cycliadas. In fact he will have realized that he had no hope of
carrying the assembly on this occasion and preferred to conserve
his forces by not even trying (cf. Aymard, *PR*, 67).

non licere . . . convocati essent: this rule probably applied to
σύγκλητοι and not to regularly convened σύνοδοι. Cf. Larsen, *Representative Government*, 94. W–M's references to Pol. xxii. 10, L. xxxix.
33. 7 are inappropriate: these passages refer to the rules for the
summoning of a σύγκλητος.

de aliis rebus: the evidence indicates that a σύγκλητος could
discuss only one topic, and the plural here is not to be taken literally. Cf. Aymard, *Assemblées*, 347 n. 5.

referre: cf. xxxii. 20. 4 n. Its precise connotation here cannot be
determined.

26. *Further attacks on Attica*

1. in Achaia: strictly speaking Argos is not in Achaea, but since
it was a member of the Achaean League, and it was a meeting of
the League that had taken place in Argos, the expression is perfectly
natural.

Thracum: probably mercenaries, cf. xxxii. 25. 10, xxxiii. 7.
11 n.

Philocles: cf. 16. 2 n.

regione Eleusinis: 'in the area near Eleusis'. For this use of
regione, common in L., cf. K–St, i. 349–50, Packard, iv. 311–12.

Cithaeronis: Mt. Cithaeron divides Attica from Boeotia.

3. castello: cf. 25. 2 n.

6. cum parte Piraeum pergit: by land, of course.

comminandaque oppugnatione: B and χ have *comminanda
oppugnatione* and with two words in each member the asyndeton is
possible.

8. muri . . . iungit: the long walls from Athens to the Piraeus.
The northern and southern walls (the latter running to Phalerum)

were built in 458/7, the 'middle wall' which made the Piraeus wall into a double wall, *c.* 444–2. The walls were destroyed at the end of the Peloponnesian war and the two northern walls were rebuilt by Conon in 393. They appear to have fallen into disrepair in the course of the third century and were not repaired when Euryclides and Micion undertook the rebuilding of the fortifications of Athens and the Piraeus *c.* 229. They were seen by Paullus in 167 (xlv. 27. 11). Cf. Judeich, 93, 155–60, Lenschau, *RE*, xix. 73, 88–9, A. W. Gomme, *Commentary on Thucydides*, i (Oxford, 1945), 312–13.

9 ff. On these comments on Philip's sacrilegious behaviour cf. 24. 18 n.

10. templa deum : the many shrines scattered throughout Attica. They are the deities called 'the other gods' in the fifth-century 'decrees of Callias' (*IG* i². 91, 92) and the names of a number are given in *IG* i². 310. Cf. also 30. 5–6.

13. ⟨erat⟩ : omitted in the MSS., but added by most editors. McDonald argues that without *erat ira satiata* would have to be taken with *deerat*. But the ellipse of *esse* is common (cf. 21. 5–6 n.) and the understanding of *erat* here would be perfectly natural.

Boeotiam : cf. xxxii. 17. 3 n.

27. *The activities of L. Apustius.* On the topography of events in northern Greece, see Hammond, *JRS* lvi (1966), 39–54. Zonaras ix. 15. 3–4 refers to this campaign and states that Sulpicius was ill for a long time. It is odd that L. has no mention of this and Zonaras may be mistaken (cf. Holleaux, *Études*, iv. 342 n. 3, Walbank, *Philip V*, 138 n. 5. Zonaras' notice is accepted by Badian, *Flamininus*, 35.)

27. 1. inter Apolloniam ac Dyrrachium ad Apsum flumen : on Apollonia cf. 18. 9 n. Dyrrachium is the Roman name for Epidamnus.

Apsum : B has *Hapsum*, which is also the form in the Peutinger table. The river is the mod. Semeni: cf. Hammond, *JRS* lvi (1966), 42. On the site of the camp cf. Walbank, *Philip V*, 138 n. 4, Hammond, l.c.

L. Apustium : cf. 4. 7 n. Zonaras ix. 15 makes him a praetor and it is possible that he was *legatus pro praetore*. Cf. Thiel, 217.

2. Corrhago et Gerrunio et Orgesso : the precise location of these forts is not known. Hammond, *JRS* lvi (1966), 42, suggests that they are on the ridge to the west of Antipatrea. Gerrunium and Orgessos are usually identified with the Gerous and Orgussos of Pol. v. 108. 8. Cf. Hammond, *JRS* lviii (1968), 16 n. 55.

ad Antipatream: Antipatrea is usually located at the modern Berat. Hammond, *JRS* lvi (1966), 42, reports that he has seen traces of Macedonian foundation courses there and refers to recent archaeological evidence of the town having been destroyed by fire (cf. § 4).

3. **ut fidei Romanorum se committerent**: i.e. they are asked to make a *deditio in fidem* to Rome. This means an unconditional surrender, after which Rome can treat the surrendered people as she pleases—though the understanding is that she will normally act with generosity. On the *deditio* procedure cf. Heuss, *Völkerrechtlichen Grundlagen* (1. 9–10 n.), 60 ff., A. Piganiol, *RIDA* v (1950), 339–47, Badian, *FC*, 4–7, V. Bellini, *RD* xlii (1964), 448–57, S. Calderone, πίστις–fides (Messina, 1964), C. Becker, *RLAC*, vii. 812 ff., W. Flurl, *Deditio in Fidem* (cf. 216–17 on this episode). On *fides Romana* cf. Merten, *passim*.

5. **Codrionem**: thus the MSS. Madvig and Harant read *Codrione*, as a nominative, Madvig (*Emendationes*, 467) arguing that an attraction into the accusative is impossible. But such attractions are found (cf. xxiii. 10. 3, xxxiv. 61. 4, xliv. 40. 1) and the accusative should be retained. Cf. Riemann, 16 n. 1, Tränkle, *Gnomon*, 371 n. 2, K–St, ii. 581: see also xxxiii. 40. 5 n.

Hammond, *JRS* lvi (1966), 43 (cf. *Epirus*, 586) identifies Codrio with Rrmait to the north-east of Antipatrea.

6. **Cnidus**: position unknown. W–M quote Callimachus, *Hymn to Demeter*, 24, who says that the Cnidians used to live in Δώτιον ἱρόν (which is near Lake Boebeis in the south of Thessaly) and Plutarch, *QGr.* 13, who says that the Aenianes migrated from this area to Illyria. Nobody says that the Aenianes went to Cnidus, and there is thus no implication that the name Cnidus went from Thessaly to Asia via our Cnidus.

in Asia: Cnidus is at the end of a long peninsula sticking out into the Aegean between Cos and Rhodes. Cf. G. E. Bean and J. M. Cook, *ABSA* xlvii (1952), 171–212, lii (1957), 85–87, Cook and D. J. Blackman, *AR* 1970–1, 52–4.

Athenagoras: a leading Macedonian general in the Second Macedonian War, cf. 35. 1, 40. 8, 43. 1, xxxii. 5. 9, xxxiii. 7. 11, Pol. xviii. 22. 2.

fluminis: i.e. the Apsus.

8. **ad classem**: cf. 44. 1.

28. *Winter 200/199: activities of Sulpicius and Philip*

28. 1. **reguli ac principes**: Zon. ix. 15. 4 says that Ἰλλυριοί τινες and Amynander joined Rome. It may be that Polybius said that

several kings and princes came to the Romans and went on to specify Pleuratus, Amynander, and Bato as the most important of them.

In Illyria and other places in this region society was still organized in a rather tribalized, feudal fashion. We can see from the events of Rome's first ventures in Illyria that though Teuta was nominally sovereign of all Illyria, in fact people like Demetrius of Pharos and Scerdilaidas had considerable independence, and the precise delineation of authority is obscure. It would thus be plausible to think that minor princes from Illyria and perhaps from Dardania as well came to Sulpicius' camp at this time. *principes* has the sense here of 'leading men'. Cf. 17. 11 n.

Pleuratus Scerdilaedi filius: Scerdilaidas had fought for Teuta at Phoenice (Pol. ii. 5. 6 ff.): in 220 he joined Demetrius of Pharos in his expedition south of Lissus (Pol. iv. 16. 6 ff.) and collaborated with the Aetolians (ibid., and iv. 29. 5): he then joined Philip (Pol. iv. 29. 2, v. 3. 3) but later quarrelled with him (Pol. v. 95, 101, 108). In 216 Scerdilaidas informed the Romans of Philip's move against Apollonia in 216 (Pol. v. 110. 8). He is last heard of in the First Macedonian War in 208 (xxviii. 5. 7, Pol. x. 41. 4). His son Pleuratus is associated with him in the kingship by 212/11 (xxvi. 24. 9, cf. xxviii. 5. 7, Pol. x. 41. 4) but appears as sole king by the time of the Peace of Phoenice in 205 (xxix. 5. 14).

The MSS. here read *Scerdilevi*. The Greek form of the name is Σκερδιλαίδας. At xxvi. 24. 9 and xxviii. 5. 7 the best MSS. have *Scerdilaedus* or *Scerdiledus* and we should clearly read *Scerdilaedi* here.

Amynander Athamanum rex: Athamania is in the south-east of Epirus. It seems to have broken away from Epirus *c*. 230 and became independent. Amynander was a relation of Scerdilaidas (Pol. iv. 16. 9). He was brought into the peace negotiations of 209 as a mediator by the Aetolians (xxvii. 30. 3) and in 207 again appears as a mediator (App. *Mac.* 3). In 206 he allowed Philip to pass through his territory and enabled him to force the Aetolians to come to terms (xxxvi. 31. 11). In 201 the Roman *legati* visited him on their way to Athens (Pol. xvi. 27. 4). See further 41. 6–7, xxxii. 13. 15 ff., 32. 11, 36. 10, xxxiii. 12. 2, 34. 11.

In the literary sources Amynander is always called king, but no coins and inscriptions refer to him in this way, and an inscription of the end of the third century (Welles, *Royal Correspondence*, no. 35) refers to 'King Theodorus and Amynander'. On the other hand, Pol. xviii. 10. 7 (cf. xxxii. 36. 10 n.) clearly implies that he was officially king. It is possible, then, that he was originally guardian of Theodorus but *c*. 200 became king in his own right. Cf. Oost, *CPh* lii (1957), 1 ff., Welwei, 118 ff., *Historia* xiv (1965), 252–6.

ex Dardanis . . . patre gesserat: the Dardanians, on the northern frontiers of Macedon, were a constant source of danger to the rulers of Macedon, and a natural ally for Rome. For other Dardanian conflicts in this period cf. Pol. iv. 29. 1 (220/19), Pol. iv. 66 (219), L. xxvi. 25. 3 (211), xxvii. 33. 1, Just. xxix. 4. 6 (209), L. xxviii. 8. 14 (208), Diod. xxviii. 2 (204). See also 43. 1–3 and Hammond, *ABSA* lxi (1966), 249.

Longari: both here and in the next sentence φ has *Langarus*, but there is no reason at all to think that there is any connection with the Langarus of the Agrianes mentioned by Arrian, *Anab.* i. 5. 2–5. The Agrianes were a Thracian tribe and lived to the east of the Dardanians. (Cf. Walbank, *Commentary*, i. 274.)

2. Demetrio: Demetrius II reigned from 239–229. He was defeated by the Dardanians towards the end of his reign (Just. xxviii. 3, Niese, ii. 277, 286–7).

3. Amynandro Aetolos concitandos: on the Aetolians cf. 15. 10. For Amynander's relations with them § 1 n.

Attali . . . Aeginae rex: evidently Attalus has just returned to Aegina. That he had not remained there all summer is shown by 16. 7–8, though he had been delayed a long time by the Aetolians (15. 9).

classem Romanam: i.e. the rest of Sulpicius' fleet together with that of Valerius (cf. W–M ad loc. and 3. 3) are to join Centho at Aegina. For the numbers sent to join Attalus in 199 cf. 44. 1 n. Philip's fleet was at Demetrias (33. 1–2) and did not dare to undertake any operations (cf. Thiel, 232–3).

sicut ante: for L.'s use of *ante* in preference to *antea* cf. Ogilvie, 585.

5. filium Persea, puerum admodum: Perseus, king of Macedon from 179 until his defeat at Pydna in 168. He was about 13 at the time. L. is wrong at xxvi. 25. 4–6 in thinking that the Perseus there referred to is Philip's son. On the issue and the date of the birth of Perseus cf. Holleaux, *Études*, iv. 115–23, Meloni, *Perseo*, 16–17, R. G. Hopital, *RD* xlii (1964), 240 n. 32.

ex amicorum numero: *amicorum* here is a technical term for the court advisers (φίλοι): on them cf. Holleaux, *Études*, iv. 116 n. 3, Walbank, *Philip V*, 3, Meloni, *Perseo*, 18 n. 3.

angustias quae ad Pelagoniam sunt: Pelagonia must be the district in the north of Macedon, not the town mentioned in xlv. 29. 9 and identical with Heraclea Lyncestis, as argued by Ober-hummer, *RE*, xix. 244. (Though the use of *ad* suggests that L. may have thought it was the town; cf. 33. 6 n.) Most writers have placed these *angustiae* in the valley of the Axius (cf. Kromayer, ii. 28 n. 1, Walbank, *Philip V*, 142 and n. 4, Meloni, *Perseo*, 20 ff.). Hammond, however (*JRS* lvi [1966], 43 and n. 16, *Epirus*, 615), argues that they are in the upper valley of the Erigon, which flows into the Axius. His reason for this is that he thinks that Philip's aim was not just to prevent a Dardanian attack (cf. 33. 3) but to prevent a junction between the Roman and Dardanian forces. There is, however, nothing in the evidence about such a junction and, while Hammond could be right, he has not produced any arguments against the traditional view.

6. Sciathum et Peparethum : these are islands off the southern tip of Magnesia: cf. P–K, iv. 41–7. Peparethos had been attacked by Attalus in 208 (xxviii. 5, Pol. x. 42). Peparethos appears to have been restored after the war; cf. *Syll.*³ 587, Herbst, *RE*, xix. 555.

29–32. Spring 199. The conference of the Aetolian League

L. takes the opportunity of the meeting of the Aetolian League to present a full-scale debate. Polybius, no doubt, also had speeches at this point, but they will have been elaborated by L. The occasion was clearly of importance. The debate concerned the vital decision by one of the two great Greek federations on whether to throw in their lot with Rome, and involved discussion of Roman motives and Roman imperialism. L. alternates direct and indirect speech. The Macedonian accusations against Rome in ch. 29 are balanced by the Roman replies in ch. 31, whilst the accusations against Philip are almost wholly contained in the *oratio obliqua* of the Athenian speech. The whole debate is thus given a carefully contrived balance.

On the debate, see especially Zancan, 87 ff., Brueggmann, 27 ff., Burck, *Wege zu Livius*, 452 ff., *Vom Menschenbild in der römischen Literatur* (Heidelberg, 1966), 330–1, Heidemann, 18 ff., 28 ff.; on the structure of the speeches cf. pp. 20–1.

29. 1. Concilium Aetolorum stata die, quod Panaetoli⟨c⟩um vocant: the details of the Aetolian assemblies are examined in a short but typically brilliant article by Holleaux (*Études*, i. 219–27). There were two regular assemblies of the Aetolians. One, held in autumn, and at which the elections took place, was called τὰ Θερμικά and always held in Thermus. L. misunderstood the name to refer to Thermopylae and hence mistranslated it *Pylaicum* (32. 4, xxxiii. 35. 8). The second was the Παναιτωλικά, held in the spring and at various places, in this instance at Naupactus (29. 8). Cf. especially 32. 3–4 and epigraphic evidence adduced by Holleaux, 223. This assembly is held in the spring of 199. Cf. also Larsen, *TAPA* lxxxiii (1952), 1–33, Walbank, *Commentary*, i. 453–4.

At 32. 3 and xxxv. 32. 7 *Panaetolicum* is used and Holleaux plausibly argues (222 n. 2) that this is what we should read here.

vocant: cf. 24. 4 n.

L. Furius Purpurio legatus: (86, 87). Quite possibly identical with the praetor of 200 (cf. 4. 4 n., 10. 5, 21–2). He had gone out of office a few months previously (the events described in 47. 6 ff. are earlier than those here). Cf. Münzer, *RE*, vii. 364, *MRR*, i. 329 n. 4, and 47. 4–49. 3, 49. 8–11 n.

2. recentissimum: i.e. the peace of 206 whilst the Romano–Aetolian alliance had been in 212/11.

3. experta . . . fecissent: a rather odd way of putting it. They had not preferred Philip to Rome, but had been deserted by Rome and left with no alternative but to make peace. Cf. 1. 8 n., 31. 18.

compositam semel pacem: for the emphatic repetition W–M rightly refer to ii. 64. 1 (cf. Ogilvie, 388).

4. licentiam, an levitatem dicam: for the *correctio* cf. 7. 8 n., Ullmann, *Étude*, 66.

Qui cum . . . fecistis: an Aetolian appeal to Rome is also mentioned by Appian, *Mac.* 4. Appian, however, places it after the Rhodian embassy in 201. Holleaux (*Rome*, 293 n. 1) argued that it was impossible for such an appeal to be rejected at the very time that the senate was preparing for war. He therefore placed the appeal in 202, and its rejection played an important part in his view that the senate had no intention of fighting Philip until it heard the news of the pact with Antiochus.

It is certainly hard to accept Appian's dating of the episode: but both Holleaux's date of 202 and attempts to reject the embassy altogether involve unnecessary violence to the evidence. The embassy could still belong to 201, but could precede the Rhodian and Attalid embassies. The senate would then have been unimpressed by news of Philip's aggressions against the faithless Aetolians: it would be appeals from Rhodes and Attalus that proved decisive. Cf. pp. 45–6.

Appian's date is defended by Bickermann, *RPh* 3ème série, ix (1935), 162 n. 4, Meloni, *Valore storico*, 45–9, Ferro, 46 ff. Holleaux's date is supported by Walbank, *CR* n.s. xii (1962), 273, and McDonald *JRS* liii (1963), 188. The episode is rejected by V. Costanzi, *Studi storici per l'antichità classica* i (1908), 423 ff., T. Walek, *Eos* xxxi (1928), 372, A. Passerini, *Ath.* n.s. ix (1931), 266 n. 1, Badian, *Latomus* xvii (1958), 208. In favour of the authenticity of the embassy, see Dorey, *CR* n.s. x (1960), 9.

5. propter vos et pro vobis: a claim repeated by the Romans in

31. 18, and attributed to them by a Rhodian envoy in 207 (Pol. xi. 6. 2). In 212 the Romans must have convinced the Aetolians that it was in their interest to join Rome. The treaty was very favourable to the Aetolians who received the towns captured and half the booty (xxvi. 24. 9 ff., *StV*, iii. 536: cf. xxxiii. 13. 9–12 n.). But they can hardly have claimed at the beginning that they were acting in Greece for the sake of the Aetolians. For similar Greek views of Roman imperialism at this time cf. Walbank, *JRS* liii (1963), 8 ff., lv (1965), 3. Cf. also i. 8, 31. 18, xxxii. 21. 18 nn.

6. Messanae: cf. 7. 3 n.

iterum ut Syracusas: Sicily had been in Roman possession since 241 and was organized as a province in 227. Syracuse was a free ally of Rome and defected to Carthage in 214 in the turmoil that followed the death of Hieron. Rome's propaganda claim, repeated in 31. 8, is that in besieging Syracuse she was trying to 'free' it from Carthaginian domination. Cf. xxv. 28. 7. On the defection of Syracuse cf. Pol. vii. 2–8, L. xxiv. 4–7. 9, 21–32, De Sanctis, iii. 2. 263 ff.

7. et Messanam et Syracusas: again misleading. Originally Messana and Syracuse were *civitates foederatae* free from tax. After the secession of Syracuse this status was retained by Tauromenium and Netum, previously part of the Syracusan state. In addition Centuripae, Halaesa, Halicyae, Panormus, and Segesta were *liberae et immunes* though not possessing treaties. Other states paid *vectigal* to the governor, being a tenth of their produce. On the organization of Sicily cf. Marquardt, *StV*, i. 242 ff., J. Carcopino, *La Loi de Hiéron et les Romains* (Paris, 1919), V. M. Scramuzza, *Economic Survey*, iii. 327 ff., Badian, *FC*, 36 ff., Toynbee, ii. 218 ff.

securibus et fascibus: the *insignia* of the *imperium* of the governors of Sicily.

8. scilicet: for this use of *scilicet* to introduce heavy irony cf. Ogilvie, 430.

Naupacti: cf. § 1 n. This passage must mean that the meeting in question took place at Naupactus. Cf. Holleaux, *Études*, i. 222 n. 4.

concilium . . . conventus: *conventus* here means 'assizes', courts conducted by the *praetor* (cf. *TLL*, iv. 849). They are not to be confused with the *conventus civium Romanorum* in Sicily (cf. Scramuzza, *Economic Survey*, iii. 338). They are also recorded at Syracuse, Lilybaeum, Agrigentum, Panormus, and Aetna (Cic. *II Verr.* 2. 63, 3. 27, 3. 38, 3. 57, 5. 16 (cf. Carcopino, *La Loi de Hiéron et les Romains*, 157). *II Verr.* 4. 55 and 5. 140, adduced by Marquardt, *StV*, i. 247, in fact refer to *conventus civium Romanorum*. Although

Messana was a *civitas foederata*, it is not improbable that *conventus* were held there. For *conventus* in free cities in Asia cf. Magie, *RRAM*, 172.

9. praetor . . . imminent: a vivid picture of the typical apparatus of a Roman governor.

sortiuntur: 'they find themselves given by lot'.

10–11. Italiae urbes . . . sine magistratibus: again the statement is misleading, as there are important differences in the status of the three cities mentioned.

Rhegium had been under Roman protection since *c.* 280 when Rome garrisoned it with Campanian troops. The Campanians subsequently massacred the Rhegines but were expelled by Rome in 270. (Cf. 31. 6–7, *per.* xii, xv, Diod. xxii. 1, D.H. xx. 4–5, 16, Zon. viii. 6, Strabo vi. p. 258c, Oros. iv. 3. 3–5. See Philipp, *RE*, iA. 500, Walbank, *Commentary*, i. 52–3). It was loyal in the Hannibalic War, and its position therefore remained unchanged. It was bound by treaty to provide military help, but otherwise independent (cf. Philipp, *RE*, iA. 500–1).

Tarentum had been an ally of Rome since surrendering in 272. Although her defection to Hannibal was the responsibility of a minority (xxv. 8 ff., Pol. viii. 24–34) her independence seems to have been considerably reduced after her recapture. (Cf. P. Wuilleumier, *Tarente des origines à la conquête romaine* [Paris, 1939], 167, Brunt, 279.)

Capua had become a *civitas sine suffragio* in 338 and retained considerable internal independence (cf. Toynbee, i. 214–15). She defected from Rome in 216 and after her recapture in 211 all traces of independence were removed, the state being administered by *praefecti* sent from Rome: cf. xxvi. 16. 10, Toynbee, i. 242 ff. The language of § 11 is in accordance with the *s.c.* recorded in xxvi. 34 providing for the whole of the population of Capua to be removed elsewhere. But the evidence suggests that this *s.c.* was never put into effect. Cf. Toynbee, i. 242, ii. 121 ff.

ne finitimas . . . nominem: L. is thinking, no doubt, of towns actually destroyed like Veii in 396 (v. 1–23) or Alba in legendary days (i. 29: cf. xxvi. 13. 16). But more generally the reference is to the many states which lost their corporate identity and became merged in the *ager Romanus*. Cf. Toynbee, i. 115 ff.

sepulcrum ac monumentum: for the *amplificatio* cf. Ullmann, *Étude*, 23.

deiecta: B, *deleta* χ. McDonald defends *deiecta* by comparing xli. 2. 11 *praetorio deiecto*. Ogilvie, *Phoenix*, 344, objects that cities, unlike tents, cannot be thrown down and supports *deleta*. But Vergil, *A.* xii. 655 *deiecturum arces Italum* seems a close enough parallel: cf. also Tac.

Ann. xv. 40, *TLL*, v. 1. 395. Whether one punctuates after *prodigium* or after *relicta* seems to me to make no difference to the argument.

12–15. For this view of Rome as barbarians cf. the speech of Agelaus in 217 (Pol. v. 104. 1), of Lyciscus in 210 (Pol. ix. 37. 6) and of Thrasycrates in 207 (Pol. xi. 4 ff.). See also Walbank, *JRS* liii (1963), 8 ff., Schmitt, *Hellenen, Römer und Barbaren* (Aschaffenburg, 1958), Deininger, 23–37. The establishment of the Trojan legend of Rome's origin helped to reinforce the idea of perpetual enmity between Greeks and Romans. When Greek elements (Odysseus) remained in the story, Rome could be regarded as a Greek city (thus Heraclides Ponticus *ap.* Plut. *Cam.* 22. 2 ff.). The striking statement in § 15 of an *aeternum bellum* has many pedigrees in Greek thought. It formed part of the sharp distinction between Greeks and barbarians that grew up after the Persian Wars. Herodotus (i. 1–4) saw the Trojan War as the origin of the Persian Wars (cf. especially i. 4. 4) and Plato spoke of Greeks and barbarians as being πολεμίους φύσει (*Rep.* v. 470c5). The idea naturally formed part of the pan-Hellenic ideas of Isocrates (cf. *Pan.* 157–8). See also Gorgias *DK* 82 B 5b, Eur. *Hec.* 1199, Dem. *Meid.* 49, Lyc. *Alex.* 1283 ff. On Macedonian claims to be fully Greek cf. Walbank, *Commentary*, ii. 176, A. Daskalakis, *The Hellenism of the Ancient Macedonians* (Thessaloniki, 1965). On the use of *barbarus* by Latin writers to refer to Rome cf. Austin, *Commentary on Vergil, Aeneid ii*, 195. Add Cic. *de r. p.* i. 58.

13. fidem . . . desiderat : for possible attacks by Philip on Aetolian allies cf. 1. 9–10 n. In asking the Aetolians to maintain *fides* towards Philip, the speaker is turning against Rome her own propaganda weapon. Cf. Burck, *Wege zu Livius*, 456.

14. socium Philippum quaeretis : a *post eventum* prediction. In 193 the Aetolians appealed to Philip to join themselves, Nabis, and Antiochus in 'freeing' Greece from Roman domination (xxxv. 12. 6).

15. eiusdem linguae : on the language of the Macedonians cf. Toynbee, *Some Problems in Greek History* (London, 1969), 64 ff.

   alienigenis : Isocrates, *Philippos*, 154, described those who were neither Greek nor Macedonian as τὸ τῶν ἄλλων γένος.

16. triennio ante : cf. 1. 8 n.

30. *The Athenian Speech*

30. 1. introducti sunt : as W–M point out, the word means 'brought forward to speak', not 'brought into the meeting'.

2. belli iura : the passage implies that these are the rights of the combatants to inflict injury, not a set of rules prohibiting certain actions. This is also the meaning of all the references to the *ius belli* in L. (cf. Packard, i. 578, ii. 1383, 1385. Ogilvie, 688 misrepresents the meaning of v. 27. 6), and of πολέμου νόμοι in Pol. ii. 58. 10, v. 9. 1, 11. 3–4. But to do more than the laws of war allowed would amount to transgressing them, as is implied by Pol. vii. 14. 3. There was, however, clearly no agreement on what actions were prohibited. To protest against acts considered excessive, appeal could be made to the more general 'laws of mankind' as in Pol. ii. 58. 6, or to the *humana iura* here (§ 4). Cf. R. von Scala, *Die Studien des Polybios* (Stuttgart, 1890), 310–16, F. Kiechle, *Historia* vii (1958), 150–3, Walbank, *Commentary*, i. 264, 549, Ducrey, 289–95, *Problèmes de la guerre en Grèce ancienne*, ed. J.-P. Vernant (Paris, 1968), 231 ff., G. Gandolfi, *Archivio Giuridico*, 6ª serie, xvi (1954), 7 ff.

3. sata exuri : for the destruction of crops as a legitimate action in war cf. Plato, *Rep.* 470a, Pol. v. 11. 3, xxiii. 15. 1, von Scala, op. cit., 313–14.

praedas hominum : for enslavement of the defeated and captured as a right of the conqueror cf. Volkmann, 7 ff.

4. verum enim vero : for this very strong phrase cf. Ogilvie, 537.

omnia . . . polluerit : for the language cf. 24. 18, xxv. 40. 2, Sall. *Cat.* 11. 6, Skard, 16.

priore . . . gesserit : the *prior populatio* is the one described in ch. 24, the *secunda* that of 26. 5 ff. (cf. *priorem populationem* in 26. 9). The *bellum cum infernis deis* refers to the desecration of graves (cf. § 5 and 24. 18), that *cum superis* to the attack on the local shrines in the second invasion (26. 10).

5. sepulcra monumentaque : deliberately taking up *sepulcrum ac monumentum* in 29. 11.

manes : here the 'shades of the buried'. It is a later development of the meaning 'spirits of the underworld'. Contrary to W–M the meaning is the same as in iii. 19. 1. Cf. Ogilvie, 429.

6. delubra : 26. 10.

quae . . . reliquerint : a striking anacoluthon. The syntax requires *consecraverint nec*. . . . But the sense is clear enough and, as editors have seen, it is clearly what L. wrote. Cf. Tränkle, *WS*, 142.

pagatim habitantes . . . reliquerint : the synoecism of Attica, legendarily attributed to Theseus (cf. especially Thuc. ii. 15. 2) but probably much later (cf. C. Hignett, *A History of the Athenian Constitution* [Oxford, 1952], 34–7, who envisages a gradual process culminating in the eighth century). The synoecism was a political unification, not a migration of population.

7. truncata : taking up *trunca* in 29. 11.

9. arcis Minervam petitam: i.e. Athena as the chief goddess worshipped on the Acropolis. The Athenians argue that if Philip had been successful in his attack on Athens he would have desecrated the Acropolis.

Eleusine Cereris: 25. 2, 26. 4. On the form of the name cf. 25. 2 n.

10. Piraei Iovem Minervamque: for the attack on the Piraeus cf. 26. 6 ff. The two temples were close together and referred to as the Disoterion. The colonnades contained many paintings. The precise location is uncertain, cf. Judeich, 453, J. G. Frazer, *Commentary on Pausanias* (London, 1898), ii. 22–4.

31. The Roman Speech

31. 1. Romanus legatus: L. Furius Purpurio (29. 1).

2. socias . . . urbes: of those listed in § 4 Rome's only *socii* (even in the weak sense of being *amici*) are the Messenians, and, in so far as they were Egyptian, Samos, Aenus, and Maronea. Cf. 1. 9–10 n.

3. inferos superosque: a hysteron-proteron, cf. Ullmann, *Étude*, 91.

4. Cianos: B has a blank here and the second hand reads *chios*. The χ group have *hechios* or *echios*. But *Cianos* must be correct. It is repeated in conjunction with Abydos in xxxii. 21. 22 (B there has *Clani*, which must represent *Ciani*; the χ group have the nonsensical *Elani* or *Elatii*) and while Philip's assault on Chios in 201 was unsuccessful (Walbank, *Philip V*, 121 and n. 2) his treatment of Cius in 202 was well known (Pol. xv. 21 ff., xviii. 3. 12, 4. 7, 5. 4, L. xxxii. 33. 16, 34. 6, Steph. Byz. s.v. Προῦσα, Strabo xii. p. 563c, Memnon *FGH* 434 F1 (19), *OGIS* 340).

Abydenos: 16. 6–18. 9.

Aenios Maronitas: 16. 4.

Thasios: captured in 202, after the capture of Cius. Pol. xv. 24. Cf. xxxiii. 30. 3.

Parios: cf. 15. 8 n.

Samios: cf. p. 37 n. 5.

Larisenses: it is clear that *Messenios* (v. i.) refers to events of 215 and 214 and hence this passage is no argument for the view that the towns of Phthiotic Achaea were attacked in 202 or 201 (cf. Holleaux, *Études*, iv. 126). If there was no such attack, the reference is to the capture of Larisa in (probably) 210. Cf. 1. 9–10 n.

The MSS. have *Lamsenses* or *Lansenses* but the correct reading is not in doubt.

Messenios: Philip's intervention in Messene took place in 215 and 214. In 215 he endeavoured to inflame already existing factional disputes: he contemplated installing a garrison in the acropolis but was dissuaded by Aratus (Pol. vii. 11. 10, 12. 9, 13. 6–7, 14. 2–5, L. xxxii. 21. 23, Plut. *Aratus* 49. 2 ff., Holleaux, *Rome*, 197 n. 5, Walbank, *Aratus*, 202, *Philip V*, 300–1). In 214 Philip ravaged Messenian territory and attempted to seize Messene itself (Pol. iii. 19. 11, viii. 8a, Plut. *Aratus* 51, Walbank, *Aratus*, loc. cit., *Philip V*, loc. cit.).

ex Achaia : an inaccurate expression, as Messene was not in Achaea geographically, nor did she become a member of the Achaean League until 191 (xxxvi. 31). Messene had become a member of the symmachy in 220 (Pol. iv. 16. 1) but had joined Rome in the First Macedonian War (Pol. ix. 30. 6) and was included in the Roman *adscripti* to the peace of Phoenice (xxix. 12. 14).

6–7. Regium . . . reddidimus : M. Gelzer (*Hermes* lxviii [1933], 136) regards these words as reflecting Fabius Pictor's defence of Rome's conduct towards Rhegium. Fabius may well have defended it in this way, but this version of events will have been that commonly accepted at Rome.

6. a nobis : B omits these words. After *nobis obiecit* in the previous sentence repetition is somewhat harsh, and omission is preferable.

8. Syracusanis : cf. 29. 6 n.

externis tyrannis : the Carthaginian agents Hippocrates and Epicydes.

cum iam ipsi . . . mallent : an interesting admission of the Syracusans' own preferences, assorting oddly with the view that they were being suppressed.

liberatam : subject to the qualifications described in §9.

9. stipendiarias nobis et vectigales : both phrases mean 'paying tribute' and there is no special reference to Roman *ager publicus* in Sicily which was let out by the censors (on this cf. Toynbee, ii. 218 n. 4).

10 ff. According to vii. 31 Capua made a *deditio* to Rome in 343 (Varr.) and a *foedus* was granted to them. (Toynbee, i. 401, wrongly rejects the possibility of a *foedus* following a *deditio*; cf. Heuss, *Klio* Bhft. xxxi (1933), 78–83, Dahlheim, 69 ff.). In 340 Capua helped the Latins in their revolt but the *equites Campani* remained loyal and were granted *civitas* (probably *sine suffragio*): cf. viii. 11. 16, Cassola, *GP*, 122 n. 4, Toynbee, i. 402 ff. In 338 the rest of the Campanians were given the same status (viii. 14. 10—Vell. Pat. i. 14. 3 dates it to 334).

Intermarrying between Roman and Campanian families was, as

L. suggests, an early feature of Romano–Campanian relations. Cf. viii. 3. 3, xxiii. 4. 7, xxvi. 33. 3, xxxviii. 36. 5, Cassola, *GP*, 122 n. 3, Salmon, *Samnium*, 329. There may have been even earlier connections—there is a case for thinking that the Atilii had come to Rome from Cales, perhaps with the support of the Fabii (Münzer, *RA*, 56 ff.), but *contra* cf. J. Beloch, *Römische Geschichte* (Berlin, 1926), 338, L. R. Taylor, *Voting Districts of the Roman Republic* (Rome, 1960), 180 n. 33, Cassola, *GP*, 153.

pro iis . . . gessissemus: the period is from 343 until the final defeat in 272. On these years see Salmon, *Samnium*, 187–292. The claim to be fighting for the Campanians, like that to be fighting for the Aetolians (§ 18) is, of course, grossly distorted.

11. deinde . . . atque inde cognationibus: B omits *inde*. McDonald defends it on the grounds that the relationships flowed from the marriages, as is implied by xxvi. 33. 3. Indeed they did, but *deinde . . . inde* is harsh, and the sense remains clear without *inde*.

12. tempore . . . defecerunt: cf. xxiii. 2 ff.
praesidio . . . interfecto: xxiii. 7. 3.
deinde . . . miserunt: Hannibal marched on Rome in 211 as a final attempt to relieve Capua, but made no serious effort to attack the city (xxvi. 7–11, Pol. ix. 3–7, for other sources *MRR*, i. 272). Cf. Salmon, *Phoenix* xi (1957), 153–63, E. W. Davis, *Phoenix* xiii (1959), 113–20. *miserunt* is ironical. Hannibal acted on his own initiative.

14. plures . . . consciverunt: xxvi. 14. 3–5.
ceteris . . . daremus: cf. 29. 10–11 n.

15. Carthagini: for the peace terms with Carthage cf. xxx. 37, Pol. xv. 18, *MRR*, i. 317.
Flamininus refers to Roman generosity to Carthage in xxxiii. 12. 7, Pol. xviii. 37. 3. Cf. also xxxvii. 34. 4, Flurl, 96 n. 1.

16. ad experiundam . . . fortunam belli: for L.'s fondness for the phrase *experiri fortunam belli* cf. Kajanto, 78.

17. domestica parricidia: anachronistic, as the reference is to the events leading up to the execution of Demetrius in 182 (cf. pp. 23–4).
cognatorum amicorumque caedes: *amicorum* can be taken in its technical sense (cf. 28. 5 n.) and the reference will be to the removal of Leontius, Megaleas, and Apelles in 218 (Pol. v. 27–9, Walbank, *Philip V*, 52–60, Errington, *Historia* xvi [1967], 19–36), and the execution of five φίλοι in 204 (Diod. xxviii. 2). None of these, however, is known to have been a *cognatus* of Philip. He is also accused of murdering both the elder and younger Aratus (xxxii.

21. 23, Pol. viii. 12. 2–8, Plut. *Aratus* 52. 1, 54. 2–3, Paus. ii. 9. 4, Walbank, *Philip V*, 79 n. 6, *Commentary*, ii. 87–8), Euryclides and Micion in Athens (Paus. ii. 9. 4, Walbank, *Philip V*, 124 n. 7) and Chariteles (xxxii. 21. 23, Walbank, *Philip V*, 79 n. 2), and of attempting to murder Philopoemen (cf. Plut. *Phil.* 12. 2, Paus. viii. 50. 4, Just. xxix. 4. 11, cf. Aymard, *PR*, 63 n. 65). The Arati and Chariteles could be described as *amici* in a non-technical sense, but again none was related to Philip.

libidinem: with particular reference to his abduction of Polycrateia (cf. xxxii. 21. 24 n.). Cf. also the description of his behaviour at the Nemean games of 209 (xxvii. 31. 5, Pol. x. 26, Plut. *Mor.* 760A–B, Walbank, *Commentary*, ii. 230).

18. Hopital (*RD* xlii [1964], 232 n. 81) points out that this is a translation of Xenophon, *Hell.* vii. 4. 40. It is not clear whether this is due to Polybius or to L. himself. Probably the former, for Polybius knew the work of Xenophon (cf. vi. 45. 1, x. 20. 7) and we know also of the fondness of Scipio Aemilianus for Xenophon (Cic. *TD* ii. 62, *ad Q.fr.* i. 1. 23).

pro vobis: cf. 1. 8, 29. 5 nn.

19. Et forsitan . . . accepisse: which was in fact the truth.
alia maiora: the invasion of Africa.

20. As in 11. 10 we have here the view that revenge is a Roman motive in going to war with Macedon, and the Peace of Phoenice is seen as merely a pause in a continuing conflict. Cf. pp. 39–40 and Balsdon, *JRS* liv (1954), 32 n. 15.

restituendi . . . societatemque: officially the *amicitia* between Rome and Aetolia had come to an end in 206 (cf. 1. 9–10 n.: xxxiii. 13. 9–12 n.).

perire . . . mavultis: taking up the language of §8.

32. *The Aetolian decision*

32. 1. Damocritus praetor: the Aetolian *strategos* for 200/199, cf. 40. 9, 41. 1, 11, 43. 6. He was an ambassador to Rome after the conference of Nicaea (Pol. xviii. 10. 9). He was later a leader of the anti-Roman movement in Aetolia, being *strategos* a second time in 193/2. Cf. xxxv. 12. 6, xxxvi. 24. 12, xxxviii. 10. 6.

2. rem . . . celeritatem: for this idea cf. Thuc. iii. 42. 1, Soph. *O.T.* 617, Publilius Syrus I. 25.

3–4. cum legibus . . . actum esset: L. may have misunderstood Polybius here. Special assemblies deal with peace and war in Pol. iv. 15. 8–9, L. xxvi. 24. 1. Cf. Larsen, *TAPA* lxxxiii (1952), 16 n. 27.

3. in Panaetolico et Pylaico: cf. 29. 1 n. The MSS. make non-sense of *Pylaico* here, but read it correctly below.

4. decernerent ut . . . actum esset: L. reproduces the decision in Roman legal language. Both *ius ratumque* and *sine fraude* are found, for example, in official documents recorded in Cael. *ap.* Cic. *fam.* viii. 8. 3 and 5.

5. nam . . . inclinaturos: the same policy of waiting to see which side was winning is ascribed to Philip at the time of the Hannibalic war (xxiii. 33. 3).

Haec . . . acta: L. thus indicates the end of the episode concerning the meeting of the Aetolian League. Cf. Witte, 380.

33–40. 6. *The campaign of Sulpicius in 199*

The campaign is briefly described in Dio fr. 58, Zon. ix. 15. 5–6.

33. 1. Demetriadem: cf. 24. 1 n. We have not heard anything of the activities of Philip's fleet since its return from Abydus.

2. principio veris: cf. 22. 4—47. 3 n.
    ab Aegina: cf. 28. 3.
    Heraclidam . . . praefecerat: cf. 16. 3 n. At 46. 8 and xxxii. 5. 7 the MSS. have *Heraclides, -en,* and the dative at 16. 3 is *Heraclidi.* But L. may not have been consistent on the point. The Greek form is Ἡρακλείδης.

3. Aetolos: by preventing them from joining Rome (29–32).
    Dardanos . . . interclusis: cf. 28. 5 n.

4. per Dassaretiorum fines: on Sulpicius' route cf. Hammond, *JRS* lvi (1966), 43, who argues convincingly that he advanced across the hills to the south of Lake Lychnitis, and not as Kromayer, ii. 13, and Walbank, *Philip V,* 142, say, up the valley of the Genusus. Dassaretis is the area to the south and west of Lake Lychnitis (cf. Walbank, *Commentary,* i. 632, Hammond, *JRS* lvi, 43 n. 19, Philippson, *RE,* iv. 2221–2).
The MSS. completely bungle the name here, but have it correctly at 40. 4.
    agris: presumably from the *horrea* (cf. § 6) and not directly as the corn would not be ripe (W–M).

6. ad Lyncum: Lyncus is not a town, but the name of an area (cf. Hammond, *JRS* lvi, 43 n. 19) though *ad* suggests that L. wrongly thought it was a town (cf. 28. 5 n.). At xxxii. 9. 9 he is clearly talking about an area.
    Bevum: Carbach's emendation for the nonsense of the MSS. The evidence for the true name is Steph. Byz. s.v. Βεύη. The precise

location of the river is unknown. Cf. Hammond, *JRS* lvi, 43 n. 19, lviii, 16 n. 55.

8. Note the short vivid sentences, typical of L.'s military narrative (cf. 23. 6–7 n.).

hostes adpropinquare: omitted in B. Weissenborn deleted, but was not followed by later editors. *fallere* is used absolutely and without a noun clause explaining what caused deception: for examples cf. *TLL*, vi. 1. 187 (of Weissenborn's examples x. 41. 6 is not parallel as *fefellit* there has a subject). Yet the *ut* clause would be rather odd at the end of the sentence, and on balance I prefer to keep *hostes adpropinquare*.

34. 4. gladio Hispaniensi: normally the short Spanish sword is the equipment of infantry (Pol. vi. 23. 6–7) and Polybius does not mention a sword at all as part of the standard equipment of *equites*. Cf. Kromayer–Veith, 325, 327, Walbank, *Commentary*, i. 704. On the other hand, this passage must come from Polybius (Nissen, *KU*, 128: the comments on mass psychology (§ 3) and military tactics are very typical of Polybius) and one must assume that in this particular case the *equites*, since they were fighting by themselves, had been equipped with infantry swords.

5. Ipsum quoque regem terror cepit: Diodorus (xxviii. 8) reports remarks by Philip to encourage his troops, which assorts oddly with the alleged terror. Walsh (*RhM* xcvii [1954], 114, *Livy*, 163) points out that in xxxiii. 7. 8 L. imputes fear to Philip when the corresponding passage of Polybius (xviii. 22) does not. Walsh has a point in respect of these two passages but he goes too far on 17. 10 (cf. n. ad loc.) and Polybius himself attributes panic to him in v. 110. 4 (cf. also xviii. 9. 2). Other cases of fear attributed to Philip are xxiv. 40. 13 and xxxii. 5. 2, 13. 2: cf. also xxxii. 12. 8. For fear attributed to Flamininus cf. xxxii. 11. 5 n.

cepit: cf. 2. 9 n.

6. faucibus Pelagoniae: cf. 28. 5 n., 33. 3.
Pleurato: cf. 28. 1 n.

7. duobus milibus: B. The chaos in the χ group is due to misunderstanding of the *sigla* used in the archetype: cf. McDonald, xvii. There is no validity in W–M's argument that the number is too small, on the grounds that their subsequent activities in 36. 1 and 37. 3 suggest a larger number.

Ataeo: ψ. *Athaeo* ϕ. B has a gap. The place is unknown and the correct spelling therefore unascertainable.

8. admiratus . . . videri posse: Philip's admiration of Roman institutions is found in his letter to Larisa in 214 praising Roman methods of extending their citizenship (*Syll.*[3] 543, cf. Toynbee, ii. 437–8, J. M. Hannick, *Antidorum Peremans* [Louvain, 1968], 97–104). The ascription of the same comment to Pyrrhus (Plut. *Pyrr.* 16) is probably a retrojection of this incident.

For the details of the Roman camp, see especially Pol. vi. 27 ff. and Walbank, *Commentary*, i, ad loc.

tendentium: as often for *tentoria tendentium*, 'rows of men encamped'.

itinerum intervallis: 'regular spaces between the paths', not with reference to the *intervallum*, the space between the palisade and the first row of tents.

barbarorum: cf. 29. 12–15 n.

9. eduxit: here χ is clearly right against B's *duxit*.

35. 1. non tam: an old crux. McDonald defends the MSS. reading by arguing that Philip wanted a pitched battle and therefore sent out a few troops to provoke the Romans whilst waiting for Perseus to arrive (cf. 34. 6). This is unconvincing: Philip is clearly only committing a small section of his troops because he wants to avoid a pitched battle. That is the situation described by Dio fr. 58. *non* must go. Cf. Tränkle, *Gnomon*, 376, Ogilvie, *Phoenix*, 346, Walsh, *CR*, 55.

Tralles: cf. xxvii. 32. 4 (the passage referred to in *alio loco*), xxxiii. 4. 4, xxxvii. 39–40. They are described as Illyrians by Steph. Byz. s.vv. Βῆγις and Τραλλία but as Thracians by Strabo xiv. p. 649c and Hesych. s.v. Τραλλεῖς. Nothing further is known of them and certainty is impossible. Cf. Polaschek, *RE*, viA. 2091–3.

Cretenses: Philip had inherited friendly connections with several Cretan cities and had cultivated them assiduously himself: in 220 he and the symmachy sent help to cities fighting Cnossos (Pol. iv. 53–5) and soon after he was proclaimed as προστάτης of the island (Pol. vii. 11. 9). In 205/4 Philip stirred up the Cretans to go to war with Rhodes (Pol. xiii. 4–5, Diod. xxviii. 1, Polyaenus v. 17. 2, cf. p. 36). Nabis was also involved in this (Pol. xiii. 8): he too had gained considerable influence in Crete and hence had Cretan soldiers. When he joined Rome Cretan soldiers were found fighting on both sides (Macedonian side: xxxiii. 14. 4, 18. 9. Roman side: xxxii. 40. 4, xxxiii. 3. 10 n.).

For the possibility that Cretan forces helped Athens against Philip cf. Paus. i. 36. 5, Walbank, *Philip V*, 131–2. On Cretan matters cf. Errington, *Philopoemen*, ch. iii.

Athenagora: cf. 27. 6 n.

purpuratis: often used in Latin for courtiers, without necessarily implying that they actually wore purple. Cf. xxxii. 39. 8, xxxiii. 8. 8,

E. Bikerman, *Institutions des Séleucides* (Paris, 1938), 42, Reinhold, *History of purple as a status symbol in antiquity*, 34–5.

2. ferme : 'about' not 'almost'. The normal cavalry contingent of a legion was 300 men (Pol. vi. 20. 9, Kromayer–Veith, 261, Brunt, 671 ff.). I see no evidence for W–M's assertion that at this time they contained 500 men each. Of the three passages of L. which they quote only x. 29. 12 mentions 500 and they are Campanians.

emissae : clearly the correct reading, as against *missae*. McDonald's report of B, however, is rather misleading. What survives is *ale missae*—the line under the *e* of *ale* is in a different ink: there is an erasure after *ale* but it is impossible to see what was originally there.

3. quo : this is the only certain example in L. of *adsuescere* with an ablative: other cases are either dative, or could be either dative or ablative. But the ablative is found in Cicero and it would be wrong to alter the MSS. reading here.

36. 1. quos peltas⟨tas⟩ vocant : the MSS. read *peltas*, as at xxxiii. 4. 4. For the use of *vocant*, cf. 24. 4 n. The *peltastai*, or lightly armed troops, were given a new importance at the beginning of the fourth century by Iphicrates; cf. Kromayer–Veith, 89, Cary, *CAH*, vi. 48.

4. elephantis . . . captos : for the capture of elephants in the Second Punic War cf. xxiii. 46. 4, 49. 13, xxiv. 42. 8, xxv. 41. 7, xxvi. 21. 9, xxx. 6. 9, 35. 3. But by the terms of the peace of 201 Carthage had to hand over all her elephants and it must be this that provided Rome with her main supply; cf. xxx. 37. 3, Pol. xv. 18. 3, Walbank, *Commentary*, ii. 468. For elephants at Cynoscephalae cf. xxxiii. 9. 6. On the use of elephants, cf. Kromayer–Veith, 313.

6. Ottolobum : *Attalobum* MSS., but almost certainly the same as *Ottolobum* in 40. 9. It is not otherwise recorded and its precise location is unknown, cf. Lenk, *RE*, xviii. 1878.

7. simul et neglegentia cum audacia : the phrase has caused a lot of difficulty, and led to a variety of emendations, some deleting *et*, others adding another noun before *et* or a second *et* and a noun after *neglegentia*. McDonald defends the MSS. reading by saying that the phrase is the reverse of *audacia et simul cum ea etiam neglegentia*. But this merely restates, rather than solves the problem. In fact it is an instance of the use of *et* to mean *etiam* (cf. *TLL*, v. 2. 913–14)—'at the same time they would even grow negligent, as well as being overbold'.

37. 4. effusos pugnantes: *pugnantes* agrees with *conferti prae-paratique* (W–M).

7. ut primo: Madvig, *Emendationes*, 467, says that *ut primo* for *ut primum* is not a Livian usage and suggests *prima*. But one case of *ubi primo* occurs (iv. 58. 9) as an exception to *ubi primum* found elsewhere in L. and since there are only eight instances of *ut primum* in the sense of 'as soon as' (Packard, iv. 1351) it is best to keep the MSS. reading.

convertit . . . versaque: for this repetition of a root in a different sense cf. Tränkle, *Gnomon*, 375 n. 1.

8. in paludes: for Kromayer, ii. 20, and Walbank, *Philip V*, 143 n. 4, these are the marshes of the Erigon. With Hammond's scheme (cf. 33. 4 n.) they are to the south of Lake Lychnitis.

Dio's statement (fr. 58. 3) that Philip was wounded is probably incorrect (cf. Walbank, *Philip V*, 143 n. 5).

10. subiecit: the *sub-* has the force of 'in his place' and the verb is not therefore used simply to mean 'lifted' as in vi. 24. 5, Vergil, *A.* xii. 288.

38. This criticism of the tactics of the two commanders is very typical of Polybius. Cf. e.g. Pol. ix. 8, x. 17, 32. 7 ff., xi. 2, 8, 19, xv. 15, xvi. 28. For other passages where L. has inserted technical military details from Polybius cf. Nissen, *KU*, 73.

4. omnibus peditum quoque copiis: i.e. not just the *caetrati* and auxiliaries (36. 1, 8, 37. 4).

7. temptasse eum fortunam: for the phrase cf. xxvi. 12. 14, xl. 27. 2, Kajanto, 78.

Pleuratum Dardanosque: cf. 34. 6. Walbank, *Philip V*, 143 n. 6, rightly points out that Philip did not take immediate action to deal with this threat and this suggests that the threat from the north was not in fact very serious at this point.

9. caduceatore: L.'s regular word for a herald seeking a truce or peace, but outside L. rarely used (cf. *TLL*, iii. 32–3).

10. frustratus . . . abit: both Dio fr. 58. 3 and Frontinus ii. 13. 8 say that he actually made a truce before disappearing. For similar ruses cf. viii. 38. 4, xxiii. 41. 11, Catin, 102.

39. The battle described in this chapter is referred to as an important Roman success by Flamininus in his speech before Cynoscephalae (xxxiii. 8. 5, Pol. xviii. 23. 3). Cf. Walbank, *Philip V*, 144.

4–5. Stuberram . . . Pluinnam . . . Bruanium: Strabo, vii. p. 327c, says that Βρυάνιον and Στύβαρα are in the neighbourhood of

143

the River Erigon: Pluinna is not otherwise mentioned, but is presumably in the same region.

Stuberra is referred to at xl. 24. 7, xliii. 18. 4, Pol. xxviii. 8. 8 (cf. Oberhummer, *RE*, ivA. 395). For an inscription of Stuberra cf. N. Vulic, *Mélanges Glotz* (Paris, 1932), 875, Walbank, *Philip V*, 143 n. 7. The name of Bruanium is corrupted in the MSS., but the correct form is guaranteed by Strabo, l.c. (Oberhummer, *RE*, iii. 916).

Pelagonia: cf. 28. 5 n.

comperto: this ablative absolute use occurs only here, in § 7, and at xxxiii. 5. 4. Cf. K. Gries, *CPh* xlvi (1951), 36.

terrorem . . . hosti: Walbank (*Philip V*, 144 n. 1) follows Kromayer, ii. 22 n. 4 in thinking that these words conceal a Roman reverse. That is by no means a necessary deduction.

Osphagum: presumably a tributary of the River Erigon; cf. Oberhummer, *RE*, xviii. 1. 1588.

6. vallo: on this passage see W. E. Thompson, *AJP* lxxxix (1968), 349–50, who argues that the construction of a palisade is an odd thing to do, and that L. has misunderstood a statement by Polybius that Philip used the river as a bulwark. L. makes just this error in xxi. 5. 9, deriving from Pol. iii. 14. 5.

7. Eordaeam: as at 40. 1 and xxxiii. 8. 5 the MSS. make chaos of the name. The true form is guaranteed by Pol. xviii. 23. 3. Eordaea is the region south of Lyncus, near Lake Ostrovo. Cf. Oberhummer, *RE*, v. 2656.

ad occupandas angustias: the Monastir gap, or pass of Kirli-Debend; cf. Walbank, *Philip V*, 144. Its identification with the pass mentioned in Thucydides iv. 127–8 (Walbank, l.c.) is doubted by Gomme, *Commentary on Thucydides*, iii. 617–18.

9. fecit: ψ, *faciat* φ, *facit* B. L. may well have followed the perfect with a historic present: cf. e.g. xxii. 42. 5. See also 42. 9 n., xxxii. 10. 12 n., xxxiii. 29. 9 n. For L's alternation of tenses in narrative cf. Chausserie-Laprée, 383–410.

10. phalangi: as W–M note, at xxxii. 17. 11 L. uses the *vocant* formula in talking about the phalanx (cf. 24. 4 n.) but here and at xxxiii. 4. 3 just the Greek word. (On xxxiii. 8. 7 cf. n. ad loc.) At xviii. 28–32 Polybius discusses the relative merits of the phalanx and the Roman legion. On the phalanx, cf. Pickard-Cambridge, *CAH*, vi. 205 ff., Kromayer–Veith, 99.

praelongis hastis: cf. xxxii. 17. 13, Pol. xviii. 29. 2, Kromayer–Veith, 134–5, Walbank, *Commentary*, ii. 586–7.

11. rumpiae: the Greek ῥομφαία and sometimes *rhomphaea* in Latin. It is a long spear used by Thracians (Gell. x. 25. 4).

12. peterent: Bχ. Later MSS. have *peteret*, but L. often uses a plural after a collective noun (Riemann, 256, Kühnast, 60 ff., K–St, i. 23). For an example of a plural after a previous singular verb cf. ii. 58. 6. Cf. also 42. 5 n., xxxii. 12. 9 n.

14. testudine: the famous tactic of locking shields together above the heads of the soldiers, especially used in siege warfare.

15. circuitu: most MSS. read *circumitu*: though *circuitu* is the more normal form, *circumitu* is found in good MSS. of Cicero, and is probably the right reading here. Cf. Neue–Wagener, ii. 825–6, to which should be added the fact that *circumitu* is read by the uncial MS. at xlii. 16. 1.

40. 1–6. For Sulpicius' route cf. Hammond, *JRS* lvi (1966), 45.

1. Eordaeam: 39. 7 n.

Elimiam: the area to the south of Eordaea, by the river Haliacmon and bordering on Thessaly. Cf. Oberhummer, *RE*, v. 2367.

⟨**consul**⟩: the supplement is probably necessary, though an anacoluthon here (L. ending the sentence as if he had begun *Sulpicius pervenit*) is not entirely impossible.

Orestidem: the area round Kastoria, as appears from this passage. Cf. Schmidt, *RE*, xviii. 960–5, Walbank, *Commentary*, ii. 616. On the subsequent position of the Orestae cf. xxxiii. 34. 6 n.

Celetrum: Kastoria at the edge of the lake of the same name. For full topographical details cf. Oberhummer, *RE*, xi. 142–6.

paeneinsula: McDonald reports B as dividing the word into *paene insula*. But the division is at the end of a line, and though there is no continuation mark, it is not significant. B omits it, for example, in the case of *conge / rie* at 39. 8.

3. imperium: here in its primary sense of 'command'. Cf. *TLL*, vii. 1. 568 ff. (the usage is not as pre-classical and post-Augustan as L–S say).

4. Dassaretios: cf. 33. 4 n.

Pelion: not otherwise known; for its position cf. Walbank, *Philip V*, 144 n. 5, Hammond, *JRS* lvi, 45.

servitia . . . abduxit: for lists of enslavements in this period cf. Toynbee, ii. 172, Volkmann, 14 ff. For distinctions in the treatment of free and slave in a captured city cf. Ducrey 284–6.

[et]: the clause is adversative and *et* is clearly inappropriate.

5. nam . . . faciendos: Sulpicius is planning to launch a new attack the following year from Pelion via Orestis; cf. Hammond, *JRS* lvi, 45.

6. in loca pacata: χ unnecessarily adds *iam* before *pacata* (cf. Tränkle, *Gnomon*, 373).

The reference is to the area between Apollonia and Antipatrea which had been overrun by Apustius the previous autumn (ch. 27). It does not mean the land of Rome's allies, as W–M say.

L. omits Dio's statement (fr. 58. 4) that Sulpicius withdrew because of lack of supplies. The notice probably stood in Polybius: at xxxii. 9. 10 a similar statement in Plutarch, *Flam.* 4 is omitted by L.

Apolloniam . . . orsus . . . erat: cf. 22. 4.

40. 7—43. *Philip against the Dardanians, Aetolians and Athamanians*

7. Athamanes . . . Dardani: cf. 28. 1–3 nn.

8. iam recipientes: after the attack referred to in 38. 7.
Athenagoran: cf. 27. 6 n.

9–10. The Aetolian decision was followed by the meeting between Pyrrhias, Apustius, and Attalus described at 46. 1–5; Larsen, *TAPA* lxxxiii (1952), 23 n. 40, *JRS* lx (1970), 219 (cf. Walbank, *Philip V*, 145) argues against this chronology on the grounds that 46. 6 implies that the attack on Oreus followed the conference with the Aetolians in 46. 1–5, while the present passage implies that the Aetolian decision followed the attack. 46. 1–5 would then be negotiations preceding the Aetolian decision. *de ratione gerendi belli* in 46. 1 would be inaccurate. But the view is not necessary: the present passage refers only to the approach of the Roman fleet towards Oreus, 46. 6 to the actual beginning of the siege.

Damocritus: cf. 32. 1 n.

auctor: Madvig (*Emendationes*, 467–8) argued that *auctor* should be deleted, on the grounds that the gerundive phrase should go with the verb, not with *morae*. It is hard to see why the gerundive phrase should not follow *morae auctor fuerat* (or why Madvig holds that it should go with *erat*, not with *morae*), and since *auctor* is found with the genitive in xxvi. 13. 2 and xxvii. 16. 3, the MSS. reading should be retained.

proximo concilio: the special assembly authorized at 32. 4, not the normal autumn assembly. For the date cf. Walbank, *Philip V*, 318.

10. post . . . pugnae: 36. 4–37. 12. On Ottolobus cf. 36. 6 n.

ad hoc . . . Oreum: for the naval warfare cf. 44–47. 3.

41. 1. restituerant: not implying a renewal of the original agreement of 212/11: cf. xxxiii. 13. 9–12 n.

Amynandro . . . Athamanum: 28. 1 n.

Cercinium: its precise location is unknown (cf. Stählin, *HTh*, 103, Walbank, *Philip V*, 146 n. 1). It is clear from § 4 that it is in the vicinity of Lake Boebe. This implies that the Aetolians have traversed the whole of southern Thessaly. W–M's suggestion that it is in the south-west of Thessaly is impossible.

obsedere: χ. *obsidere* B. A historical infinitive is quite possible after an indicative. Cf. 35. 3, K–St, i. 135 ff.

3. qui superfuerunt . . . abducti: cf. 40. 4 n.

4. Boeben paludem: the large lake on the borders of Magnesia. The Greek names vary between Βοιβηίς, Βοίβη and Βοιβίας (cf. Oberhummer, *RE*, iii. 628–9, Stählin, *HTh*, 61–2, P–K, i. 1. 120–1).

5. Perrhaebiam: Perrhaebia is the north-eastern part of Thessaly; cf. Stählin, *HTh*, 5–39.

Cyretias: the town is the modern Domeniko, in the hills near the valley of the Titaresius (Stählin, *HTh*, 25). The name in inscriptions is always Χυρετίαι, and though the MSS. of L. always have *Cyretiae* (cf. xxxvi. 10. 5, 13. 4, xlii. 53. 9), we should presume that L. transcribed Polybius correctly and read *Chyretias* here. Bürchner, *RE*, iii. 2528, and Kern, *IG* ix. 2. 338, misreport the reading of Flamininus' letter to Chyretiae in 194; cf. *Syll.*[3] 593. See also Ogilvie, *Phoenix*, 345.

Maloeam: it is at either Analipsis or Paljokastro in the valley of the Titaresius. For discussion see Stählin, *HTh*, 29–30, *RE*, xiv. 913–16, P–K, i. 1. 85. At all other mentions of its name (all in L.— xxxvi. 10. 5, 13. 4, xxxix. 25. 16, xlii. 67. 7) it is spelt *Malloea* and it would seem best to read that form here also.

deditionem societatemque: not necessarily involving a *foedus*, as asserted by Dahlheim, 72 n. 14; cf. i. 9–10 n., 31. 10 n.

6. Gomphos: for its position near, as stated here, to Athamania, cf. Stählin, *HTh*, 125 ff., *RE*, vii. 1584–5, P–K, i. 1. 56.

7. campos Thessaliae opimos: the central Thessalian plain, enclosed by the mountain ranges of Ossa, Pelion, Olympus, Pindus, and Othrys. It is the same as the *Coelen Thessaliae* of xxxii. 4. 4 and Herodotus vii. 129. 1. Larisa, the chief town of the plain, was habitually described as fertile. Cf. Nisbet and Hubbard, 100. There is thus no need to assume that L. is consciously imitating Horace, *Odes* i. 7. 11 as is argued by C. Brakman, *Mnemosyne* lv (1927), 54.

fors tulisset: for the frequent use of *ferre* with *fors* cf. Kajanto 76–7.

8. Pharcado⟨ni⟩: the MSS. read *Phaeca* or *Phaecado*. (B has *Phaeca* with *do* added in what looks like an erasure: there does not seem to be room for four letters after *Phaeca*, as McDonald states.) Phaeca (cf. xxxii. 14. 1 n.) is geographically impossible and Pharcado must be intended. On the form of the name and its position cf. Stählin, *HTh*, 117, Kirsten, *RE*, xix. 1835–8, Walbank, *Philip V*, 146, P–K i. 1. 54.

10. alii . . . advenit: Ogilvie, 302, compares a similar defeat of the Sabines in ii. 26. 3.

palati: χ, *om.* B. L. often combines *palati* and *vagi* (cf. W–M's note, Packard, iii. 748), but χ may have added it precisely because of its occurrence in other passages.

12. excitare: χ unnecessarily adds *igitur*.

13. cum sescentorum: Gelenius added *universi* after *cum*. But the text is sound as it stands in the MSS. and the addition is unnecessary.

14. quidam: χ, *om.* B. It is unnecessary and overemphatic. χ added it because he did not understand the construction.

42. 1. suis iam: χ, *iam suis* B. But the hyperbaton for emphasis is quite possible and B's reading should be retained.

fatigatos . . . celeritate: on Philip's march cf. Walbank, *Philip V*, 146.

2. turmatim . . . manipulos: W–M point out that L. uses Roman military terms to describe divisions of the Macedonian army (cf. § 4).

4. summum: 'at the most'. Cf. Packard, iv. 815.

5. receperat: Carbach. The MSS. have *receperant*. But the plural verb may follow a collective noun. Cf. 39. 12 n., Walsh, *CR*, 54.

ut defensuri: for L.'s use of *ut* with the future participle cf. Tränkle, *WS*, 139–40.

6. ad tumulum ad castra Athamanum: the double *ad* is rather harsh, but it is probably better not to alter it. The use of *dies* three times in the next section suggests a certain haste of composition in this chapter. For Amynander's camp cf. 41. 9.

8. ignotas: with *hostibus*. The reading *ignotos* arises from the word being mistakenly taken with the Aetolians.

9. videt: Bψ, *vidit* φN. Cf. 39. 9 n.

43. 1. Athenagoras: cf. 40. 8. On Athenagoras, 27. 6 n.

primo: χ. *om.* B. W–M point out that *primo* and *primum* do not always precede *dein* and *deinde* in L. Their citation of xxxv. 11. 10 in defence of B's text is as relevant as McDonald's quotation of xxxv. 1. 8 in favour of *primo*.

2. tale: χ, *om*. B. I suspect an addition by χ. The meaning without *tale* is 'no kind of auxiliary troops at all'.

Dardanos: the name is repeated four times in six lines; cf. 42. 6 n.

4. ita . . . eventu: for the praise of Philip cf. 16. 1 n.

forte: indicating that Philip could not have foreseen Scopas' action, not that Scopas' activities themselves occurred by chance. Cf. J. Champeaux, *RÉL* xlv (1967), 369–70.

5. Scopas: a leading Aetolian in the last quarter of the third century. He played a large part in the social war acting as virtual *strategos* in 221/20 (Pol. iv. 5. 1, 6. 7, 9. 8 ff., 14. 4, 16. 11, 19. 12) and being elected *strategos* for 220/19 (iv. 27. 1, cf. 37. 2, 62. 1, v. 11. 2). In these activities he collaborated closely with Dorimachus, and it was these two who were responsible for the alliance with Rome in 212/11, when Scopas was again *strategos* (L. xxvi. 24. 7). In 205 Scopas and Dorimachus were given a special commission to enact laws. They proposed the abolition of all debts, but this was successfully resisted by Alexander Isius. Scopas and Dorimachus then left Aetolia, the latter to serve as a mercenary in Egypt (Pol. xiii. 1–2; cf. Walbank, *Commentary*, ii. 413–15, showing that Scopas was not *strategos* in 205/4). Scopas was sent by Agathocles to Greece in 203 to collect mercenaries (Pol. xv. 25. 16) and was the leader of the Ptolemaic army defeated by Antiochus III at Panion in 200 (Pol. xvi. 18. 2 ff., 39, Hier. *in Dan*. xi. 15 ff. = *FGH* 260 F 46). In 196 he plotted a *coup d'état* in Egypt, but was arrested and executed (Pol. xviii. 53–5). Cf. in general Dumrese, *RE*, supp. vii. 1211–17.

princeps gentis: 'a leading Aetolian'. Cf. 17. 11 n.

magno cum pondere auri: similarly on his mission in 203, Pol. xv. 25. 16; the money was for advance payment of wages, cf. Walbank, *Commentary*, ii. 485.

Aegyptum: for the omission of the preposition with names of countries cf. K–St, i. 481.

avexit: χ, *vexit* B. Both are possible, but McDonald's reason for preferring *avexit* 'sed cf. ex Aetolia' is not compelling. *avexit* might be expected, and χ probably added the *a*.

7. an . . . cultus: 'or whether he wanted to obstruct Scopas, who had not bribed him sufficiently'. For Aetolian propensity to bribery cf. Pol. xviii. 34. 7.

44–47. 3. *The naval campaign of 199*

44. 1. terra: *erant* MSS. Madvig's case here (*Emendationes*, 468) is unanswerable. *erant* is weak, and L. often ends accounts of campaigns with a participle alone, cf. 47. 3. But deletion is not sufficient, for this is not the end of the year's campaign, only the transition to the naval sphere. *terra* (but for one letter an anagram of *erant*) must be right.

a Corcyra . . . L. Apustio: cf. 28. 3 n. Apustius (on whom cf. 4. 7 n.) had returned to the fleet after his land expedition in the autumn of 200 (cf. 27. 8). For the number of ships in Apustius' fleet cf. Thiel, 210 ff., arguing for a figure of about 30.

Maleo: the promontory at the south-eastern tip of the Peloponnese. The MSS. have the form *Maleum* here, at 47. 2, xxxii. 16. 4–5 (B there has *Malaeum*), xxxiv. 36. 3, and at xxxiv. 32. 18, though at xxxiv. 32. 19 they read *promunturium Maleae* and *Malea* also occurs at xxxvi. 41. 4, 42. 5. The normal Greek form is Μαλέα (Polybius uses this or Μαλέαι) and the usual Latin form is *Malea, Maleum*, apart from these passages, being very rare. Μάλεον is even rarer, found only in Schol. Eur. *Or.* 362 and Suid. s.v. Μάλειον ὄρος. This last instance suggests, as W–M say, that *Maleum* is meant to be an adjective with *promunturium*, though it is in that case odd that at xxxiv. 32. 18–19 we have *Maleum* followed by *promunturium Maleae*.

It seems best to conclude from the strong MSS. evidence that L. himself is responsible for the form, as being the name known to him. He did not read it in Polybius and in some passages it was altered to its more usual form.

This note is based mainly on the collection of evidence by Bölte, *RE*, xiv. 859–60.

Scyllaeum agri Hermionici: Hermione lies on the south coast of the Argolid, and Cape Scyllaion is the easternmost promontory of the Argolid; cf. P–K, iii. 1. 113 ff. According to Scylax, 52, and the implication of Paus. ii. 34. 6 it lay in the territory of Troezen not Hermione, though Strabo, x. p. 484c, agrees with L. Presumably the boundaries were different at different times and the discrepancy is no reason for altering the location of Cape Scyllaion. Cf. Geyer, *RE*, iiiA. 659–60.

Attalo regi: sailing from Aegina, cf. 28. 3.

2. Atheniensium: the tone of what follows is extremely hostile to Athens, reflecting Polybius' anti-Athenian attitude; cf. 14. 6 n.

Philippum: χ. *Philippo* B. Weissenborn defended B's reading quoting xxviii. 43. 8 and Sall. *Cat.* 51. 15. But in both these cases the meaning is 'in the case of' which is hardly possible here.

iam diu : i.e. during the attacks of the previous year (16. 2, 24–6) and while a renewal of those attacks was feared.

4. Rogationem . . . scivit : L. employs the technical language used for the workings of the Roman assemblies, cf. 32. 4 n.

statuae imagines : for the asyndeton cf. xxvii. 16. 7, xxxii. 16. 17, Sall. *Cat.* 11. 6, all referring to works of art. Emendation is unnecessary. *imagines* will be paintings or busts, as distinct from full statues.

nominaque earum : i.e. the inscriptions on them.

maiorum eius : many will date from the period of Macedonian control of Athens. This had been ended in 229 (cf. Ferguson, *Hellenistic Athens*, 206–7) but Athens remained an ally of Macedon (cf. Walbank, *Commentary*, i. 631). Documentation of the period is, of course, made difficult by the very fact of the present decision. In the event the Athenians went further than is implied here, and erased the names of members of the Antigonid family from several public inscriptions, but Ferguson's implication (*Hellenistic Athens*, 277) that all references to the Antigonids on the Athenian inscriptions were removed is misleading. Cf. Habicht, *Gottmenschentum*, 190 and n. 6. For reference in an Eleusinian inscription to φιλία and εἰρήνη with Philip himself cf. *Syll.*³ 547.

virile ac muliebre secus : B. *virilis ac muliebris sexus* φ, *viriles ac muliebres sexus* ψ. Both are misunderstandings of the idiom, which is an adverbial accusative. It is probably an archaism, found almost exclusively in historical authors; cf. Enn. *Var.* 70v, Sempronius Asellio fr. 7, Sisenna fr. 80, Sall. *Hist.* ii fr. 70, L. xxvi. 47. 1, Tac. *Hist.* v. 13, *Ann.* iv. 62, K–St, i. 306(b), Tränkle, *WS*, 128, Lebek 225.

diesque festi sacra sacerdotes : in Macedon itself the kings were not deified, either in their lifetime or after their death (cf. Tarn and Griffith, *Hellenistic Civilisation*, 51) but Athens had instituted a cult of Alexander and deified Demetrius Poliorcetes in 307. But Gonatas and his successors were not so deified, and the festivals and the priests to superintend them can only have been concerned with prayers *for* the king, not to him (cf. Ferguson, *Hellenistic Athens*, 108, 162–3, Habicht, *Gottmenschentum*, 28 ff., 44 ff., 80).

profanarentur : 'should cease to have their religious position'.

5. esse . . . placere : for the change from subjunctive to infinitive cf. xxxiii. 31. 11. W–M take *placere* as parallel to *plebes scivit*. But it surely means 'it should be wrong in the future to make a decision'.

6. sacerdotes . . . nomenque : Ferguson (*Hellenistic Athens*, 277) points out that on inscriptions of the 180s there is no mention of these imprecations, and suggests that the provision was repealed. It may simply have been ignored.

8. si quis . . . iure caesurum : for similar provisions in Attic law cf. D. M. MacDowell, *Athenian Homicide Law in the Age of the Orators* (Manchester, 1963), 77 ff., which completely removes the basis of the attempt by F. Ruhl (*N.J.f.Phil.* cxxxvii [1888], 335) to argue that there should be a lacuna before *qui occidunt*, on the grounds that it was unheard of in Attic law not to prescribe a specific penalty for an offence, or to condemn someone unheard.

quae adversus Pisistratidas : when Hippias was expelled in 511/10 the names of his family were put on a stele (Thuc. vi. 55) which presumably carried details of their banishment and other measures taken against them. But we know nothing of the detailed measures and it is not clear what they could be if they could be equally applied to Philip.

In addition the prohibition on Macedonians entering Attica (xli. 23. 1) presumably belongs to the same series of decisions: cf. De Sanctis, iv. 1. 49.

9. litteris verbisque : Polybius, no doubt, was consciously following Demosthenes, *Phil.* i. 30. ἵνα μὴ μόνον ἐν τοῖς ψηφίσμασι καὶ ταῖς ἐπιστολαῖς πολεμῆτε Φιλίππῳ, ἀλλὰ καὶ τοῖς ἔργοις. Cato at Athens in 191 said 'Antiochus epistulis bellum gerit, calamo et atramento militat' (*ORF²*, p. 19 fr. 20).

45. 1. Piraeum : here presumably Apustius joined Centho who had remained at Piraeus throughout the winter; cf. Thiel, 231, 234.

2. in ira : dett., *in iram* Bχ. But the meaning is 'to satisfy their anger against Philip', not 'passed in anger against Philip' and *in iram* is parallel to *ad honores*.

Andrum : one of the islands remaining in Philip's possession after the Rhodian successes of 201/0, cf. 15. 8 n.

3. portu : the reading of the Paris edition of 1513. *portum* Bχ. The accusative with *consistere* to mean 'came to and stopped there' is rare, but it is not impossible that L. used it here. Cf. K–St, i. 591 (γ).

Gaureion : the MSS. have *Gaurelon* or *Caurelon*. McDonald's correction is based on the assertion that Xenophon *Hell.* i. 4. 22 has Γαύρειον. But according to Marchant (in the OCT) the Xenophon MSS. have Γαύριον. The only other mention of the place is Diod. xiii. 69. 4 where the MSS. have Κάτριον and Γαύριον seems the right reading. *Gaureion* makes the best sense of the MSS. reading, but the evidence, such as it is, suggests that Polybius wrote Γαυρίον. Bürchner (*RE*, vii. 877–8) implausibly regards Gaurelos as the name of the harbour of the state of Gaureion.

4. apparatuque omni: Thiel, 235 n. 181, argues that all this equipment cannot have been carried on the warships, and that the fleet must have been accompanied by transports. Such transports are mentioned at xxxii. 16. 4.

5. plus aliquanto: i.e. 'more than the verbal offers'. The meaning is obscured by Sage's translation—'caused no small terror'.

6. cum singulis vestimentis: cf. 17. 3 n.

Delium Boeotiae: originally a shrine of Apollo on the coast of Boeotia, near Tanagra, and famous for the Athenian defeat there in 424 (Thuc. iv. 76. 4, 89–101). For its position cf. Gomme, *Commentary on Thucydides*, iii. 538, Philippson, *RE*, iv. 2443, P–K, i. 2. 516.

7. Ea . . . avexerunt: a similar division was provided for in the Romano–Aetolian treaty of 212/11, except that there if a town was captured by the Romans and Aetolians jointly the booty was shared (*StV*, iii. 536, cf. xxxiii. 13. 9–12 n.). For such divisions in general cf. Aymard, *RH* ccxvii (1957), 233–49 = *ÉHA*, 499–512, Dahlheim, 190–1, n. 31, Volkmann, 8 ff. For Pergamum's subsequent possession of Andros cf. xxxiii. 31. 3 n., Holleaux, *Études*, ii. 169 n. 1.

9. Cythnum: MSS. *Cydnum*, but of course the true reading is not in doubt. Again an island remaining in Macedonian possession, cf. 15. 8.

abscessere: they make no attempt on the third Macedonian-held island in the Cyclades, Paros (cf. Thiel, 236).

10. Prasias: on the east coast of Attica, south of Brauron. Cf. Ernst Meyer, *RE*, xxii. 1695–6, P–K, i. 3. 820.

Issaeorum: the island of Issa, off the Illyrian coast, was taken into Roman *fides* during the First Illyrian War in 229 (Pol. ii. 8. 5, 11. 12; the version of Appian [*Ill.* 7–8] in which the appeal of Issa to Rome is the cause of the war is to be rejected). It was probably now under the *de facto* control of Pleuratus. On Issa cf. Fluss, *RE*, supp. v. 346 ff.

lembi: the light craft, especially used by the Illyrians for their marauding expeditions.

Carystiorum: Carystus is on the south-western tip of Euboea. For Macedonian control of Euboea cf. 22. 7 n. Cf. von Geisau, *RE*, x. 2256 ff., P–K, i. 2. 630.

Geraestum: the true reading is preserved by ψ. Geraestus is a harbour north of Cape Geraestus, not far from Carystus (Bölte, *RE*, vii. 1233–4, P–K, i. 2. 629).

11–12. Scyrum . . . Icum . . . Sciathum: all these islands were presumably under Macedonian control, though Icos and Sciathos clearly did not have garrisons. Icos (cf. P–K, iv. 47–9) is the eastern-most of the Magnesian islands, with Peparethos and Sciathos lying to its west. On the ravaging of Sciathos and Peparethos by Philip the previous winter cf. 28. 6. On Scyros cf. xxxiii. 30. 11 n.

13. nec meruerant: as having been so badly treated by Philip.

14. Cassandream: the name given to Potidaea after its refounda-tion by Cassander in 316: cf. xliv. 11. 2, Ernst Meyer, *RE*, supp. x. 628 ff., J. A. Alexander, *Potidaea, its History and Remains* (Athens, Georgia, 1963).

Mendaeum: the Greek name is Μένδη (originally Μίνδη). Pliny, *NH* iv. 36 has *Mendae*. Suidas s.v. gives Μενδαῖος as the adjective from Μένδη and presumably L. knew of that form. Cf. note on *Maleo* in 44. 1. On the town cf. Lenk, *RE*, xv. 777–9.

promunturio: Cape Posidium to the west of Mende; cf. xliv. 11. 3.

15. ad Canastraeum: the promontory at the southern tip of Pallene.

Toronae . . . Acanthum: the MSS. read *Coronae*. The pro-montory of Torone is the tip of the Sithone peninsula, south of the city of Torone. Acanthus is at the neck of Acte. As Thiel (237) says, they do not seem to have rounded the Acte peninsula.

16. Euboeam: clearly the Macedonian troops in Euboea could not prevent the allied fleet anchoring off the northern coast of the island and getting the supplies they needed.

46. 1–6. On the chronology cf. 40. 9–10 n. These discussions pre-ceded the Aetolian invasion of Thessaly described in 41–2. Cf. the synchronism at 40. 10.

1. sinum Maliacum: the gulf between Locris and Phthiotic Achaea with Thermopylae at its head.

2. Pyrrhias Aetolus: the true form of the name (B has *Pyrrihas*, χ *sipyrrichas*) is guaranteed by xxvii. 30. 1 and Pol. v. 30. 2, 91. 3, 94. 2. Pyrrhias was active in the social war (Pol. ll.cc.) and *strategos* in 210/9 (L. l.c.). Walbank (*Commentary*, i. 561) oddly says that the Pyrrhias of the Polybius passages is not otherwise known. Cf. Ziegler, *RE*, xxiv. 1420–1.

quae: Gronovius. *qui* Bχ, wrongly thinking it went with Pyrrhias.

Heracleam: the word order suggests that Pyrrhias came to Heraclea in the company of Apustius and Attalus, when the meaning is clearly that he was to hold discussions with them (i.e. *cum* goes with *ad communicanda consilia*). Hence transpositions have been sug-gested, *Heracleam* being placed either before *ad communicanda* or after *legato*. I cannot understand McDonald's defence of the MSS.' order, and agree with Ogilvie (*Phoenix*, 346) that transposition is necessary. It is true that the sentence as a whole is not at all clearly expressed, but I cannot feel that the obscurity of the MSS. text is what L. wrote. (Weissenborn's *convenit* would be acceptable if it was the verb of the main clause but the relative seems to require description of an antecedent event.)

Heraclea is near the head of the gulf: distinguished from other towns of the name as Heraclea in Trachis, it was founded by Sparta in 426. Cf. Stählin, *RE*, viii. 424–9, Gomme, *Commentary on Thucydides*, ii. 396, P–K, i. 1. 250.

3. ex foedere ab Attalo: evidently Aetolia and Attalus concluded a formal treaty in 211 though Attalus' relationship to Rome remained one of *amicitia*: cf. 15. 9 n.

⟨**mitteret**⟩: a verb has fallen out and this suggestion of Weissenborn makes the omission easy to understand.

4. quo tempore . . . potuissent: i.e. during Philip's attack on Pergamum in 201. Cf. p. 37.

6. Oreo: cf. 25. 7 n.

quia ante fuerat temptata: the reference is to the capture of Oreus by Attalus and the Romans in 208: it was quickly recovered by Philip. Cf. xxviii. 5. 19—8, Walbank, *Philip V*, 94–7. *temptata* obscures the fact that the attempt was successful.

Andri: 45. 2–8.

Acesimbroto: the name is Acesimbrotus (Pol. xviii. 1. 4, 2. 3, *Syll.*[3] 673) but the MSS. of L. always have *Agesimbrotus*. As McDonald says, it is likely that L. would have copied the name correctly from Polybius (it is not one of which he would know of a variant form). Dorey's arguments to the contrary (*JRS* lvii [1967], 280) are unconvincing.

tectae: cf. 22. 8 n.

7. Zelasium . . . Phthiotidis: the MSS. read *Zelasium* and then B has *Phthiniae id* and *χyshinie id*, both pieces of gibberish. Gronovius read *Phalasiam . . . Istiaeae id* (or *Istiaeotidis*), Phalasia being a cape on the east coast of Euboea. But it is hard to square this with *super Demetriadem* and B's reading certainly looks like a corruption of *Phthiotidis*. Zelasium is not otherwise known but will be one of the capes south of Demetrias, probably Halmyrus (cf. Stählin, *HTh*, 170 n. 4, P–K, i. 1. 176, McDonald ad loc.). Ernst Meyer (*RE*, ixA. 2473) unconvincingly argues that *Demetriadem* should be emended to *Demetrium*, the harbour of Pyrasus, on the grounds that *super Demetriadem* makes no sense.

8. Heraclides . . . classem : the fleet had retired to Demetrias for the winter (33. 1). On Heraclides cf. 16. 3 n.

9. a maritima arce . . . inter duas . . . arces : L. gives a description of the topography of Oreus in xxviii. 6. 2. W–M's claim that L.'s account makes better sense if Attalus was attacking a fort on the second hill and the Romans the city wall is unconvincing. L.'s description of the attack makes perfectly good sense on the natural assumption that the Romans are attacking the walls of the seaward citadel, Attalus the city wall in the valley. *a maritima arce* means 'from the direction of the seaward citadel', cf. 24. 9 n.

10. faciebant : the MSS.' *iaciebant* would have to be taken with *saxa*, which would involve an intolerable anacoluthon. Emendation to *cuniculis*, with *et pondere . . . iaciebant* as a parenthesis, involves an incredibly tortuous construction. *faciebant* (Kreyssig) is simple and makes the sense run clearly.

11. castigationis : Gronovius. *castigationibus* MSS., which was kept by Drakenborch deleting the *et* before *simul*. But *castigationibus* is very harsh as a parallel to *praesentioribus animis*. Pettersson (74–5 n. 2) unconvincingly defends the MSS. reading, taking *castigationibus* as an instrumental ablative followed by *memores*.

12. ⟨militibus⟩ relictis, quod satis videbatur : Bψ have *relictis quod satis videbatur*, φ *quot* instead of *quod*. Editors have adopted one of two basic kinds of solution. One is to keep *quod* and either insert *militum* after *satis* (Weissenborn) or *militibus* before *relictis* (thus McDonald who also thinks a numeral has fallen out). The other is to read *quot* and change *videbatur* to *videbantur*, supplying *militibus* after *perficienda*.

Is B's text impossible? At xliv. 1. 1 we have *consul cum quinque milibus, quod . . . traiecturus erat*, and that proves that *quod* can refer to a body of soldiers. *relictis quod satis videbatur* then seems perfectly possible Latin for *iis relictis qui satis videbantur* and it is not necessary to say specifically that they are soldiers. McDonald argues that L. would not have omitted a number given by Polybius. But we do not know that Polybius did give a number.

in proxima continentis : for the construction cf. ii. 33. 7 (Ogilvie, 320).

Larisamque . . . Cremaste : for the political history of Larisa Cremaste cf. 1. 9–10 n. For its site Stählin, *RE*, xii. 842–5, *HTh*, 182 ff., P–K, i. 1. 208. The explanation is probably by L. himself.

praeter arcem cepit : the *arx* was all-important, and it is not surprising that Philip soon recaptured the town, as appears from the later disputes concerning it (cf. 1. 9–10 n.).

13. Pteleon: *Egeleon* MSS., but the true reading is not in doubt. Pteleon is on the coast north-east of Larisa (Kirsten, *RE*, xxiii. 1481–5, Stählin, *HTh*, 181, P–K, i. 1. 207).

15. in arcem quae super portum est: *quae super portum est in arcem* B (χ *quoque* or *quodque* for *quae*). This is obviously impossible and most editors have accepted Büttner's transposition. But doubt remains. W–M rightly say that *quae super portum est* is not a necessary explanation, as it is quite clear from the narrative which *arx* is involved. It could be a gloss.

16. urbs . . . cessere: as at Andros (cf. 45. 7 n.). On its subsequent fate cf. xxxiii. 31. 3 n., 34. 9–10.

Dedications from Attalus' capture of Oreus may be recorded in *OGIS* 284, 288.

47. 1. autumnale aequinoctium: for the chronology cf. Walbank, *Philip V*, 318.

Coela: the Κοῖλα Εὐβοίας are said by Strabo (x. p. 445c) to be the waters between the Euripus and the southern tip of Euboea, but the name may in fact have referred to the coasts of the southern part of Euboea as a whole; cf. Macan on Herodotus viii. 13. 6, G. C. Richards, *CR* xliv (1930), 61–2, J. Labarbe, *BCH* lxxvi (1952), 401–2 n. 4, A. R. Burn, *Persia and the Greeks* (London, 1962), 399 n. 42. Which meaning was intended by Polybius or understood by L. is unclear.

2. triginta . . . relictis: presumably again under Centho (Thiel, 239).

Maleum: 44. 1 n.

statum: this is its only use in L. as an apparent noun (cf. Packard, iv. 762). Presumably we must understand either *tempus* with it, or think that L. regarded *statum initiorum* as equivalent to *stata initia*.

For the date of the mysteries cf. p. 43.

Acesimbroto et Rhodiis: cf. 46. 6 n. All MSS. except L omit *et*.

domum remissis: an odd form of expression, since Attalus had no power to issue orders to the Rhodians.

3. legato: φ. *legatis* Bψ. Apustius is the only *legatus* mentioned in the summer's operations.

47. 4—50. *Events in Rome and Italy: Warfare in Spain*

These are the events of the consular year of 200, though the preceding narrative has dealt with the military history of 199, cf. 22. 4–47. 3 n.

47. 4–49. 3, 49. 8–11. *Triumph of L. Furius Purpurio*

The story of Furius' activities is continued from 22. 3; cf. Dio fr. 57. 81. Münzer's view (cf. 10–11. 3 n.) that this story really belongs to 196 is not convincing.

The politics of the episode are obscure. The *legatus* in Illyria M. Aurelius had a considerable influence on the decision to go to war (xxx. 26. 4, xxxi. 3. 4, 5. 5). Furius could be identical with Galba's envoy to the Aetolian League (29. 1 n.) and a M. Furius was Aurelius' representative sent to the senate from Greece (xxx. 42. 5).

All this might appear to suggest that both Cotta and Furius were allies of the Fulvians and Galba. Yet Furius is certainly Scipionic later: in 187 he joined L. Aemilius Paullus in giving an adverse account of the activities of the anti-Scipionic Cn. Manlius Vulso and then proposed that the inquiry into the activities of L. Scipio should be extended to cover those of Manlius (xxxviii. 44. 11, 54. 7). Furius could have changed sides later, but we do not know for certain either that he was the *legatus* of Galba, or the relationship of the M. Aurelius and M. Furius who were *legati* in Greece to the consul and the praetor. Certainty is impossible.

T. A. Dorey (*PACA* ii [1959], 9–10) arguing for an alliance of Furius and Cotta is impressed by the mildness of Cotta's complaints at the senate's decision to grant a triumph to Furius (49. 8–11). But the mildness could be heavy irony, and both L. and Dio suggest that the dispute was a major political battle, and not just a personal squabble.

Scullard's assertions (*RP*, 93, 95, 106) that Furius and Aurelius were former supporters of Scipio Africanus are entirely without foundation.

On other debates about triumphs in the fourth and fifth decades cf. Paschkowski, 156 ff.

4. absente se : Furius had acted on senatorial instructions (11. 3). He possessed *imperium* and for that reason it could be argued (48. 6 ff.) that he was *suis auspiciis* (cf. 4. 1 n.).

5. misso . . . in Etruriam : the consul's *imperium* was greater than that of the praetor, and Cotta could thus issue orders to Furius. He is sent to Etruria to take charge of the garrison there (11. 3, 21. 1).

6. ratus ⟨est⟩ : *est* is omitted by the MSS. Madvig (*Emendationes*, 469) deleted the *quem* instead of adding *est*. But Weissenborn may be right in suggesting that L. lost track of the construction here and introduced an anacoluthon.

7. in aede Bellonae : the temple was in the area of the Circus
Flaminius, though its precise location is not known for certain. For
a recent discussion cf. F. Coarelli, *Bull. Comm.* lxxx (1965–7), 37–72.
It was outside the *pomerium* and was often used for meetings of the
senate held to consider claims for triumph, since the prospective
triumphator, whether a pro-magistrate, or, as in both this case and
xxxiii. 22. 1, a magistrate in office, could not cross the *pomerium*
without forfeiting his *auspicia* and with them his right to triumph.
Cf. Mommsen, *StR*, i³. 127 n. 2, Platner–Ashby, 82–3.

48. 1. gratia : his personal influence with them, and in addition
the influence of his political supporters.

2. maiores natu : L. represents the conflict as one between age-
groups (cf. *consulares* in § 3). This seems unlikely, though as a matter
of fact there were very few pro-Scipionic consulars at this time and
this may lend weight to the view that Furius had Scipionic support.
For a similar division cf. xlii. 47. 4 ff., *JRS* liv (1964), 66 ff.

alieno exercitu : but this did not affect the issue of *auspicia*: cf.
47. 4 n.

provinciam reliquisset : Furius could argue against this that
he had not been assigned Etruria by the senate, but had only been
sent there by the consul.

nullo exemplo fecisse : for similar accusations cf. xxxvii. 47. 6
(M. Aemilius Lepidus), Plut. *CG* 2 (Gaius Gracchus). W–M say
others had left their provinces but they quote only xxviii. 9. 10
which is a case of leaving with the senate's permission, a very
different matter.

3–4. expectandum . . . consulem expectaret : Furius should
have waited for the consul to come to Gaul and the senate should
now wait for the consul's return. For such pleas to wait for the
return of a consul cf. 2. 2 n.

urbem : Cremona (21. 2).

4. extrahere—et : thus χ. B has *extraheret*, Hertz reads just *extrahere*.
But McDonald is right to follow χ, regarding *potuisse . . . extrahere* as
a parenthesis: it is in any case a better explanation of B's reading.

6. magna pars : in fact the *maior pars*.

suis quis : thus χ. B has the nonsensical *magistratus ius quis*. Most
editors read *suisque*. McDonald justifies *suis quis* by saying that the
remark is of general application. But in that case the transition to the
next sentence is very sudden and *suisque* is preferable. Cf. Ogilvie,
Phoenix, 346, Tränkle, *Gnomon*, 379.

7. ex duabus coloniis . . . una direpta : Placentia and Cremona,
una direpta being Placentia (10. 3).

8. This is the crux of the argument. The senate had authorized the praetor to act if the consul so decided, and the consul had so decided (11. 1–3, 21. 1 n.).

sicut non: B, clearly right against *si non cum* or *si cum non* of χ, cf. Madvig, *Emendationes*, 470.

senatus consulto: *senatus consultum* MSS., but the object of *finire* when not a noun clause is the content of the decision (*numerum, diem*, etc.), not the medium in which it is conveyed. The ablative is what is required as in Cic. *ad fam.* xv. 9. 2; cf. *TLL*, vi. 1. 783–4.

9. occurrerit: φ, *occurreret* B, *occurrisset* ψ. *dederit* above shows which is right. The perfect subjunctive in historic sequence in *oratio obliqua* is very common in historical writers; cf. S. A. Handford, *The Latin Subjunctive* (London, 1947), 156–7, K–St, ii. 194.

12. supplicationes: cf. 22. 1 n.

data . . . Gallica bella: the great M. Furius Camillus who was believed to have defeated the Gauls in 390. He was the *dux fatalis* destined to conquer Veii (v. 19. 2) and it was the gods who led him on to defeat the Gauls (v. 49. 1). His son L. Furius Camillus defeated the Gauls in 349 (vii. 25–6). P. Furius Philus, consul 223, was also involved in the Gallic war (sources: *MRR*, i. 232). The relationship of Purpurio to the consul of 223 is uncertain.

The phrase is reminiscent of the famous line of Naevius 'fato Metelli Romae fiunt consules'.

49. 1. frequentes: 'a full house'. Sometimes the word implies a 'quorum', and in the late republic a quorum was required for the vote on *supplicationes*, though there is no positive evidence for a quorum being required for voting a triumph; but it is in any case unlikely that such rules would have existed as early as this. For a *s.c.* being passed by a rump senate (*per infrequentiam furtim senatus*) cf. xxxix. 4. 8. On the whole matter cf. Balsdon, *JRS* xlvii (1957), 19–20.

2. trecenta . . . quingentos: B has *cccxx milia* ∞ ✗ (the final *siglum* is of a more complex form than McDonald's apparatus indicates), having omitted the intervening words because the scribe's eye slipped from the first to the second *milia*. ⟨*bigati*⟩ is the supplement of McDonald who argues that in other cases L. says whether the silver is coined or solid (xxxiii. 23. 7, 27. 2, 37. 11, xxxiv. 10. 4, xxxvi. 21. 11, 39. 2, 40. 12, xxxiii. 23. 7, 37. 11 being instances of coined silver only, so that the expression is not only used where distinction is necessary). The figure given must be of coined silver (cf. Madvig, *Emendationes*, 471) but it is possible that L. omitted the description here as he thought it would be clear which was involved. Amounts for coined silver in booty-lists occur only in the fourth and fifth decades: this is therefore the first reference, and L. may not yet have been conscious of the need to specify that the silver was coined.

As far as the figures themselves are concerned, that for the bronze is 320,000 asses. The figure for silver in χ is 170,000 plus a figure which B gives as shown above. This Madvig and McDonald plausibly take as 1,500 which gives a total of 171,500 denarii.

For comparative figures for booty in the second century cf. Tenney Frank, *Economic Survey*, i. 127–37.

49. 4–7. *Games of Scipio, distribution of land, supplementation of Venusia, Spain*

4. consul: Scipio did not cross to Africa until 204 when his consulship was at an end. But magistrates and pro-magistrates were not always distinguished and there is no need to emend; cf. xxvi. 33. 4, *TLL*, iv. 564, Mommsen, *StR*, ii³. 240 n. 5. There is no other reference to this vow.

5. de agris militum eius: in 4. 1–3 we are told of the appointment of *xviri* for the assignation of land to the African veterans; presumably the *xviri* referred to the senate the question of the amount of land and also whether the Spanish veterans (see next note) were also to be included. (Sage's note on this passage is nonsensical.)

in Hispania: 4. 1 refers only to African veterans, and the Spanish ones are now added. W–M argue that *militum eius* is inaccurate as the Spanish armies had not returned with Scipio and only the veterans had been released in 201 (xxx. 41. 5). But the Spanish armies had served under Scipio and the phrase is perfectly natural.

agri: B, *om.* χ. It is strictly unnecessary with *agrum* following; but a gloss in B omitted by χ would be extremely strange and in these brief notices, perhaps coming almost unaltered from the *annales*, such a repetition is perfectly understandable.

decemviri: in 199 the rest of their work was entrusted to the propraetor C. Sergius (xxxii. 1. 6); for reasons for this cf. n. ad loc. For the *xviri* cf. 4. 3 nn. *item* does not indicate that L. was here assuming that the *xviri* were first appointed on this occasion, as W–M argue.

6. ad supplendum . . . erant: Venusia, mod. Venosa, on the borders of Samnium, Lucania, and Apulia and famous as the birthplace of Horace (*Lucanus an Apulus anceps*), was a Latin colony founded in 291. It remained loyal to Rome in the Hannibalic war when much of the surrounding area was in Hannibal's hands. For full details cf. Radke, *RE*, viiiA. 892–6, Salmon, *Samnium*, 316,

Colonization, 96. For other cases of supplementation of colonies cf. xxxii. 2 (Narnia), xxxiii. 24 (Cosa), xxxvii. 46 (Placentia and Cremona), *CIL* i². p. 200 (Cales), Toynbee, ii. 91–2, 144.

C. Terentius Varro: (83). Cf. 11. 18 n.

T. Quinctius Flamininus: (45). Cf. xxxii. 7. 9 n. Plutarch, *Flam.* 1. 4 makes him a *iiivir* for Narnia and Cosa instead of for Venusia, but this must be a confusion; cf. Gundel, *RE*, xxiv. 1050.

P. Cornelius Cn. f. Scipio: (350). *Cn. f.* B. χ has the nonsensical *C. Fulvius*. The filiation is given to distinguish him from his cousin Africanus. The son of Cn. Cornelius Scipio, the consul of 222, he was quaestor between 204 and 199, curule aedile in 197 (xxxiii. 25. 1), praetor in 194 with *imperium* prorogued in 193, and consul in 191 with *imperium* prorogued in 190. He was a candidate for the censorship of 189 and a *iiivir* for Aquileia in 183. He is the father of P. Cornelius Scipio Corculum, consul in 155 and grandfather of Nasica Serapio, consul of 138 and murderer of Tiberius Gracchus.

As often the commission consists of one consular and two younger men (cf. Ogilvie, 549).

Venusiam adscripserunt: for the construction cf. xxxiv. 42. 6.

7. C. Cornelius Cethegus: (88). Elected curule aedile for 199 (50. 6, xxxii. 7. 14) and consul for 197 (xxxii. 27. 5, 28. 1), when he campaigned in Gaul (xxxii. 29. 5 ff.) and triumphed (xxxiii. 22. 5, 23. 1). He was censor with Sex. Aelius Paetus in 194 and a *legatus* to Carthage in 193. He is a *privatus cum imperio* but we are not told of his appointment, which was presumably made in accordance with the terms of the *s.c.* of xxx. 41. 4 (*MRR*, i. 324).

in agro Sedetano: it is clear from other references that it is in northern Spain; but whether north or south of the Ebro is uncertain; cf. xxviii. 24. 4, 31. 7, xxix. 1. 26, App. *Ib.* 77, Schlag, 28 n. 41. It is not to be confused with the land of the Edetani (cf. Hübner, *RE*, v. 1938–9). De Sanctis, iv. 1. 442 n. 123 declares this victory to be an annalistic invention.

49. 8–11. *The return of Cotta*

8. praeceperant: i.e. the senators. Cf. iii. 37. 5 (W–M).

9. et ⟨non⟩: *non* was Weissenborn's supplement. Others, including Madvig, delete *et* assuming a transposition of *nullius eorum qui bello interfuissent nisi eius* . . . McDonald says this order is too harsh, but it seems perfectly possible.

10. testes: B has a gap, χ has *virtus* and then alters *populus Romanus videret* into *publice videretur*. Madvig's emendation of *testes* is generally accepted. (B's gap is not quite large enough for six letters, but this is no objection to *testes*: B left a gap when he could not read F and the size of the gap is only an estimate.) C. Brakman's *arbitros* (*Mnemosyne* N.S. lv [1927], 56) has little to commend it.

49. 12. *Elections*

For the assignations of provinces cf. xxxii. 1. 1–2.

L. Cornelius Lentulus : (188). Cf. 20. 1 n.

P. Villius Tappulus : (10). Cf. 4. 3 n. The MSS. here read *t. appalus* though they get the name right in the case of the praetor.

L. Quinctius Flamininus : (43). Cf. 4. 5 n.

L. Valerius Flaccus : (173). Cf. 4. 5 n.

L. Villius Tappulus : (9). Plebeian aedile in 213.

Cn. Baebius Tamphilus : (41). Cf. xxxii. 7. 5. Tribune in 204 or 203, plebeian aedile in 200 (50. 3), *iiivir* for Sipontum and Buxentum in 186, and consul in 182 with command prorogued in 181. For the political position of the Baebii cf. 6. 3–4 n.

50. *Various domestic events*

50. 1. Annona . . . diviserunt : cf. 4. 6 n. This is presumably the corn sent by Carthage (19. 2), and not the remnant of the corn collected by Scipio the previous year.

M. Claudius Marcellus : (222). Military tribune in 208, plebeian tribune in 204, praetor in 198 (xxxii. 7. 13, 8. 5, 27. 3), and consul in 196 (xxxiii. 24. 1, 25. 4, 36. 4, 37. 9, 42. 5, 42. 7). He was a *legatus* to Carthage in 195 (xxxiii. 47. 7), a military *legatus* in Gaul in 193, censor in 189, and *pontifex* from 196 (xxxiii. 42. 5) until his death in 177.

Sex. Aelius Paetus : (105). A distinguished jurist, *iiivir* for the supplementation of Narnia in 199 (xxxii. 2. 6), consul in 198 (xxxii. 7. 12, 8. 1, 9. 4, 26. 1, 27. 5), censor in 194. For his political position cf. p. 33 n. 2.

2. ludos Romanos . . . instaurarunt : cf. 4. 5 n., 9. 5–10 n.

ex multaticio argento : for other cases of aediles using fines for public ornaments or public works cf. x. 23. 11–13, 33. 9, 47. 4, xxvii. 6. 19, xxx. 39. 8, xxxiii. 25. 2, 42. 10, xxxiv. 53. 4, xxxv. 10. 12, 41. 9, xxxviii. 35. 5–6. The phrase *aere multaticio* is found in inscriptions recording similar dedications both at Rome and elsewhere; cf. *ILLRP* 45, 130a, 593, 683, G. Voza, *AC* xix (1967), 101 ff. On the judicial powers of the aediles, cf. Mommsen, *StR*, ii³. 492 ff.

3. plebeii ludi : cf. 4. 7 n.

L. Terentio Massiliota : (58). One of the *x legati* to Macedonia in 196 (xxxiii. 35. 2, 39. 2), praetor in 187, and military tribune in Spain from 182 until 180. The MSS. here have *Massioliota* or *Masiliota*. At xxxviii. 42. 4 B has *Massaliota* and Mg had *Massiliota*.

At xl. 35. 3 most MSS. read *Massaliota*. It thus seems possible that the *cognomen* was Massaliota, spelt in the Greek way. The *cognomen* is not found elsewhere (I. Kajanto, *Latin Cognomina* [Helsinki, 1965], 202).

Cn. Baebio Tamphilo: 49. 12 n.

ter toti instaurati: cf. 4. 7 n., xxxii. 27. 8 n.

4. ludi funebres . . . pugnarunt: gladiatorial shows are found in private funerary games from 264 but do not occur in public festivals until 105. For evidence see Wissowa, *RuK²*, 456 n. 5, 466. Cf. Lippold, 97 n. 81.

⟨**M.**⟩ **Valeri Laevini**: cf. 3. 3 n. The MSS. omit the *praenomen* but L. would not have referred to him without a *praenomen*.

P. et M. filiis eius: P. Valerius Laevinus is not otherwise known. Marcus (210) was praetor in 182, a *legatus* in Liguria in 181 and in Macedon in 171. A third son, C. Valerius Laevinus (208), was suffect consul in 176. B has *et* after *M.*, deleted by the second hand and Weissenborn plausibly conjectured that we should read *P. et M. et C.*

5. M. Aurelius Cotta: (103). Cf. 3. 4 n. and addenda.

decemvir sacrorum: on the *xviri s.f.* cf. 8. 2 n.; originally two in number, they were raised to ten in 367 and to 15 by Sulla. Later the number was larger still though they continued to be called *quindecimviri s.f.*: cf. Wissowa, *RuK²*, 535, Latte, *RRG*, 397–8.

M'. Acilius Glabrio: (35). The MSS. have *M.*, but he is clearly the consul of 191. He was tribune in 201, plebeian aedile in 197 (xxxiii. 25. 2), praetor in 196 (xxxiii. 24. 2, 26. 1, 36. 2), and consul in 191, with command prorogued in 190. He was a supporter of Scipio Africanus (cf. p. 31).

6. C. Cornelius Cethegus: (88). Cf. 49. 7 n.

7. C. Valerius Flaccus . . . flamen Dialis: (166). The *flamen dialis* was the most important of the *flamines* and strict rules governed both his selection and his activities in office. He was forbidden to leave Rome for more than a few days and he was thus effectively debarred from a political career. Flaccus had been forced into the post against his will by the *pontifex maximus* P. Licinius Crassus (xxvii. 8. 4). According to L. he did this in an attempt to reform Flaccus' character. In fact Crassus was a supporter of Scipio (cf. 9. 7 n.) and since the Valerii were among Scipio's opponents, it is probable that Crassus' real aim was to block Flaccus' political career. Flaccus was determined to salvage something, however, as is shown by his assertion of his right to sit in the senate (L. l.c.) and his holding of this aedileship and the praetorship in 183.

Cf. Wissowa, *RuK*², 504 ff., Latte, *RRG*, 402–3, Samter, *RE*, vi.
2486 ff., Schlag, 140 ff., J.-C. Richard, *Latomus* xxvii (1968), 789,
W. Pötscher, *Mnemosyne* series 4, xxi (1968), 215 ff.

iurare: for the prohibition of the making of oaths by the *flamen
dialis*, cf. Gell. x. 15. 5, 31. Fest. p. 92L, Plut. *QR* 44. On the oath
of the magistrates, cf. H. B. Mattingly, *JRS* lix (1969), 143 n. 87.

8. si iis videretur: cf. 4. 2 n.

cum tribunis . . . ferrent: in this period the tribunes were
often used for carrying matters in the assembly instead of the consuls
or praetors. It is not clear whether the present cumbersome procedure was designed merely to give the tribunes work to do or
whether the consular year was near to an end, and the tribunes
(who entered office on 10 December) provided an element of
continuity.

9. L. Valerius Flaccus . . . designatus: cf. 49. 12.

11. L. Manlius Acidinus: (46). Praetor in 210, *legatus* to Greece
in 208, pro-magistrate in Italy in 207, and first appointed to Spain
in 206 (cf. xxviii. 38. 1, xxix. 13. 7, xxx. 2. 7, 27. 9, 41. 4–5, Schlag,
22 ff.). For his return cf. xxxii. 7. 4.

Cn. Cornelio Lentulo: the MSS. read *Lentulo* but at xxxiii.
27. 2 he is referred to as Cornelius Blasio, and it is Blasio whom the
Fasti record as celebrating an *ovatio* in 196. It is impossible to say
whether the error belongs to L. himself or the name was corrupted
in transmission. Blasio (74) was praetor in 194 after holding the
command in Spain until 197.

et.: the stop after *et* in the Oxford text is a misprint.

L. Stertinio: the first member of the *gens* known. He was one of
the *legati* for the settlement with Philip in 196. Cf. xxxiii. 27. 3, 35. 2.

The MSS. have *tercinio* here but the correct reading in the other
passages.

imperium: in both cases *privati cum imperio* are appointed; cf.
49. 7 n.

BOOK XXXII

1–2	199 B.C.	Events in Rome and Italy
3–6		The campaign in Greece in autumn/winter 199/8
7		Events in Rome and Italy
8–9, 5	198 B.C.	Events in Rome and Italy
9, 6—25		The campaign in Greece in 198
26–7		Events in Rome and Italy
28–31	197 B.C.	Events in Rome and Italy
32–40		Events in Greece in autumn/winter 198/7

199 B.C.

1–2. *Events in Rome and Italy*

1. 1–8. *Provinces and armies*

1. 1. consules praetoresque: on the consuls and praetors cf. xxxi. 49. 12 nn.

idibus Martiis: cf. xxxi. 5. 2 n.

2. Ariminum: it is clear from §§ 4–5 that in fact the consul Lentulus is to command an army in Gaul, and hence Baebius' command is restricted to the area round Ariminum. On many occasions there is only one command in Gaul. Sometimes Gaul is specially mentioned as a province, on others, as here, it is included in *Italia*. W–M's note says all that is necessary.

Sicilia: in succession to Q. Fulvius Gillo. Cf. xxxi. 8. 8 n.

Sardinia: in succession to M. Valerius Falto. Cf. xxxi. 8. 9.

3. novas legiones: cf. xxxi. 8. 5. Presumably two legions are to be enrolled by Lentulus.

in supplementum . . . permissum: Sulpicius had taken two legions (xxxi. 8. 5). Apart from the indefinite supplement here indicated, Flamininus is reported to have taken 8,000 extra infantry in 198 (8. 2, 9. 6) and to have been sent a further 6,000 in 197 (28. 10). The Roman infantry at the battle of Cynoscephalae amounted to, at the most, 22,800 and probably much less (cf. xxxiii. 4. 6 n.). Sulpicius' army contained at least 8,400 Roman infantry (perhaps more; cf. xxxiii. 1. 2 n.) and probably an equivalent number of *socii*. We thus have at least 30,800, plus the indefinite number referred to here. It seems impossible to hold that the difference could be accounted for by losses, troops held in garrison duties, and perhaps the discharge of 2,000 veterans (cf. 3. 1–7). We must therefore follow Kromayer (ii. 95 ff.) in rejecting the present notice and that in 28. 10. The supplement of 198 appears in both the non-Polybian passage 8. 2 and the Polybian 9. 6 (cf. p. 2) and is referred to by Ennius *Ann.* fr. 332v. It can therefore be accepted. Cf. also Walbank, *Philip V*, 147 n. 5. (I argue in xxxiii. 4. 6 n. that there were some 4,500 men on garrison duty at the time of Cynoscephalae, but in that case the total of Roman troops is less than 22,800. McDonald who argues for the latter figure does not believe that any substantial numbers were on garrison duty. It would be very difficult to believe in both the higher number and the existence of garrisons.)

4. consul . . . succederet : i.e. Lentulus.

5. exauctorati : *ex auctoritate* MSS., which is nonsense. The word occurs seven times in L. in reference to the discharge of veterans (viii. 34. 9, xxv. 20. 4, xxix. 1. 9, xxxvi. 40. 14, xl. 40. 15, xli. 5. 11).

quinque milia socium : probably the 5,000 who had been sent to Gaul in 200 and then transferred to Etruria (xxxi. 8. 7, 11. 3).

6. prorogata imperia : the MSS. have *prorogato imperio*. It is uncertain whether the nominative singular or the plural should be read. Both are found where more than one command is in question. Cf. Packard, iii. 1191–2.

C. Sergio : (36). Cf. xxxi. 4. 4 n. He was *praetor urbanus* in 200 (xxxi. 6. 2).

militibus . . . curaret : cf. xxxi. 49. 5 n. Sardinian veterans are now added for the first time. It appears that the job was transferred to Sergius from the existing *xviri*. The reason may be either that the problems involved seemed to require a magistrate possessing *imperium* or that the *xviri* had been depleted by death and the fact that Villius, one of their number, was now consul and Flamininus was known to be standing for the consulship, and probably holding a quaestorship (cf. 7. 9 n.). Cf. Toynbee, ii. 202.

7. Q. Minucio : (22, 55). Cf. xxxi. 4. 4 n. He continues in command in Bruttium. For the incident cf. xxxi. 12. 1–4.

1. 9. *The Latin Festival*

9. Feriae Latinae : the Latin festival was held each year at a date determined by the consuls, but most usually in the spring. The meat from the sacrifices was offered to representatives of the Latin states. For a similar omission cf. xxxvii. 3. 4. Cf. Samter, *RE*, vi. 2213–16, Wissowa, *RuK*², 124–5, Latte, *RRG*, 144–6.

Ardea : originally a town of the Rutuli, it was said to have been attacked by Tarquinius Superbus (i. 57. 1), and became a Latin colony in 442 (iv. 11). On its history and topography cf. Ashby, *Campagna*, 212, A. Boëthius, *BSM* ii (1931–2), 2. 1–17, v (1934), 1–2. 1–6, B. Tilly, *Vergil's Latium* (Oxford, 1947), ch. ii, Ogilvie, 220. For a dedication by Ardea at the Alban Mount cf. *ILLRP* 188.

1. 10–14. *Prodigies*

Cf. xxxi. 12. 5–10 n.

10. Suessa: probably Suessa Aurunca, as in 9. 3, and not Suessa Pometia in Latium. It is modern Sessa Aurunca, in northern Campania (cf. Nissen, *IL*, ii. 2. 666–7, Philipp, *RE*, ivA. 584–6, A. Maiuri, *RAAN* xxxvi [1961], 55–62).

nuntiatum est: since there is no verb with *legati* below Gronovius read *nuntiarunt* here. Actives without subjects are found in reports of prodigies (cf. xxxi. 12. 5 n.), but in this case, as McDonald says, it is as easy to understand the verb with *legati* as the subject here, and there is no need to alter the MSS. reading.

de caelo tactum: lightning is one of the most common forms of prodigy. Cf. Wülker, 9, Luterbacher, 22–3, Krauss, 35–46.

Formiani: Formiae, mod. Formia, on the coast of Latium about 80 miles south of Rome. It received *civitas sine suffragio* in 338 and full citizenship in 188. The precise location of the temple of Jupiter is not known. Cf. Nissen, *IL*, ii. 2. 659 ff., Weiss, *RE*, vi. 2857–8. Other prodigies at Formiae: Oros. iv. 4. 3 (269), xxxii. 29. 2 (197), xxxv. 21. 4 (192), xl. 2. 4 (182), Obs. 14 (163), Wülker, 97.

Ostienses aedem Iovis: R. Meiggs, *Roman Ostia* (Oxford, 1960), 352 suggests that the temple may have been one of the two built on the Decumana at Ostia, on the northern side of the forum. Other prodigies at Ostia: xxvii. 23. 2 (208), Obs. 28 (130), Wülker, 98.

Veliterni: Velitrae was a Volscian town, to which several Roman colonies were dispatched. It is the modern Velletri, some 30 miles south of Rome near the Via Appia. Cf. Nissen, *IL*, ii. 2. 2. 632–3, Radke, *RE*, viiiA. 2406–11, G. Cressedi, *Velitrae* (Rome, 1953), Ogilvie, 308–9. Other prodigies at Velitrae: xxx. 38. 8 (202), xxxii. 9. 3 (198), Wülker, 101.

Apollinis: Suetonius (*DA* 94) tells that Augustus' mother had intercourse with a serpent in the temple of Apollo at Velitrae.

Sancus: B reads *Sangus* as a genitive, and a similar reading occurs at viii. 20. 8. The true name of the god is Sancus (or fully Semo Sancus Dius Fidius) and the epigraphic evidence suggests that it is a second declension noun. But the occurrence in two places of the genitive in *-us* suggests that L. did write that (*contra* Ogilvie, *Phoenix*, 345). Sancus was worshipped at Rome on the Quirinal. Cf. Link, *RE*, iA. 2252–6, Wissowa, *RuK*², 129–31, Latte, *RRG*, 127–8.

in Herculis aede : I see no case for Walsh's statement (*CR*, 55) '*aede* should be obelized: perhaps *signo Herculis aereo*'.

capillum enatum : the instance is unique but belongs to the class of 'matter growing in strange places' (Wülker, 13). Radke (*RE*, viiiA. 2410) suggests emendation to *capellum*, there being several cases of animals born in temples (Wülker, 16–17). This seems unnecessary: *capellus*, moreover, is attested only in Priscian.

11. eculeum . . . ternis pedibus : cf. xxxi. 12. 7 n.

12. A P. Sulpicio . . . enatam : in fact in the course of the campaign described in book xxxi, which actually belongs to 199 (cf. xxxi. 22. 4–47. 3 n.). Schlag (110) oddly thinks that Sulpicius announced the prodigy in order to prevent Villius from arriving early in Macedon. Cf. p. 32 n. 3 and *Latomus* xxxi (1972), 41–2. On the prodigy cf. Krauss, 137–8.

13. senatus censuerat : for the senate acting on its own initiative in regard to prodigies cf. Wülker, 29–30, Luterbacher, 35.

maioribus hostiis . . . videretur : cf. xxxi. 5. 3 n.

14. haruspices : the *haruspices* were concerned with *divinatio* and their skills were of Etruscan origin. They were not an official part of the Roman priesthood and were consulted only as occasion demanded. Cf. Wissowa, *RuK²*, 543 ff, Latte, *RRG*, 158, 396–7, and for their consultation in regard to prodigies, Wülker, 35–7, Luterbacher, 35.

supplicatio . . . pulvinaria : cf. xxxi. 8. 2 n.

edicta : χ, *dicta* B. Weissenborn read *indicta*, but *edicere* is found in reference to *supplicationes* at xxii. 10. 8, xxxvi. 2. 5, and xlv. 16. 6 (cf. McDonald's apparatus) and should be accepted.

2. *Other decisions of the senate*

2. 1. Carthaginienses . . . advexerunt : by the terms of the peace of 201 the Carthaginians had to pay 10,000 talents in 50 years— i.e. 200 talents a year (xxx. 37. 5, Pol. xv. 18. 7, App. *Lib.* 54). In 191 the Carthaginians asked to pay off the whole of the amount outstanding, and this the Romans refused (xxxvi. 4. 7–9). The first payment was presumably due in 200 and *eo anno primum* is either an error, or in fact the money arrived at the conclusion of 200, and the events here described occurred at the beginning of 199.

2. probum . . . decocta : for debasement of coinage in Egypt at this period cf. Rostovtzeff, *SEHHW*, ii. 712, iii. 1494 n. 131.

mutua sumpta : no doubt the Carthaginians were compelled to do this rather than return to Carthage to collect the deficit—greatly to the advantage of Roman financiers.

3. obsides . . . spes facta : the information on the Carthaginian hostages at Rome is conflicting. L. (xxx. 37. 6) and Polybius (xv. 18. 8) talk of 100 hostages. Appian (*Lib.* 54) says 150 but this probably refers to hostages guaranteeing the preliminary truce. Here, however, L. seems to imply more than 100. In 181 (xl. 34. 14) L. again talks of the return of a hundred hostages and in 168 there is mention of one individual hostage (xlv. 14. 5). This gives us a total of at least 201 hostages. It seems that L. has misunderstood the situation and that hostages were exchanged, not restored. The fullest discussion is by Aymard, *Pallas* i (1953), 44–63 = *ÉHA*, 436–50 (though Aymard oddly puts the present episode in 198). Cf. also Walbank, *Commentary*, ii. 470–1.

4. Norba . . . Signiam . . . Ferentinum : Norba, in Latium, is about 32 miles south-east of Rome on the western side of the Monti Lepini (cf. Nissen, *IL*, ii. 2. 644–5, Philipp, *RE*, xvii. 925), Signia (mod. Segni) is on the eastern side of the Monti Lepini, about 7 miles north of Norba (cf. Nissen *IL*, ii. 2. 650–1, Philipp, *RE*, iiA. 2347–8), and Ferentinum (mod. Ferentino), not to be confused with the Etruscan Ferentium, is a Hernican town 12 miles east of Signia (cf. Ashby, *MDAI(R)* xxiv [1909], 1–58, Hülsen, *RE*, vi. 2208, A. Bartoli, *BA* xxxiv [1949], 293–306, G. Gullini, *AC* vi [1954], 185–216). We hear also of hostages kept at Fregellae (Nepos, *Hann.* vii. 2) and Setia (26. 5) but 26. 7–8 is not necessarily evidence for hostages at Circeii and Norba, as Aymard, *Pallas* i. 54 = *ÉHA*, 448 assumes (cf. 26. 7 n.). The hostages were clearly dispersed and it is perverse to read *Setiam* for *Signiam* here. For the practice of keeping hostages in allied states cf. Toynbee, i. 255.

5. Gaditanis . . . convenisset : the *deditio* of Gades in 206 is mentioned at xxviii. 37. 10, the conclusion of a treaty by L. Marcius and the subsequent status of that treaty by Cicero, *pro Balbo* 34 ff. The present passage is much disputed. Does *adversus id . . . convenisset* indicate that the treaty had provided for a *praefectus* to administer Gades, and the senate now cancelled this clause, or that the treaty had specified that there should be no *praefectus*, but one had nevertheless been sent? The case for the first alternative is argued by Badian (*CPh* xlix [1954], 250–2) and McDonald ad loc. Their chief arguments are (i) that if, as the second view requires, the *adversus* clause depends on *petentibus*, we should expect *sibi*, not *iis*, (ii) that the senate would not have simply broken an agreement, as the second view implies, (iii) that *remissum* implies conceding a point on which Rome had legal rights. It may be replied to (i) that the *adversus* clause is L.'s own comment, though the verb is quite naturally attracted into the subjunctive (the subjunctive is far harder to explain on the first view, where the clause depends on *Gaditanis . . . mitteretur* as a whole). As to (ii), in fact the treaty had never been ratified at Rome (Cic. l.c.): it may have been an informal agreement preceding the *deditio* of Gades, and legally was overtaken by the *deditio*. (The fact that it was made with Marcius Septimus does not mean that the latter was now in charge of Spain, and that hence the agreement comes after the departure of Scipio, as argued by Dahlheim, 58–9 n. 25, cf. Flurl, 194.) It is quite possible that its terms had been ignored and Gades now appealed to Rome on its basis. This would in itself dispose of (iii) also, though in fact *remissum* can perfectly well mean 'agree' without implying the waiving of legal rights.

Gades' treaty was ratified by the senate in 78 B.C. though it was never formally ratified by the people (Cic. l.c.). Cf. also H. Gundel, *Historia* xii (1963), 291–3, and literature quoted by Schlag, 28 n. 40, Dahlheim, 58–9 n. 25.

in fidem : the *deditio* referred to at xxviii. 37. 10.

L. Marcio Septimo : (101). At xxviii. 28. 13 he is called *Septimus Marcius* and at xxv. 37. 2 *L. Marcius Septimi filius*. B here reads *Septimo*, χ *Septimio*. The evidence favours the former quite apart from the fact that *cognomina* ending in *-ius* are rare. In 211 he took command of the Roman forces in Spain after the death of the two Scipios (sources in *MRR*, i. 275) and in 206 he played a large part in Scipio's campaign. His precise status on both occasions is uncertain—that he was a centurion in 206 as Cicero, *pro Balbo* 34 states is highly unlikely. Cf. Münzer, *RE*, xiv. 1591–5.

6. Narniensium . . . iussus : cf. xxxi. 49. 6 n. Narnia (mod. Narni) was a Latin colony founded in 299 on the site of Nequinum. It is in Umbria, on the east of the Tiber. It was one of the defaulting colonies in 209 (xxvii. 9. 7). Cf. Nissen, *IL*, ii. 1. 406, Philipp, *RE*, xvi. 1734–6, Brunt, 539. On the issue cf. Toynbee, ii. 91, 108, 144, 202, who points out that the senate's action now is a *de facto* admission that the defaulters did have a case.

immixtos . . . generis : i.e. Umbrians claiming to be colonists. But it was not impossible for local Italians to become citizens of Latin colonies: cf. xxxiii. 24. 9 n. It is an early example of urban drift (Toynbee, ii. 337).

7. P. et Sex. Aelii—Paetis : on Publius Aelius (101), consul in 201, cf. xxxi. 2. 5 n., on Sextus (105), consul in 198, xxxi. 50. 1 n.

Cn. Cornelius Lentulus : (176). Cf. xxxi. 14. 2 n. It is unusual to find two consulars on a commission of three on a comparatively minor matter.

datum erat : *erat* χ, *om.* B. It is unnecessary, and should be deleted (cf. Walsh, *CR*, 54).

Cosani : Cosa was a Latin colony on the coast of Etruria, at the modern Ansedonia. It was founded in 273. It remained loyal in 209. Cf. Hülsen, *RE*, iv. 1666–7, F. E. Brown, *Cosa* (*MAAR* xx [1951], xxvi [1960]), F. Castagnoli, *MAAR* xxiv (1956), 149 ff., Salmon, *Colonization*, 29–39. Their request was eventually granted in 197 (xxxiii. 24. 8).

3–6. *The campaign in Greece, autumn/winter 199/8*

3. *Mutiny in the Roman army*

Nissen (*KU*, 132) regarded this chapter as of annalistic origin. His arguments were (a) that it has no connection with what follows, in particular with 6. 1 where Vilius is said to have wintered at Corcyra, (b) that *in Macedoniam cum venisset* (§ 2) is an annalistic way of describing arrival in Greece: Polybius gives precise place-names, (c) that *se . . . scripturum* (§ 7) is an annalistic phrase. None of this is convincing. Villius could have dealt with the mutiny and then gone to Corcyra, *in Macedoniam* may not be the Polybian expression, but it is merely L.'s own transition to Greek affairs (cf. xxxi. 3. 2 n., 14. 2, p. 10 n. 4) and though *se . . . scripturum* is expressed in a Roman form, there is no reason why Polybius should not have referred to the fact. The whole episode is indeed expounded in rhetorical language, but that may be only L.'s reworking of what he had read in Polybius.

Nissen's view has been widely accepted. Cf. W–M ad loc., Walbank, *Philip V*, 147 n. 5, Klotz, *Livius*, 4.

For a list of cases of insubordination in the Roman army in this period cf. Toynbee, ii. 80 ff.

3. 2. P. Villius . . . venisset : he arrived at the end of Sulpicius' campaign in 199. Cf. Walbank, *Philip V*, 319.

3. ex Africa . . . transportata erant : according to L. (xxx. 45. 2) most of Scipio's army returned to Italy. Hence W–M think that there is a confusion here between Valerius' expedition (xxxi. 3) and the main army: xxxi. 8. 6 and 14. 2 do not imply that the *voluntarii* came from Sicily. But some troops did remain in Sicily, and were presumably taken from there to Brindisi. Most of them are the Cannae veterans, as § 5 suggests that they had served in Sicily before crossing to Africa with Scipio.

pro voluntariis : only volunteer veterans were to go (xxxi. 8. 6).

4. exhaustam : i.e. they had fulfilled all the obligations that could be demanded of them. The Cannae legions had served over the

16 years which were the legal requirement for an infantryman (cf. Brunt, 399).

6. consul . . . causam esse: the typical appeal to reason in dealing with a mutiny. Cf. xxv. 7, Tac. *A*. i. 25 ff.

4. *Philip's attack on Thaumaci*

On this assault cf. Walbank, *Philip V*, 146–7.

4. 1. Thaumacos: mod. Domoko, in Phthiotic Achaea, commanding the route from the Malian gulf into Thessaly as L. describes in §§ 3–5. Cf. Stählin, *HTh*, 155–7, *RE*, vA. 1331–7, G. Daux and P. de la Coste-Messelière, *BCH* xlviii (1924), 353 ff., P–K, i. 1. 197–8. See also 13. 14.

eo tempore: in the autumn of 199, following the events described in xxxi. 42.

2. Archidamo: leader of Aetolian troops under Flamininus in 197 (Pol. xviii. 21. 5). He was an Aetolian ambassador to the Achaean League in 192 (xxxv. 48. 10) and to Acilius Glabrio in 191 (Pol. xx. 9. 2). In 169 he was accused by Lyciscus of anti-Roman activities (Pol. xxviii. 4. 8) and soon joined Perseus (xliii. 21. 9, xliv. 43. 6). He was three times Aetolian *strategos*.

The form is *Archidamus* consistently in the MSS. of L., though Ἀρχέδαμος in Polybius and inscriptions. L. probably wrote the former wrongly.

Cf. Wilcken, *RE*, ii. 439, Walbank, *Commentary*, ii. 580.

3. Pylis: the MSS. have *Pyleis*, a non-existent form.

per Lamiam: Lamia is near the northern edge of the head of the Malian gulf. It is mentioned here simply to locate the road which Thaumaci commands.

imminentes . . . transeunti: the MSS. have *quam coelem* (Bψ) or *quas coele* (φ) . . . *Thessaliaeque*—i.e. *Thessaliae* is taken with what follows. Madvig (*Emendationes*, 473–4) saw that *Thessaliae* must go with the preceding sentence. The *confragosa loca*, it is clear, lie to the south of Thaumaci and are not therefore in Thessaly, while the *Coele Thessaliae* is the central Thessalian plain referred to in xxxi. 41. 7 (cf. n. ad loc.). The *fauces* cannot be this plain, and that rules out *quas*. *quam Coelen* seems the best reading, as the *vocant* formula suggests a Greek form (cf. xxxi. 24. 4 n.). Madvig first suggested *quam Coelen vocant Thessali; itaque* and later *Thessaliae; atque*. But it seems perverse to change *Thessaliae* and *quae* is the easiest explanation of the MSS. reading. The phrase is equivalent to *ei parti Thessaliae quam vocant Coelen Thessaliae*, but it is the first *Thessaliae* which is understood, and Madvig and W–M are wrong to punctuate after *vocant*.

5. ab eo . . . appellati: the origin of the name is unclear, but L.'s explanation is not very plausible.

7. hiemps . . . iam instabat: cf. xxxi. 22. 4 n. For the date cf. Walbank, *Philip V*, 319.

5. 1–5. *Philip and the Achaean League*

5. 2. angunt . . . timentem: cf. xxxi. 34. 5 n.

3. sociorum: particularly the Achaeans and Epirus (cf. 14. 5–6, xxxi. 7. 9 n.).

popularium: 'his own countrymen' (cf. § 7) but the following words suggest social revolution and this may have lead L. to use the word which has the sense of 'revolutionary' in Roman political language.

cupido novandi res: Philip had encouraged the lower classes in Greece and was now afraid that his own people would follow his lead (cf. *Past and Present*, no. 36 [April 1967], 3).

caperet: cf. xxxi. 2. 9 n.

4. ius iurandum . . . exigerent: the only other reference to this oath is at 21. 5, and it is hard to equate it with the oaths referred to in Pol. iv. 9. 4, which appear to be reciprocal. It may be that all members swore to carry out whatever the symmachy decided, and this was interpreted by L. as an oath of personal loyalty to Philip. As it stands here it assorts oddly with the concessions that follow. Cf. Aymard, *PR*, 54–5 n. 34, P. Herrmann, *Der römische Kaisereid* (Göttingen, 1968), 42 n. 75. On Philip and the Achaean League in 200 cf. xxxi. 25. 3 ff.

4–5. Achaeis . . . contributae forent: this passage raises a number of problems.

(a) *Text.* The MSS. read *Eleis Alipheran*, which makes nonsense of what follows and conflicts with xxviii. 8. 6, where Philip promises Aliphera to Megalopolis (see below). Madvig's emendation *Eleis ⟨ademptam, Megalopolitis⟩ Alipheran* makes excellent sense and squares with the facts about Triphylia.

(b) *The places involved.*

Orchomenus. Originally Achaean it had passed to the Aetolians, perhaps in the late 230s, and then been captured by Cleomenes in 229 and by Doson in 224. It then remained in Macedonian hands (cf. Walbank, *Commentary*, i. 242).

Heraea. In western Arcadia, on the east bank of the Alpheius. It had been Achaean since 236, was captured by Cleomenes in 227 and by Doson in 224. The easiest assumption is that it remained in

Macedonian possession. This has been objected to on two grounds. (a) In 197 the Aetolians claimed the possession of Heraea (Pol. xviii. 42. 7), which implies recent possession. (b) Polybius, iv. 6. 4–6, in discussing Macedonian possessions in the Peloponnese in 219 does not refer to Heraea. Hence the view that Heraea was returned to the Achaeans in 224 and captured by the Aetolians in the First Macedonian war, only to be quickly recaptured by the Macedonians (Niese, ii. 483, Aymard, *PR*, 25–8 n. 5). But Aetolia's claim does not necessarily refer to recent possessions and there is no reason why Polybius should have mentioned all the Macedonian possessions. Cf. Walbank, *Commentary*, ii. 607–8.

Triphylia. Triphylia is the general name for the area in the west of the Peloponnese between the Alpheius and the Neda. It had been captured by Philip from Elis in the winter of 219/18. Cf. Bölte, *RE*, viiA. 186–201, Walbank, *Philip V*, 45–6, *Commentary*, i. 529–31, P–K, iii. 2. 349 ff.

Aliphera. Aliphera is south of Heraea and was also captured from the Eleans by Philip in 219/18. Cf. Walbank, *Commentary*, i. 531.

Megalopolis. Megalopolis was founded by synoecism of surrounding communities *c.* 370 (cf. von Hiller, *RE*, xv. 127–40, P–K, iii. 1. 293, H. Bengtson, *Griechische Geschichte*⁴ (Munich, 1969), 280. L. here uses the Greek form Μεγάλη πόλις. The Greek form for the inhabitants is Μεγαλοπολῖται (cf. e.g. Xen. *Hell.* vii. 5. 5). L. varies between *Megale Polis* and *Megalopolis*, and *Megalopolitae* and *Megalopolitani*. Cf. Packard, iii. 237.

For the possibility that Phigaleia should be added to the list cf. Aymard, *PR*, 58–9 n. 51.

(c) *The Facts.* Did Philip actually surrender the towns now? In 208 L. says *reddidit inde Achaeis Heraeam et Triphyliam; Alipheram autem Megalopolitis . .. restituit* (xxviii. 8. 6) but he clearly did no more than promise to restore the places involved (cf. Walbank, *Commentary*, ii. 606–7, Errington, *Philopoemen*, 62 n. 1). At xxxiii. 34. 9 (cf. Pol. xviii. 47. 10) Triphylia and Heraea are *redditae* to Achaea. Are we to conclude that once again Philip only promised restoration? Against such a view Aymard (*PR*, 59–61 n. 53) argues that in xxxii. 21 there is no complaint by Aristaenus that Philip has not kept his promises. The 196 episode is then to be understood as Roman recognition of Achaean possessions rather than actual restoration.

firmabat: cf. xxxi. 14. 11 n.

5. 6–7. *Heraclides*

6. ⟨**ad**⟩: Madvig's supplement (*Emendationes*, 475) is the simplest remedy. For the usage, common in L., cf. W–M ad loc.

7. Heracliden: cf. xxxi. 16. 3 n. Diod. xxviii. 9 refers to this episode in similar language. Cf. Walbank, *Philip V*, 145.

5. 8–6. 8. *Philip and Villius at the Aous gorge*

8. unquam ante alias: cf. xxxi. 7. 3 n., Ogilvie, 576.

9–11. For L.'s brevity in topographical descriptions of strategically important sites cf. Burck, *Erzählungskunst*, 198.

9. principioque veris: spring 198.
    Athenagora: cf. xxxi. 27. 6 n.
    in Chaoniam . . . misit: recent excavations appear to have established that the site of Antigonea is not at Tepelenë, north of the confluence of the Aous and the Drin, as had been held by earlier writers, but some 16 miles to the south, near Saraginishtë. Details are reported by Hammond in *JRS* lxi (1971), 112–15. This seems to confirm Hammond's own earlier view (*JRS* lvi [1966], 45–51, *Epirus*, 278 ff., 617 ff.) that the *stena* are the Drin gorge, but that in § 10 Philip moves to a position well within the Aous gorge. Though Saraginishtë is well south of the gorge, the gorge was called *Tà παρ' Ἀντιγόνειαν στενά* at Pol. ii. 5. 6 and *ad Antigoneam fauces* here not because Antigonea was itself near the gorge, but, as Hammond says, because it was 'the largest city in the region'. For Kromayer (ii. 40 ff.) and Walbank (*Philip V*, 149–50 n. 1) Philip is at the mouth of the Aous gorge all the time, for De Sanctis (iv. 1. 60 n. 117) and Accame (*Espansione romana*, 140) north of the confluence. The site is described in detail in Plutarch, *Flam.* 3.
    Chaoniam: Chaonia is the general name for the north-eastern part of Epirus. Cf. Hammond, *Epirus*, 678 ff.
    per Epirum: this indicates that the area to the north-east of the Aous gorge was part of Epirus. Cf. Walbank, *Philip V*, 150, Hammond, *JRS* lvi, 46, *Epirus*, 679.

11. inter montes: for the omission of *duo* cf. iv. 9. 4, Ogilvie, 547.
    Meropum . . . Asnaum: these mountains are not elsewhere mentioned. For their identification cf. Hammond, *JRS* lvi, 49.

6. 1. Charopum: the Greek form is Χάροψ, but L. always has *Charopus*: cf. 11. 1 ff., 14. 5. He is the grandfather of the pro-Roman demagogue of the years following 170 (cf. Scullard, *JRS* xxxv [1945], 58–64, Briscoe, *Past and Present* no. 36 [April, 1967], 15).
    in continentem travectus: probably to Oricum, thence to the main army at Apollonia (cf. xxxi. 40. 6). Cf. Hammond, *Epirus*, 617 and n. 1 who suggests that *in continentem* is L.'s translation of εἰς τὴν Ἤπειρον in Polybius.

2. quinque milia ferme: for this phrase and the distance involved cf. Hammond, *JRS* lvi, 49, 51.

3. eodem itinere: cf. xxxi. 33. 4 ff. and nn., Walbank, *Philip V*, 148 ff., Hammond, *JRS* lvi, 46–7.

4. T. Quinctium consulem factum: 7. 8–12. L. does not imply that Villius heard of Flamininus' election, appointment, and arrival at the same time, as is claimed by Badian, *Flamininus*, 38.

5–8. For the relevance of this section, and in particular *ceteri Graeci Latinique auctores*, for the understanding of L.'s use of his sources cf. p. 9.

5. Valerius Antias: for the fragments of Valerius cf. *HRR*, i². 238 ff. On his work cf. Peter, *HRR*, i². cccv ff., Ogilvie, 12–16, Volkmann, *RE*, viiA. 2313–40, Badian, *Latin Historians*, 21–2.

recto itinere: it is far from clear what Antias thought was the *rectum iter* which was avoided by going through the *saltus*. There was no other direct route.

7. *Events in Rome and Italy*

7. 1–3. *Activities of the censors*

7. 1. L. Lentulus: (188). Cf. xxxi. 20. 1 n.

2. multis claris petentibus viris: normally only consulars sought the censorship (P. Licinius Crassus in 210 was the most recent exception) and many of the consuls of recent years were available.

   P. Cornelius Scipio Africanus: (336). For the political position of Scipio in this period cf. pp. 29 ff. *Cornelius* is omitted by B and φ, and L. often refers to *P. Scipio* (cf. Packard, iii. 733–4); but the full form is normally given at the election of magistrates.

   P. Aelius Paetus: (101). Cf. xxxi. 2. 5 n.

3. magna inter se concordia: for the political position of Paetus and the significance of this censorship cf. p. 33 n. 2.

   senatum sine ullius nota: the *nota* or mark of censure by the censors involved removal from the list of senators. Cf. xxxix. 42. 6, Mommsen, *StR*, ii³. 384.

   portoria . . . Castrum portorium: the difficulties in the text as given by the MSS. and retained by McDonald are the meaning of *portoria venalicium* and *Castrum portorium*. For McDonald both *venalicium* and *Castrum* are genitive plurals, the abbreviated form being used here because the phrase is a 'formula'. *portoria venalicium* then means 'transport dues levied on items for sale' and *Castrum* *portorium* 'transport dues levied at Castra'. But (i) there are no parallels for the alleged formula, and the abbreviated genitive plural is never found with a neuter. (ii) There is a harsh transition from the locatives *Capuae Puteolisque* to the alleged genitive *Castrum*. (iii) *venalicium* appears to mean 'a tax on sale' (Cod. Just. xii. 19. 4), and it is not certain whether it could mean *res venales* (Tränkle, *Gnomon*, 376, thinks the meaning is possible, and quotes *Dig.* ix. 2. 27. 24, xxiv. 1. 31. 10, xxiv. 1. 2. But in all these cases *venalicius* is an adjective meaning 'available for sale'). This lends support to Madvig's view that *portoria* is a gloss on *venalicium* and should be deleted. As for *Castrum*, *Castris* is perhaps the easiest emendation (Pettersson, 110 n. 1).

Portoria can refer to transport taxes in general, not only to harbour dues, so there is no difficulty in their being levied at Capua. *Castra* may be one of the *Castra Hannibalis* attested in Bruttium and Campania (cf. Hülsen, *RE*, iii. 1768 [*castra*, 20, 21]), or an otherwise unknown place in Campania. Cf. Hülsen, *RE*, iii. 1767, Toynbee, ii. 145, 355, 358, Kahrstedt, *Historia* viii (1959), 194. Salmon (*Colonization*, 180 n. 120, 184 n. 161) thinks that *Castrum portorium* is the name of the colony, and that it is equivalent to *Castrum Salerni* in 29. 3, but it is hard to see how such a view can be reconciled with the text of our passage. Moreover, if the site is in fact settled in 199, why should it be done again, apparently *de novo* in 197?

It is uncertain whether new taxes are being levied for the first time or whether Rome is taking over the collection of taxes previously levied by the local communities concerned.

See further Madvig, *Emendationes*, 476–7, S. J. de Laet, *Portorium* (Bruges, 1949), 55–7, Nisbet, *Commentary on Cicero, in Pisonem*, 157–8, Tränkle, *Gnomon*, 376–7.

Puteolis: mod. Pozzuoli, a little north of Naples. It formed part of the *ager Romanus* and justice there was probably administered by the *praefecti Capuam Cumas*. Cf. Frederiksen, *RE*, xxiii. 2036–60, Brunt, 528, 540 ff. A colony is sent there in 197 (29. 3).

colonos . . . adscripserunt: presumably a Roman colony. W–M's argument that it was not a colony because that would have required a decision by the people is not compelling. It was the senate that really decided these matters, and the people's ratification was a formality. L.'s form of expression is perfectly natural. Cf. Salmon, *Colonization*, 167.

sub Tifatis: Capua lay at the foot of Mt. Tifata. Cf. Philipp, *RE*, viA. 932–3.

agrum vendiderunt: sale of *ager publicus* is referred to in general by App. *BC* i. 7. 27, Plut. *TG* 8. 1. The only other specific instance known is in 205 (xxviii. 46. 4–5). Little was sold, as it became more profitable simply to occupy the land. I see no reason for the common assumption that the land sold technically remained the property of the Roman people (cf. Gabba, *ad* App. l.c.).

7. 4. *The return of L. Manlius Acidinus*

4. L. Manlius Acidinus : (46). Cf. xxxi. 50. 11 n.

P. Porcio Laeca : (19). He was a *iiivir epulo* from 196 and praetor in 195 (xxxiii. 42. 1, 42. 7, 43. 5). He may have been responsible for the first *Lex Porcia de provocatione* extending the right of *provocatio* to Roman citizens outside Rome (cf. McDonald, *JRS* xxxiv [1944], 19, Scullard, *RP*, 96). Manlius may have originally claimed a triumph, and been refused for the same reasons as Lentulus in 200 (xxxi. 20)—i.e. that he had been appointed to his command as a *privatus cum imperio*. No political conclusions can be drawn from the episode. Cf. Schlag, 58–9.

privatus : because the *ovatio* was refused he did not have the privilege of retaining his *imperium* within the *pomoerium*.

sex milia : McDonald believes that this is the best interpretation of the MSS. readings. In this sort of case precision is impossible. Most editors read *mille ducenta*. Lentulus in 200 brought 43,000 pounds of silver (xxxi. 20. 7).

triginta : emendation to *trecenta* to obtain a more normal ratio of gold to silver would be quite unjustified.

7. 5–8. *Gaul*

5. Cn. Baebius Tamphilus : (41). Cf. xxxi. 49. 12 n. For his appointment 1. 2.

C. Aurelio : (95). Cf. xxxi. 4. 4 n.

Insubrum : cf. xxxi. 10. 2 n.

6. quod iam timeri desierat : after the victory of Furius in 200 (xxxi. 21).

7. L. Lentulum : (188). Cf. xxxi. 20. 1 n. For his appointment xxxii. 1. 2 n.

decedere . . . iussit : by virtue of his superior *imperium* a consul could order a praetor to leave a province to which he had been assigned by the senate. Since Baebius was a Scipionic supporter (xxxi. 6. 3–4 n.) and Lentulus' brother Gnaeus had opposed Scipio as consul in 201 (cf. xxxi. 14. 2 n.) there is nothing surprising in Lentulus' treatment of Baebius.

7. 8–13. *Elections*

8. M. Fulvium : (56) or (91). It is unclear whether he is to be identified with M. Fulvius Flaccus, the *xvir* of 201 (xxxi. 4. 3) or with M. Fulvius Nobilior, the consul of 189. Cf. Münzer, *RE*, vii.

240, 265, Bleicken, 84. For the political position of the Fulvii at this time cf. p. 32.

M'. Curium : (4). The MSS. read *M.*, but Plut. *Flam.* 2. 1 has Μάλλιον which looks like a corruption of Μάνιον and the famous Curius Dentatus is *M'. M'. f. M'. n.* Two other M'. Curii are known, but no Marci. This one is not otherwise known.

tribunos plebis : Broughton (*MRR*, i. 331) makes them tribunes of 198 but the elections may have taken place before 10 December 199 (Varr.).

9. T. Quinctium Flamininum : (45). Flamininus had been military tribune in 208, propraetor at Tarentum in 205–4, a *xvir* for land assignation in 201 (xxxi. 4. 3) and a *iiivir* for the supplementation of Venusia in 200 (xxxi. 49. 6). On his early career as a whole cf. Badian, *JRS* lxi (1971), 102–11, who argues that his command at Tarentum was in fact prorogued until at least 203 and possibly 202. For his subsequent career cf. pp. 22 ff.

ex quaestura : does this indicate that he was quaestor in 199 or simply that his only previous office was the quaestorship? The usage of the phrase itself is indecisive (cf. *MRR*, i. 329 n. 2). The arguments of the tribunes are that Flamininus is omitting the praetorship and the aedileship, not that he is moving from one office to another. On the other hand *continuare* does suggest immediate continuation (cf. *TLL*, iv. 724) and the vehemence of the protest does perhaps indicate that immediate succession was in question. Cf., however, Badian, *JRS* lxi, 109, arguing for a quaestorship in 206.

Of the other five consuls of 199–7 three did not hold the praetorship, but all held the aedileship. Indeed Flamininus was the first consul since 211 who had not held either the praetorship or the aedileship. The rules laid down in the *Lex Villia Annalis* in 180 were gradually adopted informally in the early years of the second century (cf. xxxi. 4. 7 n.). Thus after 196 all consuls held the praetorship. The protests of the tribunes may thus be seen more as a step in this process than as a particular objection to Flamininus. Though if Flamininus was quaestor in 199, his action was unique.

Cf. A. E. Astin, *The Lex Annalis before Sulla* (Brussels, 1958), 26 ff., G. Rögler, *Klio* xl (1962), 99 ff., Gundel, *RE*, xxiv. 1051, Schlag, 142.

10. summa imis continuare : the phrase is quoted by Nisbet and Hubbard, 384 as parallel to such pejorative descriptions of *populares* as *infima summis paria fecit* (Cic. *legg.* iii. 19) and *summa imis miscuit* (Vell. Pat. ii. 2. 3). Our passage, however, has a different connotation: Flamininus' action is criticized as an example of the arrogance of the *nobiles*.

11. patres . . . aequum esse: the sentence is cast in the formal language of a *senatus consultum*. The view that the people is free to elect whom it wants is found also in xxiv. 8. 1, xxxix. 39. 5 and Appian, *Lib.* 112 (on the latter cf. Astin, *Scipio Aemilianus*, 65 ff.). When the man desired was disqualified by laws, dispensation from the laws could be granted. In this case there was no law (Plut. *Flam.* 2. 1 is wrong to say there was).

12. in auctoritate: i.e. they accepted the senate's decision. No doubt there was a heavy majority against them, and as usual they did not imperil the system as a whole by pressing their point of view.

Sex. Aelius Paetus: (105). Cf. xxxi. 50. 1 n.

13. L. Cornelius Merula: (270). He was a *iiivir* for the foundation of Tempsa in 194 and consul in 193.

M. Claudius Marcellus: (222). Cf. xxxi. 50. 1 n.

M. Porcius Cato: (9). The great Cato Censorius. He had been military tribune in 214, and quaestor in 204. He was consul in 195 with command prorogued in 194. He served in Greece in 191 and 189 and was censor in 184. For his political position in the 190s cf. *Latomus* xxxi (1972), 47.

C. Helvius: (1). The MSS. corrupt the name here but have it correctly at 8. 5, 9. 4, and 26. 2.

qui aediles . . . fuerant: cf. xxxi. 4. 7 n.

7. 13–14. *Games*

13. ludi plebeii instaurati: cf. xxxi. 4. 5 n. The length or number of times of the *instauratio* is usually stated and F. Ritschl (*Parerga zu Plautus und Terenz* [Leipzig, 1845], 311) reasonably suggested that some such indication has fallen out here.

epulum Iovis: cf. xxxi. 4. 7 n.

14. C. Valerio Flacco: (166). Cf. xxxi. 50. 7 n.

C. Cornelio Cethego: (88). Cf. xxxi. 49. 7 n.

ludi Romani: cf. xxxi. 9. 5–10 n.

7. 15. *Deaths of* pontifices

15. Ser. et ⟨C.⟩ Sulpicii Galbae: the MSS. read *Ser. Sulpicius et Galba*, which is nonsense. The appointments of both Ser. Sulpicius Galba and C. Sulpicius Galba as *pontifices* are recorded by L. (xxx. 26. 10, 39. 6). Ser. Galba (56) was curule aedile in 209 and a *legatus* to collect the *Magna Mater* in 205/4. Gaius (49) is not otherwise known. Münzer regards Servius as a brother of P. Sulpicius Galba, the consul of 211 and 200, and Gaius as Publius' son. But both men may be brothers of Publius.

M. Aemilius Lepidus: (68). Cf. xxxi. 2. 3 n.

Cn. Cornelius Scipio: (346). Scipio Hispallus, probably a *legatus* under the Scipios in 190, praetor in 179, and consul in 176. He is probably a brother of P. Cornelius Scipio Nasica, consul in 191.

198 B.C.

8–9. 5. *Events in Rome and Italy*

8. 1–8. *Provinces and armies*

8. 1. consules: χ, *om.* B. The sense is clear without it and it should be regarded as a gloss. L. varies his form of expression for indicating the beginning of a new consular year, and the fact that *consules inito magistratu* is found in xxxvi. 1. 1 does not prove that it is correct here, particularly as *consules* occurs later in the sentence.

senatum in Capitolio cum habuissent: for the use of the Capitol for the first meeting of the senate in a new consular year cf. Mommsen, *StR*, iii. 927 n. 4, Willems, *Le Sénat*, ii. 159 n. 1, O'Brien-Moore, *RE*, supp. vi. 704.

compararent . . . sortirenturve: from § 4 (*sortiti*) it is clear that the latter alternative was chosen. But it is highly likely that the lot was not entirely arbitary in its operation. Flamininus' election programme was based on a policy for the Macedonian war and Aelius was not a man of war. Cf. pp. 32–3, Badian, *Flamininus*, 30–1.

2. in supplementum . . . equites: cf. 1. 3 n., 9. 1 n.
sociorum Latini nominis: cf. xxxi. 8. 7 n.
novus omnis exercitus: i.e. the normal two legions.

3. L. Lentulo: (188). Cf. 7. 7. He presumably returned to the north after holding the elections.

veterem deducere exercitum: in 199 Lentulus was granted an army (1. 4) and also took over that of Baebius (7. 7). Whether both armies were now in Gaul is not clear. The senate had originally decreed that most of Baebius' army was to be disbanded on the arrival of Lentulus (1. 5).

4. sortiti: § 1 n.

5. M. Claudius Siciliam: in succession to L. Valerius Flaccus.
M. Porcius Sardiniam: in succession to L. Villius Tappulus.
Galliam: since Lentulus is to be succeeded by Aelius, presumably Helvius' command is that described as Ariminum in 1. 2 (cf. n. ad loc.).

6. praetoribus: *praetores* MSS., but the datives that follow make it clear that the consuls remain the subject.

7. socium et Latini nominis: cf. xxxi. 8. 7 n. and § 2 above.

8. 9–16. *The embassy from Attalus*

Holleaux (*Études*, iii. 331–5, cf. Niese, ii. 607 n. 4) argued that the whole of this account (together with 27. 1) is a fabrication, and that there was no invasion of Pergamum by Antiochus in the winter of 199/8. His reason is that the account assumes that Attalus was not in Pergamum at the time of the invasion while in fact he returned from Greece in the autumn of 199 (xxxi. 47. 2). Holleaux's case is unconvincing. Attalus could have left Pergamum to rejoin Roman forces in 198 and then heard of the invasion.

See against Holleaux, Badian, *CPh* liv (1959), 82–3 = *Studies*, 114–15, Schmitt, *Antiochos*, 269–70, Schlag, 76 and n. 22, Bredehorn, 139–47. Cf. also xxxiii. 20. 8 n.

10. Antiochum . . . invasisse: probably not Antiochus in person, as he was still occupied in Koile Syria, but one of his satraps (cf. W–M ad loc., Schmitt, *Antiochos*, 270).

11. sua classi suaque opera: i.e. his (Attalus') fleet etc.

13. socium et amicum populi Romani: there is no previous mention of this, but the *amicitia* will have been formed when the Roman *legati* of 201/0 visited Antiochus after delivering their ultimatum to Philip at Abydos. It has nothing to do with Suetonius' story (*Claud.* 25) of an offer of *amicitia* to Seleucus II. Cf. xxxiii. 20. 8, Badian, *CPh* liv, 82 = *Studies*, 114.

14. potestatem: thus all the MSS. except L, which has *potestate*. McDonald justifies the accusative as 'come into power and stay there', but there is no sense of 'come into power' here, even if the construction itself is a possible one. Cf. Ogilvie, 268, *Phoenix*, 345.

15. legatos . . . missuros: cf. 27. 1 and nn.

nuntient . . . absistat: if the senate could use this sort of language it must have already received substantial assurances from Antiochus that his agreements with Philip mattered little to him.

16. aequum: because *amici* had no *foedus* which could bind them not to attack other *amici* of Rome.

9. 1–4. *Prodigies*

Cf. xxxi. 12. 5–10 n.

9. 1. eos . . . milites: it is clear that as in 200 (cf. xxxi. 8. 6) they were volunteers. Plutarch (*Flam.* 3. 3) refers explicitly to 3,000

Scipionic volunteers for Flamininus' army. For the political importance of this cf. p. 32.

2. de caelo tacta: cf. 1. 10 n.

Veis: for the topography of Veii cf. J. B. Ward-Perkins, *PBSR*
xxxix (1961). Though sacked after its capture in 396, the site remained inhabited (cf. Ogilvie, 630). For other prodigies at Veii cf.
xxvii. 37. 1 (207), xli. 21. 12 (174), xlii. 2. 4 (173), xliv. 18. 6 (169),
Obs. 12 (166), Obs. 30 (125), Wülker, 101.

Lanuvi: cf. xxxi. 12. 6 n. The temple of Jupiter is not otherwise
known, though Cic. *fin.* ii. 63 refers to the multitude of shrines there.

Ardeae: cf. 1. 9 n. A prodigy is also recorded there in 133 (Obs.
27a, Wülker, 95). The temple of Hercules is not otherwise mentioned.

Capuae: cf. xxxi. 29. 10 n. For other prodigies at Capua cf.
xxii. 1. 12 (217), xxvii. 11. 2 (209), xxvii. 23. 1 (208), xxvii. 37. 3
(207), xxx. 2. 10 (203), xxxv. 9. 4 (193), xl. 45. 3 (179), xli. 9. 5
(177), Obs. 14 (163), Wülker, 96.

aedes . . . Alba: it is also referred to in xl. 45. 3. Cic. *leg. agr.* ii.
94. and Val. Max. ix. 1. ext. 1 mention the *Albana* which is presumably the street in which the *aedes* stood. It may have been the
Town Hall of Capua. Cf. Hülsen, *RE*, iii. 1561.

3. caelum ardere: cf. xxxi. 12. 5 n.

Arreti: cf. xxxi. 21. 1 n. Other prodigies at Arretium are recorded at xxxv. 21. 3 (192), Obs. 52 (92), Obs. 53 (92), Obs. 54 (91),
Wülker, 95.

Velitris: cf. 1. 10 n.

trium . . . desederat: for similar prodigies cf. Wülker, 18,
Krauss, 53–4.

Suessae Auruncae: cf. 1. 10 n.

agnum . . . capite: cf. xxxi. 12. 7 n.

4. supplicatio: cf. 1. 14.

consules: the implication seems to be that in this case the
consuls acted on their own authority. This may be a brachylogy
but there is no good reason for Wülker's assertion (30) that the
consuls could not take action with regard to prodigies on their own
initiative. Cf. Luterbacher, 35.

9. 5. *Gaul*

The information is repeated in 26. 1–2. Cf. n. ad loc.

5. Aelius cum Helvio: cf. 8. 4 n.

quem dimittere debebat: there is no clear statement in 8. 3
that the army of Lentulus was to be disbanded, and there is no
indication what army Helvius was to have.

9. 6–25. 12. *The campaign in Greece in 198*

9. 6–11. *The arrival of Flamininus*

6. T. Quinctius: the MSS. have *et T. Quinctius*. Walsh (*CR*, 54) suggests that *et* should be retained as a 'resumptive *et*'. But in the first mention of the military activities of a new consul such an *et* would be very strange indeed. L. regularly uses asyndeton in such places. Cf. e.g. xxxi. 22. 4, xxxiv. 8. 4, 46. 4.

maturius quam priores: for the dates of the arrival of Sulpicius and Villius cf. xxxi. 22. 4 n., xxxii. 3. 2 n., Plutarch also stresses Flamininus' early arrival in Greece (*Flam.* 3. 1). The actual date is May (Walbank, *Philip V*, 151, 319).

octo . . . quingentis: these are the reinforcements authorized in 8. 2. On the authenticity of the figures cf. 1. 3 n.

In 8. 2 the number of *equites* authorized is 800. But the actual figure may not have reached this, and emendation seems unwise. It is not necessarily a question of L. being inconsistent as McDonald argues.

8–9. utrum . . . intraret: the same problem as had confronted Villius (6. 3).

recto itinere: i.e. through the Aous gorge.

per Dassaretios . . . Lyncumque: as Sulpicius had in 199. Cf. xxxi. 33. 4 n.

10. ni timuisset: similar arguments are attributed to Flamininus by Plutarch, *Flam.* 4. 1, who adds that Flamininus was afraid of lack of supplies: cf. xxxi. 40. 6 n.

10. *The conference of Antigonea*

Cf. Diod. xxviii. 11.

10. 1. diesque quadraginta . . . pacis: the implication is that the conference follows the forty days *sine ullo conatu*. Plutarch makes no mention of the conference, but describes some skirmishes (4. 2) which Walbank (*Philip V*, 151) places during the forty days. Hammond (*JRS* lvi, 51–2) is right to protest at this, and equates Plutarch's battles with the skirmishes of §§ 9–12 of this chapter. Hammond thinks that Plutarch implies that these skirmishes lasted more than the one day stated by L. and he places the conference during the forty days. Neither inference is justified. L. should be followed on both matters.

per Epirotarum gentem: for the Epirote policy in the First Macedonian war cf. xxxi. 7. 9 n. As on that occasion they are eager for peace and very lukewarm allies of Philip. Cf. Oost, *RPEA*, 46: *contra* Hammond, *Epirus*, 618.

2. habitoque concilio: i.e. a meeting of an organ of the Epirote League. Hence the *concilio* of the MSS. is right, and is not to be altered to *consilio*.

Pausanias praetor: probably the *strategos* of the Epirote League. Inscriptions bear witness to the existence of the office, and there seems to have been only one at a time. Hence xxix. 12. 11 is not to be taken as evidence for three *strategoi*. Cf. Hammond, *Epirus*, 648–51, though Hammond's position on the book xxix passage does not seem to accord with the rest of his argument.

Pausanias is not otherwise known.

Alexander magister equitum: presumably a ἵππαρχος. Neither the man nor the office is elsewhere attested.

ubi . . . amnis: cf. 5. 9 n. For Walbank (*Philip V*, 151) this is near Tepelenë, for Hammond (*JRS* lvi, 51) at Dragot. The language seems to favour Hammond here.

3. praesidia . . . deduceret: as is clear from what follows, Rome is now demanding the complete evacuation of Macedonian troops from all Greek states. This is the same demand as that made at Nicaea (33. 3, Pol. xviii. 1. 13) but is a considerably more extreme demand than that made at Abydus. Cf. Badian, *FC*, 70, Walbank, *Commentary*, ii. 550–1.

Diodorus (xxviii. 11) describes the demands as ἐκχωρεῖν ἁπάσης τῆς Ἑλλάδος. But since Polybius (xviii. 1. 13) uses that phrase of the demands at Nicaea (cf. 33. 3) and it is clear that evacuation of Philip's Asiatic possessions was also being demanded then, it seems reasonable to conclude that Flamininus' demands at Antigonea were not restricted to the mainland.

Walsh (*RhM* xcvii [1954], 107–8) compares L.'s account with that of Diodorus to illustrate L.'s embellishment of Polybius. His conclusions may be right, but caution is needed as we cannot be sure how closely Diodorus was reproducing Polybius: Diodorus' phrase ὅπως ἀφρούρητος ᾖ καὶ αὐτόνομος looks like an anticipation of the Isthmus declaration of 196. Cf. Heidemann, 105 n. 2.

res . . . ceterorum: W–M rightly compare 29. 5, v. 16. 7, xxxv. 1. 12 for the conjunction of *res* with a neuter. Cf. K–St, i. 63, H–S, 431.

aequo arbitrio: the demand δίκας ὑποσχεῖν is made at Athens and Abydus (Pol. xvi. 27. 2, 34. 3). The idea of arbitration is not Roman (W–M's parallel of *recuperatores* is misleading). In all three cases it is clear that Rome regards the amount of damages as the only question available for arbitration, while Philip's offer concerns arbitration on the merits of his case. Cf. §§ 5–6 below and Walbank, *Commentary*, ii. 537.

4. Philippus . . . excessurum: Philip is ready to give up his own conquests, but not what he inherited. For the rights of succession, not a Roman conception, cf. xxxiii. 40. 4–6 n. Badian, *FC*, 70 n. 2 thinks that Philip was making very small concessions, as not much of his conquests remained. This is not the case: he still held the gains he made in the Social war and the First Macedonian war, his probable conquests after 205 (cf. xxxi. 1. 9–10 n.) and almost all his Aegean conquests of 202–200.

6. priorem vim omnibus fecisse: at Abydus (xxxi. 18. 2, Pol. xvi. 34. 5) and Nicaea (34. 7, Pol. xviii. 6. 2) Philip denied that he was the aggressor.

7. cum ageretur: presumably Philip, while not accepting Flamininus' terms, did inquire which states were involved.

Thessalos: Thessaly had been, with the smallest interruptions, under Macedonian control since the middle of the fourth century. Its mention first made clear the nature of Rome's demands.

8. se . . . proripuit: for the phrase cf. viii. 30. 11, xxii. 3. 9, xxix. 9. 4, Cic. *har. resp.* 2, Sall. *Cat.* 32. 1.

9. in planitie . . . patenti: at the entrance of the gorge (Hammond, *JRS* lvi, 52).

11. aptum: the MSS. have *amplum* which makes little sense. *aptum* is the reading of Gelenius from the *codex Spirensis*.

catapultae ballistaeque: Plutarch (*Flam.* 4. 2) refers only to ἀκοντίων καὶ τοξευμάτων.

12. fecit: χ, *facit* B, perhaps rightly. Cf. xxxi. 39. 9 n.

11. *The shepherd and the pass*

For other evidence see Ennius *Ann.* fr. 334 ff.v, Plut. *Flam.* 4. 2–6, App. *Mac.* 6, Zon. ix. 16. 1, *de vir. ill.* 51. Plutarch and *de vir. ill.* speak of several shepherds and Plutarch says that they produced Charops as witness to their good faith.

On the differences between L. and Plutarch cf. Nissen, *KU*, 135–6, Hammond, *JRS* lvi, 52 n. 1 38, p. 8 n. 1. On the route, Hammond, 52.

11. 1. Charopo: cf. 6. 1 n.

3. educturum: *deducturum* MSS., but the emendation of Gronovius is generally accepted. The scribe would have been influenced by *deducitur* in § 1. Yet the MSS. reading may be right. *educere* is often used in military contexts, but not in the sense 'lead out of (e.g. a forest) to the place they wanted to be' (cf. *TLL*, v. 2. 118). *Deducere* does not necessarily mean 'lead down' (cf. *in arcem*, Caes. *BC* ii. 19. 4) but even if it did 'lead up the mountain and down to a position above Philip's troops' would still make excellent sense.

4. suae . . . essent: 'in such a way that the over-all control of the situation should remain in Flamininus', not the shepherd's hands'.

5. metu: cf. xxxi. 34. 5 n.

6. r⟨eg⟩em: *rem* MSS., but Harant's emendation is clearly necessary.

biduo: in Plutarch (*Flam.* 4. 4) the turning-party sets out, and Flamininus then rests his army for two days; for L. he attacks for two days, and the turning-party, presumably, sets out on the third day. But *interim die tertio* in 12. 1 must mean the third day after the turning-party set out, not the day following the *biduum* here. (Hammond, *JRS* lvi, 52 n. 38 misrepresents the difference between L. and Plutarch on this point.)

9. pernox: on the word cf. Ogilvie, 690. The moon shines through the night only near full moon. The battle can thus be dated *c.* 25 June (cf. Walbank, *Philip V*, 152, 319).

10. circa: B reads *capit*, χ *capi*. There have been a variety of emendations, which may be divided into three groups:
(a) those using an infinitive after *instat* (*capere, agere*).
(b) those putting a comma after *instat* and another indicative.
(c) a preposition (*apud, circa, contra*—the last Ogilvie, *Phoenix*, 346). *Instare* with an infinitive meaning 'presses on to' is rare (*TLL*, vii. 1. 2002 ll. 62–76) and is not found at all in a military context (cf. *TLL*, vii. 1. 2000), but equally none of the prepositions suggested are found after *instare* (cf. *TLL*, vii. 1. 2003). B's *capit* is ruled out by the fact that the *stationes* would be Flamininus' own, not Philip's as the strategy requires (cf. Ogilvie, l.c.). Walsh (*CR*, 55) defends Weissenborn's *carpit* on the grounds (a) that L. often uses it (in fact in xxxi. 40. 8 it is found in proximity to *instare*), (b) that περισπᾶν in Plutarch, *Flam.* 4. 4 (which in fact means 'divert the attention of') may have been in Polybius and suggested *carpit* to L. L., however, uses *carpere* mainly with *agmen*, where it is appropriate for harassing the end of a column, and the argument from περισπᾶν is very problematical. But though Walsh's arguments do not support *carpit*, I prefer it to the other suggestions. *instare* is very often used absolutely, and *carpit* is an easy explanation of B's reading.

12. *The battle in the pass*

12. 1. interim . . . significarent: the construction is a little awkward, as *interim* really goes with the infinitives (cf. W–M).

interim die tertio: cf. 11. 6 n. The shepherds promised to turn the pass in three days (Plut. *Flam.* 4. 2, App. *Mac.* 6).

se: χ, *om.* B. The omission of an unemphatic accusative is not uncommon (K–St, i. 701) and *se* can be regarded as an addition by χ (cf. Walsh, *CR*, 54: 35. 4 n.).

fumo significarent: in Plut. *Flam.* 4. 5 Flamininus attacks before the smoke is seen.

castris; nec: Walsh (*CR*, 54) asserts that the punctuation should be *admovet. Castris*, arguing that Flamininus did not move his wings to the camp. But Philip's camp was on both sides of the river, and the two wings were moving against the two parts of the camp. In any case it is far from clear that *castris obviam eunt* is a possible Latin phrase.

3–4. Apart from the difference over when the smoke appeared, I cannot see the inconsistency between L. and Plutarch alleged in this passage by Hammond (*JRS* lvi, 52 n. 38).

8. rex . . . fugit: cf. xxxi. 34. 5 n. At xxxiii. 4. 3 Philip claims that the phalanx had stood firm in this battle.

in tumulo quodam: for the position cf. Hammond, *JRS* lvi, 53.

9. frequenti agmine: for the phrase cf. Ogilvie, 491.

petunt: for the plural after a collective singular cf. xxxi. 39. 12, 42. 5 nn.

Thessaliam: i.e. they were proceeding south-east from the eastern end of the gorge.

13–15. *Warfare in Thessaly*

On the topography of these events see particularly Stählin, *HTh*, Y. Béquignon, *BCH* lii (1928), 444 ff. For a brief geographical survey cf. also H. D. Westlake, *Thessaly in the Fourth Century B.C.* (Cambridge, 1935), ch. i.

13. 1. per ipsas . . . sequitur: the Aous gorge, cf. 14. 5 n.

2. castra Pyrrhi: Hammond (*ABSA* xxxii [1931/2], 145, *JRS* lvi, 53, *Epirus*, 280) places this near Konitsa, about 32 miles south-east of the end of the gorge.

in Triphylia terrae Molottidis: the Molossian tribe of Triphylia is also known from inscriptions (*AE* 1956, 1 ff., Ἑλληνικά xv [1957], 247–55, Hammond, *Epirus*, 525 ff.). On the extent of Molossis cf. Hammond, *Epirus*, 673 ff., 683 ff.

metus urgebat: cf. xxxi. 34. 5 n.

montes Lyncon . . . Thessaliaeque: cf. Hammond, *Epirus*, 280–1 for their identification, north-east of Konitsa. (In *ABSA* xxxii, 145 Hammond placed them near Metzovo: cf. Walbank, *Philip V*,

153 n. 2). The connection with Lyncus (cf. xxxi. 33. 6) is not clear. Cf. also Bürchner and Stählin, *RE*, xiii. 2473.

3. vestiti . . . habent: for this description cf. Hammond, *Epirus*, 39 ff.

5. Triccamque: on Tricca, *c.* 10 miles north of Gomphi (on which cf. xxxi. 41. 6 n.), cf. Stählin, *HTh*, 119–20, Kirsten, *RE*, viiA. 146–9, P–K, i. 1. 50.

9. Phacium: ESE of Tricca. On its position cf. xxxvi. 13. 3, Thuc. iv. 78. 5, Stählin, *HTh*, 133–4, Lenk, *RE*, xix. 1609–10, Gomme, *Commentary on Thucydides*, iii. 545, P–K, i. 1. 265.

⟨P⟩**iresiae**: *Iresiae* MSS. There are several ancient references to Πειρασία (or some similar form of the name) while the only references apart from this passage to Iresiae are *Hom. Hymn* iii. 32 and Pliny *NH* iv. 32, and the former seems to refer to a place on the coast. Iresiae, then, may be the name of a coastal town, but Piresiae is the correct name for this site. For the position just west of Phacium cf. Stählin, *HTh*, 134, *RE*, xix. 102–4, P–K, i. 1. 61.

Euhydrium: there is no case for emending to Methydrium (cf. Stählin, *HTh*, 143 n. 6). Stählin places it at Ktouri, 12 miles southeast of Phacium. Cf. Béquignon, *BCH* lii, 444–5, lvi (1932), 122 ff.

Eretria: 18 miles east of Pharsalus. Cf. xxxiii. 6. 10, Pol. xviii. 20. 5, Philippson, *RE*, vi. 425, Stählin, *HTh*, 174–5, P–K, i. 1. 172, Walbank, *Commentary*, ii. 579.

Palaepharsalus: for the identification of Palaepharsalus cf. Béquignon, *BCH* lvi, 89 ff., withdrawing his argument in *BCH* lii, 22 ff. that Palaepharsalus was merely the older part of Pharsalus and not a separate town. Several sources refer to the battle of 48 as having been fought at Palaepharsalus (Béquignon, *BCH* lii, 22–3).

Pheras: Pherae is about 12 miles north-east of Pharsalus. For literature on its history and topography cf. Walbank, *Commentary*, ii. 574. I do not understand Walbank's statement (*Philip V*, 153 n. 8) that Pherae's resistance does not imply revolt. xxxiii. 6 and Pol. xviii. 19 do not indicate that it was Macedonian in 197. Cf. Kirsten, *RE*, supp. vii. 1018.

in Macedoniam: presumably directly via Larisa (Walbank, *Philip V*, 153).

10. proximis: i.e. the nearest to Aetolia.

Spercheias et Macran . . . Comen: in the Spercheius valley. Their precise position is disputed. Cf. Stählin, *HTh*, 222–4, *RE*, xiv. 808–9, iiiA. 1625–6 (his views are not consistent), Béquignon, *BCH* lii, 447–52, P–K, i. 1. 244.

in Thessaliam C⟨t⟩imenes et Angeias: on the positions of these towns cf. Stählin, *HTh*, 148–9, *RE*, xi. 2081–3, Béquignon, *BCH* lii, 452–8, *La Vallée du Spercheios* (Paris, 1937), 333–6. The towns are known to be Dolopian, but L. is using *Thessaliam* loosely. It cannot be the case that they are called Thessalian because they had been captured by Philip (as suggested by Béquignon, *BCH* lii, 454), since the area round Spercheiae and Macra Come is equally not in Aetolian hands. Cf. Walbank, *Commentary*, ii. 616–17.

11. Metropoli: *c.* 10 miles south-east of Gomphi, formed in the fifth century by synoecism of surrounding villages (cf. Stählin, *HTh*, 128–9, *RE*, xv. 1491–4). For its surrender to the Romans cf. 15. 3.

Callithera: a little to the south-west of Metropolis (cf. Stählin, *HTh*, 132–3, Bölte, *RE*, x. 1749, Béquignon, *BCH*, lii, 459, P–K, i. 1. 61).

12. Teuma: its position is uncertain. *Peumata* was suggested by U. Köhler (*Ztscht. Num.* xii [1885], 113 ff.), and accepted by Holleaux (*Études*, iv. 208 n. 2: cf. G. Daux and P. de la Coste-Messelière, *BCH* xlviii [1924], 359 n. 3). But Peumata (or Peuma) is in Phthiotic Achaea and does not fit in with the rest of the information.

Celathara: its position is uncertain. Cf. Stählin, *HTh*, 133, Béquignon, *BCH* lii, 460. A. Plassart (*BCH* xlv [1921], 53 n. 1) thought it a mere doublet of Callithera (§ 11).

13. Acharras: identified by Stählin (*HTh*, 154) with Ekkara and placed in the north-west of Phthiotic Achaea but cf. Béquignon, *BCH* lii, 460–1.

Xyniae: on the eastern shore of Lake Xyniae (cf. Stählin, *HTh*, 160–1, Daux and de la Coste-Messelière, *BCH* xlviii [1924], 348 ff., P–K, i. 1. 195, Walbank, *Commentary*, ii. 188). It was probably captured by Philip in 210: cf. Pol. ix. 45. 3.

14. Thaumacum: cf. 4. 1 n. There the plural form is used and the correction of Rubens to *Thaumacos* may well be correct.

15. Cyphaera . . . castellum: Cyphaera is placed by Stählin, *HTh*, 159–60, Béquignon, *BCH* lii, 464–5, at Kaitsa, just to the west of Lake Xyniae. For its commanding position cf. Béquignon, *Vallée du Spercheios*, 337.

Amynander atque Athamanes: cf. xxxi. 28. 1 n.

14. 1. Gomphos: cf. xxxi. 41. 6 n.

Phaecam: its precise position is unclear. Cf. Stählin, *HTh*, 127, Kirsten, *RE*, xix. 1560–1.

fauces: the pass of Porta on the river Portikos.

2. adortus: there is no need to add *est*. Cf. xxxi. 21. 5 n., Pettersson, 95.

eo dem⟨um⟩: *eodem* MSS. The supplement is inevitable.

3. Pherinium . . . Lampsum: none of these places is known otherwise. On Pherinium cf. Kirsten, *RE*, xix. 2040 and on the form of Ligynae Stählin, *RE*, xiii. 535–6.

4. ab tribus simul exercitibus: i.e. Macedonian, Aetolian, Athamanian.

crederet: χ. B has *crederent*, which could be right. For plural verbs after singular place-names cf. K–St, i. 22–3.

5. faucibus . . . in regionem Epiri: this must refer to the Aoi Stena, and so it cannot be the case that Flamininus proceeded down the valley of the Drin (thus Walbank, *Philip V*, 156, Accame, *Espansione romana*, 152). Hammond (*Epirus*, 619, *JRS* lvi, 53) thinks that Flamininus himself passed down the Aous gorge, while his baggage train went down the Drin. He also holds that the name of a specific *regio* of Epirus has been omitted by L. W–M's view that *regionem Epiri* means 'the land of Epirus' is impossible.

cui parti . . . favissent: the judgement, no doubt that of Polybius, may be wrong. The Epirotes wanted peace, and tried to behave as neutrals. Charops was unique in being specially pro-Roman. Cf. xxxi. 7. 9 n., Hammond, *Epirus*, 619.

6. eos: χ, *om*. B. *aestimare* is rarely used absolutely, and then usually in parenthesis. Cf. *TLL*, i. 1105.

animos . . . conciliat: there is no question of a treaty between Rome and Epirus at this stage (cf. Hammond, *Epirus*, 619).

7. Corcyram: the Roman naval base to which the fleet had returned in the autumn of 199 (xxxi. 47. 2).

onerariae naves: Flamininus' army was being supplied from Corcyra, though the main fleet, including some supply ships, had left there earlier in the year (16. 1–17. 3). For supply difficulties cf. xxxi. 40. 6 n., Thiel, 206 ff.

sinum . . . Ambracium: on Ambracia cf. Hammond, *Epirus*, 135 ff. It had been a member of the Aetolian League since *c*. 229 (cf. Flacelière, 252).

in monte Cercetio: for its site, on the borders of Epirus and Thessaly, cf. Stählin, *HTh*, 123, Walbank, *Philip V*, 156, Hammond, *Epirus*, 619.

eodem: χ, *eo* B. *eo* may be right, *eodem* having been caused by *eodem consilio* below.

8. duces: for Amynander's knowledge of routes in Thessaly cf. xxxi. 42. 8.

15. 1. Phaloriam: for its position on the west bank of the Peneius cf. Stählin, *HTh*, 124, Kirsten, *RE*, xix. 1749. On the form of the name cf. Stählin, 124 n. 6. Cf. xxxvi. 13. 6, xxxix. 25. 3.

3. legati . . . Phaloria: these words are omitted by B, the scribe's eye having jumped from the first *Phaloria* to the next.

Metropoli: 13. 11 n.

Cierio: *piera, pirea, pierea* MSS. At xxxvi. 10. 2 and 14. 6 Cierium is mentioned in connection with Metropolis (the MSS. there read *Cierum* or *Cieria*). Since π and κ are interchangeable in Thessalian names, it is very probable that *Πιερίου* at Thuc. v. 13. 1 and *ἐν Πιέρῳ* at Aelian *NA* iii. 37 in fact refer to Cierion. The site is at Arne, about 13 miles east of Metropolis. Cf. McDonald's note and Stählin, *HTh*, 130–2, especially 132 n. 2, P–K, i. 1. 60. Kroll, *RE*, xi. 380 is wrong. (The Pieria of Pliny *NH* iv. 33 is the region of Macedonia: its association there with a town called Aeginium would appear to be coincidental.)

iis[dem]: *hisdem* or *eisdem* MSS. (*hisdem* for *iisdem* is often found in renaissance MSS.). Reference to the *legati* being the same ones seems superfluous. Walsh's defence of *iisdem* (*CR*, 55) on the grounds that it is the *legati*, not individuals from Phaloria, to whom pardon is granted, is unconvincing. M. Müller may have been right to delete it entirely.

incensa ac direpta: L.'s normal, and more logical order, is *diripere et incendere*. The reverse order occurs only here and at 33. 11. Cf. K. Gries, *CPh* xlvi (1951), 36.

4. Aeginium: placed by Stählin (*HTh*, 121–2) at Kalabaka, on the basis of an inscription found there referring to Aeginium (*IG* ix. 2. 329). But Hammond (*Epirus*, 681) thinks the stone was moved to Kalabaka, and argues that Kalabaka shows no trace of fortifications. He identifies it with Nea Koutsoufliani, *c*. 20 miles north-west of Kalabaka. But this makes Flamininus' line of march very strange since Aeginium would then be far nearer to the initial part of his route into Thessaly. Cf. also P–K, i. 1. 275 locating it at Kastraki, a little to the north of Kalabaka.

5. Gomphorum . . . campos Thessaliae: cf. xxxi. 41. 6–7 nn.

Leucadem an sinum Ambracium: cf. 14. 7. Presumably Flamininus was not certain to which places the supply ships had gone. Leucas formed part of Acarnania: it was captured in 197 (xxxiii. 17). Flamininus may have thought it could be easily won over.

6. spatio perbrevi: an exaggeration. The distance from Gomphi to the Ambracian gulf is 50 miles as the crow flies.

8. Atragem: Alifaka, south of the Peneius, and in fact about 14 miles west of Larisa. Cf. Stählin, *HTh*, 101–2, Oberhummer, *RE*, ii. 2137, P–K, i. 1. 67: on the form of the name cf. Stählin, 102 n. 3. Here the MSS. have *adrhagem* though at xxxiii. 4. 1 B has *Atragem*. The genitive in Greek is either Ἄτραγος or Ἄτρακος.

ex Perrhaebia oriundi sunt: Stählin, *HTh*, 102, takes this to mean that the town once belonged to Perrhaebia. This may be the case, but it is not what L. says. On Perrhaebia cf. xxxi. 41. 5 n.

9. intra Tempe: Tempe is the valley of the Peneius east of Larisa. The phrase means that Philip kept his army in that area north of the Peneius which was not under attack by Flamininus.

16–17. 3. *Naval events*

See also Paus. vii. 8. 1 (extremely muddled), Zon. ix. 16. 2–3.

16. 1. sub idem . . . castra: for Flamininus' arrival cf. 9. 8. In fact the *castra* had been placed by Villius, but L. is probably writing carelessly, and the sentence is not to be regarded as evidence for thinking that Lucius Flamininus arrived in Greece well before his brother. Cf. Walbank, *Philip V*, 320: *contra* Schmitt, *Antiochos*, 270 n. 4.

2. imperium: the word might suggest that he was a propraetor, having been praetor in 199. But at xxxiii. 17. 2 he is called a *legatus* and so is probably a *legatus cum imperio*. The fact that he is called στρατηγός in *Syll.*³ 591 is indecisive: the Lampsacenes could have been mistaken. It is unnecessary to hold, as do W–M and Thiel, 217–18, that Lucius was appointed by his brother on the authority of the senate. *Legati* could be appointed by the senate itself: cf. 28. 12. See W. F. Jashemski, *The Origins and History of the Proconsular and Propraetorian Imperium to 27 B.C.* (Chicago, 1950), 28.

Corcyram: cf. 14. 7 n.

3. Samen insulam: the MSS. have *Zammam* but *Samen* is far closer to this than *Zacynthum*. W–M are wrong to say that Same is in fact a city on Cephallenia, for Same is used for the island in Homer. Cf. Pliny *NH* iv. 54, Bürchner, *RE*, iA. 2126.

⟨**C.**⟩ **Livio:** we have had no previous mention of Livius and there is no subsequent one. But it is unlikely either that L. should have referred to a previously unmentioned man by his *nomen* alone, or that the MSS. reading is a corruption for *L.* and that *Apustio* has dropped out. Livius, as McDonald says, is clearly the naval commander under Villius. He is to be identified with C. Livius Salinator (29). He had been curule aedile in 204, praetor in 202, and was a *praefectus* in Gaul in 193. He held a second praetorship in 191 and was a *legatus* to Prusias in 190. He eventually reached the consulship in 188. He was a *pontifex* from 211 until his death in 170. The second praetorship is unusual, but the facts of his career, and L.'s statements about the censorships of 199 and 194 (7. 3, xxxiv. 44. 4) preclude the possibility of his being expelled from the senate, and re-entering it by a second praetorship, as sometimes occurred (cf. xxxiii. 42. 1 n.). Münzer (*RE*, xiii. 888) thinks that the replacement of Livius by Lucius Flamininus is a sign of the continuing hostility of the nobility to his father M. Livius Salinator (cf. xxxi. 12. 8 n.). But at this time all commanders were being changed annually (cf. p. 25).

4. Maleum: cf. xxxi. 44. 1 n.

5. relictas ibi ab L. Apustio: on Apustius cf. xxxi. 4. 7 n. The number of ships left was 30 (xxxi. 47. 2).

6. Attalo: cf. 8. 9–16 n. Antiochus will by now have withdrawn from Pergamum and Attalus has rejoined the Roman fleet.

Acesimbrotus: cf. xxxi. 46. 6 n.

7. Andrum: for the capture of Andros cf. xxxi. 45.

Euboeam: cf. xxxi. 22. 7 n.

8. Carystiorum: cf. xxxi. 45. 10 n.

Eretriam: cf. xxxi. 22. 7 n. For recent excavations at Eretria cf. the literature referred to by A. J. Graham, *JHS* xci (1971), 46 nn. 94–6, to which add K. Schefold, *Archaeology* xxi (1968), 272 ff.

9. iussis ut quaeque . . . petere: *iussis ut quaeque . . . peterent* Bφ, *iussitque ut quae . . . peterent* ψ. Both readings are a result of the *ut* being mistakenly taken as dependent on *iussis*.

10. trium iunctarum classium: i.e. the Rhodian, Attalid, and Roman fleets.

omnis generis tormenta: Thiel, 241 n. 218, suggests that some of this equipment will have been carried by the transports rather than by the warships themselves, as L. appears to suggest.

11. haud impigre: a long-standing crux. Bψ have *haud impigre*, φ *ut impigre*. As the words stand *haud impigre* means that the Eretrians engaged at first in only a half-hearted resistance and then inclined to peace. This seems difficult since we would expect them first to fight bravely, then to weaken in their resistance. There have been three principal ways of approaching the problem:

(a) deleting *haud*. Thus the later MSS. and Drakenborch.

(b) keeping *haud impigre*, but arguing that the negatives intensify rather than cancel each other. Thus Heraeus (*N. Jahr. für Phil.*

cxxxiii [1886], 713–20, cxliii [1891], 501–7) and Löfstedt, *Syntactica*, ii. 215.

(c) keeping *haud impigre* and arguing that the Eretrians were indeed half-hearted at the beginning, and did not really want to defend themselves. Their behaviour at the beginning of the siege thus accords with their later lethargic continuance of the defence after the promises of help from Philocles (§ 13) and their subsequent desire for peace (§ 15). Thus McDonald.

Neither of the explanations of the MSS. reading is convincing. The Heraeus–Löfstedt view is based on a passage from Sallust (*Hist.* iv fr. 41 M) which makes no sense. As for McDonald's view, it is not the case that §§ 13 and 15 are a continuation of the same attitude as shown at the beginning. The logic of the narrative is (i) resistance, (ii) many wounded—hence inclination to surrender, (iii) fear of Macedonian garrison prevents them doing so immediately, (iv) offer of help from Philocles, but basically they want to surrender. The desire to surrender, however, is a result of the initial wounds, not evidence for thinking that they did not want to fight at all at the beginning.

It follows that *haud* must be deleted. Cf. Ogilvie, *Phoenix*, 346, Tränkle, *Gnomon*, 378.

cernerent . . . ⟨ut . . .⟩ inclinarent: B and two manuscripts of the φ group have a gap after *cernerent* and this is a clear indication of a lacuna, resulting from the inability of scribes to read the uncial archetype. B normally leaves a gap equivalent to the passage he has been unable to read and in this case it is a line and a half long. B has *inclinarent*, χ *inclinarunt*. McDonald thus postulates an *ut* to govern *inclinarent*, while Tränkle, *Gnomon*, 378 argues for *et* and a clause parallel to *cum . . . cernerent*, with *inclinarunt* as the main clause. Either is possible (McDonald objects that *aliquot* would be harsh as the subject of *inclinarunt* but Tränkle rightly points to xxxvii. 38. 4 as a parallel).

12. Philocles: cf. xxxi. 16. 2 n., 26. 6. He appears to be based at Chalcis.

14. ad Attalum: they evidently preferred to deal with Attalus rather than the Romans. Hence Lucius Flamininus does not regard their action as a *deditio* to Rome: cf. Flurl, 134.

16. in deditionem venit: in 196 there was discussion over whether to give Eretria and Oreus to Eumenes (xxxiii. 34. 10). Since Oreus had been handed to Attalus (xxxi. 46. 16) it is likely that Eretria was treated in the same way. See further xxxiii. 31. 3 n.

17. pecuniae aurique et argenti: i.e. coined money, and un-coined gold and silver.

signa . . . inventa : these works of art were, no doubt, in private hands. There was, it seems, a large differential of wealth. The *per capita* wealth was small, but a few were very rich.

17. 1. Carystus inde repetita : cf. 16. 8. McDonald does not mention that B has *repetit*.

omnis multitudo : as in 16. 16. I do not understand W–M's statement that the phrase is used differently here. Presumably the Macedonian garrison is in the *arx*.

2. libertas : i.e. they were not to be sold into slavery. Lucius could not at this stage make any promises or decisions about their future political status. On this cf. xxxiii. 34. 10 n.

nummi treceni : B omits *nummi* and it is possible that some name of a Greek coin has dropped out and *nummi* has been inserted by χ. If not *nummi* probably refers to drachmae. The Roman forces would need Greek money for obtaining supplies. On ransom prices in Greece cf. Ducrey, 248 ff.

3. Boeotiam : cf. xxxi. 26. 13. Boeotia had been an ally of Macedon since 224. For the earlier relations of Boeotia and Macedon cf. M. Feyel, *Polybe et l'histoire de Béotie au iiie siècle avant notre ère* (Paris, 1942), Walbank, *Commentary*, i. 248–9: see also Deininger, 49 ff.

Cenchreas : on Cenchreae, the harbour of Corinth cf. Bölte, *RE*, xi. 167–70, H. N. Fowler and R. Stilwell, *Corinth*, i (Cambridge, Mass., 1932), 71 ff., R. L. Scranton and E. S. Ramage, *Hesperia* xxxiii (1964), 134 ff., J. G. Hawthorne, *Archaeology* xviii (1965), 191 ff. The move is preliminary to the siege of Corinth: cf. 19. 3 ff.

17. 4—18. *Land operations (continued)*

Walsh (*Livy*, 169, cf. *RhM* xcvii [1954], 99) notes that the description of the siege of Atrax is an example of L.'s habit of giving an account of the state of mind of the commander before proceeding to the action itself.

4. ⟨Atragis⟩: cf. 15. 8 n. The name is missing in the MSS. but there must be a mention of the place involved here, and it has clearly dropped out by haplography before *atrociorem*.

8. conferti . . . firmata : i.e. they packed themselves together and strengthened their line by forming more deeply and presumably shortening it. Cf. ii. 31. 2, xxxiii. 8. 14 n., Ogilvie, 307.

sensissent: 'realized'. M. Müller's emendation *sivissent* is unnecessary. For this usage of *sentire* cf. e.g. xxxiv. 14. 1, xxxv. 27. 7.

9. oppugnandae : B, *expugnandae* χ. χ's reading is probably a correction, stemming from the view that with the wall breached the siege proper was over. But L. is thinking in terms of the whole operation, and *oppugnandae* should be retained.

quod: agreeing with *universi belli*. The parallels given by Ogilvie, 622 are not all exact, as in some of them *quod* is causal.

momentis . . . penderet: for the conception here cf. xxv. 18. 3, xxvii. 9. 1, 15. 9, xxx. 34. 1, E. Dutoit, *Lettres d'humanité* v (1946), 186 ff.

10. tabulato: the 'storeys' of the tower: cf. Caes. *BG* vi. 29. 3.

11. cuneum . . . vocant: for the formula cf. xxxi. 24. 4 n., for the phalanx xxxi. 39. 10 n.

12. intervallo diruti muri: i.e. the space where the wall had been destroyed.

13. hastas ingentis longitudinis: cf. xxxi. 39. 10 n.
velut . . . testudinem: cf. xxxi. 39. 14 n.

14. praecidere: McDonald does not mention that B reads *praecedere*.

si quam: *quas* MSS., *quam* Gelenius in the 1535 edition, perhaps from the *codex Spirensis*. χ has *hastilia . . . explebant* in the following clause, presumably by emendation. *quam* is generally accepted, but it cannot be ruled out that L. wrote *quas* and then changed to a singular.

17. orbitam: 'a rut'.

trepidationemque insanam: *insanam* has been emended to *ingentem* (Madvig), *vanam* (H. J. Müller), or *magnam* (Ogilvie). McDonald explains *insanam* as a colloquial use meaning 'unreasonable'. His parallels, however, do not support him. Hor. *Sat.* ii. 2. 5 *insanis fulgoribus* means *fulgores* which produce *insania* and Pliny *NH* xvi. 115 *vites insanas* means vines which, madly as it were, flower three times in a year. In fact in prose *insanus* is very rarely used except of persons and is unparalleled with words denoting states of mind (cf. *TLL*, vii. 1832–6). Hence even an explanation of the phrase as meaning 'fear like that of a madman' would seem to be very difficult. Emendation seems required.
Cf. Ogilvie, *Phoenix*, 346, Tränkle, *Gnomon*, 372.

18. 1. minime aequo animo . . . patiebatur: the comparison was presumably being made by both the men of Atrax and the Roman troops. Flamininus could not stop the comparison being made and *patiebatur* therefore has the sense here of 'suffer' rather than 'allow'.

2. procul a mari: Atrax was 80 miles from the Ambracian gulf as the crow flies. On the importance of the supply routes cf. 14. 7 n., 15. 5.

3. tota Acarnaniae atque Aetoliae ora: on Acarnania cf. xxxi. 14. 7 n. It is of course still an ally of Macedon (cf. 15. 5 n.). The Aetolian coast is the northern shore of the gulf of Corinth.

4. Anticyra in Phocide: Anticyra is on the southern coast of Phocis, about 10 miles south of Delphi. Cf. Hirschfeld, *RE*, i. 2427–8, P–K, i. 2. 417. Phocis had been a member of the symmachy since 224 (Pol. iv. 9. 4, cf. Walbank, *Commentary*, i. 248–9) but by 217 it seems to have been taken under direct Macedonian control (cf. Walbank, *Commentary*, i. 558–9). Although not mentioned in xxix. 12. 14 they were almost certainly included among Philip's *adscripti* to the peace of Phoenice (cf. Walbank, *Philip V*, 103 n. 6). On the advantages of Anticyra and its earlier strategic use cf. F. Chamoux, *BCH* lxxxix (1965), 221–2 (Chamoux suggests that the bust from Delphi which he believes to be of Flamininus dates from a visit during Flamininus' stay at Anticyra).

5. ex adverso . . . ab tergo . . . ab lateribus: Aetolia and Acarnania are scarcely *ab tergo* of Anticyra; rather they adjoin Locris on one *latus*. L. is probably keen to describe the environs of Anticyra on all sides. Cf. Cic. *Phil.* iii. 32.

Locridem: Western, or Ozolian Locris, which belonged to Aetolia. Cf. L. Lerat, *Les Locriens de l'Ouest* (Paris, 1952).

6. Phanoteam: the Greek name is Φανοτεύς or Πανοπεύς. On the site, a little to the north of Chaeronea cf. Kirsten, *RE*, xviii. 2. 637–49, Walbank, *Commentary*, i. 625, P–K, i. 2. 431. For an inscription which probably records the dedication of a statue of Flamininus at Phanotea cf. G. Klaffenbach, *Chiron* i (1971), 167–8.

in oppugnando: *in* χ, *om*. B. I do not understand McDonald's comment 'qua de re *in oppugnando* aptius'. *in* may be an addition by χ, failing to understand that *oppugnando* is a dative. B, it is true, is particularly inaccurate in this part of the book, but *in oppugnando*, with its active sense, goes rather uneasily with *Anticyra* as the subject.

7. Ambrysus: the MSS. have *ambrussum* or *ambrussium*. The Greek form varies between -*o* and -*u* and between -*σ* and -*σσ*. L. may therefore have written *Ambryssum*. For the site cf. Hirschfeld, *RE*, i. 1815, P–K, i. 2. 437.

Hyampolis: in Eastern Phocis, near Abae. Cf. Bölte, *RE*, ix. 17–22, P–K, i. 2. 343.

receptae: on the meaning of *recipere* cf. xxxiii. 18. 22 n.

Daulis: mod. Davlia. Cf. Philippson, *RE*, iv. 2233, L. Robert, *BCH* lix (1935), 200 ff., P–K, i. 2. 402.

8. insequendoque : χ. B has *sequendoque*. *Sequi* can mean 'pursue' (cf. L–S s.v.) but in view of xxxi. 35. 3 *in vicem insequentes refugientesque* χ is probably right.

impetum Romani facerent : L. does not specifically refer to the capture of Daulis, and some editors have suspected corruption or a lacuna. This is unnecessary: L. simply leaves his readers to deduce the end result.

9. Elatia : the form of the name varies enormously in the MSS. (cf. W–M, 188, where B is wrongly reported as having *Elatea* here). Most of the readings, in one way or the other, represent *Elatia*, which is the natural Latinization of 'Ελατεῖα. Elatia, the most important Phocian town, is north of the Cephisus, very near Eastern Locris. Cf. Philippson, *RE*, v. 2236–7, P–K, i. 2. 423–4.

19–23. 3. *The meeting of the Achaean League at Sicyon*

Cf. also App. *Mac.* 7, Paus. vii. 8. 1–2, Zon. ix. 16. 3.

The decision of the Achaean League to abandon its alliance with Macedon and join Rome is of enormous importance. For the general political background to the decision see above all Aymard, *PR*, ch. i. Cf. also Lehmann, 216 ff., Deininger, 42 ff. On the date of the meeting cf. Aymard, *PR*, 80–1 n. 49.

Aristaenus was the leader of those who wanted to join Rome. Errington, *Philopoemen*, 72 ff. argues that at this time such a policy was also supported by Philopoemen, later an opponent of Aristaenus and at the time in self-imposed semi-exile in Crete. His arguments are (i) that Aristaenus prevented Megalopolis from formally exiling Philopoemen when he retired to Crete (Plut. *Phil.* 13. 4), (ii) that Aristaenus was *hipparchos* in Philopoemen's *strategia* in 208/7, (iii) that Plutarch's statement (*Phil.* 13. 2) that Philopoemen went to Crete because the Achaeans chose others as ἄρχοντες refers to the election of the pro-Macedonian Cycliadas for 200/199, not to that of Aristaenus for 199/8. As to (i) Aristaenus could well have deplored such an extreme step as the exiling of Philopoemen, even though he disagreed with him politically—which is what Plutarch says. (ii) proves nothing for the completely different circumstances of 200–198, and (iii) is circular. It is preferable to believe that Philopoemen is neither pro-Macedonian nor pro-Roman at this time. He certainly had no love lost for Philip now, but he was by no means happy about the intrusion of Rome into Greek affairs. He was in an unhappy position and that is probably at least one of the reasons for his withdrawal to Crete. (The statement of Justin xxix. 4. 11 that Philopoemen persuaded the Achaeans to join Rome is simply an error.) Cf. Deininger, 40–1.

The meeting is a σύγκλητος (cf. xxxi. 25. 2 n., Aymard, *Assemblées*, 325, Larsen, *Representative Government*, 171–2). Problems of procedure are discussed in the detailed notes.

19. 1. Elatiam obsidenti: there is no conflict between this and 24. 1 as Aymard, *PR*, 7 n. 3 alleges. In ch. 24 L. reverts to a detailed account of the siege of Elatia after his description of the Achaean meeting and the connected naval activities.

Achaeorum . . . avertendi: on Achaea and Macedon cf. xxxi. 25. 2 n.

2. Cycliadan: cf. xxxi. 25. 3 n. He fled to Philip after his expulsion (32. 10, Pol. xviii. 1. 2, Walbank, *Commentary*, ii. 549). On the date of the expulsion cf. Deininger, 41 n. 6.

Aristaenus . . . praetor erat: Aristaenus was *strategos* in 199/8 (cf. Aymard, *RÉA* xxx [1928], 4 = *ÉHA*, 3, Errington, *Philopoemen*, 251). For problems concerning his city and the name of his father cf. Errington, *Philopoemen*, 276–9.

3. classis . . . oppugnare: 17. 3.

4. Corinthum contributuros: χ had *iis* or *his* after *Corinthum*, which has all the signs of a gloss by a scribe who thought a dative necessary for the sense. Cf. Tränkle, *Gnomon*, 373.

On Corinth cf. xxxi. 22. 6 n. Aymard, *PR*, 85 ff. argues that the senate's future freedom of action could not be restricted and that the promise was (a) made only unofficially to Aristaenus and his political friends, (b) related only to the city, not to the Acrocorinth, (c) referred only to Corinth's status following its capture in the siege for which the Romans were preparing, not its final status. None of this is necessary. If Roman representatives could never make firm promises, diplomatic initiatives would have been impossible. Technically the senate could repudiate the promises but it was highly unlikely that they would actually do so. In any case, that is a risk that Flamininus was willing to take. The omission of any mention of Corinth in Aristaenus' speech is not significant, as the speech may be largely L.'s own composition.

in antiquum gentis concilium: *antiquum* has the force of 'the league as it was before the foundation of the symmachy'.

5. Atheniensibus: the reason for their inclusion is evident from § 12.

Sicyone . . . concilium: cf. xxxi. 25. 2 n. L. uses *concilium* for the meeting, though he has just used it to mean the League. This is due, no doubt, to L.'s difficulty in finding the vocabulary to translate Polybius' technical terms.

Sicyon, the city of Aratus, had been brought into the League by the latter in 250.

6. non admodum simplex: an understatement, as what follows indicates that their thoughts were extremely complex.

Walsh, *Livy*, 169 notes this passage as an example of L.'s fondness for describing the emotions and thoughts of the persons about whom he is writing.

Nabis: cf. xxxi. 25. 3 n.

7. Macedonum . . . regem ipsum: *beneficiis . . . veteribus* refers to the help of Doson against Cleomenes in the 220s and of Philip in the Social war against Aetolia, *recentibus* to the concessions made in 5. 4–5. Against this Aymard (*PR*, 87 n. 18, cf. Holleaux, *Rome*, 272 n. 3) argues that from the Achaean point of view these were only the restoration of places which Achaea regarded as her own, and that the reference of *recentibus* is to Philip's help to Achaea in the First Macedonian war. But it could equally be replied that the First Macedonian war was not of the League's choosing, and that Philip only helped them to prevent Sparta from fighting outside the Peloponnese. Moreover, if the reference is to the First Macedonian war, there is insufficient contrast between the *vetera* and the *recentia beneficia*.

The distinction between *Macedonas* and *regem ipsum* refers in part to the fact that Antigonus Doson was also involved in the *beneficia*, but also to the fact that the Macedonian people could be said to exist as an entity independently of their king, which was not the case in any other Hellenistic kingdom. Cf. Aymard, *RÉA*, 73–135.

crudelitate perfidiaque: Philip's *crudelitas* will be his sackings of towns and pillage of sacred places, his *perfidia* such things as the alleged murdering of political opponents and the secret machinations against Rhodes. Cf. p. 36, xxxi. 24. 18 n., 31. 17 n., Walbank, *Philip V*, 79, 110.

8. neque: with *aestimantes*, not with *cernebant*.

ad tempus: the concessions of 5. 4–5.

9–10. neque solum . . . satis constabat: a very obscurely expressed sentence. On the problems raised by it see Aymard, *Assemblées*, 325–31, on which the following note is heavily dependent.

(a) What does *pro sententia dicerent* mean? L. uses the phrase again in Aristaenus' speech at 21. 2, but it is not a phrase that has any technical meaning in Roman procedure, nor is it easy to see what Greek words in Polybius it could correspond to. W–M quote Tac. *A.* iii. 57 *dixit pro sententia* and Festus, p. 252L *pro sententia, ac si dicatur sententia*. (They also quote L. iv. 44. 12 but that is not parallel.) The Paulus passage may help us to understand the meaning here. *Sententiam dicere* is, of course, the phrase for expressing one's views in the Roman senate. The procedure in the League assembly is different and hence L. uses *pro sententia*.

(b) Why should the matter be discussed in the councils of the local states? The σύγκλητος was open to all citizens, and not all would be members of their local councils. Nor could such councils mandate their citizens as to how they should vote. Aymard argues that the leading citizens of each state, who would be members of their councils, in fact discussed the matter there, not by any constitutional requirement, but simply as a means of preparing themselves for the full meeting at Sicyon. They are the opinion-formers and it is they who would be expected to speak at Sicyon (cf. 21. 1 n.). Aymard may be right, but it is possible (as Aymard himself admits) that L. has misunderstood and garbled Polybius.

10. op⟨timum pu⟩tarent: *optarent* MSS. M. Müller's supplement does not seem necessary and it is not proved by 20. 6 *aut velit aut optimum putet*. Cf. T. A. Dorey, *JRS* lvii (1967), 279.

11. Romanus ... legatus: the plurals that follow may suggest that there was in fact only one Roman envoy (cf. Aymard, *PR*, 1 n. 3). But at 21. 7 Aristaenus is made to say *Philippi praeter legatum videmus nihil*, while the present passage clearly indicates that more than one Macedonian representative was present. So the point cannot be pressed.

L. Calpurnius: (13). The MSS. have *Carpunnius*, a non-existent name. Calpurnius must be right, but this man is not otherwise known. The Calpurnii were only just coming to public office, and he is almost certainly related to C. Calpurnius Piso, praetor in 211 and C. Calpurnius Piso, consul in 180. Before these three men the only Calpurnii known are a military tribune of 258 and a *legatus* of 256.

12. nulli ... passi erant: the actions of Philip in 200: cf. xxxi. 24–6, 44. 2–9.

20. This speech of Aristaenus is too short to admit of structural analysis. It is, however, composed in a rhetorical style and is probably a considerable embellishment of what Polybius had at this point. Cf. Aymard, *Assemblées*, 364–5 n. 9.

20. 1. ubi ... facta esset: the words *sicut Graecis mos est* are clearly an addition by L. Roman assemblies had no speeches at all. Even at the preliminary *contio*, or informal meeting, only magistrates or those introduced by magistrates could address the people (cf. Taylor, *RVA*, 15 ff.). Freedom of speech was regarded as typically Greek, though not all Greek states had this right. In Sparta debate at the assembly was not allowed (Ar. *Pol.* 1273 a 13).

diu silentium . . . fuit: on L.'s descriptions of silences cf. E. Dutoit, *Mélanges Marouzeau* (Paris, 1948), 141–51, Ogilvie, 486.

2. quae difficilia essent: arguments which were hard to evaluate.

3. Aristaenus: cf. 19. 2 n.

quibus: with *certamina*. The ablative is instrumental—'strife, because of which you scarcely refrained from violence'.

in conviviis et circulis: for the phrase cf. xxxiv. 61. 5, xliv. 22. 8, Cic. *pro Balbo* 57, Dutoit, *Hommages Herrmann* (Brussels, 1960), 333.

4. ad eam rem unam indicto: a σύγκλητος had to be summoned for one specific agendum. Cf. Aymard, *Assemblées*, 348 and xxxi. 25. 9 n.

cum legatorum . . . obmutuistis: cf. Dem. *de cor.* 170 (C. Brakman, *Mnem.* lv [1927], 56).

referant: L. often uses *referre* in regard to Achaean assemblies (xxxi. 25. 9, xxxii. 22. 3, 22. 8, xxxviii. 31. 2). The word is the one used of putting a matter before the senate at Rome. L. does not appear to give it a precise meaning in Achaean contexts and since it is used both here and at ch. 22, in different places in the same debate, it must have a different sense on the two occasions. Here it must refer to the matter for debate being laid before the assembly. Aymard (*Assemblées*, 363 ff.) thinks that either L. has misplaced it, and that it should precede the introduction of the foreign envoys, or that it refers simply to the invitation to speak and does not correspond to the normal Greek *probouleuma*. But there does not seem any reason why the presiding magistrates should not put the subject for decision formally before the assembly after the foreign envoys had spoken. On *referre* in 22. 3, 8 cf. 22. 3 n.

6. ubi semel . . . defendendum: a strikingly early example of the concept of 'cabinet responsibility'. One may argue freely before a decision is taken, but once taken it is binding on everybody. A confederation like the Achaean League could easily split up if differences were pursued further. Cf. Aymard, *PR*, 96 n. 60.

21. On the contents of the speech of Aristaenus cf. Aymard, *PR*, 91–3, and on its structure p. 21. See also Brueggmann, 80 ff.

21. 1. principes: on the meaning of the word cf. xxxi. 17. 11 n. The meeting is a σύγκλητος (19–23. 3 n.) and it is therefore odd that Aristaenus should use the word. There are three possible explanations. (a) Aristaenus addressed himself to the leaders who would normally speak at meetings (W–M). (b) Only the well-to-do could afford to attend the meeting and they are thus a political élite whom Aristaenus can address as *principes* (Aymard, *Assemblées*, 328 and n. 1). (c) The word is used carelessly by L. who is presenting the speech as if it were delivered before the Achaean equivalent of the Roman senate. The third explanation seems to me the most likely.

non sine responso eos dimittendos esse: B has *non sine responso eos non dimittendos esse,* χ *inde sine responso eos dimittendos non esse.* The double negative in B reverses the sense required, whilst χ's *inde* is unnecessary and over-emphatic: it is an obvious emendation. The only question, then, is which *non* in B should be deleted, and Madvig (*Emendationes,* 478) was clearly right to delete the second. The balance of the two *aut* clauses requires the negative to come at the beginning of each.

2. pro sententia . . . pro sententiis percenseamus: the MSS. have *pro sententiis dictas.* As Madvig (*Emendationes,* 479) and McDonald rightly say, this gives the sense of 'let us consider the speeches which were delivered as if they were proposals'. The point, however, which Aristaenus wants to make is that they have no proposals and so must make do with the speeches as if they were proposals. Hence Madvig inserted *ut* before *pro sententiis.* As McDonald points out, this leaves *hesterno die* hanging in the air. McDonald, therefore, returns to the old reading *dictas pro sententiis.* The difficulty with this is that *pro sententiis* then means 'as if they were *sententiae*' while *pro sententia* above (cf. 19. 9 n.) must mean actual proposals. L. could have used the phrase carelessly in different senses, but it would perhaps be better to combine Madvig's and McDonald's solutions and read *dictas ut pro sententiis.*

4. se a nobis . . . censent: the reference is probably quite general, and not specifically to the forthcoming Roman attack on Corinth, as Aymard, *PR,* 86 n. 14 thinks.

5. iuris iurandi: cf. 5. 4 n.

modo ne intersimus armis: cf. § 33. In 429 the Spartans demanded that Plataea either join them or remain neutral (Thuc. ii. 72). The *ne* is quite intelligible as depending on the demand implied in *contentum esse* (cf. *TLL,* iv. 680) and Madvig's *ni* (which gives the sense of 'unless we actually help Rome') is not necessary.

7. legatum: cf. 19. 11 n.

Cenchreas: cf. 17. 3 n.

consulem . . . pervagantes: ch. 18, for *exiguo maris spatio* cf. 18. 5.

Locridem: this must refer to eastern Locris, since Ozolian Locris is in Aetolian hands (18. 5 n.). We have not had any mention of Flamininus' activity in Locris, but it fits in perfectly naturally with the rest of his actions: cf. § 14, 32. 1. Epicnemidian Locris had, it seems, been captured by Philip in 208 (Walbank, *Commentary*, ii. 258), and Opuntian Locris was probably also in direct Macedonian possession (Feyel, 172 n. 2: *contra* Walbank, *Philip V*, 16 n. 3 and literature there cited).

8. Cleomedon: we have not previously been given his name and he is not otherwise known (cf. Olshausen, *RE*, supp. xii. 513–14).

9. Nabide: cf. xxxi. 25. 3 n.

et ab Romanis: because the attack on Corinth could be regarded as an attack on the League, or because the Romans would procede to attack the Achaean towns after capturing Corinth.

10. pollicendo: cf. xxxi. 25. 7.

11. oblitus: hardly fair, since the Achaeans refused to agree to Philip's conditions.

12. elevabat: 'made light of'.

eventumque . . . prioris belli: the First Macedonian war concluded by the Peace of Phoenice, which left Philip in possession of many of the places he had captured in the war. Cf. Walbank, *Philip V*, 103 ff.

13. Nos dico: cf. xxxi. 7. 8 n.
   Eretriam: 16. 10–17.
   Carystumque: 17. 1–2.
   capi!: the punctuation here should be a question mark (Walsh, *CR*, 56).
   Thessaliae urbes: ch. 15.

14. Locridem Phocidemque: cf. § 7 n.
   Elatiam: 18. 9.
   excessit faucibus Epiri: cf. 5. 9 n., and § 20 n. below.
   penitus in regnum abiit: Philip fled (12. 8) but initially only into Epirus, and then plundered Thessaly (ch. 13). Even after this he did not retreat *penitus in regnum*: cf. 15. 9 n.
   aut vi aut metu aut voluntate: in χ these words come between *amnem* and *relictoque* and B has *aut voluntate* there, omitting the rest. It cannot belong there, since the phrase gives three possible answers to the question in *cur*, and Madvig's transposition (*Emendationes*, 479) is clearly right.

16. maioribus . . . gesserint: the Roman force in the First war was mainly naval. Laevinus had one *legio classica* (xxiv. 11. 3, 44. 5, xxvi. 1. 12): it was withdrawn in 210 (xxvi. 28. 9) and its renewed mention in xxvii. 7. 15 is probably an error. Holleaux's doubts (*Rome*, 187 n. 2) on the authenticity of this legion are unfounded. Cf. also Toynbee, ii. 527–8. The total number of ships in the First war was 50 or 55 (xxiii. 32. 17, 34. 9, 38. 7—these passages raise problems which it is not necessary to go into here: cf. Walbank, *Philip V*, 75 n. 2, Thiel, 92 n. 169). After the withdrawal of the *legio* Sulpicius Galba had ships alone, though no doubt with marines as well. The third Roman commander, Sempronius Tuditanus, had a large force of both soldiers and extra ships, but he did not fight with it (xxix. 12). For the fleet numbers now cf. Thiel, 210 ff., and for the army 1. 3 n.

17. nec duce consulari nec exercitu: both Laevinus and Galba were *consulares* but the meaning here is that they were not consuls in office with a regular consular army.

sociorum . . . erant: for the activities of Sulpicius in 209 and 208 cf. Walbank, *Philip V*, 89 ff. For the Achaean appeals to Philip cf. xxvii. 29. 9 (209—though this refers only to an Aetolian naval attack), xxviii. 5. 6 (208).

The alliteration in *maritimae tum . . . terrore . . . tumultu* is probably deliberate. Cf. Ullmann, *Étude*, 114.

Philippus . . . depopularetur: this is Philip's expedition in 207 which forced the Aetolians to make peace (Pol. xi. 7. 2). For Roman inactivity at this time cf. xxxi. 1. 8 n.

18. per sedecim annos: 218–203 inclusive.

non praesidium Aetolis bellantibus: again a distortion of the position at the time of the Romano-Aetolian alliance. It was Rome, not Aetolia who was *bellans* then. Cf. xxxi. 1. 8, 29. 5 nn., 31. 18. B reads *n̄ in*. It is unlikely that this is a simple corruption of *non*, as McDonald states, since *n̄* is B's regular abbreviation for *non*. But that L. wrote *classem in praesidium*, as Weissenborn suggested, is improbable.

19. Sulpicius . . . depopulatus: xxxi. 33 ff. *fugavit* refers to the battle in xxxi. 37. But Aristaenus over-estimates the extent of Sulpicius' successes.

20. claustra Epiri: cf. § 14. The phrase means 'the barrier that lies in Epirus', not 'the barrier leading into Epirus', as claimed by Accame, *Espansione romana*, 141. Cf. Hammond, *JRS* lvi (1966), 54.

21–5. This hypothetical rejection of the relevance of arguments about Philip's cruelty is termed *confessio*. Cf. R. Volkmann, *Die Rhetorik der Griechen und Römer* (2nd edn., Leipzig, 1885), 495, Ullmann, *Étude*, 65.

21. ne sint vera . . . admissa: cf. 19. 12 n. Though Philip's actions in Attica are not really examples of his *avaritia* and *libido*. Cf. Aymard, *PR*, 88–9 n. 25.

22. Ciani: cf. xxxi. 31. 4 n.
   Abydenique: xxxi. 16. 6–18. 9.

23. caedes . . . factas: cf. xxxi. 31. 4 n.
   hospitem . . . occisum: this is the only evidence for this incident. Cf. Walbank, *Philip V*, 79 n. 2. Cyparissia is a town near the coast north-west of Messene (cf. Pieske, *RE*, xii. 47–50, P–K, iii. 2. 377). It probably became a member of the Achaean League *c.* 220 (cf. Niese, ii. 411 n. 1, Aymard, *PR*, 13 n. 6). Chariteles is not otherwise known.
   Aratum . . . Sicyonios: cf. xxxi. 31. 17 n. For the earlier good relations of Philip and the elder Aratus, cf. Walbank, *Philip V*, 20, 45 ff., 60, 67. The clash came over the Messene episode (cf. xxxi. 31. 4 n.). The younger Aratus is said to have been originally a lover of Philip (Walbank, *Philip V*, 73 n. 5).

24. filii . . . asportatam: this is Polycrateia, carried off to Macedon by Philip and made his wife in 213. Perseus was her son, but she was probably dead by 209 as Demetrius, half-brother of Perseus, was born the following year. Cf. xxvii. 31. 8, Plut. *Arat.* 49–51, Walbank, *Philip V*, 78–9, *Commentary*, i. 251, Meloni, *Perseo*, 1–15, Seibert, 39 n. 48. (xxxix. 53. 3 casts aspersions on Perseus' birth, but does not imply that Polycrateia was not Philip's wife.)

25. cum Antigono . . . non posset: McDonald puts a comma after *esse*, and takes the *num* clause as depending on *disceptationem*. But (a) this destroys the clause-balance, (b) we should expect *postulet* not *postularet*. The natural way of taking the sentence (W–M, Walsh, *CR*, 55) is to put a colon after *esse*, and translate 'would Antigonus be demanding that we do the impossible'. But this is not the point that Aristaenus ought to be making. He is saying that Philip's cruelty is irrelevant. If Antigonus were asking us to help him it would simply be impossible. The sense is given by taking *id* as the subject of *postularet*—'would the fact that we were disputing with a benefactor like Antigonus require us to do the impossible'.
   Antigono: Antigonus Doson, Philip's uncle. He was first regent on the death of Demetrius II in 229 and then king until 221. It was with him that the symmachy was formed in 224 and his services are those against Cleomenes. Cf. Walbank, *Aratus*, 89 ff., *Philip V*, ch. i, Will, *HP*, i. 325 ff. On Doson's regency cf. Aymard, *Aegyptus* xxxii (1952), 90 ff. = *ÉHA*, 234 ff. For Achaean honours to Antigonus cf. Pol. ii. 70. 5, v. 9. 10. On Polybius' picture of him cf. Welwei, 33 ff., *RhM* cx (1967), 306 ff.

27. centum . . . lembi: on *naves tectae* and *apertae* cf. xxxi. 22. 8 n., on the figures Thiel, 210–11. The *apertae* are allied ships, of the 100 *tectae*, 44 are allied (cf. 16. 6).

Issaici: cf. xxxi. 45. 10 n. The form there is *Issaei*, which Madvig rightly reads here. The MSS. have *Issaici* or *Hissaci*, but *Issaei* is also the MSS. reading at xxxvii. 16. 8, xlii. 26. 2, 48. 8. xliii. 9. 5 and xlv. 26. 13 have *Issenses*. There is no evidence for *Issaici* in either Greek or Latin. Cf. Fluss, *RE*, supp. v. 346.

 scilicet: cf. xxxi. 29. 8 n.

 intestino: i.e. one within the Peloponnese.

 haerente . . . visceribus: cf. xxxiii. 44. 8 n.

28. unde: 'whence shall we seek Macedonian help?' seems odd, and a mixture of 'whence shall we seek help' and 'what use will it be to beseech Macedon for help'. Madvig put a lacuna before *unde*. McDonald explains that *unde* is used because Philip will be nowhere near, but the oddity of the expression remains. L. may have written elliptically or perhaps we should read *regiamne*.

Dymas: Dyme is on the west coast of the Peloponnese on the south side of the gulf of Patras (cf. Philippson, *RE*, v. 1877–8, P–K, iii. 1. 197). It was one of the original Achaean cities. Its capture in the first Macedonian war, referred to by Paus. vii. 17. 5, is not recorded elsewhere in L. (W–M are wrong to refer to xxvii. 31. 9) and it is therefore likely that it belongs to the period after the end of L.'s narrative for 208 since he has no account of events in 207 and 206 (cf. Walbank, *Philip V*, 98 n. 1). Errington (*Philopoemen*, 59 n. 1) argues for 209 but this does not explain L.'s silence so easily.

30. summa ope petendum: χ, *summa repetendum* B. The feminine in B suggests that χ is right, and *summopere* is therefore unnecessary.

31. metu . . . terra: the construction is chiastic, *compulsi* going with *metu*, *deprensi* with *terra*.

32. quia . . . patiuntur: an obscure remark, apparently connected with what follows. 'They will force you to join them, because they do not want to destroy you and therefore will not allow you to remain neutral. If you are neutral, you will end up as *praeda victoris* (§ 34).' The logic is not impeccable.

33. Nam quod Cleomedon . . . ostendebat: cf. § 5.

34. praeterquam . . . erimus: 'apart from the fact that Rome will not allow neutrality (§ 32), it is not in your interest.'

 aspernanda: φL, *aspernenda* ψ, *spernenda* B. McDonald justifies *aspernanda* by reference to § 37 *si socios aspernamini*. But *spernenda* may be right, and the χ reading influenced by § 37.

 nusquam gratia stabili: neutrality would mean that the League had no claim to lasting gratitude from anyone.

35. nolite . . . fastidire: an almost verbatim repetition of § 30.

36. Liberare . . . audetis: it is wrong to take this as an indication that Philopoemen had already planned the League's defection from Macedon, as is done by Petzold, *Studien zur Methode des Polybios und zu ihrer historischen Auswertung* (Munich, 1969), 98 n. 6.

mare: χ, *om.* B. Walsh, *CR*, 55 plausibly suggests that *mare* is a gloss, comparing xxix. 26. 2.

22. 2. et . . . altercabantur: i.e. the members of each state acting as a whole joined in the disputes.

damiurgos vocant: for the *vocant* formula cf. xxxi. 24. 4 n. The *damiourgoi* are clearly a body of magistrates who have probouleutic functions at the assembly. On this occasion it is they alone who decide the matter, and the *strategos* has no vote. Yet there is no other evidence for such a procedure, and on other occasions the *strategos* appears to be the chairman of the committee of *damiourgoi*, and to exercise considerable influence on the conduct of business in the assembly. It seems best to follow Aymard's view (*Assemblées*, 359–61) that Aristaenus, by making a proposal himself, had debarred himself from taking part in the subsequent procedural arguments. (Although it is not specifically referred to by L. we may assume that Aristaenus did make a formal proposal: cf. Aymard, *Assemblées*, 360 n. 1.)

On the *damiourgoi* cf. also Walbank, *Commentary*, i. 219, Larsen, *Greek Federal States*, 86.

Both here and at xxxviii. 30. 4 L. has the Doric form *damiurgi*, though the only reference to them in Polybius (xxiii. 5. 16) has δημιουργοῖς. W–M rightly say that the Doric form must have stood in Polybius and Nissen and Büttner-Wobst corrected the reading in the Polybius passage.

3. relaturos: the *relatio* here must be the recital of the proposal for alliance with Rome made by Aristaenus and the taking of a vote (cf. § 5). It cannot be identified with the *relatio* introducing the debate as a whole: cf. 20. 4 n.

lege cautum: there is no reason to disbelieve that adherence to the Macedonian alliance had been sanctified by such a law. Aristaenus could have first proposed annulment of the law, but the practical effect would have been the same (cf. Errington, *Philopoemen*, 224).

5. Pisias: the MSS. have *Risias* or *Risiasus* which are not Greek names. Madvig's *Pisias* (*Emendationes*, 480) is generally accepted. It is rare for us to have the name of a *damiourgos* (cf. Aymard, *Assemblées*, 370).

Pellenensis: Pellene was one of the original Achaean cities. Cf. Meyer, *RE*, xix. 354–66, P–K, iii. 1. 168, Walbank, *Commentary*, i. 232.

decretum . . . sententias: the *decretum* is the proposal of Aristaenus (cf. §§ 2, 3 nn.). *perrogari sententias* is the equivalent of *suffragium daturos* in § 3 and therefore has no connection with the procedure of asking for *sententiae* in the Roman senate (cf. Aymard, *Assemblées*, 374 n. 3).

10. Megalopolitanos . . . Antigonus: Megalopolis was destroyed by Cleomenes in 223 (W–M confuse this with the events of 226): cf. Pol. ii. 55, 61–2, Plut. *Cleom.* 23–5, Walbank, *Commentary*, i. 258. The restoration by Doson will have taken place soon after Sellasia. Cf. Pol. v. 93. 8, von Hiller, *RE*, xv. 136.

Dymaeis . . . Romano: for its capture cf. 21. 28 n. *Nuper* does not necessarily mean the same year, as Errington, *Philopoemen*, 59 n. 1 thinks.

cum redimi . . . reddiderat: for other cases of searching out those sold into slavery and restoring them to freedom cf. Volkmann, 91 ff.

11. Argivi . . . credunt: cf. xxvii. 30. 9. The story of the Argive origin of the Macedonian royal house goes back at least to the early fifth century (cf. Hdt. v. 22, viii. 137, Thuc. ii. 99, How and Wells, *Commentary on Herodotus*, ii. 282–3, A. A. Daskalakis, *The Hellenism of the Ancient Macedonians* (Thessaloniki, 1965), pt. iii. The Antigonids were keen to establish their own connections with Argos, and Philip's marriage to the Argive Polycrateia and his naming of his son Perseus contributed to this (cf. Aymard, *PR*, 54 n. 30, Meloni, *Perseo*, 13–14).

privatis . . . amicitia: this suggests that there were other marriage ties apart from those of Philip himself.

23. 1. ceteri populi: the votes in the assembly were taken on a group basis, those present from each state determining the one vote of that state. This was to prevent the citizens of the state where the meeting was held from 'swamping' the vote. Cf. Aymard, *Assemblées*, 377 ff., U. Hall, *Historia* xiii (1964), 268.

cum ⟨Attalo⟩: the MSS. read *cum Romanis* (with deletion indicated as a variant in φ). This is nonsense, since § 2 makes it clear that as yet there was no formal agreement with Rome. There was, however, an alliance between the League and Attalus (Pol. xxii. 7. 8) and the emendation is clearly correct. Cf. Errington, *Philopoemen*, 280–1.

2. cum Romanis . . . dilata est: for the actual date of the treaty between Rome and the League cf. Badian, *JRS* xlii (1952), 76 ff. The Achaeans wanted to be sure that the terms were going to be acceptable at Rome before committing themselves to them. Cf. the delays in the ratification of the Aetolian treaty of 212/11 (xxvi. 24. 14).

3. exercitum omnem : doubtless an exaggeration: cf. Aymard, *PR*, 106 n. 6.

23. 4–13. *The Siege of Corinth*

On the topography of Corinth cf. H. W. Fowler and R. Stilwell, *Corinth*, i (Cambridge, Mass., 1932).

4. hi : the Achaeans. Most MSS. read *ii* which may be right.

portae . . . Sicyonem : the western gate.

⟨**in**⟩ **Cenchreas versam partem :** the eastern side. The *in* is omitted in the MSS. and this may be right. *Cenchreae* as a separate town could be constructed without a preposition. Omission of *in* and *ad* with names of towns is common when *versus* is used as a preposition (cf. K–St, i. 537, H–S, 221) and there seems no reason why it should not also be possible with the participle. *ab Lechaeo* is not an objection to this, as it means 'from the direction of Lechaeum'. On Cenchreae cf. 17. 3 n.

ab Lechaeo : the northern side. On Lechaeum cf. Zschietzschmann, *RE*, supp. v. 542–5, Fowler and Stilwell, *Corinth*, i. 95–6.

5. Androsthenen : cf. xxxiii. 14. 1, 15. 1. Apart from these passages he is not otherwise known.

suffragio creatum suo imperio : L. uses Roman technical vocabulary (cf. W–M).

6. ⟨**op**⟩**pugnantibus :** Gronovius's supplement is clearly necessary.

7. in quem locum . . . protegendum : the phrase appears to be a combination of *in quem locum concurrerent* and *ad quem locum protegendum*.

9. ex Hannibalis exercitu : i.e. those who fought with Hannibal at Zama: cf. xxx. 33. 6, 35. 9. Pol. xv. 11. 2 refers only to τοὺς ἐξ Ἰταλίας ἥκοντας and Walbank, *Commentary*, ii. 458 appears to doubt whether they really included Italians. But this passage, which looks Polybian, would justify L.'s interpretation in the former case. The men at Corinth cannot simply be Italians who supported Hannibal in general.

navales socii : the Greek states in southern Italy who had to provide ships and sailors rather than soldiers for Roman forces. There is no reason to think that their position *vis-à-vis* Rome was any better than that of the infantry-providing *socii* (cf. Badian, *FC*, 28–30).

ad spem honoratioris militiae: the meaning appears to be that naval service was regarded as inferior, perhaps because of the sort of people they had to associate with (cf. Thiel, 215–16, Toynbee, ii. 94, 521, Brunt, 402). But this is scarcely a good reason for actually deserting. More likely they did not want as Greeks to fight against Greeks for Rome. L. may have misunderstood what Polybius said here.

rabiem: cf. xxxi. 17. 5, 18. 6.

10. Promunturium . . . Acraeam: the headland at the north-east corner of the bay in which Corinth lies. Cf. Strabo, viii. p. 380c. Ἀκραία is the epithet of a number of goddesses worshipped on hills or headlands. Cf. Wentzel, *RE*, i. 1193.

11. Philocles: cf. xxxi. 16. 2 n. He is last heard of at Chalcis (16. 12) and presumably crossed from there.

regius et ipse praefectus: i.e. as well as Androsthenes.

12. Quinctius [Romanus] in incepto: B has *cum intus Romanus in incepto*, χ *Quintius anusini neepio*. Both are easily recognizable as *Quinctius Romanus*. But such a double description is quite out of place and either *Quinctius* or *Romanus* will have to be deleted. We thus have to decide whether it is more likely that L. wrote *Romanus* and it was glossed as *Quinctius* or that *Quinctius* became corrupted early in the transmission and *Romanus* was inserted to make sense. *Romanus* as a simple gloss, as McDonald suggests, is not likely. On the whole *Quinctius* seems the more probable addition. Cf. Tränkle, *Gnomon*, 375 n. 2.

13. Corcyram: the Roman base, as at the end of 199: cf. 14. 7 n.

24. *The siege of Elatia*

Cf. Paus. x. 34. 4.

24. 1. dum . . . geruntur: cf. 19. 1 n. The events of this chapter are concurrent with those described in 19–23.

in Phocide: ch. 18.

principes: cf. xxxi. 17. 11 n.

3. admoto cum: *admotoque* B, *admoto* χ. *cum* is necessary since *quantum . . . prorutum* is the subject of *nudasset* and the *cum* before *ingenti* must govern what immediately follows it.

⟨**duas**⟩: Madvig's addition (*Emendationes*, 480) is generally accepted, but it is possible that L. did not specify the number of towers if in fact there were only two.

4. suis quisque stationibus: cf. xxxi. 3. 5 n.

7. libertatem . . . data: L.'s veracity here is open to very serious challenge. An inscription from Stymphalus (*SEG* x. 1107 = Moretti, *ISE* 55) records that the Elatians were restored to their land by M'. Acilius Glabrio in 191. The implication must be that they were expelled after their capture by Flamininus. Cf. M. Mitsos, *RÉG* lix–lx (1946–7), 150–74, Accame, *RFIC* n.s. xxvii (1949), 217 ff., *Espansione romana*, 254 ff., G. Klaffenbach, *BCH* xcii (1968), 257–9. The attempt to argue that they were expelled by the Aetolians after 196 is not convincing (thus A. Passerini, *Ath.* n.s. xxvi [1948], 83 ff., Lehmann, 120–5, Errington, *Philopoemen*, 132 n. 1, J. and L. Robert, *RÉG* lxxii [1969], 462, no. 265). Volkmann, 22–3, attempts to reconcile L. and the inscription by arguing that 'freedom' was restored to the city but the Elatians lost their *territorium* and their slaves, which made it virtually impossible for them to continue to live in Elatia. In view of the suppression by L. of other criticisms of Flamininus (cf. p. 22 n. 4) it is quite possible that the removal of the inhabitants of Elatia was described by Polybius and deliberately omitted by L. or one of his annalistic predecessors.

25. *The secession of Argos*

It is probable that it was the actions of those Argives who were responsible for delivering Argos to Philip that were criticized by Polybius in the 'fragment on traitors' (xviii. 13–15). Cf. Aymard, *RÉA* xlii (1940), 9–19 = *ÉHA*, 354–63, Walbank, *Commentary*, ii. 564–5.

1. adventu . . . Philoclis: cf. 23. 11.

2. primo: 'first of all', not going with *die* (cf. W–M).

praetores: in § 3 it is the *praeco* who omits the name of Philip, and it is possible that we should read either *praeconem* here or *praetor* below. In uncials the words would look extremely similar. If *praetores* is right, the reference is to local magistrates of Argos. Cf. *SEG* xvi. 255 l. 20, Deininger, 47 n. 8.

pronuntiare . . . Herculem: i.e. to call on with prayers.

additum . . . adiceretur: the Antigonids were not officially worshipped as gods on the Greek mainland (cf. xxxi. 44. 4 n.) but after the battle of Sellasia Antigonus Doson and then Philip were given honours which approximated to deification. Cf. C. F. Edson, *HThR* xxvi (1933), 324–5, Aymard, *PR*, 53 n. 27, Walbank, *Commentary*, i. 290, Habicht, *Gottmenschentum*, 80–1.

lege: the MSS. have *legi*, but this ruins the sense: if it was only a *mos* to call on the gods, the inclusion of Philip could not be described as an addition to a law.

3. **pactam** : 'pledged' as § 11, because a formal alliance had not yet been made (23. 2).

praeco : cf. n. on *praetores* (§ 2). Whoever was responsible, they clearly belong to that group of Argives who did not walk out of the assembly at Sicyon (cf. 22. 9).

4. **legitimum honorem** : i.e. the *honos* conferred by a *lex*.

5. **Larisam** : lying to the west of Argos. There was a second Acropolis, the Aspis, to the north-east: cf. xxxiv. 25. 5, Geiger, *RE*, xii. 840, P–K, iii. 1. 142–3. For the topography of Argos cf. W. Vollgraff, *BCH* xxxi (1907), 144 ff., *Mnemosyne* lvi (1928), 315 ff., A. Boethius, *Strena Philologica Upsaliensis* (Upsala, 1922), 248 ff.

6. **praesidium erat Achaeorum** : the *venia* of 22. 12 certainly did not extend to allowing Argos, Megalopolis, and Dyme to pursue their own course. And since some Argives had stayed and voted for the alliance the League could claim some justification for installing a garrison.

Aenesidemus : not otherwise known.

Dymaeus : presumably Dyme, despite its walk-out at Sicyon (22. 9), now accepted the decision of the League (cf. Aymard, *PR*, 109). But it is unlikely that Aenesidemus would have been given this sensitive task if he had been less than a positive supporter of the League's position.

7. **ne Romani quidem ad Corinthum** : 23. 11–13.

8. **si pertinacior . . . subituri** : the apodosis is in the indicative, and the 'real' apodosis *et mortui fuissent* is unexpressed. The construction is very common in Tacitus (cf. e.g. *A*. i. 23). For L.'s use of the construction cf. Chausserie-Laprée, 606 ff. (his denial that the idiom is to be explained as an ellipse of the real apodosis is unconvincing). See also K–St, ii. 404, xxxiii. 5. 2 n.

9. **pactus a Philocle** : thus B, χ has *cum*. This is a clear case of *lectio difficilior*: χ did not know that *paciscor* could be constructed with *ab*. Cf. Sall. *BJ* 26. 1.

10. **nihil statu moto** : Bφ have *statu modo*, ψ *tantum modo* (also found as a variant in φ). Madvig's *statu moto* 'not moving his position' makes excellent sense and is far easier than supplementing before *tantum modo*.

Thraecibus : cf. xxxi. 26. 1 n.

26–27. *Events in Rome and Italy*

26. 1–3. *Gaul*

The information contained in §§ 1–2 has already been given in 9. 5. This may be simply an oversight by L. and is not necessarily an indication of the use of different sources, as claimed by Kahrstedt, 65.

26. 1. Sex. Aelio consule: (105). Cf. xxxi. 50. 1 n.

2. cum duos . . . adduxit: cf. 8. 2–3, 9. 5 nn.

C. Helvium: (1). Cf. 7. 13 n., 8. 5.

3. Cremonensibus Placentinisque: cf. xxxi. 10. Placentia had been sacked in 200 (l.c.) but Cremona had not. But the mere danger of the Gallic attack had no doubt caused some people to flee from the town.

26. 4–18. *Slave revolts*

Cf. also Zon. ix. 16. 6. On the revolts see particularly M. Capozza, *Movimenti servili nel mondo romano in età repubblicana* (Rome, 1966), 101–20, A. B. Bosworth, *JRS* lviii (1968), 272–4, Toynbee, ii. 251, 308, 318 ff. Toynbee's view that most of the slaves involved are 'plantation slaves' does not seem to be based on any evidence. It is uncertain whether the revolt was engineered by the hostages or the slaves. The lacunae in § 8 and §13 and the uncertainty of reading at the beginning of § 7 make it difficult to discover L.'s own view, and though Zonaras ix. 16. 6 makes the hostages responsible, that may represent only Dio's interpretation of L. See also § 16 n. That the revolt was inspired from Carthage itself, as suggested by Capozza, 113–16, is most improbable.

4. prope tumultus: it did not become a *tumultus*, though it was dealt with as if it were (cf. § 12).

5. obsides Carthaginiensium: on the hostages cf. 2. 3–4 nn.

    Setiae: mod. Sezze, about 45 miles south of Rome. It was a Latin colony, founded in 312 (Vell. Pat. i. 14. 2). It was one of the defaulting colonies in 209 (xxvii. 9. 7, xxix. 15. 5). Cf. Nissen, *IL*, ii. 2. 645–6, H. A. Armstrong, *AJA* xix (1915), 34–56, Philipp, *RE*, iiA. 1924–5.

6. ab ipsis Setinis . . . mancipia: i.e. they formed part of the booty captured from the Carthaginians. The *aerarium* will have realized their value by selling them to the citizens of Setia. Cf. F. Bona, *SDHI* xxv (1959), 309–70.

7. cum coniurationem fecissent: the lack of a subject is difficult, and supplementation seems necessary. McDonald regards the hostages as the subject, but in that case L. is being very obscure. H. J. Müller's *ii*, to refer to the hostages, is equally ambiguous. McDonald objects to Madvig's *ea*, referring to *mancipia*, on the grounds that it is the hostages who took the initiative. But this is precisely what is in dispute (cf. 4–18 n.). If the slaves are the subject, Madvig is probably right: if the hostages are intended, specific reference to them is required. (Pettersson, 46, also defends the MSS. reading.)

primum qui : McDonald considers inverting these two words, but rejects it on the grounds that these visits to stir up the slaves in the adjoining areas are the first stage of the conspiracy, to be followed by the projected attack at the *ludi*. But the inversion of the relative pronoun is so common in L. (cf. the list in W–M) that it is perfectly natural even where the *primum* is followed by a *deinde* inside the relative clause. To take *primum* with what precedes and not with *deinde* is impossible.

Norbam : cf. 2. 4 n.

Cerceios : about 60 miles south of Rome on the coast. It was a Latin colony attributed to Tarquinius Superbus (i. 56. 3) though assigned to 393 by Diodorus, xiv. 102. Cf. Nissen, *IL*, ii. 2. 636–7, Hülsen, *RE*, iii. 2565–6, Ogilvie, 215–16. The later form is *Circeii* but several MSS. of classical authors give *Cerceii* (cf. Hülsen, l.c.).

8. There is a large lacuna here, indicated as such by gaps in B and A. McDonald fills it by assuming that there is a reference to an attempt to release the hostages as described in *per.* xxxii. But the latter could just be a general summary of the whole affair. There is no need to posit a reference either here, or in the lacuna in § 13, to the man whose services are mentioned in § 14 (thus Walsh, *CR*, 55).

L. Cornelium Lentulum praetorem urbanum : he is really L. Cornelius Merula (cf. 7. 13 n., 8. 5) and *Lentulum* is an error, either by L. himself or his source. Zon. ix. 16. 6 also refers to Lentulus.

9. acta futuraque : thus the MSS., but the phrase *facta futuraque* is idiomatic (cf. W–M ad loc., *TLL*, vi. 1. 133) and Lentz's correction is probably right.

10. quaerendam : i.e. he was to establish a *quaestio*: cf. xxxi. 12. 3 n.

iussus : technically the senate could not issue instructions to magistrates.

11. sacramento rogatos : apparently a technical term for exacting an oath. Cf. xxxv. 2. 8, xl. 26. 7, Caes. *BG* vi. 1. 2. It is an adaptation of the customary oath taken by an army to their commander at the beginning of a campaign (cf. Pol. vi. 21. 1–3) and was clearly designed to strengthen this irregular levy.

12. tumultuario dilectu : cf. xxxi. 2. 5 n.

13. A lacuna is indicated here in several MSS. McDonald's supplement is based on the statement in *per.* xxxii that 2,500 were killed; 500 of these are accounted for in § 16 below.

14. centum milia gravis aeris : 100,000 asses, at this time the qualification for the Roman *prima classis* (cf. Walbank, *Commentary*, i. 706). The man was presumably a Latin, but he could obtain

Roman citizenship *per migrationem et censum. gravis aeris* implies *asses* of libral standard, though in fact the sextantal *as* was current at this date (cf. M. H. Crawford, *JRS* liv [1964], 29 ff.). It is improbable that the senate would have given him old *asses* to provide him with the capital for the *prima classis* qualification, as it would have been far more profitable to have them melted down and re-minted as sextantal *asses*. L. is probably writing carelessly. This is the only passage where *gravis aeris* is used of the period when the post-libral standards were in operation (for use in a similar context cf. xxii. 33. 2, of 217, the time when the libral standard was being abandoned).

I am grateful to Mr. Crawford for advice on this matter.

vicena quina milia : the property qualification for the *quarta classis* (cf. i. 43. 5).

15. Praeneste : mod. Palestrina, about 30 miles east of Rome. Cf. Nissen, *IL*, ii. 2. 620 ff. Though joining in the Latin war, it remained of Italian status until after the Social war (cf. Sherwin-White, *RC*, 31, L. R. Taylor, *Voting Districts of the Roman Republic* [Rome, 1960], 81).

16. in timore . . . moliri : the reference is purely to the trouble at Praeneste, and is not to be taken as indicating that there was no definite evidence that the hostages had been involved in the Setia uprising, as Bosworth, *JRS* lviii (1968), 273, argues. (Capozza, 112 n. 33 also takes *ea* to refer to all the attempts at revolt.)

17. minores magistratus : technically the *minores magistratus* are those elected in the tribal, as opposed to the centuriate assembly (cf. Mommsen, *StR*, i³. 19). But it seems that it was the plebeian aediles who were especially concerned with security duties and the reference may be to them alone (cf. iii. 6. 9 and Ogilvie ad loc.).

triumviri : the *iiiviri capitales*, in charge of the prisons and executions.

carceris lautumiarum : a prison on the Capitol, probably in the rocks on its southern side: cf. xxvi. 27. 3, xxxvii. 3. 8, xxxix. 44. 7. They were so named after the quarries of Syracuse (Varro, *LL* v. 151). They were regarded as a less restrictive prison than the *carcer* (Sen. *Contr.* ix. 4. 21, *Dig.* iv. 6. 9, xi. 5. 1. 4): hence the order for extra precautions. Cf. Platner–Ashby, 316, J. Le Gall, *MEFR* lvi (1939), 76–80, M. Blake, *Ancient Roman Construction in Italy* (Washington, 1947), 23–4.

There is no need to take *carceris lautumiarum* as a paratactical phrase, as is done by Mommsen, *Strafrecht*, 302 n. 3.

18. captivi : it is hard to believe that the ex-prisoners already sold could be kept in a public prison. The reference, therefore, is presumably to prisoners of war who had not been sold, and whom the senate now decided were not to be sold.

27. 1. *Embassy from Attalus*

For the antecedents cf. 8. 9–16 and nn.

27. 1. coronam auream : Ogilvie, 444, wrongly includes this in his list of crowns dedicated from spoil: it should belong to the category of donations by allied states.

ducentum quadraginta sex pondo : Schmitt, *Antiochos*, 275 n. 3 notes that such precision over weight is unusual in L. and suggests that it is a calculation to give the equivalent of 3 talents at the rate of 82 talents to the pound.

Antiochus . . . deduxisset : Schmitt, *Antiochos*, 271–6 argues that in 196 Antiochus' army must have proceeded to Abydus by land, and that to do this it must have marched through land occupied by Attalus since 216. Hence he plausibly suggests that in fact Attalus and Antiochus reached a compromise, and that it is to this that the συνθῆκαι of Pol. xxi. 17. 6, (cf. 43. 20ff., L. xxxvii. 45. 15, xxxviii. 38. 14, App. *Syr.* 38) refers. His further suggestion, however, that the envoys of 8. 15 never set out, and that Attalus' thank-offering is an annalistic invention is not probable.

27. 2–4. *Supplies from Massinissa, Sicily, and Sardinia:*
Cato's governorship of Sardinia

2. elephanti : B has *elephantes*. The form *elephas* is found in the nominative singular, but though often attested in the oblique cases —several times in the MSS. of L.—it is generally held to be a mistake. Cf. Neue-Wagener, i. 492–4, *TLL*, v. 2. 354.

Masinissa : cf. xxxi. 11. 4–18 n. For other gifts of corn from Massinissa cf. xxxi. 19. 4 n.

item ex Sicilia Sardiniaque : it is not clear whether this is tithecorn, or voluntary gifts over and above the tithe, or corn bought from the two provinces. Toynbee, ii. 338 assumes it is an additional tithe, as in xxxvi. 2. 12–13, xxxvii. 2. 12, 50. 9–10, xlii. 31. 8.

3. Siciliam M. Marcellus : cf. xxxi. 50. 1 n., xxxii. 7. 13, 8. 5.

Sardiniam M. Porcius Cato : cf. 7. 13 n., 8. 5. The comments on Cato occur in what might otherwise appear as a section of purely 'archival' material. Cf. p. 11.

Cato at this period was making a parade of his simple way of life and demonstrating his virtue. As a provincial governor he was concerned to set an example. But the contrast implied is more suggestive of the evils of provincial government at a later date, and the almost religious tone of *sanctus et innocens* suggests some of the later 'Catosaga'. For other sources on Cato in Sardinia cf. Nep. *Cato* 1. 4, Plut. *Cato mai.* 6, *vir. ill.* 47. 1, Scullard, *RP*, 112, D. Kienast, *Cato der Zensor* (Heidelberg, 1954), 42.

asperior: 'too harsh'.

in faenore coercendo: Cato's professions about usury and his actual practice did not always coincide, at least in the later part of his life. (Cf. Frank, *Economic Survey*, i. 207–8, Scullard, *RP*, 112 n. 3, 222: Wegner, 52–3 unconvincingly rejects the evidence of Plut. *Cato mai.* 21. 6.) There is no reason to think that the money-lenders involved were Punic (thus Frank, l.c.: cf. Kienast, *Cato der Zensor*, 42–3).

4. sumptus ... sublati: the *Lex Porcia de sumptu provinciali* may be a praetorian law of 198 (cf. Scullard, *RP*, 112 n. 4).

27. 5–8. *Elections. The aediles of 198. Ludi Romani*

5. Sex. Aelius: (105). Cf. xxxi. 50. 1 n.
ex Gallia: 26. 1–3.
C. Cornelium Cethegum: (88). Cf. xxxi. 49. 7 n.
Q. Minucium Rufum: (22, 55). Cf. xxxi. 4. 4 n.
biduo post: probably 'two days later'. Cf. Nisbet, *Commentary on Cicero, in Pisonem*, 67, xxxi. 1. 8 n.

6. sex praetores ... imperio: the aim, in particular, was to provide praetors in office to govern the two Spanish provinces, which had hitherto been governed by *privati cum imperio* (cf. xxxi. 20. 1 n.). In addition, the appointment of praetors to places like Bruttium and Ariminum, as had happened recently, had meant that there had not been a *praetor peregrinus* as well as a *praetor urbanus* (cf. xxxi. 6. 2 n.). In 181 the *Lex Baebia* provided for alternation of six and four praetors, but this provision was soon dropped. Cf. Scullard, *RP*, 173.

The raising of the number of praetors to six seems to have been associated with the informal adoption of a number of rules governing the *cursus honorum*: cf. 7. 9 n., xxxi. 4. 7 n.

One would expect that a change in the number of praetors would be sanctioned by a *lex*. But there is no trace of one, and it is not inconceivable that the change was introduced on senatorial authority alone.

7. L. Manlius Volso: (93). The *praenomen* is missing in the MSS. but he must be identical with the brother of Cn. Manlius Vulso, consul in 189, under whom he served as a *legatus* in 189 and 188. For his identity with the T. Manlius of Cic. *II Verr.* ii. 123 cf. *MRR*, i. 334 n. 2, Toynbee, ii. 211 n. 11.

C. Sempronius Tuditanus: (90). Plebeian aedile in 198 (§ 8). Cf. xxxiii. 25. 9, 27. 1. He was a *pontifex* (xxxiii. 42. 5). His relationship to the consul of 204 is not known.

M. Sergius Silus: (40). Cf. 28. 2, 31. 6, xxxiii. 21. 9, 24. 4. For a speech delivered during his praetorship cf. *ORF*[2], 97–8.

M. Helvius: (4). Plebeian aedile in 198 (§ 8). His Spanish command was prorogued in 196 and 195 (cf. xxxiii. 21. 7, 25. 9 n.).

M. Minucius Rufus: (53). He was a *iiivir* for the colonization in Bruttium from 194 to 192 and a *legatus* to Carthage in 193.

L. Atilius: (16). He is not known apart from his praetorship. The MSS. here and at 28. 2 read *Acilius* and there is no real way of determining which is correct (a L. Acilius occurs as a *legatus* in 181).

8. curules aediles: as it stands it looks as if these are the curule aediles elected now. But 197 is a year for patrician curule aediles and we know who they are (xxxiii. 25. 1). So Minucius and Sempronius are clearly the aediles of 198, and L. is led to name them because he has just mentioned the plebeian aediles. It would be better to punctuate only with a comma after *erant*.

Q. Minucius Thermus: (65). He was a military tribune in 202, tribune of the plebs in 201, a *iiivir* for the foundation of Campanian colonies from 197 to 194 (29. 3–4), praetor in 196 (xxxiii. 24. 2, 26. 2, 43. 8, 44. 4) with command prorogued in 195. He was consul in 193, with command prorogued until 190. He was one of the *x legati* for the Apamea settlement, and was killed in Thrace during his return from Asia. He was a supporter of Scipio Africanus and an opponent of Cato. Cf. McDonald, *JRS* xxviii (1938), 161–2, Scullard, *RP*, 81, 133–4.

Ti. Sempronius Longus: (67). Cf. xxxi. 20. 5 n.

ludi Romani: cf. xxxi. 9. 5–10 n.

quater instaurati: cf. xxxi. 4. 5 n. It is not clear whether L. means that the whole of the games were repeated four times (as with *ter toti* in xxxi. 4. 7, 50. 3, xxxiii. 25. 1, 42. 9) or whether the omission of *toti* means that four individual items were repeated, as is argued by S. Monti, *RAAN* xxiv–xxv (1949–50), 171.

197 B.C.

28–31. *Events in Rome and Italy*

28. *Provinces and armies*

28. 2. res . . . poterat: the phrase is odd because it is not the case either that there was some aspect of the praetorian assignations that could not be settled by lot, or that praetorian, as opposed to consular provinces were normally assigned by lot. The meaning must be that in the case of the praetors it was politically possible to complete the matter without the arguments that occurred in the case of the consular provinces.

peregrina iurisdictio: L. alternates between this expression and *iurisdictio inter cives et peregrinos* (cf. xxxiii. 21. 9, 26. 1). But it is possible that at this date the peregrine praetor dealt only with cases between peregrines and that cases between peregrines and citizens came before the urban praetor. Cf. D. Daube, *JRS* xli (1951), 66–70.

Sardiniam Atilius : in succession to Cato.

Siciliam Manlius : in succession to Marcellus.

Hispanias : 27. 6 n.

3–9. *The Macedonian command.* It was fear of being superseded, according to Polybius, that led Flamininus to agree to Philip sending ambassadors to Rome after the conference of Nicaea, despite the inadequacy of the terms offered by Philip (Pol. xviii. 10. 1–7, 11. 1). L. suppresses most of Polybius' critical remarks about Flamininus' conduct of the Nicaea negotiations and gives the facts about the decision not to supersede him in this 'Roman' section, rather than in his account of the sequel to the Nicaea negotiations. Cf. 32–7 n., 36. 10 n., 37 n., pp. 24–6.

From Polybius xviii. 11. 1–2 it appears that Flamininus' friends discovered before the actual debate that Flamininus was not going to be superseded (cf. Holleaux, *Études*, v. 71 n. 1, Walbank, *Commentary*, ii. 563). This is hard to square with L.'s account of the proceedings, but it may be true, and would perhaps help to explain why the tribunes gave their agreement so easily to letting the senate make the decision (cf. § 8 n.). No doubt their canvassing had been more accurate than that of the consuls.

This debate, then, takes place after that described in ch. 37.

3. L. Oppius : (32, cf. 19). L. Oppius Salinator, plebeian aedile in 193, in charge of the fleet off Sicily in 192, and praetor in 191 with command prorogued in 190.

Q. Fulvius : (28, 60). It is not clear whether he is to be identified with the Q. Fulvius Flaccus who became plebeian aedile in 189, praetor in 187 and *consul suffectus* in 180 or whether the latter is rather the Q. Fulvius who is sent to Rome by Flamininus as a *legatus* after Nicaea (36. 10). The tribune and the *legatus* cannot, of course, be identical. Cf. Schlag, 112–14, and on the political position of this Fulvius p. 32.

I see no reason for Gelzer's suggestion (*Historia* i [1950], 637 = *Kleine Schriften*, i. 204) that the names of these two tribunes are a late annalistic invention.

3–4. quod . . . revocaretur : for the political significance of the dispute cf. p. 33. In the case of Sulpicius L. may be thinking in terms of his own false chronology, according to which all of Sulpicius' campaign is placed in 200 (cf. xxxi. 22. 4–47. 3 n.). With regard to Villius it could be replied that it was the late date of his arrival that was the cause of his ineffectiveness. It is perhaps awareness of this that leads to exaggeration in § 6.

prior consul revocaretur: 'the consul already there'. The phrase has nothing to do with *consul prior* meaning the consul who held the *fasces* in January and *revocaretur* has nothing to do with elections, as claimed by J. Linderski (and apparently L. R. Taylor) in *Historia* xiv (1965), 433 n. 41.

5. quartum iam annum: counting inclusively from 200.

quaerendo . . . absumpsisse: xxxi. 33–40. 6. Cf. the completely opposite picture presented by Aristaenus in 21. 19.

Villium . . . revocatum: chs. 3–6.

6. rebus divinis: the prodigies (9. 1–4).

maiorem partem anni: not true. Flamininus arrived in Greece about May (9. 6 n).

7. prope: 'had almost gone into his winter quarters'. There is no need for emendation or deletion, nor should it be taken to mean 'Flamininus had set out so late that he had almost gone straight into his winter quarters', as argued by Walker, *Supplementary Annotations*, 192, and W–M.

8. consules . . . consultationem: there is a limit beyond which members of the governing class are unwilling to press their point by using their powers of veto or holding up other business. Cf. 7. 12 n. But in this case both sides may have believed that their view would command a majority in the senate (cf. 3–9 n.).

9. donec successor . . . venisset: an apparent extension, not a limitation of the prorogation. But it made little practical difference, as the senate could change its mind the following year. For a similar prorogation in 209 for Scipio and M. Iunius Silanus cf. xxvii. 7. 17 (xxx. 1. 10, also quoted by W–M, is rather different).

binae legiones: cf. 8. 2 n.

defecissent: cf. xxxi. 10. The reference is to the tribes who had combined in 200 and though defeated had not yet submitted to Rome. But it is far from clear that they posed an actual threat at this time (cf. Schlag, 42).

sex . . . equites: cf. 1. 3 n. It is not made clear whether they are to be citizens or allies.

11. L. Quinctius Flamininus: cf. 16. 2 n.

socium ac nominis Latini: cf. xxxi. 8. 7 n.

veterem ex Hispaniis militem: the commanders in Spain had been there since 200 but many of the soldiers for far longer. Only a part had been dismissed in 201 (xxx. 41. 5). On the Spanish armies in the second century cf. Toynbee, ii. 61 n. 2, 131, Brunt, 661 ff.

terminare iussi.. . . . servaretur : though there had been two commanders in Spain for several years it seems that their commands had not been clearly defined. It is odd to find the senate leaving such a decision to the praetors, but perhaps they knew little themselves of the geography, and felt that any decision would be arbitrary. On the boundary cf. K. Götzfried, *Annalen der römischen Provinzen beider Spanien* (Erlangen, 1907), 43, E. A. Schulten, *CAH*, viii. 306, C. H. V. Sutherland, *The Romans in Spain* (London, 1939), 48 and 224 n. 5, Schlag, 31. See addenda.

29. 1–2. Prodigies

Cf. xxxi. 12. 5–10 n.

29. 1. aedes Volcani Summanique Romae : the temple of Volcanus was in the Campus Martius (Platner–Ashby, 584), that of Summanus in the Circus Maximus (Platner–Ashby, 502). Summanus appears to have been originally a name of Jupiter. After a statue of Jupiter Summanus in the Capitoline temple was struck by lightning in 278, a separate temple was founded. *summanium* or *fulgur summanium* was the name given to lightning at night-time. Cf. Wissowa, *RuK*², 53, 122, 135, Latte, *RRG*, 208–9.

et quod : the *quod* is not repeated in the following clauses. *quod et* is impossible, because both the Rome and the Fregenae episodes are included in *tacta erant* and the *et* could not join *Fregenis* and *Frusinone*. This sort of inconsistency in a prodigy section is not surprising.

Fregenis : mod. Maccarese, the wine-growing area by the coast 9 miles north of Ostia. A Roman colony was founded there in 245 (cf. *per.* xix, Vell. Pat. i. 14. 8, Nissen, *IL*, ii. 1. 350, Weiss, *RE*, vii. 94–5, Ashby, *Campagna*, 219).

de caelo tacta : cf. 1. 10 n.

2. Frusinone : cf. xxxi. 12. 7 n.

inter noctem lux orta : for similar prodigies cf. Wülker, 7–8, Luterbacher, 21, Krauss, 78.

Aefulae : B reads *Aefulo*, χ *Efulo*. The *arx Aefulana* is mentioned at xxvi. 9. 9. Horace, *Odes* iii. 29. 6 refers to *Aefula* and it seems probable that apparent references to *Aesulum* or *Aesula* at Vell. Pat. i. 14. 8, Pliny *NH* iii. 69 are MSS. corruptions: in that case the Velleius passage will tell us that a colony was founded at Aefula in 247. It probably lay to the south of Tibur. Cf. Nissen, *IL*, ii. 2. 614, Hülsen, *RE*, i. 475–6, Ashby, *Campagna*, 122, Salmon, *Colonization*, 180 n. 120.

agnus . . . natus : cf. 9. 3, xxxi. 12. 7 n.

Formiis : cf. 1. 10 n.

lupi : for similar prodigies cf. Wülker, 17, Luterbacher, 28, Krauss, 107–10.

29. 3–4. *Campanian colonies*

3. C. Atinius tribunus plebis: we know of a C. Atinius tribune in 196 (xxxiii. 22. 2, 25. 6) and Broughton assumes that the present man is in fact the tribune for 197/6, and that he carried his proposals at the end of the consular year (*MRR*, i. 336, 339 n. 3). L. has two sections of domestic material for the year and if Broughton is right it might have been expected that Atinius' proposals would have been included in the second of these (xxxiii. 21. 6–25. 3)—though admittedly L. may have had no very secure basis for his division. There is a C. Atinius who is praetor in 195 and another in 190, so there is no difficulty in finding a second tribune. On the other hand, an argument for Broughton's view might be drawn from the fact that these colonies were, with additions, settled in 194 (xxxiv. 45. 1). This action in 194 is usually, and rightly, ascribed to fear of the advances of Antiochus and a wish to protect the coast against him (cf. Scullard, *RP*, 117, who, however, ignores the fact that several of the colonies were planned in 197). If the planning now also had Antiochus in mind, it must follow news of his Asiatic advances in 197, and so could not be earlier than the end of the year. Yet Atinius may not have been concerned with Antiochus at all at this stage. There is no need to believe that small citizen colonies were purely defensive in character. Equally, the fact that the *iiiviri* were appointed for three years (§ 4) does not prove that they were appointed at the end of 197, and that the *triennium* was 196–194. Their term of office could have been extended in 194.

It may have proved difficult to find colonists for these sites, which were unattractive ones. Cf. xxxix. 23. 3, Val. Max. v. 3. 2, Salmon, *Colonization*, 185 nn. 166, 167.

ostia fluminum Volturni Liternique: the Volturnus is the main river of Campania and forms a fertile valley (cf. Radke, *RE*, ixA. 861–3). The Liternus is in fact a lagoon into which the river Clanis runs. The colonies were named Volturnum and Liternum respectively. The former is the modern Castelvolturno. On the ruins of Liternum, on the shores of the Lago di Patria, cf. A. Maiuri, *Passeggiate Campane*[3] (Florence, 1957), 89 ff. See also Nissen, *IL*, ii. 2. 712–14, Philipp, *RE*, xiii. 746–7, Radke, *RE*, ixA. 858–9.

Puteolos: cf. 7. 3 n.

Castrum Salerni: mod. Salerno. The name suggests that it was scarcely inhabited before the settlement of the colony. Cf. Nissen, *IL*, ii. 2. 825–6, Philipp, *RE*, iA. 1869, Brunt, 278.

Buxentum: mod. Polikastro, in Lucania. It lay on the site of the former Greek town of Pixus. It quickly became deserted and in 185 a fresh *deductio* was ordered. Cf. xxxix. 23. 3, Vell. Pat. i. 15. 3,

Nissen, *IL*, ii. 2. 897–8, Hülsen, *RE*, iii. 1093, Kahrstedt, *Historia* viii (1959), 190.

4. per triennium . . . haberent: although the three-year period of office for the settling of colonies is attested only here and in xxxiv. 53. 2 (194), it was probably the normal practice. Cf. Salmon, *Colonization*, 19.

    M. Servilius Geminus: (78). Cf. xxxi. 4. 3 n.
    Q. Minucius Thermus: (65). Cf. 27. 8 n.
    Ti. Sempronius Longus: (67). Cf. xxxi. 20. 5 n.

29. 5—31. *The Gallic war*

For Gaul in 198 cf. 9. 5, 26. 1–3. On this campaign cf. G. Mezzar-Zerbi, *RSC* vi (1958), 11 ff., Toynbee, ii. 269 ff., Schlag, 42–4. Schlag argues with some plausibility that the consuls provoked the conflict on this occasion. Cf. also 28. 9 n.

5. divinis: i.e. the prodigies.

6. Insubres . . . Cenomanis: cf. xxxi. 10. 2 n.
Genuamque exercitu ducto: presumably along the coast. The difficulties raised by Toynbee, ii. 678–9 n. 9 are not serious. On Genua (mod. Genova) cf. Weiss, *RE*, vii. 1204–6, on its importance Toynbee, ii. 261. For later connections of the Minucii Rufi with Genua cf. *ILLRP* 517.

7. Clastidium: mod. Casteggio, about 7 miles east of Voghera. It was the site of a famous victory of Marcellus in 222. Cf. Nissen, *IL*, ii. 1. 271, Hülsen, *RE*, iii. 2649, M. Baratta, *Clastidium* (Pavia, 1932).
    Litubium: the site is uncertain. Nissen, *IL*, ii. 1. 271 n. 4, Toynbee, ii. 269 identify it with Retorbido, a little to the south of Voghera.
    utraque Ligurum: in fact Clastidium was a town of the Anares who were a Gallic people. Cf. Hülsen, *RE*, i. 2055–6, iii. 2049, Walbank, *Commentary*, i. 183.
    Celeiates: cf. xxxi. 10. 2 n.
    Cerdiciates: not otherwise known.
    Boios, Ilvates: cf. xxxi. 10. 2 n.

30. 1. traicerat . . . Cenomanis: i.e. they crossed to the north of the Po.

2. rem gesturos ut: *ut* depends, somewhat harshly, on *iunxeratque*. We should, therefore, punctuate with a comma after *gesturos*.

3. alterum consulem: Minucius (29. 8).

4. super amnis Minci ripam: the Mincius (mod. Mincio) flows from Lake Garda and forms three lagoons at Mantova. It flows thence to join the Po.

5. duo milia passum : B has ∞ ∞, χ *mille passuum milia*. But the omission of *passuum* is very common (cf. *TLL*, viii. 979) and χ has probably added it.

6. Brixiamque : mod. Brescia. Cf. Nissen, *IL*, ii. 1. 196–7, Hülsen, *RE*, iii. 884–5.

9. animis : to be taken with *suspicio*.

10. aedem Sospitae Iunoni : for the temple of Juno Sospita at Lanuvium cf. xxxi. 12. 6 n. This temple was dedicated in 193 (xxxiv. 53. 3) but is there said to be to *Juno Matuta*. This must be wrong, since Matuta is not known as an epithet for Juno, whilst Sospita is known, and is indeed extremely suitable for the present occasion. Latte (*RRG*, 168 n. 5) suggested emending the latter passage to *Matris Reginae Sospitae*, though he admitted that L. himself may have been responsible for the mistake.

11. Quidam . . . auctores sunt : cf. p. 9.

12. Hamilcarem : cf. xxxi. 10. 2, 21. 18 nn.

carpenta supra : B and two MSS. of the χ group indicate a lacuna here. All supplements remain quite conjectural.

31. 2. hosti : the Romans. Cf. e.g. xxxi. 45. 6.

4. Clastidium incensum : cf. 29. 7 n. It is not clear whether Clastidium is burnt by the Boii, or by the Romans. The context suggests the latter, but since Clastidium had made a *deditio* to Minucius already (29. 7) we should have to assume that it had defected. There is certainly no need to posit a change of source between 29. 7 and here, as is done by Zimmerer, *Qu. Claudius Quadrigarius* (Munich, 1937), 29, G. Mezzar-Zerbi, *RSC* vi (1958), 13.

inde : if Clastidium was burnt by the Boii, *inde* will mean 'from the land of the Boii' not 'from Clastidium'.

Ligustinos Ilvates : 29. 8.

6. prospere gestis : *gestis prospere* MSS. Madvig (*Emendationes*, 481–2) suggested *prope*, but McDonald seems right to prefer Kreyssig's transposition.

M. Sergius : (40). Cf. 27. 7 n.

praetor urbanus : B has *pr. urbis* (with a capital R after *p*), χ *praefectus urbis*. This suggests that the archetype had *PR.URB.*

supplicatio in quadriduum decreta : cf. xxxi. 22. 1 n.

32–40. *Events in Greece: winter 198/7 B.C.*

32–7. *The conference of Nicaea*

For this section we have the narrative of Polybius, xviii. 1–12. Other sources are Plut. *Flam.* 5. 6, 7. 1–2, App. *Mac.* 8, Just. xxx. 3. 8–10,

Zon. ix. 16. 4. L. omits Polybius' criticisms of Flamininus (cf. p. 22 n. 4), though he does not conceal Polybius' theme—that Flamininus was prepared to make peace on terms well below Rome's demands if his command was not prorogued (32. 7–8). For the interpretation of Flamininus' behaviour at Nicaea cf. pp. 24–6. On points of detail cf. Walbank, *Commentary*, ii. 548–64.

On L.'s adaptations of Polybius in this section cf. Witte, 283–4, Lambert, 63 ff., Walsh, *RhM* xcvii (1954), 103 ff., McDonald, *JRS* xlvii (1957), 161, Brueggmann, 91 ff.

32. 1. Hiems iam eo tempore: a false link, as L. has just been describing events in the summer of 197. What follows, however, belongs to the winter of 198/7. L. has taken events described by Polybius under the Olympiad year 198/7 and attached them to the consular year 197. Cf. p. 3. For the date of the conference cf. Walbank, *Commentary*, ii. 548–9.

  capta Elatia: 24. 7.

  in Phocide ac Locride: cf. ch. 18, 21. 7 n.

  Opunte: Opus is *c.* 16 miles east of Elatia: cf. Meyer, *RE*, xviii. 812–19, P–K, i. 2. 355.

2–3. seditio . . . tenuit urbem: it is clear that both parties in Opus wanted to be rid of the Macedonians, but the poor naturally looked to Aetolia as their champion, the rich to Rome. The senate's class-preferences were clearly already well known in Greece. Cf. *Past and Present* no. 36 (April, 1967), 5.

4. decederent: B reads *decerent* with *de* written above it, not *decererent* as McDonald's apparatus may suggest.

5. caduceator: cf. xxxi. 38. 9 n.

6. gravate: 'unwillingly'. Holleaux, *Études*, v. 32 n. 1, followed by Walbank, *Philip V*, 159 n. 4, interprets this as an assumed unwilling-ness, so as not to appear over-eager for negotiations. McDonald, however, thinks that Flamininus agreed unwillingly because he wanted to delay the negotiations until he knew for certain whether or not his command was to be prorogued. Balsdon, *Phoenix* xxi (1967), 180 n. 12 thinks that Flamininus was simply unwilling to abandon the siege of Opus. (Balsdon is unfair to Holleaux in attributing to him the assertion that *gravate* was an addition by L. himself. Holleaux raised the possibility, but left the question open.)

McDonald's interpretation seems too complex. It involves taking *necdum . . . prorogaretur* as explaining *gravate*, *aptum . . . inclinare* as elucidating *concessum*. But the *quin* clause must explain *gravate*, and hence it is very difficult not to take all that follows as also being an explanation of *gravate*. Balsdon, on the other hand, simply ignores all that follows *gravate concessum*. L. feels he has to explain *gravate*, and his explanation has nothing to do with the siege of Opus. The argument, which is certainly expressed in a very compressed fashion, is as follows (cf. Holleaux, *Études*, v. 65–6 n. 2). *non quin . . . bellum* explains that though Flamininus appeared to agree with reluctance, this did not mean that he was averse to a negotiated peace. *necdum . . . prorogaretur* expands this by stressing that as he did not yet know whether he was to remain in Greece, he could not be sure whether or not he would need to negotiate. *aptum autem . . . inclinare* concludes the explanation by saying that he nevertheless thought a conference would be useful because he could push the discussion in either direction as events demanded. It follows that Holleaux was right to take *gravate* as an assumed reluctance. For a similar assumed reluctance to agree to a request which a Roman representative clearly wanted to agree to cf. xlii. 43. 2–3, pointed out by K. Niemeyer, *N. Jahr. f. Phil.* cxli (1890), 710–12.

9. in sinu Maliaco prope Nicaeam : Pol. xviii. 1. 5: συνεγγίσαντες δὲ κατὰ Νίκαιαν πρὸς τὴν θάλατταν. For the site of Nicaea cf. Oldfather, *RE*, xvii. 222 ff., P–K, i. 2. 344, Walbank, *Commentary*, ii. 257.

Eo rex . . . venit : Pol. xviii. 1. 1: ὁ μὲν Φίλιππος ἐκ Δημητριάδος ἀναχθεὶς εἰς τὸν Μηλιέα κόλπον, πέντε λέμβους ἔχων καὶ μίαν πρίστιν, ἐφ᾽ ἧς αὐτὸς ἐπέπλει.

nave rostrata : a πρίστις was apparently a beaked ship, but *nave rostrata* perhaps suggests that L. imagined it to be a larger vessel than it actually was. Cf. Pol. xvi. 2. 9, Walbank, *Commentary*, ii. 549. At xxxv. 26. 1 L. simply transliterates πρίστις (cf. McDonald and Walbank, *JRS* lix [1969], 34 n. 22).

10. erant cum eo . . . Cycliadas : Pol. xviii. 1. 2: συνῆσαν δ᾽ αὐτῷ Μακεδόνες μὲν Ἀπολλόδωρος καὶ Δημοσθένης οἱ γραμματεῖς, ἐκ Βοιωτίας Βραχύλλης, Ἀχαιὸς δὲ Κυκλιάδας, ἐκπεπτωκὼς ἐκ Πελοποννήσου διὰ τὰς πρότερον ὑφ᾽ ἡμῶν εἰρημένας αἰτίας.

L. appears to have been rather free here, since γραμματεῖς are not *principes*. At 35. 8 he refers to *duobus quos pridie adhibuerat* where Polybius (xviii. 8. 7) has παραλαβὼν Ἀπολλόδωρον καὶ Δημοσθένην but that may mean 'with two men whom he had brought with him on the previous day' and not 'the two (Macedonians) whom . . .'. It is, then, unwise to insert *duo* before *principes* or to make any other additions to bring L. into line with Polybius.

On Cycliadas cf. xxxi. 25. 3 n., xxxii. 19. 2 n.

11. cum imperatore . . . Xenophon : Pol. xviii. 1. 3–4: μετὰ δὲ τοῦ Τίτου παρῆν ὅ τε βασιλεὺς Ἀμύνανδρος καὶ παρ᾽ Ἀττάλου Διονυσόδωρος, ἀπὸ δὲ τῶν ἐθνῶν καὶ πόλεων τῶν μὲν Ἀχαιῶν Ἀρίσταινος καὶ Ξενοφῶν, παρὰ δὲ Ῥοδίων Ἀκεσίμβροτος ὁ ναύαρχος, παρὰ δὲ τῶν

Αἰτωλῶν Φαινέας ὁ στρατηγός, καὶ πλείους δ᾽ ἕτεροι τῶν πολιτευομένων. L. alters the order and omits the last phrase.

Amynander : cf. xxxi. 28. 1 n.

Dionysodorus : cf. Walbank, *Commentary*, ii. 550.

Acesimbrotus : cf. xxxi. 46. 6 n.

Phaeneas princeps Aetolorum : he was in fact *strategos* for 198/7, as Polybius says and L. is aware (§ 16). He was *strategos* again in 192/1 and attempted on several occasions to reach a settlement with Rome. Cf. Hoffmann, *RE*, xix. 1563–5, Walbank, *Commentary*, ii. 550, Flurl, 27–8.

Achaei . . . Xenophon : on Aristaenus cf. 19–23. 3 n., on Xenophon, Walbank, *Commentary*, ii. 550, Schmitt, *RE*, ixA. 1568. Aristaenus is evidently no longer in his *strategia*.

12. inter hos . . . processisset : Pol. xviii. 1. 5: οἱ μὲν περὶ τὸν Τίτον ἐπέστησαν παρ᾽ αὐτὸν τὸν αἰγιαλόν, ὁ δὲ Φίλιππος ἐγγίσας τῇ γῇ μετέωρος ἔμενε, xviii. 1. 6: διαναστὰς ἐκ τῆς νεώς . . . L. here portrays the scene in a little more detail.

extremum litus : 'the edge of the shore'. Cf. Ogilvie and Richmond, *Commentary on Tacitus' Agricola*, 171.

13. commodius . . . times : Pol. xviii. 1. 6–7: τοῦ δὲ Τίτου κελεύοντος αὐτὸν ἀποβαίνειν, διαναστὰς ἐκ τῆς νεὼς οὐκ ἔφησεν ἀποβήσεσθαι. τοῦ δὲ πάλιν ἐρομένου τίνα φοβεῖται . . . L. expands this into *oratio recta* remarks by Flamininus.

14. ad hoc . . . animo : an addition by L. himself. Cf. Walsh, *AJP* lxxvi (1955), 373.

neminem . . . Aetolis : Pol. xviii. 1. 7: φοβεῖσθαι μὲν ἔφησεν ὁ Φίλιππος οὐδένα πλὴν τοὺς θεούς, ἀπιστεῖν δὲ τοῖς πλείστοις τῶν παρόντων, μάλιστα δ᾽ Αἰτωλοῖς.

15. istuc quidem . . . fides sit : Pol. xviii. 1. 8: τοῦ δὲ τῶν Ῥωμαίων στρατηγοῦ θαυμάσαντος καὶ φήσαντος ἴσον εἶναι πᾶσι τὸν κίνδυνον καὶ κοινὸν τὸν καιρόν.

si nulla fides sit : thus B. Madvig in his 1863 edition (= *Emendationes*, 482 n. 2) argued that the subjunctive is inappropriate and suggested (but did not print) *ne nulla fides sit*. But Flamininus uses the subjunctive because he does not admit the possibility that the Romans, at least, are lacking in *fides*. *Fides* (as in § 14) has its usual sense of 'trustworthiness', not 'trusting in other people' (cf. E. Fraenkel, *RhM* lxxi [1916], 187 ff. = *Kleine Beiträge zur klassischen Philologie* [Rome, 1964], i. 15 ff.).

16. non tamen . . . substituant : Pol. xviii. 1. 8–9: μεταλαβὼν ὁ Φίλιππος οὐκ ἔφησεν αὐτὸν ὀρθῶς λέγειν· Φαινέου μὲν γὰρ παθόντος τι πολλοὺς εἶναι τοὺς στρατηγήσοντας Αἰτωλῶν, Φιλίππου δ᾽ ἀπολομένου

κατὰ τὸ παρὸν οὐκ εἶναι τὸν βασιλεύσοντα Μακεδόνων. Perseus was only
14, but a regent would have been appointed.

33. 1. Secundum haec . . . acciperet: Pol. xviii. 1. 10–11: ὅμως
δὲ λέγειν αὐτὸν ἐκέλευεν ὁ Τίτος ὑπὲρ ὧν πάρεστιν. ὁ δὲ Φίλιππος οὐκ ἔφη
τὸν λόγον αὐτῷ καθήκειν, ἀλλ' ἐκείνῳ· διόπερ ἠξίου διασαφεῖν τὸν Τίτον
τί δεῖ ποιήσαντα τὴν εἰρήνην ἄγειν. L. omits Polybius' ἐδόκει μὲν οὖν πᾶσι
φορτικῶς κατάρχεσθαι τῆς ὁμιλίας. The silence (cf. 20. 1 n.) is L.'s
addition, as is his attribution of the reasons for each side thinking
that the other should speak first.

qui daret pacis leges: as at Antigonea Philip makes no offers
on his own initiative. Rome had declared war and it was for Rome
to specify the terms on which she would desist from it. Philip's
attitude does not imply that he is accepting that Rome has achieved
military superiority.

2. tum Romanus . . . condicio: Pol. xviii. 1. 12: ὁ δὲ τῶν
Ῥωμαίων στρατηγὸς αὐτῷ μὲν ἁπλοῦν τινα λόγον ἔφη καθήκειν καὶ
φαινόμενον.

3. deducenda . . . esse: Pol. xviii. 1. 13: κελεύειν γὰρ αὐτὸν ἐκ μὲν
τῆς Ἑλλάδος ἁπάσης ἐκχωρεῖν. This is the same demand as that made
at Antigonea. Cf. 10. 3 n.

captivos . . . reddendos: Pol. xviii. 1. 13: ἀποδόντα τοὺς αἰχμαλώτους καὶ τοὺς αὐτομόλους ἑκάστοις οὓς ἔχει. sociis corresponds to
ἑκάστοις and Walbank (Commentary, ii. 551) is right to reject Holleaux's
view (Études, v. 36–7 n. 8) that this is an error by Polybius and that
Flamininus was in fact speaking for Rome alone.

restituenda . . . occupasset: Pol. xviii. 1. 14: τοὺς δὲ κατὰ τὴν
Ἰλλυρίδα τόπους παραδοῦναι Ῥωμαίοις, ὧν γέγονε κύριος μετὰ τὰς ἐν
Ἠπείρῳ διαλύσεις. On the problems raised by this passage cf. xxxi.
1. 9–10 n. restituenda is an inexact rendering of παραδοῦναι (Walbank,
Commentary, ii. 551, Petzold, Historia xx [1971], 211 n. 51) though the
implication that the Illyrian protectorate was a Roman possession
does not misrepresent the contemporary view (cf. Pol. vii. 9. 13).

pacem in Epiro: the peace of Phoenice.

4. Ptolomaeo . . . occupavisset: Pol. xviii. 1. 14: ὁμοίως δὲ καὶ
Πτολεμαίῳ τὰς πόλεις ἀποκαταστῆσαι πάσας, ἃς παρῄρηται μετὰ τὸν
Πτολεμαίου τοῦ Φιλοπάτορος θάνατον. On the date of the death of
Ptolemy Philopator cf. p. 36 n. 5. On the towns of Ptolemy in Philip's
possession cf. Walbank, Commentary, ii. 552.

suas . . . verum esse: Pol. xviii. 2. 1: ταῦτα δ' εἰπὼν ὁ Τίτος
αὐτὸς μὲν ἐπέσχε, πρὸς δὲ τοὺς ἄλλους ἐπιστραφεὶς ἐκέλευε λέγειν ἅπερ
ἑκάστοις αὐτῶν οἱ πέμψαντες εἴησαν ἐντεταλμένοι. For verum esse 'right
and proper' cf. the passages quoted by W–M.

231

5. Attali regis . . . capta essent: Pol. xviii. 2. 2: πρῶτος δὲ
Διονυσόδωρος ὁ παρ' Ἀττάλου μεταλαβὼν τὸν λόγον τάς τε ναῦς ἔφη
δεῖν αὐτὸν ἀποδοῦναι τὰς τοῦ βασιλέως τὰς γενομένας αἰχμαλώτους ἐν τῇ
περὶ Χίον ναυμαχίᾳ καὶ τοὺς ἅμα ταύταις ἄνδρας.
ad Chium navali proelio : the battle of Chios in 201 (Pol. xvi.
2–9, cf. Holleaux, *Études*, iv. 234 ff. For the chronology cf. p. 37).
et Nicephorium . . . restitui: Pol. xviii. 2. 2: ἀποκαταστῆσαι
δὲ καὶ τὸ τῆς Ἀφροδίτης ἱερὸν ἀκέραιον καὶ τὸ Νικηφόριον, ἃ κατ-
έφθειρε. The reference is to Philip's attack on Pergamum in 201 after
the battle of Lade. On the buildings involved cf. Walbank, *Commentary*, ii. 501.

6. Rhodii . . . repetebant: Pol. xviii. 2. 3: μετὰ δὲ τοῦτον ὁ τῶν
Ῥοδίων ναύαρχος Ἀκεσίμβροτος τῆς μὲν Περαίας ἐκέλευεν ἐκχωρεῖν τὸν
Φίλιππον, ἧς αὐτῶν παρῄρηται. The note of explanation is added by
L. for Roman readers. For the extent and history of the Peraea cf.
Fraser and Bean, *RPI*, chs. i–iv, Bean and Cook, *ABSA* lii (1957),
58 ff. Philip attacked the Peraea after the battles of Lade and Chios
in 201 (Pol. xvi. 11. 2, cf. Holleaux, *Études*, iv. 255–6, Walbank,
Commentary, ii. 513).
Here, at 34. 8, 35. 10, and xxxiii. 18. 2 and 20 MSS. readings are
all of forms in *Pir-*. But it is unlikely that L. spelt it like this and it
is probably an error which came early into the tradition because of
confusion with the Piraeus. At xxxvii. 21. 4, 22. 3 the form is *Per-*.
At 34. 8 and 35. 10 B has the form ending in -*n* and McDonald
seems justified in printing it here also.

6–7. postulabantque . . . portusque: Pol. xviii. 2. 3–4: τὰς δὲ
φρουρὰς ἐξάγειν ἐξ Ἰασοῦ καὶ Βαργυλίων καὶ τῆς Εὐρωμέων πόλεως,
ἀποκαταστῆσαι δὲ καὶ Περινθίους εἰς τὴν Βυζαντίων συμπολιτείαν,
παραχωρεῖν δὲ καὶ Σηστοῦ καὶ Ἀβύδου καὶ τῶν ἐμπορίων καὶ λιμένων
τῶν κατὰ τὴν Ἀσίαν ἁπάντων.
Iaso : for its position cf. Walbank, *Commentary*, ii. 513. For recent
excavations cf. *ASAA* xliii–xliv (1965–6), 401 ff., xlv–xlvi (1967–8),
537 ff. For the capture of Iasus in 201 cf. Holleaux, *Études*, iv. 257.
See also p. 36 n. 4.
Bargyliis : for its position cf. Walbank, *Commentary*, ii. 529. It was
captured after Iasus and Philip was besieged there in the autumn of
201. Cf. Pol. xvi. 24 and p. 37.
Euromensium : for its position cf. Walbank, *Commentary*, ii. 553.
For its capture in 201 cf. Holleaux, *Études*, iv. 258–9. Pedasa was
probably captured by Philip at the same time as Euromus (cf. xxxiii.
30. 3, Pol. xviii. 44. 4, Holleaux, l.c.).
Sesto atque Abydo : for the capture of Sestus, almost certainly
in 200, cf. Pol. xvi. 29. 3, Holleaux, *Rome*, 290, *Études*, iv. 129 n. 4,

Walbank, *Philip V*, 306, *Commentary*, ii. 539. For Abydus cf. xxxi. 16–18.

Perinthum . . . restitui : Perinthus was probably captured in 202 (cf. p. 36). For its relations with Byzantium cf. Walbank, *Commentary*, ii. 553.

Rhodes' claims on behalf of Byzantium, and Byzantine presence at Chios (Pol. xvi. 2. 10) do not prove that there was a formal alliance with Rhodes (for the earlier war between Rhodes and Byzantium cf. Pol. iv. 38–52). As the final Rhodian demand shows, she was making a wide series of claims and not restricting herself to places where she could claim a *locus standi*. For an Athenian inscription of the time honouring a number of Byzantines cf. *IG* ii². 884.

8. Achaei . . . repetebant : Pol. xviii. 2. 5: ἐπὶ δὲ τοῖς Ῥοδίοις Ἀχαιοὶ Κόρινθον ἀπῇτουν καὶ τὴν τῶν Ἀργείων πόλιν ἀβλαβῆ. On Corinth cf. xxxi. 22. 6 n., on Argos ch. 25. Given the Roman policy as expounded by Flamininus there is no reason to think that the Achaeans were not demanding the Acrocorinth as well as the city itself (cf. Holleaux, *Études*, v. 54 n. 2: *contra* Aymard, *PR*, 118–20, Walbank, *Commentary*, ii. 553. See also 19. 4 n.).

praetor Aetolorum . . . fuissent : Pol. xviii. 2. 6: μετὰ δὲ τούτους Αἰτωλοὶ πρῶτον μὲν τῆς Ἑλλάδος ἁπάσης ἐκέλευον ἐξίστασθαι, καθάπερ καὶ Ῥωμαῖοι, δεύτερον αὐτοῖς ἀποκαθιστάναι τὰς πόλεις ἀβλαβεῖς τὰς πρότερον μετασχούσας τῆς τῶν Αἰτωλῶν συμπολιτείας. On the towns in Greece involved cf. xxxi. 1. 9–10 n. From §§ 15–16 = Pol. xviii. 3. 11–12 it appears that the Propontis states are also included. Polybius applies the term συμπολιτεία to both, though the Propontis towns were almost certainly not members of the Aetolian League: cf. Walbank, *Commentary*, ii. 478, 555. L.'s *iuris ac dicionis* is too strong for the relations with the Propontis towns. He has been misled by Polybius.

The MSS. read *aut* between *iuris* and *dicionis* but there is no point in such a disjunction.

9. excepit . . . facundus : Pol. xviii. 3. 1: ταῦτα δ' εἰπόντος τοῦ Φαινέου τοῦ τῶν Αἰτωλῶν στρατηγοῦ, μεταλαβὼν Ἀλέξανδρος ὁ προσαγορευόμενος Ἴσιος, ἀνὴρ δοκῶν πραγματικὸς εἶναι καὶ λέγειν ἱκανός. *vir ut inter Aetolos facundus* is an addition by L., though Polybius would probably not have dissented from the view that the Aetolians were not naturally good at oratory (for Polybius' poor view of the Aetolians cf. Walbank, *Commentary*, i. 12). On Alexander Isius cf. Walbank, *Commentary*, ii. 554, Briscoe, *Past and Present*, no. 36 (April 1967), 7–8, Deininger, 61 n. 15.

10. iam dudum . . . interpellet : an addition by L.

nec de pace . . . gessisse: Pol. xviii. 3. 2: οὔτε διαλύεσθαι νῦν ἔφησε τὸν Φίλιππον ἀληθινῶς οὔτε πολεμεῖν γενναίως.

11. in conloquiis . . . captare: Pol. xviii. 3. 2: ἀλλ' ἐν μὲν τοῖς συλλόγοις καὶ ταῖς ὁμιλίαις ἐνεδρεύειν καὶ παρατηρεῖν καὶ ποιεῖν τὰ τοῦ πολεμοῦντος ἔργα. Here L. abbreviates Polybius.

in bello . . . corrumpere: Pol. xviii. 3. 2–3: κατ' αὐτὸν δὲ τὸν πόλεμον ἀδίκως ἵστασθαι καὶ λίαν ἀγεννῶς· ἀφέντα γὰρ τοῦ κατὰ πρόσωπον ἀπαντᾶν τοῖς πολεμίοις, φεύγοντα τὰς πόλεις ἐμπιπράναι καὶ διαρπάζειν καὶ διὰ ταύτης τῆς προαιρέσεως ἡττώμενον τὰ τῶν νικώντων ἆθλα λυμαίνεσθαι.

incendere ac diripere: cf. 15. 3 n.

12. at non . . . imperium: Pol. xviii. 3. 4: καίτοι γε τοὺς πρότερον Μακεδόνων βεβασιλευκότας οὐ ταύτην ἐσχηκέναι τὴν πρόθεσιν, ἀλλὰ τὴν ἐναντίαν· μάχεσθαι μὲν γὰρ πρὸς ἀλλήλους συνεχῶς ἐν τοῖς ὑπαίθροις, τὰς δὲ πόλεις σπανίως ἀναιρεῖν καὶ καταφθείρειν. Much of what follows in Polybius—examples of the behaviour of earlier kings of Macedon—is omitted by L., though *quo opulentius haberent imperium* is similar to Pol. xviii. 3. 7: χάριν τοῦ τοὺς νικήσαντας ἡγεῖσθαι τούτων καὶ τιμᾶσθαι παρὰ τοῖς ὑποταττομένοις.

⟨**rem ita gessisse**⟩: these words are a supplement by M. Müller. W–M print the MSS. reading and understand *fecisse*. But this is incredibly harsh (their parallels of i. 23. 8, v. 43. 2, and xxii. 58. 2 are not exact) and supplementation seems necessary.

13. nam de quorum . . . consilium esse: Pol. xviii. 3. 8: τὸ δ' ἀναιροῦντα περὶ ὧν ὁ πόλεμός ἐστι τὸν πόλεμον αὐτὸν καταλιπεῖν μανίας ἔργον εἶναι, καὶ ταύτης ἐρρωμένης, ὃ νῦν ποιεῖν τὸν Φίλιππον. On what Polybius means here cf. Walbank, *Commentary*, ii. 554. W–M are wrong to say that L.'s *sibi* is inappropriate, on the grounds that it is both sides that will have no possessions left. The supposition is made that Philip's policy is directed to winning the war, and is looked at from that angle.

14. plures . . . fuerint: Pol. xviii. 3. 9: τοσαύτας γὰρ διεφθαρκέναι πόλεις ἐν Θετταλίᾳ, φίλον ὄντα καὶ σύμμαχον, καθ' ὃν καιρὸν ἐκ τῶν ἐν Ἠπείρῳ στενῶν ἐποιεῖτο τὴν σπουδήν, ὅσας οὐδείς ποτε τῶν Θετταλοῖς πεπολεμηκότων διέφθειρε. For Philip's destruction of Thessalian towns in 198 cf. 13. 4–9.

evastasse: B, *vastasse* χ. *Evastare* is found often in L. but only three times otherwise. Cf. *TLL*, v. 2. 1003, Packard, ii. 414–15.

15. ipsis . . . ademisse: the emphasis is due to L. Polybius (xviii. 3. 12) says merely φίλος ὑπάρχων Αἰτωλοῖς. L. omits Polybius' reference to a varied collection of complaints by Alexander (xviii. 3. 10).

Lysimachiam . . . occupasse eum: Pol. xviii. 3. 11: ἤρετο γὰρ τὸν Φίλιππον διὰ τί Λυσιμάχειαν μετ' Αἰτωλῶν ταττομένην καὶ στρατηγὸν ἔχουσαν παρ' αὐτῶν ἐκβαλὼν τοῦτον κατάσχοι φρουρᾷ τὴν πόλιν. Lysimachia was captured by Philip in 202 (Pol. xv. 23. 8). On its history and position cf. Walbank, *Commentary*, ii. 478–9, add G. Longega, *Arsinoe II* (Rome, 1968), 23 n. 52.

16. Cium . . . delesse: Pol. xviii. 3. 12: διὰ τί δὲ Κιανούς, παραπλησίως μετ' Αἰτωλῶν συμπολιτευομένους ἐξανδραποδίσαιτο. On Cius cf. xxxi. 31. 4 n., on *dicionis* § 8 n.

eadem . . . Pharsalum: Pol. xviii. 3. 12: τί δὲ λέγων κατέχει νῦν Ἐχῖνον καὶ Θήβας τὰς Φθίας καὶ Φάρσαλον καὶ Λάρισαν. Cf. xxxi. 1. 9–10 n., Walbank, *Commentary*, ii. 555–6.

Thebas Phthias: B has *thias Thebas*, not *Thebas thias* as McDonald's apparatus suggests. L. probably spelt the second word *Pthias* (cf. W. Schulze, *Orthographica* [Marburg, 1894], 34 ff., 51 = *Orthographica et Graeca Latina* [Rome, 1958], 49 ff., 75).

34. Philip's speech is considerably adapted by L. from Polybius. L. abbreviates, and gives the points in a different order from that of Polybius. But some phrases are his own, and he suppresses all references to Flamininus' reaction to what Philip is saying.

34. 1–2. motus . . . maxime: L. abbreviates and summarizes Pol. xviii. 4. 1–2, though he adds the detail that Philip was affected (*motus*) by Alexander's speech and also gives the motive for Philip's coming closer to the shore. But he omits Polybius' dramatic detail about standing up in the ship.

2. violenter . . . esse: Pol. xviii. 4. 3: ὑπέκρουε τὸν Φίλιππον, φάσκων αὐτὸν ληρεῖν· δεῖν γὰρ ἢ μαχόμενον νικᾶν ἢ ποιεῖν τοῖς κρείττοσι τὸ προσταττόμενον.

interfatus: *interfari* is found six times in L. but in earlier or contemporary literature only in Vergil, *A.* i. 386 (cf. Tränkle, *WS*, 121).

3. apparet . . . temperans: Pol. xviii. 4. 4: ὁ δὲ Φίλιππος, καίπερ ἐν κακοῖς ὤν, ὅμως οὐκ ἀπέσχετο τοῦ καθ' αὑτὸν ἰδιώματος, ἀλλ' ἐπιστραφείς "τοῦτο μὲν" ἔφησεν "ὦ Φαινέα, καὶ τυφλῷ δῆλον." ἦν γὰρ εὔθικτος καὶ πρὸς τοῦτο τὸ μέρος εὖ πεφυκὼς πρὸς τὸ διαχλευάζειν ἀνθρώπους. Polybius refers to Phaeneas' bad sight earlier, ἠλαττωμένος τοῖς ὄμμασιν ἐπὶ πλεῖον (xviii. 4. 3). L. adapts considerably here and change Polybius' factual comments about Philip's skill at repartee into a critical comment. Cf. A. Bauer, *Stromateis* (Graz, 1909), 58 ff. (with other examples of the different views that L. and Polybius took of kings), Walsh, *AJP* lxxvi (1955), 371, Ogilvie, 4.

4. Indignari . . . non esse: from a later part of Philip's speech in Polybius (xviii. 5. 5–8): "τὸ δὲ δὴ πάντων δεινότατον, οἱ ποιοῦντες ἑαυτοὺς ἐφαμίλλους Ῥωμαίοις καὶ κελεύοντες ἐκχωρεῖν Μακεδόνας

ἁπάσης τῆς Ἑλλάδος· τοῦτο γὰρ ἀναφθέγξασθαι καὶ καθόλου μέν ἐστιν
ὑπερήφανον, οὐ μὴν ἀλλὰ Ῥωμαίων μὲν λεγόντων ἀνεκτόν, Αἰτωλῶν
δ' οὐκ ἀνεκτόν· ποίας δὲ κελεύετέ με" φησὶν "ἐκχωρεῖν Ἑλλάδος καὶ
πῶς ἀφορίζετε ταύτην; αὐτῶν γὰρ Αἰτωλῶν οὐκ εἰσὶν Ἕλληνες οἱ πλείους·
τὸ γὰρ τῶν Ἀγραῶν ἔθνος καὶ τὸ τῶν Ἀποδωτῶν, ἔτι δὲ τῶν Ἀμφιλόχων,
οὐκ ἔστιν Ἑλλάς." On the peoples involved cf. Walbank, *Commentary*,
ii. 557. On Macedonian claims to be fully Greek cf. xxxi. 29. 12–15 n.

5. an quod . . . habeant: adapted from Polybius xviii. 4. 7–5. 4.
Philip's claim is that in attacking Cius, an ally of Aetolia, he was
only doing what the Aetolians themselves did in allowing their
citizens to fight, in a private capacity, against allies of Aetolia. Cf.
Walbank, *Commentary*, ii. 557.

6. Neque ego . . . adiuvi: Pol. xviii. 4. 7: Κιανοῖς δ' ἐγὼ μὲν οὐκ
ἐπολέμησα, Προυσίου δὲ πολεμοῦντος βοηθῶν ἐκείνῳ συνεξεῖλον αὐτούς.
    Prusiam: Prusias I of Bithynia. He was a relation of Philip by
marriage (Pol. xv. 22. 2, Walbank, *Commentary*, ii. 475–6), and had
been included among Philip's *adscripti* to the peace of Phoenice
(xxix. 12. 14). He also received Myrleia from Philip at the same time
as Cius (Strabo, xii p. 563c, Hermippus, *FHG* iii. 51). Prusias later
supported Rome against Antiochus and in 183 was forced by
Flamininus to agree to surrender Hannibal who had taken refuge
with him (cf. p. 23). For full details of his career cf. Habicht, *RE*,
xxiii. 1086–1107. See also Magie, *RRAM*, i. 312–15.
    et Lysimachiam . . . habent: Pol. xviii. 4. 6: ἵνα μὴ διὰ τὴν
ὑμετέραν ὀλιγωρίαν ἀνάστατος ὑπὸ Θρᾳκῶν γένηται, καθάπερ νῦν γέγονεν
ἡμῶν ἀπαγαγόντων τοὺς στρατιώτας διὰ τοῦτον τὸν πόλεμον. On the
Thracians cf. Walbank, *Commentary*, ii. 556.
    sed quia: the MSS. have *et quia* but a disjunction is necessary for
the sense.

7. et Aetolis haec: L. omits the fact that Flamininus laughed at
Philip's cracks about the Aetolians not being Greeks (Pol. xviii. 6. 1).
    Attalo autem . . . ortum est: Pol. xviii. 6. 1–2: πρὸς δὲ
Ῥοδίους καὶ πρὸς Ἄτταλον ἐν μὲν ἴσῳ κριτῇ δικαιότερον ἂν νομισθείη
τούτους ἡμῖν ἀποδιδόναι τὰς αἰχμαλώτους ναῦς καὶ τοὺς ἄνδρας ἥπερ
ἡμᾶς τούτοις· οὐ γὰρ ἡμεῖς Ἀττάλῳ πρότεροι καὶ Ῥοδίοις τὰς χεῖρας
ἐπεβάλομεν, οὗτοι δ' ἡμῖν ὁμολογουμένως. Philip had made the same
claim at Abydos as far as Rhodes was concerned (Pol. xvi. 34. 5,
cf. xxxi. 18. 2 n.).

8. Romanorum autem . . . restituam: Pol. xviii. 6. 3: οὐ μὴν
ἀλλὰ σοῦ κελεύοντος Ῥοδίοις μὲν ἀποδίδωμι τὴν Περαίαν, Ἀττάλῳ δὲ τὰς
ναῦς καὶ τοὺς ἄνδρας τοὺς διασῳζομένους.
    Peraean: cf. 33. 6 n.

qui comparebunt: Polybius has διασῳζομένους which means simply 'those who survive'. L.'s phrase, however, must mean 'those who can be found'—i.e. have not been irretrievably dispersed: cf. 22. 10 n.

9–10. Nam quod . . . placet: Pol. xviii. 6. 4: τὴν δὲ τοῦ Νικη-φορίου καταφθορὰν καὶ τοῦ τῆς Ἀφροδίτης τεμένους ἄλλως μὲν οὐκ εἰμὶ δυνατὸς ἀποκαταστῆσαι, φυτὰ δὲ καὶ κηπουροὺς πέμψω τοὺς φροντιοῦντας θεραπείας τοῦ τόπου καὶ τῆς αὐξήσεως τῶν ἐκκοπέντων δένδρων. L. adds the ironical comment at the end, but again omits the fact that Flamininus laughed at Philip's remarks (Pol. xviii. 6. 5).

11–12. extrema . . . descivissent: Pol. xviii. 6. 5–7: μεταβὰς ὁ Φίλιππος ἐπὶ τοὺς Ἀχαιοὺς πρῶτον μὲν τὰς εὐεργεσίας ἐξηριθμήσατο τὰς ἐξ Ἀντιγόνου γεγενημένας εἰς αὐτούς, εἶτα τὰς ἰδίας· ἑξῆς δὲ τούτοις προηνέγκατο τὸ μέγεθος τῶν τιμῶν τῶν ἀπηντημένων αὐτοῖς παρὰ τῶν Ἀχαιῶν. τελευταῖον δ' ἀνέγνω τὸ περὶ τῆς ἀποστάσεως ψήφισμα καὶ τῆς πρὸς Ῥωμαίους μεταθέσεως.

Antigoni: Antigonus Doson: cf. 21. 25 n.

divinos: an addition by L. On Achaean honours to the Antigonids cf. 25. 2 n.

recens . . . descivissent: formal renunciation of the Macedonian alliance was the necessary corollary of the decision to join Rome, though there is no explicit mention of it in L.'s account of the decisions taken at Sicyon (23. 1–3).

invectusque . . . dixit: Pol. xviii. 6. 7–8: ᾗ χρησάμενος ἀφορμῇ πολλὰ κατὰ τῶν Ἀχαιῶν εἰς ἀθεσίαν εἶπε καὶ ἀχαριστίαν. ὅμως δ' ἔφη τὸ μὲν Ἄργος ἀποδώσειν.

13. de Corintho . . . accepisset: Pol. xviii. 6. 8–7. 1: περὶ δὲ τοῦ Κορίνθου βουλεύσεσθαι μετὰ τοῦ Τίτου. ταῦτα δὲ διαλεχθεὶς πρὸς τοὺς ἄλλους ἤρετο τὸν Τίτον, φήσας πρὸς ἐκεῖνον αὐτῷ τὸν λόγον εἶναι καὶ πρὸς Ῥωμαίους, πότερον οἴεται δεῖν ἐκχωρεῖν ὧν ἐπέκτηται πόλεων καὶ τόπων ἐν τοῖς Ἕλλησιν, ἢ καὶ τούτων ὅσα παρὰ τῶν γονέων παρείληφε. L. omits to mention Flamininus' silence at this question (Pol. xviii. 7. 2).

35. 1. parantibus . . . respondere: Pol. xviii. 7. 2: ἐκ χειρὸς ἀπαντᾶν οἷοί τ' ἦσαν ὁ μὲν Ἀρίσταινος ὑπὲρ τῶν Ἀχαιῶν, ὁ δὲ Φαινέας ὑπὲρ τῶν Αἰτωλῶν.

cum prope occasum . . . redierunt: this is very much abbreviated from Pol. xviii. 7. 3–7. L. omits Philip's request for the demands of the allies to be reduced to writing, and the badinage between Philip and Flamininus. The motive of the latter, at least, is to suppress mention of Flamininus' less formal behaviour and Polybius' suggestion that Flamininus enjoyed Philip's jokes but did not want to show that he did so. On the other hand the details of where the two sides went to is an addition by L. Philip may not in fact have spent the night at sea (cf. Walbank, *Commentary*, ii. 559) and it is hardly likely that Flamininus returned to the main camp near Opus. But it is highly unlikely that L. had any evidence for these statements and there is no point in speculating about them.

2. Quinctius . . . naves : Pol. xviii. 7. 7–8. 1: ταξάμενοι κατὰ τὴν ἐπιοῦσαν εἰς Νίκαιαν πάλιν ἀπαντήσειν· τῇ δ' αὔριον οἱ μὲν περὶ τὸν Τίτον ἧκον ἐπὶ τὸν ταχθέντα τόπον ἐν ὥρᾳ πάντες, ὁ δὲ Φίλιππος οὐ παρεγίνετο. τῆς δ' ἡμέρας ἤδη προαγούσης ἐπὶ πολὺ καὶ σχεδὸν ἀπεγνωκότων τῶν περὶ τὸν Τίτον, παρῆν ὁ Φίλιππος δείλης ὀψίας ἐπιφαινόμενος μεθ' ὧν καὶ πρότερον.

Nicaeam : cf. 32. 9 n.

3–4. atque ipse . . . respondendum : Pol. xviii. 8. 2: κατατετριφὼς τὴν ἡμέραν, ὡς μὲν αὐτὸς ἔφη, διὰ τὴν ἀπορίαν καὶ δυσχρηστίαν τῶν ἐπιταττομένων, ὡς δὲ τοῖς ἄλλοις ἐδόκει, βουλόμενος ἐκκλεῖσαι τῷ καιρῷ τήν τε τῶν Ἀχαιῶν καὶ τὴν τῶν Αἰτωλῶν κατηγορίαν.

gravia et indigna : for the phrase cf. Ogilvie, 647.

diem se consumpsisse : B omits *se* and it should be regarded as an insertion by χ: cf. 12. 1 n. (The omission of *se* in E is presumably coincidental.)

5. et eam . . . conloqui : Pol. xviii. 8. 4: διὸ καὶ τότε συνεγγίσας ἠξίου τὸν τῶν Ῥωμαίων στρατηγὸν ἰδίᾳ πρὸς αὐτὸν διαλεχθῆναι περὶ τῶν ἐνεστώτων, ἵνα μὴ λόγοι γένωνται μόνον ἐξ ἀμφοτέρων ἀψιμαχούντων, ἀλλὰ καὶ τέλος τι τοῖς ἀμφισβητουμένοις ἐπιτεθῇ.

6–7. id primo . . . litus processit : Pol. xviii. 8. 5–6: πλεονάκις δ' αὐτοῦ παρακαλοῦντος καὶ προσαξιοῦντος, ἤρετο τοὺς συμπαρόντας ὁ Τίτος τί δέον εἴη ποιεῖν. τῶν δὲ κελευόντων συνελθεῖν καὶ διακοῦσαι τῶν λεγομένων, παραλαβὼν ὁ Τίτος Ἄππιον Κλαύδιον χιλίαρχον ὄντα τότε, τοῖς μὲν ἄλλοις μικρὸν ἀπὸ τῆς θαλάττης ἀναχωρήσασιν εἶπεν αὐτόθι μένειν, αὐτὸς δὲ τὸν Φίλιππον ἐκέλευσεν ἐκβαίνειν.

Ap. Claudio tribuno militum : (245). He is clearly the same man as the *legatus* of 36. 10 (= Pol. xviii. 10. 8) and is therefore Appius Claudius Nero, who was praetor in 195 and one of the x *legati* for the Apamea settlement in 189–8. Cf. *MRR*, i. 332 n. 4, Walbank, *Commentary*, ii. 558, Schlag, 112–13. I am unconvinced by Badian's denial of the identity (*Flamininus*, 44–5) on the grounds that Polybius added ἐπικαλούμενον Νέρωνα in xviii. 10. 8 in order to distinguish the two Claudii.

extremum litus : cf. 32. 12 n.

8–9. rex . . . socios : Pol. xviii. 8. 7–8: ὁ δὲ βασιλεὺς παραλαβὼν Ἀπολλόδωρον καὶ Δημοσθένην ἀπέβη, συμμίξας δὲ τῷ Τίτῳ διελέγετο καὶ πλείω χρόνον. τίνα μὲν οὖν ἦν τὰ τότε ῥηθέντα παρ' ἑκατέρου, δυσχερὲς εἰπεῖν· ἔφη δ' οὖν ὁ Τίτος μετὰ τὸ χωρισθῆναι τὸν Φίλιππον, διασαφῶν τοῖς ἄλλοις τὰ παρὰ τοῦ βασιλέως . . . This is an important alteration by L. Polybius says that no one knew what was said, only what Flamininus reported. For L. it is the contents of Philip's report-back that are in doubt. Again an imputation against Flamininus is removed.

cum duobus : cf. 32. 10 n.

9–11. On these offers of Philip see p. 26. L. alters the order of the individual points as given by Polybius.

9. Romanis . . . captivi : Pol. xviii. 8. 10: Ῥωμαίοις δὲ τὰ κατὰ τὴν Ἰλλυρίδα φάναι παραδώσειν καὶ τοὺς αἰχμαλώτους πάντας.

perfugas : added by L., as deserters and prisoners are often joined together, and indeed had been in Flamininus' original demand (33. 3 = Pol. xviii. 1. 13).

Illyrici ora : cf. xxxi. 1. 9–10 n.

10. Attalo . . . non cessurum : Pol. xviii. 8. 9: Ῥοδίοις δὲ τῆς μὲν Περαίας παραχωρεῖν, Ἰασοῦ δὲ καὶ Βαργυλίων οὐκ ἐκχωρεῖν, and xviii. i. 10: Ἀττάλῳ δὲ τάς τε ναῦς ἀποκαταστήσειν καὶ τῶν ἀνδρῶν τῶν ἐν ταῖς ναυμαχίαις ἁλόντων ὅσοι περίεισι.

navales socios : L. here uses, somewhat inappropriately, the Roman technical term (cf. 23. 9 n.). It may be true that men of Pergamum's so-called allies in northern Asia Minor did fight at Chios, but L. will not have had any independent evidence for his addition. Cf. xxxiii. 38. 14 n.

On the Peraea, Iasus, and Bargylia cf. 33. 6 nn.

11. Aetolis . . . cessurum : Pol. xviii. 8. 9: Αἰτωλοῖς μὲν ἀποδοῦναι Φάρσαλον καὶ Λάρισαν, Θήβας δ' οὐκ ἀποδιδόναι . . . Ἀχαιοῖς δὲ παραδιδόναι τὸν Κόρινθον καὶ τὴν τῶν Ἀργείων πόλιν.

Corintho : but not the Acrocorinth; cf. Walbank, *Commentary*, ii. 559.

12–13. Nulli . . . defore : Pol. xviii. 9. 1: πάντων δὲ τῶν παρόντων δυσαρεστουμένων τῇ διαλύσει καὶ φασκόντων δεῖν τὸ κοινὸν ἐπίταγμα πρῶτον ποιεῖν—τοῦτο δ' ἦν ἁπάσης ἐκχωρεῖν τῆς Ἑλλάδος—εἰ δὲ μή, διότι τὰ κατὰ μέρος μάταια γίνεται καὶ πρὸς οὐδέν. Flamininus may well have showed displeasure himself even if he did not feel it: *contra* Holleaux, *Études*, v. 55 n. 2, Walbank, *Commentary*, ii. 559.

36. 1. cum haec . . . est perlata : Pol. xviii. 9. 2: θεωρῶν ὁ Φίλιππος τὴν ἐν αὐτοῖς ἀμφισβήτησιν καὶ δεδιὼς ἅμα τὰς κατηγορίας . . . Altered by L. for dramatic effect.

2. itaque . . . passurum : Pol. xviii. 9. 2: ἠξίου τὸν Τίτον ὑπερθέσθαι τὴν σύνοδον εἰς τὴν αὔριον διὰ τὸ καὶ τὴν ὥραν εἰς ὀψὲ συγκλείειν· ἢ γὰρ πείσειν ἢ πεισθήσεσθαι τοῖς παρακαλουμένοις.

3. Litus . . . conventum est : Pol. xviii. 9. 3 : τοῦ δὲ συγχωρήσαντος, ταξάμενοι συμπορεύεσθαι πρὸς τὸν κατὰ Θρόνιον αἰγιαλόν, τότε μὲν ἐχωρίσθησαν, τῇ δ' ὑστεραίᾳ πάντες ἧκον ἐπὶ τὸν ταχθέντα τόπον ἐν ὥρᾳ.
Thronium : on its position cf. Walbank, *Commentary*, ii. 185.

3–4. ibi Philippus . . . accepturum : Pol. xviii. 9. 4–5 : ὁ Φίλιππος ἠξίου πάντας, μάλιστα δὲ τὸν Τίτον, μὴ διακόψαι τὴν διάλυσιν, τῶν γε δὴ πλείστων εἰς συμβατικὴν διάθεσιν ἠγμένων, ἀλλ' εἰ μὲν ἐνδέχεται δι' αὐτῶν συμφώνους γενέσθαι περὶ τῶν ἀντιλεγομένων· εἰ δὲ μή, πρεσβεύσειν ἔφη πρὸς τὴν σύγκλητον, κἀκείνην πείσειν περὶ τῶν ἀμφισβητουμένων, ἢ ποιήσειν ὅ τι ποτ' ἂν ἐπιτάττῃ. L. omits Philip's first suggestion that they try to reach agreement themselves. Philip says that he will accept the senate's decision whatever it is, and though Flamininus says that this is unlikely (Pol. xviii. 9. 7—omitted by L.) it was no doubt designed to persuade the Greeks to accept the suggestion of reference to the senate. On the question of Flamininus' responsibility for Philip's request cf. p. 25.

5. id ceteris . . . quaeri : Pol. xviii. 9. 6 : ταῦτα δ' αὐτοῦ προτείνοντος, οἱ μὲν ἄλλοι πάντες ἔφασαν δεῖν πράττειν τὰ τοῦ πολέμου καὶ μὴ προσέχειν τοῖς ἀξιουμένοις. L. gives the allies' protests a more concrete form, to which Polybius merely alludes in Flamininus' reply (Pol. xviii. 9. 10: τῶν γὰρ στρατοπέδων οὐδ' ὡς δυναμένων οὐδὲν πράττειν διὰ τὸν χειμῶνα) and in his comments on Flamininus' policy (xviii. 10. 3)—which L. omits altogether.

6. Quinctius . . . mittendos : this clause has no very close verbal correspondence to Polybius. Cf. Pol. xviii. 9. 8: τῷ δ' ἁπλῶς μηδὲν ἐμποδίζειν τὰς σφετέρας πράξεις τὴν αἰτουμένην χάριν ὑπὸ τοῦ βασιλέως ἐκποιεῖν ἔφη χαρίζεσθαι, and 9. 10: τοῦτον ἀποθέσθαι τὸν χρόνον εἰς τὸ προσανενεγκεῖν τῇ συγκλήτῳ περὶ τῶν προσπιπτόντων, οὐκ ἄθετον, ἀλλ' οἰκεῖον εἶναι πᾶσι.

7. nam neque . . . pepigissent : Pol. xviii. 9. 9: κυρωθῆναι μὲν γὰρ οὐδ' ὡς εἶναι δυνατὸν οὐδὲν τῶν νῦν λεγομένων ἄνευ τῆς συγκλήτου . . . This is perfectly valid in itself, but it was not usual for reference to be made to the senate before the Roman commander and the enemy in question had reached a provisional agreement. Cf. Walbank, *Commentary*, ii. 559. For a similar procedure with the Aetolians in 191 and 190 cf. xxxvi. 35. 6, xxxvii. 7. 4 ff.

nam : W–M rightly say that this sentence is not really an explanation of what precedes, and that *nam* is probably taken from Polybius' γάρ which has a different antecedent clause.

et explorari . . . posse: Pol. xviii. 9. 9: πρὸς δὲ τὸ λαβεῖν πεῖραν τῆς ἐκείνων γνώμης εὐφυῶς ἔχειν τὸν ἐπιφερόμενον καιρόν.

8. in hanc sententiam . . . placuit: Pol. xviii. 10. 1–2: ταχὺ δὲ συγκαταθεμένων ἁπάντων διὰ τὸ θεωρεῖν τὸν Τίτον οὐκ ἀλλότριον ὄντα τῆς ἐπὶ τὴν σύγκλητον ἀναφορᾶς, ἔδοξε συγχωρεῖν τῷ Φιλίππῳ πρεσβεύειν εἰς τὴν Ῥώμην, ὁμοίως δὲ καὶ παρ' αὐτῶν πέμπειν ἑκάστους πρεσβευτὰς τοὺς διαλεχθησομένους τῇ συγκλήτῳ καὶ κατηγορήσοντας τοῦ Φιλίππου, and xviii. 10. 4: δοὺς γὰρ ἀνοχὰς διμήνους αὐτῷ τὴν μὲν πρεσβείαν τὴν εἰς τὴν Ῥώμην ἐν τούτῳ τῷ χρόνῳ συντελεῖν ἐπέταξε. L. omits Polybius' statement that the allies agreed because they saw that Flamininus was in favour, and the subsequent implied criticism of Flamininus in xviii. 10. 3.

et ceteri: no other *principes* of the Greeks have been mentioned. For the idiom cf. xxxi. 1. 9–10 n.

singulos: presumably a misinterpretation of Polybius' ἑκάστους. In fact the Aetolians sent six representatives (Pol. xviii. 10. 9).

9. additum . . . deducerentur: Pol. xviii. 10. 4: τὰς δὲ φρουρὰς ἐξάγειν παραχρῆμα τὰς ἐκ τῆς Φωκίδος καὶ Λοκρίδος ἐκέλευσε. These will be the remaining garrisons in Phocis and Locris, much of which was already in Flamininus' hands. Cf. ch. 18, 21. 7 n., 32. 1, Walbank, *Commentary*, ii. 560.

10. Et ipse . . . misit: Pol. xviii. 10. 7–8: καὶ τὸν μὲν Ἀμύνανδρον εἰς τὴν Ῥώμην ἐξέπεμπε παραχρῆμα, γινώσκων αὐτὸν εὐάγωγον μὲν ὄντα καὶ ῥᾳδίως ἐξακολουθήσοντα τοῖς ἐκεῖ φίλοις, ἐφ' ὁπότερ' ἂν ἄγωσιν αὐτόν, φαντασίαν δὲ ποιήσοντα καὶ προσδοκίαν διὰ τὸ τῆς βασιλείας ὄνομα. μετὰ δὲ τοῦτον ἐξέπεμπε τοὺς παρ' αὐτοῦ πρέσβεις, Κόιντόν τε τὸν Φάβιον, ὃς ἦν αὐτῷ τῆς γυναικὸς ἀδελφιδοῦς, καὶ Κόιντον Φολούιον, σὺν δὲ τούτοις Ἄππιον Κλαύδιον ἐπικαλούμενον Νέρωνα. L. again omits Polybius' comments which do not reflect well on the way Flamininus was securing his own interests.

Amynandrum: cf. xxxi. 28. 1 n.

speciem: a far more complimentary word than Polybius' φαντασίαν . . . καὶ προσδοκίαν.

Q. Fabium: (57?). He may be Q. Fabius Buteo, praetor in 196 (cf. xxxiii. 24. 2, 26. 1, 43. 7).

uxoris Quincti sororis filius erat: Polybius' phrase τῆς γυναικὸς ἀδελφιδοῦς can mean either 'son of his wife's brother' or 'son of his wife's sister' and it is very doubtful whether L. had any independent evidence for choosing the latter alternative (cf. p. 8 n. 1). If the former, Flamininus married a Fabia, if the latter it was only his wife's sister who was married to a Fabius. Balsdon gives no argument for his assertion that Livy 'had better be believed' (*Phoenix*, xxi [1967], 181 n. 19). Walbank, *Commentary*, ii. 561 inverts the argument and Schur, *SA*, 138 strangely thought that Flamininus' sister married a Fabius. Cf. Münzer, *RA*, 117, Scullard, *RP*, 98 n. 1, Badian, *Flamininus*, 32–3. For the political implications of the choice of the *legati* cf. pp. 32–3.

    Q. Fulvium : (26, 60). Cf. 28. 3 n.
    Ap. Claudium : cf. 35. 7 n.
    L. omits the names of the Greek ambassadors given by Polybius xviii. 10. 9–11. Cf. p. 18 n. 5.

37. L. omits Polybius xviii. 11. 1–2 in which the φίλοι of Flamininus discover that there is a majority in the senate against succeeding him. He also omits the actual senatorial decision and Polybius' subsequent comments on Flamininus' ability to reconcile the best interests of himself and the state (Pol. xviii. 12). On the chronology cf. 28. 3–9 n.

37. 1. cetera . . . consumpta est : Pol. xviii. 11. 2 : πάντες κατηγόρουν ἀποτόμως τοῦ Φιλίππου.

2–4. moverunt . . . appellare : Pol. xviii. 11. 4–5 : τοῦτο δ᾽ ἐπιμελῶς ἐντίκτειν ἐπειρῶντο τῇ συγκλήτῳ πάντες, διότι τῆς Χαλκίδος καὶ τοῦ Κορίνθου καὶ τῆς Δημητριάδος ὑπὸ τῷ Μακεδόνι ταττομένων οὐχ οἷόν τε τοὺς ῞Ελληνας ἔννοιαν λαβεῖν ἐλευθερίας. ὃ γὰρ αὐτὸς Φίλιππος εἶπε, τοῦτο καὶ λίαν ἀληθὲς ἔφασαν ὑπάρχειν· ὃς ἔφη τοὺς προειρημένους τόπους εἶναι πέδας ῾Ελληνικάς, ὀρθῶς ἀποφαινόμενος. L. omits the rest of Polybius' report of the allies' speeches, in which they elaborate on the importance of the fetters (xviii. 11. 6–11)—though this is summarized in *maris terrarumque regionis eius situm*.

    moverunt eo maxime : *eo* B, *eum* χ. McDonald defends *eo* as an instrumental ablative, to which *demonstrando* stands in apposition. But such a usage is unparalleled and very harsh. Weissenborn's *cum—cum maxime* being a common phrase—seems right. (McDonald's assumption that abuse of Philip carried no weight with the senate is not justified.)

    3. Demetriadem : cf. xxxi. 24. 1 n.
    Chalcidem : cf. xxxi. 22. 7 n.
    Corinthum : cf. xxxi. 22. 6 n.

    4. compedes eas Graeciae : cf. Walbank, *Commentary*, ii. 563.

    5. Legati . . . quicquam : Pol. xviii. 11. 12–13 : οἱ δὲ παρὰ τοῦ Φιλίππου παρεσκευάσαντο μὲν ὡς ἐπὶ πλεῖον ποιησόμενοι τοὺς λόγους, ἐν ἀρχαῖς δ᾽ εὐθέως ἐκωλύθησαν· ἐρωτηθέντες γὰρ εἰ παραχωροῦσι Χαλκίδος καὶ Κορίνθου καὶ Δημητριάδος, ἀπεῖπαν μηδεμίαν ἔχειν περὶ τούτων ἐντολήν. For the reason for the envoys' reply cf. pp. 25–6.

    sic infecta pace . . . permissum : Pol. xviii. 12. 1 : τὸν δὲ πρὸς τὸν Φίλιππον πόλεμον ἐψηφίσατο κατάμονον εἶναι, δοῦσα τῷ

Τίτῳ τὴν ἐπιτροπὴν ὑπὲρ τῶν Ἑλληνικῶν. liberum arbitrium exaggerates Flamininus' freedom of action: cf. Aymard, *PR*, 131 n. 61.

For L.'s omissions at this point cf. note at the beginning of the chapter. The extract from Polybius ends after the sections omitted by L.

6. Cui . . . conloquium : this takes up the language of 32. 8 where L. had referred to Flamininus' motives. L. was fully aware of what he was suppressing.

Cui : the MSS. have *quod* which makes no sense. *Qui* would be possible.

38–40. *Nabis and Argos*

Cf. Just. xxx. 4. 5, Zon. ix. 16. 5. On these events cf. Aymard, *PR*, 132 ff.

38. 1. cum . . . videret : at xxxiii. 3. 1 L. reports Philip's activities as *primo vere postquam legati ab Roma nihil pacati rettulerant*. It seems probable, then, that Philip's approach to Nabis precedes the return of the envoys from Rome: Polybius will have indicated that Philip had little confidence in the outcome of the negotiations.

regionis ab se diversae : geographically distant, and hence difficult to control himself.

2. Nabidi . . . tyranno : cf. xxxi. 25. 3 n.

velut fiduciariam : L. qualifies the legal technical term, which refers to something given 'as security'. Cf. A. Watson, *The Law of Obligations in the Later Roman Republic* (Oxford, 1965), 172 ff. For the use of *fiduciarius* in political contexts cf. *TLL*, vi. 1. 703, H. Heinen, *Rom und Ägypten* (Tübingen, 1966), 117 n. 3.

ut victori . . . haberet : Aymard, *PR*, 133–4 n. 9, pointed out that if Philip's terms were as L. expresses them here, Nabis would have had an interest in Philip's defeat. Aymard plausibly suggests that Philip offered Nabis certain Achaean territories in the case of a Macedonian victory.

Philocli : cf. 16. 12 n., xxxi. 16. 2 n. He now appears to be based in the Peloponnese (cf. 40. 5).

2–3. scribit . . . adicit : this should not be taken to mean that Philip gave no precise instructions to Philocles and that the offer of a marriage alliance was made entirely on Philocles' own initiative (thus Seibert, 41).

filias suas : their names and number are not known. We know of the marriages later of two daughters of Philip. Cf. Walbank, *Philip V*, 261 n. 3.

5. nomen tyranni: the concept of an autocratic ruler, not the name of Nabis personally.

6. superiora loca: on the topography of Argos cf. 25. 5 n.

7. principum: here it is clear that the word does refer to the rich men in Argos. Cf. *Past and Present* no. 36 (1967), 6 n. 17.

9. contione . . . accendendam: Nabis thus introduced at Argos the sort of revolution he had instituted at Sparta, though there is no specific evidence for the abolition of debt at Sparta. Cancellation of debts and redistribution of land (γῆς ἀναδασμός and χρεῶν ἀποκοπή) were the standard pair of revolutionary cries in Greece and debt and land were also the two social issues in the traditional account of the struggle of the orders at Rome. But L. uses Roman political language with formal promulgation of bills, and the language of the last sentence—though the idea behind it may be Polybian—reflects the political propaganda of the late Republic.

39. 1. in quam condicionem: cf. 38. 2 n. Aymard (*PR*, 137 n. 17) argues quite unconvincingly that Nabis did not in fact accept the conditions, on the grounds that Philocles' agreement to Nabis seeking an inviting vote of the Argives implied his withdrawal of the conditions.

2. Elatiam ad Quinctium: Flamininus presumably returned to Elatia after the conference of Nicaea.

Attalum Aeginae hibernantem: Attalus returned to Piraeus at the end of the summer's naval campaign (23. 13) and presumably passed from there to Aegina. On Aegina cf. xxxi. 14. 11 n. Whether Nabis himself invited Attalus to the conference (as argued by Aymard, *PR*, 141 n. 34) is uncertain.

3. Sicyonem: cf. 19. 5 n.

4. Anticyra: cf. 18. 4 n.

forte: 'as it happened'. For L.'s use of *forte* in expressions to indicate relative chronology, without any sense of chance, cf. J. Champeaux, *RÉL* xlv (1967), 374. See also xxxiii. 20. 9, 48. 5.

L. Quinctius . . . Corcyrae: for Lucius' return to Corcyra cf. 23. 13.

6. Mycenica: *regio* is to be understood. McDonald refers to Madvig, *Emendationes*, 463, but that concerns only the use of *vocatur* (cf. xxxi. 2. 6). Polybius may have said ἡ Μυκηνική.

L. appears ignorant of the earlier glories of Mycenae. Though not impressive (cf. Thuc. i. 10) remains were still visible to Pausanias (ii. 16. 5 ff.): cf. Gomme, *Commentary on Thucydides*, i. 111. On

Mycenae in the Hellenistic age cf. C. A. Boethius, *ABSA* xxv (1921–3), 408–29.

Mycenae formed part of the territory of Argos: Nabis' control of it is attested by *Syll.*³ 594.

7. Nicostratus: *strategos* in 198/7. Cf. 40. 4, xxxiii. 14–15. He continued the policy of close co-operation with Rome. For his *strategia* cf. Aymard, *RÉA* xx (1928), 3, 22 = *ÉHA*, 3, 17, Errington, *Philopoemen*, 251. The Achaeans are represented because of the fact that they are at war with Nabis and it is an Achaean city that is under discussion. The meeting is also on Achaean territory. Cf. Aymard, *PR*, 142–3 n. 38.

8. ex purpuratis: the courtiers of Attalus (§6 *regio comitatu*). Cf. xxxi. 35. 1 n.

9. inermes . . . regemque: the rest of the Roman party were also apparently unarmed.

10. de condicionibus amicitiae: formally the alliance made with Sparta in 210 had not been abandoned (xxxiv. 31. 5, 32. 1, 16) though Rome could doubt the legitimacy of Nabis as king of Sparta. The situation had changed so much that a new agreement had to be made: but *amicitia* does not refer to a new formal treaty. Cf. Heuss, *Klio* Bhft. xxxi (1933), 44 ff., Larsen, *CPh* xxx (1935), 210–12, Badian, *FC*, 58, Dahlheim, 221 ff.

11. bellum cum Achaeis . . . indutiae impetratae: cf. xxxi. 25. 3 n. For speculations on Nabis' motives in agreeing to a truce cf. Aymard, *PR*, 145–6 n. 48.

40. 1. ab Attalo: Attalus is opposed to Argos being simply handed over to Nabis and no doubt is at a loss to understand how the Romans, normally favourable to the upper classes, can countenance an agreement with someone with the political views of Nabis. Cf. p. 29.

ille . . . accitum: he had hoped for this, but had been disappointed (38. 4–5). The Romans and Attalus must have been ignorant of what actually happened if Nabis could make this claim without it being immediately rejected.

4. sescentis Cretensibus: cf. xxxi. 35. 1 n., xxxiii. 3. 10 n.

in quattuor menses: Aymard, *PR*, 148 n. 54 (followed by Walbank, *Philip V*, 166 n. 2) does not think that a truce would be made for only four months. They hold that it was in fact made for the length of the war, as stated originally (39. 11) and this was in fact four months. L. will have misunderstood Polybius. But truces were often made for a limited period of time, and could be renewed.

Nabis and Nicostratus clearly had separate talks about the truce, and there is no difficulty in believing that these led to a modification of the earlier agreement.

5. Philocli praefecto urbis: cf. 38. 2 n.

6. transiret: the chance of Philocles betraying Philip and joining Rome must have been very remote indeed.

7. A Corintho . . . Anticyram: apparently Flamininus sailed directly from Corinth, not from his point of arrival at Sicyon (39. 4). Cf. Aymard, *PR*, 152 n. 66.

Acarnanum gentem: cf. xxxi. 14. 7 n. For Lucius' activities in Acarnania in 197 cf. xxxiii. 16–17.

8–9. Ibi . . . redit: Pol. xviii. 16: ὁ βασιλεὺς Ἄτταλος ἐτιμᾶτο μὲν καὶ πρότερον ὑπὸ τῆς τῶν Σικυωνίων πόλεως διαφερόντως, ἐξ οὗ τὴν ἱερὰν χώραν τοῦ Ἀπόλλωνος ἐλυτρώσατο χρημάτων αὐτοῖς οὐκ ὀλίγων, ἀνθ' ὧν καὶ τὸν κολοσσὸν αὐτοῦ τὸν δεκάπηχυν ἔστησαν παρὰ τὸν Ἀπόλλωνα τὸν κατὰ τὴν ἀγοράν. τότε δὲ πάλιν αὐτοῦ δέκα τάλαντα δόντος καὶ μυρίους μεδίμνους πυρῶν, πολλαπλασίως ἐπιταθέντες ταῖς εὐνοίαις εἰκόνα τε χρυσῆν ἐψηφίσαντο καὶ θυσίαν αὐτῷ συντελεῖν κατ' ἔτος ἐνομοθέτησαν. Ἄτταλος μὲν οὖν τυχὼν τῶν τιμῶν τούτων ἀπῆρεν εἰς Κεγχρεάς.

8. novis . . . honores: L. summarizes what Polybius describes in detail. Cf. Walbank, *Commentary*, ii. 571.

rex . . . redemerat: the land had probably been mortgaged to secure a loan. Cf. Walbank, *Commentary*, ii. 570–1.

quondam: in fact only a few months earlier. Cf. Walbank, *Commentary*, ii. 570. *Contra* Aymard, *PR*, 143 n. 41.

9. Cenchreas: 17. 3 n.

10–11. Et Nabis . . . ademit: Pol. xviii. 17. 1–5: Νάβις ὁ τύραννος ἀπολιπὼν ἐπὶ τῆς τῶν Ἀργείων πόλεως Τιμοκράτην τὸν Πελληνέα διὰ τὸ μάλιστα τούτῳ πιστεύειν καὶ χρῆσθαι πρὸς τὰς ἐπιφανεστάτας πράξεις, ἐπανῆλθεν εἰς τὴν Σπάρτην, καὶ μετά τινας ἡμέρας ἐξέπεμψε τὴν γυναῖκα, δοὺς ἐντολὰς παραγενομένην εἰς Ἄργος περὶ πόρον γίνεσθαι χρημάτων. ἡ δ' ἀφικομένη πολὺ κατὰ τὴν ὠμότητα Νάβιν ὑπερέθετο· ἀνακαλεσαμένη γὰρ τῶν γυναικῶν τινὰς μὲν κατ' ἰδίαν, τινὰς δὲ κατὰ συγγένειαν, πᾶν γένος αἰκίας καὶ βίας προσέφερε, μέχρι σχεδὸν ἁπασῶν οὐ μόνον τὸν χρυσοῦν ἀφείλετο κόσμον, ἀλλὰ καὶ τὸν ἱματισμὸν τὸν πολυτελέστατον.

10. firmato praesidio: with Timocrates of Pellene in charge (Pol. xviii. 17. 1).

uxorem: Apega. Cf. Pol. xiii. 7. 2 ff.

11. blandiendo: an addition by L. Polybius refers only to force.

For the conjunction of persuasion and threats of force cf. Tac. *Agr.* 42. 1.

aurum . . . vestem . . . mundum : Pol. xviii. 17. 5 refers to gold ornaments and clothes. L. may have misunderstood him.

domum : *om.* B. Probably an addition by χ. Cf. Walsh, *CR,* 55.

BOOK XXXIII

1–21. 5	197 B.C.	The campaign of 197 in Greece
21. 6–25. 3		Events in Rome—including report of war in Spain
25. 4–27. 5	196 B.C.	Events in Rome and Italy
27. 5—35		Events in Greece, winter 197/6 and 196
36–7		Events in Italy
38–41		The activities of Antiochus and the conference of Lysimacheia
42		Events in Rome
43–45. 5	195 B.C.	Events in Rome
45. 6–49. 7		The flight of Hannibal from Carthage
49. 8		Senatorial reply to Aetolia

The text of 1–17. 6 rests on the authority of the Bambergensis alone. The Mainz edition of 1519 (Mog.), based on the now lost MS. Mg, begins with *artis faucibus* at 17. 6.

1–21. 5. *The campaign of 197 in Greece*

1–2. *Boeotia*

Cf. Plut. *Flam.* 6, Zon. ix. 16. 9, Aymard, *PR*, 154–6, P. Cloché, *Thèbes de Béotie* (Namur, 1954), 253 ff., Deininger, 49 ff.

1. 1. Haec per hiemem gesta: the winter of 198/7. 1–21. 5 describe the events of the summer of 197 and continue directly from xxxii. 32–40. Together they represent Polybius' narrative of the Olympiad year 198/7 in book xviii. 1–41. Cf. xxxii. 32. 1 n. and p. 3.

Attalo Elatiam excito: the only possible route, given the territory still held by Philip or loyal to him, is for Attalus to have crossed from Aegina (cf. 39. 3) to the Argolid and to have proceeded thence to Sicyon, to cross the gulf by boat.

Boeotorum: cf. xxxii. 17. 3 n. Flamininus was no doubt encouraged by pro-Roman elements in Boeotia: cf. § 7 and 27. 5 ff.

Thebis: this is the first mention of Boeotian Thebes in L. Thebes, destroyed by Alexander in 335, was refounded by Cassander in 316 (cf. Will, *HP*, i. 46).

quod caput est Boeotiae: doubtless L.'s own comment (cf. xlii. 44. 3). In fact the regular meeting-place of the federal assembly at this time was Onchestus, though the council may normally have met in Thebes (cf. Roesch, 125–6, Will, *RPh* 3ème série, xli [1967], 297).

2. unius signi: at this time the *signum* was carried by the maniple (Kromayer–Veith, 323).

legationibusque: presumably representatives of Boeotian towns friendly towards Rome. As the assembly of the League is primary (§ 7 n.) they cannot be delegates to the meeting.

legionis hastatis: emendations have been made to insert *unius* or the number of a legion, or to alter to *legionum* (with or without inserting *duarum*). The motive for the emendations was the feeling that *legionis* needed further definition, and in the case of the change to the plural, the view that one legion could not produce 2,000 *hastati*. But *legionis* quite naturally means 'a legion'. As to the second point, we know from Polybius (vi. 21. 6–9) that in a legion of 4,200 there were 1,200 *hastati* (the front line), 1,200 *principes*, 600 *triarii*, and 1,200 *velites*. If the legion was larger, the *triarii* remained at 600, the others were increased. Hence there would be no difficulty in having 2,000 *hastati*, probably including their assignment of *velites*, in a larger legion. Such large legions are often attested in this period. Cf. Afzelius, *Die römische Kriegsmacht* (xxxi. 8. 7 n.), 48 ff., Walbank, *Commentary*, i. 702–3, ii. 584–5, Brunt, 671 ff.

3. Boeotorum praetor Antiphilus: Antiphilus is not otherwise known (cf. Deininger, *RE*, supp. xi. 61). He was probably the *strategos* of the Boeotian League. Cf. Larsen, *Greek Federal States*, 179–80. I am not convinced by the attempt of Roesch, 112–21, to deny that there was a *strategos* of the Boeotian League at this time.

5. tardius incedebat: for this technical term for a slow march cf. Ogilvie, 384.

6. ante lictorem: Gronovius emended to *lictorum turba acti*—'driven on by the crowd of lictors'. But description of lictors as a *turba* is surely impossible. The objection to the text of B was that there should be twelve lictors, not one, for a proconsul. W–M and McDonald explain that *ante lictorem* was a technical formula used to refer to people being led in front of a lictor (cf. xxiii. 10. 6). This is acceptable, but the precise position remains unclear. McDonald says that the *turba* is the *oppidani*. They will have left Thebes, and the meaning will be that they could not see the *hastati* because they were so close to the lictor (and hence to Flamininus). But it could mean that the people in Thebes could not see the soldiers because of the mass of people (in fact also *oppidani*) massed in front of the lictor.

7. dolo Antiphili: L. does not make it clear, either here or in § 3, whether Antiphilus was really involved or himself taken in.

concilio: it appears that this is a primary assembly with the votes taken by cities (cf. 2. 6 n.). Cf. Larsen, *Greek Federal States*, 178 ff. Will's argument (*RPh* 3ème série xli [1967], 295 ff.) that L. has confused the proceedings of council and assembly is not convincing.

2. 1. maiorum . . . meritis: cf. Pol. xviii. 17. 6: ὑπεμίμνησκεν αὐτοὺς τῆς ἀνέκαθεν τῶν προγόνων ἀρετῆς. For Attalus' benefactions to Athens cf. xxxi. 14. 11 n., to Aetolia xxxi. 15. 9 n., to Delphi, Hansen, 292 ff. For benefactions of Philetaerus and Attalus to Boeotia cf. Hansen, 19, 192, McShane, 40, P. M. Fraser, *RÉA* liv (1952), 233 ff.

3. reficiunt: this is Gronovius's emendation for the nonsensical *perfecunt* of B. The 1616 edition made the easy change to *perferunt*, which is read by W–M, but *auferunt perferuntque* lacks both point and taste.

4. Aristaenus . . . Achaeorum praetor: in fact Nicostratus is now *strategos*: cf. xxxii. 39. 7 n.

   quae Achaeis suaserat: Aristaenus' speech in xxxii. 21.

6. Plataeensi Dicaearcho: Plataea is a member of the Boeotian League (cf. Roesch, 50). Dicaearchus is not otherwise known. He may have been one of the Boeotarchs: cf. Niese, ii. 627 n. 2, Roesch, 106, Deininger, 52 n. 29.

   lata: 'brought forward', not 'carried'.

   civitatum suffragiis: the votes are now taken by cities. There is no reason to doubt this, and think that L. has applied Achaean practices (cf. xxxii. 23. 1 n.) to the Boeotian League, as W–M do. Cf. Larsen, *Greek Federal States*, 180, who thinks it possible that the votes were weighted, and that each city did not necessarily have one vote.

   dicere: B has *adicere*, not *addicere* as McDonald's apparatus may suggest.

9. quoniam: Gronovius. B has *quō*. The 1616 edition read *quando*. *quando* is quite possible (cf. K–St, ii. 383, H–S, 607) but *quoniam* perhaps explains B's reading better.

   ab tergo: L. thinks of Thessaly and Macedon as lying to Flamininus' front, and hence of Boeotia and the Peloponnese as being to the rear.

3–5. *The prelude to Cynoscephalae*

3. 1. postquam . . . rettulerant: on the chronology cf. xxxii. 38. 1 n.

2–3. absumpserant . . . numerus: it is not clear how long a period L. (and Polybius) had in view. Continual warfare was a normal feature of all Greek states. After the end of the Chremonidean war (262) the reign of Antigonus Gonatas was relatively peaceful, but both Demetrius II and Antigonus Doson had serious wars. As far as Philip himself is concerned, L. appears to refer only to the Second Macedonian war, though this was preceded by the Social war and the First Macedonian war. On the Macedonian army cf. Walbank, *Philip V*, 289 ff., Launey, 101–2, Toynbee, i. 67 ff.

navalibus . . . Attalumque: the battles of Lade and Chios in 201.

5. Dium: on the northern side of Mount Olympus. Cf. Philippson, *RE*, v. 833, P–K, i. 1. 105. The adoption of this position does not in itself mean that Philip was taking the offensive, as claimed by Walbank, *Philip V*, 167.

6. Thronium: cf. xxxii. 36. 3 n.

Scarphaeam: a little to the west of Thronium on the Malian gulf. Cf. Oldfather, *RE*, iiiA. 460–5, P–K, i. 2. 344.

7. concilium . . . indictum: as the meeting is in the spring this could be the regular Παναιτωλικά (cf. xxxi. 29. 1 n.) though Holleaux, *Études*, i. 227 n. 3 would leave open the question whether this is a regular or an extraordinary meeting. Cf. Larsen, *TAPA* lxxxiii (1952), 24–5.

On Heraclea cf. xxxi. 46. 2 n. For the use of *tenere* cf. xxxi. 15. 9 and for the omission of the object cf. xxxiv. 39. 7.

8. Xynias: cf. xxxii. 13. 13 n.

Aenianum: the Aenianes are a people living to the south of Thessaly and the east of Aetolia, and belonging to the Aetolian League. In 167 they became a κοινόν of their own. Cf. Hirschfeld, *RE*, i. 1027–8, Stählin, *HTh*, 219 ff., Béquignon, *Vallée du Spercheios* (xxxii. 13. 10 n.), 148 ff., Flacelière, 17–18, 191, P–K, ii. 2. 307.

9. Phaenea: cf. xxxii. 32. 11 n.

sex milia peditum: B has ōc *pedites*. The Aetolians later boasted that they had won the battle (xxxv. 12. 15, Pol. xviii. 34. 2, 48. 8) and though their cavalry were far more impressive than their infantry (7. 13, Pol. xviii. 22. 5) it is hard to think that the boast could have been made on the basis of a contingent of only 1,000 men in all. Hence Plutarch's figure (*Flam.* 7. 2) of 6,000 is preferable. Cf. De Sanctis, iv. 1. 78–9, n. 159, Walbank, *Commentary*, ii. 585: *contra* Lehmann, 372–4.

10. in Phthioticum agrum: Xyniae is in Phthiotic Achaea, but it does not seem possible to take *Xynias praegressus* in §8 as 'advancing towards Xyniae' as W–M do. Rather Xyniae is on the borders of Phthiotic Achaea and Flamininus then proceeded north-east into the heart of Phthiotic Achaea.

quingenti Gortynii . . . Apolloniatae: Aymard (*PR*, 147–8 n. 52 and 431) followed by Walbank (*Philip V*, 167 n. 4) argued that these Cretans were the balance of those promised by Nabis at xxxii. 40. 4. Hence the men of Apollonia were from Illyria (cf. xxxi. 18. 9 n.) not from the Cretan Apollonia, a little to the west of Cnossus. But L. says that the Cretans were given by Nabis, not promised, and Aymard's arguments that he could not have spared them are based on probability alone. Moreover, Errington (*Philopoemen*, 34 ff.) has shown that it is extremely unlikely that Nabis had friendly relations with Gortyn, the city which invited Philopoemen to Crete (Plut. *Phil.* 13, Paus. viii. 50. 6). But it may still be true that the Apolloniates came from Illyria. The comment on the similarity of arms (a Herodotean touch) would be unnecessary if both were Cretan—in that case their armour would not be expected to vary.

Cydante: for his possible identification cf. Errington, *Philopoemen*, 42 n. 2.

Amynander cum Athamanum: cf. xxxi. 28. 1 n.

11–4. 3. We have here the customary address to soldiers by their general before battle, with the customary theme of not being downcast by previous defeats (cf. e.g. Thuc. ii. 87). On speeches before battle in the fourth and fifth decades cf. Paschkowski, 35 ff.

12. ⟨erigi⟩: B has a gap here. For the use of *erigere* with *in spem* cf. iii. 1. 2, xxvii. 38. 6, xxix. 14. 1, xxx. 15. 14, Ogilvie, 392.

4. 1. acceptae . . . cladi: xxxii. 11–12.

⟨i⟩terum . . . Romanos: cf. xxxii. 17.

⟨i⟩terum a: B has *terra* which makes no sense. Gronovius read *ter a*. McDonald objects to this that in xxxii. 17 the Romans are repulsed twice, not three times, and Dorey's justification of *ter* as suiting the rhetorical tone (*JRS* lvii [1967], 279) does not make the case any better. Hence McDonald reads *iterum a* saying we can either understand *bis* with *pulsos* or *pugnando* with *iterum*. But one cannot just 'understand' *pugnando* and it is very doubtful if *iterum* can be taken in the sense of *bis* in L. (for such usages cf. *TLL*, vii. 2. 556).

I feel something more radical may be needed. There are three clues. (i) Although we can find two repulses in xxxii. 17, these phases are not clearly marked and it would be more natural just to talk of it as a Roman repulse. (ii) The clause balance in this section seems to require a simple opposition of the Aous and Atrax. (iii) The strong statement about the phalanx in § 3 is considerably weakened by its mention here. Hence I would delete *terra Macedonum phalange*. The scribe recalled the reference to the phalanx in xxxii. 17. 11, and *terra* noted that Philip was talking about land engagements.

2. culpam . . . servassent: in failing to spot the party that, led by the shepherd, turned the pass.

3. secundam . . . stetisse: this distinction was not made in L.'s account of the battle of the pass in xxxii. 12. Cf. Walbank, *Philip V*, 153 n. 1.

et loco aequo . . . invictam: as Walbank (*Philip V*, 168 n. 3) says, this was a perfectly valid point. There had been no pitched battle between Philip's phalanx and the Roman legions.

4. peltas⟨tas⟩: cf. xxxi. 36. 1 n.

Thracumque et Illyriorum: probably also mercenaries: cf. 7. 11 n.

Tralles: cf. xxxi. 35. 1 n. B has *trailis*. Either nominative or dative is possible in this idiom (cf. K–St, i. 420, H–S, 90–1) and in view of B's reading McDonald may be right to read the nominative.

6. par numerus erat; qui tum: thus B. *equitum* was the emendation of Gronovius, almost universally followed. McDonald (apart from the long note in the text cf. also *JRS* lviii [1968], 235) returns to *qui tum*. His argument is that Philip's army (§§ 4–5) totals 23,500 infantry and 2,000 cavalry. The Roman army he estimates at between 22,000 and 22,800 infantry and 2,000 cavalry. The Aetolian contingent of 6,000 infantry and 400 cavalry (cf. 3. 9 n.) thus allowed it to be larger than that of Philip, and this applied to both infantry and cavalry. Plutarch, *Flam.* 7. 2, in giving 26,000 as the total wrongly included the Aetolians in this figure.

The principal objection to McDonald's reading is the text it produces. It seems impossible that L. should have included the Cretans and Illyrians of 3. 10 in *Romanis ferme par numerus erat*, but deliberately excluded the Aetolians. Or, in other words, that he should first appear to say that the Roman army was more or less the same size as Philip's and then contradict that proposition in the next sentence (cf. Ogilvie, *Phoenix*, 346). *qui tum*, moreover, is extremely inelegant (cf. Tränkle, *Gnomon*, 379).

Palaeographically *equitum* is the obvious explanation. Can we square it with the actual figures of the Roman forces? If we accepted the figure of 600 for the Aetolian infantry contingent there would be little problem. But the arguments for reading 6,000 are very strong (cf. 3. 9 n.) and I am unwilling to reject them simply to help the case here. The two Roman legions (cf. 1. 2 n.) cannot be less than 10,000 in all, or 20,000 with their allied contingents. The Gortynians, Apolloniates, and Athamanians number 2,000 (3. 10), making a total of 22,000 and 28,000 with the Aetolian contingent. Philip's infantry numbers 23,500. We shall have to believe then that *c.* 4,500 men were left on garrison duty and did not take part in the battle. I see no difficulty in this assumption (cf. Walbank, *Commentary*, ii. 585). The fact that at Magnesia the legions were at full strength (xxxvii. 39. 7–9) does not mean that the same must have been the case at Cynoscephalae, as McDonald implies.

5. 1. Thebas Phthioticas: cf. xxxii. 33. 16 n.
Timonem: not otherwise known.
principem civitatis: probably just 'a leading man in Thebes'. Cf. xxxi. 17. 11 n.

2. erumpentibus: presumably the Macedonian garrison.

subiret . . . evenissent: *subiret* in the consecutive clause represents an indicative and W–M's parallel of ix. 19. 5 is not therefore accurate. For the construction cf. xxxii. 25. 8 n.

3–4. quidem . . . ceterum: the contrast indicates that Flamininus was still engaged in positive activity.

4–12. *Greek and Roman stakes.* This section comes from Polybius xviii. 18. L. shortens and adapts. Where Polybius describes the Greek and Roman customs in relation to each point, L. collects all the Greek customs together first and then describes Roman methods. L.'s exposition is perfectly clear and indeed somewhat easier to understand than that of Polybius. The discussion is an example of Polybius' fondness for digressions on technical military matters (cf. Walbank, *Commentary*, i. 2).

4. ceterum satis gnarus . . . parare iubet: Pol. xviii. 18. 1: ὁ δὲ Τίτος οὐ δυνάμενος ἐπιγνῶναι τοὺς πολεμίους ᾗ στρατοπεδεύουσι, τοῦτο δὲ σαφῶς εἰδὼς ὅτι πάρεισιν εἰς Θετταλίαν, προσέταξε κόπτειν χάρακα πᾶσιν ἕνεκα τοῦ παρακομίζειν μεθ' αὐτῶν πρὸς τὰς ἐκ τοῦ καιροῦ χρείας.

comperto: cf. xxxi. 39. 4 n.
vallum caedere: 'to cut stakes for a palisade'. *Vallus* is a stake, *vallum* the palisade formed from the stakes.

5. vallo . . . aptaverunt: this sentence summarizes the contents of the section. Cf. Pol. xviii. 18. 17–18: διὸ καὶ μεγάλης οὔσης διαφορᾶς τῷ καὶ τὴν εὕρεσιν ἑτοίμην εἶναι τοῦ τοιούτου χάρακος καὶ τὴν κομιδὴν εὐχερῆ καὶ τὴν χρείαν ἀσφαλῆ καὶ μόνιμον, φανερὸν ὡς εἰ καί τι τῶν ἄλλων πολεμικῶν ἔργων ἄξιον ζήλου καὶ μιμήσεως ὑπάρχει παρὰ Ῥωμαίοις, καὶ τοῦτο, κατά γε τὴν ἐμὴν γνώμην.

6. nam et maiores . . . posset: Pol. xviii. 18. 3: οἱ μὲν γὰρ Ἕλληνες μόλις αὐτῶν κρατοῦσι τῶν σαρισῶν ἐν ταῖς πορείαις καὶ μόλις ὑπομένουσι τὸν ἀπὸ τούτων κόπον, and xviii. 18. 6: οἱ μὲν γὰρ Ἕλληνες τοῦτον ἡγοῦνται χάρακα βέλτιστον, ὃς ἂν ἔχῃ πλείστας ἐκφύσεις καὶ μεγίστας πέριξ τοῦ πρέμνου.

et cum . . . valli erat: Pol. xviii. 18. 9: ὁ μὲν γὰρ τῶν Ἑλλήνων ὅταν τεθῇ πρὸ τῆς παρεμβολῆς, πρῶτον μέν ἐστιν εὐδιάσπαστος.

7–8. nam et quia . . . obmolirentur: Pol. xviii. 18. 10–11: ὅταν γὰρ τὸ μὲν κρατοῦν καὶ πιεζούμενον ὑπὸ τῆς γῆς ἐν ὑπάρχῃ μόνον, αἱ δ' ἀποφύσεις ἐκ τούτου πολλαὶ καὶ μεγάλαι, κἄπειτα δύο παραστάντες ἢ τρεῖς ἐκ τῶν ἀποφύσεων ἐπισπάσωνται τὸν αὐτὸν χάρακα, ῥᾳδίως ἐκσπᾶται. τούτου δὲ συμβάντος εὐθέως πύλη γίνεται διὰ τὸ μέγεθος καὶ τὰ παρακείμενα λέλυται. . . .

7. et quia: there is no second causal clause, and Madvig considered the deletion of *et*. McDonald says 'cf. § 8 *nec*' but that clause is parallel to the previous main clause (*duo . . . evellebant*) not to the causal clause, and it would be quite impossible to take *et* with *evellebant*. L. may have begun as if he intended to write a second causal clause and then failed to do so. But the simplest change would be *quia et*, with the *-que* of *multique* taking up the *et*.

8. qua evulsa: B has *que vulsa*, with a faint line under the *-e*.

9. Romanus . . . miles: Pol. xviii. 18. 4: Ῥωμαῖοι δὲ τοὺς μὲν θυρεοὺς τοῖς ὀχεῦσι τοῖς σκυτίνοις ἐκ τῶν ὤμων ἐξηρτηκότες, ταῖς δὲ χερσὶν αὐτοὺς τοὺς γαίσους φέροντες, ἐπιδέχονται τὴν παρακομιδὴν τοῦ χάρακος, and xviii. 18. 7–8: παρὰ δὲ Ῥωμαίοις δύο κεραίας ἢ τρεῖς ἔχουσιν οἱ χάρακες, ὁ δὲ πλείστας τέτταρας . . . ὁ γὰρ εἷς ἀνὴρ φέρει τρεῖς καὶ τέτταρας συνθεὶς ἐπ' ἀλλήλους.

et trium: for Polybius it is a stake with two, or at most three or four branches. L. conceives of one main fork, with three or four separate branches. There is no case for emending *et* to *vel* to make L. consistent with Polybius.

ab tergo: for Polybius it is hung from the shoulders (cf. Walbank, *Commentary*, ii. 572).

10. et ita densos . . . possit: Pol. xviii. 18. 12: τιθέασι γὰρ εὐθέως ἐμπλέκοντες εἰς ἀλλήλους οὕτως ὥστε μήτε τὰς κεραίας εὐχερῶς ἐπιγνῶναι, ποίας εἰσὶν ἐκφύσεως τῶν ἐν τῇ γῇ κατωρυγμένων, μήτε τὰς ἐκφύσεις, ποίων κεραιῶν.

ramis: B has *ramos*. McDonald says 'sed adhuc de *vallis*' but the point is equally well made by saying 'they bind together the branches' as 'they bind the stakes with their branches'. *densos*, of course, agrees with *vallos* in § 9.

⟨quis . . . neque⟩: an addition is necessary to give sense to the previous *neque* and the text of Polybius (which is clear in general meaning despite difficulties of detailed interpretation—cf. Walbank, *Commentary*, ii. 573–4) shows what is required.

11–12. et adeo . . . possit: Pol. xviii. 18. 13–15: λοιπὸν οὔτ' ἐπιλαβέσθαι παρείραντα τὴν χεῖρα δυνατόν, ἅτε πυκνῶν οὐσῶν καὶ προσπιπτουσῶν αὐταῖς, ἔτι δὲ φιλοπόνως ἀπωξυμμένων τῶν κεραιῶν, οὔτ' ἐπιλαβόμενον ἐκσπάσαι ῥᾴδιον ... διὰ τὴν εἰς ἀλλήλους ἐμπλοκήν.

11. adeo: taken up by *ut*. There is no case for deleting it.
rami: B has *radii* which has no meaning in this context.

12. et si ... perfacile est: Pol. xviii. 18. 16: ἐὰν δέ ποτε καὶ κατακρατήσας ἐκσπάσῃ τις ἕνα καὶ δεύτερον, ἀνεπιγνώστως γίνεται τὸ διάστημα. L. adds, paradoxically, *alium reponere perfacile est* (cf. Nissen, *KU*, 31–2).

6–10. The battle of Cynoscephalae

Other sources: Pol. xviii. 19–27, Plut. *Flam*. 7–8, Just. xxx. 4, Oros. iv. 20. 5–6, Zon. ix. 16. 9–10.

I have not attempted a discussion of the topographical problems concerning the battle, on which see Walbank, *Commentary*, ii. 574 ff. To Walbank's bibliography add Accame, *Espansione romana*, 170 ff., W. K. Pritchett, *Studies in Ancient Topography*, ii (Berkeley and Los Angeles, 1969), 133–44. On L.'s adaptations of Polybius in this section cf. Witte, 382 ff., Brueggmann, 111 ff., K. Lindemann, *Beobachtungen zur livianischen Periodenkunst* (Marburg, 1964) 128 ff.

6. 1–2. Quinctius ... misit: Pol. xviii. 19. 1–2: Πλὴν ὅ γε Τίτος ἑτοιμασάμενος ταῦτα πρὸς τὰς ἐκ τοῦ καιροῦ χρείας, ... ἀποσχὼν δὲ περὶ πεντήκοντα στάδια τῆς τῶν Φεραίων πόλεως αὐτοῦ παρενέβαλε. κατὰ δὲ τὴν ἐπιοῦσαν ὑπὸ τὴν ἑωθινὴν ἐξέπεμπε τοὺς κατοπτεύσοντας καὶ διερευνησομένους, εἴ τινα δυνηθεῖεν λαβεῖν ἀφορμὴν εἰς τὸ γνῶναι ποῦ ποτ' εἰσὶ καὶ τί πράττουσιν οἱ πολέμιοι. On Pherae cf. xxxii. 13. 9 n.

3. Circa ... castra: Pol. xviii. 19. 3–4: Φίλιππος δὲ κατὰ τὸν αὐτὸν καιρὸν πυνθανόμενος τοὺς Ῥωμαίους στρατοπεδεύειν περὶ τὰς Θήβας, ἐξάρας ἀπὸ τῆς Λαρίσης παντὶ τῷ στρατεύματι προῆγε, ποιούμενος τὴν πορείαν ὡς ἐπὶ τὰς Φεράς. ἀποσχὼν δὲ περὶ τριάκοντα στάδια, τότε μὲν αὐτοῦ καταστρατοπεδεύσας ... Thus in Polybius Philip moves from Larisa to Pherae when he hears that Flamininus is at Phthiotic Thebes, whilst for L. he does so on hearing that Flamininus has moved to Pherae. Walbank (*Commentary*, ii. 574) calls this a mistranslation but it is probably a deliberate change by L., who did not realize that Philip's actions in Pol. xviii. 19. 3 were concurrent with those of Flamininus described in xviii. 19. 1–2. It cannot, however, be ruled out that L.'s text of Polybius had Φεράς for Θήβας. *defungi ... pergit* is L.'s own addition, in order to motivate Philip's action.
Larisam: Thessalian Larisa. Cf. xxxi. 46. 12.

4–5. Inde ... opperientes: Pol. xviii. 19. 5–7: ὑπὸ δὲ τὴν ἑωθινὴν ἐξεγείρας τὴν δύναμιν τοὺς μὲν εἰθισμένους προπορεύεσθαι τῆς δυνάμεως προεξαπέστειλε, συντάξας ὑπερβάλλειν τὰς ὑπὲρ τὰς Φερὰς ἀκρολοφίας, αὐτὸς δὲ τῆς ἡμέρας διαφαινούσης ἐκίνει τὴν δύναμιν ἐκ τοῦ χάρακος. παρ᾽ ὀλίγον μὲν οὖν ἦλθον ἀμφοτέρων οἱ προεξαπεσταλμένοι τοῦ συμπεσεῖν ἀλλήλοις περὶ τὰς ὑπερβολάς· προϊδόμενοι γὰρ σφᾶς αὐτοὺς ὑπὸ τὴν ὄρφνην ἐκ πάνυ βραχέος διαστήματος ἐπέστησαν, καὶ ταχέως ἔπεμπον, ἀποδηλοῦντες ἀμφότεροι τοῖς ἡγεμόσι τὸ γεγονὸς καὶ πυνθανόμενοι τί δέον εἴη ποιεῖν. It is not clear whether L. realizes that the Roman advance party is identical with those sent out by Flamininus in § 2. L.'s sentence is unusually complex in structure.

tumulos . . . iugo : for their identification cf. Walbank, *Commentary*, ii. 575.

6. et illo . . . revocati sunt : Polybius (xviii. 19. 8) has a lacuna, followed by ἐπὶ τῶν ὑποκειμένων στρατοπεδειῶν κἀκείνους ἀνακαλεῖσθαι.

postero die . . . compulsi sunt : L. considerably abbreviates from Pol. xviii. 19. 9–12 and exaggerates the Romano-Aetolian success.

non minimum : adverbial = οὐχ ἥκιστα. Cf. W–M ad loc. L. is unwilling to give quite as much credit to the Aetolians as does Polybius. Cf. Hoch, 50.

7. magnum . . . interclusa : Pol. xviii. 20. 1 : διὰ τὸ καταφύτους εἶναι καὶ πλήρεις αἱμασιῶν καὶ κηπίων. L. expands, giving the picture of *horti suburbani* such as those he knew in Rome.

8. itaque . . . frumenta : Pol. xviii. 20. 1–3 : κατὰ δὲ τὴν ἐπιοῦσαν ἀμφότεροι δυσαρεστούμενοι τοῖς περὶ τὰς Φερὰς τόποις . . . ἀνέζευξαν. ὁ μὲν οὖν Φίλιππος ἐποιεῖτο τὴν πορείαν ὡς ἐπὶ τὴν Σκοτοῦσσαν, σπεύδων ἐκ ταύτης τῆς πόλεως ἐφοδιάσασθαι, μετὰ δὲ ταῦτα γενόμενος εὐτρεπὴς λαβεῖν τόπους ἁρμόζοντας ταῖς αὐτοῦ δυνάμεσιν· ὁ δὲ Τίτος ὑποπτεύσας τὸ μέλλον ἐκίνει τὴν δύναμιν ἅμα τῷ Φιλίππῳ, σπεύδων προκαταφθεῖραι τὸν ἐν τῇ Σκοτουσσαίᾳ σῖτον. L. does not mention that this occurred on the day following the skirmish.

velut ex praedicto : this is L.'s own comment. *praedictum* is taken by L–S and Sage to mean 'agreement', a unique usage. It seems best to interpret it as 'as if they had previous information'.

Scotusam : on its site cf. Walbank, *Commentary*, ii. 575–6.

9. per diem totum . . . ierunt : Pol. xviii. 20. 4 : τῆς δ᾽ ἑκατέρων πορείας μεταξὺ κειμένων ὄχθων ὑψηλῶν, οὔθ᾽ οἱ Ῥωμαῖοι συνεώρων τοὺς Μακεδόνας, ποῖ ποιοῦνται τὴν πορείαν, οὔθ᾽ οἱ Μακεδόνες τοὺς Ῥωμαίους. On the routes of the marches cf. Walbank, *Commentary*, ii. 576–8.

10. Romani . . . castra : Pol. xviii. 20. 5 : ταύτην μὲν οὖν τὴν ἡμέραν ἑκάτεροι διανύσαντες, ὁ μὲν Τίτος ἐπὶ τὴν προσαγορευομένην Ἐρέτριαν τῆς Φθιώτιδος χώρας, ὁ δὲ Φίλιππος ἐπὶ τὸν Ὀγχηστὸν ποταμόν, αὐτοῦ κατέζευξαν. On Eretria cf. xxxii. 13. 9 n., on the river

Onchestus cf. Walbank *Commentary*, ii. 576, 579, Pritchett, *Studies*, ii. 135–9.

11. ne postero . . . habuerunt: Pol. xviii. 20. 6: τῇ δ' ὑστεραίᾳ προελθόντες ἐστρατοπέδευσαν, Φίλιππος μὲν ἐπὶ τὸ Μελάμβιον προσαγορευόμενον τῆς Σκοτουσσαίας, Τίτος δὲ περὶ τὸ Θετίδειον τῆς Φαρσαλίας, ἀκμὴν ἀγνοοῦντες ἀλλήλους.

quod vocant Scotusae⟨i⟩ agri: the district is added not to distinguish it from another Melambium as with Eretria in § 10, but to locate a very small place. On its site cf. Walbank, *Commentary*, ii. 576, Pritchett, *Studies*, ii. 139–40.

Thetideum: B has *Thetidem* here, but *Thetideum* correctly at 7. 4. As with *Melambium* above the correct form is guaranteed by Polybius. On the site cf. Walbank, *Commentary*, ii. 578, Pritchett, *Studies*, ii. 141.

12. tertio . . . tenuit: Pol. xviii. 20. 7: ἐπιγενομένου δ' ὄμβρου καὶ βροντῶν ἐξαισίων, πάντα συνέβη τὸν ἀέρα τὸν ἐκ τῶν νεφῶν κατὰ τὴν ἐπιοῦσαν ἡμέραν ὑπὸ τὴν ἑωθινὴν πεσεῖν ἐπὶ τὴν γῆν. Fear of an ambush at this point is an addition by L. and an anticipation of 7. 4.

nimbus: a poetic word, found five times in L. (cf. Tränkle, *WS*, 117).

nocti: B has *noctis*, but L. always uses the dative of things with *similis* (cf. Wölfflin, *Livianische Kritik und livianischer Sprachgebrauch* [Berlin, 1864], 14).

7. 1. Philippus . . . iussit: Pol. xviii. 20. 8: οὐ μὴν ἀλλ' ὅ γε Φίλιππος κατανύσαι σπεύδων ἐπὶ τὸ προκείμενον, ἀναζεύξας προῄει μετὰ πάσης τῆς στρατιᾶς.

2. sed tam . . . turbaretur: Pol. xviii. 20. 7: ὥστε διὰ τὸν ἐφεστῶτα ζόφον μηδὲ τοὺς ἐν ποσὶ δύνασθαι βλέπειν . . . and xviii. 20. 9 δυσχρηστούμενος δὲ κατὰ τὴν πορείαν διὰ τὴν ὀμίχλην. L. elaborates to give a graphic picture.

3. supergressi . . . castra: Pol. xviii. 20. 9: βραχὺν τόπον διανύσας τὴν μὲν δύναμιν εἰς χάρακα παρενέβαλε, τὴν δ' ἐφεδρείαν ἀπέστειλε, συντάξας ἐπὶ τοὺς ἄκρους ἐπιβαλεῖν τῶν μεταξὺ κειμένων βουνῶν. L. evidently thinks that Philip's army has just crossed the mountains in which he now places his ambush party, when he has in fact marched to the north of them.

Cynoscephalae: on the actual site of the battle cf. Walbank, *Philip V*, 169–70, *Commentary*, ii. 576–9, Pritchett, *Studies*, 142–4. The name is not given by Polybius until xviii. 22. 9.

4. Romanus . . . praecaverent: Pol. xviii. 21. 1: ὁ δὲ Τίτος στρατοπεδεύων περὶ τὸ Θετίδειον, καὶ διαπορούμενος ὑπὲρ τῶν πολεμίων

ποῦ ποτ' εἰσί, δέκα προθέμενος οὐλαμοὺς καὶ τῶν εὐζώνων εἰς χιλίους
ἐξαπέστειλε, παρακαλέσας εὐλαβῶς ἐξερευνωμένους ἐπιπορεύεσθαι τὴν
χώραν. L. again emphasizes the mist, Polybius refers to it in connection with the meeting between the two parties (xviii. 21. 2).

5. ubi ventum . . . abstinuere: Pol. xviii. 21. 2–3: οἳ καὶ προ-
άγοντες ὡς ἐπὶ τὰς ὑπερβολὰς ἔλαθον ἐμπεσόντες εἰς τὴν τῶν Μακεδόνων
ἐφεδρείαν διὰ τὸ δύσοπτον τῆς ἡμέρας. οὗτοι μὲν οὖν ἐν ταῖς ἀρχαῖς ἐπὶ
βραχὺ διαταραχθέντες ἀμφότεροι μετ' ὀλίγον ἤρξαντο καταπειράζειν
ἀλλήλων, διεπέμψαντο δὲ καὶ πρὸς τοὺς ἑαυτῶν ἡγεμόνας ἑκάτεροι τοὺς
διασαφήσοντας τὸ γεγονός. In Polybius the skirmishing begins before
the messengers are sent back to headquarters, in L. afterwards.

quieverunt: both sides are the subject: cf. 6. 4.

6. principio . . . premi sese: Pol. xviii. 21. 4: ἐπειδὴ δὲ κατὰ τὴν
συμπλοκὴν οἱ Ῥωμαῖοι κατεβαροῦντο καὶ κακῶς ἔπασχον ὑπὸ τῆς τῶν
Μακεδόνων ἐφεδρείας, πέμποντες εἰς τὴν ἑαυτῶν παρεμβολὴν ἐδέοντο
σφίσι βοηθεῖν. L. elaborates the detail of the battle in traditional form,
and emphasizes the difficulties of the Romans in *alios super alios* (the
phrase recurs in 8. 1, where, however, it is influenced by ἕτερος
ἐφ' ἑτέρῳ in Polybius).

7–8. quingenti . . . implorabant: L. abbreviates Polybius' account in xviii. 21. 5–8, shortening his description of the fighting and
omitting the names of the Aetolian commanders (cf. p. 18 n. 5) and
the statement that the Macedonians fought bravely.

maxime Aetolorum: Polybius does not say that the force was
mainly Aetolian, though the cavalry may well have been (cf. § 13
below).

8. rex . . . trepidavit: Pol. xviii. 22. 1: ὁ δὲ Φίλιππος οὐδέποτ' ἂν
ἐλπίσας κατ' ἐκείνην τὴν ἡμέραν ὁλοσχερῆ γενέσθαι κίνδυνον διὰ τὰς
προειρημένας αἰτίας, ἀφεικὼς ἔτυχε καὶ πλείους ἐκ τῆς παρεμβολῆς ἐπὶ
χορτολογίαν. L. adds that Philip was afraid and did not know what
to do. Cf. xxxi. 34. 5 n.

rex: B has *sed*, which was defended by Weissenborn (and kept by
W–M: cf. also Pettersson, 46–7) on the grounds that with *regis* in
the previous sentence mention of the king is unnecessary. But the
emphatic adversative, separated by two long subordinate clauses
from its main clause, is extremely inelegant, and Jacobs' emendation
seems inevitable.

offusam: Gronovius's emendation for B's *effusam*. *offusam* would
make excellent sense, but there is nothing wrong with *effusam*—'widespread'.

9–10. deinde . . . fieret: Pol. xviii. 22. 2: τότε δὲ πυνθανόμενος
τὰ συμβαίνοντα παρὰ τῶν διαποστελλομένων, καὶ τῆς ὁμίχλης ἤδη

διαφαινούσης. L. elaborates, and adds that Philip decided to risk a pitched battle. This seems to conflict with 8. 1, but L. may mean that Philip decided to send reinforcements, realizing that he might be drawn into a pitched battle. When things went well, he became more hesitant.

detexerat nebula : i.e. the dispersal of the mist enabled the tops of the mountains to be seen. For *postquam* with the pluperfect rather than the perfect cf. Ogilvie, 479.

11. Athenagoram . . . mittit : Pol. xviii. 22. 2: παρακαλέσας Ἡρακλείδην τε τὸν Γυρτώνιον, ὃς ἡγεῖτο τῆς Θετταλικῆς ἵππου, καὶ Λέοντα τὸν τῶν Μακεδόνων ἱππάρχην ἐξέπεμψε, σὺν δὲ τούτοις Ἀθηναγόραν ἔχοντα πάντας τοὺς μισθοφόρους πλὴν τῶν Θρακῶν. Polybius has 'all the mercenaries except the Thracians', L. 'all the auxiliaries except the Thracians'. But it is probable that the Thracians and Illyrians of 4. 4 are mercenaries (cf. Walbank, *Commentary*, ii. 581) and L. has not therefore made a mistake in his apparent alteration of Polybius. L. omits the names of Heraclides and Leon (cf. §§ 7–8 n.).

Athenagoram : cf. xxxi. 27. 6 n.

12. eorum . . . perventum est : Pol. xviii. 22. 3: συναψάντων δὲ τούτων τοῖς ἐν ταῖς ἐφεδρείαις, καὶ προσγενομένης τοῖς Μακεδόσι βαρείας χειρός, ἐνέκειντο τοῖς πολεμίοις. καὶ πάλιν οὗτοι τοὺς Ῥωμαίους ἤλαυνον ἐκ μεταβολῆς ἀπὸ τῶν ἄκρων, and xviii. 22. 6: διὸ καὶ τότε τούτων παρακατασχόντων τὴν ἐπιφορὰν τῶν πολεμίων, οὐκέτι συνηλάσθησαν ἕως εἰς τοὺς ἐπιπέδους τόπους, βραχὺ δ' ἀποσχόντες ἐκ μεταβολῆς ἔστησαν. Polybius says that they were not driven as far as the level ground, L. that they did not resist until they reached it. On the location of this level ground cf. Walbank, *Commentary*, ii. 581.

13. ne effusa . . . vincebantur : Pol. xviii. 22. 4–5: μέγιστον δ' αὐτοῖς ἐμπόδιον ἦν τοῦ μὴ τρέψασθαι τοὺς πολεμίους ὁλοσχερῶς ἡ τῶν Αἰτωλικῶν ἱππέων φιλοτιμία· πάνυ γὰρ ἐκθύμως οὗτοι καὶ παραβόλως ἐκινδύνευον. Αἰτωλοὶ γάρ, καθ' ὅσον ἐν τοῖς πεζικοῖς ἐλλιπεῖς εἰσι καὶ τῷ καθοπλισμῷ καὶ τῇ συντάξει πρὸς τοὺς ὁλοσχερεῖς ἀγῶνας, κατὰ τοσοῦτον τοῖς ἱππικοῖς διαφέρουσι πρὸς τὸ βέλτιον τῶν ἄλλων Ἑλλήνων ἐν τοῖς κατὰ μέρος καὶ κατ' ἰδίαν κινδύνοις. For this comment cf. Pol. iv. 11. 8, Walbank, *Commentary*, i. 460.

8. 1–2. Laetior res . . . in aciem : L. considerably abbreviates Pol. xviii. 22. 8–10, changing the direct speech of the Macedonians to indirect, but verbalizing Philip's thoughts. Cf. Lambert, 58–9, Walsh, *RhM* xcvii (1954), 106, 109.

alii super alios : cf. 7. 6 n.

⟨**Philippum**⟩ : B has a space at the end of the line, and it cannot therefore be ascertained how large a gap is involved: hence decision between *Philippum* and *regem* is not possible.

3. Idem . . . fecit: Pol. xviii. 22. 7: ὁ δὲ Τίτος, θεωρῶν οὐ μόνον τοὺς εὐζώνους καὶ τοὺς ἱππέας ἐγκεκλικότας, ἀλλὰ διὰ τούτους καὶ τὴν ὅλην δύναμιν ἐπτοημένην, ἐξῆγε τὸ στράτευμα πᾶν καὶ παρενέβαλε πρὸς τοῖς βουνοῖς, and xviii. 23. 1 ὁ δὲ Τίτος παρεμβαλὼν τὴν αὑτοῦ στρατιὰν ἑξῆς ἅπασαν.

Dextrum . . . vadit: Pol. xviii. 23. 7: οὗτος μὲν οὖν ταῦτ' εἰπὼν τὸ μὲν δεξιὸν μέρος ἐκέλευε μένειν κατὰ χώραν καὶ τὰ θηρία πρὸ τούτων, τῷ δ' εὐωνύμῳ μετὰ τῶν εὐζώνων ἐπῄει σοβαρῶς τοῖς πολεμίοις. In Polybius this follows Flamininus' speech, in L. it precedes it. The consequence, as W–M point out, is that in L.'s version the right wing will not have heard the speech. On L.'s methods here cf. Lambert, 59–60.

4–5. simul admonens . . . vicissent: Pol. xviii. 23. 3–4: "Οὐχ οὗτοι Μακεδόνες εἰσίν, ὦ ἄνδρες, οὓς ὑμεῖς προκατέχοντας ἐν Μακεδονίᾳ τὰς εἰς τὴν Ἐορδαίαν ὑπερβολὰς ἐκ τοῦ προφανοῦς μετὰ Σολπικίου βιασάμενοι πρὸς τόπους ὑπερδεξίους ἐξεβάλετε, πολλοὺς αὐτῶν ἀποκτείναντες; οὐχ οὗτοι Μακεδόνες εἰσίν, οὓς ὑμεῖς προκατέχοντας τὰς ἀπηλπισμένας ἐν Ἠπείρῳ δυσχωρίας ἐκβιασάμενοι ταῖς ἑαυτῶν ἀρεταῖς φεύγειν ἠναγκάσατε ῥίψαντας τὰ ὅπλα, τέως εἰς Μακεδονίαν ἀνεκομίσθησαν;" L. elaborates the description of the Aous gorge. Cf. Walsh, *RhM* xcvii (1954), 112.

ad Epiri fauces: the battle of the Aous pass (xxxii. 11–12). For the phrase cf. xxxii. 21. 14 n.

P. Sulpicii . . . vicissent: the battle described in xxxi. 39. On Eordaea cf. xxxi. 39. 7 n., and on Sulpicius xxxi. 4. 4 n.

fama . . . evanuisse: L.'s own addition, but he omits the rest of Flamininus' speech reported by Polybius in xviii. 23. 5–6.

6. iam perventum . . . hostem: Pol. xviii. 23. 8: οἱ δὲ προκινδυνεύοντες τῶν Ῥωμαίων, προσλαβόντες τὴν τῶν πεζῶν στρατοπέδων ἐφεδρείαν, ἐκ μεταβολῆς ἐνέκειντο τοῖς ὑπεναντίοις.

in ima valle: Ogilvie, 184 suggested correction to *infima* on the grounds that *imus* is a colloquial use which only later became established as the usual form. But as McDonald rightly points out, L. uses *imus* elsewhere (cf. Packard, ii. 987–8, 993, 1021). McDonald weakens his case, however, by agreeing with Ogilvie that the use is colloquial and claiming that this battle-description is colloquial. There is no reason why L. should be writing colloquially here—all that is necessary is said by Tränkle, *Gnomon*, 377. (Löfstedt, *Syntactica*, ii. 345–8, whose discussion of *imus* and *infimus* is fundamental, did not consider the usage of L.)

7. Philippus . . . vadit: Pol. xviii. 24. 1: Φίλιππος δὲ κατὰ τὸν αὐτὸν καιρόν, ἐπειδὴ τὸ πλέον μέρος ἤδη τῆς ἑαυτοῦ δυνάμεως ἑώρα παρεμβεβληκὸς πρὸ τοῦ χάρακος, αὐτὸς μὲν ἀναλαβὼν τοὺς πελταστὰς καὶ τὸ δεξιὸν τῆς φάλαγγος προῆγε, σύντονον ποιούμενος τὴν πρὸς τοὺς λόφους ἀνάβασιν.

quam phalangem vocabant: there are three peculiarities about this phrase. (i) L. has been talking about the phalanx (4. 3) and this fresh introduction seems unnecessary. (ii) Neither the right wing of the infantry nor the army as a whole are the phalanx. (iii) It is not L.'s practice to attract the relative in clauses using the *vocant* formula and a Greek word, though such attraction is common elsewhere (cf. K–St, i. 38–9). It seems improbable that L. has misunderstood τὸ δεξιὸν τῆς φάλαγγος in Polybius and I suspect that the phrase is a gloss.

prope cursu: B has *propere cursu*. For the phrase cf. 33. 1.

8. Nicanori . . . imperat: Pol. xviii. 24. 2: τοῖς δὲ περὶ τὸν Νικάνορα τὸν ἐπικαλούμενον ἐλέφαντα συνέταξε φροντίζειν ἵνα τὸ λοιπὸν μέρος τῆς δυνάμεως ἐκ ποδὸς ἕπηται. Nicanor led the Macedonian raid on Athens when the Roman *legati* were present in the winter of 201–200 (Pol. xvi. 27. 1), an incident omitted by L. (cf. p. 41).

purpuratis: cf. xxxi. 35. 1 n.

9. Primo . . . est elatus: Pol. xviii. 24. 6: ὁ δὲ βασιλεὺς ἐν μὲν ταῖς ἀρχαῖς, ὅτε παρεγίνετο, θεωρῶν οὐ μακρὰν τῆς τῶν πολεμίων παρεμβολῆς συνεστῶτα τὸν τῶν εὐζώνων κίνδυνον περιχαρὴς ἦν. L. omits Polybius' detailed description (xviii. 24. 3–5) of Philip's march and of the rout of the Macedonians on the lower ground, and concentrates on the emotions of Philip.

10. mox . . . trepidavit: Pol. xviii. 24. 7: ὡς δὲ πάλιν ἐκ μεταβολῆς ἑώρα κλίνοντας τοὺς ἰδίους καὶ προσδεομένους ἐπικουρίας. Cf. xviii. 24. 3–5. It is L.'s addition that Philip thought of returning to his camp. In fact that option was already closed to him.

11–14. deinde . . . iungerentur: Pol. xviii. 24. 7–9: ἠναγκάζετο βοηθεῖν καὶ κρίνειν ἐκ τοῦ καιροῦ τὰ ὅλα, καίπερ ἔτι τῶν πλείστων μερῶν τῆς φάλαγγος κατὰ πορείαν ὄντων καὶ προσβαινόντων πρὸς τοὺς βουνούς. προσδεξάμενος δὲ τοὺς ἀγωνιζομένους, τούτους μὲν ἤθροιζε πάντας ἐπὶ τὸ δεξιὸν κέρας, καὶ τοὺς πεζοὺς καὶ τοὺς ἱππέας, τοῖς δὲ πελτασταῖς καὶ τοῖς φαλαγγίταις παρήγγελλε διπλασιάζειν τὸ βάθος καὶ πυκνοῦν ἐπὶ τὸ δεξιόν. γενομένου δὲ τούτου, καὶ τῶν πολεμίων ἐν χερσὶν ὄντων, τοῖς μὲν φαλαγγίταις ἐδόθη παράγγελμα καταβαλοῦσι τὰς σαρίσας ἐπάγειν, τοῖς δ' εὐζώνοις κερᾶν. For L.'s alterations see the detailed notes.

11. praeterquam . . . receptus erat: again the motivation is

supplied by L. Polybius simply says that Philip was compelled to
fight.

12. iuxta caetratos : B has *locatus caetratas* which is nonsense. The
1616 editors read *locat, caetratos et* . . . meaning that the *caetrati* as
well as the phalanx are included in the order of the next sentence.
This is not what Polybius says, though since L. makes such a howler
here (cf. next note) such a mistake is perfectly possible (McDonald's
argument to the contrary is a simple assertion). McDonald follows
those who want L. to be giving the position relative to the peltasts
of those who have retreated from conflict with the Romans, and
reads *iuxta* on the grounds that it is more easily derived from B's
reading. This is far from certain and Tränkle (*Gnomon*, 379) points out
that *iuxta* occurs only twice as a preposition in L.—and then not in
a spatial sense. I prefer Lachmann's *cum caetratis*.

hastis positis . . . iubet : a famous mistake (cf. Walsh, *G & R*
v [1958], 84–5). Polybius said that they were to lower their spears for
the charge and L. took him to mean they were to put them down on
the ground. L. then added the alleged motivation for this action.

Pianezzola, 85–8, argues that the change was deliberate. He con-
nects it with 9. 3 where L. omits Polybius' mention of the superiority
of their armour as a reason for the temporary victory of the Macedonian right. He argues that L. was unwilling to admit that the
normal phalanx armour was superior, and held that the Macedonians were successful only because they were using their swords.
This is extremely implausible.

14. dimidium . . . duplicat : Philip is the subject, not *dimidium*
with *aciem* as the object, as W–M and McDonald say. Philip takes
half of the front of the phalanx and 'doubles' it—i.e. places it behind
the other half. L. found it difficult to express such technical details,
and it is unwise to emend. For *introrsus* in descriptions of this sort of
manœuvre cf. xxxii. 17. 8 n.

vir viro, arma armis : almost certainly influenced by Polybius'
quotation of Homer, *Il.* xiii. 131–3, xvi. 215–17 at xviii. 29. 6.
L. need not have had Vergil, *A.* x. 361 in mind, as claimed by
C. Brakman, *Mnemosyne* N.S. lv (1927), 54.

9. 1. Quinctius . . . signum : Pol. xviii. 24. 10: κατὰ δὲ τὸν αὐτὸν
καιρὸν καὶ Τίτος, δεξάμενος εἰς τὰ διαστήματα τῶν σημαιῶν τοὺς προ-
κινδυνεύοντας, προσέβαλε τοῖς πολεμίοις. L. uses the conventional *tuba
dat signum* which does not correspond to anything in Polybius.

inter signa et ordines : 'between the ranks'. For the phrase, cf.
Ogilvie, 384.

2. raro . . . veniebant : Pol. xviii. 25. 1: γενομένης δὲ τῆς ἐξ ἀμφοῖν συμπτώσεως μετὰ βίας καὶ κραυγῆς ὑπερβαλλούσης, ὡς ἂν ἀμφοτέρων ὁμοῦ συναλαλαζόντων, ἅμα δὲ καὶ τῶν ἐκτὸς τῆς μάχης ἐπιβοώντων τοῖς ἀγωνιζομένοις, ἦν τὸ γινόμενον ἐκπληκτικὸν καὶ παραστατικὸν ἀγωνίας. For L.'s fondness for emphasizing the uniqueness of important events cf. Bornecque, 144.

3. dextero . . . vincebat: abbreviated from Pol. xviii. 25. 2. L. omits the superiority of the formation and armour of the phalanx as reason for its initial success (cf. 8. 13 n.).

3–4. sinistro . . . intenta: Pol. xviii. 25. 3: τὰ δὲ λοιπὰ μέρη τῆς δυνάμεως αὐτῷ τὰ μὲν ἐχόμενα τῶν κινδυνευόντων ἐν ἀποστάσει τῶν πολεμίων ἦν, τὰ δ' ἐπὶ τῶν εὐωνύμων ἄρτι διηνυκότα τὰς ὑπερβολὰς ἐπεφαίνετο τοῖς ἄκροις. L. has been criticized (cf. W–M ad loc., Walsh, *Livy*, 161) for treating this battle as a conventional one with a left, a right, and a middle when in fact, because of the disorganization of the phalanx, it was not such. But the distortion is not all that great. There is certainly no proper middle but τὰ ἐχόμενα τῶν κινδυνευόντων are indeed between the left and the right (cf. Walbank, *Commentary*, ii. 583) and L. makes it abundantly clear that the left wing of the phalanx was still coming up the hill.

stabat . . . intenta: again giving the feelings of the troops rather than the plain fact as stated by Polybius.

5. Phalanx . . . evaserat: Pol. xviii. 25. 3, quoted above, and xviii. 25. 5: τὰ δ' ἐκ τῶν ἄκρων ἀκμὴν ἐπικαταβαίνοντα, τὰ δ' ἔτι τοῖς ἄκροις ἐφεστῶτα. *phalanx* here must mean that part of the phalanx which was still approaching. In a sense it was not a real phalanx until it was all there.

6. in hos . . . tracturam: Pol. xviii. 25. 4–5: ὁ δὲ Τίτος, θεωρῶν . . . ἐκπιεζουμένους τοὺς ἐπὶ τῶν εὐωνύμων, καὶ τοὺς μὲν ἀπολωλότας ἤδη, τοὺς δ' ἐπὶ πόδα ποιουμένους τὴν ἀναχώρησιν . . . προθέμενος τὰ θηρία προσῆγε τὰς σημαίας τοῖς πολεμίοις. L. omits Polybius' comments on what was possible, but adds Flamininus' hopes of what would follow.

dextro: Philip's right, but the Roman left. To avoid confusion L. continued to describe it from the Macedonian side. Emendation is therefore undesirable.

7. Non dubia . . . sequebantur: abbreviated from Pol. xviii. 25. 6–26. 1.

8. unus . . . invadit: Pol. xviii. 26. 2–3: εἷς δὲ τῶν χιλιάρχων τῶν ἅμα τούτοις σημαίας ἔχων οὐ πλείους εἴκοσι . . . ἀπολιπὼν τοὺς ἐπὶ τοῦ δεξιοῦ νικῶντας ἤδη καταφανῶς, ἐπιστρέψας ἐπὶ τοὺς ἀγωνιζομένους καὶ κατόπιν ἐπιγενόμενος προσέβαλλε κατὰ νώτου τοῖς Μακεδόσι. For this action, and the possibility that it was in fact inspired by

Flamininus and not taken on the tribune's own initiative cf. Walbank, *Commentary*, ii. 583–4.

ex tempore: B has *extemplo*, but the sense is weak and the *-o* repetition inelegant. Duker's *ex tempore* seems to be what is needed.

9–10. Nullam aciem . . . patiebantur: Pol. xviii. 26. 4–5: τῆς δὲ τῶν φαλαγγιτῶν χρείας ἀδυνάτου καθεστώσης ἐκ μεταβολῆς καὶ κατ' ἄνδρα κινδυνεύειν . . . συνεπιθεμένων αὐτοῖς ἐκ μεταβολῆς καὶ τῶν κατὰ πρόσωπον ἐγκεκλικότων. L. elaborates on the difficulties.

⟨**tre**⟩**pidationem**: B has *reparatiorem*. Between *trepidationem* and *desperationem* it is impossible to decide. Both are easy palaeographically and McDonald's parallels show nothing.

hoc: i.e. turn round. I see no oddity here, as alleged by Walsh, *CR*, 55 and no case for his emendation *hostes*.

11. ad hoc . . . circumducto: an addition by L., but one which shows that he had a perfectly clear idea of the nature of the battle.

paulisper . . . fugam: Pol. xviii. 26. 4–5: οὗτος μὲν ἐπέκειτο κτείνων τοὺς ἐν ποσίν, οὐ δυναμένους αὐτοῖς βοηθεῖν, ἕως οὗ ῥίψαντες τὰ ὅπλα φεύγειν ἠναγκάσθησαν οἱ Μακεδόνες.

omissis plerique armis: cf. xxxi. 3. 5 n.

10. 1–2. Philippus . . . excessit: Pol. xviii. 26. 7–8: τότε δὲ συνθεασάμενος ἄφνω ῥιπτοῦντας τὰ ὅπλα τοὺς Μακεδόνας . . . βραχὺ γενόμενος ἐκ τοῦ κινδύνου μετ' ὀλίγων ἱππέων καὶ πεζῶν συνεθεώρει τὰ ὅλα. κατανοήσας δὲ τοὺς Ῥωμαίους κατὰ τὸ δίωγμα τοῦ λαιοῦ κέρως τοῖς ἄκροις ἤδη προσπελάζοντας, ἐγίνετο ⟨πρὸς τὸ φεύγειν⟩. L. adds mention of the hillocks, but again it is an intelligent extension.

tum: thus B (corrected). It is perfectly clear that *signis atque armis* refers to the Romans, and Jacobs' *hostium* is not only unnecessary but undesirable: the position of *hostium* would be too emphatic.

3–4. Quinctius . . . habebat: Pol. xviii. 26. 9–11: Τίτος δὲ τοῖς φεύγουσιν ἑπόμενος . . . ἐπέστη, τῶν πολεμίων ὀρθὰς ἀνασχόντων τὰς σαρίσας, ὅπερ ἔθος ἐστὶ ποιεῖν τοῖς Μακεδόσιν, ὅταν ἢ παραδιδῶσιν αὑτοὺς ἢ μεταβάλλωνται πρὸς τοὺς ὑπεναντίους· μετὰ δὲ ταῦτα πυθόμενος τὴν αἰτίαν τοῦ συμβαίνοντος παρακατεῖχε τοὺς μεθ' αὑτοῦ φείσασθαι κρίνων τῶν ἀποδεδειλιακότων.

novitate: the change from B's *novitatem* is extremely simple, as B regularly abbreviates *-m* endings. For *novitate rei* cf. iv. 14. 1.

5. ceterum . . . dissipati sunt: Pol. xviii. 26. 12: ἀκμὴν δὲ τοῦ Τίτου ταῦτα διανοουμένου τῶν προηγουμένων τινὲς ἐπιπεσόντες αὐτοῖς ἐξ ὑπερδεξίου προσέφερον τὰς χεῖρας, καὶ τοὺς μὲν πλείους διέφθειρον, ὀλίγοι δέ τινες διέφυγον ῥίψαντες τὰ ὅπλα. For Polybius the majority are killed, for L. only the first ones. This is probably a deliberate suppression of Roman brutality. Cf. § 6 and Walsh, *Livy*, 152.

6. Rex . . . petit: Pol. xviii. 27. 1: παντᾳχόθεν δὲ τοῦ κινδύνου συντέλειαν εἰληφότος καὶ κρατούντων τῶν Ῥωμαίων, ὁ μὲν Φίλιππος ἐποιεῖτο τὴν ἀποχώρησιν ὡς ἐπὶ τὰ Τέμπη. L. exaggerates the head-long nature of the flight. Similar language is used after the Aous battle (xxxii. 12. 8). On Tempe cf. xxxii. 15. 9 n.

ibi . . . superessent: Pol. xviii. 27. 2: καὶ τῇ μὲν πρώτῃ περὶ τὸν Ἀλεξάνδρου καλούμενον πύργον ηὐλίσθη, τῇ δ᾽ ὑστεραίᾳ προελθὼν εἰς Γόννους ἐπὶ τὴν εἰσβολὴν τῶν Τεμπῶν ἐπέμεινε, βουλόμενος ἀναδέξασθαι τοὺς ἐκ τῆς φυγῆς ἀνασῳζομένους. L. omits the stop at the Tower of Alexander and the fact that the stop at Gonni was on the next day.

Gonnos: on the site of Gonni cf. Walbank, *Commentary*, ii. 584, P-K, i. 1. 111.

Romani victores . . . inveniunt: Pol. xviii. 27. 3–4: οἱ δὲ Ῥωμαῖοι . . . οἱ δὲ πλείους ὥρμησαν ἐπὶ τὴν διαρπαγὴν τοῦ τῶν πολεμίων χάρακος. ἔνθα δὴ καταλαβόντες τοὺς Αἰτωλοὺς προεμπεπτωκότας καὶ δόξαντες στέρεσθαι τῆς σφίσι καθηκούσης ὠφελείας, ἤρξαντο κατα-μέμφεσθαι τοὺς Αἰτωλοὺς καὶ λέγειν πρὸς τὸν στρατηγὸν ὅτι τοὺς μὲν κινδύνους αὐτοῖς ἐπιτάττει, τῆς δ᾽ ὠφελείας ἄλλοις παρακεχώρηκε. A significant change by L. In Polybius the Romans are deprived of their chance of loot, and then express their anger at the Aetolians. Cf. Walsh, *Livy*, 152.

⟨**inrumpunt**⟩: B has a gap. Ogilvie, *Phoenix*, 346 says that *inrumpunt* is too short for the gap. But the gaps left by B are only an approximation for words that the scribe could not read in F. We are not supplementing a papyrus.

7. Caesa . . . ceciderunt: Pol. xviii. 27. 6: ἔπεσον δὲ τῶν Ῥωμαίων πρὸς τοὺς ἑπτακοσίους· τῶν δὲ Μακεδόνων ἀπέθανον μὲν οἱ πάντες εἰς ὀκτακισχιλίους, ζωγρίᾳ δ᾽ ἑάλωσαν οὐκ ἐλάττους πεντακισχιλίων.

8. Si Valerio qui credat: cf. xxxii. 6. 5 n. On Valerius Antias' exaggeration of figures cf. p. 11.

9. Claudius: for the fragments of Q. Claudius Quadrigarius cf. *HRR* i². 205 ff. On him cf. Peter, *HRR* i². cclxxxv ff., Zimmerer, *Qu. Claudius Quadrigarius* (Munich, 1937), Badian, *Latin Historians*, 18 ff.

10. Polybium . . . gestarum: for the significance of this remark cf. p. 10.

11–13. *The negotiations after Cynoscephalae*

Cf. Pol. xviii. 33–9, Plut. *Flam.* 9, App. *Mac.* 9. 1–2, Dio fr. 60.

At this point Polybius inserts his famous digression on the legion and the phalanx (xviii. 28–32) which L. omits entirely (though cf. 8. 14 n.).

11. The problems of this chapter were discussed by Holleaux in

Études, v. 86–103. Between xviii. 33. 8 and 34. 1 there is a lacuna in Polybius. The sending of a *caduceator* by Philip (§ 3) is not found in what survives of Polybius. L., on the other hand, has no mention of the meeting of Flamininus with the three ambassadors sent by Philip, described by Polybius in xviii. 34. 4–5. Holleaux showed that L. cannot have distorted the latter into the former and that the *caduceator* episode must have occurred in the lacuna in Polybius. Holleaux then proceeds to argue that L. has created a major distortion of Polybius' account of the origin of the quarrel between Flamininus and the Aetolians. He alleges that while Polybius had seen the origin in the welcome given by Flamininus to the Macedonian herald, for L. it arises from Flamininus' justified aloofness towards the Aetolians after the battle of Cynoscephalae. When L. reports Flamininus' reasons for his attitude (§§ 8–9), he does it in the wrong place.

This analysis appears to me to be mistaken. Polybius' account of Flamininus' motives for annoyance with the Aetolians probably occurred in the context of his explanation of Aetolian annoyance after the reception of the *caduceator* (cf. Holleaux, 96–8). Polybius will have said that the Aetolians were annoyed with Flamininus because of his aloof attitude, of which his conversation with the herald without consulting the Aetolians was an example. Flamininus had been acting like this (a) because he did not want to let the Aetolians become too powerful, (b) because of his dislike of Aetolian greed and boastfulness.

L., by omitting the ambassadors, combines the two stages of Aetolian hostility (cf. Pol. xviii. 34. 6 διπλασίως ἐξεκάετο τὰ τῆς ὑποψίας). His narrative then says: the Aetolians were already annoyed with Flamininus before the herald's visit, after it they were even more annoyed. They were upset at Flamininus' new attitude and thought he was being bribed. Flamininus' reasons are then given. This is merely stylistic variation, not distortion.

What, then, of L.'s omission of the ambassadors? Holleaux (100) argued that this was because L. wanted to omit Flamininus' failure to consult his allies. This could be so, and would have parallels in L.'s treatment of the conference of Nicaea. But it may be that L. simply thought the meeting, which merely agreed on a fifteen-day truce (12. 1), was not of great importance.

11. 1. Philippus . . . concessit: Pol. xviii. 33. 1–2: Φίλιππος δέ, . . . ἀναδεξάμενος ὅσους ἐδύνατο πλείστους τῶν ἐκ τῆς μάχης ἀνασῳζομένων, αὐτὸς μὲν ὥρμησε διὰ τῶν Τεμπῶν εἰς Μακεδονίαν. εἰς δὲ τὴν Λάρισαν ἔτι τῇ προτεραίᾳ νυκτὶ διεπέμψατό τινα τῶν ὑπασπιστῶν, ἐντειλάμενος ἀφανίσαι καὶ κατακαῦσαι τὰ βασιλικὰ γράμματα. Polybius then digresses on Philip's presence of mind in burning the records (xviii. 33. 3–7).

2. Quinctius . . . pararet: Pol. xviii. 33. 8: *Τίτος δὲ μετὰ τὴν μάχην ποιησάμενος τὴν καθήκουσαν πρόνοιαν περί τε τῶν αἰχμαλώτων καὶ τῶν ἄλλων λαφύρων, ᾔει πρὸς Λάρισαν.* L.'s specification of the details of the division is due to his knowledge of the normal procedure, on which cf. P. Fraccaro, *Opuscula*, i (Pavia, 1956), 367 ff., Scullard, *RP*, 292–3, Vogel, *RE*, xxii. 1200–13.

partim: the supplement is far better here (Madvig) than after *venumdatis* (Hertz). A chiastic construction would not be expected in this sort of straightforward narrative.

3. caduceator: cf. xxxi. 38. 9 n.

sepulturam . . . cecidissent: the dead of Cynoscephalae were not in fact buried now, and the burial was eventually carried out at the instance of Antiochus in 192 (xxxvi. 8. 3–5, App. *Syr.* 16, Holleaux, *Études*, v. 92). But that is no reason to distrust L.'s account of the herald's request. As L. makes clear, it was not the real purpose of his mission (cf. Holleaux, *Études*, v. 92–3).

5. ante pugnam . . . agere: Pol. xviii. 34. 3: *διὸ καὶ κατά τε τὰς ἐντεύξεις ἀγερωχότερον αὐτοῖς ἀπήντα καὶ περὶ τῶν κοινῶν ἀπεσιώπα, τὰ δὲ προκείμενα συνετέλει καὶ δι᾽ αὐτοῦ καὶ διὰ τῶν ἰδίων φίλων.* L. adds that before the battle Flamininus consulted the Aetolians in all matters (cf. Holleaux, *Études*, v. 97 n. 2) but that does no more than bring out the implications of Polybius' statement. In any case, a more detailed account of Aetolian complaints may have occurred in the lacuna in Polybius. L. tones down Polybius' *ἀγερωχότερον*.

6. cum Philippo . . . vertat: this too could have stood in the lacuna. It is not likely to be an adaptation of Roman complaints in Pol. xviii. 27. 4, omitted by L. (cf. 10. 6 n.).

7. donis . . . virum: cf. Pol. xviii. 34. 7 ff. Polybius (xviii. 35) then digresses on Roman incorruptibility.

invicti . . . animi: for the phrase cf. xxii. 15. 1, 26. 7, xxxix. 40. 10, Sall. *BJ* 43. 5, Skard, 25.

8. sed et . . . offendebat: Pol. xviii. 34. 1: *καθόλου τῇ περὶ τὰ λάφυρα πλεονεξίᾳ τῶν Αἰτωλῶν . . . δυσχερῶς δ᾽ ἔφερε καὶ τὴν ἀλαζονείαν αὐτῶν, θεωρῶν ἀντεπιγραφομένους ἐπὶ τὸ νίκημα καὶ πληροῦντας τὴν Ἑλλάδα τῆς αὐτῶν ἀνδραγαθίας.* For the justification of the Aetolian claims concerning Cynoscephalae cf. Walbank, *Commentary*, ii. 593 and 3. 9 n.

9. et Philippo . . . cernebat: Pol. xviii. 34. 1: *εἴτ᾽ οὐκ ἐβούλετο*

Φίλιππον ἐκβαλὼν ἐκ τῆς ἀρχῆς Αἰτωλοὺς καταλιπεῖν δεσπότας τῶν
Ἑλλήνων. Cf. App. *Mac.* 9. 1, Dio fr. 60. *Philippo sublato* in itself
could mean 'removed from Greece' but the language of Polybius
here, and the later arguments, make it clear that Polybius was
talking about the removal of Philip from the throne of Macedon
(cf. Holleaux, *Études*, v. 97 n. 4) and there is no reason to think that
L. has misunderstood him.

12. On L.'s adaptation of Polybius in this chapter cf. Witte, 296–9.

12. 1. indutiae . . . conloquium: Pol. xviii. 34. 5: πεντεκαιδεχ-
ημέρους ἀνοχὰς ἐποιήσατο παραχρῆμα, συνετάξατο δὲ καὶ συμπορεύεσθαι
τῷ Φιλίππῳ κοινολογησόμενος ὑπὲρ τῶν καθεστώτων ἐν ταύταις, and
xviii. 36. 1: ὁ δὲ Τίτος ταξάμενος ἡμέραν πρὸς τὸν Φίλιππον. Placed
here because of L.'s omission of the visit of the three Macedonian
ambassadors.

cuius . . . dici: Pol. xviii. 36. 1–2: τοῖς μὲν συμμάχοις ἔγραψε
παραχρῆμα, διασαφῶν πότε δεήσει παρεῖναι πρὸς τὸν σύλλογον . . .
ἀναστὰς ὁ τῶν Ῥωμαίων στρατηγὸς ἐκέλευε λέγειν ἕκαστον ἐφ᾽ οἷς
δεῖ ποιεῖσθαι τὰς πρὸς τὸν Φίλιππον διαλύσεις.

consilium: Polybius refers to a σύλλογος both here and in 38. 1.
Both the latter meeting and this one are referred to as a *concilium* in
13. 1–2, and it would perhaps be better to read *concilium* here.
Strictly speaking *concilium* is the actual meeting, *consilium* the ab-
stract 'taking of advice', though the latter was often used in the
former sense. There is certainly no case for reading *consilium* at 13. 1.

rettulit: L. uses the language of Roman senatorial debate.

2. Amynander . . . esset: Pol. xviii. 36. 3–4: Ἀμύνανδρος μὲν
οὖν ὁ βασιλεὺς βραχέα διαλεχθεὶς καὶ μέτρια κατέπαυσε τὸν λόγον·
ἠξίου γὰρ πρόνοιαν αὐτοῦ ποιήσασθαι πάντας, ἵνα μὴ χωρισθέντων
Ῥωμαίων ἐκ τῆς Ἑλλάδος εἰς ἐκεῖνον ἀπερείδηται τὴν ὀργὴν ὁ Φίλιππος.
L. generalizes Amynander's request and omits his subsequent
reference to his country's particular difficulties. It is clear from his
speech that the Greeks assumed, or wished it to appear that they
assumed, that Roman forces would leave Greece after a settlement
had been reached.

On Amynander cf. xxxi. 28. 1 n.

paucis . . . absolvit: the phrase is common in Sallust, but otherwise found only in Pacuvius (cf. *TLL*, i. 177, Skard, 72).

tuendae: B has *tu dae*. There is a hole in the page between *tu* and
dae but the adjoining lines and the reverse side of the page show that
this was there before the codex was written, so that *tuendae* cannot
have stood in B.

3–4. Aetolorum . . . vellet: cf. Pol. xviii. 36. 5–8. L. has shortened

Polybius' version but has retained the main points. He omits the name of the speaker (cf. p. 18 n. 5) and Polybius' references to Rome's policy and Flamininus' promises. He adds, however, the possibility of killing Philip.

asperior: there is nothing to correspond to this in Polybius, but it is the opposite of μέτρια which Polybius uses to describe Amynander's contribution—a word which is not taken up by L.

aiunt: Madvig. B has *autem*, which is explained by W–M either as an anacoluthon or by understanding *dixerunt* after *praefati* and taking *recte . . . consilia* and the *autem* clause as the two parts of the speech proper. But *recte . . . consilia* is clearly in apposition to *pauca*. The only other possibility would be to understand *sunt* with *praefati* (which would be highly unusual in a relative clause) and let the *autem* clause be governed by a *dixerunt* understood from *praefati*. But in that case there would be no contrast between the *praefatio* and the rest of the speech. Madvig's emendation seems the right answer.

5–6. ad haec . . . disseruisse: Pol. xviii. 37. 1 ὁ δὲ Τίτος ἀναδεξάμενος ἀστοχεῖν αὐτὸν ἔφησεν οὐ μόνον τῆς ῾Ρωμαίων προαιρέσεως, ἀλλὰ καὶ τῆς αὐτοῦ προθέσεως καὶ μάλιστα τοῦ τῶν ῾Ελλήνων συμφέροντος, and xviii. 37. 4–5: καὶ μὴν οὐδ᾽ αὐτὸς οὐδέποτε ταύτην ἐσχηκέναι τὴν αἵρεσιν, ὅτι δεῖ πολεμεῖν πρὸς τὸν Φίλιππον ἀδιαλύτως· ἀλλ᾽ εἴπερ ἐβουλήθη ποιεῖν τὰ παρακαλούμενα πρὸ τῆς μάχης, ἑτοίμως ἂν διαλελύσθαι πρὸς αὐτόν. διὸ καὶ θαυμάζειν ἔφη πῶς μετέχοντες τότε τῶν περὶ τῆς διαλύσεως συλλόγων ἅπαντες νῦν ἀκαταλλάκτως ἔχουσιν. The content of § 6 makes it clear that *sibi ipsis convenientem* must mean 'a view inconsistent with their own earlier position' and not 'a view against their own interests'. Thus it cannot represent Polybius' τοῦ τῶν ῾Ελλήνων συμφέροντος and it is unclear whether L. has mistakenly taken αὐτοῦ to refer to the Aetolian speaker rather than to Flamininus himself, or is elaborating on what Polybius says in xviii. 37. 5.

[et] . . . ⟨non⟩: both the deletion of *et* and the insertion of *non* are necessary for the sense.

7. et Romanos . . . data: Pol. xviii. 37. 2–3: οὔτε γὰρ ῾Ρωμαίους οὐδενὶ τὸ πρῶτον πολεμήσαντας εὐθέως ἀναστάτους ποιεῖν τούτους· πίστιν δ᾽ ἔχειν τὸ λεγόμενον ἐκ τῶν κατ᾽ Ἀννίβαν καὶ Καρχηδονίους. For the theme cf. xxxi. 31. 15 n. It is so common that there is no need to think that L. is consciously thinking of Virgil's *parcere subiectis et debellare superbos* (*A.* vi. 853).

8. omittere se Carthaginienses: L. himself is responsible for the rhetorical *omissio*.

cum Philippo . . . actum esse: Pol. xviii. 37. 4 (quoted above).

an quia . . . factum: Pol. xviii. 37. 6: ἢ δῆλον ὅτι νενικήκαμεν; ἀλλὰ τοῦτό γ᾽ ἐστὶ πάντων ἀγνωμονέστατον.

9. cum armato . . . habere: Pol. xviii. 37. 7: πολεμοῦντας γὰρ δεῖ τοὺς ἀγαθοὺς ἄνδρας βαρεῖς εἶναι καὶ θυμικούς, ἡττωμένους δὲ γενναίους καὶ μεγαλόφρονας, νικῶντάς γε μὴν μετρίους καὶ πραεῖς καὶ φιλανθρώπους.

adversus . . . habere: 'towards the defeated it is the most merciful who show the greatest spirit'. Emendation is unnecessary.

10–11. libertati . . . facerent: Pol. xviii. 37. 8–9: ἀλλὰ μὴν καὶ τοῖς Ἕλλησι ταπεινωθῆναι μὲν ἐπὶ πολὺ συμφέρει τὴν Μακεδόνων ἀρχήν, ἀρθῆναί γε μὴν οὐδαμῶς. τάχα γὰρ αὐτοὺς πεῖραν λήψεσθαι τῆς Θρᾳκῶν καὶ Γαλατῶν παρανομίας· τοῦτο γὰρ ἤδη καὶ πλεονάκις γεγονέναι. L. inappropriately adds the Illyrians. Much of Illyria was in Rome's alliance, the rest was in Philip's possession. Some Thracians and Illyrians were fighting on Philip's side (cf. 4. 4, 7. 11 n.). Cf. Holleaux, *CAH*, viii. 177 n. 1, though I cannot see why Holleaux calls the Thracians Roman allies. On the Gallic incursions into Greece *c*. 280 cf. Walbank, *Commentary*, i. 49–51. For the argument cf. Pol. ix. 35. 3–4, for Philip's claims to be protecting Cius from Thracians cf. xxxii. 34. 6 n. The reasons adduced here are not his real ones—in fact he wanted to maintain a balance of power in Greece: the truth is given in 11. 9 (cf. Holleaux, l.c.).

L. now omits Flamininus' statement (Pol. xviii. 37. 10) that he will make peace if Philip will agree to the terms offered earlier, but if the Aetolians want to remain at war, that is up to them.

12–13. interfanti . . . possit: Pol. xviii. 37. 11–12: τοῦ δὲ Φαινέου μετὰ ταῦτα βουλομένου λέγειν ὅτι μάταια πάντα τὰ πρὸ τοῦ γέγονε· τὸν γὰρ Φίλιππον, ἐὰν διολίσθῃ τὸν παρόντα καιρόν, ἤδη πάλιν ἀρχὴν ἄλλην ποιήσεσθαι πραγμάτων· ὁ Τίτος αὐτόθεν ἐξ ἕδρας καὶ θυμικῶς "Παῦσαι" φησὶ "Φαινέα, ληρῶν. ἐγὼ γὰρ οὕτως χειριῶ τὰς διαλύσεις ὥστε μηδὲ βουληθέντα τὸν Φίλιππον ἀδικεῖν δύνασθαι τοὺς Ἕλληνας." For Polybius it is Flamininus who interrupts Phaeneas, for L. vice versa.

interfanti: cf. xxxii. 34. 2 n.

Phaeneae: cf. xxxii. 32. 11 n.

desistite: B has *desistit et*. Walsh, *CR*, 55 suggests *desiste tu. tu tumultuari* could easily be corrupted (though the change to *desistite* is simpler) but *tu tumultuari* is a jingle which it would not be wise to import into the text. The plural, addressed to the Aetolian delegation as a whole, is perfectly natural.

non iis . . . possit: B has *pax* which is not a possible subject for *inligabitur*. The sentence is an odd way of saying 'he will be bound by such conditions that he will not be able to wage war'.

13. 1–2. Hoc . . . concilium: Pol. xviii. 38. 1: καὶ τότε μὲν ἐπὶ τούτοις ἐχωρίσθησαν. τῇ δ' ὑστεραίᾳ παραγενομένου τοῦ βασιλέως,

καὶ τῇ τρίτῃ πάντων εἰς τὸν σύλλογον ἀθροισθέντων. Polybius had mentioned the venue in connection with the meeting of Flamininus with
the allies (xviii. 36. 1).

    concilio: cf. 12. 1 n.

    Tempe: cf. xxxii. 15. 9 n.

    tertio die: i.e. two days after the conference of Flamininus and
the allies.

3–4. ibi . . . dixit: Pol. xviii. 38. 1–2: εἰσελθὼν ὁ Φίλιππος . . . ἔφη
γὰρ τὰ μὲν πρότερον ὑπὸ ῾Ρωμαίων καὶ τῶν συμμάχων ἐπιταττόμενα πάντα
συγχωρεῖν καὶ ποιήσειν, περὶ δὲ τῶν λοιπῶν διδόναι τῇ συγκλήτῳ τὴν
ἐπιτροπήν. L. elaborates on Philip's motives.

    potius . . . quam . . . extorquerentur: equivalent to *ne
extorquerentur*. Cf. K–St, ii. 300–1, H–S, 594.

5. Quamquam . . . tacentibus: a neat combination of Pol.
xviii. 38. 1: εὐστόχως καὶ συνετῶς ὑπετέμετο τὰς πάντων ὁρμάς and
xviii. 38. 3: τούτων δὲ ῥηθέντων οἱ μὲν ἄλλοι πάντες ἀπεσιώπησαν, ὁ δὲ
τῶν Αἰτωλῶν Φαινέας.

6. Quid . . . Phthias: Pol. xviii. 38. 3: "Τί οὖν ἡμῖν οὐκ ἀποδίδως,
Φίλιππε", ἔφη, "Λάρισαν τὴν Κρεμαστήν, Φάρσαλον, Θήβας τὰς Φθίας,
Ἐχῖνον"; On the history of these towns cf. xxx. 1. 9–10 n.

    Phthias: B has the spelling *Pthias* here (cf. xxxii. 33. 16 n.).

7. cum Philippus . . . Thebis: Pol. xviii. 38. 4: ὁ μὲν οὖν
Φίλιππος ἐκέλευε παραλαμβάνειν αὐτούς, ὁ δὲ Τίτος τῶν μὲν ἄλλων οὐκ
ἔφη δεῖν οὐδεμίαν, Θήβας δὲ μόνον τὰς Φθίας. L. appears to have completely misunderstood this. Flamininus allowed the Aetolian claim
to Thebes, but rejected it in respect of Larisa Cremaste, Echinus, and
Pharsalus. In this sentence L. appears to reverse the situation.
McDonald argues that emendation is wrong as L.'s account, though
mistaken, is self-consistent. This is hardly the case, for in §§ 7–8 L.
appears to imply that Flamininus is refusing to grant Thebes to
Aetolia but accepts their claim to the other towns, whilst §§ 8–12
represent what Polybius says accurately enough, and carry the
implication that Flamininus' refusal applied to all the towns. L. may
simply have been confused by the complexities of the situation, but
it is possible that there is a lacuna in the text. The argument of Flurl
(109–10) that the change is deliberate, and designed to make sense
of the distinction between Thebes and the other cities, is absurd.

8. nam eas . . . praeposuissent: Pol. xviii. 38. 5: Θηβαίους γὰρ
ἐγγίσαντος αὐτοῦ μετὰ τῆς δυνάμεως καὶ παρακαλοῦντος σφᾶς εἰς τὴν
῾Ρωμαίων πίστιν οὐ βουληθῆναι· διὸ νῦν, κατὰ πόλεμον ὑποχειρίων
ὄντων, ἔχειν ἐξουσίαν ἔφη βουλεύεσθαι περὶ αὐτῶν ὡς ἂν προαιρῆται. For
the attempt on Phthiotic Thebes cf. 5. 1–3. In fact all four towns had

probably come into Roman control in the same way—as a result of Philip's defeat at the battle of Cynoscephalae. All except Thebes, no doubt, had made a *deditio* to Rome, though it was scarcely a voluntary one. Flamininus, however, chooses to regard Thebes as being in a separate category because it had made a previous positive resistance. In fact it lay in his power, by virtue of the *deditio*, to grant the other three towns also to Aetolia if he had so chosen.

9–12. Phaeneas . . . venerunt: Pol. xviii. 38. 6–9: τῶν δὲ περὶ τὸν Φαινέαν ἀγανακτούντων, καὶ λεγόντων ὅτι δέον αὐτοὺς εἴη, πρῶτον μέν, καθότι συνεπολέμησαν νῦν, κομίζεσθαι τὰς πόλεις τὰς πρότερον μεθ' αὐτῶν συμπολιτευομένας, ἔπειτα κατὰ τὴν ἐξ ἀρχῆς συμμαχίαν, καθ' ἣν ἔδει τῶν κατὰ πόλεμον ἑλόντων τὰ μὲν ἔπιπλα Ῥωμαίων εἶναι, τὰς δὲ πόλεις Αἰτωλῶν, ὁ Τίτος ἀγνοεῖν αὐτοὺς ἔφη κατ' ἀμφότερα. τήν τε γὰρ συμμαχίαν λελύσθαι, καθ' ὃν καιρὸν τὰς διαλύσεις ἐποιήσαντο πρὸς Φίλιππον ἐγκαταλείποντες Ῥωμαίοις, εἴ τε καὶ μένειν ἔτι τὴν συμμαχίαν, δεῖν αὐτοὺς κομίζεσθαι καὶ παραλαμβάνειν, οὐκ εἴ τινες ἐθελοντὴν σφᾶς εἰς τὴν Ῥωμαίων πίστιν ἐνεχείρισαν, ὅπερ αἱ κατὰ Θετταλίαν πόλεις ἅπασαι πεποιήκασι νῦν, ἀλλ' εἴ τινες κατὰ κράτος ἑάλωσαν. On the serious difficulties raised by this section, or rather by Polybius' account, see the literature cited in *StV*, iii. no. 536, to which add: Walbank, *JRS* lviii (1968), 253–4, Badian, *HZ* ccviii (1969), 637 ff., *Flamininus*, 48 ff., Deininger, *Gnomon* xlii (1970), 65 ff., J. Muylle, *AC* xxxviii (1969), 408–29. Flurl, 107 ff. does not discuss the inscription in his treatment of the passage. A full discussion of the issue is out of place here, and the following comments are merely a brief statement of my own position.

The Aetolians made two points—(a) they were entitled to the towns as a moral right because of their part in the war, (b) they were entitled to them by the terms of the earlier treaty. Flamininus ignores (a) and makes a double reply to (b)—(i) the treaty is no longer in force; (ii) even if it were the Aetolian claim would not be justified. (i) is the strong point. The Romans regarded the Aetolians as having abandoned their alliance by their separate peace with Philip in 206 (cf. xxxi. 1. 8 n. Badian's attempt to deny that the treaty was no longer operative [*Flamininus*, 50 ff.] is quite unconvincing). No formal treaty had been made when the Aetolians rejoined Rome in 199. Controversy centres on (ii). As long as the Livian text of the treaty (xxvi. 24) was all we possessed, Flamininus' claim seemed to be quite unjustified. But the inscription recording the treaty (*StV*, iii. 536) has a last clause which could be restored in such a way that it would give states that surrendered to Rome of their own accord the choice of whether or not to join the Aetolian League (cf. McDonald, *JRS* xlvi [1956], 155). Walbank, *Commentary*, ii. 598–601, objects to this on the grounds that Polybius' citation of the clause about booty would have to be Polybius' own comment, not part of Phaeneas' speech, for Phaeneas would not have cited the clause which did not cover the claim. But Phaeneas could well have thought that the *deditio* of the towns of Phthiotic Achaea, being made after Cynoscephalae, was not a genuine *deditio*—as we know from the events of 191, he did not fully grasp what the Romans meant by *deditio*—and that the Aetolian claim was therefore justified under the terms of the original treaty. But in any case Phaeneas may have been well aware that Rome regarded the treaty as no longer operative, and was only making debating points.

9. ante bellum: a misleading phrase. It was not the case that Aetolia held these towns when the war began. Cf. xxxi. 1. 9–10 n.

10. belli praeda . . . Romanos: cf. xxvi. 24. 11. The inscription adds that if a town were captured jointly by Rome and Aetolia, the booty is to be divided. It is presumably taken for granted that if the Aetolians alone are responsible for the capture, they keep all the booty.

11. 'Vos' inquit 'ipsi' Quinctius: on this word-order cf. G. W. Williams, *Tradition and Originality in Roman Poetry* (Oxford, 1968), 715.

13. Haec . . . fuerunt: Pol. xviii. 39. 1–2: τοῖς μὲν οὖν ἄλλοις ὁ Τίτος ἤρεσκε ταῦτα λέγων, οἱ δ' Αἰτωλοὶ βαρέως ἤκουον καί τις οἷον ἀρχὴ κακῶν ἐγεννᾶτο μεγάλων· ἐκ γὰρ ταύτης τῆς διαφορᾶς καὶ τούτου τοῦ σπινθῆρος μετ' ὀλίγον ὅ τε πρὸς Αἰτωλοὺς ὅ τε πρὸς Ἀντίοχον ἐξεκαύθη πόλεμος. This was the origin of the quarrel that led to the Aetolians inviting Antiochus to invade Greece in 192. Polybius is specific, L. leaves his readers to understand what is meant.

14. cum Philippo . . . essent: Pol. xviii. 39. 5: διὸ συνεχωρήθη τῷ βασιλεῖ, καθάπερ ἠξίου, λαβόντα τετραμμένους ἀνοχὰς παραχρῆμα μὲν δοῦναι τῷ Τίτῳ τὰ διακόσια τάλαντα καὶ Δημήτριον τὸν υἱὸν εἰς ὁμηρείαν καί τινας ἑτέρους τῶν φίλων, περὶ δὲ τῶν ὅλων πέμπειν εἰς τὴν Ῥώμην καὶ διδόναι τῇ συγκλήτῳ τὴν ἐπιτροπήν.

Demetrium . . . obsides: cf. Walbank, *Commentary*, ii. 601. It would appear that pending ratification of the peace by senate and people in Rome, the hostages remained in Greece. For Demetrius' release in 191 cf. xxxvi. 35. 13, Pol. xxi. 3; for the events leading to his death cf. pp. 23–4.

amicorum: cf. xxxi. 28. 5 n.

ducenta talenta: Polybius has τὰ διακόσια τάλαντα but there has been no previous mention of this money and Schweighäuser was right to suspect that the article should be deleted.

15. Si pax . . . receptum est: Pol. xviii. 39. 6: ἐὰν μὴ συντελῆται

τὰ κατὰ τὰς διαλύσεις, ἀποδοῦναι Φιλίππῳ τὰ διακόσια τάλαντα καὶ τοὺς
ὁμήρους.

causa . . . constabat: Pol. xviii. 39. 3: τὸ δὲ συνέχον ἦν τῆς
ὁρμῆς τῆς τοῦ Τίτου πρὸς τὰς διαλύσεις, ἐπυνθάνετο τὸν Ἀντίοχον ἀπὸ
Συρίας ἀνῆχθαι μετὰ δυνάμεως, ποιούμενον τὴν ὁρμὴν ἐπὶ τὴν Εὐρώπην.
L. omits Polybius' further statement that Flamininus was afraid
that Philip would try to hold out until Antiochus would help him
and that another commander would be appointed to succeed him.
On the ascription of the selfish motive by Polybius cf. pp. 26–7, on
Antiochus' advances 19. 6 ff. and nn.

14–15. *The Achaean victory over Androsthenes*

Cf. Zon. ix. 16. 11. For the Roman attack on Corinth in 198 cf.
xxxii. 23; for the attempt by Flamininus to persuade Philocles to
betray the city, xxxii. 40. 5–6. On these events cf. Aymard, *PR*,
164 ff.

14. 1. ut quidam tradidere, eodem die: the authorities involved
are uncertain. They are probably not Roman annalists, who would
not have mentioned this purely Greek incident. They may have
been mentioned by Polybius himself (cf. Klotz, *Livius*, 94: *contra*
Nissen, *KU*, 141).

The exact synchronism of two battles which fell in the same year
as part of the same war is an old motif and is highly suspect.
Cf. Salamis and Himera in 480 (Hdt. vii. 166. 1), Plataea and Mycale
in 479 (Hdt. ix. 90). For such synchronisms cf. Bengtson, *Griechische
Geschichte*4 (Munich, 1969), 185 n. 2.

Androsthenem: cf. xxxii. 23. 5 n. Philocles, described as *praefectus
urbis* at xxxii. 40. 5, had probably returned to Chalcis (Walbank,
Philip V, 175 n. 2).

2. pro arce . . . civitates: it was one of the 'fetters of Greece': cf.
xxxii. 37. 3.

et principes: co-ordinate with the *et praeter* clause (§ 3).

4. mille ac ducentos: Kreyssig's alteration to *mille octingentos* is
quite unnecessary.

qui . . . militabant: L. is referring to this particular engage-
ment, not to the war as a whole. For Thracians in the Achaean army
cf. 15. 6, 13. For Illyrians, Thracians, and Cretans in Philip's army
at other times cf. 4. 4, 18. 9, xxxi. 35. 1; for Cretans and Illyrians
in the Roman army 3. 10 n.

5. Boeoti: cf. xxxii. 17. 3 n.
Thessali: cf. xxxii. 10. 7 n.
Acarnanes: cf. xxxi. 14. 7 n.

These are all contingents of Macedonian allies, not mercenaries (Launey, i. 204, Klaffenbach, *IG* ix. 1². 2. p. xxvi).

⟨**septingenti ex**⟩: evidently a number has dropped out and this generally accepted supplement is arrived at by deducting the numbers already mentioned from the total of 6,000. For the comparatively rare use of *implere* meaning 'to make up a number' cf. *TLL*, vii. i. 635.

6. Nicostratus: cf. xxxii. 39. 7 n.

duobus . . . equitibus: perhaps all mercenaries; cf. Aymard, *PR*, 166 n. 25.

7. Pellenensem: on Pellene cf. xxxii. 22. 5 n.

Phliasium: Phlius is about 14 miles south-west of Corinth. On it cf. Meyer, *RE*, xx. 269–90, P–K, iii. 1. 159.

Cleonaeum: Cleonae is a little to the east of Phlius. Cf. Bölte, *RE*, xi. 721–8, P–K, iii. 1. 91.

8. circumvecti: along the north coast of the Peloponnese. *Circumvehi* is used for both παραπλεῖν and περιπλεῖν.

10. nuntium . . . quo die et quot: sc. *ut nuntiaret*.

Apelaurum—Stymphaliae: Stymphalus is about 11 miles west of Phlius. Apelaurum is a mountain to the south-east of the town. Cf. Pol. iv. 69. 1, Walbank, *Commentary*, i. 523, P–K, iii. 1. 232.

12. †armaturae levis: evidently a numeral has dropped out before *armaturae*.

15. 1. Nemeam . . . agrum: the stream, mod. Kutsomodi, flowing to the gulf of Corinth between Nemea and Sicyon. It is called ἡ Νεμεὰς χαράδρα or simply ἡ Νεμέα. Cf. Meyer, *RE*, xvi. 2322, P–K, iii. 1. 159.

2. ibi partem . . . divisit: B has *parte dimidia exercitus dimissa dimidiam trifariam divisit* (the last word corrected from *dimsit*). It is clear, however, from § 3 and the context as a whole that the part of the army that was *dimissa* was also the part that was *divisa*. Hence Madvig (*Emendationes*, 485–6) read *partem dimidiam exercitus dimissam, divisam trifariam* . . . McDonald (anticipated by Walker, *Supplementary Annotations*, 196) keeps *divisit* as a parenthesis. This certainly explains B's text better, but Madvig's solution is smoother and, on balance, preferable. Walsh's *dimidiam exercitus divisam trifariam—divisit et omnes equites* (*CR*, 55) has little to commend it. The chiastic anaphora of *divisit* is quite alien to this sort of narrative style.

Pellenensem Sicyoniumque agros et Phliasium: it is hard to see the point of this unusual word-order.

3. mercennariorum: on Achaean use of mercenaries, cf. G. T. Griffith, *Mercenaries of the Hellenistic World* (Cambridge, 1935), 99 ff., xxxi. 25. 3 n.

saltum: the valley of the Longo Potamos; cf. P–K, iii. 1. 91–2.

5. illarum gentium: the Achaeans. B has the nonsensical *aliarum*.

6. castris: the Macedonian camp.

7. trepidare dux: cf. xxxi. 34. 5 n.

ab Cleonis: B has *ad Cleonis* and the Rome edition read *ad Cleonas*. The latter is surely right. *accedere* has the sense of motion towards and I can find no case of it being used literally with *ab*. Moreover Androsthenes did not know that the Achaeans had moved to Cleonae (14. 11, 15. 1).

9. ⟨su⟩per: B has 'p' = *pro*. *prope* is palaeographically easier but *super amnem* perhaps the more natural phrase.

13. Thracumque auxiliis: cf. 14. 4 n.

utrobique: B has *ibique*. Gronovius's *utrobique* is neat in itself but *ubique* is the simplest change and most likely reading.

14–15. B has a number of nonsensical corruptions in this section; see McDonald's apparatus.

ex discursu: the commotion of both the Achaean and Macedonian troops.

16. ceciderunt: B has 'ced ϒĩ.' The end is clearly meant to be the ligature for *-tur* and the letter before could originally have been a *u*, but there is no trace of the correction to *cederunt* reported by McDonald.

16–17. *Lucius Flamininus in Acarnania*

Cf. Zon. ix. 16. 11. The fragment Pol. xviii. 40. 5 probably belongs to Polybius' account of these events (cf. Walbank, *Commentary*, ii. 602). *ILLRP* 321 is probably a dedication by Flamininus of spoils for his victory. On the Acarnanians cf. xxxi. 14. 7 n. Lucius was sent to try and win over Acarnania by his brother at the end of the winter of 198/7; cf. xxxii. 40. 7.

16. 1. priusquam . . . Cynoscephalas: no precise date between March and June 197 can be arrived at for this episode (Walbank, *Philip V*, 323).

Acarnanum principibus: not an official delegation but those leading Acarnanians who, actually or potentially, were inclined towards Rome.

sola . . . manserat: not that any positive attempt to win over Acarnania had yet been made.

2. fides: as W–M point out, Polybius also referred to Acarnanian devotion to duty in iv. 30. 4.

metus odiumque Aetolorum: this is certainly the main reason. The Romano-Aetolian treaty of 212/11 had specifically provided for attacks on Acarnania (xxvi. 24. 11).

3. The proceedings are very puzzling. We are evidently dealing with a meeting of the primary assembly of the Acarnanian federation, in which votes are taken by cities (Larsen, *Greek Federal States*, 270 n. 5). The attempt by G. E. W. van Hille, *Mnem.* n.s. xlv (1917), 310–18 to deny this, and argue that L. has misunderstood Polybius, is quite unconvincing. But what is the *privatum decretum*? It is far from clear that the decree was invalid. Certainly it is later repealed, which implies it had validity (§ 5, cf. § 11). Larsen argues that for important decrees the cities had to be unanimous, but this is an unlikely provision. It is possible that the number of states voting for the decree was a minority of the total states of the federation, even though a majority of those present. This may never have occurred before—the meeting had clearly been gerrymandered and it would be highly unusual for any city to be completely unrepresented at an assembly. It could thus be argued that the decision was no decree but only the expression of the private views of those present. It is not likely that *privatum decretum* represents any technical term; it may reflect a phrase of Polybius to the effect that the decision was not really one of τὸ κοινόν but only of ἴδιοι. The pro-Macedonians, however, preferred to have the decree annulled rather than argue on constitutional grounds. For the institutions of the league, cf. Larsen, *Greek Federal States*, 269–70.

Leucadem: cf. 17. 1, 5–8 nn.

duo principes et magistratus: B has *et principes*. The correction is based on the two *principes* responsible for the decree in § 5. The emended text then presumably means 'two leading men who were magistrates'. But it is not clear from § 5 that they were magistrates. W–M's suggestion that *magistratus* is singular and refers to the *strategos* Zeuxidas (§ 5) is improbable. It is unlikely that L. would refer to the *strategos* as 'the magistrate'; nor does 'two leading men and (all) the magistrates' make much sense. It seems better to delete the *et*, so that the sense is 'the leading men (those of § 1) and the magistrates'. L. could easily refer to *principes* as in § 1 though aware that some took the opposite view. Archelaus and Bianor were specially condemned because they actually moved the decree.

4–5. Androcles . . . Echedemus . . . Archelaus . . . Bianor . . .

Zeuxidae : Echedemus may be the *hipparchos* of *IG* ix. 1². 2. 583 l. 2 (*c.* 216). Bianor also occurs in the same inscription (l. 20). For an earlier Acarnanian Bianor cf. Arr. *An.* ii. 13. 2.

6. nam⟨que⟩ : B has *nam* but the position demands *namque* which is often used by L. (Packard, iii. 401).

9. quantum : presumably this is a mere misprint in the OCT for *quantam* (Walsh, *CR*, 56).

17. 1. caput . . . conveniebant : though the assembly could meet elsewhere in Acarnania; cf. Larsen, *Greek Federal States*, 270.

2. ad legatum Flamininum : cf. xxxii. 16. 2 n.

Heraeum : the precise site of this shrine or temple of Hera is not known.

5–8. Polybius was fond of these geographical excursuses. See in general Pédech, ch. xii.

6. Leucadia . . . Acarnaniae : the name of Leucas island appears variously as Λευκάς and Λευκαδία (Bürchner, *RE*, xii. 2213).

It seems incredible that L. can really have intended to say that Leucas was a peninsula in 197 but an island by the time he was writing. Polybius must have said in accordance with the normal view that Leucas was once a peninsula but now an island, and L. has repeated this carelessly (cf. Pol. v. 5. 12).

The ancient view (for sources cf. Walbank, *Commentary*, i. 541) was that a narrow piece of land joining Leucas to the mainland was severed by the building of a canal at the time of their colonization of Leucas by the Corinthians in the tyranny of Cypselus. It seems probable, however, that Leucas was never a real peninsula and the Corinthians merely cut through the sand bar at the north of the island and made a navigable channel. Cf. W. M. Leake, *Travels in Northern Greece* (London, 1835), iii. 10 ff., J. Partsch, *Petermanns Mitteilungen* liii (1907), 269 ff., Maull, *RE*, xii. 2220 ff., P–K, ii. 2. 474 ff.

paeninsula : elsewhere (xxvi. 42. 8, xxxi. 40. 1, xxxii. 21. 26) the MSS. have the form *paeneinsula*.

occidentis regione : oddly expressed from the point of view of the mainland. It was to the east of Leucas.

7. in iis angustiis : in fact not on them, but at the very end of them.

10. die ac nocte : Mog. B has *diem ac noctem*. Madvig (*Emendationes*, 487 n. 1) argued that the latter means 'for one day and night': but the accusative occurs in the sense of 'by day and night' at xxvii. 45. 11, xxxvi. 25. 4, xlii. 54. 3, Cic. *leg. agr.* ii. 68, *de div.* ii.

59, and corruption in all these places is improbable. Cf. Preuss, 34.

11. exules . . . habitantes : not political exiles, but Italian traders living at Leucas. Italian penetration east of the Adriatic was increasing considerably at this time. Cf. A. J. N. Wilson, *Emigration from Italy in the Republican Age of Rome* (Manchester, 1966), 95: *contra* Brunt, 208–9.

13. per stragem lapidum : 'over heaps of stones strewn on the ground'.

18. The Rhodians in the Peraea

18. 1. omnia . . . fortuna : taken by itself, the language might suggest that L. is here picturing *fortuna* as the capricious τύχη, a conception which is common in Polybius and found elsewhere in L. (cf. Kajanto, 79 ff., Walsh, *AJP* lxxix [1958], 364 ff., *Livy*, 55 ff.). But when the passage is taken in conjunction with 19. 2 it becomes evident that in both places Polybius was thinking of τύχη as a power punishing Philip's earlier misdeeds (cf. Pol. xxiii. 10. 2). On this view of Polybius cf. Walbank, *JHS* lviii (1938), 55 ff., *Commentary*, i. 24.

Peraean : cf. xxxii. 33. 6 n.

possessam a maioribus suis : the phrase suggests that L. is not aware, at this point at least, that the area had only recently been acquired by Philip.

For earlier attempts, partly successful, to recapture the lost lands cf. *Syll.*³ 586, C. Blinkenberg, *Lindos*, ii. 1. (Copenhagen–Berlin, 1941), no. 151, *SGDI* 4269. For the date cf. Fraser and Bean, *RPI*, 99 n. 1.

2. Pausistratum praetorem : probably not as *nauarchos* for campaigns of this sort. He was *nauarchos* in 191 (xxxvi. 45. 5) and 190, in which year he was killed after being tricked by Antiochus' admiral Polyxenidas (xxxvii. 9–11). Cf. Lenschau, *RE*, xviii. 2. 2423–5.

Achaeis : these are probably mercenaries, but the contingent of § 5 may be troops sent officially by the Achaean League. Cf. Aymard, *PR*, 162–3 nn. 11, 12, Launey, i. 135.

3. Galli : probably Galatian mercenaries. Cf. Launey, i. 518–19, J. and L. Robert, *La Carie*, ii (Paris, 1954), 378–9 n. 4.

et Mniesutae : the name is omitted by B and Mog. has *et Nisuetae*. The latter are unknown in this locality, though the mention of Nisya in Africa by Ptolemy (iv. 3. 7) led Gronovius and others to transpose it to after *Pisuetae* and to take them, together with the *Tamiani*, as being African. Holleaux (*Études*, i. 417–18) saw that they must be the people from whom came *Φάϋλλος Διονυσίου Μνιεσύτης* in *SGDI* 4276 l. 10.

Pisuetae : from Pisye, mod. Pisiköy: cf. Fraser and Bean, *RPI*, 73. It had already been recaptured (*Syll.*³ 586, *Lindos Inscriptions*, 151), but these men also may be mercenaries.

Tarmiani : B and Mog. have *Tamiani*, but evidence of a κοινὸν *Ταρμιανῶν* makes the correction certain. Cf. L. Robert, *Études anatoliennes* (Paris, 1937), 563 n. 3, Magie, *RRAM*, ii. 1029, Fraser and Bean, *RPI*, 73–4.

Theraei ex Peraea : B has *Trahi ex Africa*, Mog. *Arei ex Africa*. The presence of African mercenaries would not in itself be impossible (cf. Launey, i. 589 ff.): but since the previous three names can be shown to be Carian, and a Peraean Thera is known (cf. Robert, *Études anatoliennes*, 499 n. 3, Fraser and Bean, *RPI*, 72, Magie, *RRAM*, ii. 1032), the Roberts' correction makes excellent sense. *ex Peraea* is added to distinguish them from the better-known island.

 Laudiceni : Laodiceia-on-the-Lycus was founded by Antiochus II. In both Greek and Latin inscriptions the form in *Λαυ-* is found. Cf. Ruge, *RE*, xii. 722–4, Magie, *RRAM*, i. 127, ii. 986–7.

4. Tendeba : B has *tenebat*, Mog. *tendebat*. Tendeba is described as a Carian city by Steph. Byz. s.v.

Stratonicensi agro : for Stratonicea cf. § 22 n.

Therae erant : cf. § 3 n. Here B and Mog. have *tenuerant*. The presence of Therean mercenaries is not incompatible with their town being in Macedonian occupation.

5. Achaei : cf. § 2 n.

Theoxenus : he and his troops made a dedication at Delos, no doubt for this victory (*Inscriptions de Délos*, 442 l. 68: cf. Geyer, *RE*, vA. 2259). He is not known apart from this episode, though he may be the father of the pro-Roman Callicrates (cf. *Syll.*³ 634, Aymard, *PR*, 163 n. 14).

6. Dinocrates : not otherwise known.

ad ipsa Tendeba : cf. § 4 n. Here B has *tenpe ad*, Mog. *tendebat*.

Astragon : nothing further is known of it.

7. eo : *ex* MSS. Correction is preferable to deletion, as an easier explanation of the MSS. reading.

Alabanda : Alabanda is *c.* 30 miles north of Stratonicea, and this seems too far from the scene of the rest of the operations. Hence the Roberts (*La Carie*, ii. 378–9 n. 4) suggested reading *Lobolda*, the name of a deme of Stratonicea (cf. *BCH* xi [1887], 33). McDonald prefers to see an error by L. himself.

 The difficulty is that Alabanda would not seem to have been a well-enough known place to have occurred as a corruption, and though L. mentions it on other occasions (xxxviii. 13. 2, xliii. 6. 5, xlv. 25. 13), he also is unlikely to have altered Lobolda to Alabanda.

Alabanda had been guaranteed by Antiochus *c.* 203 (cf. *OGIS* 234) and attacked by Philip in 201 (Pol. xvi. 24. 6). It is not unlikely that a Macedonian garrison was left there: in which case perhaps the truth is that the Thessalian auxiliaries were summoned from Alabanda and Dinocrates then marched to Stratonicea. L. will have misinterpreted Polybius.

On the later history of Alabanda cf. Magie, *RRAM*, ii. 994–5.

8. detractaverunt: B. Mog. has *detrectaverunt*. Both forms are found in MSS. (*TLL*, v. 1. 834).

9. Agrianas: *Agrianos* B, *Acrianos* Mog. The Agrianes were often used as light-armed troops. They came from the area of the Strymon. Cf. Walbank, *Commentary*, i. 274, ii. 257.

contractos . . . praesidiis: cf. § 7.

Cares: Carians from the area overrun by Philip in 201.

Cretensium . . . Thracumque: cf. 14. 4 n.

10. Rhodii . . . habuere: B omits *dextro cornu, sinistro mercennarios* and Madvig argued that these words were an interpolation in Mg. His case is that the Achaeans were themselves mercenaries and that the *lectam peditum manum* must refer to the Achaeans. He sees the alleged interpolation as an attempt to provide information about the two wings by a scribe who did not see that this was in fact given in the words *mixta . . . circumiectum*. It is, however, not certain that all the Achaeans were mercenaries (cf. § 2 n.). But what is decisive against Madvig's view is that in § 15 the Achaeans attack the Agrianes. These were on the Macedonian left, and these Achaeans must therefore be those said by Mog. here to be on the Rhodian right. Moreover L. does not describe the wings of an army in the language of *mixta . . . circumiectum*. These are the troops surrounding the wings. It remains true that there is confusion in the passage, no doubt due to L. himself. The two detachments of Achaeans (§§ 2, 5) must have been on opposite wings, the right wing, described as *mille* in §16, being the 1,000 of § 5, the left the 800 of § 2. The *lectam peditum manum* was thus exclusively Achaean, and this fact is obscured by L.

12. ripam . . . torrentis: B has *torrens*, Mog. *quae tenui aqua interfluebat torrentis*. I find the word-order accepted by McDonald extremely strange (his parallel of § 9 is not relevant) and prefer H. J. Müller's transposition of *torrentis* to follow *ripam*.

13. terna milia: the total Rhodian infantry forces are given as 2,600 (§2) + 1,000 (§5). But troops left to defend the camp (W–M), or places already captured (McDonald), easily explain the discrepancy. (H. Sauppe, *Ausgewählte Schriften* [Berlin, 1896], 826, wanted to delete *octingentis Achaeis peditibus* in § 2 in order to reconcile the figures.)

16. **Achaei, mille**: cf. § 10 n.

17. **veluti stipata phalanx**: because it was not a real phalanx.

19. **Bargylias**: cf. xxxii. 33. 6 n. The Greek name is *Βαργύλια* but L. clearly treated it as a feminine: cf. 35. 1.

20. **castellis vicisque recipiendis**: *recipiendis* is not itself evidence for earlier Rhodian possession of all the places now captured (cf. § 22 n.) though such possession is probable enough: cf. Fraser and Bean, *RPI*, 98.

22. **nec recipi . . . potuit**: on Stratonicea, probably founded by Antiochus I, cf. Magie, *RRAM*, i. 131, ii. 995 ff., Fraser and Bean, *RPI*, 102. The interpretation of the present passage is central to the problem of Rhodian possession of Stratonicea. Polybius, xxx. 31. 6 says (Rhodian envoys are speaking) *Στρατονίκειαν ἐλάβομεν ἐν μεγάλῃ χάριτι παρ᾽ Ἀντιόχου καὶ Σελεύκου* (we may ignore Niebuhr's emendation *Ἀντιόχου τοῦ Σελεύκου*). The pair in question can be either Antiochus I and his son Seleucus—in which case the acquisition is dated to 279–268, or Seleucus II and Antiochus Hierax, in which case it belongs to 240, or Antiochus III and his son Seleucus, in which case it was given to Rhodes after its capture referred to by L. here. The last is the simplest solution, but it depends on rejecting the argument that *recipi* implies recapture of something previously possessed.

It is, in fact, clear that *recipere* is widely used for 'take into possession something one is trying to get' without the implication of previous possession. Cf. e.g. ii. 39. 4, xxxii. 18. 7, 24. 7, Caes. *B. Alex.* 32. 4, *CIL* i². p. 223.

Seleucus will thus be the future Seleucus IV. He was not associated with Antiochus on the throne until 189 (cf. R. A. Parker and W. H. Dubberstein, *Babylonian Chronology*, 626 B.C.–A.D. 75 [Providence, 1956], 22), but Polybius' words do not require us to believe that Seleucus was co-regent at the time of the cession of Stratonicea. For Seleucus' activities in these years cf. 19. 9 n., 40. 6 n., 41. 4, Pol. xviii. 51. 8.

On the problem see Holleaux, *Études*, v. 107, Walbank, *CQ* xxxvi (1942), 141 n. 2, Magie, *RRAM*, ii. 879–80, Fraser and Bean, *RPI*, 102–7, Schmitt, *Rom und Rhodos*, 112 n. 1, J. and L. Robert, *Mélanges Isidore Levy* (*Annuaire de l'Institut de philologie et d'histoire orientales et slaves* xiii [1953]), 564–5.

19. 1–5. *Philip against the Dardanians*

For these sections we have photographs of the fragments of F, the fragments themselves having now, apparently, been lost. Cf. H. Fischer, *SB Bay. Ak.*, 1907, 97 ff.

1. **Dardanos :** cf. xxxi. 28. 1 n.

2. **exigente fortuna :** cf. 18. 1 n.

3. **Stobos Paeoniae :** Stobi, mod. Pustogradsko, is at the junction of the Axius and the Erigon: cf. Saria, *RE*, ivA. 47–54. Paeonia, the district immediately to the north of Macedon, had been annexed by Antigonus Gonatas after a series of conflicts, but partly lost again *c.* 230. Philip captured Bylazora in 217 (Pol. v. 97. 1) but lacked complete control over Paeonia as a whole. Cf. Lenk, *RE*, xviii. 1. 2403–8.

5. **Thessalonicam :** Thessalonica was founded by Cassander by synoecism of surrounding towns. Cf. Oberhummer, *RE*, viA. 143–63, A. H. M. Jones, *The Greek City* (Oxford, 1940), 10.

19. 6—20. *The advance of Antiochus*

Apart from a brief scrap of Polybius (cf. 20. 3 n.) the only other source for these events is Hier. *in Dan.* xi. 15–16 (= *FGH* 260 F 46). See Holleaux, *Études*, v. 156 ff., O. Leuze, *Hermes* lviii (1923), 187 ff., Passerini, *Ath.* N.S. x (1932), 115 ff., Walbank, *Philip V*, 177 ff., *Commentary*, ii. 615 ff., Schmitt, *Rom und Rhodos*, 74 ff., *Antiochos*, 278 ff., Badian, *CPh* liv (1959), 84 ff. = *Studies*, 116 ff., Will, *HP*, ii. 157–8.

6–7. This collocation of events in East and West, pointing forward to the Spanish section in 21. 6–9, is probably due to L. himself. Polybius, of course, believed in the unity of Mediterranean history at this time, but it seems unlikely that he would have referred to Spanish matters in his introduction to the activities of Antiochus. Nor is Polybius likely to have thought the warfare in Spain important enough at this stage to have made such a comparison in his introduction to book xviii as a whole. Cf. p. 10.

6. ne simul . . . bellandum : in fact Rome would have refrained from declaring war on Philip if the war with Carthage had still been in progress.

Antiocho ex Syria movente bellum : thus B. Mog. has *in Syria moliente bellum*, which is preferred by Tränkle, *Gnomon*, 374 n. 1 on the grounds that *bellum moliri* is a good Livian expression altered to the common *bellum motum* in the tradition represented by B (he believes that *bellum motum* at 26. 5 and 45. 5 is also wrong). He may have a case for *moliente*—though there is nothing wrong with *movente*—but *in Syria* cannot stand. The war was being organized from Syria, but was not taking place in it.

8. priore aestate . . . redactis : although the Fifth Syrian war was really settled by Antiochus' victory at Panium in 200, the mopping-up operations continued until 198. Cf. Holleaux, *Études*, iii. 317–35, Will, *HP*, ii. 101–2, Walbank, *Commentary*, ii. 523.

Coele Syria : the name may have applied originally to a small piece of land between Mounts Lebanon and Anti-Lebanon, but it now referred to all that area to the south of Syria—including Phoenicia and Judaea—down to the Nile delta, which was the subject of dispute between Egypt and Syria. Most of it had been in Egyptian possession since 301. Cf. Beer, *RE*, xi. 1050–2, Walbank, *Commentary*, i. 564–5. W. Brandenstein (*AAHG* viii [1955], 61 ff.) argues implausibly that Κοίλη did not mean 'hollow' but comes from κοῖλυ = 'beautiful'.

Antiochiam : Antiochia-on-the-Orontes, built as the capital of the kingdom by Seleucus I. See G. Downey, *A History of Antioch in Syria from Seleucus to the Arab Conquest* (Princeton, 1961).

9. ingentes copias : no doubt over-estimated at Rome, in their usual fear of the might of the orient.

filiis duobus Ardye⟨que⟩ ac Mithridate: the *-que* is Holleaux's addition to B's text (the gibberish in Mog. can be seen to be a corruption of the same reading). Holleaux showed (*Études*, iii. 183–93) that the two sons must be the young Antiochus, who died in 193, and the future Seleucus IV, and that Ardys and Mithridates were not sons of Antiochus III. He argued (i) that Antiochus would not have given his children oriental names, (ii) that they would not have been old enough to command in 197, (iii) that the complete absence of later references to them would be very odd. In fact Ardys must be the officer mentioned by Pol. v. 53. 2 and Mithridates the nephew of Antiochus attested in Pol. viii. 23. 3.

The historical arguments are overwhelming, but the resulting change is rather inelegant. Thus Ogilvie (*Phoenix*, 345) posits an error by L. himself. Holleaux refers to a suggestion of Guillot that we should read *cum Ardye ac Mithridate*. This is just possible, though the repeated *cum* is rather harsh. I am attracted by Schmitt's suggestion (*Antiochos*, 14 n. 4) of *duobus ⟨ducibus⟩* (*et ducibus* was in fact suggested by C. Brakman, *Mnem.* lv [1927], 56).

10. centum : on the authenticity of this figure cf. Thiel, 273 n. 343, against the doubts of De Sanctis, iv. 1. 121 n. 16.

cercurisque : ships originating from Cyprus (Pliny *NH* vii. 208). They are described by Nonius p. 533M as *pergrandes*, so they are presumably larger than *lembi*. On their use cf. McDonald and Walbank,

JRS lix (1969), 32 n. 10, to which should be added a reference to xxiii. 34. 4.

11. simul . . . adiuturus : this may have been genuinely believed at Rome and Rhodes, though it is in fact highly unlikely. Cf. xxxii. 8. 15 n.

20. 1–2. Polybius was clearly dependent on Rhodian sources for these events. Neither Polybius nor L. saw any inconsistency between this encomium and Rhodes' virtual withdrawal in § 10.

2. Chelidonias . . . Persarum : the Chelidonian islands are off the south-eastern tip of Lycia: cf. Ruge, *RE*, iii. 2227–8. The *foedus* is the much-disputed Peace of Callias, said to have been concluded between Athens and Artaxerxes in 449. This would not be the place to discuss the peace. For modern discussions see H. T. Wade-Gery, *HSCP* supp. vol. i (1940), 121 ff. = *Essays in Greek History* (Oxford, 1958), 201 ff., Gomme, *Commentary on Thucydides*, i. 331 ff., R. Sealey, *Historia* iii (1954/5), 325 ff., D. L. Stockton, *Historia* viii (1959), 61 ff., A. Andrewes, *Historia* x (1961), 1 ff., H. B. Mattingly, *Historia* xiv (1965), 273 ff.

regibus : if there is any special significance in the plural, it may refer to the fact that the treaty was renewed in 424 with Darius II (cf. Wade-Gery, *HSCP*, 127–32 = *Essays*, 207–11—this too is disputed).

3. non . . . Graeciam : Pol. xviii. 41a. 1: κωλύειν δὲ τὸν Ἀντίοχον παραπλεῖν, οὐκ ἀπεχθείας χάριν, ἀλλ᾽ ὑφορώμενοι μὴ Φιλίππῳ συνεπισχύσας ἐμπόδιον γένηται τῇ τῶν Ἑλλήνων ἐλευθερίᾳ. Cf. 19. 11 n. The Rhodians would have been extremely worried about complete control of the Asia Minor coast by Antiochus, whatever his intentions in regard to Philip. The actual language of the ultimatum may have been milder than is portrayed here: cf. De Sanctis, iv. 1. 121, Schmitt, *Rom und Rhodos*, 76 n. 1, Passerini, *Ath.* n.s. x (1932), 118, Badian, *CPh* liv (1959), 84 = *Studies*, 116.

4. On the geography of southern Asia Minor cf. in general Magie, *RRAM*, i. 266 ff.

Coracesium : in western Cilicia: cf. Ruge, *RE*, xi. 1371.

Zephyrio : in eastern Cilicia, a little south-west of Tarsus.

Solis : Soli is to the west of Zephyrium: cf. Ruge, *RE*, iiiA. 935–8. For a dedication to Antiochus there, probably shortly after these events, cf. *OGIS* 230, J. and L. Robert, *RÉG* lxxxiii (1970), 470.

Aphrodisiade : on the Zephyrium promontory (not to be confused with the town of Zephyrium). Cf. Wilhelm, *RE*, i. 2726.

Coryco : in fact east of Aphrodisias: cf. Ruge, *RE*, xi. 1452. Corycus is omitted from Schmitt's list in *Antiochos*, 278.

Anemurio: the south-western promontory of Cilicia. Cf. Hirschfeld, *RE*, i. 2182.

Selinunte: north-west of the Anemurium promontory. Cf. Ruge, *RE*, iiA. 1308-9.

recepto: cf. 18. 22 n. Though in this case Antiochus was capturing places which had in the past been in Seleucid possession. Ptolemaic control in the area dated at least from the Laodicean war. Cf. J. Beloch, *Griechische Geschichte*², iv. 2 (Berlin–Leipzig, 1927), 333-4, Magie, *RRAM*, i. 278, ii. 1156, Will, *HP*, i. 227.

5. aliis . . . castellis: the only other Cilician name preserved is Mallus (Hier. *in Dan.* xi. 15-16) but this is in the far east of Cilicia, in an area probably already in Antiochus' possession. Cf. Magie, *RRAM*, ii. 1156. For the names of other towns on the coast cf. Magie, ii. 1142-3.

7. vestusta iura: no details are known of the precise relationship between Rhodes and the Seleucids after 281. Rhodes had mediated in the Fourth Syrian war (Pol. v. 63. 5).

8. amicitiam: cf. xxxii. 8. 13 n.

recentem . . . reponsaque: this passage and 34. 2 are the evidence for an embassy of Antiochus to Rome in the winter of 198/7 and it should be seen as a response to the senate's request that he should desist from his attacks on Pergamum (cf. xxxii. 8. 9-16, 27. 1 nn.). Cf. Holleaux, *Études*, v. 156-9, Badian, *CPh* liv (1959), 83-4 = *Studies*, 115-16. The embassy is unnecessarily rejected by Passerini, *Ath.* N.S. x (1932), 116 ff. as a Rhodian fabrication to show Rome's complaisance towards Antiochus.

9. forte: cf. xxxii. 39. 4 n.

ut tempus . . . belli: the comment is an interpretation, perhaps L.'s own, made with the benefit of hindsight.

10. legati regis: not, of course, identical with the *legati* to Rome of § 9, as is strangely argued by Schlag, 90-1; cf. p. 27.

11-12. illam . . . Samiisque: these states were technically allies, *de facto* subjects of Egypt. For payments of tribute cf. A. H. M. Jones, *Anatolian Studies presented to W. H. Buckler* (Manchester, 1939), 105, Magie, *RRAM*, ii. 929 and for Ptolemaic ships and garrisons in Samos and Caunus respectively, cf. Pol. v. 35. 11, xxx. 31. 6. But with the decline of Ptolemaic power the degree of control may have lessened. The result of Rhodes' actions was to bring them under Rhodian control, though they may have formally remained in the Egyptian alliance (cf. n. on Caunus below).

Samos, Halicarnassus, and perhaps Caunus too appear as mediators between Miletus and Magnesia-on-the-Maeander in 196 (*Syll.*³

588). But this does not show that they are now genuinely free. If tribute-paying states could be described as free, they could presumably act as mediators as if they were independent. Cf. Magie, *RRAM*, ii. 946 n. 49, Fraser and Bean, *RPI*, 106 n. 1, Schmitt, *Rom und Rhodos*, 76 n. 3, *Antiochos*, 280 n. 2, 282, 287, Walbank, *Commentary*, ii. 615.

Cauniis: Caunus is on the Carian coast almost opposite the northern tip of Rhodes. Cf. Bürchner, *RE*, xi. 86–8, G. E. Bean, *JHS* lxxiii (1953), 10–35, lxxiv (1954), 85–110. The Rhodians later bought it from the Ptolemaic generals in charge of the garrison there (Pol. xxx. 31. 6; for the date cf. Fraser and Bean, *RPI*, 105–7, Schmitt, *Rom und Rhodos*, 112 n. 1). The purchase shows that Caunus was still regarded as Ptolemaic (see above).

Myndiis Halicarnassensibusque: both are on the north shore of the gulf of Cos. On Myndus cf. Ruge, *RE*, xvi. 1075–9, on Halicarnassus Bürchner, *RE*, vii. 2253–64. See also G. E. Bean and J. M. Cook, *ABSA* l (1955), 85 ff., lii (1957), 87 ff., Cook and D. J. Blackman, *AR* 1970–1, 48–9.

13. non operae . . . sufficiam: L. thus omits mention of Antiochus' further conquests in Lycia, Caria, and Ionia. For the details of these cf. Schmitt, *Antiochos*, 278–88. On the sentiment cf. the similar comments in xxxix. 48. 6, xli. 25. 8. L. was writing the history of Rome, not of the whole Hellenistic world (cf. also viii. 24. 18, xxxv. 40. 1). But these comments should be seen more as a sign of L.'s desperation of living to complete his work than of a lack of interest in non-Roman matters. Cf. xxxi. 1. 5 n., Tränkle, *WS*, 136–7; *contra* Holleaux, *Études*, iv. 122, Toynbee, i. 286, Salmon, *Samnium*, 2.

operae est: on L.'s use of the phrase—apart from L. used commonly only by Plautus—cf. Tränkle, *WS*, 112.

21. 1–5. *Death and obituary of Attalus*

This section is abbreviated from Polybius xviii. 41. Polybius gave a number of short obituaries on the deaths of leading figures (xviii. 41. 1 καθάπερ περὶ τῶν ἄλλων): cf. Walbank, *Commentary*, ii. 603. The practice goes back to Thucydides (i. 138, ii. 65). The earliest extant example in Roman historiography is Pollio's obituary of Cicero (Sen. *Suas.* vi. 24). L. developed the practice, Tacitus took it further still. Cf. Sen. *Suas.* vi. 21, I. Bruns, *Die Persönlichkeit in der Geschichtschreibung der Alten* (Berlin, 1898), 53–61, R. Syme, *Tacitus* (Oxford, 1958), 312, A. D. Leeman, *Orationis Ratio* (Amsterdam, 1963), 188 ff.

21. 1. ab Thebis: Boeotian Thebes. For Attalus' stroke there cf. 2. 2–3. Mog. omits *ab*, but for L.'s usage of prepositions with names of towns cf. Kühnast, 186–7, Riemann, 274, K–St, i. 476.

altero . . . regnasset: Pol. xviii. 41. 8: βιώσας ἔτη δύο πρὸς τοῖς ἑβδομήκοντα, τούτων δὲ βασιλεύσας τετταράκοντα καὶ τέτταρα. Polybius says that he was 72, while L., if taken strictly, says 71. But L. is writing carelessly. Attalus was born in 269 or 268 and succeeded Eumenes in 241 (cf. Walbank, *Commentary*, ii. 604).

2. Huic . . . regno: Pol. xviii. 41. 2: ἐκείνῳ γὰρ ἐξ ἀρχῆς ἄλλο μὲν οὐδὲν ἐφόδιον ὑπῆρξε πρὸς βασιλείαν τῶν ἐκτός, πλοῦτος δὲ μόνον and xviii. 41. 5: διὸ καὶ τοῦ προειρημένου ἄξιον ἀγασθῆναι τὴν μεγαλοψυχίαν, ὅτι πρὸς οὐδὲν τῶν ἄλλων ἐπεβάλετο χρήσασθαι τοῖς χορηγίοις ἀλλὰ πρὸς βασιλείας κατάκτησιν. L. omits Polybius' general reflections on wealth.

fortuna: here more in the sense of 'fate', not 'luck' (Kajanto, 76) or *natura* (Walsh, *JRS* xlviii [1958], 193).

aliis non indignus: in the Hellenistic world, outside Macedon itself, kingship was a personal thing and depended on certain qualities in the person claiming to be a king. See above all the articles of Aymard collected together in *ÉHA*, 73 ff.

3. victis . . . aequavit: Pol. xviii. 41. 7: νικήσας γὰρ μάχῃ Γαλάτας, ὃ βαρύτατον καὶ μαχιμώτατον ἔθνος ἦν τότε κατὰ τὴν Ἀσίαν, ταύτην ἀρχὴν ἐποιήσατο καὶ τότε πρῶτον αὐτὸν ἔδειξε βασιλέα. In fact the victory was probably over the Gauls and Antiochus Hierax, followed by one over the Gauls alone, and is to be dated *c.* 237. Cf. Bikerman, *Berytus* viii (1944), 76–8, Will, *HP*, i. 266–8. *recenti* is not inexact as W–M claim: L. was aware of the truth (cf. xxxviii. 16), and *recens* is not inappropriate for a period of about 40 years. For the facts cf. Walbank, *Commentary*, ii. 603–4.

4. summa . . . fuit: Pol. xviii. 41. 8–10: σωφρονέστατα μὲν ἐβίωσε καὶ σεμνότατα πρὸς γυναῖκα καὶ τέκνα, διεφύλαξε δὲ τὴν πρὸς πάντας τοὺς συμμάχους καὶ φίλους πίστιν . . . τέτταρας υἱοὺς ἐν ἡλικίᾳ καταλιπών. The sentence reads like the conventional language of epitaphs.

unicam: on L.'s use of *unicus* cf. E. Dutoit, *Latomus* xv (1956), 481–8.

comis uxori ac liberis: B has *comis uxor ac liberos*, Mog. *uxorem ac liberos* (omitting *comis*). McDonald explains *liberos* as a corruption caused by its being taken as the object of *habuit*. *comis* is normally used with the dative (*TLL*, iii. 1786) but Horace (*Ep.* ii. 2. 133) has *comis in uxorem* and in view of that and the MSS. tradition Goeller's *comis in uxorem ac liberos* may be right (cf. A. Zingerle, *Ztscht. f. öst. Gymn.* xxxix [1888], 701).

quattuor superstites habuit: for their names cf. Walbank, *Commentary*, ii. 604. B and Mog. have *duos*. It is better to assume a simple numerical corruption rather than an error by L. himself.

Kreyssig's *quos* is too weak and L.'s fondness for parenthesis tells against Madvig's *quos quattuor*.

5. regnum . . . descenderit: Pol. xviii. 41. 10: οὕτως ἡρμόσατο τὰ κατὰ τὴν ἀρχὴν ὥστε παισὶ παίδων ἀστασίαστον παραδοθῆναι τὴν βασιλείαν. Attalus III was the grandson of Attalus I.

21. 6–25. 3. *Events in Rome, including report of war in Spain*

21. 6–9. *Spain*

L.'s scattered references to Spanish events before 195 are not fully coherent. But there is no need to think either that inconsistencies arise from the use of conflicting sources, or that the notices themselves are untrustworthy.

At 26. 5 L. says *bellum in Hispania quinto post anno motum est quam simul cum Punico bello fuerat finitum*. The fifth year must be 197, when the fighting described here and in 25. 8–9 took place. Presumably the conflicts described in xxxi. 49. 7 and the events which justified the *ovatio* of Cn. Cornelius Blasio (27. 1) are not regarded as a *bellum*. In fact L. does not relate any details of Spanish events between 205 (xxix. 2–3) and 200. His source(s), however, must have been aware of fighting in Spain continuing until 201.

Fighting in 197 is reported here and at 25. 8–9, and the appointment of praetorian governors for 196 at 26. 3–4. Under 196, however, there is no further mention of Spain. In 43. 1–5 the senate decides that one of the consuls of 195 shall govern Hispania Citerior, and the lot gives it to Cato. Then, at 44. 4, comes news of a victory by one of the governors of 196.

The conflict is throughout presented as a major danger—*Hispania . . . magno tumultu ad bellum consurrexit* at 19. 7, *ingens bellum* here and at 44. 5, *tantum glisceret bellum* at 43. 2. Yet at 44. 4 we read *mirantibus iam volgo hominibus quod Hispania movisset bellum neglegi*. The apparent inconsistency can be explained. The previous statements will reflect the view of the danger from Spain that was generally held at the time. That danger may well have been taken over-seriously, and perhaps exaggerated by Cato himself to justify his own activities. At the time of the assignation of consular provinces for 195 the position was still regarded as serious. Cato himself, however, may have been aware of the real situation, and hence did not leave immediately for Spain. (But the fact that the events of 196 are not reported under that year cannot be used as an indication that those events were not all that important: cf. 44. 4 n.)

On Spanish events cf. K. Götzfried, *Annalen der römischen Provinzen beiden Spanien, 218–154* (Erlangen, 1907), 37 ff., Klotz, *Hermes* l (1915), 484 ff., E. A. Schulten, *CAH*, viii. 306 ff., Schlag, 22 ff.

6. cum hic . . . bellum: cf. 19. 6.

Hispania ulteriore: for the formal division of Spain into two provinces this year cf. xxxii. 28. 11 and addenda.

7. M. Helvius: (4). Cf. xxxii. 27. 7 n.

Culcham: evidently identical with the Culchas who helped Scipio in 206 (xxviii. 13. 3).

Luxinium: not otherwise known.

8. Carmonem: mod. Carmona, a city of the Turdetani east of the river Baetis. Cf. Hübner, *RE*, iii. 1597.

Bardonem: thus Mog. B has *Baldonem*. Neither name is known, but they have been justified by reference to Pliny *NH* iv. 118 (Barduli) and Strabo iii. p. 141C (’Οβούλκων) respectively. Schlag, 31, identifies it with Baelo, on the coast (cf. Hübner, *RE*, ii. 2759), but the following sentence precludes reference to a coastal town here.

in maritima ora . . . omnem: B has *Etruriam* for *Baeturiam*. Mog. has an abbreviated version *et maritimam oram omnem quae*, which is clearly an attempt to emend a corrupt text (cf. Tränkle, *Gnomon*, 374).

Malacinos Sexetanosque: both Malaga and Sexi are Phoenician colonies on the southern coast of Spain. On them cf. Schulten, *RE*, xiv. 823–4 and Hübner, *RE*, iiA. 2027–8 respectively.

Baeturiam: the north-western part of the later province of Hispania Baetica. Cf. Hübner, *RE*, ii. 2764–5.

nudaverant: for L.'s use of the indicative in subordinate clauses in *oratio obliqua* cf. Kühnast, 235 ff., Riemann, 290, K–St, ii. 544 ff.

9. M. Sergio praetore . . . erat: cf. xxxii. 27. 7 n. In fact Sergius was *praetor urbanus* (xxxii. 28. 2). The error is probably L.'s own. On *inter cives et peregrinos* cf. xxxii. 28. 2 n.

ut . . . referret: for the postponement of an important decision to await new magistrates cf. *per.* xlviii. It is very odd for a praetor to be instructed to make a *relatio* himself concerning his province, but there is no reason to doubt L.'s statement. *primo quoque tempore* must mean 'as soon as possible in the new consular year', not 'immediately after the praetorian elections'.

22–23. *The debate on the triumph of the consuls*

For the consuls' activities in Gaul cf. xxxii. 29. 5–31. For the conditions for a triumph cf. xxxi. 20. 3 n., 48. 6. On the source problems raised by this section cf. p. 5 n. 2.

22. 1. in aede Bellonae: cf. xxxi. 47. 7 n.

2. C. Atinius Labeo: (8). Cf. xxxii. 29. 3 n. Whatever the truth about the identity of the tribune mentioned in the latter passage, the present tribune must be identical with the C. Atinius Labeo of 25. 6, and he and Afranius are therefore tribunes of 197/6. The advance of the calendar (cf. p. 42) means that the tribunes will have entered office about September/October, 197 (Jul.).

C. Afranius: (3, 15). He is probably to be identified with C. Afranius Stellio, praetor in 185 and *iiivir* for the foundation of Saturnia in 183.

3. utrique . . . obtigisse: xxxii. 28. 8.

4. Boios . . . auxilio essent: xxxii. 30. 1.
depopulante vicos eorum: xxxii. 31. 1.

5. honore . . . habendo: I cannot see why W–M deny that this refers to the *supplicatio* already granted (xxxii. 31. 6). It is true that the triumph is itself a 'Dankfest' but to take the phrase as referring to the triumph leaves no sense for the *magis . . . quam* comparison.

7. magnum . . . amisisse: there is no reference to this in L.'s own account of the campaign.

8. T. Iuventium: (9). Not otherwise known. Since he was killed, the apparent implication of *MRR*, ii. 578 that he is identical with the praetor of 194 is impossible! Nor is Münzer (*RE*, x. 1362) likely to be right in making him the father of that praetor. They would be of equivalent age.
Cn. Ligurium . . . cecidisse: note the extraordinarily deep corruption in Mog. here.
Cn. Ligurium: (2). Not otherwise known.
quartae: the Gallic legions at this time were presumably II, IV, V, VI (cf. 36. 5), those in Greece I and III. For the alleged inconsistency between this passage and xxxi. 21. 10 cf. p. 4. There is no need to doubt that the legions did have official numbers at this period. Cf. A. Klotz, *RhM* lxxxi (1932), 143 ff., Walbank, *Commentary*, i. 375.

23. 1–2. Placentini . . . exemptos: there is nothing to correspond to this in L.'s account in xxxii. 29–31, but it represents precisely the events of 200: cf. xxxi. 10–11. 3 n.

3. in monte Albano . . . dixit: L. himself gives only two other cases of triumphs on the Alban mount, Marcellus in 211 (xxvi. 21. 6) and C. Cicereius in 172 (xlii. 21. 7). The first Alban triumph was by C. Papirius Maso in 231 (*Fasti Triumph.*, Piso, *HRR* i². 135, fr. 31, Val. Max. iii. 6. 5). As *iure imperii consularis* indicates, it would appear that the senate could not refuse a triumph *tout court* but only the funds for the expenses (cf. § 8 below). The Alban Mount (Monte Cavo) was a considerable distance from Rome, and the climb to the summit far from easy, so the number of spectators is unlikely to have been all that large.

See further Walbank, *Commentary*, i. 689 and literature there cited. Add Lippold, 313–14, 319, L. B. Warren, *JRS* lx (1970), 50–1, J. Jahn, *Interregnum und Wahldiktatur* (Kallmunz, 1970), 104.

5. Hamilcarem: cf. xxxi. 21. 18 n., xxxii. 30. 12.

6. pilleatorum: the *pilleus* was a soft cap worn by freed slaves at their manumission. The people of Placentia and Cremona were thus indicating that their release from Gallic captivity was tantamount to being freed from slavery. Cf. the similar action by Q. Terentius Culleo at the triumph of Scipio Africanus (xxx. 45. 5). See addenda.

7. duplex equiti centurionique: thus B. Mog. has *duplex equiti*, *triplex centurioni*. The latter is impossible—a centurion would not be given more booty than an *eques*. Hence Duker read *duplex centurioni*, *triplex equiti*. Ogilvie, *Phoenix*, 344, argues in favour of this on the grounds that other passages show the *equites* getting three times as much as the infantry (37. 12, xxxiv. 46. 3, 52. 11). But the amounts were a matter for the discretion of the commander, and it is not necessary for all divisions to have been the same. Duker's transposition, moreover, makes it difficult to explain B's text. (Brunt, 394, is unaware of B's reading and hence sees 37. 12 as a unique, and hence dubious, example of centurions and *equites* getting equal amounts.)

8. Q. Minucius . . . triumphavit: fragments of the entry on Minucius survive in the *Fasti Triumphales*: . . .]DE G[. . .]ALBAN[(*I.I.* xiii. 1. 78–9, 552).

24. 1–2. *Elections*

24. 1. L. Furius Purpurio: (86). Cf. xxxi. 4. 4 n.

M. Claudius Marcellus: (222). Cf. xxxi. 50. 1 n. Like Ti. Sempronius Longus in 194, Cn. Domitius Ahenobarbus in 192, and Q. Marcius Philippus in 186 he has only a one-year praetor-consul gap. Cf. Roegler, *Klio* xl (1962), 104.

2. Q. Fabius Buteo: (57). Perhaps the *legatus* of Flamininus in 198 (cf. xxxii. 36. 10 n.). Nothing more is heard of him after his praetorship.

Ti. Sempronius Longus: (67). Cf. xxxi. 20. 5 n. The *praenomen* has to be corrected from the *T.* of B and Mog.

Q. Minucius Thermus: (65). Cf. xxxii. 27. 8 n.

M'. Acilius Glabrio: (35). Cf. xxxi. 50. 5 n. The *praenomen* has to be corrected from the *M.* of B and Mog.

L. Apustius Fullo : (5). Cf. xxxi. 4. 7 n.

C. Laelius : (2). The famous friend of Scipio Africanus. He had served under Scipio in Spain and Africa and was quaestor in 202 and plebeian aedile in 197 (25. 2). He was consul in 190 with command prorogued in 189. He was a *legatus* to Macedon in 174–3 and to Gaul in 170.

Laelius and Acilius proceeded directly from the plebeian aedile-ship to the praetorship: cf. xxxi. 4. 7 n.

24. 3–7. *Decisions on Macedon*

L.'s account raises serious chronological difficulties. The news of Cynoscephalae is said to arrive *exitu ferme anni* (§ 3). The battle took place in June (cf. Walbank, *Philip V*, 322) and though the Roman calendar was perhaps two to three months in advance at the time (cf. p. 42), it cannot have taken five or six months for the news to reach Rome. In addition the *ludi Romani* are said to have followed news of the Roman victory (25. 1). These *ludi* normally took place in the Roman month of September (cf. xlv. 1. 6, *CIL* i². 1. 328–9) but because of the advance of the calendar will in fact have taken place in July. And the fact that the dispatch was read to the senate by the *praetor urbanus* (cf. 21. 9 n.) suggests that the consuls had not yet returned from the north. It therefore appears that there must have been a gap between the receipt of the news and the actual arrival of the envoys from Flamininus and Philip. This is quite natural. The news of the battle would be sent immediately. The conference of Tempe arranged about the dispatch of envoys. Cf. Walbank, *Philip V*, 323, Accame, *Espansione romana*, 187 ff.

But if L. places the news of the battle too late, he would appear to have placed the debate on the peace too early. He splits this from his account in 25. 4–7 of Marcellus' opposition to the peace and the final ratification by the people. Polybius (xviii. 42) makes Marcellus oppose the granting of peace immediately after the senatorial debate. Polybius states that this was after the beginning of Marcellus' consular year, and though Polybius can be wrong about domestic events, it is more likely, in view of the other difficulties in L.'s account, that he is right here. There is no case for emending Polybius to make him say that Marcellus had not yet taken up office, as urged by Nissen, *KU*, 143. (Walbank, *Philip V*, 177 n. 7 agrees with L., but at *Commentary*, ii. 604–5 he is non-committal.) For other differences between the accounts of L. and Polybius cf. 25. 5 n.

4. ⟨M.⟩ Sergio : cf. xxxii. 27. 7 n. The insertion of the *praenomen* is necessary.

in dies quinque supplicationes : cf. xxxi. 22. 1 n.

5. legati . . . Philippo: Mog. omits *Philippo*, perhaps correctly. For the arrangement of the dispatch of envoys cf. 13. 14, Pol. xviii. 39. 5.

villam publicam: in the Campus Martius; it was originally built for the official use of the censors (iv. 22. 7). Cf. Platner–Ashby, 581, Ogilvie, 570.

lautia: this word, in the sense of 'official entertainment', appears to be used only by L. among literary sources, and always together with *locus*. Cf. Mommsen, *RF*, i. 344. For its etymology cf. Walde–Hofmann, *Lateinisches etymologisches Wörterbuch* (Heidelberg, 1938), i. 324–5.

6. Macedones . . . dicerent: it is highly unlikely that they actually said this. At Tempe Philip had agreed to all earlier Roman demands and 'to leave other matters to the senate' (13. 4, 14, Pol. xviii. 38. 2, 39. 5). That was far from saying that he would do whatever the senate required.

7. decem legati more maiorum: the appointment of ten *legati* to organize the settlement after a major war or the arrangements for a new province became regular. It is first attested after the First Punic war (Pol. i. 63. 1) and is also found after the Second Punic war (xxx. 43. 4). Cf. Balsdon, *JRS* lii (1962), 137.

ex consilio . . . daret: but within the terms of the *senatus consultum*. Their function was concerned with the detailed implementation of the terms and any matters which the senate left to their discretion (cf. 31. 5 n.).

P. Sulpicius et P. Villius: cf. xxxi. 4. 3, 4. 4 nn. Normally all the *legati* would be chosen together by the senate (cf. Willems, *Le Sénat*, ii. 491–4: the view of Mommsen, *StR*, ii³. 677 and A. A. Thurm, *De Romanorum legatis* [Leipzig, 1883], 13–14, that *legati* of this type were normally appointed by the consuls is not tenable). On this occasion the appointment of Sulpicius and Villius was included in the *s.c.* ratifying the peace on the grounds that the two previous commanders above all ought to be included. For the names of the rest, as far as they are known, cf. *MRR*, i. 337–8, p. 35.

L. has no mention of the representations of various Greek states reported by Polybius xviii. 42. 6–8.

24. 8–9. *Cosa*

For the rejection of the earlier appeal for reinforcement, in 199, cf. xxxii. 2. 7 n.

8. eo tem⟨pore⟩: B and Mog. have *eo die*. This is most improbable since L., as often, is adding brief details of other domestic events and it is very unlikely that Cosa should have been dealt with on the same day as the peace with Macedon, or that L. should have thought that it was. Of the emendations offered I prefer H. J. Müller's *eodem anno* (cf. xxxi. 49. 7, xxxii. 7. 5, 27. 1), which makes for a better explanation of the paradosis than McDonald's *eo tempore*. I see no force in Klotz's objection (*Livius*, 31 n. 1) that *eodem anno* would not be used to join mention of two different matters considered by the senate.

9. ne quis . . . fuisset: the clear implication of this is that Italians would be allowed to become citizens of a Latin colony. Cf. xxxii. 2. 6 n., Toynbee, ii. 108, Salmon, *Samnium*, 318, *Colonization*, 101, Brunt, 84 n. 4, 538 ff.

P. Cornelium et Ti. Sempronium: the consuls of 218, P. Cornelius Scipio (330), the father of Africanus, and Ti. Sempronius Longus (66), father of the Longus of § 2.

25. 1–3. *Aedilician activities*

25. 1. Ludi Romani . . . scaenaque: cf. xxxi. 4. 5 n. Accius asserted that 197 was the year when Livius Andronicus produced the first Roman play (cf. xxxi. 12. 10 n.).

P. Cornelio Scipione: (350). Nasica: cf. xxxi. 49. 6 n.

Cn. Manlio Volsone: (91). A leading opponent of the Scipios (cf. *Latomus* xxxi [1972], 52). He was praetor in 195 (42. 7) and consul in 189 with command prorogued in 188.

magnificentius: T. A. Dorey (in unpublished notes which he kindly showed me) suggests that since all the aediles were political opponents of Flamininus, the ostentation of the games was a deliberate attempt to counter Flamininus' popularity. The premiss may be true, but the conclusion is far more uncertain.

instaurati: cf. xxxi. 4. 5 n., xxxii. 27. 8 n. Here it is natural to understand *toti* with *septiens*.

2. M'. Acilius Glabrio et C. Laelius: cf. 24. 2 n.

3. de argento multaticio: cf. xxxi. 50. 2 n.

Cererem Liberumque et Liberam: the temple of these deities, at the foot of the Aventine and the side of the Circus Maximus, was dedicated in 493 (D.H. vi. 17. 2–4, 94. 3, Pliny, *NH* xxxv. 154). It was a special object of plebeian religious attention. Cf. Wissowa, *RuK*², 297 ff., Platner–Ashby, 109–10, Latte, *RRG*, 161–2, Ogilvie, 502, Nash, i. 227, H. Le Bonniec, *Le Culte de Cérès à Rome* (Paris, 1958), especially 254 ff. on the date of the temple and 266 ff. on the site.

196 B.C.

25. 4–27. 5. *Events in Rome and Italy*

25. 4–7. *Objection of Marcellus to the peace with Macedon*

On the chronology and facts cf. 24. 3–7 n.

4. L. Furius et M. Claudius Marcellus: Polybius (xviii. 42) refers only to Marcellus in this context and the apparent implication of Furius may be due only to the conjunction of a dating indication with the narrative. For the political position of L. Furius Purpurio cf. xxxi. 47. 4–49. 3, 49. 8–11 n., on that of Marcellus, p. 34.

5. pacem . . . regem: this would suggest that Marcellus is objecting not to the peace itself, as in Polybius' account, but to the withdrawal of the Roman army. The latter was no doubt known to be the policy of Flamininus, and if Marcellus was successful, it would be a sign that the senate intended to keep the army there. But though this makes political sense, it does not square with the actions of the tribunes who are concerned with the peace itself (§ 6), and it seems best, therefore, to continue to follow Polybius. Cf. Gelzer, *Hermes* lxx (1935), 298(=*Kleine Schriften*, iii. 252).

Another difference between L. and Polybius is that in the latter the senate ratifies the peace, and Marcellus objects when the matter is put before the people. It is possible that on this point L.'s more detailed version is correct.

dubios sententiae: W–M's statement that this expression is poetic is not true: cf. *TLL*, v. 1. 2106.

6. Q. Marcius Ralla: (87). He was a *iivir* for the dedication of temples in 194 and 192 (cf. xxxi. 21. 12 n.). The only other Marcius Ralla known is the praetor of 204, and the two men are probably brothers. Whether Marcius' action has any connection with the relations of the Marcii Philippi with the Macedonian royal house (cf. xlii. 38. 9), as argued by Bleicken, 92, is quite uncertain.

The cognomen is given as *Rala* in B, and appears in Mog. as *Rex*, the well-known cognomen of one branch of the Marcii. *Ralla* is the form preserved by the MSS. at xxx. 38. 4 and xxxv. 41. 8. (It is hopelessly corrupted at xxxiv. 53. 5.)

C. Atinius Labeo: cf. 22. 2 n.

ipsi . . . pacem esse: similarly the peace with Carthage was ratified by the people on a proposal by two tribunes (xxx. 43. 2–3).

7. in Capitolio: for meetings of the tribal assembly on the Capitol cf. Taylor, *RVA*, 132 n. 38. The purpose may have been to restrict attendance in the narrow space available.

omnes quinque et triginta tribus: the voting in tribal deliberative assemblies was successive and it might have been expected that the voting would have stopped when the majority was reached. The evidence suggests, however, that all the tribes did vote, and their votes were made known. Cf. P. Fraccaro, *Opuscula*, ii (Pavia, 1957), 249–50, U. Hall, *Historia* xiii (1964), 285.

uti rogas: cf. xxxi. 8. 1 n.

25. 8–9. *News from Spain*

For the news from Hispania Ulterior cf. 21. 6–9. This notice is far vaguer, and gives no indication of the location of the battle or the identity of those against whom it was fought. The style of the report reflects that of the military bulletin: cf. xxxi. 23. 6–7 n.

9. volgataeque litterae: the phrase suggests that this was not the official dispatch, though no doubt one came in due course.

C. Sempronium Tuditanum: (90). Cf. xxxii. 27. 7 n.

proconsulem: he was still in his year as *praetor* but like other commanders in Spain was *praetor pro consule*. On L.'s terminology concerning commanders in Spain cf. pp. 5–6.

fusum fugatum: for the asyndeton cf. xxiii. 11. 10, xl. 48. 6, Preuss, 96–8.

Schlag, 31, may be right to think that xxxiv. 10. 5–6 refers to action taken by M. Helvius, the governor of Ulterior, to restore peace in Citerior, and that it is for this, not for the battle described in xxxiv. 10. 1–2, that he received his *ovatio*.

25. 10–26. 5. *Provinces and armies*

10. urbanas: cf. xxxi. 8. 11.

11. [cum duabus legionibus]: redundant with *eodem exercitu* and clearly a gloss. Its presence in both B and Mog. indicates that F and Mg shared a common archetype (Tränkle, *Gnomon*, 373 n. 4).

imperium . . . videri esse: cf. xxxii. 28. 9, where Flamininus' command is prorogued until a successor is appointed. A further *s.c.* for prolongation was therefore unnecessary.

26. 1. inter cives et peregrinos: cf. xxxii. 28. 2 n.

2. Q. Fabius Buteo: in succession to M. Helvius.

Q. Minucius Thermus: in succession to the dead C. Sempronius Tuditanus (25. 9).

C. Laelius Siciliam: in succession to L. Manlius Vulso.

Ti. Sempronius Longus Sardiniam: in succession to L. Atilius.

3. legiones singulas: the two specified in 25. 10 *duas . . . mitterentur*. It is not made clear whether Fabius Buteo himself consulted the senate on the matter, as prescribed in 21. 9.

5–6. Here L. inserts a historical reflection between the account of the distribution of provinces and the section on prodigies. Cf. xxxii. 27. 3 n. and p. 11.

5. bellum . . . finitum: cf. 21. 6–9 n.

motum: Tränkle (*Gnomon*, 374 n. 1) prefers Mg's *exortum* as being a good Livian usage: cf. 19. 6 n. It should be observed that Mg appears to have been very inaccurate in this passage.

26. 6–9. *Prodigies*

Cf. xxxi. 12. 5–10 n.

7. P. Villius eques Romanus: perhaps related to the family of the consul of 199. *eques Romanus*, at this date at least, must designate a member of the eighteen equestrian centuries. Mog. has the extraordinary corruption *L. Iulius Sequestris*.

fulmine . . . exanimati: for similar prodigies cf. Krauss, 37–8.

8. Capenati: sc. *agro*. Capena is a little to the north of Rome. *Lucus Feroniae* is a separate town in the ager Capenas. Cf. Ogilvie, 644 and for full details G. D. B. Jones, *PBSR* xxx (1962), 116–207, xxxi (1963), 100–58. For other prodigies at Capena cf. xxii. 1. 10, Oros. iv. 15. 1 (217), xxvii. 4. 14 (210), Wülker, 96.

de caelo tacta: cf. xxxii. 1. 10 n.

Monetae: the temple of Juno Moneta on the Capitol. Cf. Platner–Ashby, 289–90, Marbach, *RE*, xvi. 113 ff., Nash, i. 515.

hastarum spicula arserant: for similar prodigies cf. Wülker, 20, Krauss, 89.

9. lupus: cf. xxxii. 29. 2 n.

Esquilina . . . evaserat: the Porta Esquilina is on the eastern side of the city (Platner–Ashby, 407). The Vicus Tuscus ran on the west side of the Palatine between the Forum and the Circus Maximus (Platner–Ashby, 579). The Cermalus has usually been regarded as the western part of the Palatine (Platner–Ashby, 111, V. Groh, *Ath.* N.S. vii [1929], 316–62), but F. Castagnoli, *AC* xvi (1964), 173 ff., locates it at the foot of the Palatine. The Porta Capena is the exit for the Via Appia in the south-east of the city. It did not face Capena (§ 8) and the two names may be unconnected (Platner–Ashby, 405).

maioribus hostiis: cf. xxxi. 5. 3 n.

27. 1–5. *The return of Spanish governors*

Both these men had in fact been superseded at the beginning of 197. We know of their successors' activities (21. 6–9, 25. 9), and it is best to think that disputes about Blasio's triumph (see below) took some time, rather than that they only returned at the end of 197, as Broughton, *MRR*, i. 333–4 assumes.

1. Cn. Cornelius Blasio: (74). Cf. xxxi. 50. 11 n.

ovans: this *ovatio* is recorded in the *Fasti Triumphales* for 196 (on

the reading of the entry cf. G. V. Sumner, *Phoenix* xix [1965], 24–6).
We have not been informed of the activities which merited the
ovatio: cf. 21. 6–9 n. The statement that Stertinius did not even try
to get a triumph suggests that Blasio in fact asked for a triumph, and
was refused on technical grounds, as in the case of L. Cornelius
Lentulus in 200 (cf. xxxi. 20. 1 ff., Schlag, 60).

3. L. Stertinius: cf. xxxi. 50. 11 n.

ne temptata . . . spe: see above. Presumably Stertinius did not
try for an *ovatio* either.

4. foro bovario: the Forum Boarium, the cattle-market of Rome,
lay between the Circus Maximus and the Tiber. The form *Bovarium*
is found several times in MSS. of L. Cf. Platner–Ashby, 223–4, *TLL*,
ii. 2056.

Fortunae . . . Matutae: on the identification of these temples
cf. Platner–Ashby, 214–15, 330–1, Nash, i. 411.

27. 5—35. *Events in Greece in winter 197/6, and 196*

27. 5—29. *Boeotia*

Cf. Pol. xviii. 43 and 40. 1–4 (on the latter passage cf. Aymard,
Pallas iv [1956], 27–37 = *ÉHA*, 364–72, Walbank, *Commentary*, ii.
27). See also P. Cloché, *Thèbes de Béotie*, 253 ff., Briscoe, *Past and
Present*, no. 36 (April, 1967), 10, Deininger, 54 ff. On the frequency
of murder in Boeotia cf. *GGM* i. 103 § 16, Niese, ii. 647 n. 4.

5. hibernabat . . . restituerentur: Pol. xviii. 43. 1: Τίτου παρα-
χειμάζοντος ἐν Ἐλατείᾳ Βοιωτοί, σπουδάζοντες ἀνακομίσασθαι τοὺς
ἄνδρας τοὺς παρ' αὐτῶν στρατευσαμένους παρὰ τῷ Φιλίππῳ, διεπρεσβεύ-
οντο περὶ τῆς ἀσφαλείας αὐτῶν πρὸς Τίτον. L. gives the request and its
result at the same time.

Elatiae: cf. xxxii. 18. 9 n., for its capture xxxii. 24. Flamininus
had also spent the winter of 198/7 there (xxxii. 39. 1, xxxiii. 1. 1).

Boeoti: for their submission cf. chs. 1–2.

qui . . . Philippum: whether these men were volunteers (thus
Aymard, *PR*, 117 n. 11, Deininger, 51) or an official Boeotian force
is not clear.

6. Id . . . erat: Pol. xviii. 43. 2: ὁ δὲ βουλόμενος ἐκκαλεῖσθαι τοὺς
Βοιωτοὺς πρὸς τὴν σφετέραν εὔνοιαν διὰ τὸ προορᾶσθαι τὸν Ἀντίοχον,
ἑτοίμως συνεχώρησεν. Fear of Antiochus is similarly given as a reason
for making peace with Philip (13. 15). For Flamininus it is Greek
goodwill, not Roman armed force, that is the best defence against
Antiochus.

7. Restitutis . . . miserunt: Pol. xviii. 43. 4: ἔπεμψαν δὲ καὶ πρεσβείαν πρὸς τὸν Φίλιππον τὴν εὐχαριστήσουσαν ἐπὶ τῇ τῶν νεανίσκων ἐπανόδῳ, λυμαινόμενοι τὴν τοῦ Τίτου χάριν. L. alters the order of Polybius' narrative.

8–9. et comitiis . . . fuerant: Pol. xviii. 43. 3: Βραχύλλης, τοῦτον μὲν εὐθέως βοιωτάρχην κατέστησαν and xviii. 43. 5: οἱ περὶ τὸν Ζεύξιππον καὶ Πεισίστρατον, καὶ πάντες οἱ δοκοῦντες εἶναι Ῥωμαίοις φίλοι. W–M follow Nissen, *KU*, 12, in thinking that a clause representing *quod . . . fuisset* has fallen out from our texts of Polybius. It is possible, however, that L. simply assumed that Brachylles had been the leader of the Boeotian contingent.

Boeotarchen: on the Boeotarchs cf. Walbank, *Commentary*, ii. 608. Brachylles is one of several Boeotarchs and not the federal *strategos*, on whom cf. 1. 3 n. Larsen, *Greek Federal States*, 386 wrongly implies that Brachylles became head of the confederacy.

Brachyllem: Antigonus Doson had appointed him *epistates* of Sparta in 222 and he had been with Philip at Nicaea (Pol. xviii. 1. 2). Cf. Wilcken, *RE*, iii. 806–7, Walbank, *Commentary*, ii. 549.

Zeuxippo et Pisistrato: not otherwise known.

aliisque: such as Dicaearchus and, probably, Antiphilus, who are mentioned in chs. 1–2.

10. id . . . ceperunt: Pol. xviii. 43. 5: ἃ συνορῶντες . . . δυσχερῶς ἔφερον, προορώμενοι τὸ μέλλον καὶ δεδιότες περὶ σφῶν αὐτῶν καὶ τῶν ἀναγκαίων.

cum ad portas . . . fuissent: Pol. xviii. 43. 6: σαφῶς γὰρ ᾔδεισαν ὡς, ἐὰν μὲν οἱ Ῥωμαῖοι χωρισθῶσιν ἐκ τῆς Ἑλλάδος, ὁ δὲ Φίλιππος μένῃ παρὰ πλευράν, συνεπισχύων αἰεὶ τοῖς πρὸς σφᾶς ἀντιπολιτευομένοις, οὐδαμῶς ἀσφαλῆ σφίσιν ἐσομένην τὴν ἐν τῇ Βοιωτίᾳ πολιτείαν.

28. *The murder of Brachylles.* It is clear from §§ 11 and 14 that the murder took place at Thebes and not at Elatia, as stated by A. W. Lintott, *Violence in Republican Rome* (Oxford, 1968), 12.

28. 1. Dum . . . statuerunt: in this one sentence L. passes over and suppresses what Polybius says in xviii. 43. 7–12. Zeuxippus and his friends approach Flamininus who says αὐτὸς μὲν οὐκ . . . κοινωνεῖν τῆς πράξεως ταύτης, τοὺς δὲ βουλομένους πράττειν οὐ κωλύειν (xviii. 43. 10). Flamininus refers them to Alexamenus, the Aetolian *strategos*, who produces the assassins. For similar suppressions cf. p. 22 n. 4.

2. celebri: 'at which many people were present'.

3. tres Italici, tres Aetoli: Pol. xviii. 43. 12: τρεῖς μὲν τῶν Αἰτωλικῶν . . . τρεῖς δὲ τῶν Ἰταλικῶν.

Aetoli: B has *Aetoli*, Mog. *Aetolici*. L.'s practice is to use *Aetoli* for the people, *Aetolicus* as an epithet (cf. Packard, i. 276–81). Polybius sometimes uses the form *Αἰτωλικός* and it is conceivable that on this occasion L. followed him.

quiritatio: this seems to be a Roman term for the process of calling for help to fellow-citizens when attacked (calling on *Quirites*). *Quiritare* is found several times in this sense though the present passage appears to be the only occurrence of *quiritatio*. Cf. Lintott, *Violence in Republican Rome*, 11 ff., P. Garnsey, *Social Status and Legal Privilege in the Roman Empire* (Oxford, 1970), 191.

4. in theatro: for theatres as the meeting-place for Greek assemblies cf. Taylor, *RVA*, 123 n. 42.

7. constanti animo: *et constanti* B, *consimili* Mog. Deletion of *et* is preferable to positing a lacuna before it.

8. argumentatur: B and Mog. have *argumentatus*. Omission of *est* is possible (cf. xxxi. 21. 5 n., Pettersson, 95) but confusion of *-s* and *-r* is easy, and the change seems preferable.

9. nihil, opinione omnium pro indicio . . . nominaverunt: thus B. Mog. has *opinionem omnium, ea pro indicio usi . . . nominaverunt*. McDonald takes *pro indicio nominare* as a formula, and presumably regards *opinione omnium* as an instrumental ablative. But there are no parallels for the alleged formula. Mg was certainly emending after omitting *nihil* (cf. Tränkle, *Gnomon*, 374) but *usi* may not be part of that emendation. I think Kreyssig was right to insert it after *indicio*, otherwise keeping B's text.

10. Stratonida: not otherwise known.

Tanagram: about 15 miles east of Thebes. Cf. Fiehn, *RE*, ivA. 2154–62, P–K, i. 2. 514–15.

suam magis . . . metuens: cf. Pol. xviii. 43. 13: οὐδεὶς γὰρ οὕτως οὔτε μάρτυς ἐστὶ φοβερὸς οὔτε κατήγορος δεινὸς ὡς ἡ σύνεσις ἡ κατοικοῦσ’ ἐν ταῖς ἑκάστων ψυχαῖς. *conscientiam* and *consciorum* are deliberately used in different senses.

11. servus erat: the phrase serves to introduce a new character and a new element in the narrative. It is thus similar to the *est locus* formula (cf. Ogilvie, 103, G. W. Williams, *Tradition and Originality in Roman Poetry* [Oxford, 1968], 640 ff.). Cf. e.g. vii. 26. 2, ix. 36. 1, xxiv. 48. 2, xxv. 34. 2, xxxii. 22. 5, xliv. 24. 9. See also A. Bloch, *MH* i (1944), 250 ff., Nisbet, *CR* N.S. xxi (1971), 63.

The episode is similar both to the Bellerophon legend (Hom. *Il.* vi. 155 ff.) and, more closely, to the story of Pausanias' messenger (Thuc. i. 132–3). But the source is Polybius, and it is scarcely possible to question its truth. Indeed Polybius himself (xviii. 40. 2) says the incident had many precedents.

14. conscientia: the slave's knowledge of the crime. Polybius (xviii. 40. 1–4) condemns the slave's action as treachery, L. understands it. Cf. xxxi. 17. 11 n.

Anthedonem: on the coast a little north of the Euripus. It is odd that Zeuxippus could hope to go into exile here, as it was part of the Boeotian League. Perhaps he intended to cross to Euboea, and L. has abbreviated the story.

On Anthedon cf. Hirschfeld, *RE*, i. 2360–1, P–K, i. 2. 496, on its harbour H. Schlaeger–D. J. Blackman–J. Schaefer–G. Anger–M. H. Jameson, *AA* lxxxiii (1968), 21 ff.

29. 1. credentes . . . conscisse: having omitted Polybius' account of Flamininus' connivance at the murder, L. can present the Boeotians' beliefs without committing himself as to whether or not they are true.

principem gentis: cf. xxxi. 17. 11 n. As a leading man in Boeotia he would not have organized the murder without the agreement of Flamininus.

2. proximum bello: guerilla warfare.

in hospitiis . . . per hiberna: evidently a number of Roman troops were wintering in Boeotia, but those killed *in hospitiis* were probably there on their own initiative.

3. deversoria: = *hospitiis*.

deducti: B. Mog. has *devecti deductique*, indicating that variants must have occurred in the archetype of Mg (cf. Tränkle, *Gnomon*, 374).

4. negotiandi . . . causa: perhaps actually trading themselves, rather than just 'shopping'. Cf. W–M's note.

5. castris: L. seems to have forgotten that the main camp is at Elatia in Phocis.

6. Copaidem paludem: Lake Copais is to the north-east of Thebes. Cf. Geiger, *RE*, xi. 1346–60, P–K, i. 2. 466 ff.

Acraephiae: just to the east of Lake Copais. Cf. Hirschfeld, *RE*, i. 1194, P–K, i. 2. 488. Its name as attested in inscriptions is τὰ Ἀκραίφια (cf. M. Feyel, *BCH* lx [1936], 11 n. 1).

Coroneae: a little to the west of the Lake. Cf. Pieske, *RE*, xi. 1425–31, P–K, i. 2. 449–50.

7 ff. Technically the Boeotians were allies of Rome (chs. 1–2) so Flamininus had little legal basis for acting in this way.

8. pioque se bello: B. Mog. has *pioque bello se*, which is a clear emendation of what seemed an unusual word-order. It is in fact a case of Wackernagel's law, with *iusto pioque* regarded as a single unit.

(Cf. J. Wackernagel, *Kleine Schriften*, i. 1 ff., K–St, ii. 592 ff., Nisbet, *Commentary on Cicero, in Pisonem*, 52).

9. Ap. Claudio : (294). Almost certainly identical with the *legatus* of xxxiv. 28. 10, 50. 10, and he cannot therefore be the Ap. Claudius Nero of xxxii. 35. 7, 36. 10, as the latter was praetor in 195 (cf. 42. 7, 43. 5). He is therefore Ap. Claudius Pulcher, who will have served as a *legatus* in Greece from 196 to 194. He served again in Greece in 191, was praetor in 188 or 187, and reached the consulship in 185. He was a *legatus* in Macedonia and the Peloponnese in 184 and in Aetolia in 174–3. Cf. Schlag, 112–13, xxxii. 35. 7 n.

circumsidit : B. Mog. has *circumsedit*. Ogilvie, *Phoenix*, 344 says that the aorist is necessary. But for L.'s alternation of tenses cf. xxxi. 39. 9 n. With *mittunt* in the next sentence we need not hesitate to keep the present.

11. plus . . . decreverant : they had agreed to fight on Rome's side and therefore their loyalty could not be in doubt.

For a later attempt by Flamininus to secure the recall of Zeuxippus cf. Pol. xxii. 4.

30–35. *The settlement of the Isthmus*

L.'s main source is Pol. xviii. 44–8. See also Plut. *Flam*. 10–12, App. *Mac*. 9. 3–4, Just. xxx. 4. 17–18, Val. Max. iv. 8. 5, Zon. ix. 16. 12 (on Plutarch's account cf. C. P. Jones, *Plutarch and Rome* [Oxford, 1971], 97 ff.). For literature cf. Walbank, *Philip V*, 179 n. 1, *Commentary*, ii. 609–10, to which add Dahlheim, 83 ff., Accame, *Espansione romana*, 199 ff. On L.'s adaptation of Polybius in this section cf. Brueggmann, 145 ff.

30. 1. paucos . . . est : Pol. xviii. 44. 1: κατὰ τὸν καιρὸν τοῦτον ἧκον ἐκ τῆς Ῥώμης οἱ δέκα, δι' ὧν ἔμελλε χειρίζεσθαι τὰ κατὰ τοὺς Ἕλληνας, κομίζοντες τὸ τῆς συγκλήτου δόγμα τὸ περὶ τῆς πρὸς Φίλιππον εἰρήνης. What Polybius reports as the *senatus consultum* governing the actions of the *x legati* L. describes as the actual terms of peace. Polybius does not claim to be reporting the whole of the *s.c.*, only τὰ συνέχοντα (xviii. 44. 2).

paucos post dies : in this case a genuine chronological link; κατὰ τὸν καιρὸν τοῦτον in Polybius probably refers to the events in Boeotia; cf. Walbank, *Philip V*, 324.

decem legati : cf. 24. 7 nn.

2. ut omnes . . . tempus : Pol. xviii. 44. 2–3: τοὺς μὲν ἄλλους Ἕλληνας πάντας, τούς τε κατὰ τὴν Ἀσίαν καὶ κατὰ τὴν Εὐρώπην, ἐλευθέρους ὑπάρχειν καὶ νόμοις χρῆσθαι τοῖς ἰδίοις· τοὺς δὲ ταττομένους ὑπὸ Φίλιππον καὶ τὰς πόλεις τὰς ἐμφρούρους παραδοῦναι Φίλιππον Ῥωμαίοις πρὸ τῆς τῶν Ἰσθμίων πανηγύρεως. L. has misunderstood

Polybius here. Freedom for the Greeks was granted for all except those under Philip's direct control. The latter were to be handed over to Rome and their ultimate status was left in doubt. There could, of course, have been no serious question of those in the first category not remaining free: but the statement was probably designed to serve as a manifesto against Antiochus as well as a settlement with Philip. L. has made all the states free, and then added the provision that those of them in Philip's control were to be evacuated by him. (It is conceivable that L. understood Polybius perfectly well, but chose to portray Rome as granting freedom to all without question.)

3. quae in Asia . . . esse : Pol. xviii. 44. 4: Εὔρωμον δὲ καὶ Πήδασα καὶ Βαργύλια καὶ τὴν Ἰασέων πόλιν, ὁμοίως Ἄβυδον, Θάσον, Μύριναν, Πέρινθον, ἐλευθέρας ἀφεῖναι τὰς φρουρὰς ἐξ αὐτῶν μεταστησάμενον. L. has added *quae in Asia essent*, wrongly, for Myrina, Thasos, and Perinthus are not in Asia: though at xviii. 45. 4 (cf. 31. 3) Polybius makes the Aetolians complain that all the states specifically freed are in Asia.

Euromo : cf. xxxii. 33. 6 n. It became Rhodian after Apamea and so may already have been captured by Antiochus (cf. Fraser and Bean, *RPI*, 108 n. 1, Schmitt, *Antiochos*, 281).

Pedasisque : cf. xxxii. 33. 6 n. For its site cf. Walbank, *Commentary*, ii. 610.

B conflated *Euromo Pedasisque* into *Burū ope dasis*.

Bargyliis : cf. xxxii. 33. 6 n. Whether or not it was later captured by Antiochus is not clear (Schmitt, *Antiochos*, 280).

Iaso : cf. xxxii. 33. 6 n. It was captured by Antiochus in 197 (Schmitt, *Antiochos*, 287–8) and granted αὐτονομία by him (*OGIS* 237).

Myrina : on Lemnos. In 35. 2 Hephaestia, the other town on the island, is freed and it seems certain that the whole of Lemnos was under Philip's control. The date of its acquisition by Macedon is uncertain. Cf. Walbank, *Commentary*, ii. 611.

Abydo : cf. xxxi. 16. 6 ff. It also had been captured by Antiochus by this time (cf. 38. 1 n., Schmitt, *Antiochos*, 284).

Thaso : cf. xxxi. 31. 4 n.

Perintho : cf. xxxii. 33. 7 n.

The absence of any reference to Sestus and Chalcedon may be due to an omission by Polybius, but it is conceivable that they had already been abandoned by Philip and that the senate knew this at the time the *s.c.* was passed. But the absence of any mention of the Ptolemaic cities in Thrace captured by Philip in 200 (cf. xxxi. 16) is deliberate, and not an omission by Polybius, as argued by Holleaux, *Études*, iv. 320. The senate did not intend to return them to

Egypt, as that would have been a flagrant contrast with her policy of Greek freedom. But it did not want to advertise this abandonment of Ptolemaic interests too widely. The inclusion of towns which were already in Antiochus' possession may be due to the fact that at the time the *s.c.* was passed the senate was not aware of the real situation. It is not necessarily to be seen as a warning to Antiochus, as argued by Holleaux, *Études*, iv. 309 n. 2, Walbank, *Commentary*, ii. 611.

eas quoque: in fact they alone at this stage.

4. de Cianorum . . . placuisset: Pol. xviii. 44. 5: περὶ δὲ τῆς τῶν Κιανῶν ἐλευθερώσεως Τίτον γράψαι πρὸς Προυσίαν κατὰ τὸ δόγμα τῆς συγκλήτου. L.'s addition of *decem legatis* introduces a mistake. The senate had clearly agreed in principle that Cius should be freed, but did not see how to enforce its decision without going to war with Prusias. On Philip's capture of Cius cf. xxxi. 31. 4 n., on Prusias xxxii. 34. 6 n., and on the subsequent fate of Cius, Walbank, *Commentary*, ii. 611.

5. captivos . . . agebant: Pol. xviii. 44. 6: τὰ δ' αἰχμάλωτα καὶ τοὺς αὐτομόλους ἅπαντας ἀποκαταστῆσαι Φίλιππον Ῥωμαίοις ἐν τοῖς αὐτοῖς χρόνοις, ὁμοίως δὲ καὶ τὰς καταφράκτους ναῦς πλὴν πέντε σκαφῶν καὶ τῆς ἑκκαιδεκήρους. L. adds details of the ship, for which cf. xlv. 35. 3, Walbank, *Commentary*, ii. 611–12, D. J. Blackman, *GRBS* x (1969), 215–16, who doubts whether this ship was identical with the one built by Demetrius Poliorcetes. The provision about the ships is an addition by the senate to the terms provisionally agreed with Flamininus (cf. App. *Mac.* 9. 3).

The *captivi* probably included those of Rome's allies. Cf. Walbank, *Commentary*, ii. 611, Ducrey, 270, xxxii. 33. 3 n.

6. ne plus . . . gereret: these two clauses are not in Polybius, and have long been recognized as annalistic fabrications. Philip never had any elephants, and his activities after the peace show that he was not forbidden to wage war outside Macedonia. Both provisions have been imported from the treaty with Carthage.

Cf. Täubler, i. 228–39, 432 ff., Klotz, *Hermes* l (1915), 523–5, Holleaux, *Études*, v. 104 ff., De Sanctis, iv. 1. 95–6 n. 185, Petzold, 92 ff., Meloni, *Perseo*, 187, *Valore storico*, 152, Walbank, *Commentary*, ii. 609–10. *Contra* L. Bivona, *Kokalos* ii (1956), 50 ff. On the relevance of this passage for the question of L.'s use of his sources cf. p. 7.

7. mille talentum . . . annorum: Pol. xviii. 44. 7: δοῦναι δὲ καὶ χίλια τάλαντα, τούτων τὰ μὲν ἡμίση παραυτίκα, τὰ δ' ἡμίση κατὰ φόρους ἐν ἔτεσι δέκα. Appian, *Mac.* 9. 3 sees this too as a senatorial addition to Flamininus' terms. But the 200 talents paid at the time of the negotiations with Flamininus were clearly only a deposit (cf. 13. 14–15) and the details were left for the senate to decide. Cassola (*Labeo* vi [1960], 119) thinks that Flamininus regarded them as a final payment.

8. Valerius Antias: cf. xxxii. 6. 5 n.

quaternum . . . tradit: if Antias was using a calculation of 80 lb. to a talent (cf. xxxviii. 38. 13) the total is 500 talents, which suggests that he has omitted the initial payment from his calculations.

Claudius: cf. 10. 9 n.

in annos . . . pondo: this must be completely false. Cf. Holleaux, *Études*, v. 109–12 against the suggestion of Klotz (*Hermes* l [1915], 524) that it represents an earlier stage in the negotiations.

9. idem . . . gereret: Klotz (*Hermes* l, 525) and Holleaux (*Études*, v. 118) argue that *nominatim* indicates Claudius had also mentioned the general prohibition. But the word could easily be L.'s own, to bring harmony to his account as a whole.

Eumene . . . rex erat: Eumenes II succeeded Attalus in 197 and reigned until 159.

10. in haec . . . filius: not reported by L. as being from Antias or Claudius, but equally false. They were in fact given at Tempe: cf. 13. 14 n. The *s.c.* may have said that the hostages were to remain at Rome.

Antias Valerius: B. Mog. has the usual *Valerius Antias*. For the inversion cf. xl. 29. 8. It is common in Cicero: cf. H. L. Axtell, *CPh* x (1915), 392 ff.

Attalo . . . datos: Attalus was no longer alive and Aegina was in fact acquired by Attalus in 210 (cf. xxxi. 14. 11 n.). On the elephants cf. § 6 n. Klotz's view (*Hermes* l, 524) that *absenti* means 'dead' and that the elephants were Roman elephants given to Eumenes is quite impossible. Cf. Holleaux, *Études*, v. 112–17.

11. Rhodiis . . . tenuisset: Stratonicea and several Carian cities were already in Rhodian possession (cf. ch. 18 and especially 18. 22 n.). *Cariae urbes* could refer to all the Carian cities taken by Philip, or to those recaptured by Rhodes in 197. If the former, it is an anticipation of the settlement of Apamea, if the latter, the reference, like those to Aegina and Stratonicea, could be justified on the grounds that the senate did permit Eumenes and Rhodes to keep these possessions. But the senate would not have said so publicly (the *s.c.* was clearly not secret) and it is more likely that in the case of Stratonicea Antias was seeking to justify Rome's removal of it in 167 (Pol. xxx. 21. 3) by claiming that it was an earlier Roman gift (cf.

Schmitt, *Rom und Rhodos*, 217) and that the Carian reference is simply a mistake. Cf. De Sanctis, iv. 1. 121 n. 19.

Atheniensibus . . . Scyrum : Delos and Lemnos were in fact given to Athens in 167 (Pol. xxx. 20. 7). There is no mention of Imbros and Scyros in this connection but they were Athenian later and so their acquisition by Athens may also date to 167. Cf. Niese, iii. 189 n. 6, Ferguson, *Hellenistic Athens*, 315–16, Holleaux, *Études*, v. 108 n. 1.

31. 1–2. omnibus . . . adumbratas esse : Pol. xviii. 45. 1 : τούτου δὲ τοῦ δόγματος διαδοθέντος εἰς τοὺς Ἕλληνας οἱ μὲν ἄλλοι πάντες εὐθαρσεῖς ἦσαν καὶ περιχαρεῖς, μόνοι δ' Αἰτωλοί, δυσχεραίνοντες ἐπὶ τῷ μὴ τυγχάνειν ὧν ἤλπιζον, κατελάλουν τὸ δόγμα, φάσκοντες οὐ πραγμάτων, ἀλλὰ γραμμάτων μόνον ἔχειν αὐτὸ διάθεσιν. L. continues to regard the *s.c.* as the peace itself as announced by the *x legati*: cf. 30. 1 n.

mussantes : a poetic word found twice in Sallust and three times in L. (vii. 25. 1, xxviii. 40. 2). Cf. Tränkle, *WS*, 131–2.

2–3. cur enim . . . Demetriade : Pol. xviii. 45. 3–5 : ἔφασκον γὰρ εἶναι δύο γνώμας ἐν τῷ δόγματι περὶ τῶν ὑπὸ Φιλίππου φρουρουμένων πόλεων, τὴν μὲν μίαν ἐπιτάττουσαν ἐξάγειν τὰς φρουρὰς τὸν Φίλιππον, τὰς δὲ πόλεις παραδιδόναι Ῥωμαίοις, τὴν δ' ἑτέραν ἐξάγοντα τὰς φρουρὰς ἐλευθεροῦν τὰς πόλεις. τὰς μὲν οὖν ἐλευθερουμένας ἐπ' ὀνόματος δηλοῦσθαι, ταύτας δ' εἶναι τὰς κατὰ τὴν Ἀσίαν, τὰς δὲ παραδιδομένας Ῥωμαίοις φανερὸν ὅτι τὰς κατὰ τὴν Εὐρώπην. εἶναι δὲ ταύτας Ὠρεόν, Ἐρέτριαν, Χαλκίδα, Δημητριάδα, Κόρινθον. L. reports Polybius faithfully here and sees no inconsistency with his mistaken interpretation of 30. 1–2. The Aetolian charge is that the states handed over to Rome will not in fact be freed.

 quae in Asia : cf. 30. 3 n.
 Corinthus . . . Chalcis . . . Demetriade : cf. xxxii. 37. 3 n.
 Oreus cum Eretria : both had been captured in the course of the war. Oreus was given to Attalus (xxxi. 46. 16), and it is likely that Eretria suffered the same fate (cf. xxxii. 16. 16 n.). Since they are now under consideration (cf. 34. 9–10) they cannot any longer be in Attalid hands, as were Aegina and Andros about whom no questions were raised. They had presumably been recaptured by Philip. Cf. Walbank, *Commentary*, ii. 612 and bibliography there quoted (except that in 'Aymard, *PR*, 11 n. 24' read n. 29).

4. Nec tota . . . erat : cf. Pol. xviii. 45. 2 : καί τινας ἐλάμβανον πιθανότητας ἐξ αὐτῶν τῶν ἐγγράπτων . . . In what follows L. alters the order of Polybius' narrative and reports the senate's instructions about the 'fetters' before the debate on them between Flamininus and the *legati*. This is a sensible transposition and makes the account more intelligible.

4–5. Dubitabatur . . . iussi erant: Pol. xviii. 45. 10: ταύτην δὲ συνέβαινε γίνεσθαι τὴν ἀπορίαν ἐν τῷ συνεδρίῳ διὰ τὸ περὶ μὲν τῶν ἄλλων ἐν τῇ Ῥώμῃ προδιειλῆφθαι καὶ ῥητὰς ἔχειν τοὺς δέκα παρὰ τῆς συγκλήτου τὰς ἐντολάς, περὶ δὲ Χαλκίδος καὶ Κορίνθου καὶ Δημητριάδος ἐπιτροπὴν αὐτοῖς δεδόσθαι διὰ τὸν Ἀντίοχον, ἵνα βλέποντες πρὸς τοὺς καιροὺς βουλεύωνται περὶ τῶν προειρημένων πόλεων κατὰ τὰς αὐτῶν προαιρέσεις.

ceterae . . . liberantur: as in Polybius, but clearly discussion was possible about other places than the 'fetters'. Polybius has stressed the 'fetters' because of their importance and because it was about them that the first and longest debate took place.

e re publica fideque sua: a technical formula: cf. viii. 4. 12, xxii. 39. 2, xxv. 7. 4, xxix. 10. 3, xxxviii. 8. 5, Flurl, 153–5.

6. Antiochus . . . nolebant: Pol. xviii. 45. 11: ὁ γὰρ προειρημένος βασιλεὺς δῆλος ἦν ἐπέχων πάλαι τοῖς κατὰ τὴν Εὐρώπην πράγμασιν.

Antiochus rex erat: a striking form of expression 'It was King Antiochus whom . . .'.

7. ab Elatia . . . agitabantur: Pol. xviii. 45. 7: ὁ δὲ Τίτος ὁρμήσας ἐκ τῆς Ἐλατείας μετὰ τῶν δέκα καὶ κατάρας εἰς τὴν Ἀντίκυραν, παραυτίκα διέπλευσεν εἰς τὸν Κόρινθον, κἀκεῖ παραγενόμενος συνήδρευε μετὰ τούτων καὶ διελάμβανε περὶ τῶν ὅλων. *per dies totos* is L.'s own phrase based on Pol. xviii. 45. 8.

Elatia: cf. 27. 5 n.

Anticyram: cf. xxxii. 18. 4 n.

8–9. identidem . . . traiecisse: adapted from Pol. xviii. 45. 6, 8–9. L. takes remarks attributed to the Aetolians in Polybius and fits them into his report of Flamininus' arguments. The charge is not a criticism by L. of Rome's lack of *fides*, as argued by Merten, 85 ff.

caritatem ac maiestatem: a conjunction of two different ideas. *caritas* is affection for the Romans, but *maiestas* is the dignity of Rome, which is *vera* either as being justified or as being really acknowledged as such.

fidem facere: on the phrase, in which *fides* has an active sense, cf. Fraenkel, *RhM* lxxi (1916), 188 ff. (= *Kleine Beiträge*, i. 16 ff.).

10. nihil . . . accipere: Polybius does not give the reactions or the motives of the *legati* as such (cf. Walsh, *RhM* xcvii [1954], 106–7). Some may have disagreed about the principle of *libertas* too: cf. p. 34.

11. postremo . . . decessisset: Pol. xviii. 45. 12: οὐ μὴν ἀλλὰ τὸν μὲν Κόρινθον ὁ Τίτος ἔπεισε τὸ συνέδριον ἐλευθεροῦν παραχρῆμα καὶ τοῖς Ἀχαιοῖς ἐγχειρίζειν διὰ τὰς ἐξ ἀρχῆς ὁμολογίας, τὸν δ' Ἀκροκόρινθον καὶ

Δημητριάδα καὶ Χαλκίδα παρακατέσχεν. In fact the possession of the Acrocorinth meant control of Corinth as well (cf. xxxi. 22. 6 n.). Formally, though, Corinth was restored to the Achaean League as Flamininus had promised (xxxii. 19. 4 n.).

redderetur . . . retineri : for the change of construction cf. xxxi. 44. 5 n.

32. *The declaration of the Isthmus.* On L.'s adaptation of Polybius in this chapter cf. Witte, 281 ff., McDonald, *JRS* xlvii (1957), 162, J. A. de Foucault, *RÉL* xlvi (1968), 210–13.

32. 1–2. Isthmiorum . . . mercatus erat: nothing corresponds to this in Polybius, and L. may be drawing on his own knowledge of Greek festivals. Perhaps he had read a book on the subject (cf. *FGH* III B p. 383). On the Isthmian games cf. Schneider, *RE*, ix. 2248–55.

artium viriumque et pernicitatis : *artium* refers to musical and poetical competitions, *virium* to wrestling, boxing, and the discus, and *pernicitatis* to racing.

concilium . . . erat: 'the market was the meeting-place for Greece and Asia'.

3. Tum vero . . . cessuros: abbreviated from Pol. xviii. 46. 1–3.

4. Ad spectaculum . . . pronuntiat: Pol. xviii. 46. 4: ἀθροισθέντος τοῦ πλήθους εἰς τὸ στάδιον ἐπὶ τὸν ἀγῶνα, προελθὼν ὁ κῆρυξ καὶ κατασιωπησάμενος τὰ πλήθη διὰ τοῦ σαλπικτοῦ τόδε τὸ κήρυγμα ἀνηγόρευσεν. *unde . . . solet* is L.'s own addition. There is no other specific evidence for it.

5. Senatus . . . Phthiotas: Pol. xviii. 46. 5: Ἡ σύγκλητος ἡ Ῥωμαίων καὶ Τίτος Κοΐντιος στρατηγὸς ὕπατος, καταπολεμήσαντες βασιλέα Φίλιππον καὶ Μακεδόνας, ἀφιᾶσιν ἐλευθέρους, ἀφρουρήτους, ἀφορολογήτους, νόμοις χρωμένους τοῖς πατρίοις, Κορινθίους, Φωκέας, Λοκρούς, Εὐβοεῖς, Ἀχαιοὺς τοὺς Φθιώτας, Μάγνητας, Θετταλούς, Περραιβούς. The senate and the commander alone are mentioned. The people sanctioned the peace with Philip but were not consulted on the details of the settlement.

Philippo rege Macedonibusque : cf. xxxi. 6. 1 n.

liberos . . . legibus esse : the concept of freedom had become so diluted that its content needed further definition (cf. in general Heidemann, *passim*). In fact even this freedom was only from Macedon and Rome. Phocis and Locris became Aetolian (cf. 34. 8).

Corinthios : cf. 31. 11 n.

Phocenses : cf. xxxii. 18. 4 n.

Locrensesque omnes : L. adds *omnes* because he knows of the divisions of Locris. But he is wrong. Ozolian Locris had remained Aetolian (cf. xxxii. 18. 5 n.) and it was only Eastern Locris that was concerned. The view that Epicnemidian Locris was also Aetolian already is untenable: cf. G. Klaffenbach, *Klio* xx (1926), 82, Walbank, *Commentary*, ii. 258: *contra* Oldfather, *RE*, xiii. 1227 ff., Flacelière, 308 n. 1, Accame, *Espansione romana*, 217 ff.

Magnetas, Thessalos, Perrhaebos : Perrhaebia and Magnesia were sometimes regarded as part of Thessaly (cf. Walbank, *Commentary*, ii. 613). On Perrhaebia cf. xxxi. 41. 5 n.

Achaeos Phthiotas : cf. xxxi. 1. 9–10 n.

6. percensuerat . . . fuerant : that is all those who had been directly under Philip's control, not his allies, whether they had joined Rome or, like Acarnania, surrendered. The latter category were already covered by the *s.c.* (Pol. xviii. 44. 2). There is no need for Oost's assumption (*RPEA*, 53 ff.) that Acarnania's status had been separately confirmed before the Isthmus meeting.

Walbank, *Commentary*, ii. 613 points to the omission of Dolopia and Orestis, which were also freed (34. 6). But Dolopia may have been regarded as part of Thessaly (perhaps at this point the *legati* intended to leave it as part of the new Thessalian κοινόν) while Orestis, having revolted from Macedon, was not in the same category as the other states.

6–9. audita voce . . . libertatem esse : adapted from Pol. xviii. 46. 6–9. L. gives special prominence to the feelings of the audience. He omits Polybius' statement that some had not even heard what the herald said.

10. Ludicrum . . . voluptatium : Pol. xviii. 46. 10: ὡς δέ ποτε κατέληξεν ὁ κρότος, τῶν μὲν ἀθλητῶν ἁπλῶς οὐδεὶς οὐδένα λόγον εἶχεν ἔτι, πάντες δὲ διαλαλοῦντες, οἱ μὲν ἀλλήλοις, οἱ δὲ πρὸς σφᾶς αὐτούς, οἷον εἰ παραστατικοὶ τὰς διανοίας ἦσαν. L. adds that the games were performed rapidly.

animi : with *nullius* one would expect *animus*. But L. is impressed by the phrase *animi et oculi* and emendation is not necessary. Cf. xxi. 33. 3, xxii. 48. 4, xxv. 38. 9, xxvii. 1. 8, xxviii. 6. 4, xxxii. 24. 5, xlii. 49. 2, xlv. 19. 1. *oculis animoque* and *oculorum animique* are found at ii. 40. 3 and xliv. 6. 8 respectively, but the first refers to a specific individual, and in the second L. would naturally avoid *oculorum animorumque*.

33. On L.'s adaptation of Polybius in this chapter cf. Witte, 362–3, Lambert, 60.

33. 1–2. Ludis . . . fuerit : Pol. xviii. 46. 11–12: ᾗ καὶ μετὰ τὸν

ἀγῶνα διὰ τὴν ὑπερβολὴν τῆς χαρᾶς μικροῦ διέφθειραν τὸν Τίτον εὐχαρι-
στοῦντες· οἱ μὲν γὰρ ἀντοφθαλμῆσαι κατὰ πρόσωπον καὶ σωτῆρα προσ-
φωνῆσαι βουλόμενοι, τινὲς δὲ τῆς δεξιᾶς ἅψασθαι σπουδάζοντες, οἱ δὲ
πολλοὶ στεφάνους ἐπιρριπτοῦντες καὶ λημνίσκους, παρ' ὀλίγον διέλυσαν
τὸν ἄνθρωπον. L. omits Polybius' statement that they wanted to call
Flamininus σωτήρ (on which cf. Walbank, *Commentary*, ii. 613–14).

ludis dimissis: by metonymy for the people attending the
games.

lemniscosque: the true reading is restored from Polybius. Mog.
has *lemnis quosque iacentium*, B the same but *liminis*.

3. sed erat . . . suppeditabat: L.'s own comment. Polybius
(xviii. 12. 5) says that at the time of the conference of Nicaea
Flamininus πλείω . . . τῶν τριάκοντ' ἐτῶν οὐκ εἶχε, and Plutarch
(*Flam.* 2. 2) says that at the time of his election to the consulship
Flamininus was not yet 30. It is hard to reconcile these statements
with what L. says here, even if we interpret Polybius to mean that
he had not reached 31 by November 198 and allow L. to imply that
he was a little short of 33 in June/July 196. This is the sort of case
in which L.'s information may have been more accurate than that
of Polybius. There is no need to assume that Polybius was L.'s only
source of information on the matter (thus Badian, *JRS* lxi [1971],
108 n. 35). Cf. p. 8 n. 1.

insigni: in sense goes with *gloriae*, but it is made to agree with
fructu.

4. nec praesens . . . renovata: here L. departs a long way from
Pol. xviii. 46. 13.

5–7. esse . . . potentissima sint: a fine rhetorical passage, and
a considerable elaboration on what Polybius says in xviii. 46. 14. On
the thoughts that lie behind it cf. A. Rostagni, *Scritti minori*, ii. 2
(Turin, 1956), 245.

6. terris continentibus iunctis: thus B. Mog. has *continenti*.
Madvig (*Emendationes*, 489–90) and W–M seem right to take *iunctis* as
dative with *hominibus* and *terris continentibus* as ablative.

7. una voce . . . urbes: Pol. xviii. 46. 15: ὥστε διὰ κηρύγματος
ἑνὸς ἅπαντας καὶ τοὺς τὴν Ἀσίαν κατοικοῦντας Ἕλληνας καὶ τοὺς τὴν
Εὐρώπην ἐλευθέρους, ἀφρουρήτους, ἀφορολογήτους γενέσθαι, νόμοις
χρωμένους τοῖς ἰδίοις. The freedom of *all* Greeks did not depend on
this announcement, but rhetorical exaggeration is quite understandable (cf. Walbank, *Commentary*, ii. 614, Dahlheim, 94 n. 47).

8. hoc . . . ingentis: the idea comes from Pol. xviii. 46. 14–15:
μέγα δὲ καὶ τὸ δύναμιν ἀκόλουθον τῇ προαιρέσει προσενέγκασθαι· τούτων
δὲ μέγιστον ἔτι τὸ μηδὲν ἐκ τῆς τύχης ἀντιπαῖσαι πρὸς τὴν ἐπιβολήν, ἀλλ'
ἁπλῶς ἅπαντα πρὸς ἕνα καιρὸν ἐκδραμεῖν.

audacis animi: Sallust (*Cat.* 5. 4) had described Catiline as having an *animus audax* (Skard, 25).

et virtutis et fortunae: *virtus* and *fortuna* are frequently collocated in L. (cf. Kajanto, 72-3). Polybius is thinking of the absence of a capricious τύχη working against Rome, while L.'s *fortuna* is nearer to positive fate (cf. 18. 1 n.).

34. 1-2. Secundum Isthmia . . . legati sunt: Pol. xviii. 47. 1: Διελθούσης δὲ τῆς πανηγύρεως πρώτοις μὲν ἐχρημάτισαν τοῖς παρ' Ἀντιόχου πρεσβευταῖς.

gentium civitatiumque: thus Mog.: B has *gentiumque*. As in § 5 *civitatium* refers to city-states, *gentium* to people not organized in cities. *civitatium* is therefore necessary. For similar abbreviations standing already in F cf. Tränkle, *Gnomon*, 375.

2-3. iis . . . Philippo erant: the reference must be to the embassy from Antiochus to Rome in the winter of 198/7 mentioned in 20. 8-9. But there is no reference to it in Polybius here, and it is not necessary to follow Nissen (*KU*, 12, 149) and Walbank, *Commentary*, ii. 614 in thinking that 'there is compression in our text of P(olybius) at this point'. L. may have inserted this statement simply on the basis of the passage in Polybius from which he derived his statement in 20. 8-9. But it could equally well come from a non-Polybian source (cf. p. 8).

The ambassadors are Lysias and Hegesianax (Pol. xviii. 47. 4).

nihil iam perplexe ut ante: this certainly looks annalistic. Before Philip was defeated the senate was in no position to make any kind of threat or demand to Antiochus, veiled or not. At the time of the embassy from Antiochus to Rome, he had come to an agreement with Pergamum (cf. xxxii. 27. 1 n.) and had not yet begun his attacks on the towns of the Asia Minor seaboard.

iis eadem . . . egerant: *pace* Badian, *CPh* liv (1959), 97 n. 23 (= *Studies*, 136 n. 23) these words do imply that Lysias and Hegesianax had also gone to Rome. But L. could be wrong.

3-4. sed aperte . . . traiceret: Pol. xviii. 47. 1-2: διακελευόμενοι τῶν ἐπὶ τῆς Ἀσίας πόλεων τῶν μὲν αὐτονόμων ἀπέχεσθαι καὶ μηδεμιᾷ πολεμεῖν, ὅσας δὲ νῦν παρείληφε τῶν ὑπὸ Πτολεμαῖον καὶ Φίλιππον ταττομένων, ἐκχωρεῖν. σὺν δὲ τούτοις προηγόρευον μὴ διαβαίνειν εἰς τὴν Εὐρώπην μετὰ δυνάμεως· οὐδένα γὰρ ἔτι τῶν Ἑλλήνων οὔτε πολεμεῖσθαι νῦν ὑπ' οὐδενὸς οὔτε δουλεύειν οὐδενί.

quae Philippi . . . fuissent: for the details of these cities cf. 19. 8-20 nn. Walbank's statement (*Commentary*, ii. 615) that Antiochus 'had virtually no possessions between Patara and Ephesus' ignores his captures in Caria, some of which Walbank himself tabulates. Cf. Schmitt, *Antiochos*, 280-1.

abstineret liberis civitatibus: it seems that this refers only to Lampsacus and Smyrna (cf. 38. 3 ff.), though by this time Antiochus had already captured a number of other 'free cities' in northern Asia Minor. Cf. 38. 1–2 nn.

neu quam: B's *ne umquam* (Mog. is hopelessly corrupt in this sentence) makes little sense and Madvig's correction is necessary.

ante omnia . . . traiceret: in fact Antiochus was probably already in Europe (cf. 38. 1 n., Walbank, *Commentary*, ii. 615).

L. omits Polybius' statement (xviii. 47. 3) that Hegesianax and Lysias were told that Roman envoys would soon visit Antiochus himself.

5. Dimissis...pronuntiabantur: Pol. xviii. 47. 5: μετὰ δὲ τούτους εἰσεκαλοῦντο πάντας τοὺς ἀπὸ τῶν ἐθνῶν καὶ πόλεων παραγεγονότας, καὶ τὰ δόξαντα τῷ συνεδρίῳ διεσάφουν. B has *decreto . . . pronuntiabantur*, Mog. *decreta . . . pronuntiabant*: but *civitates nominatim pronuntiare* cannot mean 'mention the states by name' and Crévier's supplement is clearly necessary.

6. Orestis . . . redditae: Pol. xviii. 47. 6: Μακεδόνων μὲν οὖν τοὺς Ὀρέστας καλουμένους διὰ τὸ προσχωρῆσαι σφίσι κατὰ τὸν πόλεμον αὐτονόμους ἀφεῖσαν. On the Orestae and their revolt cf. Walbank, *Commentary*, ii. 616, Hammond, *Epirus*, 620. Cf. also 32. 6 n.

Magnetes . . . pronuntiati: Pol. xviii. 47. 6: ἠλευθέρωσαν δὲ Περραιβοὺς καὶ Δόλοπας καὶ Μάγνητας. On these peoples cf. Walbank, *Commentary*, ii. 616–17, 32. 5–6 nn.

7. Thessalorum . . . reiecerunt: Pol. xviii. 47. 7–9: Θετταλοῖς δὲ μετὰ τῆς ἐλευθερίας καὶ τοὺς Ἀχαιοὺς τοὺς Φθιώτας προσένειμαν, ἀφελόμενοι Θήβας τὰς Φθίας καὶ Φάρσαλον. οἱ γὰρ Αἰτωλοὶ περί τε τῆς Φαρσάλου μεγάλην ἐποιοῦντο φιλοτιμίαν, φάσκοντες αὐτῶν δεῖν ὑπάρχειν κατὰ τὰς ἐξ ἀρχῆς συνθήκας, ὁμοίως δὲ καὶ περὶ Λευκάδος. οἱ δ' ἐν τῷ συνεδρίῳ περὶ μὲν τούτων τῶν πόλεων ὑπερέθεντο τοῖς Αἰτωλοῖς τὸ διαβούλιον πάλιν ἐπὶ τὴν σύγκλητον. Phthiotic Thebes was given to Aetolia, as Flamininus had agreed at Tempe (cf. 13. 7–13 nn.). Presumably the Aetolians had dropped for the moment their demands in respect of Echinus and Larisa Cremaste, and were concentrating on Pharsalus (which was not strictly in Phthiotic Achaea—cf. Walbank, *Commentary*, ii. 617). In Rome, however, they seem to have renewed their demands for all the towns. The fate of Pharsalus is thus left undecided for the moment. For the senate's decision cf. 49. 8 n.

Leucade: cf. ch. 17. There is no evidence for previous Aetolian possession of Leucas, and the Aetolian claims can have been based only on the terms of the 212/11 treaty, which specially provided for attacks on Acarnania (xxvi. 24. 11, cf. Walbank, *Commentary*, ii. 617).

8. Phocenses . . . contribuerunt: Pol. xviii. 47. 9: τοὺς δὲ Φωκέας καὶ τοὺς Λοκροὺς συνεχώρησαν αὐτοῖς ἔχειν, καθάπερ εἶχον καὶ πρότερον, ἐν τῇ συμπολιτείᾳ. Cf. 32. 5 n., G. Klaffenbach, *Klio* xx (1926), 82 ff., Walbank, *Philip V*, 182 n. 2, *Commentary*, ii. 617–18, Accame, *Espansione romana*, 228–30. That Opus was excluded, as argued by Lehmann, 109 n. 132, is scarcely credible: cf. Walbank, *JRS* lviii (1968), 254.

adiecta decreti auctoritate: L.'s own rather puzzling addition. It was the *decretum* alone that gave Phocis and Locris to Aetolia.

34. 9–37. 6. For this section fragments of F survive.

9. Corinthus . . . Achaeis: Pol. xviii. 47. 10: Κόρινθον δὲ καὶ τὴν Τριφυλίαν καὶ ⟨. . . The lacuna in Polybius is filled from our text of L. On Corinth cf. 31. 11 n., on Triphylia and Heraea xxxii. 5. 4 n. The Eleans had claimed Triphylia in Rome, the Aetolians Heraea, and both matters had been referred by the senate to the *legati*. The Messenians had then claimed Asine and Pylos, but both were probably left in Achaean hands (cf. Walbank, *Philip V*, 182 n. 3). For all this cf. Pol. xviii. 42. 6–8, omitted by L.

redditae: F. B and Mog. have *reddita*, but the fact that so easy a mistake is made independently by B and Mog. does not alter the case for thinking that B is copied directly from F but Mg is independent of F.

10. Oreum . . . adiecta: Pol. xvii. 47. 10–11: . . .⟩ ἔτι δὲ τὴν Ἐρετριέων πόλιν ἐδόκει μὲν τοῖς πλείοσιν Εὐμένει δοῦναι· Τίτου δὲ πρὸς τὸ συνέδριον διαστείλαντος οὐκ ἐκυρώθη τὸ διαβούλιον· διὸ καὶ μετά τινα χρόνον ἠλευθερώθησαν αἱ πόλεις αὗται διὰ τῆς συγκλήτου καὶ σὺν ταύταις Κάρυστος. On Oreus and Eretria cf. 31. 3 n. The addition of Carystus at this stage of the debate is puzzling. It had been captured in 198, immediately after the capture of Eretria (xxxii. 17. 1–2). It may never have been held by Pergamum, but since the senate was debating other places which had been captured by the allied fleet, Eumenes may have asked for Carystus also to be considered.

Schlag, 90, oddly thinks that Oreus and Eretria received temporary Roman garrisons.

11. Pleurato . . . ademisset: Pol. xviii. 47. 12–13: ἔδωκαν δὲ καὶ Πλευράτῳ Λυχνίδα καὶ Πάρθον, οὔσας μὲν Ἰλλυρίδας, ὑπὸ Φίλιππον δὲ ταττομένας. Ἀμυνάνδρῳ δὲ συνεχώρησαν, ὅσα παρεσπάσατο κατὰ πόλεμον ἐρύματα τοῦ Φιλίππου, κρατεῖν τούτων. If L. were right in identifying Parthus with the Parthini, this passage would be evidence for thinking that the Parthini had been conquered by Philip between 205, when they remained under Roman protection (xxix. 12. 13) and 201, and they would be one, at least, of the peoples referred to in xxx. 26. 2, 42. 2. But L.'s identification is probably incorrect: cf. Walbank, *Commentary*, ii. 618–19, xxxi. 1. 9–10 n., xxxii. 33. 3. On Pleuratus cf. xxxi. 28. 1 n., on Lychnidus, Walbank, l.c., on Amynander's captures xxxii. 14. 1–3.

35. 1–2. Dimisso . . . ad Philippum: Pol. xviii. 48. 1–3: ταῦτα δὲ διοικήσαντες ἐμέρισαν σφᾶς αὐτούς, καὶ Πόπλιος μὲν Λέντλος εἰς Βαργύλια πλεύσας ἠλευθέρωσε τούτους, Λεύκιος δὲ Στερτίνιος εἰς Ἡφαιστίαν καὶ Θάσον ἀφικόμενος καὶ τὰς ἐπὶ Θράκης πόλεις ἐποίησε τὸ παραπλήσιον. πρὸς δὲ τὸν Ἀντίοχον ὥρμησαν Πόπλιος Οὐίλλιος καὶ Λεύκιος Τερέντιος, οἱ δὲ περὶ Γνάιον τὸν Κορνήλιον πρὸς τὸν βασιλέα Φίλιππον.

P. Lentulus: (214). P. Cornelius Lentulus Caudinus. Perhaps curule aedile in 209, he was praetor in 203 with command prorogued in 202. He was also a member of the *x legati* for the Apamea settlement.

Bargylias: cf. 30. 3 n.

L. Stertinius: (5). Cf. xxxi. 50. 11 n. The correct praenomen is given by F and Gelenius. B has *P*. (Walbank's note, *Commentary*, ii. 619, is incorrect).

Hephaestiam: on Lemnos (cf. Fredrich, *RE*, xii. 1929). See 30. 3 n.

Thasum: cf. 30. 3, xxxi. 31. 4 n.

Thraeciae urbes: the Ptolemaic possessions not mentioned in the *s.c.* Cf. 30. 3 n.

P. Villius: (10). Cf. 24. 7 n., xxxi. 4. 3 n.

L. Terentius: (58). Massiliota: cf. xxxi. 50. 3 n.

Cn. Cornelius: probably Lentulus (176), the consul of 201: cf. xxxi. 14. 2 n., *MRR*, i. 339 n. 7. If so, he is not a friend of Scipio (cf. p. 32) and his actions here are of no relevance for the understanding of Scipio's policy. Polybius' οἱ δὲ περὶ Γνάιον and the plurals that follow suggest that Cornelius was accompanied by others of the *legati*.

3–7. Qui de minoribus . . . conventus: Pol. xviii. 48. 4: ᾧ καὶ συμμίξαντες πρὸς τοῖς Τέμπεσι περί τε τῶν ἄλλων διελέχθησαν ὑπὲρ ὧν εἶχον τὰς ἐντολάς, καὶ συνεβούλευον αὐτῷ πρεσβευτὰς πέμπειν εἰς τὴν Ῥώμην ὑπὲρ συμμαχίας, ἵνα μὴ δοκῇ τοῖς καιροῖς ἐφεδρεύων ἀποκαραδοκεῖν τὴν Ἀντιόχου παρουσίαν. L. elaborates on the meeting and gives life to the reported dialogue. Cf. Walsh, *RhM* xcvii (1954), 109.

5. societatem amicitiamque: a full *foedus* is envisaged. Cf. Walbank, *Commentary*, ii. 620, Dahlheim, 149 n. 63.

7. Tempe: cf. xxxii. 15. 9 n.

8. Qui cum . . . venit: Pol. xviii. 48. 5: τοῦ δὲ βασιλέως συγκαταθεμένου τοῖς ὑποδεικνυμένοις, εὐθέως ἀπ' ἐκείνου χωρισθέντες ἧκον ἐπὶ τὴν τῶν Θερμικῶν σύνοδον. L. has mistakenly made the Aetolian meeting into an Amphictyonic one and, as in xxxi. 32. 4, confused Thermopylae with Thermus. Cf. xxxi. 29. 1 n.

9. Aetolos . . . permanerent: Pol. xviii. 48. 6: καὶ παρελθόντες εἰς τὰ πλήθη παρεκάλουν τοὺς Αἰτωλοὺς διὰ πλειόνων μένειν ἐπὶ τῆς ἐξ ἀρχῆς αἱρέσεως καὶ διαφυλάττειν τὴν πρὸς Ῥωμαίους εὔνοιαν.

10–11. Aetolorum . . . potuisse: Pol. xviii. 48. 7–8: πόλλων δὲ παρισταμένων, καὶ τῶν μὲν πρᾴως καὶ πολιτικῶς μεμψιμοιρούντων αὐτοῖς ἐπὶ τῷ μὴ κοινωνικῶς χρῆσθαι τοῖς εὐτυχήμασι μηδὲ τηρεῖν τὰς ἐξ ἀρχῆς συνθήκας, τῶν δὲ λοιδορούντων καὶ φασκόντων οὔτ' ἂν ἐπιβῆναι τῆς Ἑλλάδος οὐδέποτε Ῥωμαίους οὔτ' ἂν νικῆσαι Φίλιππον, εἰ μὴ δι' ἑαυτούς. Aetolian complaints about the change in Roman attitudes after the defeat of Philip are probably justified (cf. ch. 11 n.), but of course they are quite wrong in claiming any part in Rome's coming to Greece in the first place (cf. xxxi. 1. 8 n.).

12. adversus ea . . . habuit: Pol. xviii. 48. 9–10: τὸ μὲν ἀπολογεῖσθαὶ πρὸς ἕκαστα τούτων οἱ περὶ τὸν Γνάιον ἀπεδοκίμασαν, παρεκάλουν δ' αὐτοὺς πρεσβεύειν εἰς τὴν Ῥώμην, διότι πάντων παρὰ τῆς συγκλήτου τεύξονται τῶν δικαίων· ὃ καὶ πεισθέντες ἐποίησαν. καὶ τὸ μὲν τέλος τοῦ πρὸς Φίλιππον πολέμου τοιαύτην ἔσχε διάθεσιν. For the senate's reply cf. 49. 8.

excederet: Mog. B has *cresceret* and the corrector of F wrote a word beginning with *c*. McDonald is right to see *cresceret* as a gloss on *excederet*.

36–37. *Events in Italy*

As in 200 L. has three 'domestic' sections for the year 196. This is because Polybius' description of the advance of Antiochus and the conference of Lysimachia (= chs. 38–41) occurred in his Asiatic section, separate from his account of events in Greece. L. thus used this division to insert his account of the slave rising and the fighting in the north.

36. 1–3. *Slave rising in Etruria*

The notice is too short for it to be possible to decide whether the rising was of real slaves, or of the 'serf' class in the cities of northern Etruria. All the possibilities are canvassed at length by M. Capozza, *Movimenti servili nel mondo romano in età repubblicana* (Rome, 1966), 123–41.

2. M'. Acilius Glabrio: cf. xxxi. 50. 5 n. For his appointment as *praetor peregrinus* cf. 26. 1.

una . . . legione urbana : cf. 25. 10. For the construction cf. Sall. *BJ* 19. 7.

alios ⟨. . . alios⟩ : there must be a lacuna here, as *alios* cannot be correlated with the *alios* in § 3: the latter are subdivisions of those captured.

36. 4–37. 12. *Gaul*

Cf. Oros. iv. 20. 11.

I cannot understand the discussion of these events by Schlag, 44–6. She first produces a diagram which indicates that the activities of Marcellus and Furius should not be taken consecutively. The meeting of the two consuls (37. 2) is placed immediately after Marcellus' defeat by the Boii, and the crossing of the Po by the Boii (37. 6) is a pursuit of Marcellus. She then proceeds, however, to relate the events in the order described by L., doubting only (i) whether Marcellus was really present at the *deditio* of 37. 4, on the grounds that at that time he was still in the land of the Insubres, (ii) whether the battle of 37. 7–8 was really a Roman victory (cf. n. ad loc.). There is, in fact, no difficulty in accepting L.'s narrative as it stands. By the time of the events described in ch. 37 Marcellus had returned to the south of the Po. On the conflict of sources in 36. 15 cf. n. ad loc.

4. Marcellum : cf. xxxi. 50. 1 n.

Boiorum : cf. xxxi. 2. 5 n.

in tumulo quodam : Mog. B's *inter tumulos quosdam* is equally possible.

Corolamus : not otherwise known.

quidam : a little harsh after *quodam* or *quosdam* and omitted by Mog. But L. may have written it, especially in the non-literary style of this passage.

5. praefecti socium : cf. xxxi. 2. 6 n.

T⟨i.⟩ Sempronius Gracchus : (60). *T.* MSS. There is no other case of a Titus among the Sempronii Gracchi and McDonald is clearly right to emend (cf. xxxi. 20. 5 n.). He is perhaps a cousin of the father of the Gracchi, consul in 177. Cf. *MRR*, i. 339 n. 8 (the doubts of Münzer there referred to are unjustified).

M. Iunius Silanus : (168). Not otherwise known.

secunda : cf. 22. 8 n.

M. Ogulnius : (3). He is probably to be identified with the *legatus* in Etruria in 210 (xxvii. 3. 9). After the two famous Ogulnii, tribunes in 300, one of whom was consul in 269, only this man and the praetor of 182 are known to have held any public office.

P. Claudius : (28). Not otherwise known.

7. ⟨a⟩ tanto terrore . . . reficeret : *reficere ab* is found at xxi. 26. 5,

xxxix. 30. 7, but *reficere ex* at xxx. 29. 1, xxxix. 49. 4, so that *e* would be an equally possible supplement, and palaeographically rather easier.

8. ut . . . patiens: a typically superior comment. On Caesar's allegations of Gallic lack of steadfastness cf. A. N. Sherwin-White, *Racial Prejudice in Imperial Rome* (Cambridge, 1967), 18 ff.

9. Pado . . . traiecto: to the northern side.

   agrum Comensem: the town of Comum was not at the site of modern Como, on the southern shore of Lake Como, but in the hills to the south-west of Como, in the vicinity of Grandate. The modern town is on the site of the Roman military camp probably established soon after this time, and later developed into Novum Comum by Caesar.

   For information on this I am indebted to an article by C. Bignami in *Qui Ratti*, the house magazine of the silk firm of Ratti at Como. Cf. also Nissen, *IL*, ii. 1. 185 ff., Hülsen, *RE*, supp. i. 326–7, F. Frigerio, *Atti e memorie del primo Congresso storico lombardo* (Milan, 1937), 1–6.

   Insubres: cf. xxxi. 10. 2 n.

10. cohortem Marsorum: a cohort of Italian auxiliaries. The Marsi, a people living to the north of the Samnites, were renowned for their bravery. Cf. Philipp, *RE*, xiv. 1977–9, Salmon, *Samnium*, index, s.v. *Marsi*, Nisbet and Hubbard, 32–3.

13. Valerius Antias: cf. xxxii. 6. 5 n. L. does not on this occasion explicitly query the figures, but he implies some scepticism.

   octoginta: *octingenta* B, *et quingenta* Mog. Clearly the capture of 807 *signa* is impossible and the correction is necessary.

   carpenta septingenta: F has *carpentaria capta capta* with *-ria* and the second *capta* dotted for deletion. The archetype therefore had *carpenta capta*. But the repetition of *capta* is harsh and Mog.'s omission of it is to be accepted.

   Claudius: cf. 10. 9 n.

14. Comum oppidum: cf. § 9 n.

15. id quoque . . . accepta sit: the difference may have arisen because of confusion between the battle with the Boii in 36. 4–5 and the events in ch. 37. Schlag, 46, may be right in thinking that L.'s order is correct and that Marcellus tried to erase the memory of his defeat by attacking the Comenses. The reverse order is accepted by Tenney Frank, *CAH*, viii. 327, Toynbee, ii. 270 n. 3.

37. 1. L. Furius Purpurio: cf. xxxi. 4. 4 n.
   tribum Sapiniam: cf. xxxi. 2. 6 n.

2. Castro Mutilo: cf. xxxi. 2. 6 n.

eadem via . . . pervenit: the mention of Mutilum excludes Schlag's view (45) that Furius reached the eastern part of Liguria before turning back. But she is probably right to think that he started from Ariminum. He then retired there and advanced across the plains of the Po valley to meet Marcellus.

3. Felsinam: mod. Bologna. The colony of Bononia was founded there in 189 (xxxvii. 57. 7–8). Cf. Nissen, *IL*, ii. 1. 262 ff., Hülsen, *RE*, iii. 701–2, vi. 2171–2, P. Ducati, *Storia di Bologna*, i (Bologna, 1928).

4. urbs ceteraque circa castella: for the idiom cf. xxxi. 1. 9–10 n.

5. Boi: i.e. the *iuventus* of § 4.

6. Laevos Libuosque: the Laevi are a Ligurian tribe (v. 35. 2) but the Libui, probably to be identified with the Libicii, are Gallic in v. 35. 1 and xxi. 38. 7. But the present passage does not mean that L. regarded them as Ligurian. Ogilvie, 714, rightly says that the fighting was taking place on the borders of Gallic and Ligurian lands. (Polybius ii. 17. 4 makes the Λάοι Gallic, and Ogilvie, l.c. hence denies their identity with the Laevi. But Polybius' error is quite explicable—cf. Walbank, *Commentary*, i. 182.) The area in question is between the Po and the Ticino.

8. nam . . . relinquerent: Schlag, 46, sees the fact that neither Marcellus nor Furius triumphed over the Boii as a sign that this battle too was really a defeat for Rome. But there could be all sorts of reasons why Furius did not triumph, among them the fact that he had already done so in 200 (cf. xxxi. 47. 4–49. 3, 49. 8–11 nn.).

10. triumphavit . . . Comensibusque: in fact on *a.d. iv Non. Mart.* (*Fast. Cap.*), so that, even allowing for the advance of the calendar (cf. p. 42), there was considerable delay in dealing with Marcellus' triumph.

11. trecenta viginti milia: B has *cccxx*, but omits the thousands sign, and then omits *ducenta triginta quattuor*.

12. in pedites . . . centurionique: cf. 23. 7 n.

38–41. *The activities of Antiochus and the conference of Lysimachia*

38. *Antiochus' advance across the Hellespont*

38. 1. eodem anno: the implication of L. is that Antiochus wintered at Ephesus and that all his conquests in northern Asia Minor belong to 196. In fact it seems certain that these events took place in the autumn and winter 197/6; Antiochus then returned to Ephesus, and went directly from there to the Hellespont in the spring of 196. *eodem anno* is thus the Olympiad year 197/6 taken over from Polybius as if it were the consular year of 196. *initio veris* in § 8, on the other hand, is a true date. For the detailed arguments cf. Schmitt, *Antiochos*, 289–95, Will, *HP*, ii. 157, Walbank, *Commentary*, ii. 620.

Ephesi: Ephesus was a Ptolemaic possession, probably acquired at the time of the Laodicean war. On its capture cf. Pol. xviii. 41a. 2, Hier. *in Dan.* xi. 15–16 (= *FGH* 260 F 46), Front. iii. 9. 10, Schmitt, *Antiochos*, 282, Walbank, *Commentary*, ii. 603. On Ephesus cf. the literature cited by Walbank, l.c., to which add J. M. Cook and D. J. Blackman, *AR* 1964/5, 46 ff., G. E. Bean, *Aegean Turkey* (London, 1966), 160 ff., Knibbe, *RE*, supp. xii. 248 ff., Alzinger, ibid., 1588 ff. Excavation reports for years after 1960 are in *AAWW*, since 1965 also in *JÖAI—Grabungen*.

antiquam imperii formulam: as it applied after Seleucus' victory at Corupedium in 281.

2. et ceteras . . . accepturas: L.'s narrative implies that Antiochus concerned himself only with Lampsacus and Smyrna and did not actually attack the other places. But it is in fact clear that many of these were in his possession. For the cities involved cf. Schmitt, *Antiochos*, 282–4. L. must have compressed Polybius' account.

3. Zmyrna et Lampsacus: for Lampsacus cf. Bürchner, *RE*, xii. 590–2, Magie, *RRAM*, ii. 903, for Smyrna Bürchner *RE*, iiiA, 930–64, Magie, *RRAM*, ii. 888–9, Bean, *Aegean Turkey*, 41 ff.: the name is usually spelt with *Z-* in Latin MSS. Both appealed to the Romans in the autumn of 197. Cf. App. *Syr.* 2. 5, and for Lampsacus *Syll.*³ 591: for literature cf. Walbank, *Commentary*, ii. 614 (who, however, wrongly refers to the inscription as *Syll.* 529): add Dahlheim, 104 ff.

libertatem usurpabant: 'announced their claim to be free', without any implication that they had previously been under Ptolemaic control, as W–M wrongly suggest. They were in fact independent states loyal to Pergamum. Cf. Heuss, *Stadt u. Herrscher*, 183–4 n. 2, Magie, *RRAM*, ii. 940. Dahlheim, 104 n. 74, is misleading.

4. Abydi: cf. xxxi. 16. 6 ff. It now had no inhabitants and its Macedonian garrison (xxxi. 18. 8) may already have been withdrawn before the arrival of Antiochus.

6–7. ab rege . . . paterentur: the difference was not just one of timing. Any *libertas* granted by Antiochus would have a number of strings attached. Cf. Jones, *Buckler Studies* (20. 11–12 n.), 103 ff., Heuss, *Stadt u. Herrscher*, 229 ff., Heidemann, 49 ff.

8. initio . . . veris: cf. § 1 n.

traici . . . ad Madytum: B has *Abydo . . . ad Abydum*, which is nonsense, Mog. simply *ad Abydum traicit, Chersonesi urbem* (with *iunxit* *et* instead of *iunxisset*). The change to *Madytum* makes excellent sense (cf. xxxi. 16. 6).

Chersonesum: cf. xxxi. 16. 5–6 n. This area too had probably been evacuated by Philip.

9. Sestum: cf. xxxii. 33. 7 n.

10. Lysimachiam: cf. xxxii. 33. 15 n.

navalibus terrestribus: both here and in § 12 *tecta muros* Mog. inserts a -*que*. This is clearly a correction and the asyndeta of B should be read. For such asyndeta cf. Preuss, *passim*, Kühnast, 285, K–St, ii. 149–50.

11. cepit: cf. xxxi. 2. 9 n.

12. et partim . . . contrahere: cf. xxxii. 22. 10 n.

14. navalesque . . . socios: L. here uses the Roman technical term and it may be that Polybius referred only to Antiochus' navy in general, not to allies. Cf. xxxii. 35. 10 n., Schmitt, *Antiochos*, 272 n. 3.

39–41. *The conference of Lysimachia*

For other sources on the conference cf. Pol. xviii. 49–52, Diod. xxviii. 12, App. *Syr.* 2–3. On the date cf. Walbank, *Philip V*, 325. On L.'s adaptation of Polybius here cf. Hoch, 9–10, Walsh, *RhM* xcvii (1954), 104, *Livy*, 232.

39. 1. sub hoc tempus . . . substitit: Pol. xviii. 49. 2–3: κατ-έπλευσαν εἰς Σηλυβρίαν οἱ περὶ Λεύκιον Κορνήλιον. οὗτοι δ᾽ ἦσαν παρὰ τῆς συγκλήτου πρέσβεις ἐπὶ τὰς διαλύσεις ἐξαπεσταλμένοι τὰς Ἀντιόχου καὶ Πτολεμαίου. Appian (*Syr.* 2. 8–9) has a story of an Egyptian embassy to Rome complaining of Antiochus' aggressions, which results in this embassy of Cn. (*sic*) Cornelius. It is unclear whether this is really the embassy of 203/2 (Pol. xv. 25. 14), as Holleaux (*Rome*, 50 n. 3, 71 ff.) thought, or a fresh embassy after Antiochus' victories in the Fifth Syrian war. The latter can certainly not be ruled out.

L. Cornelius: (188). L. Cornelius Lentulus. Cf. xxxi. 20. 1 n.

missus . . . certamina: sent by the senate particularly for this purpose, while the *x legati* were supposed to deal with the matters resulting from the victory over Philip. But the two problems were in fact inseparable, and Lentulus spoke on all (Pol. xviii. 50. 5). It appears from Polybius (xviii. 49. 2) that Lentulus was accompanied by other *legati*, whose names are not preserved.

Selymbriae: cf. Walbank, *Commentary*, ii. 621.

2. et decem . . . convenerunt: Pol. xviii. 50. 1–2: κατὰ δὲ τὸν αὐτὸν καιρὸν ἧκον καὶ τῶν δέκα Πόπλιος μὲν Λέντλος ἐκ Βαργυλίων, Λεύκιος δὲ Τερέντιος καὶ Πόπλιος Οὐίλλιος ἐκ Θάσου. ταχὺ δὲ τῷ

βασιλεῖ διασαφηθείσης τῆς τούτων παρουσίας, πάντες ἐν ὀλίγαις ἡμέραις
ἠθροίσθησαν εἰς τὴν Λυσιμάχειαν. L. omits the statement that Lysias
and Hegesianax were also present (Pol. xviii. 49. 3): cf. 34. 2 n.
P. Lentulus a Bargyliis: cf. 35. 1.
P. Villius et L. Terentius ab Thaso: cf. 35. 2. Villius and
Terentius were dispatched only to Antiochus, Stertinius to Thasos.
But they probably simply called at Thasos on the way.
  For the possibility that P. Sulpicius Galba and P. Aelius Paetus
were also present cf. Walbank, *Commentary*, ii. 621.

3. Primus congressus . . . exasperati sunt: Pol. xviii. 50. 4:
αἱ μὲν οὖν κατ' ἰδίαν ἐντεύξεις τοῦ τε βασιλέως καὶ τῶν Ῥωμαίων τελέως
ἦσαν ἀφελεῖς καὶ φιλάνθρωποι· μετὰ δὲ ταῦτα γενομένης συνεδρείας κοινῆς
ὑπὲρ τῶν ὅλων ἀλλοιοτέραν ἔλαβε τὰ πράγματα διάθεσιν.

4. Romani . . . censebant: Pol. xviii. 50. 5: ὁ γὰρ Λεύκιος ὁ
Κορνήλιος ἠξίου μὲν καὶ τῶν ὑπὸ Πτολεμαῖον ταττομένων πόλεων, ὅσας
νῦν εἴληφε κατὰ τὴν Ἀσίαν, παραχωρεῖν τὸν Ἀντίοχον, τῶν δ' ὑπὸ Φίλιππον
διεμαρτύρετο φιλοτίμως ἐξίστασθαι. Problems of content and text are
here linked. L. omits reference in this section to the towns previously
occupied by Philip, and converts (as does App. *Syr.* 3. 10) a demand
that Antiochus simply evacuate the places previously held by Egypt
to one that he restore them to Ptolemy. The textual difficulties are
that *et Ptolomaeo* has no correlate and that *nam* in the following
sentence has only a very loose connection with what precedes. It
looks as if L., though departing from Polybius, was still influenced
by his actual words, and thus took over καὶ τῶν ὑπὸ Πτολεμαῖον
in xviii. 50. 5 and γελοῖον γὰρ in xviii. 50. 6. On Roman policy
towards the Egyptian possessions cf. 30. 3 n.

5–6. nam quod . . . habere: Pol. xviii. 50. 6: γελοῖον γὰρ εἶναι
τὰ Ῥωμαίων ἆθλα τοῦ γεγονότος αὐτοῖς πολέμου πρὸς Φίλιππον Ἀντίοχον
ἐπελθόντα παραλαμβάνειν. L. elaborates for effect.
  L. now omits Polybius' reference (Pol. xviii. 50. 7) to Lentulus'
demand that Antiochus leave the independent states alone too.
Diodorus and Appian also omit this demand, and this raises the
possibility that the sentence in question was missing from the text of
Polybius used by all three authors.

7. sed ut . . . facere: Pol. xviii. 50. 8–9: καθόλου δ' ἔφη θαυμάζειν
τίνι λόγῳ τοσαύταις μὲν πεζικαῖς, τοσαύταις δὲ ναυτικαῖς δυνάμεσι
πεποίηται τὴν εἰς τὴν Εὐρώπην διάβασιν· πλὴν γὰρ τοῦ προτίθεσθαι
Ῥωμαίοις ἐγχειρεῖν αὐτόν, οὐδ' ἔννοιαν ἑτέραν καταλείπεσθαι παρὰ τοῖς
ὀρθῶς λογιζομένοις. Again L. elaborates (cf. p. 8 n. 1).
  quid: B, *om.* Mog. Madvig (*Emendationes*, 491 n. 2) argued that
it should be deleted as the phrase *quid, quod* always introduces a new

sentence. Ogilvie, *Phoenix*, 344 and Tränkle, *Gnomon*, 378 n. 4 agree.
McDonald, however, follows W–M in leaving *quid* as an exclama-
tion. But his parallel of xxxiv. 32. 13 is not relevant and W–M's
examples (v. 5. 4, vi. 40. 12) are of *quid* beginning a sentence. Walsh's
potuerit, quid quod . . . transierit? quantum . . . (*CR*, 55) fails to meet
Madvig's point. Madvig, then, seems to have been right to delete
quid. It will have been a variant in the archetype.

 omnibus : an exaggeration. Cf. Schmitt, *Antiochos*, 272 n. 2.

40. L. makes considerable changes in the order of the points in
Antiochus' speech as reported by Polybius.

40. 1–2. Adversus ea . . . faciat : Pol. xviii. 51. 1–2: ὁ δὲ βασιλεὺς
πρῶτον μὲν διαπορεῖν ἔφη κατὰ τίνα λόγον ἀμφισβητοῦσι πρὸς αὐτὸν
ὑπὲρ τῶν ἐπὶ τῆς Ἀσίας πόλεων· πᾶσι γὰρ μᾶλλον ἐπιβάλλειν τοῦτο
ποιεῖν ἢ 'Ρωμαίοις. δεύτερον δ' ἠξίου μηδὲν αὐτοὺς πολυπραγμονεῖν
καθόλου τῶν κατὰ τὴν Ἀσίαν· οὐδὲ γὰρ αὐτὸς περιεργάζεσθαι τῶν κατὰ
τὴν 'Ιταλίαν ἁπλῶς οὐδέν. Antiochus claims that all Asia is his, and
has nothing to do with Rome. One is reminded of the claims of
Kings of Persia (cf. e.g. Thuc. viii. 58. 2). The Greeks naturally
accepted Rome's rule over Italy—I cannot understand Salmon's
statement (*Samnium*, 304) that this passage is unhistorical.

3. quod ad Ptolomaeum . . . iungatur : Pol. xviii. 51. 10: τὰ δὲ
πρὸς Πτολεμαῖον αὐτὸς ἔφη διεξάξειν εὐδοκουμένως ἐκείνῳ· κρίνειν γὰρ
οὐ φιλίαν μόνον, ἀλλὰ καὶ μετὰ τῆς φιλίας ἀναγκαιότητα συντίθεσθαι πρὸς
αὐτόν. L. has misunderstood Polybius here. Antiochus and Ptolemy
have not yet made peace with each other. For the date of the
betrothal and marriage of Ptolemy and Cleopatra cf. Walbank,
Commentary, ii. 623, Seibert, 65–6, Will, *HP*, ii. 161–3. Appian *Syr.*
3. 13 makes Antiochus say that he is already a συγγενής of Ptolemy,
which, if it is not a misunderstanding of Polybius, presumably refers
to the connection established by the marriage of Antiochus II to
Berenice.

4–6. Ne ex Philippi . . . habeat : cf. Pol. xviii. 51. 3–8. L. has
effectively re-arranged the argument.

 Antiochus' argument is that he is entitled to all the lands which
had belonged to Lysimachus and passed to Antiochus' great-great-
grandfather Seleucus I by his victory at Corupedium. The conflict
is one of different legal conceptions. Rome did not recognize rights
derived from such victories. Cf. E. Bickermann, *Hermes* lxvii (1932),
47–76 (with Badian's warning in *CPh* liv [1959], 98 n. 62 = *Studies*,
137 n. 62), Walbank, *Commentary*, ii. 622, Schmitt, *Antiochos*, 86.

4. ne . . . quidem : Bekker's correction for the MSS.' *nec . . . quidem*.
'Not even from Philip's misfortunes' makes no sense here: *ne . . .*

quidem in the sense of 'not either' is possible (cf. 44. 7 n.) but *nec* gives perfect sense—'and it was not indeed from Philip's misfortunes'. Walsh (*CR*, 54) also reads *nec* but he appears to regard *nec* . . . *quidem* as equivalent to *ne* . . . *quidem*. In fact when *nec* . . . *quidem* occurs in Classical Latin *nec* and *quidem* are to be interpreted as separate words. Cf. K–St, ii. 45, H–S, 450.

Lysimachi: Lysimachus had been given control of Thrace on the death of Alexander. He acquired Asia Minor after the battle of Ipsus and in 288, together with Pyrrhus, drove Demetrius Poliorcetes out of Macedon. In 285 he got rid of Pyrrhus too, but was defeated and killed at Corupedium in 281. On his career cf. Geyer, *RE*, xiv. 1 ff., G. Saitta, *Kokalos* i (1955), 62 ff., Will, *HP*, i, passages cited at ii. 528, G. Longega, *Arsinoe II* (Rome, 1968), 15–55.

5. occupatis . . . tenuisse: for Ptolemy Euergetes' occupation of Thrace cf. xxxi. 16. 4 n.

usurpandae alienae possessionis causa tenuisse: thus B. Mog. omits *causa tenuisse*. Madvig (*Emendationes*, 492) argued that reference to Philip's motives was inappropriate and the discussion was about his rights. He therefore read *usurpanda aliena possessionis causa tenuisse*, and appears to take this to mean 'Philip held them, using for himself the excuse of the possession which had belonged to someone else (i.e. Ptolemy)'. This is extremely obscure Latin. More important, it is quite unnecessary. Antiochus is concerned simply with the history of Thrace. His legal argument is based on Seleucus' victory and reference to Philip's motives is perfectly appropriate. (Sage's note and translation are nonsense.)

Chersonesus: B has *Chersonesum* (Mog. is hopelessly corrupt here). One could take this as an attraction (cf. xxxi. 27. 5 n.) but *dubitare* rarely takes a direct object except for pronouns or with a gerundive (cf. *TLL*, v. 1. 2084–5) and such attractions are usually found only where the accusative could be a direct object of the verb. Thus Scipio Aemilianus, *ORF²*, p. 127 and Columella vi. 3. 3 are not parallels.

6. Lysimachiam . . . condere: 38. 10–12.

Seleucus filius: cf. 18. 22 n., Walbank, *Commentary*, 622, Schmitt, *Antiochos*, 20–1.

L. omits Antiochus' reference to the free cities (Pol. xviii. 51. 9) as he had earlier (cf. 39. 5–6 n.) and to the speeches of the representatives of Lampsacus and Smyrna (Pol. xviii. 52). Appian, however (*Syr.* 3. 12), does report Antiochus' reply in regard to the free cities.

41. Polybius xviii. 52 ends καὶ τότε μὲν ἐπὶ τούτοις διέλυσαν τὸν σύλλογον, οὐδαμῶς εὐδοκήσαντες ἀλλήλοις (cf. Diod. xxviii. 12). Hence E. Villa (*Il mondo classico* N.S. vi (xix) [1952], 93 ff.) argued that the rumour of the death of Ptolemy did not appear in Polybius, and was invented by the *legati* when they returned to Rome so that they could point to Antiochus' designs on Egypt as proof of his aggressive intentions. But διέλυσαν τὸν σύλλογον marks the end of the first stage of negotiations, and is not an indication of the conclusion of the whole conference. Indeed τότε μὲν suggests that something more was to follow. The rumour is also reported by App. *Syr.* 4. 14.

41. 1. His . . . effecit: the conference was a diplomatic disaster for Rome. It seems that the Roman *legati* were unsure of all the facts of the situation in Asia and unable to reply to Antiochus. The different verbs used in Polybius xviii. 50. 5–6 may reflect this uncertainty.

2. dissimulabat: Mog. B has the perfect. The latter is defended by Walsh (*CR*, 54) as *variatio* on the imperfect in *petebat*. Such a *variatio* is certainly common in L. (cf. Chausserie-Laprée, 383 ff.) but the perfect is not really appropriate here.

> **cui . . . erat**: cf. 39. 1 n.
> **petebat**: i.e. openly.

3. Antiochus . . . censebat: it may be doubted whether Antiochus really intended to occupy Egypt itself.

4. Seleuco filio . . . Lysimachiam: cf. 40. 6 n.

5. Ephesum: cf. 38. 1 n.

> **legatis . . . agerent**: they did not arrive until spring 195 (xxxiv. 25. 2) and so Holleaux (*Études*, v. 164 n. 3) is probably right in thinking that L. has misinterpreted a statement that Antiochus expressed an intention of sending *legati*.

> **Lyciam, Patarisque**: cf. 19. 11. For his capture of Patara, not mentioned by L. earlier, cf. 20. 13 n., Hier. *in Dan.* xi. 15–16 = *FGH* 260 F 46. On Patara cf. Radke, *RE*, xviii. 2. 2555–61.

6. Cyprum: Cyprus was under the control of Ptolemy Soter from *c.* 316 until it was captured by Demetrius Poliorcetes in 306. It was regained by Ptolemy in 295. It was captured by Antiochus Epiphanes in the Sixth Syrian war, but surrendered after Epiphanes' accession to the ultimatum of Eleusis. Cf. Will, *HP*, i. 35, 52, G. Hill, *A History of Cyprus*, i (Cambridge, 1940), 156 ff.

> **petens**: B. Mg had *tendens*, which is strongly defended by Tränkle, *Gnomon*, 374 n. 1. He quotes xl. 4. 11 for *tendere* used intransitively of a ship.

> **seditione remigum**: whether mercenaries or natives of the Seleucid empire is unclear.

> **Chelidoniarum promunturium**: cf. 20. 2 n.

> **Pamphylia**: the area in the recess between Cilicia and Lycia. For

its degree of domination by the Seleucids cf. B. Levick, *Roman Colonies in Southern Asia Minor* (Oxford, 1967), 17–19.

Eurymedontem: a river of Pamphylia famous for Cimon's defeat of the Persians there *c*. 467.

7. ad capita quae vocant Sari fluminis: the Sarus runs into the sea a little to the south-east of Tarsus; cf. Ruge, *RE*, iiA. 34. The *quae vocant* formula indicates that L. is translating a Greek word, and it may be that he first used *caput* to mean the mouth of a river, as argued by Ogilvie, *Eranos* lv (1957), 201–2 (it is found in Caesar *BG* iv. 10. 5 but Ogilvie treats that passage as a later addition). Polybius presumably referred to Σάρου κεφαλαί. The *Stadiasmus Magni Maris* 166 (*GGM* i. 481) refers to the κεφαλή of the neighbouring river Pyramus (Ogilvie is wrong in his statement that the Sarus and the Pyramus were joined inland, or were compared by Strabo (i. p. 53c) to the Nile delta) and for the use of κεφαλή in Greek in this sense cf. Callimachus 43. 46 (Pfeiffer).

multae naves eiectae: Mog. The word order is odd and Jacobs' transposition *eiectae naves* may well be right (xxvi. 27. 12 quoted by W–M is not an exact parallel). B omits *eiectae*, and this raises the possibility that the word was in the margin at one stage of the transmission, leading to omission in B and misplacement in Mg.

enarit: *enaret* B, *enaverit* Mog. The perfect is needed and the abbreviated form explains the paradosis better.

8. regis amicorum: in a technical sense: cf. xxxi. 28. 5 n., E. Bikerman, *Institutions des Séleucides* (Paris, 1938), 40 ff.

9. Seleuciam: Selucia Pieria on the coast near Antiochia, and like Antiochia a foundation of Seleucus I: cf. Honigmann, *RE*, iiA 1184–1200, A. H. M. Jones, *Cities of the Eastern Roman Provinces*[2] (Oxford, 1971), 241 ff.

hiems instabat: cf. xxxi. 22. 4 n.
Antiochiam: cf. 19. 8 n.

42. *Events in Rome*

42. 1. Romae . . . epulones facti: on the establishment of this college cf. Wissowa, *RuK*[2], 423, Latte, *RRG*, 398–9, Schlag, 147 ff. Their number was later increased to seven, then to ten by Caesar (Dio xliii. 51. 9).

The responsibility for the *epulum* at sacrifices had originally belonged to the *pontifices* (Cic. *de or.* iii. 73) and later passed to curule magistrates in office at the time (cf. Schlag, 147 n. 25). Schlag may be correct in thinking that the *pontifex maximus* instigated the law (the *nomen* of the tribune responsible could be significant). But her further speculations on the political positions of the first *epulones* and the significance of the fact that two of them, it seems, were not in Rome the following year are without foundation.

C. Licinius Lucullus: (99). He is otherwise known only as a *iivir* for the dedication of the temple of Iuventus in 191.

qui legem . . . tulerat: the *Leges Licinia* and *Aebutia* mentioned by Cicero (*de Leg. agr.* ii. 21) forbidding the carrier of a law to serve in any board set up under it must be later than this date. Both Tiberius Gracchus in 133 (*MRR*, i. 495) and Livius Drusus in 91 (*I.I.* xiii. 3. 74) served on their own land commissions. Cf. Gabba, *Commentary on Appian, BC i*, 40; *contra* G. Niccolini, *I fasti dei tribuni della plebe* (Milan, 1934), 411. But in view of the other misrepresentations in the speeches *de Lege agraria* Cicero may be misleading even about the content of the laws (cf. his own proposal on Gabinius in *Leg. Man.* 58).

P. Manlius: (31). He is almost certainly the praetor of 195 (§ 7): the latter was praetor a second time in 182 and is probably identical with the Manilius expelled from the senate in 184 (Plut. *Cato Mai.* 17. 7, *MRR*, i. 383 n. 1). The fact that his successor as *epulo* was a plebeian is not a sufficient reason for holding that Manlius was not a patrician (thus *MRR*, i. 339 n. 9). We do not know the names of enough *epulones* to be sure that it was a purely plebeian office, as argued by Mommsen, *RF*, i. 90–1.

P. Porcius Laeca: (19). Cf. xxxii. 7. 4 n.

iis . . . habendae ius: the *toga praetexta*, with a purple stripe, was worn by boys and then only by curule magistrates and the members of the main priestly colleges. By the first century B.C. the tunic with a purple stripe—*latus clavus*—was worn by all senators, and by the end of the republic it was probably being assumed by those who proposed to stand for magisterial office. Later those not of senatorial family had to be granted the *latus clavus* by the emperor before they could stand for office. Cf. Mommsen, *StR*, i³. 410 n. 5, 418 ff., iii. 466, 887 ff., A. H. M. Jones, *Studies in Roman Government and Law* (Oxford, 1960), 30–2.

2. quaestoribus urbanis: I cannot understand why *MRR*, i. 336 should say 'perhaps *quaestores urbani*'.

Q. Fabio Labeoni: (91). He was praetor in 189 with command prorogued in 188, a *iivir* for the foundation of Potentia and Pisaurum in 184 and of Saturnia in 183. In the latter year he was consul, with command prorogued in 182. He was a *pontifex* from 180.

L. Aurelio: (18). Not otherwise known. He is unlikely to be the military tribune of 181 (97).

The quaestors lacked *imperium* and may have been instructed by the consuls to proceed in this matter (cf. Schlag, 156 n. 53).

3. ultimam pensionem . . . privatis : cf. xxxi. 13 nn. Those who had accepted land then would not be paid on this occasion unless they wished to return the land. Toynbee, ii. 346 seems to think that all the creditors had accepted land in 200.

4. quod stipendium . . . petebant : it is unclear whether there was any general custom to justify the priests' action, or they had simply not paid; there was clearly no law on the subject. Cf. Schlag, 156–7.

omnium . . . exactum est : W–M deduce from this that it was only for some years that they had not paid. This is improbable.

5. M. Marcellus consul : cf. xxxi. 50. 1 n.
C. Sempronii Tuditani . . . decesserat : cf. 25. 9.
praetor : cf. 25. 9 n., pp. 5–6.
L. Valerius Flaccus : (173). Cf. xxxi. 4. 5 n.
M. Corneli Cethegi : (92). He was curule aedile in 213, praetor in 211, censor in 209, and consul in 204 with command prorogued in 203. He had been a *pontifex* since 213. He is almost certainly a friend of Scipio.

6. Q. Fabius Maximus augur : (104). His relation to the Cunctator is uncertain, but he may be his grandson (cf. Münzer, *RE*, vi. 1790). See addenda.

nec . . . suffectus : presumably, as at xxvi. 23. 8, because his death came near the end of the year.

7. L. Valerius Flaccus : (173). Cf. xxxi. 4. 5 n.
M. Porcius Cato : (9). Cf. xxxii. 7. 13 n. For the political importance of this election cf. *Latomus* xxxi (1972), 47.
Cn. Manlius Volso : (91). Cf. 25. 1 n.
Ap. Claudius Nero : (245). Cf. xxxii. 35. 7 n., 36. 10.
P. Porcius Laeca : (19). Cf. § 1 n. B gives the *praenomen* as *M*. but it is *P*. at 43. 5 and there can be no doubt about the identification.
C. Fabricius ⟨Luscinus C. Atinius⟩ Labeo : for the names cf. 43. 5. B has *C. Fabricius Labeo*. Mog. had simply the names of the other four praetors, and subsequent editors, before the discovery of B, inserted the names before that of Volso on the basis of 43. 5. Fabricius (10) is known otherwise only as a *legatus* under L. Scipio in 190: on Atinius (8) cf. xxxii. 29. 3 n.
P. Manlius : (31). Cf. § 1 n.

8. M. Fulvius Nobilior : (91). B has *C.* (not mentioned by McDonald) but there is no C. Fulvius Nobilior known at this time and he is clearly the enemy of the Scipios, who was praetor in 193 with command prorogued in 192 and 191, consul in 189, commanding in Greece until 187, and censor in 179. On his political position cf. *JRS* liv (1964), 73–7, *Latomus* xxvii (1968), 149–56.

C. Flaminius: (3). He had been quaestor in 209 and was praetor in 193 with command prorogued until 190. He was consul in 187 and a *iiivir* for the foundation of Aquileia in 183. For his political position see below.

tritici . . . discripserunt: cf. xxxi. 4. 6 n., 50. 1.

id . . . Romam: a striking tribute to C. Flaminius, consul in 223 and 217, who was killed at Trasimene, and subsequently completely blackened in the historical tradition. He had been the first governor of Sicily when it was organized as a province in 227 (Solinus v. 1).

Flaminius . . . cum collega: thus both would gain the political credit. Since Fulvius is so bitter an enemy of the Scipios this suggests that though the elder Flaminius may well have been supported by the Scipios (Scullard, *RP*, 44 ff.; for the views of Cassola, *GP*, cf. *CR* N.S. xiii [1963], 321–4), his son was not (Scullard, *RP*, 120, regards him as Scipionic, but expresses doubts at pp. 140–1).

cum collega: B has *collegae*. *communicare* with the dative, however, appears not to be used in the active in good Latin (K–St, i. 330, *TLL*, iii. 1955; Caes. *B.C.* iii. 18. 3 is usually emended).

9. Ludi Romani: cf. xxxi. 9. 5–10 n.

ter toti instaurati: cf. xxxi. 4. 5, 7 nn., xxxii. 27. 8 n.

10. Cn. Domitius Ahenobarbus: (18). He was praetor in 194 and consul in 192 with command prorogued in 191. In 190 he may have been a *legatus* under the Scipios.

C. Scribonius Curio [maximus]: (8). He was praetor in 193. In 174 he became *curio maximus* (xli. 21. 9). Clearly at some stage of the transmission someone thought that *curio* referred to his office and added *maximus*. In fact the *cognomen* Curio was probably adopted only after 174 (cf. Münzer, *RA*, 69).

multos . . . condemnati sunt: the fact that the condemnation of only three men was sufficient to provide enough money to build a temple suggests that these were not humble shepherds. We are dealing, rather, with large-scale operators; they had, presumably, either occupied *ager publicus* without permission, or broken the law concerning the number of animals that could be grazed (cf. App. *BC* i. 8. 33). If the former, it may be that the general permission to occupy otherwise unallocated *ager publicus* (App. *BC* i. 7. 27) had not yet been made. Further condemnations are reported in 193 (xxxv. 10. 12) and then nothing further. There is no reason for thinking that those condemned were Italians as well as Romans (thus Salmon, *Samnium*, 70). Cf. also Brunt, 371 n. 2.

ex eorum . . . fecerunt: for similar action cf. xxxi. 50. 2 n. On
the *Insula* in the Tiber, cf. Platner–Ashby, 281–2, M. E. Hirst, *PBSR*
xiv (1938), 137–51, Nash, i. 508, and on the temple of Faunus,
Platner–Ashby 205–6. For the dedication of the temple cf. xxxiv.
53. 4. For the word order of *aedem in insula Fauni* cf. xxiv. 10. 9, xxx.
3. 3, xxxix. 8. 5, Nisbet and Hubbard, 390.

11. ludi . . . causa: cf. xxxi. 4. 5, 7 nn.

195 B.C.

43–45. 5. *Events in Rome*

43. *Provinces and armies*

1–2. quoniam in Hispania . . . sortiri: cf. 21. 6–9 n., 25. 8–9,
26. 3–4. L. has not yet given any information on what happened in
Spain in 196. Cf. 44. 4.

3. socium Latini nominis: cf. xxxi. 8. 7 n.

4. fractis . . . animis: cf. 36. 4—37. 12.

5. Cn. Manlius Volso Siciliam: in succession to Laelius.

Ap. Claudius Nero: in succession to Q. Fabius Buteo, cf. § 7
and 44. 4 n.

P. Porcius Laeca Pisas: Pisa is the base for his troops, not itself
a province, as with Ariminum (cf. xxxii. 2. 2). On Pisa cf. Luisa
Banti, *RE*, xx. 1756–72, N. Toscanelli, *Pisa nell'antichità* (Pisa, 1933–4),
i–iii. Toynbee, ii. 661 suggests that the use of Pisa as a base
indicates that the Via Aurelia had been built by this time; *contra* cf.
H. E. Herzig, *Epigraphica* xxxii (1970), 61–2, Brunt, 569.

ab tergo: the Ligurians are seen as facing the east, and threaten-
ing to attack eastwards.

P. Manlius . . . consuli datus: not a job invented to get
Manlius out of Rome, as Schlag, 149, claims (cf. 42. 1 n.).

6. suspectis . . . tyranno: on Aetolian dissatisfaction cf. 35. 10–12,
on Nabis xxxi. 25. 3 n., and on his possession of Argos xxxii. 38–40.
Since he joined Rome we have heard nothing of him. In fact if left
alone he would not be a danger to Rome. But that was not possible
as his possession of Argos was too blatant a contradiction of Rome's
principles of freedom. Cf. further 44. 8–45. 4 and, on the situation,
Walbank, *Philip V*, 187. The fear is as much of the three potential
enemies combining as of them in isolation.

prorogatum . . . imperium est: cf. 25. 11 n. The special grant
was specifically made this time because the war with Philip, for

which Flamininus had been appointed, was now over (cf. Bredehorn, 149).

duas legiones : as he had had from 198, but they were 'heavy' legions. Cf. 1. 2 n., 4. 6 n., xxxii. 1. 3 n.

7. Q. Fabius : (57). Q. Fabius Buteo. Cf. 24. 2 n., 26. 3.

duo milia ⟨peditum⟩ : *peditum* must have dropped out. 2,200 *equites* and no infantry is impossible.

8. Q. Minucio : (65). Cf. 26. 3, xxxii. 27. 8 n.

9. ad Etruriam : Madvig (*Emendationes*, 493 n. 1) deleted this on the grounds that *ad* and the name of a province could not be used with *decernere*. H. J. Müller inserted *tuendam*. McDonald's defence that *ad Etruriam* equals *in Etruriam* simply ignores Madvig's argument (cf. Tränkle, *Gnomon*, 379, quoting *TLL*, v. 1. 149, Ogilvie, *Phoenix*, 346). I would prefer deletion. Porcius' job was to keep an eye on the Ligurians, who were a threat to Gaul, not to Etruria itself, cf. § 5.

ex Gallico exercitu : the army already in Gaul.

Ti. Sempronio Longo : (67). Cf. xxxi. 20. 5 n.

44. 1–3. *Religious matters*

1–2. ver sacrum : the *ver sacrum* was an ancient Sabellic rite; originally it was a vow to sacrifice all that was born the following spring: the human born, however, were not killed, but were obliged to leave their native land and find fresh ones. In this case, however, the human element is lacking entirely. Cf. Eisenhut, *RE*, viiiA. 911 ff., Latte, *RRG*, 124–5, 378, Salmon, *Samnium*, 35–6.

2. A. Cornelius Mammula . . . consulibus : the vowing of the *ver sacrum* is described by L. at xxii. 9–10. Mammula is not mentioned there, but he occurs as a propraetor in 216 (xxiii. 21. 4). His *praenomen* is given there as *A.*, here as *C.* or *Cn.* There is no certain way of deciding, but since the praetor of 191 is Aulus, and probably the son of the former, Aulus is more likely to be correct.

Cn. Servilio : (61). Cn. Servilius Geminus, consul in 217 with command prorogued in 216.

C. Flaminio : (2). Cf. 42. 8 n. He was praetor in 227, consul in 223, and censor in 220.

annis . . . votum : 21 full years between 217 and 195. In 194 the *pontifex maximus* declared the *ver sacrum* had not been properly conducted, and it was repeated (xxxiv. 44. 1–3).

3. C. Claudius Appi filius Pulcher : (300). He was praetor in 180 and consul in 177 with command prorogued in 176. A military tribune in 171, he was censor in 169 and one of the *x legati* for Macedon in 167. On his political position cf. *JRS* liv (1964), 76–7,

Latomus xxvii (1968), 154–6. His father Appius is the consul of 212 (293). (The filiation of the consul of 177 is wrongly given as *Ap. f. C. n.* in *MRR*, ii. 547.)

in Q. Fabi . . . inauguratusque est: cf. 42. 6.

4. mirantibus . . . neglegi: cf. 43. 2. People are surprised that Cato is still in Rome.

litterae . . . sunt: Schlag, 32, argues that the mention in this way of the events of 196 is an indication that the importance of the war had been exaggerated. She may well be right about the exaggeration (cf. 21. 6–9 n.) but L.'s method of reporting it may be due to nothing more than a quirk of one of his sources.

Q. Minucio: cf. 43. 8 n.

Turdam: the town is not otherwise known and its name is given as Turbam by Mog. McDonald follows those who place it in Hispania Ulterior on the grounds that that is where the Turdetani are found (cf. Schulten, *RE*, viiA. 1378–80, *CAH*, viii. 312, De Sanctis iv. 1. 446 n. 135). But since they are sometimes heard of in Citerior (xxi. 6. 1, xxviii. 39. 8), and the name of the town is uncertain, it seems unwise to suppose that Minucius is fighting outside his province: L. is quite clear about his province in 26. 2 and 43. 8, and the reference to Minucius as Helvius' successor in xxxiv. 10. 6 is either simply a mistake or explained by the fact that Helvius did fight in Citerior after the death of Tuditanus (cf. 25. 9 n.). Otherwise Minucius should have been denied a triumph on the same grounds as Helvius (xxxiv. 10. 5–6). Cf. Klotz, *Hermes* l (1915), 491 n. 1, Fraccaro, *Opuscula*, i. 224 n. 15, Schlag, 33 n. 58. See addenda.

Budare et Baesadine: not otherwise known.

44. 5–45. 5. *Decisions on Greece*

5–9. On the sources of this passage cf. p. 11.

5. post adventum decem legatorum: they will have returned in the winter of 196/5. Cf. Walbank, *Philip V*, 324, Aymard, *PR*, 196–7 n. 1. There is no conflict between this passage and xxxiv. 33. 12, indicating that Villius was in the East again in 195. He presumably returned to Greece after the senatorial debate.

6. quibus legibus data pax: in fact they probably reported on the details of the settlement of Greece as a whole. Cf. 30. 1 n.

7. ingenti . . . exercitu: an exaggeration, but one that the *legati*, as usual over-impressed by the might of the East, themselves believed; cf. 19. 9, 39. 7 nn.

vana spes . . . invadendae: 41. 1 ff.

neque enim ne Aetolos quidem: 'nor would the Aetolians

either remain quiet'. *neque enim ne* . . . *quidem*, with the negatives strengthening each other, is found at xxix. 12. 10, xxx. 30. 7, xxxi. 38. 6, xliv. 36. 8.

ingenio inquietam : L. naturally thinks of a people as having innate characteristics: though Polybius would not have dissented from the view of the Aetolians (cf. ἔμφυτον ἀλαζονείαν of the Aetolians in iv. 3. 1).

8. haerere . . . in visceribus : the phrase suggests that the passage may derive from Polybius. Cf. xxxii. 21. 27, xxxiv. 41. 4, 48. 6. The first, in the speech of Aristaenus, could be attributed to L. himself, but the latter two occur in a clearly Polybian passage. For similar language in Polybius himself cf. Pol. xviii. 43. 6. The view of Nabis is particularly that of the Achaean League, cf. Aymard, *PR*, 184 ff., Briscoe, *Past and Present*, no. 36 (April 1967), 8 ff.

fama celebratos tyrannos : the notoriously cruel tyrants of archaic Greece such as Phalaris or Periander.

9. Argos : cf. xxxii. 38–40.

45. 1. tam gravibus : because of their rank: at least three of the ten *legati* were consulars.

tum qui : the *tum* following a *cum* with which it is not correlated is awkward. M. Müller's *ut* may well be right (cf. Ogilvie, *Phoenix*, 346).

2. maior res . . . visa est : 'the matters concerning Antiochus seemed of greater importance, but since the King had for some reason retreated into Syria, the discussion on Nabis appeared of greater urgency.' The asyndeton is perfectly natural and Walsh's suggestion (*CR*, 55) of *at* after *attineret* is quite unnecessary.

rex . . . concessisset : L. appears surprised, forgetting, as often with Greek and Roman writers, that the rulers of Asia had more to think about than the western parts of their Empire.

3–4. Cum diu . . . rem publicam esset : at xxxiv. 22. 5 L. appears to say, in a Polybian passage, that the senate and people did declare war on Nabis. But in this case the annalistic report may record the *s.c.* accurately. Cf. De Sanctis, iv. 1. 105 n. 209, Aymard, *PR*, 196 ff., Walbank, *Philip V*, 188 n. 1, Scullard, *RP*, 115 n. 2; *contra* Petzold, 103–4 n. 72.

non ita magni momenti : assorts oddly with *maturanda magis* in § 2.

5. magis id animadvertendum esse . . . essent : a transition to the section on Hannibal, as in 19. 6–7 (cf. n. ad loc.). The transition is perfectly natural, despite W–M's statement that it is harsh. Bredehorn's view (152–4) that it represents an amendment moved in the Senate is absurd.

bellum motum : Mog. has *ortum* which is preferred by Tränkle, *Gnomon*, 374 n. 1. Cf. 19. 6, 26. 5 nn.

45. 6–49. 7. *The flight of Hannibal from Carthage*

Other sources on this episode are Nepos, *Hann.* 7, App. *Syr.* 4, Just. xxxi. 1. 7—2. 8, Zon. ix. 18. 11–12, Val. Max. iv. 1. 6.

(a) *Chronology*

L. places the episode in 195, Nepos and Appian in 196. The principal arguments in favour of L.'s date are (i) Hannibal went first to Antiochia, where he heard that Antiochus had left for Asia Minor: he finally met him at Ephesus (49. 6–7). But Antiochus spent the whole of the winter of 197/6 at Ephesus (38. 1) and did not return to Antiochia at all until the end of 196. (ii) It is odd that there is no mention of the meeting with Hannibal when L. refers to Antiochus' return to Ephesus in 196 (41. 5). (iii) It is very probable that the Roman mission contained two consulars, and that M. Claudius Marcellus (47. 7) is the consul of 196, who would not have been available until 195. (iv) We now have evidence which seems to indicate that Antiochus celebrated games at Daphne in 197 (cf. 49. 6 n.). It is highly unlikely that such games were annual, and this would exclude 196 for the date of Hannibal's meeting with Antiochus the son. Hannibal's year as *sufete* probably belongs to 196, the flight itself to 195. Cf. Holleaux, *Études*, v. 180–3, with subsequent literature at 183 n., Scullard, *RP*, 284, *MRR*, i. 342 n. 3.

(b) *Source*

It has generally been agreed that L.'s account stems from Polybius (e.g Nissen, *KU*, 152–3, Holleaux, *Études*, v. 181, Pédech, 166, Schlag, 117 n. 134). In favour of such a view is the wealth of constitutional and topographical detail, the clear acknowledgement of the uncertainty of the rumours about Hannibal's actions, the conflict between 49. 7 and 44. 5 ff. on Antiochus' intentions. In addition the notice about the senatorial decision on Aetolia (49. 8), isolated from the account in 44. 5–45. 4, suggests that that passage comes from Polybius, and the inclusion of so short a notice would make better sense if the preceding section were also of Polybian origin.

There are, however, difficulties. The whole story has a peculiar resemblance to Thucydides' account of the flight of Themistocles (Thuc. i. 135–8). The great war leader, wanting to introduce democratic reforms, is exiled, partly due to accusations coming from another state; his escape is nearly frustrated by his meeting Carthaginian ships. When he reaches Asia, he meets not the king, but his son. Again Hannibal's method of prosecuting an individual adherent of the *iudices* as a way of attacking the council as a whole is reminiscent of the attacks on individual Areopagites ascribed to Ephialtes and Themistocles (anachronistically as far as Themistocles is concerned) in *Ἀθ. Πολ.* 25. 4. Of course, the similarities cannot be pressed too closely. Hannibal did flee to Asia because of accusations to Rome by his political enemies, and it may simply be a historical coincidence that his adventures were so similar to those of Themistocles. The similarity of the *iudices* to the Areopagus is just a historical fact. And though Polybius wrote so soon after the events, his account of Hannibal elsewhere contains a number of errors and exaggerations; the present story naturally lent itself to 'writing-up'.

It may still be the case, however, that L. has incorporated into a basically Polybian account details from annalistic sources. It is significant that in xxxiv. 61–2 there is again a very detailed account of events in Carthage, which yet contains one point (xxxiv. 62. 2) which conflicts with Polybius xxxi. 21 (cf. Walsh, *JRS* lv [1965], 157).

(c) *Carthaginian constitutional terms*

The chief magistrates of Carthage at this time were the two *sufetes* (*praetor* 46. 3). The assembly originally had very limited powers, but these may have been increased after the First Punic war. There were two councils, one of about 300, one smaller, perhaps of 30. The judges (*iudices* 46. 1), who were the main object of Hannibal's reforms, numbered 104 and had acquired wide-ranging powers, not dissimilar to those of the Areopagus at Athens before the reforms of Ephialtes (cf. Ar. *Pol.* 1272 b 35, Just. xix. 2. 5 ff.). The *quaestor* (46. 4) was presumably a financial official, but nothing more is known of him.

On the constitution of Carthage and Hannibal's reforms cf. W. L. Newman, *Politics of Aristotle*, ii (Oxford, 1887), 401 ff., Meltzer–Kahrstedt, ii. 36 ff., iii. 584 ff., S. Gsell, *Histoire ancienne de l'Afrique du Nord*, ii (Paris, 1920), 183 ff., 274 ff., E. Groag, *Hannibal als Politiker* (Vienna, 1929), 114 ff., W. Hoffmann, *Antike und Abendland* vi (1957), 19 ff., *Hannibal* (Göttingen, 1962), 114 ff., V. Ehrenberg, *RE*, ivA. 643 ff., B. H. Warmington, *Carthage* (London, 1960), 119 ff., G. Ch. Picard, *RÉL* xli (1963), 269–81, *Conférences de la Société d'Études Latines de Bruxelles, 1965–66* (Brussels, 1968), 113–30, G. Ch. and C. Picard, *The Life and Death of Carthage* (New York, 1968), 210 ff., 272 ff., Schlag, 116 ff.

(d) *The charges against Hannibal*

L.'s account itself makes it clear how fragile were the charges against Hannibal. The fact that he eventually fled to Antiochus and urged the latter to war does not mean that he had been intriguing with Antiochus before his flight—any more than Themistocles' flight to Persia proves the charge of Medism brought against him. Cf. e.g. Scullard, *RP*, 114, Hoffmann, *Antike und Abendland*, l.c., Schlag, l.c.: *contra* Passerini, *Ath.* N.S. X (1932), 331 n. 1.

6. adversae . . . factionis: the long-standing opponents of the Barcid family.

hospitibus: B has *hostibus* which is nonsense, and Mog.'s *amicis*, as McDonald says, may well be a gloss on *hospitibus*. The pro-Roman faction had obviously established personal contacts at Rome.

7. immitem et implacabilem: as in Polybius' story of Hannibal's oath to observe undying hatred towards Rome (Pol. iii. 11–12).

marcescere . . . posse: the view attributed to Hannibal is parallel to one version of the reasons for Nasica's opposition to the Third Punic war (cf. Astin, *Scipio Aemilianus*, 276 ff.). The sentence is expressed in a strikingly poetic fashion. *Marcere* and *marcescere*, not found in Caesar or in Cicero, appear in L. only in the third and fourth decades: *situs* with the meaning of 'inactivity' is not found in pre-Augustan literature. Cf. Tränkle, *WS*, 125.

8. probabilia: to Rome. But the *animos* in the next sentence are those of the Carthaginians. The chapter division here distorts the sense.

moti: this reflects the view of Fabius Pictor, rejected by Polybius, that the Barcids alone were responsible for the Second Punic war. Cf. Pol. iii. 8. The view may have originated from the present conflict; cf. Walbank, *Commentary*, i. 311.

46. 1. iudicum ordo: on the 'judges' cf. 45. 6–49. 7 n. (c).

3. impotenti: 'unlimited'.

civiliter: 'as a citizen should', in contrast with the behaviour of an authoritarian regime.

praetor: the *sufete*: *praetor* is L.'s usual word for the chief magistrate of a foreign republican state, cf. e.g. 1. 3, 14. 6, xxxi. 32. 1, xxxii. 19. 2.

quaestorem: cf. 45. 6–49. 7 n. (c).

5. viatorem . . . misit: L. uses technical Roman language; cf. A. W. Lintott, *Violence in Republican Rome* (Oxford, 1968), 101 n. 3.

6. legem . . . pertulitque: it is unclear whether Hannibal consulted either or both of the councils before putting his law before the assembly. In Aristotle's time (*Pol.* 1273 a 6 ff.) the kings and the *gerontes* decided what was to be placed before the people, if they were unanimous: otherwise the people could decide for themselves whether to discuss the matter. The constitutional position may have changed by this time, but even if it had not, it is likely that the councils would not have been unanimously opposed to Hannibal's proposal. There is certainly no need to think that Hannibal was acting unconstitutionally (cf. G. Ch. and C. Picard, *The Life and Death of Carthage*, 276: *contra* Meltzer–Kahrstedt, iii. 586; Gsell, ii. 276).

7. in singulos annos iudices legerentur: it seems that at this time the judges were elected for life, though this may not have been the case earlier (cf. Meltzer–Kahrstedt, ii. 52).

8. quo: B and Mog. have *quod*, which may be right, as *se* in a subordinate clause can refer to the subject of a main clause (cf. K–St, i. 613–14).

9. quin: Mog., *om.* B. The emphatic use of *quin* in a non-negative sense is not really appropriate here and B's text (kept by W–M) is probably right.

> **pecunia ... penderetur:** cf. xxxii. 2. 1 n.
>
> **stipendium ... tributum:** W–M claim that it was a *stipendium*, a reimbursement, from the Roman point of view, but a tribute from the point of view of Carthage. But *stipendium* is used to mean a tribute, while *tributum* refers to the tax on individuals that would have to be levied to meet the payments due to Rome. The chapter division is misleading. The break in thought comes after 46. 7.

47. 2. tributo privatis remisso: this means 'and not imposing a tax on private citizens' and does not contradict 46. 9 which implies that a tax was only a threat.

3. publicus peculatus: 'embezzlement of public funds'. *peculatus* always refers to public embezzlement, so *publicus* merely gives emphasis.

> **manubiis:** B and Mog. have *manibus*, but to describe stolen property as *bona* is impossible and Madvig's emendation is clearly right. For *manubiae* as loot in general cf. *TLL*, viii. 336.

4. subscribere odiis accusatorum: 'to sign the accusation in support', cf. L–S, 1780. In this section L. uses Roman legal language.

5. calumniam ... iurarent: 'swear that the prosecution is undertaken in good faith'. For the phrase cf. *TLL*, iii. 186, Mommsen, *Strafrecht*, 386.

7. Cn. Servilius: probably Caepio, the consul of 203 (44). He was curule aedile in 207, praetor in 205. He was a *legatus* to Greece in 192 and a *pontifex* from 213 until his death in 174. His actions as consul suggest that he was an opponent of Scipio; cf. Scullard, *RP*, 78 ff.: *contra* Lippold, 210 ff.

> **M. Claudius Marcellus:** (222). Cf. xxxi. 50. 1 n. On his identity cf. 45. 6–49. 7 n. (a).

Q. Terentius Culleo: (43). He had been freed from captivity by
Scipio (xxx. 43. 11, 45. 5) and is to be regarded as a Scipionic supporter. (For possible counter-evidence from his actions in 187 cf.
Scullard, *RP*, 294). He was tribune in 189, praetor in 187, and a
legatus to Carthage again in 171. There is nothing surprising in one
Scipionic supporter being found on this embassy; embassies were
often composed of different political factions, and included persons
hostile to the policy which the embassy represented (cf. p. 35 n. 2,
xxxi. 2. 3 n.). In addition, Culleo's years of captivity in Carthage
may have made him seem a particularly appropriate choice.

8. controversias . . . dirimendas: the disputes between Carthage
and Massinissa over their boundaries dragged on for the first half
of the second century, and eventually led to the Third Punic war.
The clause in the 201 treaty that was supposed to have settled them
was obscure, and Roman interventions appear to have done their
best to keep the dispute going. Cf. Badian, *FC*, 125 ff., Walsh, *JRS*
lv (1965), 149 ff., with references to earlier literature.

9. inexpiabile bellum: if the story of Hannibal's oath (45. 7 n.)
is true, it was Hannibal who had an undying hatred for Rome. This
passage is markedly pro-Hannibalic in tone.

10. vestitu forensi: not the robes of the *sufete* as W–M say.
Hannibal's year of office is probably now over. Cf. 45. 6–49. 7 n. (a).

48. 1. Byzacium: for this region of Carthaginian territory cf. Dessau,
RE, iii. 1114–16, Walbank, *Commentary*, ii. 317–18, J. Desanges,
Les Cahiers de Tunisie xliv (1963), 7–22, Ch. Saumagne, ibid. 47 ff.
    vocant: xxxi. 24. 4 n.
    Acyllam et Thapsum: on the position of Acylla to the south of
Thapsus cf. G. Picard, *CRAI* (1947), 557 ff. The form of *Acylla* cannot
be determined with any certainty. The Greek name is Ἀχόλλα which
is found also in Pliny *NH* v. 30. *Acylla* is B's reading and is found in
Bell. Afr. 33 and 43. *Achulla* is found on coins of the Augustan period.
Cf. Schmidt, *RE*, i. 250, Meltzer–Kahrstedt, i. 99–100, Gsell, ii.
130; on Thapsus cf. Treidler, *RE*, vA. 1281–7, Meltzer–Kahrstedt,
iii. 84–5, Gsell, ii. 133–4.
    suam turrem: i.e. *turris Hannibalis*. But it was almost certainly
so called only after this event: it is referred to otherwise only in the
parallel narrative in Just. xxxi. 2. Cf. Windberg, *RE*, viiA. 1448.

3. Cercinam insulam: in fact two islands off the coast to the south
of Acylla. Cf. Dessau, *RE*, iii. 1968, Meltzer–Kahrstedt, iii. 92–3,
Gsell, ii. 126.
    Tyrum: cf. 49. 5. On it cf. Bölte, *RE*, viiA. 1876–1908. It had
passed under Seleucid control as a result of the Fifth Syrian war.

4. Hadrumetum : to the north of Thapsus. Cf. Dessau, *RE*, vii. 2178–80, Meltzer–Kahrstedt, iii. 86 ff., Gsell, ii. 136 ff., L. Foucher, *Hadrumetum* (Paris, 1964).

iusso . . . iussit : an unstylistic repetition, but it would be rash to emend.

5. media aestas forte erat : cf. xxxii. 39. 4 n.

7. cum primum : the correction for the *quod* of B and *quam* of Mog. is unavoidable. It occurs in a sixteenth-century edition, but cannot have any manuscript authority.

9–10. Carthagine [et] . . . ut non comparere : the text can clearly not stand as it is. The *et* cannot conceivably be taken up by *et Romani* in 49. 1 (McDonald's *vix* is too weak) or by *et alii* in § 10. Drakenborch's inversion of *et* and *ut* is attractive, and gives a smooth, but loose construction which fits this kind of narrative (F. Walter, *PhW* xxxviii [1918], 934, suggests *inquietae multitudinis*, but this makes it difficult to explain the corruption).

multitudinis . . . frequentare : L. imagines the situation of the visit of Roman *clientes* to their *patronus*.

principem civitatis : 'their foremost citizen' (Sage). The phrase is not an indication that Hannibal was still *sufete*.

11. idque magis : they shouted the louder.

in civitate . . . discordi : 'in a state containing different groups supporting one party or the other and split into disunited factions.'

49. 1. Philippum regem . . . fecisse : for the facts cf. xxxi. 1. 8 n. The clear implication of the sources is that the initiative was taken by Philip, though Holleaux (*Rome*, 182 and n. 4) was willing to consider the possibility that it came from Hannibal.

et Aetolos : a new element in the allegations; cf. 45. 6.

2. nec alio . . . profectum : cf. 45. 6–49. 7 n. (d).

haud quieturum antequam bellum: B has *aut quieturum eum quam bellum antequam*. McDonald (who does not mention the *aut*) is right in explaining this as the scribe writing *eum quam* for *antequam* and then repeating *antequam* later: he was influenced by *eum quam* in the previous sentence, and we should not therefore read *eum ante quam*.

3. id ei . . . vellent : 'if the Carthaginians wanted to satisfy Rome, then Hannibal must not remain unpunished'—i.e. by Carthage.

sua voluntate : in general, not with special reference to the Carthaginian senate, as W–M say.

4. responderunt : the main verb after the *oratio obliqua* depending on *cum exposuissent*. The construction is cumbersome.

5. conditoribus Carthaginis : on the foundation of Carthage, probably *c.* 800, cf. Meltzer–Kahrstedt, i. 90 ff., Gsell, i. 359 ff., G. Ch. and C. Picard, *Life and Death of Carthage*, 28 ff.

omni genere honorum : with *exceptusque.* The comma after *patria* is misleading, though the position of *vir tam clarus* makes for a certain harshness of expression.

Antiochiam : cf. 19. 8 n.

6. profectum . . . in Asiam : for Antiochus' activities in 195 cf. xxxiv. 33. 12, and for the possibility of a meeting of Roman *legati* with him in that year Walbank, *Commentary*, ii. 621.

filiumque eius : Antiochus the son. Cf. 19. 9 n. and for this episode Schmitt, *Antiochos*, 15.

sollemne . . . celebrantem : the inscription published in *AJA* lxviii (1964), 178–9, probably refers to the celebration of games at Daphne in 197; cf. J. and L. Robert, *RÉG* lxxviii (1965), 176–7. For Antiochus Epiphanes' famous celebration in 167 cf. Pol. xxx. 25–6, Downey, *History of Antioch*, 97–8. On Daphne, a suburb near Antiochia cf. Benzinger, *RE*, iv. 2136–8, Downey, *History of Antioch*, 29 ff.

7. Ephesi : cf. 38. 1 n. On the implications of these events for the date of the episode as a whole, cf. 45. 6–49. 7 (a).

fluctuantem . . . fecit : at this stage Antiochus was certainly not contemplating an aggressive war on Rome. But he may have been uncertain how far he would maintain his European claims. This passage is far less definite about Antiochus' intentions than 44. 5 ff. (cf. 45. 6–49. 7 n. (b)).

49. 8. *Senatorial reply to Aetolia*

On the source of this passage cf. 45. 6–49. 7 n. (b).

8. Aetolorum . . . alienati : for the sending of the embassy cf. 34. 7, 35. 12.

Pharsalum et Leucadem et quasdam alias civitates : presumably they now renewed their claim to Echinus and Larisa Cremaste also; cf. 34. 7 n. It is unlikely that Phthiotic Thebes was also under discussion at this point, as claimed by Flacelière, 349.

ex primo foedere : cf. 13. 9–12 n.

ad T. Quinctium reiecit : which was as good as a refusal.

ADDENDA

ABBREVIATIONS

The following should be added:

IBM   *The Collection of Ancient Greek Inscriptions in the British Museum*
          (Oxford, 1874–1916).

IC   *Inscriptiones Creticae*, ed. M. Guarducci (Rome, 1935–50).

IGRR   *Inscriptiones Graecae ad res Romanas pertinentes*, ed. R. Cagnat
          (Paris, 1911–27).

ILS   *Inscriptiones Latinae Selectae*, ed. H. Dessau (Berlin, 1892–
          1916).

p. 6. On L.'s use of Polybius see Tränkle, *Gymnasium* lxxix (1972),
13–39.

pp. 16–17. For L.'s care in the presentation of annalistic material
cf. N. Zorzetti, *Studi di storiografia antica* (Turin, 1971), 115–25.

p. 33 n. 2. On Sex. Aelius Paetus cf. F. d'Ippolito, *Labeo* xvii (1971),
271–83. Cicero *de r.p.* i. 30 provides evidence of friendship between
Paetus and Africanus.

pp. 37–8 n. 9. On the pact of the Kings cf. R. M. Errington,
Athenaeum N.s. xlix (1971), 336–54.

p. 49. **xxxi. 1. 1–5.** On the structure of L.'s work cf. P. A. Stadter,
Historia xxi (1972), 287–307, arguing for pentadic division throughout the history.

p. 52. **xxxi. 1. 8. triennio:** cf. also the use of *biduo post* at xxxii. 27. 5
(p. 220).

p. 55. **xxxi. 1. 9–10.** In line 8 after 'Badian, *PBSR* xx (1952),
91 n. 102' add '= *Studies*, 33 n. 102'.

p. 64. **xxxi. 4. 3–4.** In the notes on P. Villius Tappulus and P.
Sulpicius Galba add a reference to their appointment as *legati* to
Flamininus in 197 (xxxii. 28. 12).

In the note on C. Aurelius Cotta add a reference to J. Jahn,
Chiron ii (1972), 171–4, discussing *ILLRP* 75.

p. 71. **xxxi. 6. 5–6. damno dedecorique:** for further examples of
damnum dedecus cf. Wölfflin, *Ausgewählte Schriften*, 257 (drawn to my
attention by Professor Nisbet).

p. 77. **xxxi. 8. 4. extra senatum:** for arguments to show that M.

Aemilius Lepidus, who delivered the ultimatum at Abydus, was not a member of the senate at this time cf. Walbank, *JRS* xxvii (1937), 195–6.

p. 79. **xxxi. 9. 5–10.** On *ludi magni votivi* cf. S. Weinstock, *Divus Julius* (Oxford, 1971), 311.

p. 83. **xxxi. 10. 2. Placentiam:** for Tenney Frank's argument that the original site of Placentia was not at Piacenza cf. Walbank, *Commentary*, i. 401.

p. 85. **xxxi. 11. 11. dona ampla:** on the *toga purpurea* and the *sella curulis* cf. Weinstock, *Divus Julius*, 271 n. 9 and 273 n. 5 respectively.

pp. 86–7. **xxxi. 12. 1.** On the temple of Proserpina at Locri cf. G. Zuntz, *Persephone* (Oxford, 1971), 159–60.

p. 90. **xxxi. 12. 9. carmen . . . iusserunt:** on the significance of the *virgines* numbering 27 cf. G. Maddoli, *PP* xxvi (1971), 159.

pp. 96–7. **xxxi. 14. 11. Rhodiique . . . Aeginam venissent:** Hansen, *Attalids*, 57 n. 141 adopts Niese's suggestion (ii. 591) that the Rhodians anchored at the Piraeus and that it was only Attalus who stayed at Aegina.

On Attalid government of Aegina cf. R. E. Allen, *ABSA* lxvi (1971), 1–12.

pp. 99–100. **xxxi. 15. 9.** On Attalus' portico at Delphi cf. Hansen, *Attalids*, 292–5.

p. 105. **xxxi. 18. 1. minimus natu:** cf. addendum to p. 77.

p. 108. **xxxi. 20. 1. L. Cornelius Lentulus:** G. V. Sumner, *Arethusa* iii (1970), 89, argues that L. Lentulus was curule aedile in 209 and that the aedile of 205 was P. Cornelius Lentulus, praetor in 203 (cf. xxxiii. 35. 1–2 n.).

p. 109. **xxxi. 20. 1. ex Hispania rediit:** on the appointment of Cethegus cf. Sumner, op. cit. 90–1.

xxxi. 20. 5. ovans: on the *ovatio* add a reference to Weinstock, *Divus Julius*, 326 ff.

p. 113. On Veiovis cf. Weinstock, *Divus Julius*, 8 ff.

p. 122. **xxxi. 25. 2.** On the Achaean assemblies see also Larsen, *CPh* lxvii (1972), 178–85.

p. 126. **xxxi. 27. 6. in Asia:** for excavations at Cnidus in 1969 cf. *AJA* lxxiv (1970), 149–55. On Cnidus cf. G. E. Bean, *Turkey beyond the Maeander* (London, 1971), 135 ff.

p. 131. **xxxi. 29. 6–11.** For similar arguments cf. xxxv. 16, xxxix. 37. 10.

p. 137. **xxxi. 31. 16.** Weinstock, *Divus Julius*, 235, is wrong to suggest that Furius is here disapproving of Scipio's policy towards Carthage.

p. 141. **xxxi. 34. 8. admiratus . . . posse:** on *Syll.*³ 543 add a reference to Habicht, *Ancient Macedonia* (Thessaloniki, 1970), 273–9.

xxxi. 35. 1. Cretenses: for a treaty between Attalus and two Cretan cities *c.* 200 cf. P. Ducrey, *BCH* xciv (1970), 637 ff., J. and L. Robert, *RÉG* lxxxiv (1971), 481 no. 125.

p. 142. **xxxi. 35. 6. parmam:** on the *parma* cf. W. K. Pritchett, *Ancient Greek Military Practices* (Berkeley–Los Angeles–London, 1971), 148 n. 21.

p. 143. **xxxi. 38. 6. neque enim ne . . . quidem:** cf. xxxiii. 44. 7 n.

p. 147. **xxxi. 41. 5. Cyretias:** for *Syll.*³ 593 cf. Sherk, no. 33.

p. 151. **xxxi. 44. 4. diesque festi sacra sacerdotes:** add to the list of references to Habicht, *Gottmenschentum*, '246 ff., 255' (addenda in the second edition of Habicht's book).

p. 154. **xxxi. 45. 14. Cassandream:** on Cassandrea cf. Alexander, *Ancient Macedonia* (Thessaloniki, 1970), 127–46.

p. 157. **xxxi. 47. 1. Coela:** on the Κοῖλα Εὐβοίας cf. H. J. Mason and M. B. Wallace, *Hesperia* xli (1972), 136 ff.

pp. 160–1. **xxxi. 49. 2.** *Denarii* were often referred to as *bigati* because a *biga* was frequently (but by no means always) represented on them.

p. 162. **xxxi. 49. 7. C. Cornelius Cethegus:** on the appointment of Cethegus to Spain cf. xxxi. 20. 1 n. and addendum thereto.

p. 164. **xxxi. 50. 5. M. Aurelius Cotta:** Cotta was plebeian aedile in 216, and had been a *xvir s.f.* since 204.

pp. 164–5. **xxxi. 50. 7.** On the *flamen Dialis* cf. Weinstock, *Divus Julius*, 307.

p. 167. **xxxii. 1. 9. Feriae Latinae:** on the Latin festival cf. Weinstock, *Divus Julius*, 320 ff.

p. 172. **xxxii. 2. 7. Cosani:** on Cosa add references to Brown, *BA* lii (1967), 37–41, A. M. McCann and J. D. Lewis, *Archaeology* xxiii (1970), 201–11, W. V. Harris, *Rome in Etruria and Umbria* (Oxford, 1971), 147–8.

p. 178. **xxxii. 7. 3.** At end of third paragraph add 'cf. Cassola, *GP*, 389'.

p. 181. **xxxii. 7. 13. C. Helvius:** Helvius was a *legatus* in Asia in 189. **xxxii. 7. 15. Ser. et ⟨C.⟩ Sulpicii Galbae:** Scullard, *RP*, 87–8

n. 3, identifies C. Sulpicius Galba with C. Sulpicius, praetor in 211.

p. 191. **xxxii. 13. 11. Metropoli:** for a recently-discovered inscription from Metropolis belonging to this period cf. Habicht, *Klio* lii (1970), 139–47.

p. 196. **xxxii. 16. 16. in deditionem venit:** for evidence indicating that the destruction of Eretria was more severe than L. suggests cf. P. M. Fraser, *AR* 1968/9, 8.

p. 197. **xxxii. 16. 17. signa tabulae:** for the asyndeton cf. xxxi. 44. 4 n.

p. 208. **xxxii. 21. 25. Antigono:** on Antigonus Doson add a reference to M. T. Piraino, *Atti della Accademia di Scienze Lettere e Arti di Palermo*, serie quarta, xiii. 2. 3 (1953), 301 ff.

p. 210. **xxxii. 22. 5. Pisias Pellenensis erat:** cf. xxxiii. 28. 11 n.

p. 214. **xxxii. 24. 7.** Larsen, *Greek Federal States*, 405–6, also supports the view of Passerini.

p. 215. **xxxii. 25. 5.** On the topography of Argos cf. R. A. Tomlinson, *Argos and the Argolid* (London, 1972), 15 ff., F. Croissant, *BCH* xcvi (1972), 137 ff.

p. 221. **xxxii. 27. 7. L. Atilius:** for L. Acilius cf. also p. 28 n. 2.

pp. 222, 224. **xxxii. 28. 2, 11.** G. V. Sumner, *Arethusa* iii (1970), 92 ff. argues, in my view unconvincingly, that a formal division of Spain into two provinces was not made in 197 and that Spain continued, as in previous years, to have two proconsuls both empowered to operate over the whole province.

p. 224. **xxxii. 28. 12. Macedoniae . . . adiecerunt:** the appointment of Sulpicius and Villius, the two previous commanders, is not to be regarded as evidence of political agreement between them and Flamininus, as argued by Balsdon, *Phoenix* xxi (1967), 185. The move was probably sponsored by the Fulvians with the object of keeping an eye on what Flamininus was doing.

p. 225. **xxxii. 29. 3–4.** At xxxiv. 45. 2 L. appears to indicate that the five colonies were planted on land confiscated from the Campanians, though this can scarcely be true in the case of Buxentum (cf. W–M ad loc.).

p. 227. **xxxii. 30. 10. aedem Sospitae Iunoni:** since the temple of Juno Sospita was in the *Forum Holitorium* and that of Mater Matuta in the *Forum Boarium* L. may well have confused the two at xxxiv. 53. 3. For the possibility that there was also a pre-existing temple of Juno Sospita on the Palatine cf. M. Guarducci, *MDAI(R)* lxxviii (1971), 111–12.

p. 232. **xxxii. 33. 6.** On the Peraea, Iasus, Bargylia, and Euromus cf. Bean, *Turkey beyond the Maeander*, 153 ff., 69 ff., 82 ff., 45 ff. respectively.

pp. 244–5. **xxxii. 39. 6.** On Mycenae cf. Tomlinson, *Argos and the Argolid*, 31 ff.

p. 256. **xxxiii. 6. 1–2.** The quotation from Polybius should include, after χρείας in the second line, the words προῆγε παντὶ τῷ στρατεύματι βάδην.

p. 264. **xxxiii. 9. 8.** The quotation from Polybius should include, after εἴκοσι in the second line, the words καὶ παρ' αὐτὸν τὸν τῆς χρείας καιρὸν συμφρονήσας ὃ δέον εἴη ποιεῖν.

p. 268. **xxxiii. 11. 2. Quinctius . . . pararet:** on the Roman general's responsibility for booty cf. now I. Shatzman, *Historia* xxi (1972), 177 ff.

p. 271. **xxxiii. 12. 9. adversus . . . habere:** on the common association of *magnitudo animi* with *clementia* cf. T. Adam, *Clementia Principis* (Kiel, 1970), 82–3 and literature there cited.

p. 276. **xxxiii. 14. 7. Phliasium:** for recent excavations at Phlius cf. W. R. Biers, *Hesperia* xl (1971), 424 ff.

Cleonaeum: on Cleonae cf. Tomlinson, *Argos and the Argolid*, 29 ff.

p. 281. **xxxiii. 18. 3. Pisuetae . . . Theraei:** on Pisye and Thera cf. Bean, *Turkey beyond the Maeander*, 154.

Laudiceni: on Laodiceia-on-the-Lycus cf. J. des Gagniers, *Laodicée du Lycos, le nymphée* (Quebec–Paris, 1969), 1–11, Bean, *Turkey beyond the Maeander*, 247 ff.

pp. 281–2. **xxxiii. 18. 7.** On Alabanda cf. Bean, *Turkey beyond the Maeander*, 180 ff.

p. 283. **xxxiii. 18. 22.** On Stratonicea cf. Bean, *Turkey beyond the Maeander*, 88 ff.

p. 286. **xxxiii. 20. 2.** On the peace of Callias see now R. Meiggs, *The Athenian Empire* (Oxford, 1972), 129–51, 487–95, G. E. M. de Ste Croix, *The Origins of the Peloponnesian War* (London, 1972), 310–14.

xxxiii. 20. 4. Zephyrio: cf. Treidler, *RE*, xA. 227–8.

p. 288. **xxxiii. 20. 12.** On Caunus, Myndus, and Halicarnassus cf. Bean, *Turkey beyond the Maeander*, 166 ff., 116 ff., 101 ff. respectively.

p. 290. **xxxiii. 21. 6–9.** For the inconsistency discussed in the fourth paragraph of the note cf. the similar case in 193 (xxxv. 7. 6).

p. 291. **xxxiii. 21. 6. Hispania ulteriore:** cf. addendum to pp. 222, 224.

p. 293. **xxxiii. 23. 4. Cenomanisque:** *I.I.* xiii. 3. 64 may refer to Cethegus' defeat of the Cenomani.

xxxiii. 23. 6. For further instances of the wearing of the *pilleus* to celebrate release from captivity, and for the association of the *pilleus* with the goddess *Libertas* cf. Weinstock, *Divus Julius*, 135 ff.

xxxiii. 23. 7. bigati: cf. addendum to pp. 160–1.

pp. 295–6. **xxxiii. 24. 8–9.** On the supplementation of Cosa see the literature quoted by Harris, *Rome in Etruria and Umbria*, 158 n. 6.

p. 296. **xxxiii. 25. 1. magnificentius:** the view of Dorey referred to will now be found in his and C. W. F. Lydall's school edition of book xxxiii (London, 1972), p. 111.

p. 298. **xxxiii. 25. 8–9.** Sumner, *Arethusa* iii (1970), 93–4, argues that Sempronius was in fact killed in southern Spain in the same area where Helvius was operating (cf. 21. 6–9).

p. 299. **xxxiii. 26. 8. Monetae:** on the temple of Juno Moneta cf. also Ogilvie, 545.

pp. 299–300. **xxxiii. 27. 1–3. citeriorem Hispaniam . . . ulteriore Hispania:** Sumner, *Arethusa* iii (1970), 91, holds that these designations are anachronistic (cf. addendum to pp. 222, 224).

p. 300. **xxxiii. 27. 4. Fortunae . . . Matutae:** on these two temples cf. also Ogilvie, 680–1.

p. 303. **xxxiii. 28. 14. Anthedonem:** for a new inscription from Chalcis, possibly dating from the time of the Second Macedonian war, honouring a citizen of Anthedon who had ransomed Chalcidian captives, cf. Ducrey, *BCH* xciv (1970), 133–7.

p. 305. **xxxiii. 30. 3. Pedasisque:** on Pedasa cf. Bean, *Turkey beyond the Maeander*, 119 ff.

Iaso: for a new inscription of Iasus in honour of Antiochus III cf. G. Pugliese Carratelli, *ASAA* xlv–xlvi (1969), 445 ff., J. and L. Robert, *RÉG* lxxxiv (1971), 502 ff. (no. 621). The Roberts also argue that the fragment published by Pugliese Carratelli and D. Levi in *ASAA* xxxix–xl (1963), 578 is part of *OGIS* 237.

p. 316. **xxxiii. 35. 1–2. P. Lentulus:** cf. addendum to p. 108.

p. 317. **xxxiii. 36. 1–3.** Harris, *Rome in Etruria and Umbria*, 142, assumes that the rising is of the Etruscan serf class.

p. 319. **xxxiii. 36. 9. agrum Comensem:** on the original site of Como cf. F. Rittatore Vonwiller, *Studi sulla città antica* (Bologna, 1970), 275–8.

p. 329. **xxxiii. 42. 6. Q. Fabius Maximus augur:** Sumner,

Arethusa iii (1970), 96–7, argues, quite unconvincingly, that the augur was really Q. Fabius Buteo, the praetor of 196. The latter was appointed to command in Spain (26. 3), but, Sumner holds, died before he could proceed to his province. This would explain why M. Helvius, who should have left Spain in 196, was still there in 195 (xxxiv. 10).

p. 331. **xxxiii. 42. 10. ex eorum . . . fecerunt:** on the *Insula* cf. now M. Guarducci, *RAL* 8, xxvi (1971), 267 ff.

xxxiii. 43. 5. P. Porcius Laeca Pisas: on the date of the Via Aurelia see now T. P. Wiseman, *PBSR* xxxviii (1970), 133–4, M. Sordi, *Athenaeum* N.S. xlix (1971), 304 n. 7, Harris, *Rome in Etruria and Umbria*, 163 ff.

p. 333. **xxxiii. 44. 4. Turdam:** for Sumner, *Arethusa* iii (1970), 94, there is no problem in Minucius fighting in Ulterior since he believes that no formal division of the provinces had yet been made. Cf. addendum to pp. 222, 224.

INDEXES

1. GENERAL

Abydus, 7, 13, 16, 41–2, 56, 95, 101–8, 135, 186–7, 208, 219, 232, 236, 305, 321.
Academy, 119–20.
Acanthus, 154.
Acarnania, Acarnanians, 41–4, 95–6, 103, 193, 199, 246, 275, 277–80, 311, 314.
L. Accius, 296.
Acesimbrotus, 155, 157, 195, 230.
Achaean League, 23, 29, 44, 136, 334; appeal of Philip to in 200, 18, 121–4; concessions of, to by Philip, 174–5; conference of, 17–19, 200–12, 215, 237; and Nabis, 122–3, 243, 245; victory over Macedonians, 275–7; Achaeans in service of Rhodes, 280–2.
Acharrae, 191.
L. Acilius, 28 n. 2, 221.
M'. Acilius Glabrio (cos. 191), 31, 66, 164, 173, 293, 296, 317.
Acraea, promontory, 213.
Acraephia, 303.
Acrocorinth, 24, 74, 116, 201, 233, 239, 310.
Acte, 154.
Acylla, 339.
aediles, jurisdiction of, 163, 331.
— plebeian, 67.
Aefula, 224.
Aegina, 29, 34, 96–7, 99, 120–1, 128, 150, 244, 248, 307–8.
Aeginium, 193.
Aegium, 122.
P. Aelius Paetus (cos. 201), 33 n. 2, 56, 58–9, 64, 78, 171, 177, 323.
Sex. Aelius Paetus (cos. 198), 33 n. 2, 162–3, 171, 181–2, 184, 216, 220.
P. Aelius Tubero (pr. 201), 78.
M. Aemilius Lepidus (cos. 187, 175), 7, 41, 56–7, 105–6, 159, 182.
L. Aemilius Paullus (cos. 182, 168), 23, 71, 125, 158.
Aenesidemus, 215.
Aenianes, 126, 251.
Aenus, 101, 135.

Aetna, 131.
Aetolian League, 44, 71, 103, 128, 174–5, 192, 199, 202, 207, 214, 240; alliance with Rome in First Macedonian war, 52, 96, 100, 130–1, 138, 147, 149, 153, 207, 273–4, 278; peace with Philip in 206, 53, 127; claims on Phthiotic Achaea, 53–4, 233, 272–4, 314, 341; appeal to Rome in 201, 45, 100, 130; relations with Attalus, 99–100, 155, 250; conference of in 199, 17–22, 31, 129–39; decision to join Rome, 154–5; campaign in 199, 146–9; at conference of Nicaea, 236, 241; part in battle of Cynoscephalae, 251, 253, 257, 259; relations with Rome after battle of Cynoscephalae, 29, 34, 269–75, 305, 308–10, 314–15, 317, 331, 333–5, 340–1.
C. Afranius Stellio (pr. 185), 292.
Africa, 66, 138, 281.
Agathocles, of Egypt, 149.
ager publicus, 62, 90, 93, 136, 178, 330.
ager Sedetanus, 162.
ager Thurinus, 67.
Agrianes, 128, 282.
Alabanda, 38, 281–2.
alae, 112.
Alba, 132.
Alban mount, 292–3.
Albingaunum, 60.
Alexamenus, 301.
Alexander Isius, 149, 233–5.
— of Epirus, 186.
— the Great, 51.
Aliphera, 74, 174–5.
allies in Roman army, 78, 112.
Alopeconnesus, 101.
Ambracia, 31.
Ambracian gulf, 192–3, 198.
Ambryssus, 199.
amici, Macedonian, 128, 137–8, 274; Seleucid, 327; in Rome, 25.

349

amicitia, 53.
Amphictyones, 317.
C. Ampius (*praef.* 201), 58.
Amynander of Athamania, 24, 126–8, 146–8, 192, 230, 241, 252, 269, 316.
Anagnia, 75.
Anares, 226.
Andros, 29, 34, 99, 152–3, 155, 157, 195, 308.
Androsthenes, 212–13, 275–7.
Anemurium, 287.
Angeiae, 190–1.
annales maximi, 11–12, 17, 88.
annalists, 2–12, 47, 65, 275, 306–7, 334.
Anthedon, 303.
Anticyra, 199, 244, 309.
Antigonea, site of, 176; conference of, 18, 185–7, 231.
Antigonus Doson, 74, 174, 202, 208, 211, 214, 237, 251, 301.
— Gonatas, 151, 251, 284.
Antiochia-on-the-Orontes, 285, 327, 335, 341.
Antiochus I, 283.
— II, 281, 324.
— Hierax, 283, 289.
— III, 133, 236, 268, 274, 283; pact with Philip V, 37–9, 45, 55, 72, 95, 130; Fifth Syrian war, 56, 149, 183; *amicitia* with Rome, 183, 287, 313; attack on Pergamum in 198, 183, 195, 219; advances of in 197/6, 26–7, 34–5, 225, 275, 284–8, 300, 305–6, 309, 313–14, 317, 320–2; conference of Lysimachia, 2, 317, 322–7; meeting with Hannibal, 335–6, 341.
— son of Antiochus III, 285, 341.
— IV Epiphanes, 326, 341.
Antipatrea, 126, 146.
Antiphilus, 249, 301.
Aoi Stena, 176–7, 185–9, 192, 252–3, 261, 266.
Apamea, peace of, 64, 221, 305, 307.
Apega, 246.
Apelaurum, 276.
Apelles, 137.
Aphrodisias, 286.
Apollo, 113.
Apollonia, in Crete, 252.
— in Illyria, 108, 116, 125, 127, 146, 176, 252.
Apsus, river, 125–6.
Apulia, 62–3.
L. Apustius Fullo (*pr.* 196), 1, 67, 125–6,

146, 150–7, 195, 294.
Aratus, the elder, 121, 136–8, 201, 208.
— the younger, 137–8, 208.
arbitration, 186–7.
Archelaus, 278.
Archidamus, 173.
Ardea, 167–8.
Ardys, 285.
Argos, 27, 29, 74, 124, 211, 214–15, 233, 243–7, 331, 334.
Ariarathes V of Cappadocia, 85.
Ariminum, 83–4, 166, 220, 320, 331.
Ariovistus, 85.
Aristaenus, 17, 21–2, 200–12, 223, 230, 250, 334.
army figures, Roman, 166–7, 249, 253–4.
Arretium, 84, 110, 184.
Artaxerxes I, 286.
Artemisium, 118.
Asine, 315.
C. Asinius Pollio, 288.
Asnaus, mt., 176.
Aspis, 215.
Astragos, 281.
Athamania, 127, 253; *see also* Amynander.
Athena, 135.
Athenagoras, 126, 141, 146, 148, 260.
Athens, Athenians, 77, 79, 201, 250, 286, 308; in peace of Phoenice, 69; changes in tribal cycle, 43 n. 1, 98; execution of Acarnanians, 95–6; Philip's attacks on, 40–4, 55, 70, 73–4, 118–21, 124–5, 141; Roman ambassadors at, 7, 44; Attalus and Rhodians at, 96–9, 117; speech at meeting of Aetolian League in 199, 18, 133–5; decisions against Philip in 199, 150–2.
Atilii, 137.
L. Atilius (*pr.* 197), 221, 298.
C. Atinius (*pr.* 195), 225, 292, 297, 329.
C. Atinius (*pr.* 190), 225.
Atrax, 194, 197–8, 252.
Attalus I, relations with Aetolia, 99–100, 155; in First Macedonian war, 86, 129, 155; conflict with Philip in 201, 37, 105; at Athens, 41, 44, 96–100; criticism of inactivity of, 100–1; possession of Aegina, 97, 120–1; possession of Oreus, 124; activities in 199, 128, 146, 150–7; embassy to Rome in 198, 183, 219;

activities in 198, 195–6; alliance with Achaean League, 211; at conference with Nabis, 244–6; in Boeotia in 197, 248, 250; death and obituary, 288–90, 307–8.
— III, 290.
Attica, synoecism of, 134.
L. Aurelius (*qu.* 196), 328.
M. Aurelius (*legatus* in Greece), 40–1, 61, 158.
C. Aurelius Cotta (*cos.* 200), 64, 68, 83, 110, 115, 158–63, 179.
M. Aurelius Cotta (*aed. pl.* 216), 164.
auspicia, 62, 158–9.
Aventine, 90.
Axius, river, 129, 284.

Baebii, 70–1.
Cn. Baebius Tamphilus (*cos.* 182), 71, 163–4, 179, 182.
Baelo, 291.
Baesadines, 333.
Baeturia, 291.
Baldo (? Bardo), 291.
Barcids, 337.
Barduli, 291.
Bargylia, 26, 37–8, 42–4, 96, 232, 239, 283, 305, 316, 323.
Bato, 127.
belli indictio, 47, 77, 105.
Bellona, temple of, 159.
Berenice, wife of Antiochus II, 324.
Bevus, river, 139–40.
Bianor, 278–9.
Boebeis, lake, 126, 147.
Boeotia, 125, 197, 248–50, 275, 300–4.
Boii, 58, 82–3, 226–7, 292, 318–20.
Bononia, 320.
booty, 110, 160–1, 179, 216, 268, 293, 320.
Brachylles, 22 n. 4, 24, 28–9, 301.
Brauron, 153.
Brixia, 82, 227.
Bruanium, 143–4.
Brundisium, 60, 95.
Bruttium, 70, 75, 77–8, 84, 220.
Budares, 333.
Buxentum, 225–6.
Bylazora, 284.
Byzacium, 339.
Byzantium, 233.

M. Caecilius Metellus (*pr.* 206), 35, 112.
Q. Caecilius Metellus (*cos.* 206), 35, 63, 80, 112.

calendar, Roman, 2, 42.
Cales, 137.
Callias, peace of, 286.
Callicrates, 281.
Callimedes, 101.
Callipolis, 101.
Callithera, 191.
Calpurnii, 203.
L. Calpurnius (*leg.* 198), 203.
L. Calpurnius Piso Frugi (*cos.* 133), 3, 9, 12.
Campania, 78, 132, 136–7, 178, 225.
Canastraeum, 154.
Capena, 299.
Capitol, the, 113–14.
captured cities, 145.
Capua, 132, 136–7, 178, 184.
Caria, 37–8, 282, 288, 307–8, 313.
Carmo, 291.
Carthage, Carthaginians, 84, 284, 335–41; peace with Rome, 68, 137, 142, 169, 297, 339; hostages, 170, 216–18.
Carystus, 153, 195, 197, 206, 314.
Cassander, 154, 284.
Cassandrea, 154.
L. Cassius Hemina, 9.
Castra, 178.
Castra Pyrrhi, 189.
Caunus, 287–8.
cavalry in Roman army, 142.
Celathara, 191.
Celeiates, 82, 226.
Celetrum, 145.
Celines, 82.
Cenchreae, 197, 205, 212, 246.
Cenomani, 82, 226.
Centuripae, 131.
Ceos, 96, 99.
Cephallenia, 194.
Cephisodorus, 44, 95.
Ceramicus, 121.
Cercina, 339.
Cercinium, 147.
cercuri, 285–6.
Cerdiciates, 226.
Ceres, Liber, Libera, temple of, 296.
Cermalus, 299.
Chalcedon, 36, 53, 305.
Chalcis, 24, 116–19, 196, 242, 275, 308.
Chaonia, 176.
Chariteles, 138, 208.
Charops, 176, 192.
Chelidonian islands, 286, 326.

Chersonese, Thracian, 101, 322.
Chios, 135; battle of, 37, 95, 106, 232, 239, 251.
Chremonidean war, 250–1.
Chyretiae, 147.
C. Cicereius (*pr.* 173), 292.
Cierium, 193.
Cilicia, 286–7, 326.
Cimon, 120.
Circeii, 170, 217.
Circus Flaminius, 159.
Cithaeron, mt., 124.
Cius, 36, 42, 53, 106, 135, 208, 235–6, 271, 306.
Clastidium, 226–7.
P. Claudius (*tr. mil.* 196), 318.
Ap. Claudius Caudex (*cos.* 264), 50.
C. Claudius Centho (*leg.* 200–199), 41, 95, 116–17, 128, 152, 157.
M. Claudius Marcellus (*cos.* 222, 214, 210, 208), 30, 91, 292.
M. Claudius Marcellus (*cos.* 196), 11, 34, 163, 181–2, 219, 222, 293–4, 296–8, 318–20, 329, 335, 338.
Ap. Claudius Nero(*pr.* 195), 24, 33, 238, 242, 303, 329, 331.
C. Claudius Nero (*cos.* 207), 56, 90.
Ap. Claudius Pulcher (*cos.* 185), 303–4.
C. Claudius Pulcher (*cos.* 177), 332–3.
Q. Claudius Quadrigarius, 3, 6–11, 15, 266, 307.
Cleomedon, 206, 209.
Cleomenes III of Sparta, 174, 202, 208, 211.
Cleonae, 276–7.
Cleopatra, daughter of Antiochus III, 324.
C. Clodius Licinus (*cos.* A.D. 4), 5 n. 1, 87.
Cnidus, 126.
Cnossus, 141.
Codrio, 126.
Coele Syria, 38–9, 183, 285.
L. Coelius Antipater, 14 n. 5.
coinage, 169, 217–18.
Colonus, 120.
comitia centuriata, 71.
comitia tributa, 297.
Comum, 319.
Conon, 125.
consuls, 68, 166, 223.
contio, 72, 203.
conventus, 131–2.
Copais, lake, 303.

Coracesium, 286.
Corcyra, 108, 116, 150, 192, 213, 244.
Corinth, 74, 116, 121, 205–6, 212–13, 233, 239, 242, 246, 275, 308, 310.
corn, 66–7, 108, 163, 219.
Cornelii Lentuli, 35.
Cn. Cornelius Blasio (*pr.* 194), 4, 165, 290, 299–300.
C. Cornelius Cethegus (*cos.* 197), 4, 33 n. 1, 82, 109, 115, 162, 164, 181, 220, 291–3.
M. Cornelius Cethegus (*cos.* 204), 329.
Cn. Cornelius Lentulus (*cos.* 201), 32, 56, 60, 94, 109, 171, 179, 316.
L. Cornelius Lentulus (*cos.* 199), 32, 35, 108–10, 163, 166–7, 177, 179, 182, 184, 300, 322.
P. Cornelius Lentulus Caudinus (*pr.* 203), 316, 323.
A. Cornelius Mammula (*pr.* 217), 332.
A. Cornelius Mammula (*pr.* 191), 332.
L. Cornelius Merula (*cos.* 193), 181, 217.
P. Cornelius Scipio (*cos.* 218), 109, 296.
P. Cornelius Scipio Aemilianus (*cos.* 147, 134), 138.
P. Cornelius Scipio Africanus (*cos.* 205, 194), 28, 30–5, 45–6, 57, 62–3, 70–1, 80, 87, 109–10, 161, 172, 177, 221, 223, 296.
L. Cornelius Scipio Asiaticus (*cos.* 190), 63, 67, 158.
Cn. Cornelius Scipio Hispallus (*cos.* 176), 182.
P. Cornelius Scipio Nasica (*cos.* 191), 31, 162, 182, 296.
P. Cornelius Scipio Nasica Corculum (*cos.* 155), 162, 337.
P. Cornelius Scipio Nasica Serapio (*cos.* 138), 162.
L. Cornelius Sisenna (*pr.* 78), 15.
Corolamus, 318.
Coronea, 313.
Corrhagus, 125.
Corupedium, battle of, 321, 324–5.
Corycus, 286.
Cos, 37–8, 126.
Cosa, 162, 172, 295–6.
Cremona, 58, 65, 83–4, 110, 159, 162, 216.
Crete, Cretans, 36–7, 61, 123, 141, 200, 245, 252–3, 275, 282.
Croton, 86.
Ctimene, 190–1.
Culchas, 291.

M'. Curius (*tr. pl.* 199 or 198), 180.
Cyclades, 37, 99, 101.
Cycliadas, 123–4, 200–1, 229.
Cydas, 252.
Cynosarges, 120.
Cynoscephalae, battle of, 16, 22 n. 4, 26, 115, 142, 166, 256–66, 294.
Cyparissia, 208.
Cyphaera, 191.
Cyprus, 326.
Cypsela, 101.
Cypselus, 279.
Cythnos, 99, 153.
Cyzicus, 103.

damiourgoi, 210.
Damocritus, 138.
Daphne, 335, 341.
Dardanians, 36, 127–9, 139, 143, 146, 284.
Darius II, 286.
Dassaretis, 139, 145, 185.
datives in -*e*, 92.
Daulis, 199–200.
deditio, 7 n. 4, 86, 102, 126, 136, 147, 171, 196, 274.
Delium, 153.
Delos, 117, 308.
Delphi, 88, 99.
Demetrias, 24, 26, 71, 116, 118, 128, 139, 155–6, 242, 308.
Demetrius Poliorcetes, 118, 151, 306, 325–6.
— II, 128, 251.
— son of Philip V, 22 n. 4, 24, 100, 137, 208, 274.
— of Pharos, 127.
devotio, 107.
Dicaearchus, agent of Philip V, 36, 61, 116.
— of Plataea, 250, 301.
Dinocrates, of Macedonia, 281.
— of Messene, 23.
Dionysodorus, 230.
Dioxippus, 119.
Dipylon, 119–21.
Dium, 251.
Dolopia, 191, 311.
Cn. Domitius Ahenobarbus (*cos.* 192), 293, 330.
Dorimachus, 149.
Doriscus, 101.
Dyme, 209, 211, 215.
Dyrrachium, 125.

Echinus, 53–4, 272–4, 314, 341.
Egypt, 56–8, 79; *see also* Ptolemy, Ptolemies.
Elatia, 7, 29, 200–1, 213–14, 228, 244, 300–1, 303, 309.
Elaus, 99.
Eleates, 83.
elephants, 142, 306.
Eleusinian mysteries, 41, 43, 96, 121.
Eleusis, 120–1, 124.
— in Egypt, 326.
Elimia, 145.
Elis, 174–5, 315.
Q. Ennius, 14, 31.
Eordaea, 144–5, 261.
Ephesus, 313, 320–1, 335, 341.
Ephialtes, 336.
Epicydes, 136.
Epidamnus, 125.
Epirus, 62, 74, 108, 176, 185–6, 192, 206–7.
epulones, 327–8.
epulum Iovis, 67, 181, 331.
Eretria, in Euboea, 27, 29, 34, 195–7, 206, 308, 315.
— in Thessaly, 190, 257.
Erigon, river, 129, 143–4, 284.
Etruria, 65, 77, 84, 158–9, 167, 317–18, 332.
Euboea, 116–17, 153–4, 157, 195, 303.
Euhydrium, 190.
Eumenes I, 289.
— II, 19, 85, 307, 315.
Euripus, 116–17, 157, 303.
Euromus, 37–8, 232, 305.
Euryclides, 79, 125, 138.
Eurymedon, river, 327.

Fabii, 30, 137.
Q. Fabius Buteo (*pr.* 196, ? *leg.* 198–7), 8 n. 1, 33, 241, 293, 331–2.
Q. Fabius Labeo (*cos.* 183), 328.
Q. Fabius Maximus (*cos.* 233, 228, 215, 214, 209), 30, 80, 85, 87.
Q. Fabius Maximus (*augur*, 203–196), 329, 333.
Q. Fabius Pictor, 136, 337.
C. Fabricius Luscinus (*pr.* 195), 329.
Faenza, 59.
Faesulae, 59.
C. Fannius (*cos.* 122), 14 n. 5.
Faunus, temple of, 331.
Felsina, 58, 320.
Ferentinum, 4, 170.

fetial procedure, 77.
'fetters of Greece', 24–7, 29, 34, 242, 275, 309–10.
fides, 126.
fines imperii, 69.
flamen Dialis, 164–5.
C. Flaminius (*cos.* 223, 217), 330, 332.
C. Flaminius (*cos.* 187), 330.
Formiae, 168, 224.
Fortuna, temple of, 300.
Forum Boarium, 300.
freedom of speech, 203.
Fregellae, 170.
Fregenae, 224.
Frusino, 89, 224.
Fulvians, 30–5.
Fulvii, 30 n. 2.
M. Fulvius (*tr. pl.* 199 or 198), 32, 64, 179–80.
Q. Fulvius (*tr. pl.* 197), 32, 222.
Q. Fulvius (*leg.* 198–7), 32–3, 222, 242.
M. Fulvius Flaccus (*xvir*, 201), 64.
Q. Fulvius Flaccus (*cos.* 237, 224, 212, 209), 30, 80, 85.
Q. Fulvius Flaccus (*cos. suff.* 180), 222.
Q. Fulvius Gillo (*pr.* 200), 65, 78, 166.
M. Fulvius Nobilior (*cos.* 189), 31, 179, 329–30.
Furii, 160.
M. Furius (*leg.* 200), 112.
M. Furius (*leg.* 201), 158.
L. Furius Purpurio (*cos.* 196), 21–2, 65, 78, 82, 84, 110–15, 130, 135, 158–60, 179, 293, 297, 318–20.

A. Gabinius (*cos.* 58), 328.
Gades, 170–1.
Galatians, 280.
Gaul, Gauls, 66, 77–8, 82–4, 110–15, 160, 166–7, 182, 184, 215–16, 226–7, 271, 289, 291–3, 318–20, 332.
Gaureion, 152.
Cn. Gellius, 9.
Genua, 226.
Genusus, river, 139.
Geraestus, 153.
Gerrunium, 125.
gladiatorial shows, 164.
Gomphi, 147, 190–1.
Gonni, 266.
Gortyn, 252–3.
Graecus ritus, 76.

Hadrumetum, 340.

Halaesa, 131.
Haliacmon, river, 145.
Halicarnassus, 287–8.
Halicyae, 131.
Halmyrus, 155.
Hamilcar, 5 n. 2, 82–4, 108, 115, 227, 293.
Hannibal, 17, 23, 52, 70, 72–5, 82, 85, 137, 212, 236, 334–41.
haruspices, 69, 169.
Hasdrubal, 83.
Hebrus, river, 101.
Hegesianax, 313–14, 323.
Hellenic symmachy, 74.
Hellespont, 36.
C. Helvius (*pr.* 198), 181–2, 184, 216.
M. Helvius (*pr.* 197), 221, 291, 298, 333.
Hephaestia, 305, 316.
Heraclea Lyncestis, 128.
— in S. Italy, battle of, 75.
— in Trachis, 154–5, 251.
Heraclides, of Gyrton, 260.
— of Tarentum, 36, 61, 100, 116, 139, 156, 176.
Heraea, 74, 174–5, 315.
Hercules, temple of at Athens, 120.
hermaphrodites, 89–90.
Hermione, 150.
Hiero of Syracuse, 73, 86, 131.
Himera, battle of, 275.
Hippias, 152.
Hippocrates, 136.
Histiaea, 123.
A. Hostilius Cato (*pr.* 207), 63.
L. Hostilius Cato (*xvir*, 201), 63.
Hyampolis, 199.

Iasus, 26, 37–8, 232, 239, 305.
Icos, 153–4.
Illyria, Illyrians, 45, 54–5, 60–1, 85, 90, 127, 141, 231, 253, 260, 271, 275, Ilvates, 83, 226–7.
Ingauni Ligures, 60.
instauratio, 66–7, 164, 181, 221, 269, 330.
Insubres, 82, 115, 179, 226, 319.
Insula Tiberina, 331.
Ionia, 288.
Iphicrates, 142.
Ipsus, battle of, 325.
Iresiae, 190.
Issa, 153, 209.
Isthmian games, 7, 310.

Isthmus, proclamation of, 16, 28, 310–11.
Italians in Latin colonies, 171, 296.
iura belli, 133–4.

C. Julius Caesar, the dictator, 319, 327.
M. Junius Pennus (*pr.* 201), 62.
M. Junius Silanus (*pr.* 212), 223.
Juno Moneta, temple of, 299.
— Sospita, temple of, 89, 227.
Jupiter, and Veiovis, 113.
— Summanus, 224.
T. Juventius (*pr.* 194), 292.
T. Juventius (*tr. mil.* 197), 292.

Kingship, Hellenistic, 289.

Lade, battle of, 37, 95, 232, 251.
C. Laelius (*cos.* 190), 84, 294, 296, 298, 331.
C. Laetorius (*pr.* 210), 112
Laevi, 320.
Lamia, 173.
Lampsacus, 27, 314, 321, 325.
Lampsus, 192.
land, price of, 93.
Lanuvium, 89, 184, 227.
Laodicean war, 101, 287, 321.
Laodiceia-on-the-Lycus, 281.
Larisa, Cremaste, 53–4, 135, 156–7, 272–4, 314, 341.
— in Argos, 215.
— in Thessaly, 140–1, 147, 190, 194, 256.
latifundia, 93.
Latin colonies, 171, 296.
— festival, 167.
— revolt, 136.
latus clavus, 328.
lautumiae, 218.
Lechaeum, 212.
lectisternium, 76.
legati, selection of, 295.
Leges Licinia et Aebutia, 328.
legions, size of, 249, 332; numbers of, 292, 318.
Lemnos, 305, 308, 316.
Leon, 260.
Leontius, 137.
Leucas, 193, 278–80, 314.
Lex Baebia, 220.
— *Genucia*, 63.
— *Porcia de provocatione*, 179.
— *Porcia de sumptu provinciali*, 220.

— *Villia Annalis*, 67, 180.
Libicii, 320.
Libui, 320.
P. Licinius Crassus Dives (*cos.* 205), 80, 91, 164, 177, 327–8.
Licinius Imbrex, 91.
C. Licinius Lucullus (*tr. pl.* 196), 328.
P. Licinius Tegula, 91.
Liguria, Ligurians, 60, 83, 226, 320, 331–2.
Cn. Ligurius (*tr. mil.* 197), 292
Ligynae, 192.
Lilybaeum, 131.
Lissus, 127.
Liternum, Liternus (river), 225.
Litubium, 226.
Livius Andronicus, 91, 296.
M. Livius Drusus (*tr. pl.* 91), 328.
C. Livius Salinator (*cos.* 188), 194–5.
M. Livius Salinator (*cos.* 219, 207), 90, 195.
Livy, sources, 1–12, 172, 266, 306, 312, 335–6; use of Polybius, 6–8, 11, 94–107, 146, 172, 186, 228–43, 254–75, 284, 300–17, 322–6; misunderstandings of Greek, 6; chronology, 2–3, 115, 248, 320–1; removal of criticisms of Flamininus, 7, 11, 22 n. 4, 214, 222, 228–43, 301; omission of Eastern events, 288; explanation of Greek terms, 1; omission of *cognomina*, 1; account of outbreak of Second Macedonian war, 39–47, 138; division of books, 49; dates A.U.C., 68; figures for enemy losses, 114; accounts of elections, 2, 11, 16; obituaries of leading figures, 288.
— view of Philip V, 100, 140, 149, 235; attitude to prodigies, 88; descriptions of emotions, 202, 311; descriptions of silences, 204, 231; *humanitas*, 105, 303.
— speeches, 17–22; *amplificatio*, 132; *confessio*, 207; *correctio*, 74, 130, 206; *omissio*, 270.
— style, 12–17, 110, 117–18, 140, **298**, 318, 337, 340–1; signs of lack of interest in composition, 110, 148–9; archaisms, 15–16; word-order, 16, 96, 116, 148, 274, 331; alliteration, 71, 79, 207; expression for beginning of a year, 182; *ecphrasis* technique, 302; historical infinitive, 147; variation of

355

Livy (*cont.*):
tenses, 104, 304, 326; plural after collective noun, 145, 148; indicative in subordinate clauses in *oratio obliqua*, 291; omission of *esse*, 111, 123, 125, 171, 192; asyndeton, 61, 108, 151, 298, 322, 334; change of construction, 151, 310; anacoluthon, 134, 158; local ablative, 89.
Lobolda, 281–2.
Locri, 86–7.
Locris, Eastern, 154, 205–6, 228, 241, 310–11, 315.
— Western, 199, 205, 311.
Longarus, 128.
Lucania 75.
Sp. Lucretius (*pr.* 205), 86.
Lucus Feroniae, 299.
ludi magni votivi, 79, 81–2.
— *plebeii*, 67, 79, 163, 181, 331.
— *Romani*, 65–6, 79, 181, 221, 294, 296, 330.
— *saeculares*, 91.
Luxinius, 291.
Lychnidus, 316.
Lychnitis, lake, 139, 143.
Lycia, 288, 326.
Lyciscus, of Acarnania, 133.
— of Aetolia, 173.
Lycium, 120.
Lyncon montes, 189–90.
Lyncus, 139, 144, 185, 190.
Lysias, representative of Antiochus III, 313–14, 323.
Lysimachia, 235; capture by Philip V, 36, 53, 234–5; conference of, 18, 35, 109, 317, 322–7.
Lysimachus, 324–5.

Macedonian war, First, 32, 36, 45, 52, 58, 74, 121, 127, 187, 202, 206–7, 209, 251.
— — Second, outbreak of, 7, 36–47; Roman politics during, 22–35.
Macedonians, claims to be Greek, 133, 136; language, 133; relationship to king, 202; *see also* Philip V of Macedon.
Machanidas, 122.
Macra Come, 190.
Madytus, 101, 322.
Magnesia, *ad Sipylum*, battle of, 254.
— in Thessaly, 26, 29, 311.
— on-the-Maeander, 287.

Mago, 83.
Malaga, 291.
Malea, 150, 157, 195.
Malloea, 147.
Mallus, 287.
Mamertines, 73.
Mandrioli pass, 59.
P. Manlius (*pr.* 195, 182), 328–9, 331.
L. Manlius Acidinus (*pr.* 210), 109, 165, 179.
T. Manlius Torquatus (*cos.* 235, 224), 80.
Cn. Manlius Vulso (*cos.* 189), 31, 158, 220, 296, 329, 331.
L. Manlius Vulso (*pr.* 197), 220, 298.
Marathon, 116.
Marcii Philippi, 297.
Q. Marcius Philippus (*cos.* 186, 169), 293.
M. Marcius Ralla (*pr.* 204), 297.
Q. Marcius Ralla (*tr. pl.* 196), 297.
L. Marcius Septimus (*leg.* 206), 170–1.
Maronea, 101, 135.
Marsi, 319.
Marzeno, river, 59.
Masada, 103.
Massinissa, 40, 84–6, 108, 219, 339.
Massyli, 84.
Mater Matuta, temple of, 300.
Mediolanium, 82.
Megaleas, 137.
Megalopolis, 174–5, 200, 211, 215.
Megara, 116, 121.
Melambium, 258.
Mende, 154.
mercenaries, 119, 123–4, 253, 260, 276–7, 326.
Meropus, mt., 176.
Messana, 131–2.
Messene, Messenians, 23, 135–6, 208, 315.
Metaurus, battle of, 115.
Metropolis, 191, 193.
Micion, 79, 125, 138.
Miletus, 287.
Mincius, river, 226.
minores magistratus, 218.
Minucii Rufi, 226.
M. Minucius Rufus (*cos.* 221), 64–5.
M. Minucius Rufus (*pr.* 197), 221.
Q. Minucius Rufus (*cos.* 197), 33 n. 1, 64, 67, 70, 78, 84, 167, 220, 226–7, 291–3.
Q. Minucius Thermus (*cos.* 193), 64, 221, 226, 293, 298, 332–3.

Mithridates, nephew of Antiochus III, 285.
Mniesutae, 280–1.
Modigliana, 59.
Molossis, 189.
Monastir gap, 144.
Mutilum, 59, 320.
Mutina, 83.
Mycale, battle of, 275.
Mycenae, 244–5.
Myndus, 288.
Myrina, 305.
Myrleia, 236.

Nabis, 27, 29, 35, 122–3, 133, 141, 202, 206, 243–7, 252, 331, 334.
Narnia, 58, 94, 162, 171.
Naupactus, 129, 131.
naves apertae, tectae, 117, 155, 208–9.
Nemean brook, 276.
neologisms, 14–16.
Netum, 131.
Nicaea, conference of, 18, 22 n. 4, 24–6, 106, 138, 186–7, 222, 227–43, 301.
Nicanor, 41, 44, 56, 77, 100, 262.
Nicostratus, 245–6, 250, 276.
Nisya, 280.
Nisyros, 37.
Norba, 170, 217.
Novum Comum, 319.
Numidia, 108; see also Massinissa, Vermina.

Oath formulae, 104.
obituaries in historiography, 288.
Cn. Octavius (pr. 205), 60, 86.
Ogulnii, 318.
M. Ogulnius (tr. mil. 196), 318.
Olympias, 74.
Onchestus, in Boeotia, 248.
— river in Thessaly, 258.
L. Oppius Salinator (pr. 191), 222.
Opus, 228–9, 238.
Orchomenus, 74, 174.
Orestis, 145–6, 311, 314.
Oreus, 27, 29, 34, 123–4, 146, 155–6, 196, 308, 315.
Orgessus, 125.
Oricum, 176.
Osphagus, river, 144.
Ostia, 168.
Ottolobus, 142, 146.
ovatio, 109.

Paeonia, 284.
Palaepharsalus, 190.
Pamphylia, 326–7.
Panium, battle of, 149, 285.
Panormus, 131.
C. Papirius Maso (cos. 231), 292.
Paros, 99, 135, 153.
Parthini, 54, 315–16.
Parthus, 315–16.
Patara, 313, 326.
patrum auctoritas, 68.
Pausanias, of Epirus, 186.
Pausistratus, 280.
peculatus, 90, 338.
Pedasa, 37–8, 232, 305.
Pelagonia, 128, 140, 144.
Pelion, 145–6.
Pellene, 211, 246, 276.
peltasts, 142, 253.
Peneius, river, 193–4.
Peparethos, 129, 153–4.
Peraea, Rhodian, 232, 236, 239, 280–3.
Pergamum, 29, 37, 45, 183, 313, 321; see also Attalus, Eumenes.
Pericles, 120.
Perinthus, 36, 233, 305.
Perrhaebia, 147, 194, 311.
Perseus, 24, 128, 208, 211, 231.
Persia, kings of, 324.
Peumata, 191.
Phacium, 190.
Phaeca, 148, 191.
Phaeneas, 230, 235, 251, 271–4.
phalanx, Macedonian, 144, 198, 253, 262, 264, 266.
Phalasia, 155.
Phalerum, 124.
Phaloria, 193.
Phanotea, 199.
Pharcado, 148.
Pharsalus, 53–4, 190, 272–4, 314, 341.
Pherae, 190, 256.
Pherinium, 192.
philhellenism among Romans, 28, 31.
Philip II of Macedon, 74.
— V of Macedon, alliance with Hannibal, 52, 73, 85, 139, 340; in First Macedonian war, 61, 155, 202; attacks on Messene, 135–6; and Polycrateia, 138, 208, 211; actions 205–1, 36–45, 53–5, 106, 133, 135, 141, 155, 202, 232; pact with Antiochus III, 37–9, 45, 55, 95, 130; and Ptolemaic possessions, 38–9, 100, 231; relations

Philip V of Macedon (*cont.*):
with Crete, 141; actions in summer of 200, 95, 100–8; attacks on Athens in 200, 118–21, 124–5, 134, 151, 202–3, 207; Athenian decrees against, 151–2; appeal to Achaean League in 200, 18, 121–4; campaign of 199, 139–49; recapture of Oreus, 124; campaign of winter 199/8, 173–7; concessions to Achaean League, 174–5, 202; campaign of 198, 185–94, 234; at conference of Nicaea, 227–43; and Nabis, 243–4; campaign of 197, 250–66; speech before battle of Cynoscephalae, 18, 252–3; negotiations after battle of Cynoscephalae, 266–75, 295; campaign against Dardanians in 197, 284; peace with Rome, 7, 34, 294–8, 304–17, 322, 333–4; sacrilege by, 120, 134, 202; alleged murders by, 137–8; admiration of Roman institutions, 140–1; cult for, 151, 214; Livy's view of, 100, 140, 149, 235; fear ascribed to, 7, 104, 140.
Philippides, 119.
Philocles, 41, 43–4, 69, 75, 100, 124, 196, 213–14, 243.
Philopoemen, 23, 122–3, 138, 200, 252.
Phlius, 276.
Phocis, 103, 199–200, 206, 213, 228, 241, 303, 315.
Phoenice, peace of, 36, 39 n. 6, 52, 54, 69, 96, 121, 127, 136, 138, 199, 206, 231, 236.
Phthiotic Achaea, 53–4, 135, 154, 233, 251, 272–4, 311.
— Thebes, *see* Thebes, Phthiotic.
piacula, 88.
Pierium, 193.
pilleus, 293.
Piraeus, 124–5, 135, 152.
Piresiae, 190.
Pisa, 331.
Pisias, 210.
Pisistratids, 120.
Pisistratus, of Boeotia, 301.
Pisuetae, 281.
Pixus, 225.
Placentia, 58, 65, 83, 159, 162, 216, 292.
Plataea, 205, 250; battle of, 275.
Plautus, language of, 13.
Q. Pleminius (*leg.* 205), 5, 87.
Pleuratus, 55, 127, 140, 143, 153, 316.

Pluinna, 143–4.
Plutarch, sources of, 8 n. 1.
Po, river, 58, 110, 318–20.
Polybius, chronology, 2, 115; division of year, 115–16; Rhodian sources, 286–7; bias against Flamininus, 23; view of Athens, 95, 150; view of Philip V, 120, 125; view of Hannibal, 335–6; view of Nabis, 122; interest in military details, 143, 254; geographical excursuses, 279; view of τύχη, 280; use of by annalists, 8; *see also* Livy, use of Polybius.
Polycrateia, 138, 208, 211.
Polyxenidas, 280.
M. Pomponius Matho (*pr.* 204), 87–8.
M. Porcius Cato (*cos.* 195), 9, 11, 14, 15, 28, 31, 65, 181–2, 219–22, 290, 329, 333.
P. Porcius Laeca (*pr.* 195), 179, 328–9, 331–2.
porta Capena, 299.
porta Esquilina, 299.
portoria, 178.
Posidium, cape, 154.
Postumii, 30 n. 2.
praefectus socium, 58–9, 318.
Praeneste, 75, 218.
praenomina, corruption of in MSS., 65.
praetor peregrinus, 70, 221–2, 291, 298.
praetor pro consule, 5.
praetor urbanus, 70.
praetors, number of, 220; presiding at elections, 62.
praetorship, held directly after aedileship, 67; repeated, 195, 328.
Prasiae, 153.
Prinassus, 37.
privati cum imperio, 108–9, 162, 165, 179.
Privernum, 88–9.
prodigies, 2, 11 n. 4, 16–17, 88–91, 168–9, 183–4, 224, 299.
Propontis, 36, 233.
Prusa, 37.
Prusias I of Bithynia, 23, 37, 195, 236, 306.
Pteleon, 157.
Ptolemais, Attic tribe, 79.
Ptolemies, 86; possessions in Thrace, 100–1, 305–6, 316, 325; possessions in Asia Minor, 38, 287–8, 321, 323; control of Cyclades, 99.
Ptolemy I Soter, 326.
— III Euergetes, 325.

— IV Philopator, 36, 54, 95, 231.
— V Epiphanes, 56, 323–6.
— son of Sosibius, 38.
— of Mauretania, 85.
publicani, 91.
pulvinaria, 76–7, 169.
Punic war, First, 49, 73, 336.
—— Second, 30, 72, 337.
—— Third, 337, 339.
Puteoli, 178, 225.
Pylos, 315.
Pyramus, river, 327.
Pyrasus, 155.
Pyrrhias, 146, 154.
Pyrrhus, 20, 62, 74–5, 325.
Pythagoras, 92.

Quaestiones, 87.
Quinctii, 30.
L. Quinctius Flamininus (*cos.* 192), 65, 163, 194–7, 223, 244, 246, 277–80.
T. Quinctius Flamininus (*cos.* 198), and Roman politics, 22–35, 296; early career, 180; alleged aedileship in 201, 4; *xvir* in 201, 64, 167; quaestorship, 180; campaign for consulship, 32, 180–2; campaign in Greece in 198, 2, 185–215; size of army, 166–7, 253–4; conference of Nicaea, 24–6, 227–43; prorogation for 197, 3, 24–6, 222–3; and Nabis, 243–7; campaign of 197, 248–66; speech before battle of Cynoscephalae, 18, 143, 261; negotiations after battle of Cynoscephalae, 137, 266–75; prorogation for 196, 26–7, 298; and Boeotia, 24, 300–4; peace with Philip and settlement of Greece, 34–5, 124, 297, 304–17; prorogation for 195, 27, 331–2; Aetolians referred back to in 195, 341; age, 7–8, 312; relationship to Fabii, 8 n. 1, 30, 241–2; bust at Delphi, statue at Phanotea, 199.

relatio, relatio de re publica, 68.
Rhegium, 132, 136.
Rhodes, Rhodians, 19, 36–7, 40–1, 44–5, 55, 61, 70, 96, 98–101, 105, 117, 120, 126, 130–1, 141, 157, 195, 202, 232–3, 280–3, 286–8, 307–8.
Rome, foundation date, 50; foundation legend, 133; Romans viewed as barbarians, 133, 141.
ruler cult, 151, 214, 237.

P. Rutilius Rufus (*cos.* 105), 9.

Sabines, 65, 89.
sacrificial victims, 68–9.
Saguntum, 20, 72, 103, 107.
Salamis, battle of, 275.
Salernum, 178, 225.
Sallust, 15–16, 288.
Same, 194.
Samnium, Samnites, 62, 75, 115.
Samos, 37–8, 135, 287.
Sancus, 168.
Sapinia tribus, 59, 319.
Sardinia, 66, 77–8, 219.
Sarsinates, 59.
Sarus, river, 327.
Scarphaea, 251.
Scerdilaidas, 127.
Sciathos, 129, 153–4.
Scipios, the, 30–1; trials of, 3; *see also* Cornelius Scipio.
Scopas, 149.
Scotusa, 257.
C. Scribonius Curio (*pr.* 193), 330.
Scyllaeum, cape, 150.
Scyros, 153–4, 308.
Segesta, 131.
Seleucia Pieria, 327.
Seleucus I, 285, 321, 324–5, 327.
— II, 183, 283.
— son of Antiochus I, 283.
— IV, 283, 285, 325.
Selinus, in Cilicia, 287.
sella curulis, 85.
Sellasia, battle of, 211, 214.
Selymbria, 322.
Sempronius Asellio, 9 n. 3.
C. Sempronius Gracchus (*tr. pl.* 123–122), 66, 159.
Ti. Sempronius Gracchus (*praef.* 196), 318.
Ti. Sempronius Gracchus (*tr. pl.* 133), 93.
Ti. Sempronius Longus (*cos.* 218), 109, 296.
Ti. Sempronius Longus (*cos.* 194), 109–10, 221, 226, 293, 296, 298, 332.
T. Sempronius Musca, 109.
T. Sempronius Rutilus, 109.
C. Sempronius Tuditanus (*pr.* 197), 5–6, 220, 329.
C. Sempronius Tuditanus (*cos.* 129), 9.
P. Sempronius Tuditanus (*cos.* 204), 57, 207.

senate, composition of, 25.
senatus consultum de Bacchanalibus, 14.
sententiae, in Roman senate, 68.
C. Sergius Plautus(*pr.* 200), 65, 161, 167.
M. Sergius Silus (*pr.* 197), 4, 220, 227, 291, 294.
Serrheum, 101.
P. Servilius (*xvir*, 201), 63.
Cn. Servilius Caepio (*cos.* 203), 338.
C. Servilius Geminus (*iiivir*, 218), 63.
C. Servilius Geminus (*cos.* 203), 63.
Cn. Servilius Geminus (*cos.* 217), 332.
M. Servilius Geminus (*cos.* 202), 63, 226.
P. Servilius Geminus (*cos.* 252, 248), 63.
Sestus, 101, 232, 305.
Setia, 4, 170, 216, 218.
Sexi, 291.
Sibylline books, 76, 90.
Sicily, 66, 77–8, 131–2, 219, 330.
Sicyon, 122, 201, 244, 246, 248, 276; meeting of Achaean League at, 201–12.
Signia, 4, 170.
Sinuessa, 89–90.
Sithone, peninsula, 154.
slave revolts, 2, 216–18, 317–18.
Smyrna, 314, 321, 325.
Social war (220–217), 187, 202, 251.
societas, socius, 53, 316.
socii navales, 212–13, 239, 322.
Soli, 286.
Sopater, of Acarnania, 118.
— of Macedonia, 55, 118.
Spain, 2, 66, 77, 109, 161, 220, 223–4, 284, 290–1, 298–300, 331, 333; title of governors of, 5–6.
Sparta, Spartans, 29, 86, 122, 205, 245, 301; *see also* Nabis.
Spercheiae, 190.
L. Stertinius (*procos.* 199–197), 165, 300, 316.
Stobi, 284.
Stoics, 92.
Stratonicea, 37–8, 281–3, 307–8.
Stratonidas, 302.
Stuberra, 143–4.
Stymphalus, 276.
Suessa Aurunca, 168, 184.
Sulpicii, 30 n. 2.
C. Sulpicius Galba (*pont.* 202–199), 181.
P. Sulpicius Galba (*cos.* 211, 200), 1–2, 17, 19–20, 26, 29 n. 8, 31, 40–2, 54, 57, 60, 64, 68, 71–6, 80–1, 94–5, 116, 125, 127–8, 139–46, 158, 166, 169,

181, 185, 207, 222, 261, 295, 323.
Ser. Sulpicius Galba (*aed. cur.* 201), 181.
Summanus, temple of, 224.
Sunium, 117.
supplicationes, 76–7, 115, 160, 169, 227, 294.
synchronism of battles, 275.
Syphax, 84–6, 115.
Syracuse, 92, 131, 136.
Syrian war, Fourth, 287.
—— Fifth, 79, 149, 285, 322, 339.
—— Sixth, 326.

Tacitus, 288.
Tanagra, 153, 302.
Tarentum, 75, 132.
Tarmiani, 281.
Tarquinius Priscus, 81.
— Superbus, 168.
Tarsus, 327.
Tauromenium, 131.
Tempe, 194, 266, 316; conference of, 18, 269–75, 295, 307.
Tendeba, 281.
Tenedos, 101–2.
Terence, language of, 13.
Q. Terentius Culleo (*pr.* 187), 35, 293, 339.
L. Terentius Massiliota (*pr.* 187), 35, 163–4, 316, 323.
C. Terentius Varro (*cos.* 216), 35, 70, 86, 162.
M. Terentius Varro, the antiquarian, 11 n. 4.
testudo, 145, 198.
Teuma, 191.
Teuta, 127.
Thapsus, 339–40.
Thasos, 37, 135, 305, 323.
Thaumaci, 173–4, 191.
Thebes, Boeotian, 248–9, 288, 301, 303.
— Phthiotic, 26, 53–4, 235, 254, 272–4, 314, 341.
Themistocles, 335–6.
Theodorus of Athamania, 127.
Theoxenus, 281.
Thera, in Caria, 281.
Thermopylae, 118, 129, 317.
Thermus, 129.
Theseus, 134.
Thessalonica, 284.
Thessaly, Thessalians, 26, 28, 103, 117–18, 126, 147–8, 154, 173, 187, 189–94, 206, 234, 250, 275, 311.

1. GENERAL

Thetideum, 258.
Thrace, Thracians, 36, 41, 100–1, 124, 141, 215, 236, 253, 260, 271, 275, 277, 282, 305–6, 316.
Thrasycrates, 133.
Thronium, 240, 251.
Thucydides, 288.
Ticino, river, 320.
Tifata, mt., 178.
Timocrates of Pellene, 246.
Timon, 254.
Titaresius, river, 147.
P. Titinius (*leg.* 200), 112.
toga praetexta, 85, 328.
Torone, 154.
Tralles, 141, 253.
transitio ad plebem, 63.
Trasimene, battle of, 330.
Tricca, 190.
trientabula, 91–3, 329.
Triphylia, in Epirus, 189.
— in the Peloponnese, 74, 174–5, 315.
triremes, 95.
triumphs, 85, 109, 158–60, 162, 179, 291–3, 300, 320, 333.
triumviri capitales, 218.
Troezen, 150.
tumultus, 58, 216–17.
tunica palmata, 85.
Turda, Turdetani, 333.
turris Hannibalis, 339.
Tyre, 339.

Valerii Laevini, 30 n. 2.
Valerius Antias, 3, 5 n. 1, 6–9, 11, 177, 266, 307, 319.
M. Valerius Falto (*pr.* 201), 78, 166.
C. Valerius Flaccus (*pr.* 183), 164, 181.
L. Valerius Flaccus (*cos.* 195), 65, 112, 163, 165, 182, 329.
C. Valerius Laevinus (*cos. suff.* 176), 181.

M. Valerius Laevinus (*cos.* 210), 40–1, 45, 57, 60–1, 73, 128, 164, 206–7.
M. Valerius Laevinus (*pr.* 182), 164.
P. Valerius Laevinus, 164.
Veii, 132, 184.
Veiovis, 113–14.
Veliates, 83.
Vclitrac, 168, 184.
Venusia, 161–2, 180.
ver sacrum, 332.
Vermina, 84, 108.
Verona, 82.
Vespasian, 65.
L. Veturius Philo (*cos.* 206), 80.
Via Aurelia, 64, 331.
Vibo, 61.
Vicus Tuscus, 299.
Villa publica, 295.
P. Villius, *eques*, 299.
L. Villius Tappulus (*pr.* 199), 64, 163, 182.
P. Villius Tappulus (*cos.* 199), 1–2, 26, 29 n. 8, 32, 64, 163, 167, 169, 172–7, 185, 194, 222, 295, 316, 323, 333.
Volcanus, temple of, 224.
Volturnum, Volturnus (river), 225.

Wackernagel's law 304.

x legati, 295; for settlement of 196, 34–5, 295.
Xenophon, of Achaea, 230.
— the historian, 138.
xviri sacris faciundis, 76, 90, 164.
Xyniae, 191, 251.

Zama, battle of, 45, 55, 115, 212.
Zelasium, 155.
Zephyrium, 286.
Zeuxidas, 278–9.
Zeuxippus, 29, 301–4.
Zeuxis, 28.

2. AUTHORS AND PASSAGES

A. LITERARY

For reasons of space references are, for the most part, given only to chapters, not to sections. The references to Livy exclude, for obvious reasons, passages in books xxxi–xxxiii themselves. The figures in larger type indicate the pages of this book.

Aelian, *NA* iii. 37, 193; vii. 41, 75.
Aeneas Tactitus, 4, 117; 6, 119.
Ampelius, 28, 45, 75.
Appian, *BC* i. 7, 93, 178, 330; i. 8, 330.
 Hann. 55, 87.
 Ib. 77, 162.
 Ill. 7–8, 153.
 Lib. 32, 185; 49, 83; 54, 169–70; 59, 83; 112, 181.
 Mac. 1, 52; 3, 58, 127; 4, 37 nn. 5, 10, 55, 130; 6, 187, 189; 7, 32 n. 1, 64, 200; 8, 227; 9, 34 n. 4, 266, 269, 304, 306.
 Samn. 10, 75.
 Sic. 1, 57.
 Syr. 2–3, 321–5; 4, 326, 335; 11, 23 n. 5; 16, 268; 38, 219.
Aristotle, *Ath. Pol.* 25, 336.
 Pol. 1272b, 336; 1273a, 203, 337.
 Rhet. 1358b, 20.
Arrian, *Anab.* i. 5, 128; ii. 13, 279.
Asconius, p. 3c, 83.
[Asconius], p. 217St., 81.
Augustine, *CD* iii. 17, 76.
Augustus, *RG* 26, 69.

Caelius, *ap.* Cic. *fam.* viii. 8, 139.
Caesar, *B. Afr.* 33, 43, 339.
 B. Alex. 32, 283.
 BC i. 1, 68; ii. 19, 188; iii. 18, 330.
 BG i. 43, 85; iv. 10, 327; vi. 1, 217; 29, 198; vii. 44, 111.
Callimachus, *Hymns* vi. 24, 126.
 fr. 43. 46, 327.
L. Calpurnius Piso Frugi, fr. 31P, 292; fr. 34P, 9 n. 3.
Cato, M. Porcius, fr. 20M, 152.
Cicero, *ad Att.* xiii, 4, 5, 6, 30, 32–3, 11 n. 4.
 ad fam. vii. 13, 92; xv. 9, 160.
 ad Q. fr. i. 1, 138.
 Brutus 72, 65.
 de div. i. 97, 99, 89; ii. 59, 279.
 de domo 14, 66.
 de finibus ii. 63, 184; v. 1, 120.

de har. resp. 2, 187.
de imp. Cn. Pomp. 2, 71; 44, 66; 58, 328.
de leg. agr. ii. 21, 328; 49, 52; 68, 279; 94, 184.
de legibus iii. 19, 180.
de natura deorum i. 82, 89; ii. 14, 88.
de oratore iii. 73, 327.
de re publica i. 58, 133; iii. 24, 69.
de senectute 50, 65.
in Catilinam iii. 13, 68.
in Pisonem 2, 71; 65, 65.
in Verrem ii. 2. 63, 131; 2. 123, 220; 3. 27, 3. 38, 3. 57, 4. 55, 5. 16, 5. 140, 131.
Philippics iii. 32, 99.
post reditum ad Quirites 18, 67.
pro Balbo 34 ff., 170–1; 57, 204.
pro Sestio 116, 65.
pro Sulla 67, 52.
Tusc. disp. i. 3, 31 n. 3, 65; ii. 62, 138.
Codex *Justiniani* xii. 19. 4, 178.
L. Coelius Antipater, fr. 47P, 14 n. 5.
Columella, vi. 3. 3, 325.
P. Cornelius Scipio Aemilianus, fr. 17M, 14 n. 5, 325; fr. 27M, 14 n. 5.
L. Cornelius Sisenna, fr. 80P, 151.

Demosthenes, *de corona* 170, 204.
 Meidias 49, 133.
 Phil. i. 30, 152.
de viris illustribus 35, 74–5; 47, 219; 51, 187.
Digest iv. 6. 9, 218; ix. 2. 27, 178; xi. 5. 1, 218; xxiv. 1. 2, 31, 178.
Dio, frs. 41, 57; 47, 89; 57, 87, 158; 58, 82–3, 139, 141, 143, 146; 60, 29 n. 3, 266, 269; 62, 29 n. 4; xliii. 51. 9, 327.
Diodorus, xiii. 47, 118; 69, 152; xiv. 102, 217; xvi. 34, 102; xxii. 1, 132; xxvii. 1, 122; 3, 36 n. 2; 4, 87; xxviii. 1, 36 nn. 2–3, 141; 2, 36 n. 3, 128, 137; 7, 120; 9, 176; 11, 185–6; 12, 322, 325; xxxii. 12, 89; xxxvii. 11, 104.

Dionysius of Halicarnassus, iii. 61, v. 35, 85; vi. 17, 94, 326; vii. 71, 81; xii. 9, 76; xx. 4–5, 16, 132; 14, 57.

Ennius (ed. Vahlen), *Ann.* 334 ff., 187; 336, 167; *Var.* 70, 151.
Euripides, *Hec.* 1199, 133.
Schol. *Or.* 362, 150.
Eusebius (ed. Schöne), ii. p. 125, 91.
Eutropius, ii. 12, 75; 15, 57; iii. 12, 52.

Festus (ed. Lindsay), p. 92, 165; p. 252, 202; pp. 446, 500, 91.
FGH III B p. 383, 310.
Florus, i. 13, 75; 22, 91; 23, 52.
Frontinus, ii. 3, 55; 13, 43; iii. 9, 321.
Fronto (ed. Naber), p. 62, 14 nn. 4, 5.

Gellius, iv. 6, 68; x. 15, 165; 25, 145; xii. 8, 67; xvi. 10, 58; xvii. 21, 65.
Gorgias, DK 82 B 5b, 133.
Granius Licinianus, p. 21, 89.

Hermippus, *FHG* iii. 51, 236.
Herodotus i. 1–4, 133; v. 22, 211; 63, 120; vi. 105, 118–19; vii. 129, 147; 166, 275; 175, 118; 183, 192, 119; viii. 13, 157; 27–8, 103; 137, 211; ix. 12, 119; 90, 275.
Hesychius, *s.v.* Τραλλεῖς, 141.
Hieronymus, *in Dan.* xi. 13–14, 38 n. 10; 15–16, 149, 284, 287, 321, 326.
Homer, *Il.* vi. 155 ff., 302; xiii. 131–3, xvi. 215–17, 263.
Homeric Hymns iii. 32, 190.
Horace, *Ars Poetica* 56–9, 14 n. 4.
Epistles i. 2. 40, 51; ii. 2. 133, 289.
Odes i. 4. 12, 68; i. 7. 11, 147; iii. 29. 6, 224.
Ps.-Acro *ad Odes* i. 37. 3, 77.
Satires ii. 2. 5, 198.

Isocrates, *Panegyricus* 157–8, *Philippus* 154, 133.

Justin, xviii. 1, 75; 2, 57; xix. 2, 336; xxv. 5, 74; xxviii. 1, 96; 3. 128; xxix. 4, 52, 128, 138, 200; xxx. 2, 38 n. 10; 3. 57, 227; 4, 243, 256, 304; xxxi. 1–2, 335, 339.

Laus Pisonis 245, 111.
Livy, *praef.*, 51; i. 23, 234; 29, 132; 34,

106; 35, 79; 43, 218; 56, 217; 57, 168; ii. 15, 53; 18, 71; 25–6, 118; 26, 148; 31, 197; 33, 156; 36, 81; 39, 283; 40, 311; 43, 75; 58, 145; 64, 130; iii. 1, 252; 5, 11; 6, 218; 7, 76, 83; 19, 134; 24, 156; 37, 162; 63, 76, 115; iv. 7, 50; 10, 53; 11, 168; 12, 81; 13, 71; 14, 265; 16, 66; 22, 295; 27, 81; 41, 53; 44, 202; 58, 71, 143; v. 1–23, 132; 4, 53; 5, 80, 324; 13, 76; 15, 88; 16, 186; 17, 53; 19, 81, 160; 23, 115; 27, 134; 30, 109; 31, 81; 35, 82, 320; 39, 53; 41, 92; 43, 234; 49, 118; 160; 54, 50; vi. 7, 106; 24, 143; 27, 71; 29, 75; 40, 324; 42, 72; vii. 2, 65; 11, 81; 12, 75; 15, 81; 18, 50; 25, 160, 307; 26, 302; viii. 3, 137; 4, 309; 6, 72; 9, 75; 11, 14, 136; 17, 119; 20, 168; 21, 53; 24, 288; 29, 75; 30, 187; 34, 167; 38, 143; ix. 3, 97; 4, 103, 17–19, 51; 19, 254; 36, 302; 45, 53; x. 21, 115; 23, 163; 29, 142; 33, 163; 38, 104; 41, 104, 140; 45, 115; 47, 163; *per.* xii, 132; *per.* xiv, 57; *per.* xv, 132; *per.* xix, 224; *per.* xx, 83; xxi. 5, 144; 6, 68, 333; 10, 71; 12–13, 102; 14, 103; 15–16, 72; 17, 68; 19, 72; 25, 82–3; 26, 318; 27, 53; 28, 92; 33, 311; 38, 74, 320; 41, 73; 55, 82; 62, 80–1, 88–9; 63, 75; xxii. 1, 68, 90, 184, 299; 3, 187; 6, 102; 9–10, 332; 9, 81; 10, 75, 81, 169; 15, 75, 268; 16, 118; 26, 268; 33, 218; 36, 89; 39, 309; 42, 144; 48, 311; 52, 102; 58, 234; 61, 62, 75; xxiii. 4, 137; 6, 103; 10, 126, 249; 11, 75, 298; 15, 101–2; 20, 103; 21, 332; 31, 89–90; 32, 207; 33–4, 52; 33, 73; 34, 207, 286; 38–9, 52, 73; 38, 45 n. 5, 60, 207; 41, 143; 46, 142; 48, 52; 49, 91, 142; xxiv. 4–7, 131; 8, 181; 9, 131; 10, 80, 88–9, 331; 11, 206; 18, 91; 20, 62; 21–32, 131; 40, 140; 42, 142; 44, 206; 48, 302; xxv. 3, 70; 7, 62, 89, 309; 8 ff., 132; 18, 198; 20, 167; 23, 52; 28, 131; 34, 302; 37, 171; 38, 311; 40, 134; 41, 142; xxvi. 1, 206; 7–11, 137; 10, 68; 12, 143; 13, 132, 146; 14, 137; 16, 132; 21, 142, 292; 23, 329; 24, 52, 96, 127, 131, 138, 149, 212, 273–4, 278, 311; 25,

Livy (cont.):
128; 26, 54; 27, 68, 218, 327; 28,
206; 33, 137, 161; 34, 132; 35–6,
91; 37, 107; 42, 54–5, 279; 47,
151; xxvii. 1, 311; 3, 318; 4, 58,
85, 90, 299; 6, 163; 7, 206, 223; 8,
164; 9, 171, 198, 216; 11, 89–90,
184; 15, 198; 16, 146, 151; 23, 88,
168; 29, 207; 30, 58, 127, 154, 211;
31, 123, 138, 208–9; 32, 141; 33,
81, 128; 36–51, 83; 37, 90–1,
184; 45, 279; 51, 115; xxviii. 5–8,
155; 5, 127, 129, 207; 6, 156, 311; 7,
58, 118, 124; 8, 61, 128, 174; 9, 109,
159; 11, 88, 90; 13, 291; 22–3, 103;
24, 162; 28, 171; 31, 162; 37, 171;
38, 62, 109, 165, 252; 39, 333; 40,
30 n. 1, 85, 307; 43, 150; 44, 80;
45, 28 n. 2, 30 n. 1; 46, 60; xxix.
1, 162, 167; 4, 84; 5, 60, 127; 8–9,
87; 9, 187; 10, 309; 11, 56; 12,
40 n. 3, 52, 69, 96, 121, 136, 186,
199, 207, 236, 315, 334; 13, 165;
14, 88–9, 252; 15, 216; 16–22, 87;
16, 92; 18, 87; 19, 88; 20, 63; 21,
88; 22, 5 n. 1; 26, 210; 27–8, 75;
29, 84; 38, 67; xxx. 1, 223; 2, 81,
89–90, 165, 184; 3, 331; 6, 142;
15, 85, 252; 17, 115; 18–19, 83; 19,
11, 60; 23, 56, 63; 24, 62; 26, 12, 54,
66, 118, 158, 181; 27, 63, 165; 29,
319; 30, 334; 33, 55, 212; 34, 198;
35, 142, 212; 37, 84–5, 137, 142,
169–70; 38, 66, 89, 168, 297; 39,
163, 181; 40, 31 n. 5, 55, 58, 62,
64, 77–8, 115; 41, 60, 77–8, 109,
161–2, 165, 223; 42, 12, 54–5,
112, 118, 158; 43, 31 n. 5, 64, 295,
297, 339; 44, 49, 60; 45, 10 n. 1,
35 n. 6, 49, 172, 293, 339; xxxiv. 8,
185; 10, 160, 298, 333; 14, 197; 15,
9; 22, 12, 334; 25, 215, 326; 28,
303; 31, 122, 245; 32, 150, 245,
324; 33 ff., 29 n. 1; 33, 53, 333; 34,
26 n. 5; 36, 150; 39, 251; 41, 334;
44, 5, 81, 87, 195, 332; 45, 4, 225;
46, 185, 293; 48, 117; 50, 303;
52, 293; 53, 62, 82, 112–14, 163,
226–7, 297; 54, 5, 50; 57–9,
29 n. 6; 61, 126, 204; 62, 336;
xxxv. 1, 149, 186; 2, 217; 7, 173; 9,
89, 184; 10, 163, 330; 11, 149; 12,
133, 138, 251; 21, 168, 184; 24,
108; 25 ff., 29 n. 2; 27, 197; 32,
103, 130; 36, 106; 40, 61; 41,
113–14, 163, 297; 47, 23 n. 3; 49,
173; 51, 59; xxxvi. 1, 68–9, 182;
2, 82, 169, 219; 4, 108, 169; 8, 268;
10, 147, 193; 13, 147, 190, 193;
14, 193; 17, 18 ; 19, 11; 21, 160;
24, 138; 25, 279; 27–8, 31 n. 5;
31–2, 29 n. 2; 31, 127, 136; 34,
29 n. 4; 35, 29 n. 2, 103, 240, 274;
38, 11; 39, 160; 40, 160, 167; 41,
70, 150; 42, 150; 45, 280; xxxvii.
2, 219; 3, 167, 218; 7, 240; 9–11,
280; 16, 209; 21–2, 232; 34, 137;
35, 320; 37, 106; 38, 196; 39–40,
141; 39, 254; 45, 219; 46, 162; 47,
159; 50, 219; 53–4, 19; 55–6,
12 n. 1; xxxviii. 8, 309; 10, 138;
13, 282; 15, 106; 16, 289; 17, 18;
23, 11; 30, 210; 31, 204; 32, 119;
35, 27 n. 2, 163; 36, 137; 38, 219,
307; 42, 163; 44, 54, 158; 57, 67;
xxxix. 4, 56, 160; 6, 9 n. 3; 8, 331;
9, 109; 22, 89; 23, 225; 25, 147,
193; 30, 319; 32, 60; 33, 103, 124;
39, 181; 40, 268; 41, 11; 42, 177;
44, 218; 47, 22 n. 4, 24 n. 1; 48,
288; 49, 319; 50, 9; 51, 23 n. 5;
52, 9; 53, 24 n. 1, 208; xl. 2, 168;
4, 326; 5–16, 24 n. 1; 19, 89;
20–4, 24 n. 1; 20, 116; 24, 144; 25,
60; 26, 217; 27, 143; 28, 60; 29,
307; 34, 170; 35, 164; 37, 90; 40,
167, 288; 41, 60; 45 ff., 35 n. 7;
45, 184; 46, 68; 48, 298; 54–5,
24 n. 1; xli. 5, 167; 9, 184; 10, 94;
13, 75; 20, 123; 21, 89–90, 184,
330; 23, 152; 25, 288; 28, 89; xlii.
2, 89, 184; 14, 85; 16, 145; 20, 69;
21, 292; 26, 209; 28, 81–2, 92; 30,
69; 31, 219; 38, 297; 43, 229; 47,
103, 159; 48, 95, 209; 49, 311;
50, 106; 53, 147; 54, 279; 65, 59;
67, 147; xliii. 2, 52; 3, 123; 6, 108,
282; 9, 209; 10, 59; 13, 88, 90; 18,
144; 21, 73, 173; xliv. 1, 156; 6,
311; 10, 59; 11, 154; 12, 59; 18,
184; 22, 204; 24, 302; 29, 107;
36, 334; 40, 126; 43, 173; xlv. 1,
294; 12, 121; 13, 109; 14, 170; 16,
89, 169; 19, 311; 22, 55; 25, 103,
282; 27, 125; 31, 71; 37, 72; 39,
94; per. xlvii, 50; per. xlviii, 291;
per. xlix, 50, 68.
Lycophron, Alexandra 1283 ff., 133.

2. AUTHORS AND PASSAGES

Memnon, *FGH* 434 F1 (19), 135.

Nepos, *Cato* 1, 219.
    Hannibal 7, 335.
Nonius, p. 533M, 285.

Obsequens, 6, 11, 89; 12, 89, 184;
    14, 89–90, 168, 184; 15, 89; 20,
    89; 22, 89–90; 24, 90; 27a, 89–90;
    28, 90, 168; 30, 184; 31, 90; 32,
    89–90; 34, 36, 89–90; 38, 89; 43,
    90; 46–8, 50, 89–90; 52, 184; 53,
    89–90, 184; 54, 184.
Orosius, iv. 2, 75; 3, 132; 4, 168; 15,
    299; 17, 91; 20, 82, 256, 318;
    v. 4, 89.
Ovid, *Ars Amatoria* iii. 455, 111.
    Fasti i. 293–4, iii. 429–30, 113.
    Schol. *Ibis* 303, 74.

Pausanias, i. 13, 74; 36, 44 n. 3, 79,
    141; ii. 9, 138; 16, 244; 34, 150;
    vii. 8, 194, 200; 17, 209; viii. 50,
    138, 252; 51, 23 n. 3, 29 n. 2; x. 1,
    103; 34, 213.
Phlegon, *FGH* 257 F36 (x), 89–90.
Plato, *Rep.* v. 470, 133–4.
Pliny, the elder, *NH* iii. 69, 224; iv. 32,
    190; 33, 193; 36, 154; 54, 194;
    118, 291; v. 30, 339; vii. 15–16,
    34–6, 89; 208, 285; viii. 221, 89;
    xvi. 115, 198; 216, 113; xxxv. 154,
    296.
Pliny, the younger, *Ep.* iii. 5, 10 n. 2.
Plutarch, *Aratus* 42, 74; 49–51, 136,
    208; 52, 54, 138.
    Camillus 22, 133.
    Cato maior 6, 219; 17, 328; 21, 220.
    Cleomenes 19, 74; 23–5, 211.
    Fabius 4, 81; 25, 80.
    Flamininus 2, 32 nn. 5, 8, 180, 312;
    3, 32 n. 8, 176, 183, 185; 4, 146,
    187–9; 5, 227; 6, 248; 7–8, 256;
    7, 227, 251, 253; 9, 266; 10–12,
    304; 12, 28 n. 1; 13, 23 n. 3, 29
    n. 1; 15, 29 n. 4; 16, 28 n. 1, 29 n. 2,
    31 n. 5; 20, 23 n. 5.
    Gaius Gracchus 2, 159.
    Moralia 275 C–D, 165; 293F, 126;
    760 A–B, 138.
    Philopoemen 12, 138; 13, 200, 252;
    15–16, 23 n. 3.
    Pompey 14, 109.

Pyrrhus 13, 75; 16, 141; 17, 75; 32 ff.,
    74.
    Tiberius Gracchus 8, 178.
Polyaenus, v. 17, 36 n. 2, 141; viii. 68,
    74.
Polybius, i. 7 ff., 73; 63, 295; ii. 5, 127,
    176; 8, 11, 153; 12, 69; 15, 66;
    20, 22–31, 58; 23–4, 32, 34, 82;
    52, 74; 54, 116; 55, 211; 58, 134;
    61–2, 211; 70, 208; iii. 8, 11–12,
    337; 14, 144; 15, 17, 72; 19, 136;
    20, 47 n. 4, 72; 40, 83; 56, 74; 60,
    82; 118, 62; iv. 3, 334; 5, 149; 6,
    149, 175; 9, 74, 149, 199; 11, 260;
    14, 149; 15, 138; 16, 127, 136,
    149; 19, 27, 149; 29, 127–8; 30,
    278; 37, 149; 38–52, 233; 53–5,
    141; 62, 120, 149; 65, 99; 66, 128;
    69, 176; v. 3, 127; 5, 279; 9, 120,
    134, 208; 11, 134, 149; 27–9, 137;
    30, 154; 34, 101; 35, 287; 53, 285;
    63, 287; 91, 154; 93, 211; 94, 154;
    95, 127; 97, 284; 99, 53; 101, 127;
    104, 133; 106, 79, 95; 108, 125,
    127; 110, 127, 140; vi. 14, 47 n. 3;
    20, 142; 21, 217, 249; 23, 140; 26,
    112; 27 ff., 141; 43–4, 95; 45, 138;
    vii. 2–8, 131; 9, 52, 73; 11–14, 136;
    11, 141; 14, 120, 134; viii. 8a, 136;
    12, 138; 23, 285; 24–34, 132; ix. 3–7,
    137; 8, 143; 11a, 58, 66; 23, 95;
    30, 56, 136; 32–9, 96; 35, 271;
    37, 133; 41, 53; 42, 32 n. 1, 64, 97;
    x. 17, 143; 20, 26, 138; 32, 143;
    41, 127; 42, 129; xi. 2, 143; 4 ff.,
    133; 5, 97; 6, 131; 7, 120, 207; 8,
    143; 18, 122; 19, 143; xiii. 1–2,
    149; 4–5, 36 n. 2, 100, 141; 7, 246;
    8, 36 n. 2, 122; xv. 11, 55, 212;
    15, 143; 18, 84–5, 137, 142,
    169–70; 20, 38 nn. 4, 10; 21 ff.,
    135; 22, 236; 23, 36 n. 6, 37 n. 2,
    235; 24, 37 n. 2, 135; 25, 38 n. 2,
    149, 322; xvi. 1, 38 n. 4, 120; 2,
    37 n. 5, 233; 7, 37 n. 5; 10, 37 n. 4,
    95; 11, 232; 14–15, 95; 15, 100;
    18, 149; 22, 38 n. 3; 24, 37 n. 7,
    42, 44 n. 4, 55, 232, 282; 25–34, 46;
    25–7, 41–2; 25–6, 1; 25, 43 n. 1,
    97; 26, 97–9; 27, 44, 77, 100, 127,
    186, 262; 28–34, 1; 28, 100–1, 143;
    29–34, 102–7; 34, 41–2, 56–7,
    186–7, 236; 36–7, 122; 38, 115,
    121; 39, 149; xviii. 1–12, 1, 24

Polybius (*cont.*):
n. 3, 227–43; 1, 54, 155, 186, 201,
301; 2, 36 n. 6, 37 n. 5, 38 n. 6,
155; 3, 36 n. 6, 53, 135; 4, 36 n. 6,
135; 5, 135; 6, 106, 187; 7, 25
n. 2, 36 n. 6; 8, 53; 9, 140; 10,
24 n. 4, 127, 138, 222; 11, 26 n. 4,
33 n. 1, 116, 222; 12, 312; 13–15,
214; 16–17, 1, 246–7; 17, 250;
18–27, 1, 254–66; 19–20, 190; 21,
173; 22, 126, 140, 251; 23, 143;
27, 268; 28–32, 144, 266; 29, 144,
263; 33–4, 36–41, 1; 33–9, 266–75;
34, 29 n. 3, 149, 251; 37, 137; 38,
53, 295; 39, 26 n. 5, 34 nn. 1, 5,
295; 40, 277, 300, 303; 41, 288–90;
41a, 286, 321; 42, 34 n. 3, 175,
294–5, 315; 43–51, 1; 43, 34 n. 5,
300–1, 334; 44–8, 304–17; 44, 232;
45, 27 n. 1, 34 nn. 7, 8; 47, 27 n. 1,
34 n. 6, 124, 175; 48, 35 n. 1, 251;
49–52, 322–6; 49–50, 35 n. 8; 49,
35 n. 3; 51, 101, 283; 53–5, 149;
54, 36 n. 3; xx. 9, 173; 10, 31 n. 5;
xxi. 3, 274; 17, 219; 24, 12 n. 1;
43, 219; xxii. 8, 97; 10, 124; xxiii.
1–3, 7–10, 24 n. 1; 5, 23 nn. 3, 6,
210; 10, 280; 15, 134; xxviii. 4,
173; 8, 144; xxx. 5, 56; 20, 95,
308; 21, 307; 25–6, 341; 31, 283,
287; xxxi. 21, 336; xxxii. 1, 85.
Ptolemy, iv. 3. 7, 280.
Publilius Syrus, I. 25, 138.

Quintilian, v. 11, 75; x. 1, 15 n. 3; xii,
prooem., 50.

Sallust, *Cat.* 5, 313; 11, 134, 151; 32,
187; 51, 150.
Jug. 19, 318; 26, 215; 43, 268.
Hist. (ed. Maurenbrecher), i. fr. 11,
53; fr. 55. 27, 75; ii. fr. 70, 151;
iv. fr. 41, 196.
Scylax, 52, 150.
Sempronius Asellio, fr. 7P, 151.
C. Sempronius Gracchus, frs. 35, 43M,
14 n. 5.
Seneca the elder, *Contr.* ix. 1, 2, 15 n. 3;
4, 218.
Suas. vi. 17, 22, 14 n. 1; 21, 24, 288.
M. Sergius Silus, *ORF*² pp. 97–8, 220.
Servius, *ad* Virgil *Aen.* vi. 839, 75.
Silius Italicus, xvii. 418 ff., 55.

Solinus. v. 1, 330.
Sophocles, *O.T.* 617, 138.
Stadiasmus Magni Maris 166, 327.
Stephanus of Byzantium, *s.vv.* Βεύη, 139;
Βῆγις, 141; Προῦσα, 135; Τένδηβα,
281; Τραλλία, 141.
Strabo, i. p. 53C, 327; iii. p. 141C, 291;
v. p. 216C, 82; vi. p. 258C, 132;
vii. p. 327C, 143; viii. p. 376C, 74;
p. 380C, 213; ix. p. 403C, 118;
x. p. 445C, 157; p. 484C, 150; xii.
p. 563C, 135, 236; xiv. p. 649C, 141.
Suetonius, *Divus Augustus* 86, 15 n. 2.
Divus Claudius 25, 183.
de grammaticis 15, 15 n. 2.
Vita Terentii 4, 31 n. 3.
Suidas, *s.vv.* Μάλειον ὄρος, 150; Μενδαῖος,
154.

Tacitus, *Agricola* 42, 247.
Annals i. 23, 215; 25 ff., 173; iii. 57,
202; iv. 26, 85; 62, 151; xii. 23,
69; xv. 40, 133.
Histories ii, 78, 69; iii. 34, 83; v. 13,
151.
Thucydides, i. 10, 244; 132–3, 302;
135–8, 335; 138, 288; ii. 15, 134;
65, 288; 70, 102; 72, 205; 87, 252;
99, 211; iii. 42, 138; iv. 76, 153;
78, 190; 89–101, 153; v. 13, 193;
vi. 55, 152; viii. 58, 324.
Trogus, *prol.* xxx, 38 n. 10.

Valerius Maximus, i. 1. 21, 87; 6. 5, 90;
ii. 8. 1, 5, 109; iii. 6. 5, 292; iv. 1. 6,
335; 3. 9, 57; 8. 5, 304; v. 1. ext. 4,
75; 3. 2, 225; vi. 6. 1, 57; ix. 1.
ext. 1, 184.
Varro, *de lingua Latina* v. 151, 218; vi.
60, vii. 37, 94; vii. 88, 76.
Velleius Paterculus, i. 14, 83, 136, 216,
224; 15, 225; ii. 2, 180.
Virgil, *Aeneid* i. 386, 235; vi. 853, 270;
xii. 288, 143; 655, 132.
Vitruvius, iii. 2. 3, 113.

Xenophon, *Hellenica* i. 4. 22, 152; ii.
3. 6, 102; vii. 4. 40, 138; 5. 5, 175.

Zonaras, viii. 6, 57, 132; ix. 4, 52; 11,
87; 13, 84; 15, 82–3, 117–18,
125–6, 139; 16, 187, 194, 200,
216–17, 228, 243, 248, 256, 275,
277, 304; 19, 29 n. 4.

2. AUTHORS AND PASSAGES

B. INSCRIPTIONS

The figures in larger type indicate the pages of this book.

AE 1956, 1 ff., 189.

AJA lxviii (1964), 178–9, 341.

Chiron i (1971), 167–8, 199.

CIL i². p. 200, 162; p. 223, 283; pp. 328–9, 294; iii. 6076, 92.

Ἑλληνικά xv (1957), 247 ff., 189.

FIRA i. 104, 62; i. 110, 93.

IBM iii. 441, 36 n. 4.

IC ii. 3. 5, 28 n. 2.

IG i². 91, 92, 310, 125; ii². 884, 233; 2362, 43 n. 1; ix². 1. 208, 28 n. 2; 583, 279; ix. 2. 329, 193; 338, 147; xii. 9. 931, 28 n. 1.

IGRR iii. 137, 104; iv. 1049, 28 n. 1.

I.I. xiii. 1. pp. 78–9, 293; xiii. 2. pp. 2, 6, 111, 121, 113; xiii. 3. 74, 228.

ILLRP 45, 130a, 593, 683, 163; 75, 64; 321, 277; 517, 226.

ILS 190, 104.

Inscriptions de Délos 442, 281.

Inscriptions of Cos 10–11, 37 n. 8.

ISE 55, 214.

Labraunda, iii. 1. no. 7, 36 n. 4.

Lindos, ii. 1. no. 151, 280–1.

MDAI(A) lxxii (1957), 233 ff., 37 n. 5.

OGIS 229, 104; 230, 286; 234, 38 n. 5, 54, 282; 237, 305; 266, 104; 284, 288, 157; 340, 135.

SEG i. 144, 28 n. 2; x. 1107, 214; xi. 923, 28 n. 1; xvi. 255, 214.

SGDI 3656, 28 n. 1; 3749, 37 n. 8; 4269, 280.

StV, iii. no. 536, 153, 273–4.

*Syll.*³ 543, 141; 547, 151; 564, 54; 568–70, 572, 37 n. 8; 582, 117; 585, 28 nn. 1, 2; 586, 280–1; 587, 129; 588, 287–8; 591, 27 n. 3, 194; 321; 592, 28 n. 1; 593, 147; 594, 245; 607 ff., 28 n. 2; 616, 28 n. 1; 617, 28 n. 2; 634, 281; 673, 37 n. 8, 155.

Tituli Calymnii xii, 38 n. 7.

Welles, *Royal Correspondence*, no. 35, 127.

3. LATIN

Entries in this Index refer to notes which deal with the usage or meaning of a word or phrase. References to notes dealing with matters of substance will be found in the General Index.

animi et oculi, 311.
animos facere, 106.
ante alias, alias ante, 72.
antiquus, 201.
autumnus, 115–16.

bellum movere, 284–5, 299, 335.
biduo, 220.

caduceator, 143.
calumniam iurare, 338.
capellus, 169.
capere, 59, 322.
caput, 327.
circumvehi, 276.
comis, 289.
communicare, 330.
continuare, 180.

diem ac noctem, 279.
divus, 75.
dubitare, 325.

educere, 187.
elephas, 219.
eques Romanus, 299.
e re publica fidequa sua, 309.
et (= *etiam*), 142.
evastare, 234.
exauctorare, 167.

facta futuraque, 167.
fidem facere, 309.
fides, 230.
fiduciarius, 243.
fidus, 53.
forte, 149, 244, 287, 340.
fortiter feliciterque, 109.
fortuna, 280, 284, 289, 313.
frequens, 160.

imperium, 145.
implere, 276.
imus, 261.
infidus, 53.
infimus, 261.
insanus, 198.
instare, 188.

interfari, 16, 235, 271.
introrsus, 263.
invictus animus, 16, 268.
iuxta, 263.

lautia, 295.
legationem renuntiare, 103.
letum, 16, 107.
litus, 51.

Macedonia, 10 n. 4.
manubiae, 338.
marcere, 337.
marcescere, 16, 337.
mussare, 16, 308.

namque, 279.
ne . . . quidem, nec . . . quidem, 324–5.
nec (= *ne . . . quidem*), 116.
neque enim ne . . . quidem, 334.
nimbus, 16, 258.
non modo . . . sed iam, 75.

operae est, 16, 288.

paludatus, 94.
paucis absolvere, 16, 269.
pollicitatio, 124.
praedictum, 257.
praetor, 337.
princeps, 105, 127, 204–5.
proconsul, pro consule, 61, 109.
propraetor, 61.
pro sententia, 202–3, 205.
purpuratus, 141–2, 245, 262.

quid, quod, 323–4.
quiritatio, 302.

recipere, 199, 283, 287.
referre, 124, 204, 210.
reficere, 318–19.

scilicet, 131, 209.
sentire, 197.
sequi, 200.
similis, 258.

3. LATIN

situs, 337.

socii ac nomen Latinum, socii nominis
Latini, 77, 182–3, 223, 331.

socius, 53.

sors, 69.

speculator, 118–19.

subitarius, 58.

subscribere, 338.

tendere, 326.

timere, 111.

traicere, 94–5.

tribus, 59.

triennio, 52.

unicus, 289.

vallum, vallus, 254.

venalicium, 178.

versus, 212.

virile ac muliebre secus, 16, 151.

vocare, 1 n. 2, 59, 119.

votum nuncupare, 94.

4. GREEK

ἀδελφιδοῦς, 241–2.
ἄφρακτοι, κατάφρακτοι, 117.
Βασιλεὺς Φίλιππος καὶ Μακεδόνες, 70.
δαμιουργός, 210.
ἐπιγαμία, 99.
ἡμεροδρόμος, ἡμεροσκόπος, 118–19.
Θερμικά, 129.
ἰσοπολιτεία, 99.
κατάστασις, 21.
κεφαλή, 327.

Κοῖλα Εὐβοίας, 157.
Παναιτωλικά, 129.
πρίστις, 229.
ῥομφαία, 145.
στρατηγὸς ἐπὶ τὰ ὅπλα, 119.
σύγκλητος, σύνοδος, 121–2, 124, 201, 204
τύχη, 280, 313.
φίλοι, 25 n. 3, 128.
φορτικόν, 97.